RAC
Road Atlas
Britain & Ireland

G000054347

CONTENTS

Key to map pages ii

Britain distance chart iii

Key to map symbols iv-v

Route planning map vi-vii
(40 miles to 1 inch)

Road map section 2-109
Britain (4.2 miles to 1 inch)

Ireland road maps 110-113
(15.8 miles to 1 inch)

M25 London orbital motorway map 114-115

London urban map 116-117
(1.1 miles to 1 inch)

London central map 118-119
(5.1 inches to 1 mile)

Urban area maps and city centre plans 120-133
(1.25 miles to 1 inch)
Southampton and Portsmouth 120-121
Cardiff and Newport 122
Bristol 123
West Midlands 124-125
Merseyside 126-127
Greater Manchester 128-129
Newcastle upon Tyne 130
Edinburgh 131
Glasgow 132-133

Index to place names in Britain 134-162

Index to place names in Ireland 162

Published by Collins
An imprint of HarperCollinsPublishers
77-85 Fulham Palace Road, Hammersmith, London W6 8JB

www.collins.co.uk

Copyright © HarperCollinsPublishers Ltd 2003

Collins® is a registered trademark of HarperCollinsPublishers Limited

Mapping generated from Collins Bartholomew digital databases

The grid on this map is the National Grid taken from the Ordnance Survey map with the permission of the Controller of Her Majesty's Stationery Office.

The contents of this publication are believed correct at the time of printing. Nevertheless, the publisher can accept no responsibility for errors or omissions, changes in the detail given, or for any expense or loss thereby caused.

The representation of a road, track or footpath is no evidence of a right of way.

Printed in Great Britain

ISBN paperback 0 00 717338 5 imp 001
      wiro 0 00 717339 3 imp 001

QC11660 / QC11661 BDM

e-mail: roadcheck@harpercollins.co.uk

KEY TO MAP PAGES

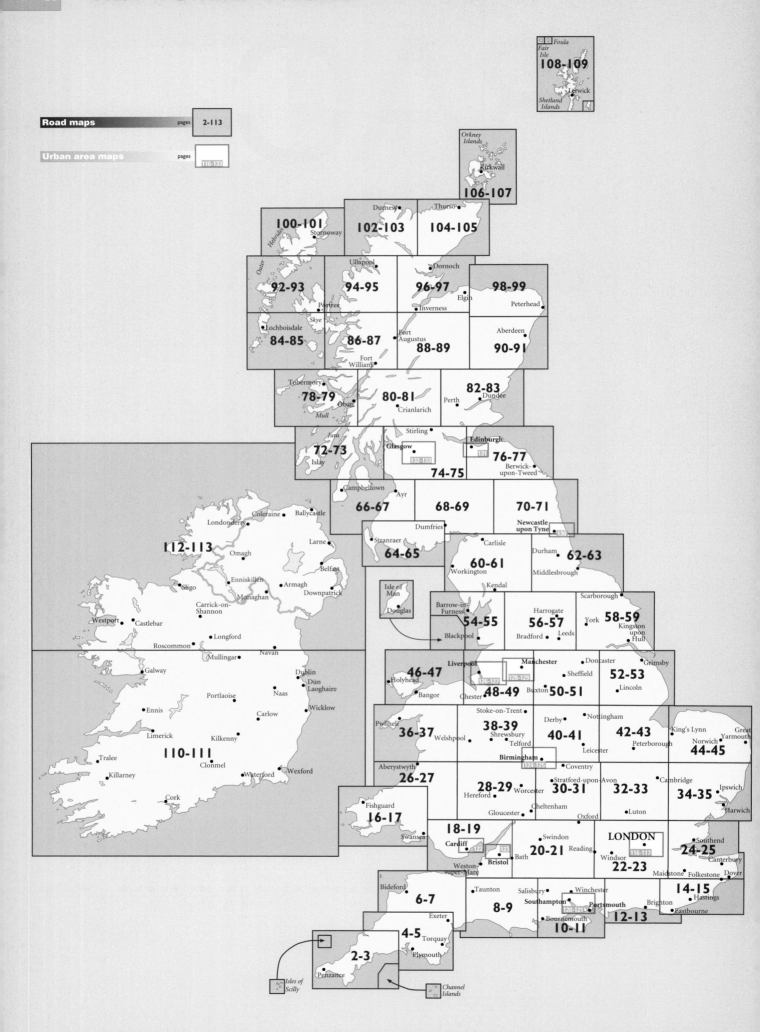

Road maps pages **2-113**

Urban area maps pages **116-133**

Distances between two selected towns in this table are shown in miles and kilometres. In general, distances are based on the shortest routes by classified roads.

DISTANCE IN KILOMETRES

DISTANCE IN MILES

KEY TO MAP SYMBOLS

Road maps (pages 2-109)

ROAD INFORMATION

 Motorway

Motorway junction with full / limited access

Motorway service area with off road / full / limited access

 Primary dual / single carriageway

 With passing places

 'A' road dual / single carriageway

 With passing places

 'B' road dual / single carriageway

With passing places

Minor road

Restricted access due to road condition or private ownership

Road proposed or under construction

Multi-level junction (occasionally with junction number)

 Roundabout

 Road distance in miles between markers

Road tunnel

Steep hill (arrows point downhill)

 Level crossing / Toll

OTHER TRANSPORT INFORMATION

Car ferry route with journey times; daytime and (night-time)

Railway line / Station / Tunnel

Airport with scheduled services

Heliport

Park and Ride site (operates at least 5 days a week)

CITIES, TOWNS & VILLAGES

Built up area

□ □ □ Town / Village / Other settlement

 Peterhead Primary route destination

Primary route destinations are places of major traffic importance linked by the primary route network. They are shown on a green background on direction signs.

St Ives Seaside destination

OTHER FEATURES

 National boundary

County / Unitary Authority boundary

 National / Regional park

Forest park boundary

 Military range

 Woodland

 Spot height in metres

Summit height in metres

 Lake / Dam / River / Waterfall

 Canal / Dry canal / Canal tunnel

 Beach

 Adjoining page indicator

TOURIST INFORMATION

A selection of tourist detail is shown on the mapping. It is advisable to check with the local tourist information office regarding opening times and facilities available.

Tourist information centre (all year / seasonal)

Ancient monument

Battlefield

Castle

Country park

Ecclesiastical building

Garden

Golf course

Historic house

Major shopping centre / Outlet village

Major sports venue

Motor racing circuit

Museum / Art gallery

Nature reserve

Preserved railway

Racecourse

Theme park

Wildlife park or Zoo

Other interesting feature

National Trust property

National Trust for Scotland property

London central map (pages 118-119)

Dual A4	Primary route	Main / Other railway station		i	Tourist information centre
Dual A302	'A' road	LRT / Bus or coach station			Cinema / Theatre
B240	'B' road	Leisure and tourism			Major hotel
Other road / Track / Path		Shopping		USA	Embassy
Street market / Pedestrian street		Administration and law		+	Church
Congestion Charging Zone		Health and welfare			Mosque
One way street / Access restriction		Education			Synagogue
Ferry		Industry and commerce		Mormon	Other place of worship
Borough boundary		Public open space		P WC	Car park / Public toilet
Postal district boundary		Park / Garden / Sports ground		POL Fire Sta PO	Police station / Fire station / Post office

Urban area maps (pages 120-133)

Symbol	Description	Symbol	Description	Symbol	Description
M4	Motorway number	B7078	'B' road number		Railway line / Station / Tunnel
12 13	Motorway junctions with full access		Dual carriageway	U	Underground station
13 14	Motorway junctions with limited access		Single carriageway	•	Light rail station
LEICESTER SERVICES	Motorway service area with off road / full / limited access		Minor road dual carriageway	P	Park and Ride site (operates at least 5 days a week)
			Minor road single carriageway		Airport with scheduled services
A316	Primary route number		Road under construction		County / Unitary Authority boundary
	Dual carriageway		Road tunnel		Public building
	Single carriageway		Roundabout / Toll	362 ▲	Spot height in metres
A4054	'A' road number		One way street / Level crossing		Woodland
	Dual carriageway		Car ferry with destination		Park
	Single carriageway				Congestion Charging Zone (London only)

City and town centre plans (pages 120-133)

Symbol	Description	Symbol	Description	Symbol	Description
	Motorway		Restricted access		One way street
dual	Primary route		Pedestrian street	i	Tourist information centre
dual	'A' road		Tourist building	P	Car park
dual	'B' road		Important building	P	Park and Ride site (operates at least 5 days a week)
dual	Through route		Higher education building		Railway line / Station
dual	Other road		Hospital	U M •	Underground / Metro / Light rail station
	Footpath / Footbridge	† †	Cemetery		Foot ferry
			Recreational area / Open space	+	Ecclesiastical building

ROUTE PLANNING MAP OF GREAT BRITAIN AND IRELAND

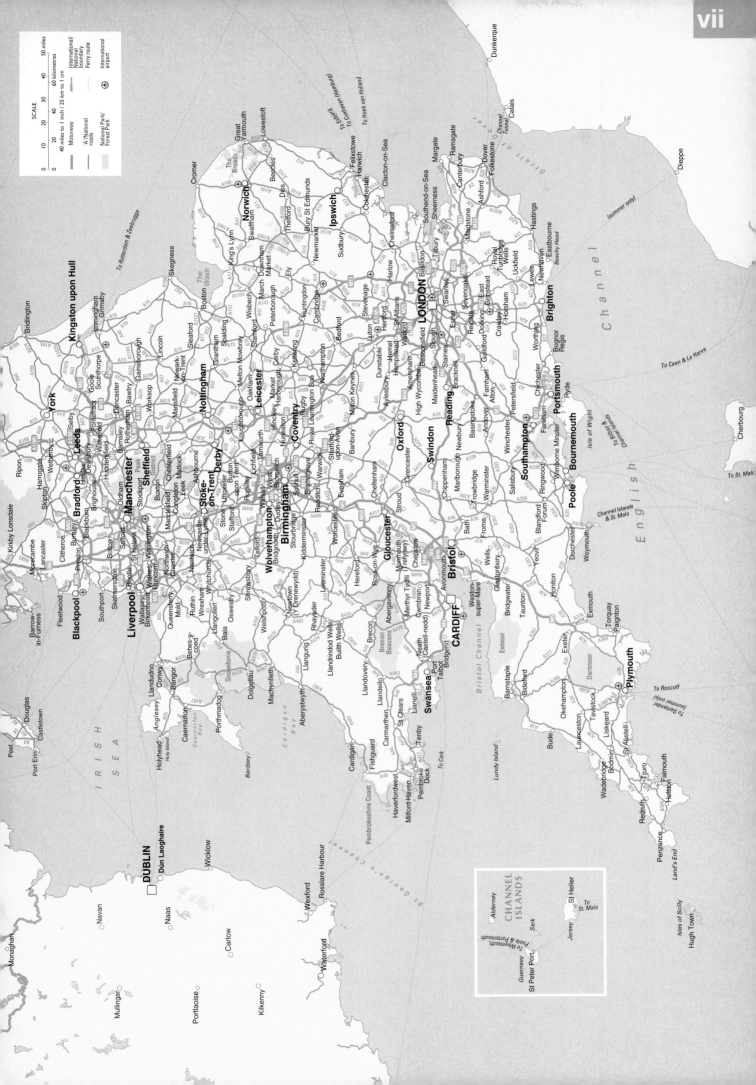

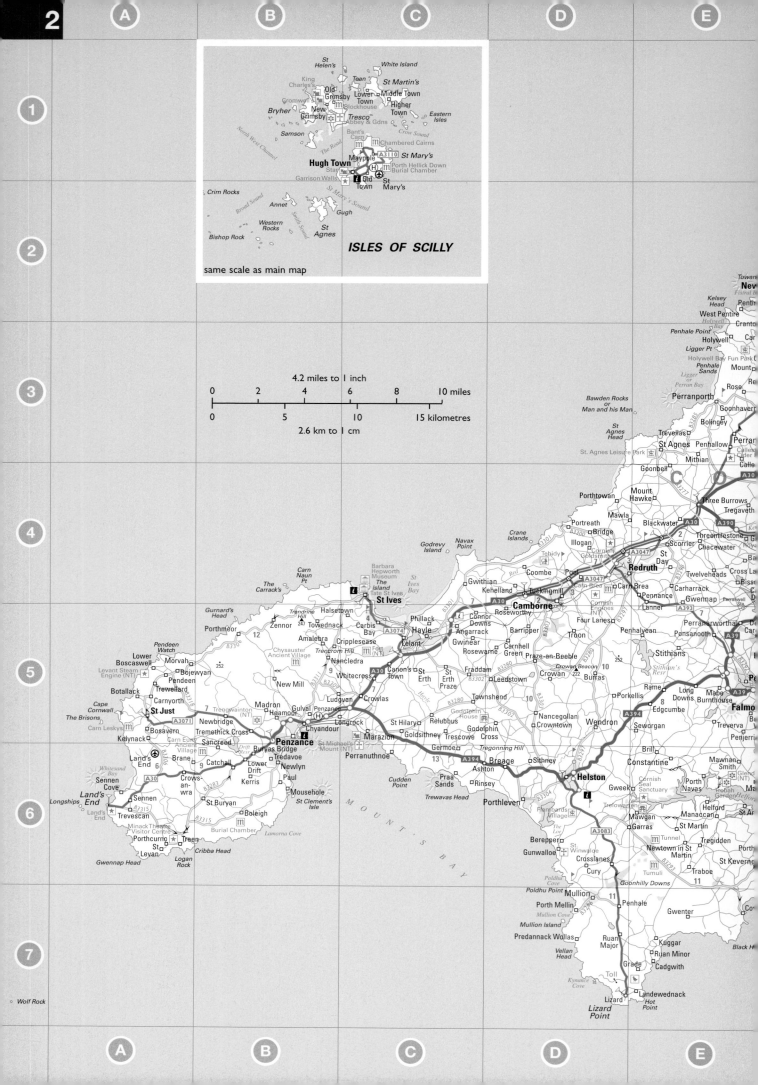

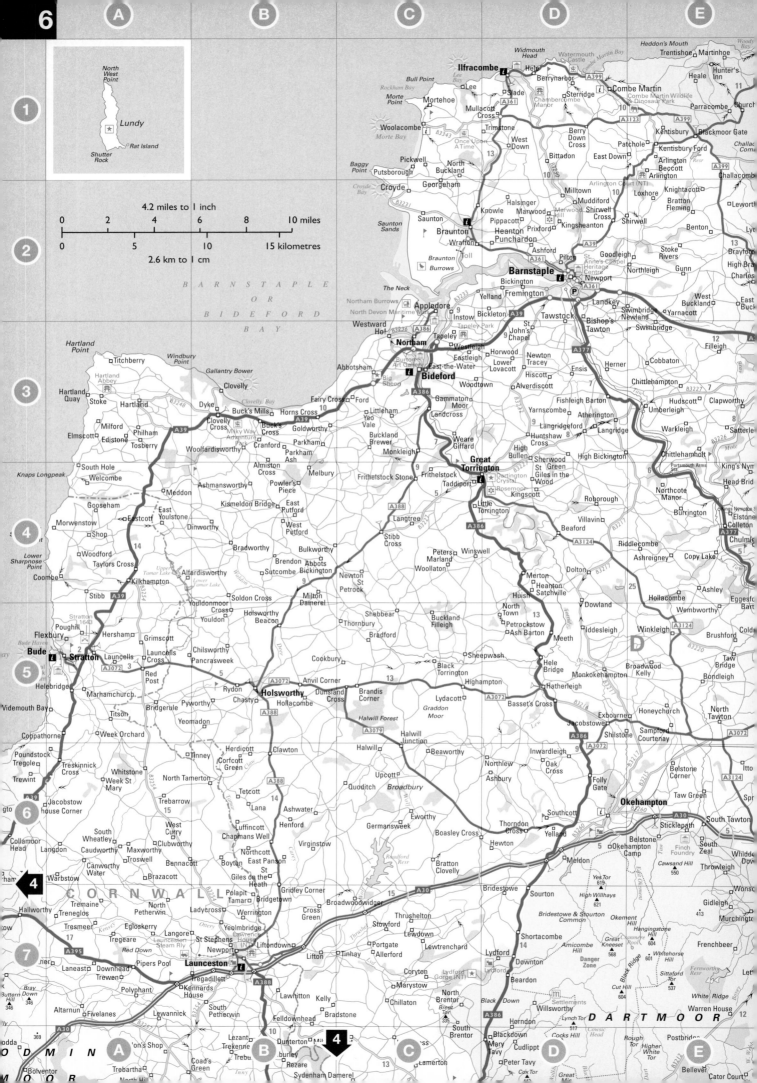

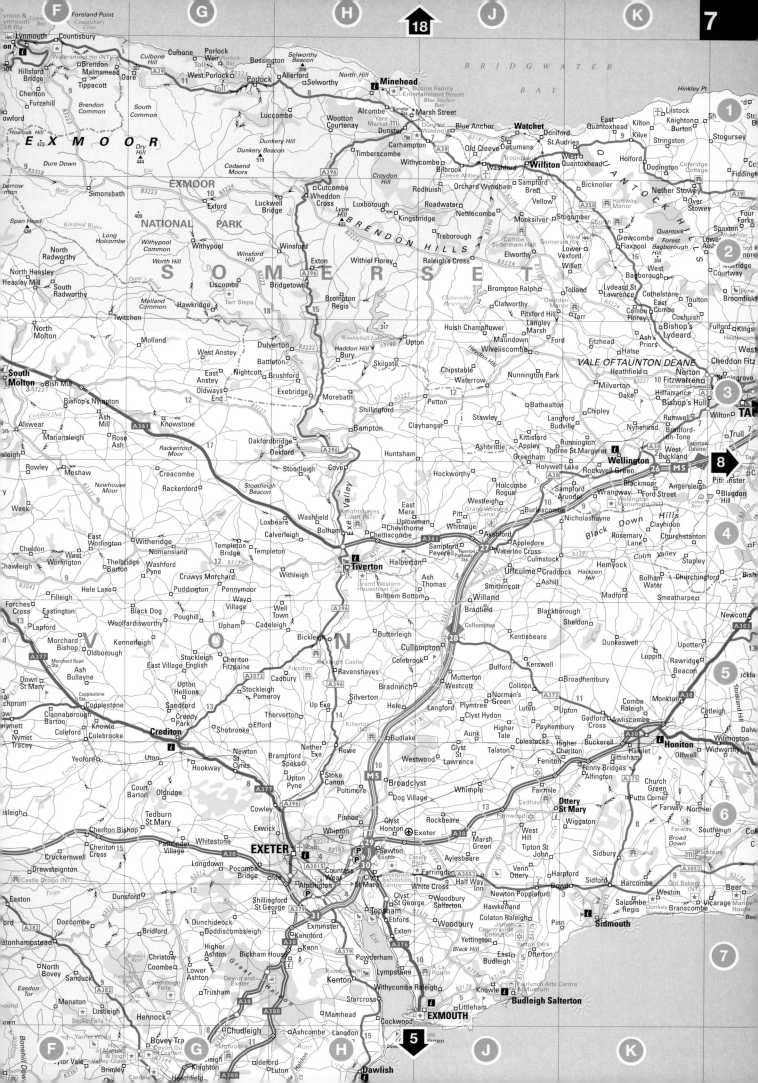

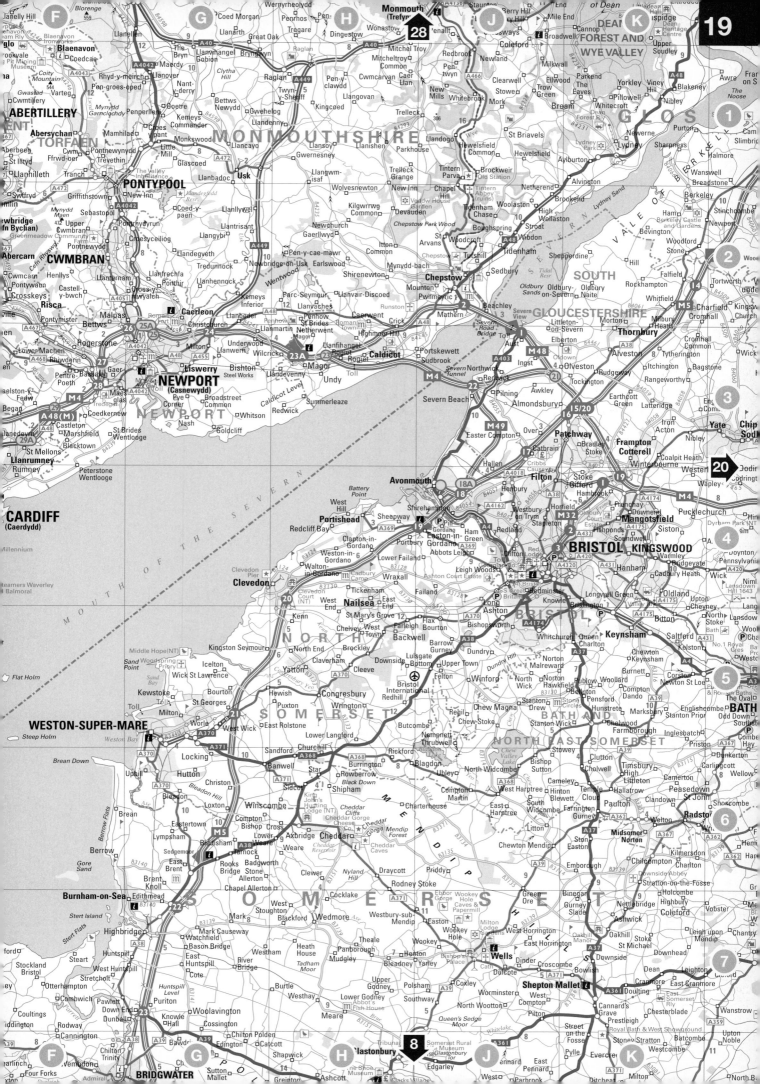

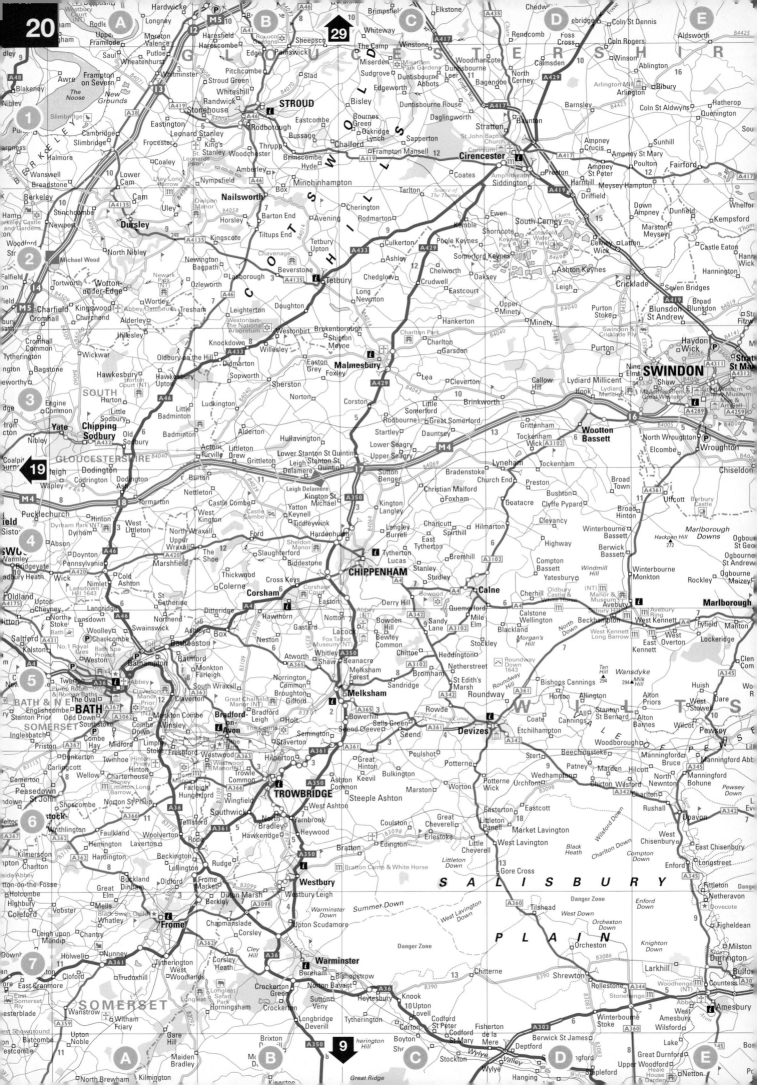

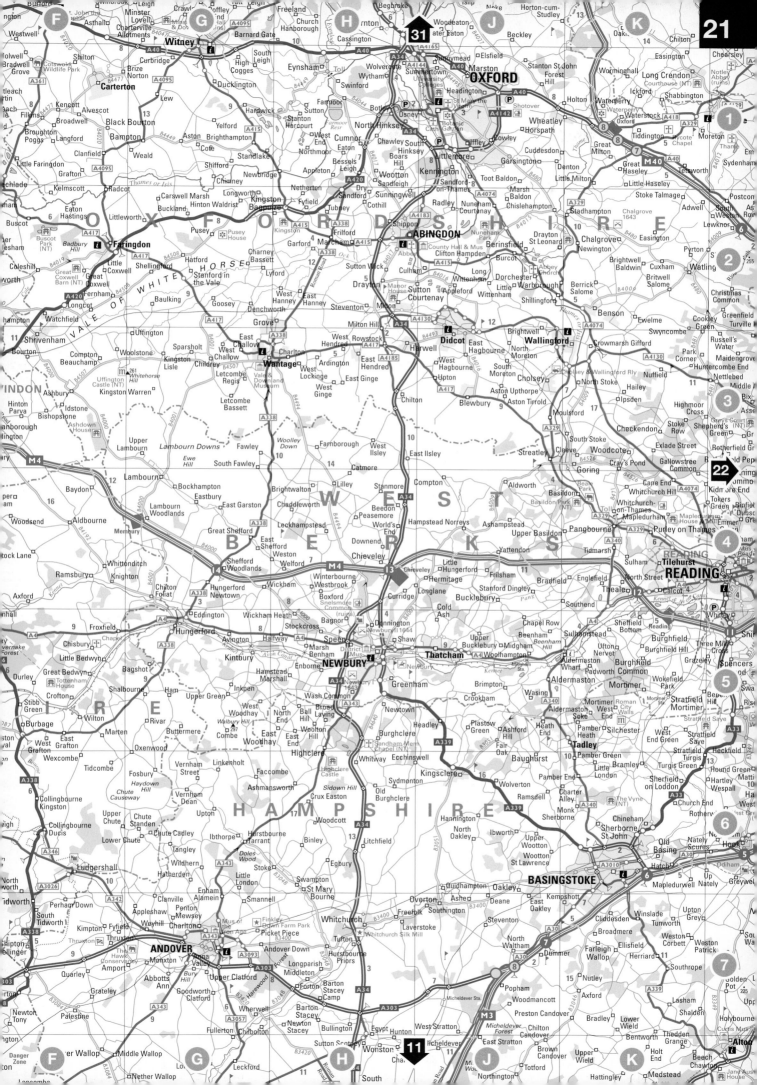

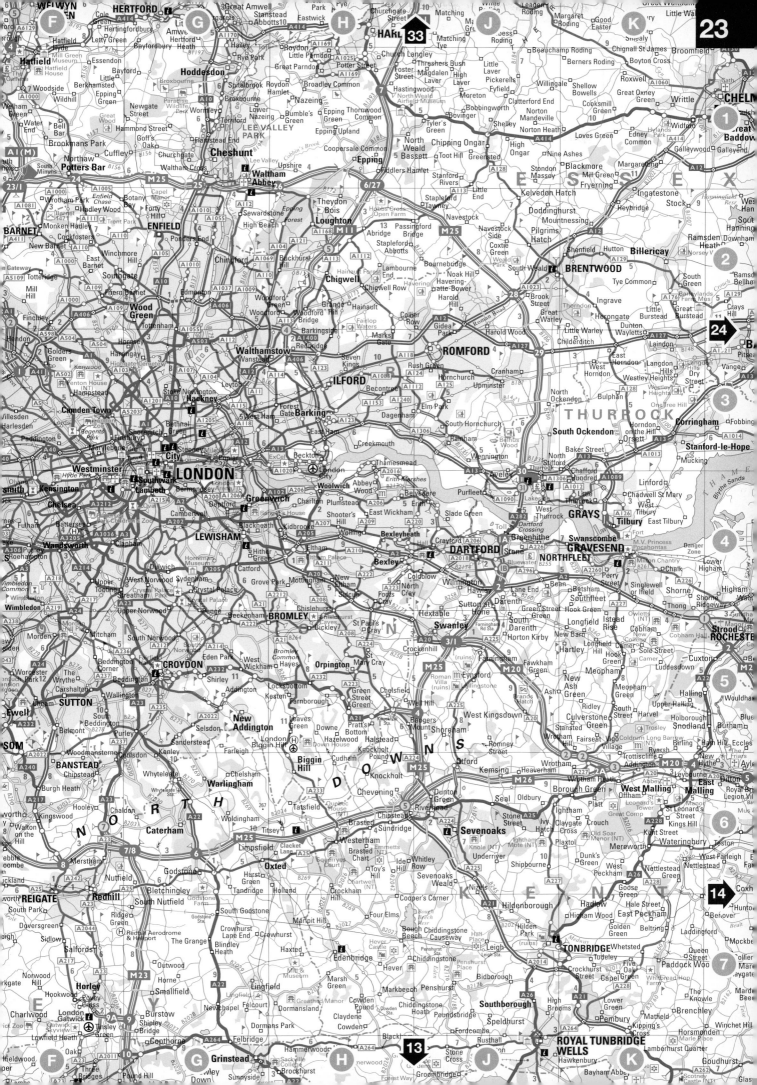

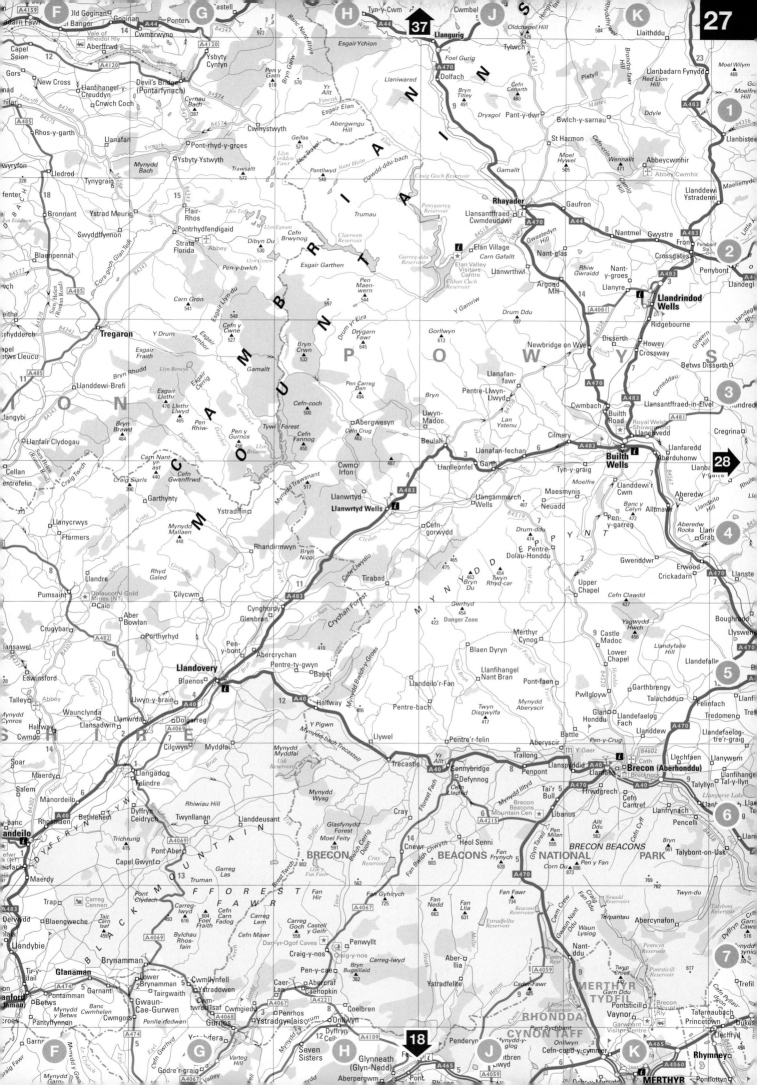

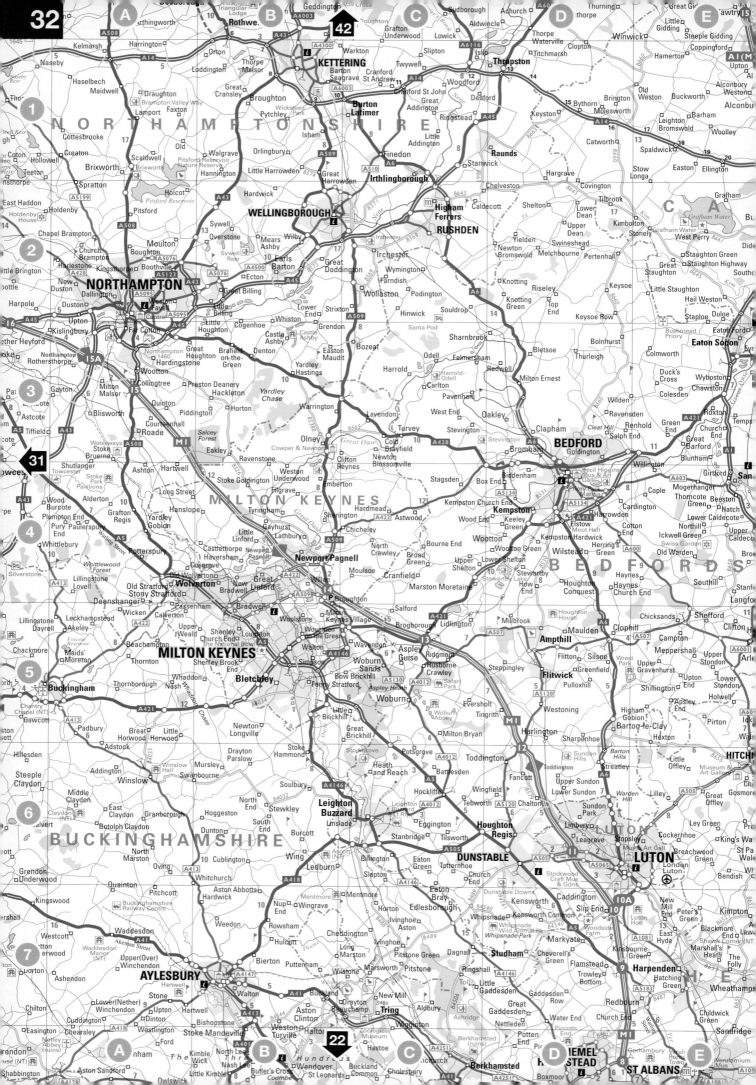

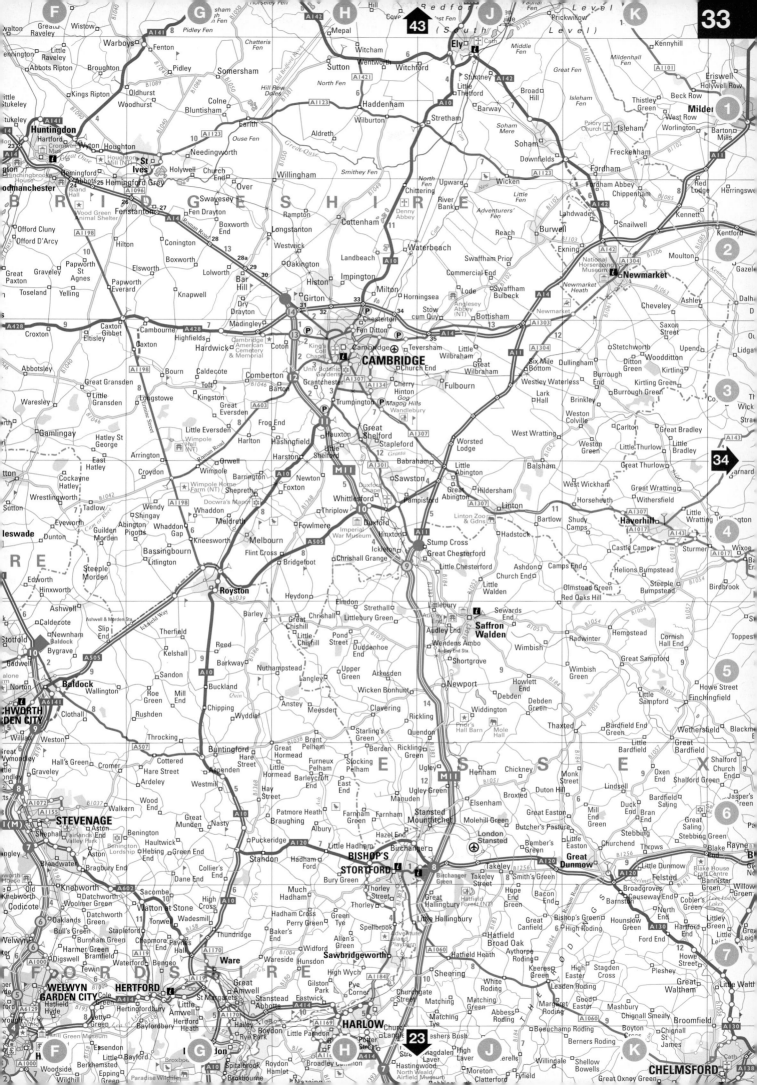

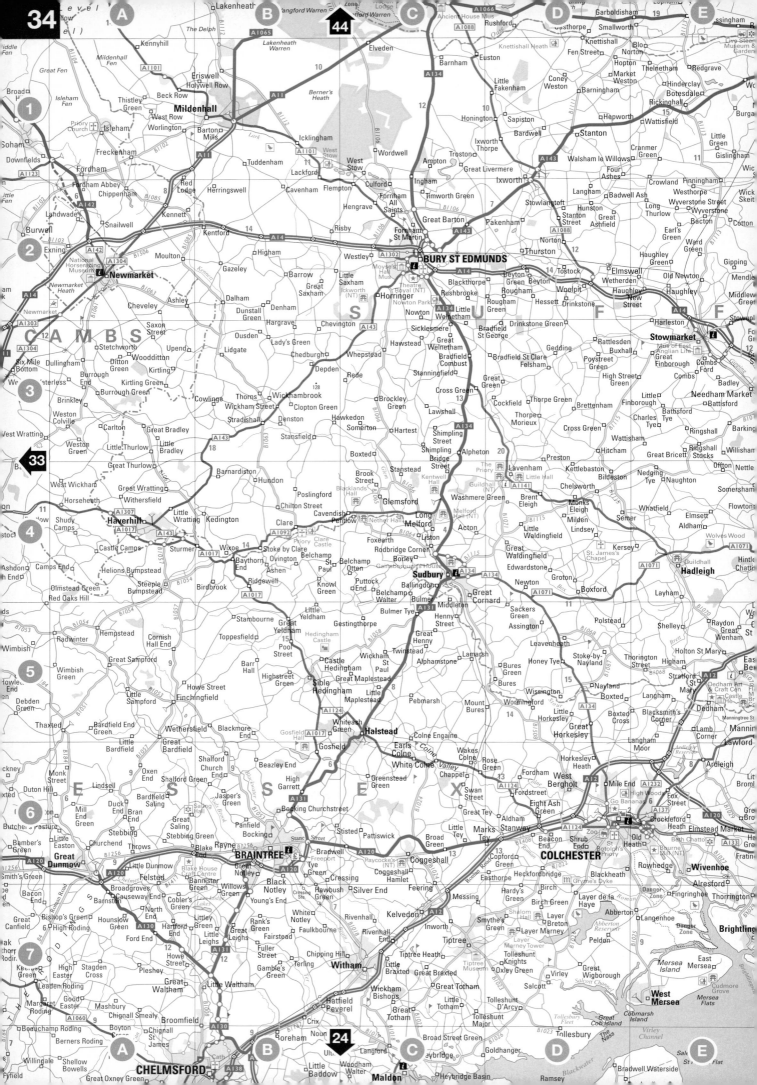

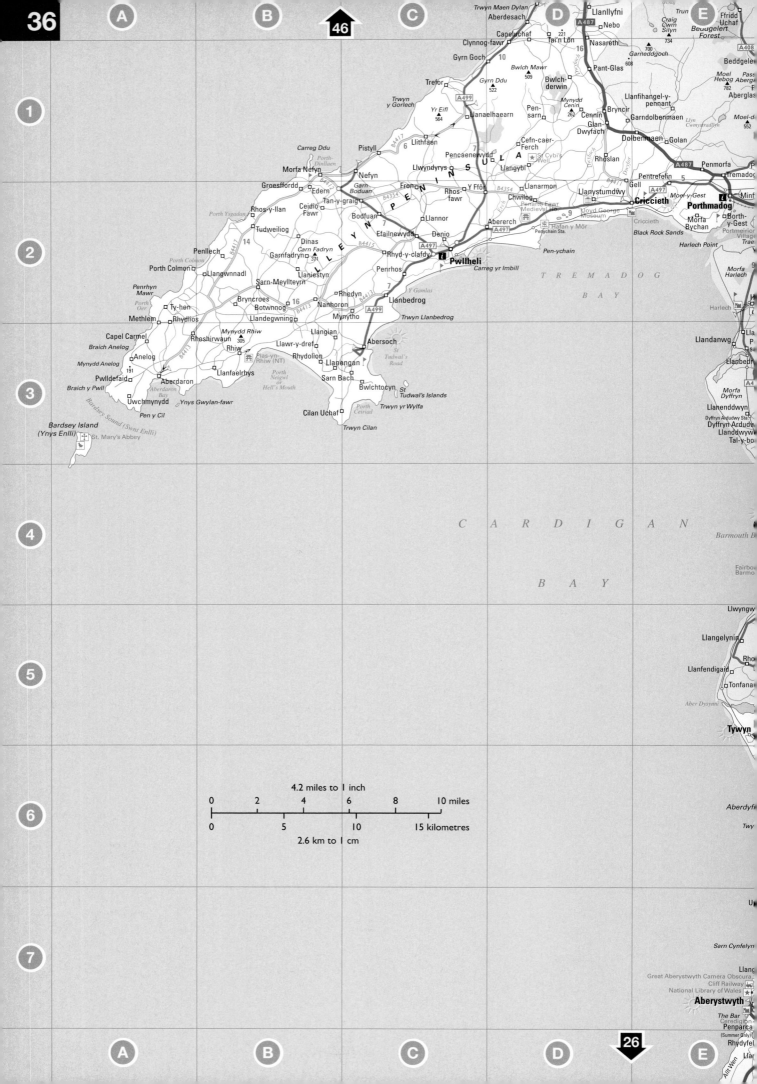

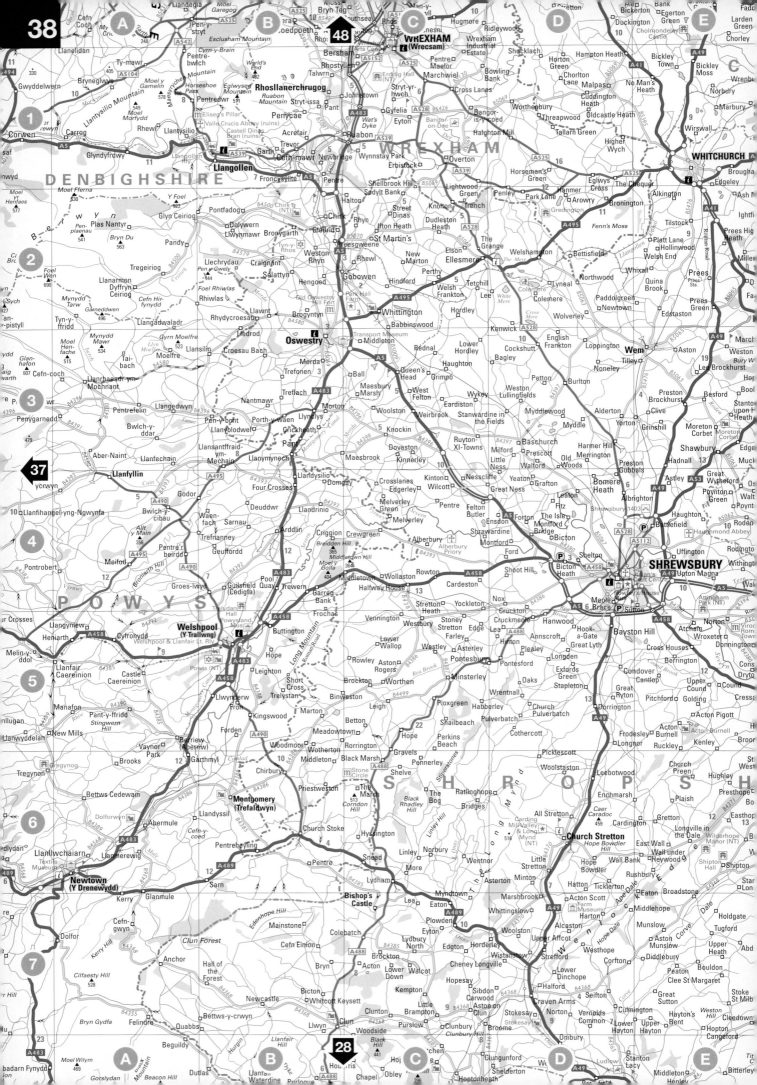

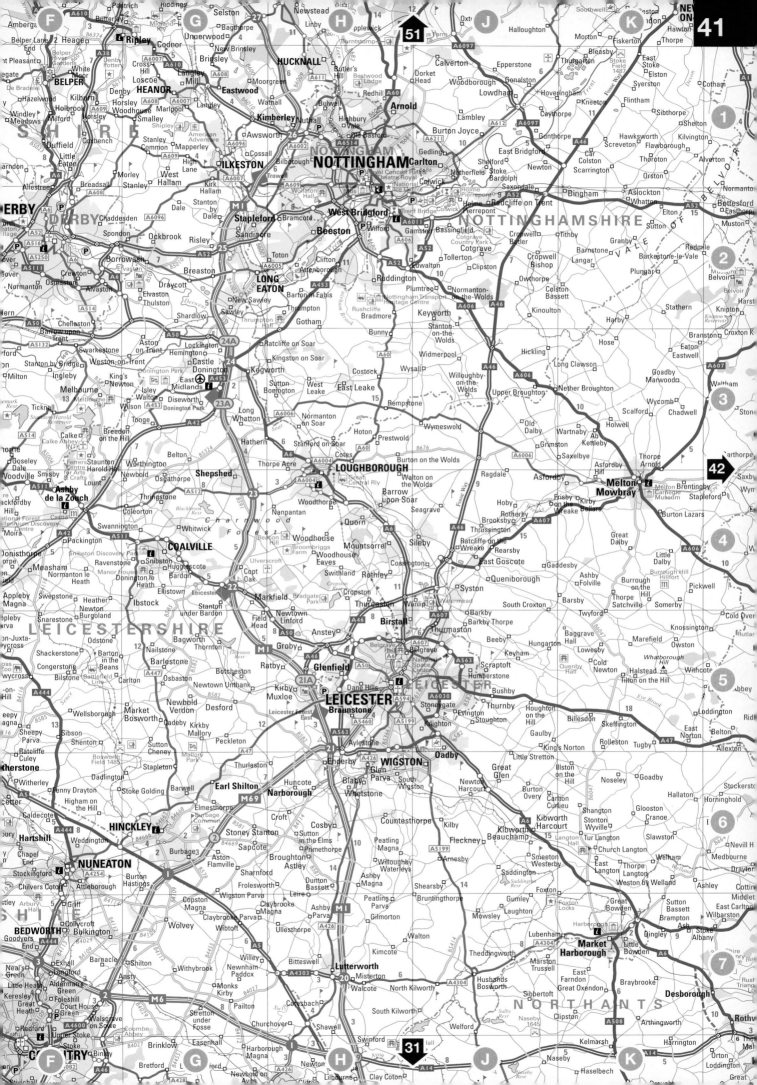

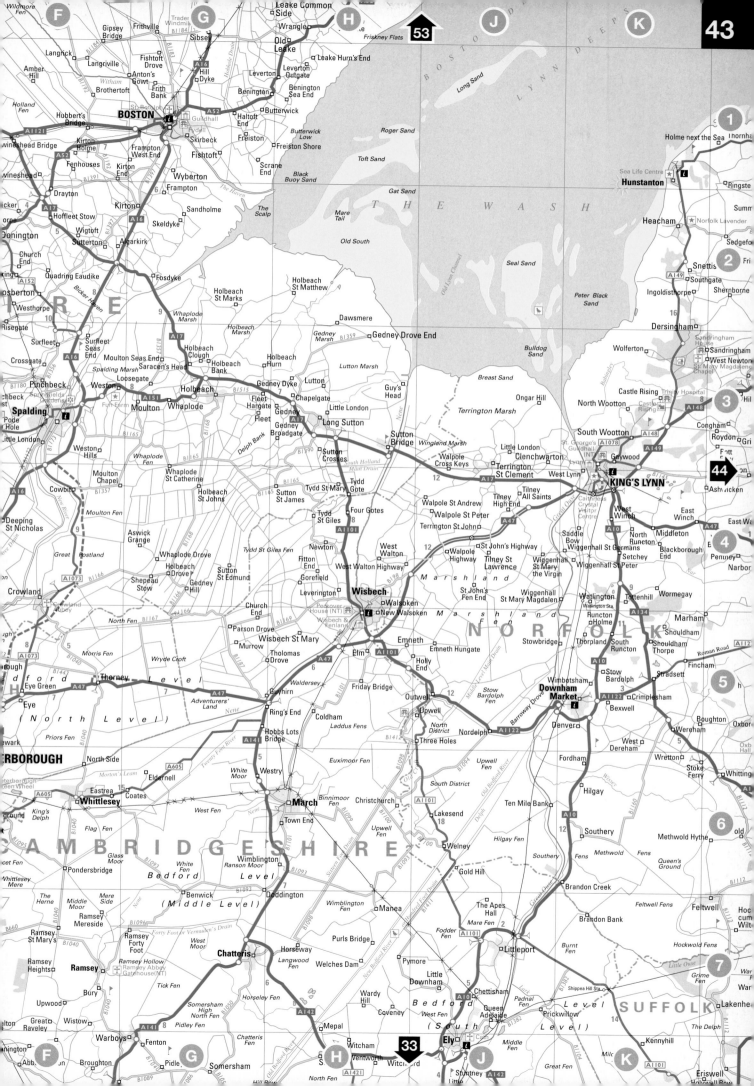

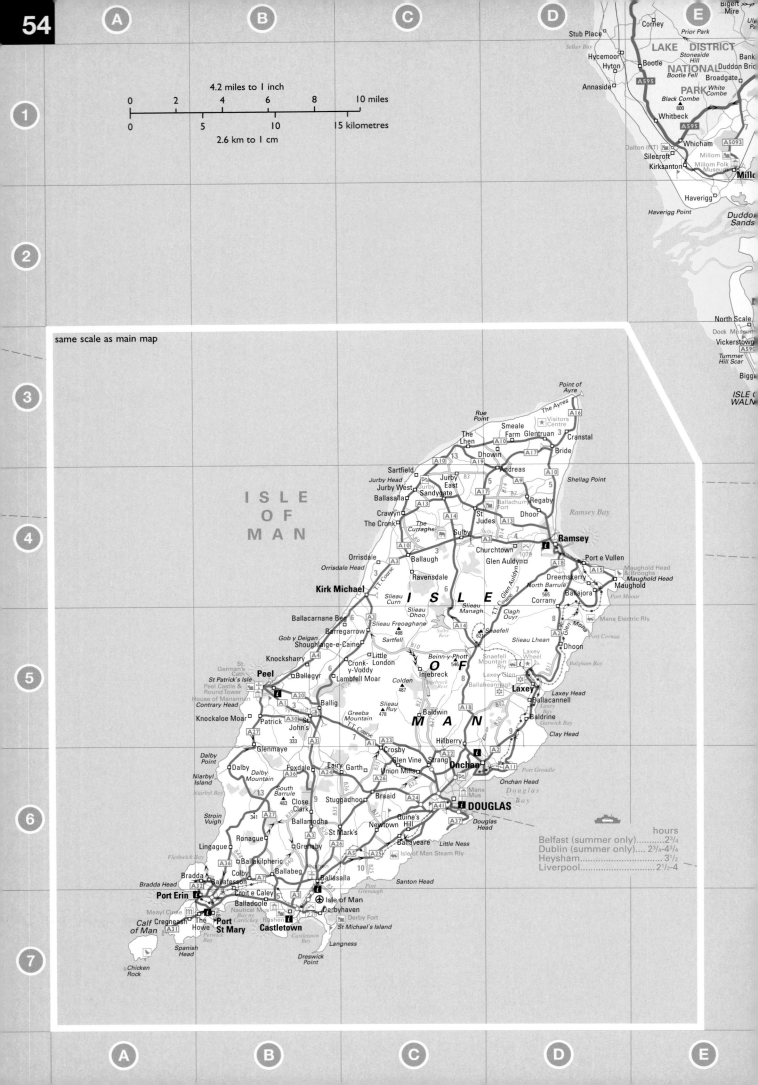

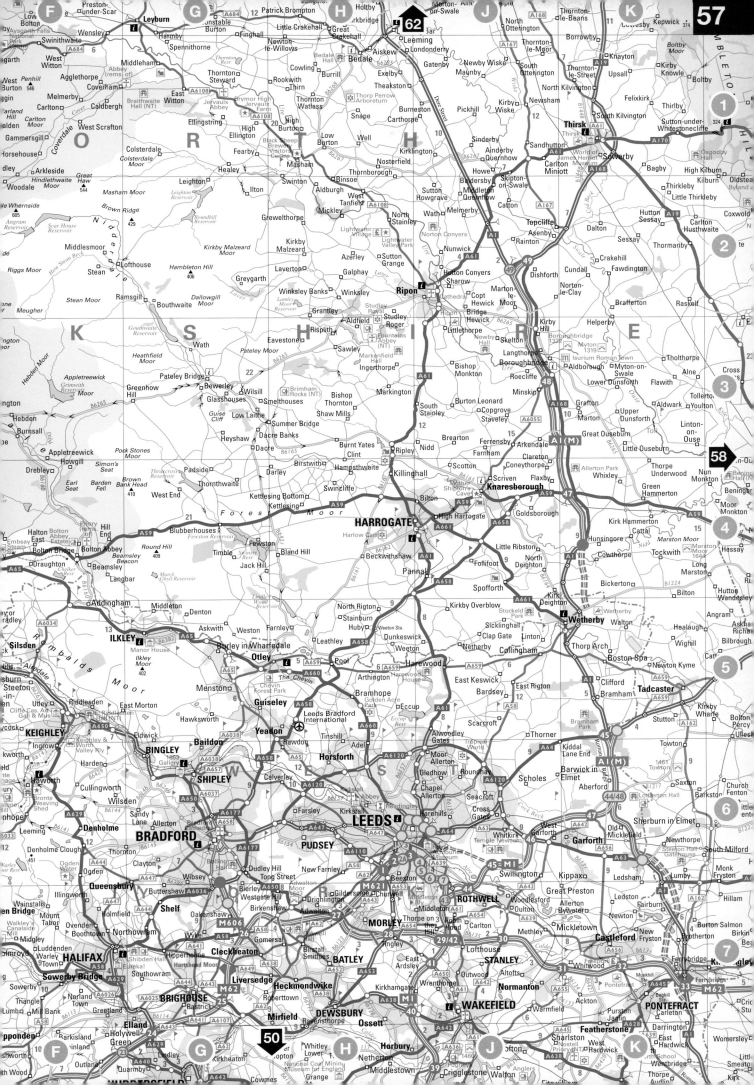

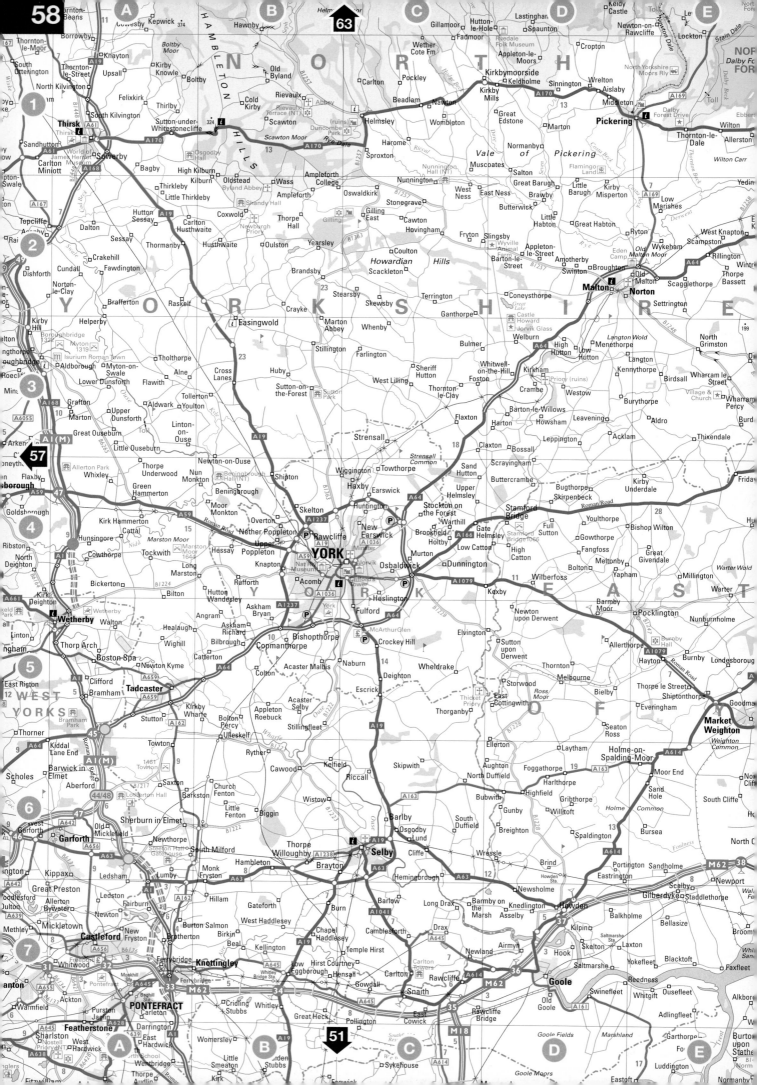

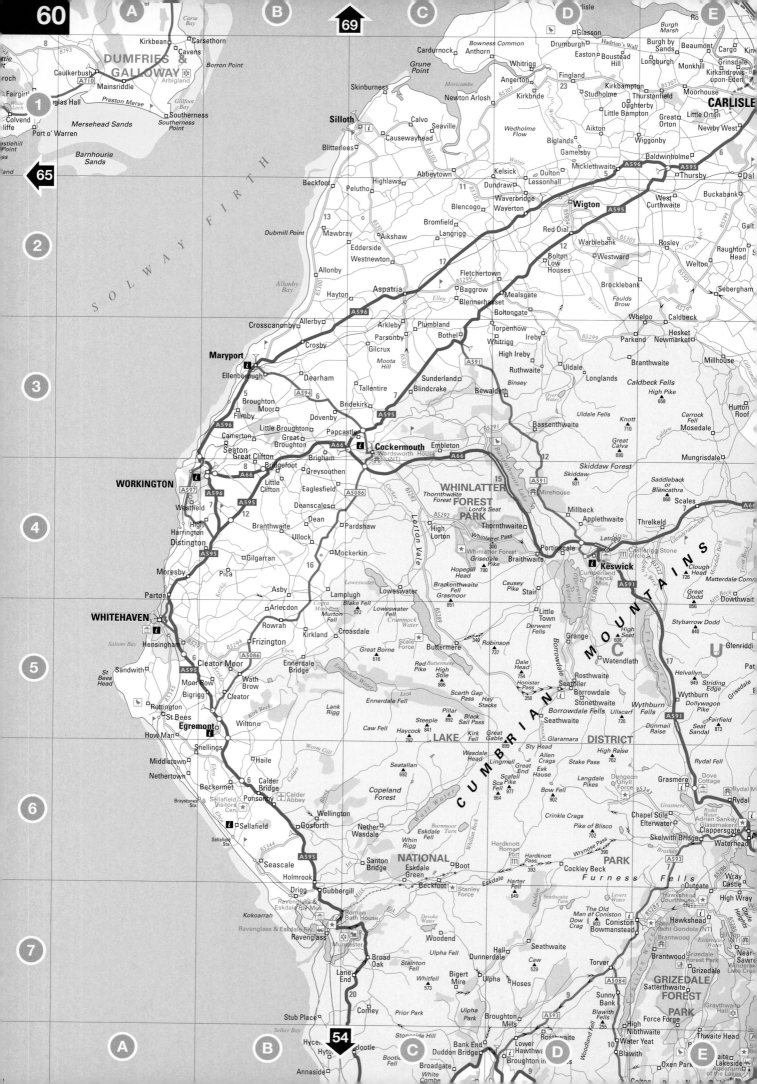

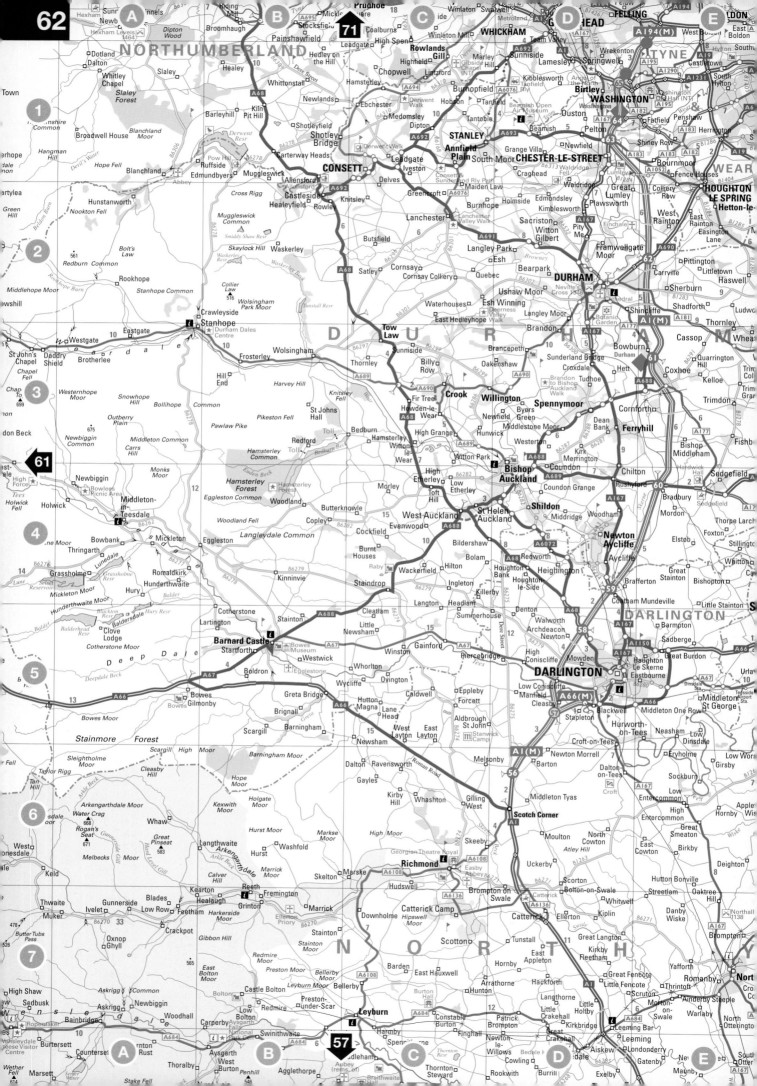

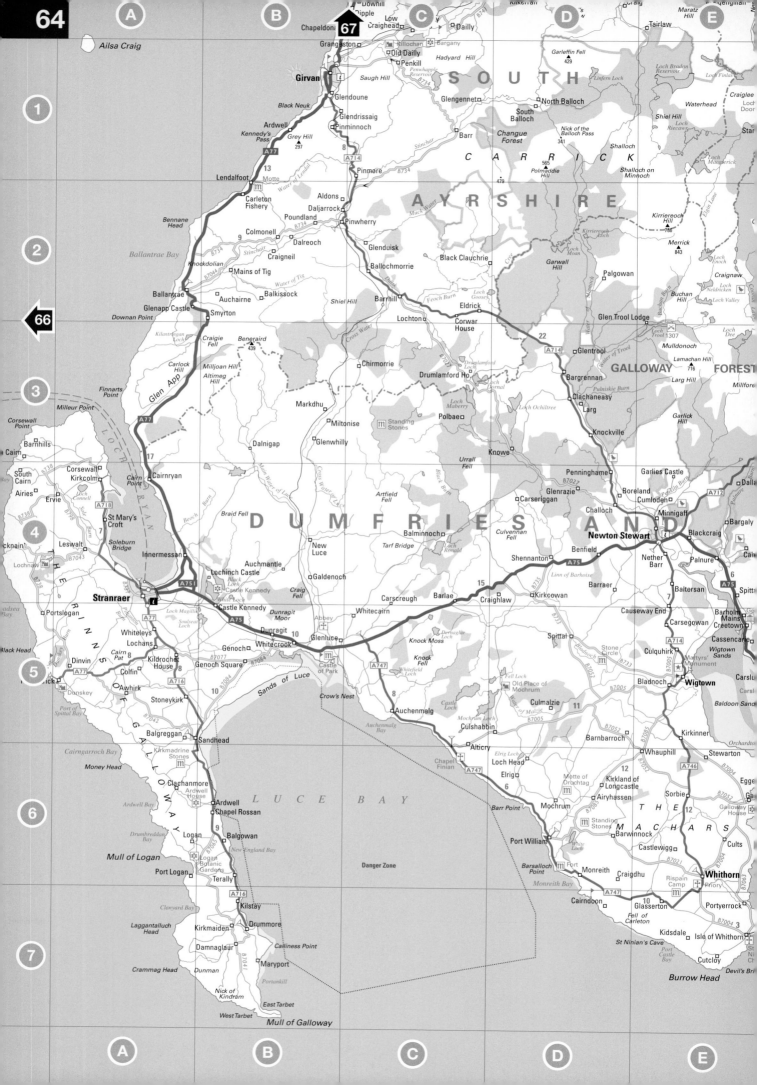

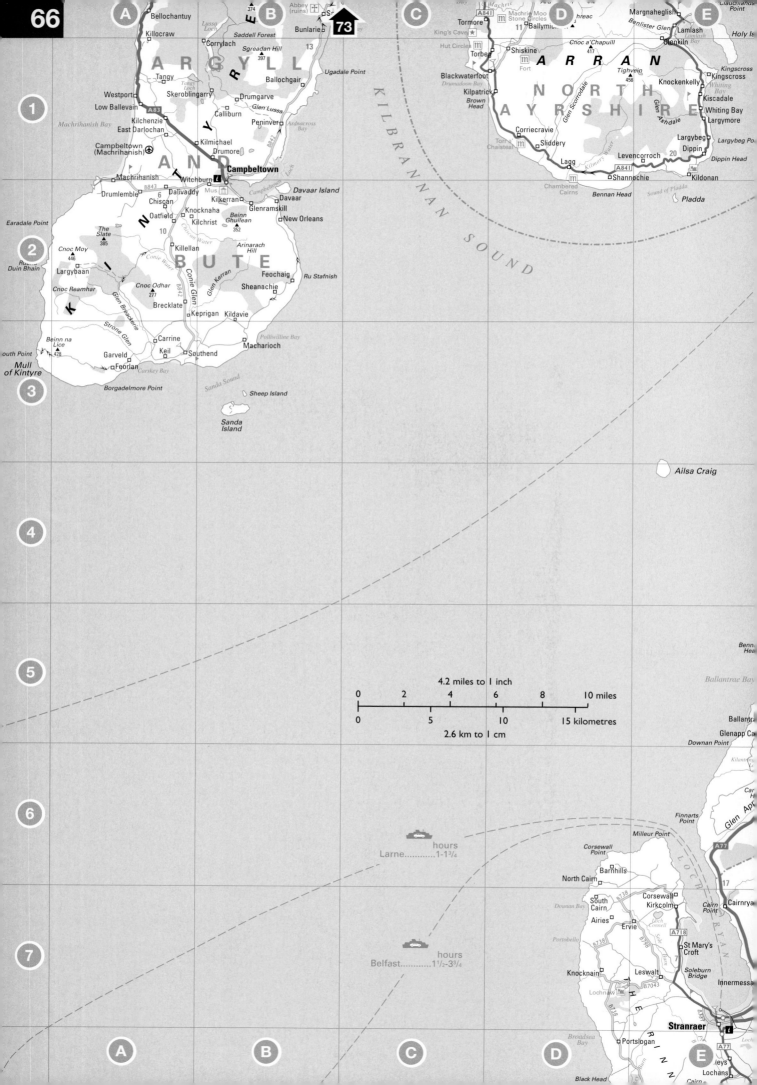

73

A · B · C · D · E

1
2
3
4
5
6
7

Bellochantuy
Killocraw
Corrylach
Tangy
Skeroblingarry
Ballochgair
Westport
Drumgarve
Low Ballevain
Glen Lussa
Kilchenzie
Calliburn
Peninver
East Darlochan
Kilmichael
Campbeltown
(Machrihanish)
Drumore
Machrihanish
Witchburn
Campbeltown
Dalivaddy
Davaar Island
Drumlemble
Dalivaddy
Davaar
Chiscan
Kilkerran
Knocknaha
Glenramskill
Oatfield
Kilchrist
New Orleans
The Slate
385
Beinn
Ghuilean
352
Killellan
Arinarach
Hill
Cnoc Moy
446
Feochaig
Ru Stafnish
Largybaan
Sheanachie
Cnoc Reamhar
Cnoc Odhar
277
Glen Kerran
Brecklate
Keprigan
Kildavie
Beinn na
Lice
428
Carrine
Mull
of Kintyre
Garveld
Keil
Southend
Macharioch
Feorlan
Borgadelmore Point
Carskey Bay
Sanda Sound
Sheep Island
Sanda
Island

ARGYLL
Saddell Forest
Sgreadan Hill
397
Abbey
(ruins)
Bunlarie
13
Ugadale Point
Lussa
Loch
Tangy
Loch
A83
Machrihanish Bay
Earadale Point
Rubha
Duin Bhain
KINTYRE
B842
Conie Water
Conie Glen
B842
Strone Glen
Glen Breackerie
outh Point
Polliwilline Bay
Ru Stafnish

Tormore
Machrie Moor
Stone Circles
Ballymi
Margnaheglish
Lamlash
Holy Is
King's Cave
Hut Circles
Shiskine
Torbeg
Cnoc a'Chapuill
417
ARRAN
Glenkin
Lamlash
Bay
Blackwaterfoot
Kilpatrick
Fort
Tighvein
458
Knockenkelly
Brown
Head
NORTH
AYRSHIRE
Kingscross
Kiscadale
Whiting Bay
Largymore
Drumadoon Bay
Torr a
Chaisteal
Corriecravie
Glen Scorrodale
Sliddery
Largybeg
Largybeg Po
Dippin
Lagg
A841
Levencorroch
20
Dippin Head
Chambered
Cairns
Shannochie
Kildonan
Bennan Head
Sound of Pladda
Pladda

KILBRANNAN SOUND

Ailsa Craig

Ballantrae Bay

Benn
Hea

Ballantra
Glenapp Ca
Downan Point

4.2 miles to 1 inch

| 0 | 2 | 4 | 6 | 8 | 10 miles |

| 0 | 5 | 10 | 15 kilometres |

2.6 km to 1 cm

Larne............1-1¾
hours

Belfast............1½-3¾
hours

Finnarts
Point
Glen App
Milleur Point
Corsewall
Point
A77
Barnhills
North Cairn
17
Corsewall
South
Cairn
Kirkcolm
Cairn
Point
Cairnrya
Airies
Ervie
A718
St Mary's
Croft
Knocknain
Leswalt
Soleburn
Bridge
Innermessa
Lochnaw
B7043
Stranraer
A77
Broadsea
Bay
Portslogan
Black Head
Lochans
leys
Cairn

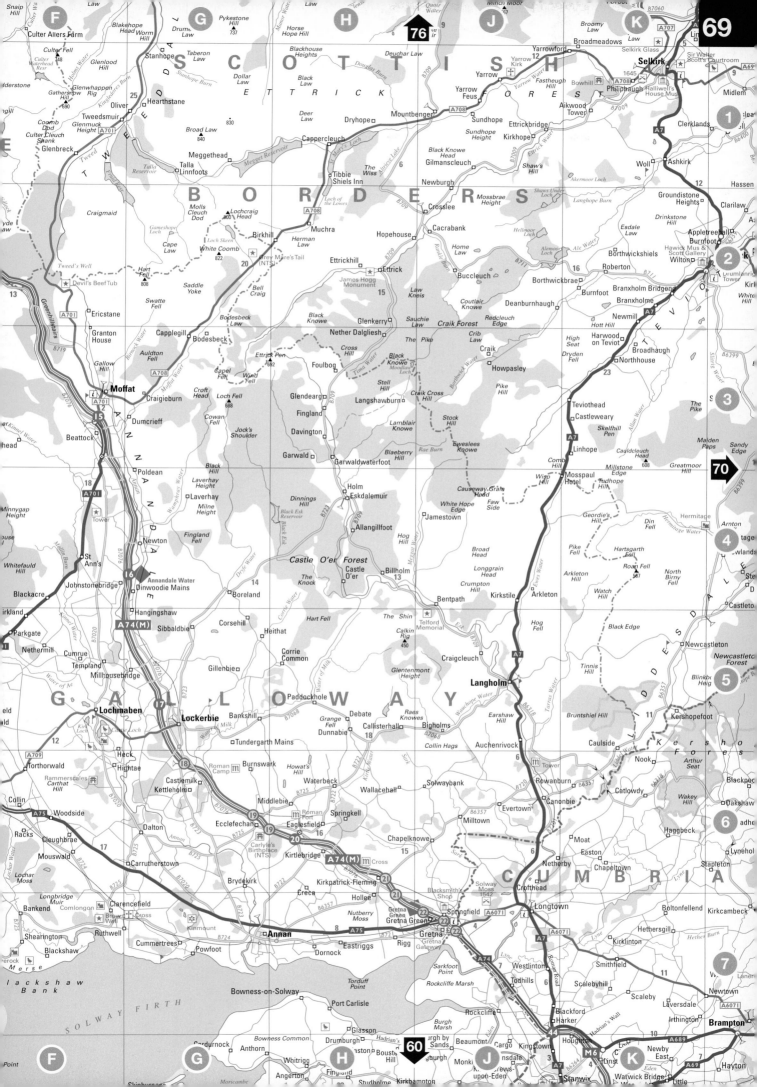

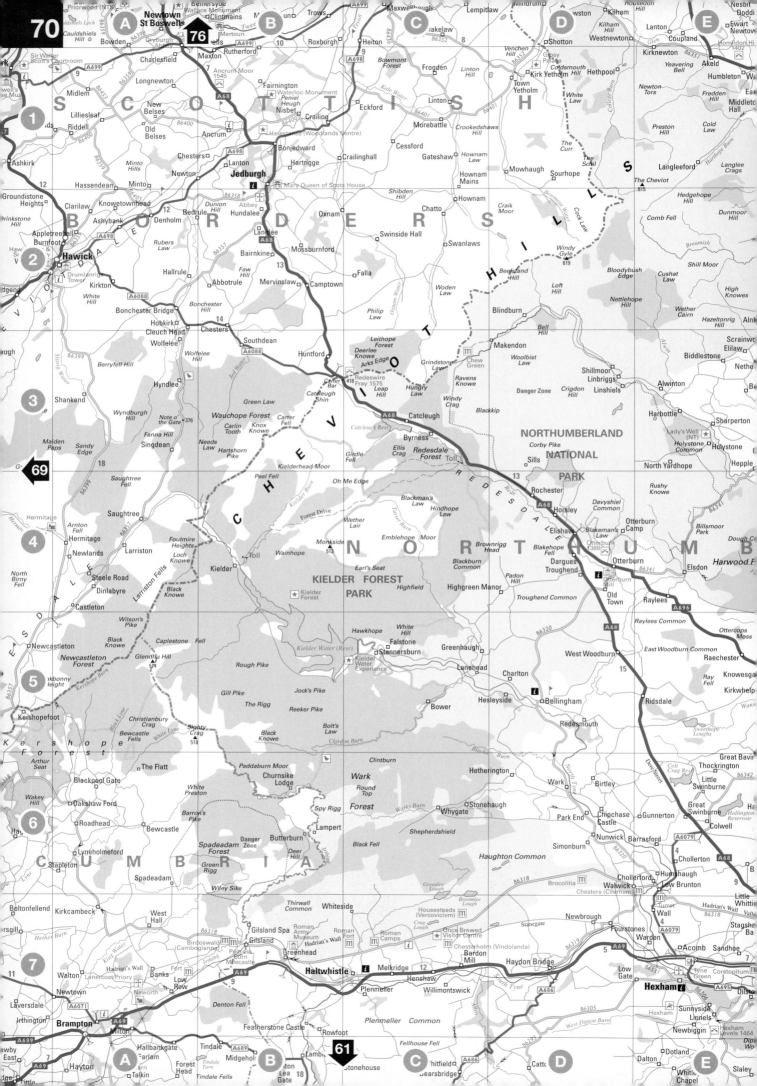

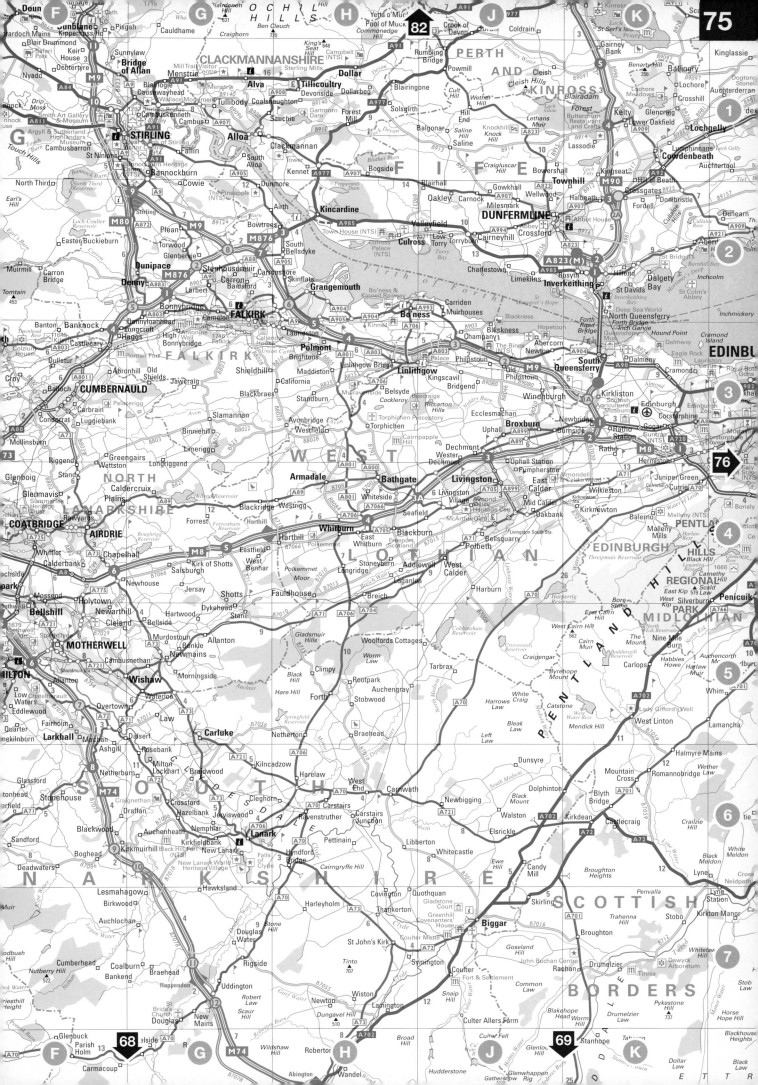

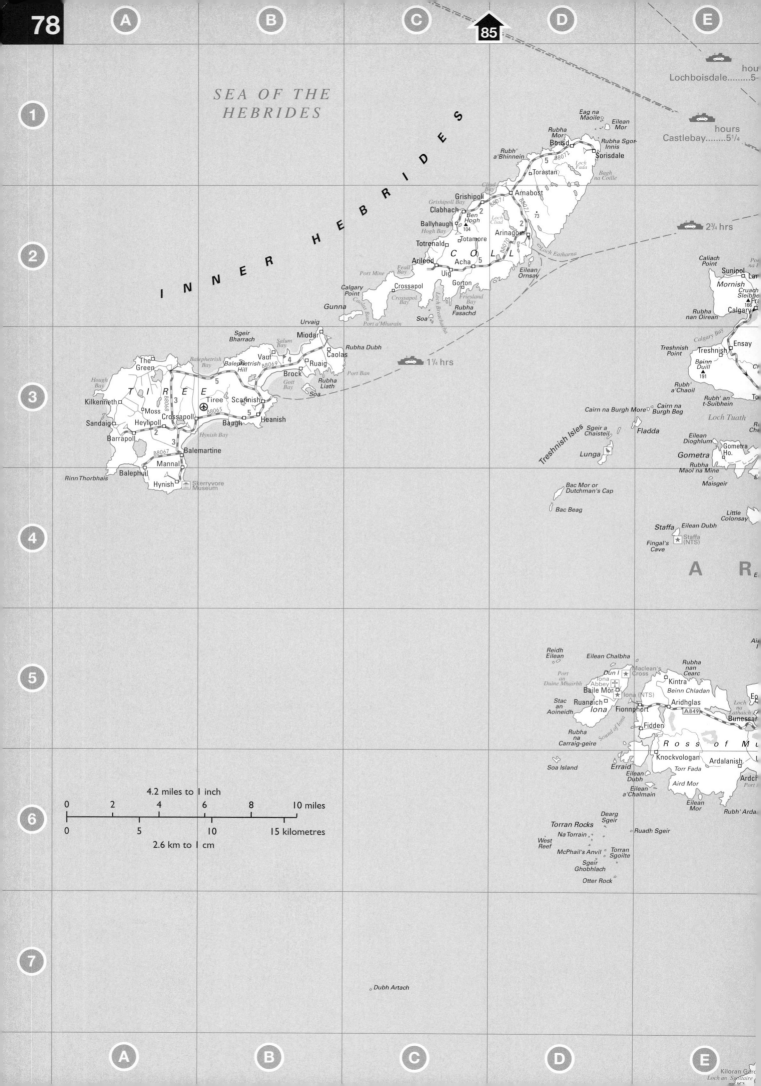

A   B   C   D   E

85

SEA OF THE HEBRIDES

1

INNER HEBRIDES

Lochboisdale.........5-

hour

Castlebay........5¼ hours

Eag na
Maoile
Eilean
Mor

Rubha
Mor

Bousd

Rubha Sgor
Innis

Sorisdale

Torastan

2¾ hrs

Grishipoll

Grishipoll Bay

Clabhach

Arnabost

Ben
Hogh

Ballyhaugh

104

Hogh Bay

Totamore

COLL

73

Arinagour

Totronald

Arileod

Acha   5

Loch Eatharna

Uig

Eilean
Ornsay

Port Mine

*Feall
Bay*

Gorton

Caliach
Point

Sunipol

Mornish

Cruach
Sleibhe

186

*Calgary
Point*

Crossapol

*Crossapol
Bay*

Rubha
nan Oirean

Calgary

Gunna

*Friesland
Bay*

Rubha
Fasachd

Soa

Calgary Bay

Port a'Mhurain

Urvaig

Miodar

Sgeir
Bharrach

*Salum
Bay*

Rubha Dubh

Treshnish
Point

Treshnish

Ensay

*Balephetrish
Bay*

Vaul

Caolas

Beinn
Duill

191

2

*The
Green*

Balephetrish
Hill

Brock

Ruaig

Port Ban

Rubha
a'Choaill

Rubh'
a'Choaill

Rubh'
a't-Suibhein

*Hough
Bay*

4

Gott Bay

Rubha
Liath

1¼ hrs

TIREE

5

Soa

Loch Tuath

3

Kilkenneth

Tiree

Scarinish

Cairn na Burgh More

Cairn na
Burgh Beg

Moss

5

Sgeir a
Chaisteil

Eilean
Dioghlum

Gometra
Ho.

Crossapol

Heanish

Fladda

Sandaig

Heylipoll

Gometra

Treshnish Isles

Baugh

Lunga

Rubha
Maol na Mine

Barrapoll

Maisgeir

Mannal

Balemartine

Hynish Bay

Bac Mor or
Dutchman's Cap

Balephuil

Bac Beag

Rinn Thorbhais

Hynish

Skerryvore
Museum

Staffa

Eilean Dubh

Little
Colonsay

4

Fingal's
Cave

Staffa
(NTS)

A   R

Reidh
Eilean

Eilean Chalbha

Rubha
nan
Cearc

5

*Port
an
Duine Mhairbh*

Dun I

Maclean's
Cross

Iona
Abbey

Kintra

Baile Mor

Beinn Chladan

Iona (NTS)

Stac
an
Aoineidh

Ruanaich

Iona

Fionnphort

Aridhglas

A849

Bunessan

Fidden

Rubha
na
Carraig-geire

Ross   of   Mu

Soa Island

Erraid

Knockvologan

Torr Fada

Ardalanish

Eilean
Dubh

Aird Mor

Eilean
a'Chalmain

Ardch

Eilean
Mor

Rubh' Arda

Dearg
Sgeir

6

Torran Rocks

Na Torrain

Ruadh Sgeir

West
Reef

McPhail's Anvil

Torran
Sgoilte

Sgeir
Ghobhlach

Otter Rock

4.2 miles to 1 inch

0   2   4   6   8   10 miles

0   5   10   15 kilometres

2.6 km to 1 cm

7

Dubh Artach

A   B   C   D   E

Kiloran Gar
Loch an Sgolaire

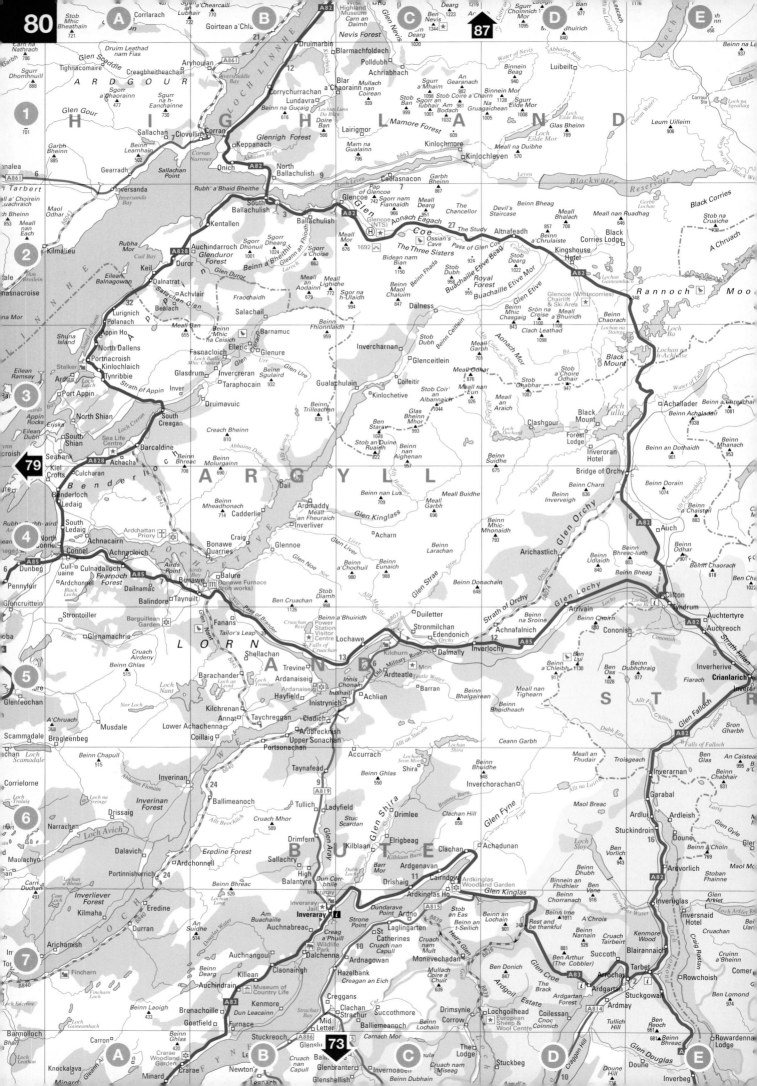

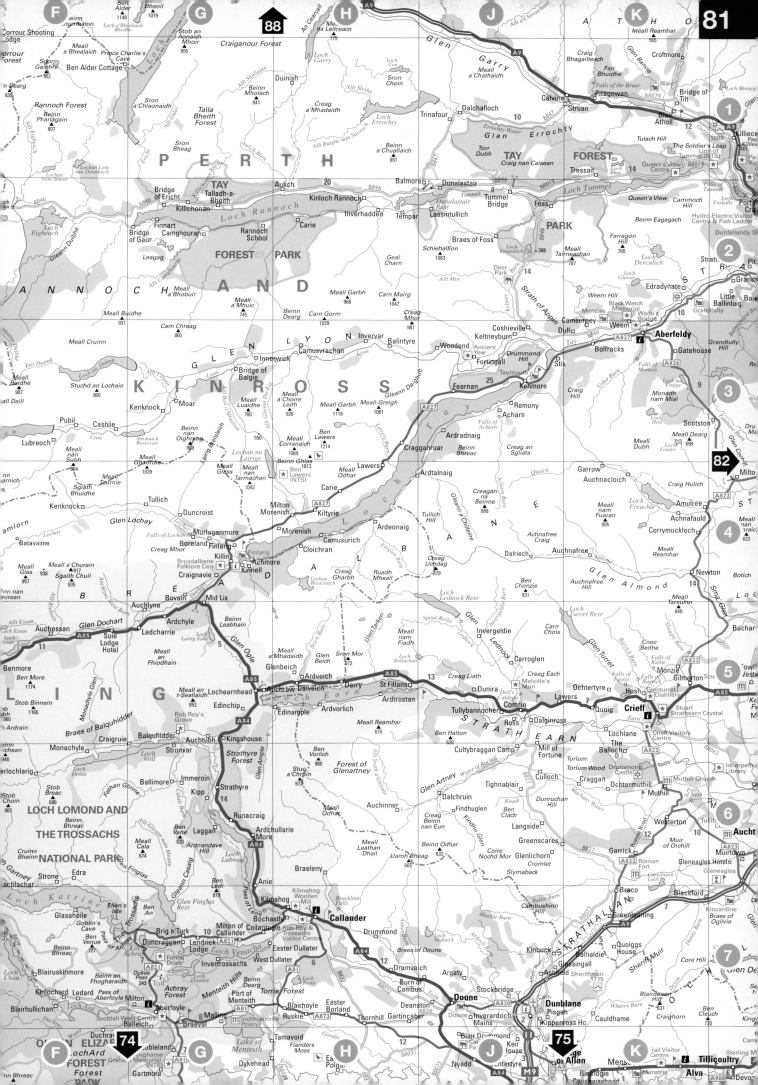

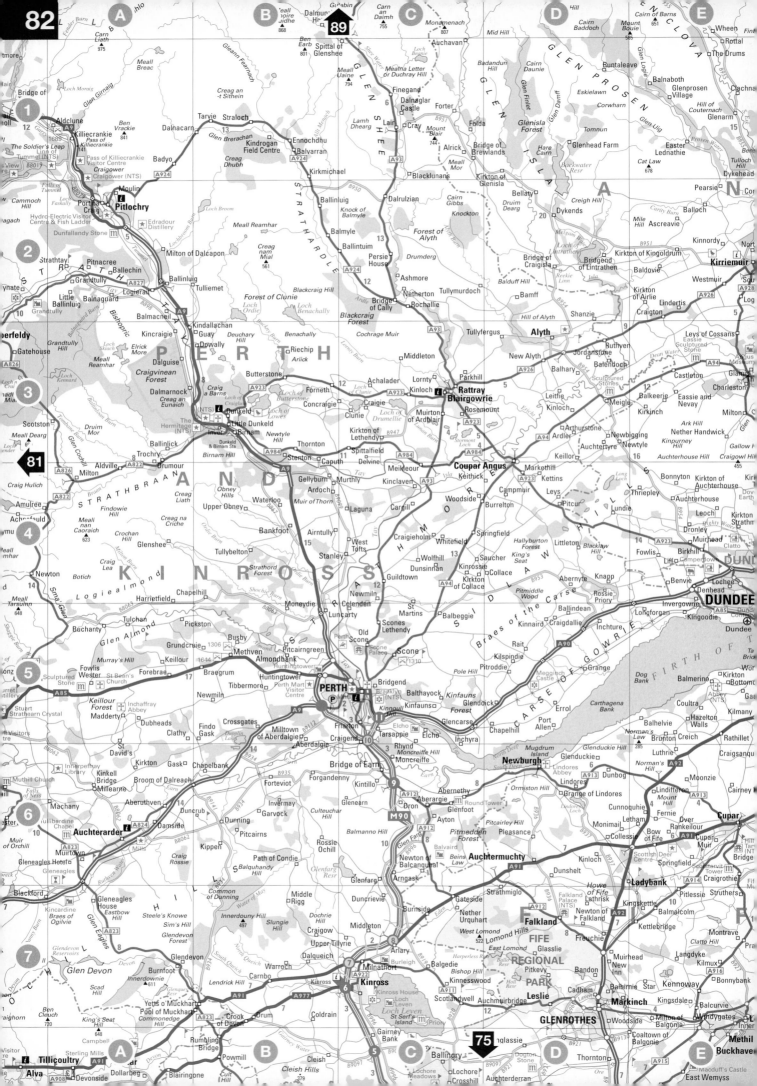

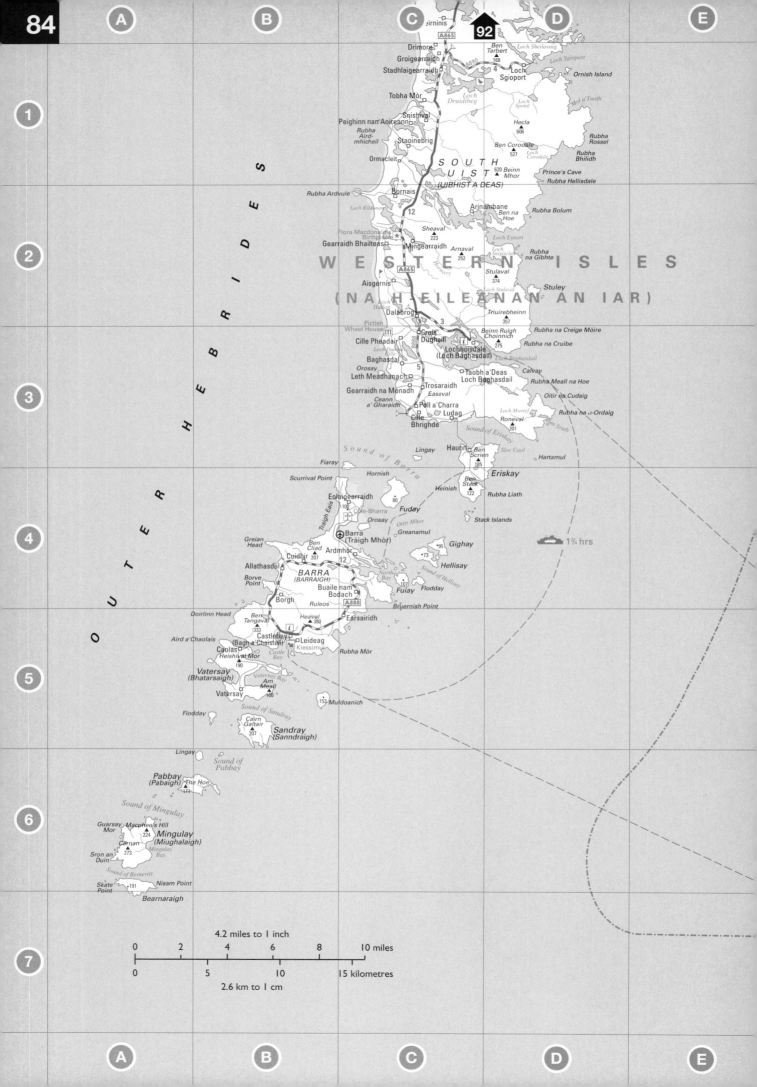

93

The Hoe
233
Lorgill
(Macleod's
Table South)
488
Balmore
Glen Osc
Ose
Ose
Glen
na
cloiche
232
Am Maol
212
Beinn
na
Beinne
K
Camastian

Ben Connan
244
Beinn na Boineid
371
Harlosh
Point
A863
Dun
Beag
Bracadale
Ben Duagrich
304
Stroc-
bheinn
400
Mugeary
Glenmore
A87
Lower Ollach

Ben Idrigill
340
Harlosh
Island
Tarner
Island
Ullinish
Strdan
Coillore
S   **K**   **Y**   **E**
1
Upper

An
Dubh
Sgeir
MacLeod's
Maidens
Loch
Bracadale
Idrigill Point
Wiay
Oronsay
Ardtreck
Point
Portnalong
Fernilea
A863
Beinn
Totaig
Roineval
439
Meall
an
Fhuarain
7
Ben Lee
445
Peinchorran

Rubha nan
Clach
Arnaval
369
Gleann Oraid
Carbost
6
Drynoch
B8009
Glen Drynoch
A863
Broc-bheinn
6
Glen Varragill
Scor

I
N
N
E
R
Talisker
Bay
Talisker
Stockval
416
Talisker
Beinn
Bhreac
370
Alli Dearg Mor
Glen Sligachan
Sligachan
Glamaig
775

H
E
B
R
I
D
E
S
Biod
Mor
383
Beinn Bhreac
445
HIGHLAND
Beinn
Dearg
2

Eynort
Beinn
a'Bhraghad
461
Cuillin Hills
Am
B

Minginish
Beinn Staic
411
Sgurr
Thuilm
879
Bruach
na Frithe
958
Sgurr
a'Mhadaidh
918
Sgurr
nan
Gillean
935 965
Harta
Corrie
Garbh
8

Loch Eynort
An Cruachan
435
Sgurr a'Ghreadaidh
973
Sgurr Mhic Choinnich
948
Sligachan
Bla Bhein
92

Glenbrittle
Bualintur
Sgurr Dearg
(Inaccessible Pinnacle)
986
Sgurr na Banachdich
986
Sgurr
Dubh
Mor
944
Loch
Coruisk
Sgurr
na Stri
497
Str
Camasu
K

Beinn an Eoin
312
Culnameán
Sgurr Alasdair
993
Sgurr nan Eag
924
Gars-
bheinn
895
Loch na
Creitheac

Rubha Thearna
Sgurr
Ceann
na
Beinne
Loch Brittle
Camas
3

Rubh' an
Dunain
Leac
nam
Faoileann
Soay Sound
Beinn
Bhreac
141
Loch Scavaig
Elgol

Soay
Camas
nan Gall
Prince
Charles's
Cave
R

Mol-
chlach

CUILLIN SOUND
86

CANNA
Carn
a'Ghaill
210
Compass
Hill
140
Rubha
Shamhnan Insir
4

Camas Tharbernish
Garrisdale Point
Canna
(NTS)
A'Chill
Canna
Harbour
Kilmory
Kilmory

Sron
Ruail
Tarbert Bay
Sanday
Sound of Canna
Sgaorishal
278
Mullach
Mor
304
Rubha
na
Roinne

Humla
Bloodstone Hill
388
National
Nature
Reserve
Kinloch
Kinloch

A'Bhrideanach
Orval
571
R U M
Bagh
na h-Uamha

Garbh Sgeir
Oigh-
sgeir
Sgor Reidh
An Dornabac
263
Barkeval
591
5

Harris
Hallival
723
Askival
812

Rubha
Sgor
an t-Snidhe
Ruinsival
528
Ainshval
781
Sgurr nan Gillean
764

Rubha nam Meirleach
SOUND OF RUM

Cleadale
An
Cruachan
299
6

Rubha
an
Fhasaidh
Bay of Laig
Beinn
Tighe
315
Laig

EIGG
An
Sgurr
393
Kildonnan

Eilean
nan Each
Godag
Sound of Eigg
Galmisdale

Rubh'
Leam na Laraich
Beinn
Airein
137
Port Mor
7

Muck

hours
Oban...............5-7

hours
Oban...............5¼

Sanna Point
Fascadale
Achateny
Kil

78

Point of
Ardnamurchan
Achnaha
Meall
nan
Con
437
Beinn na L
Achosnich
Meall an

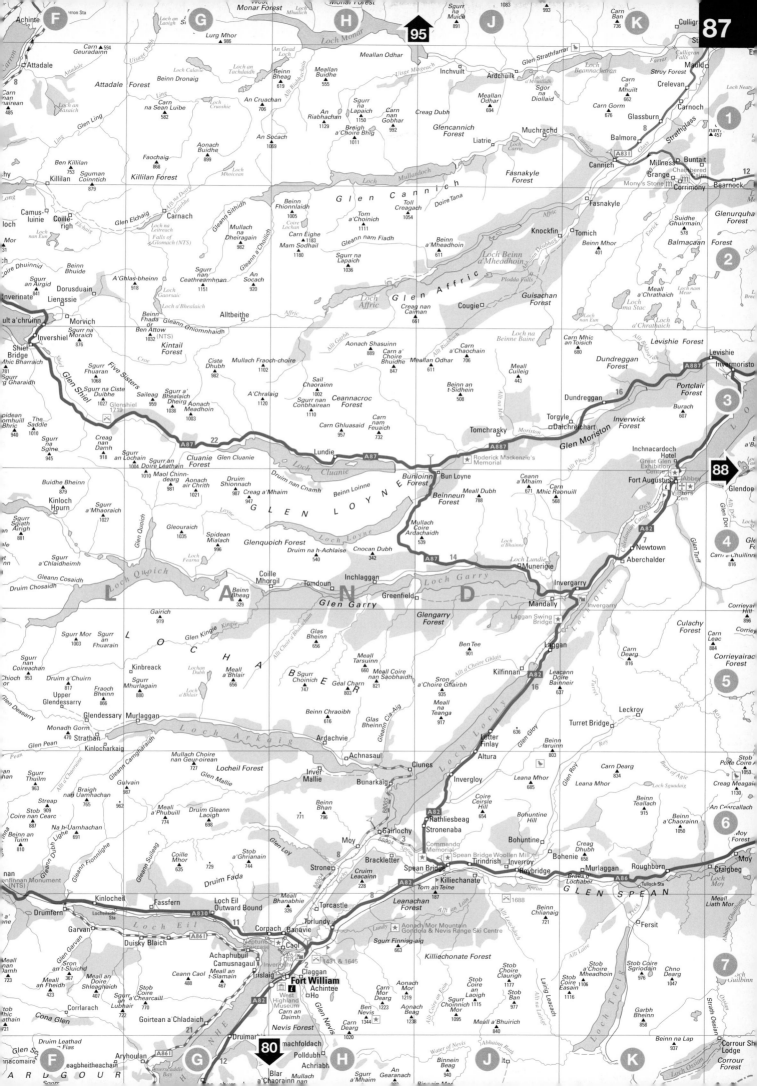

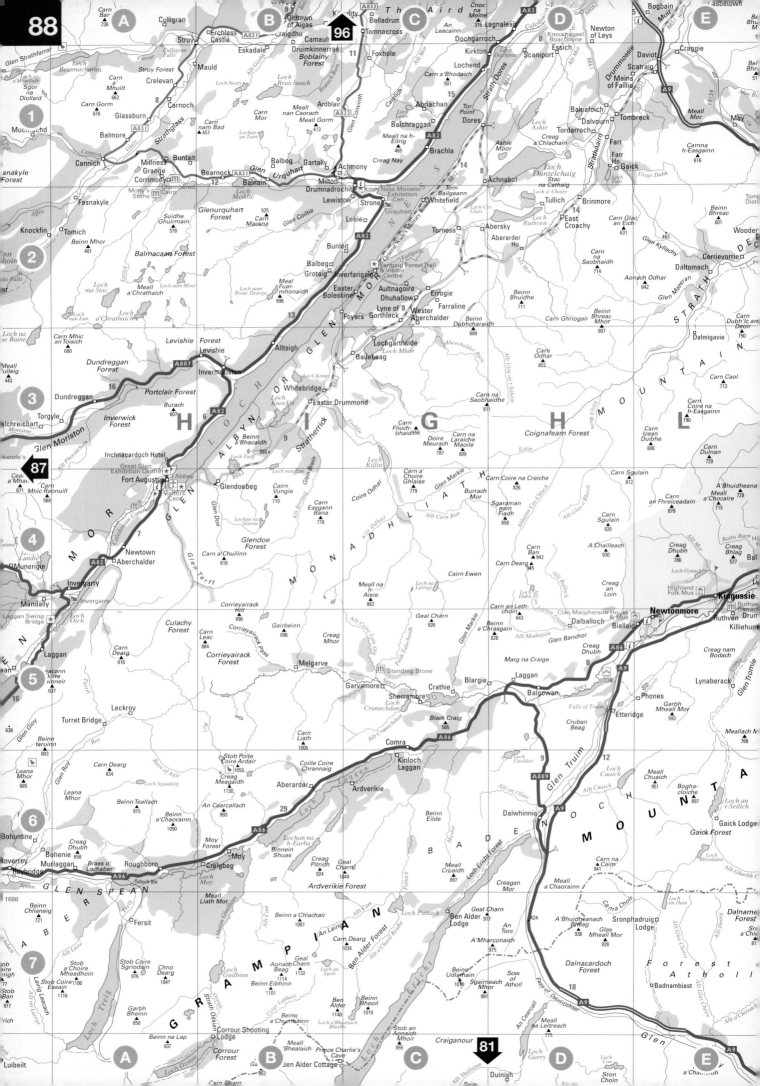

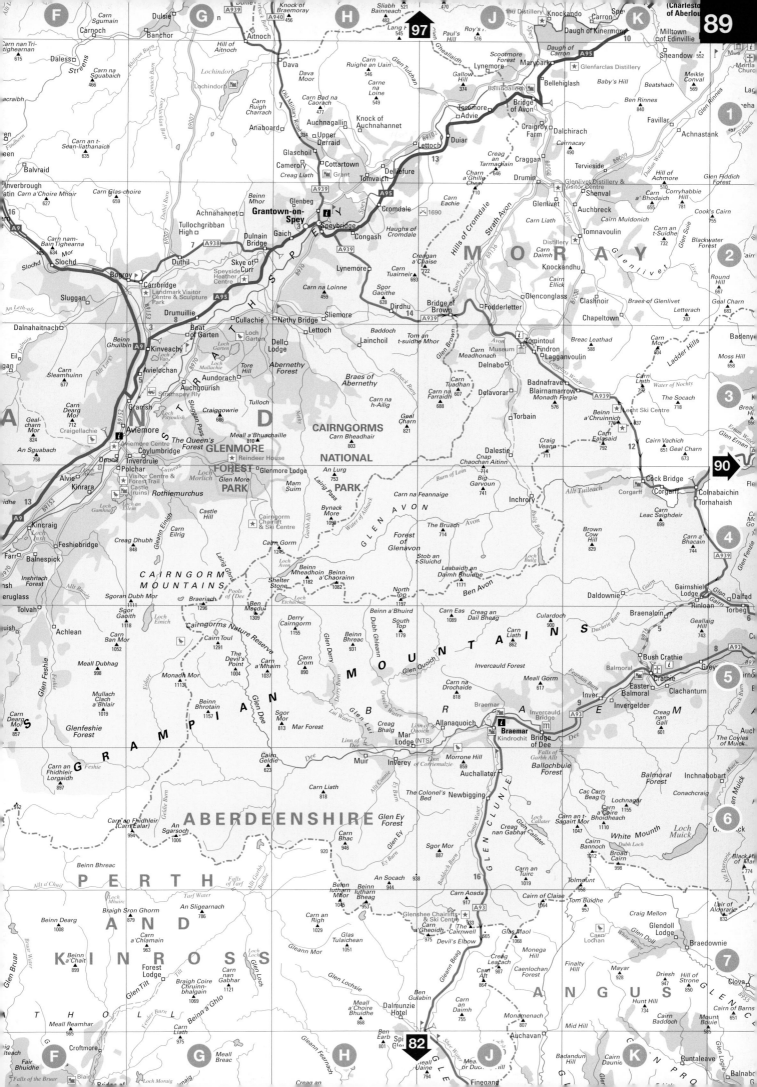

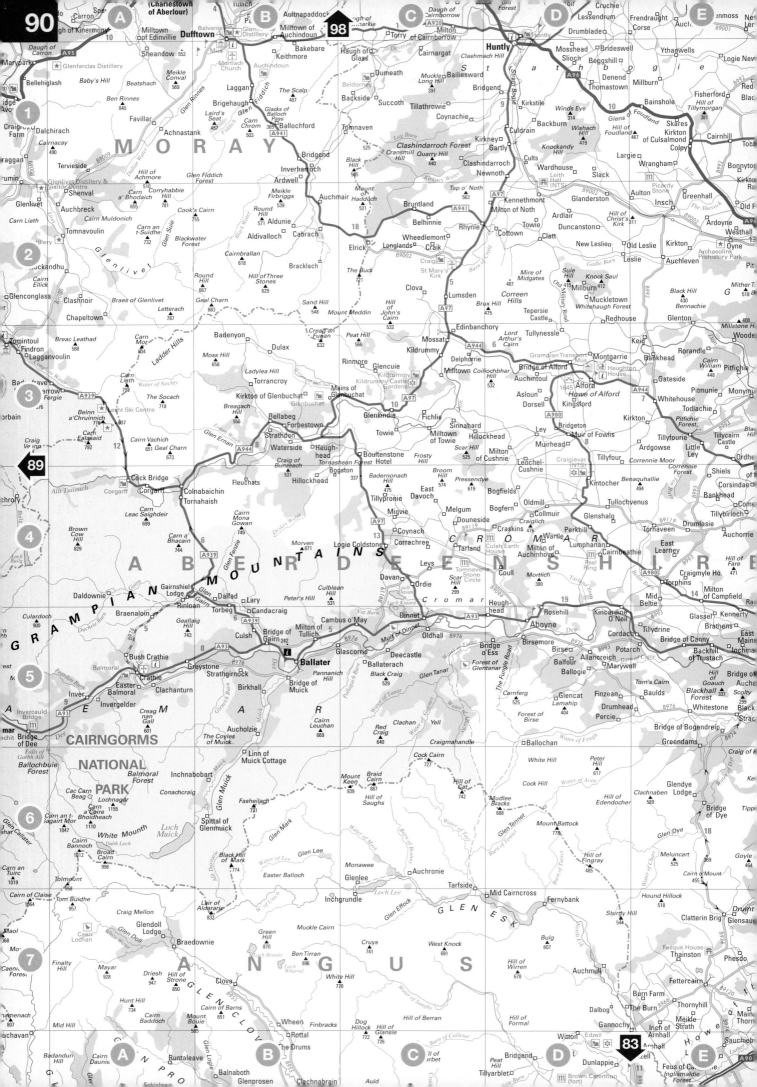

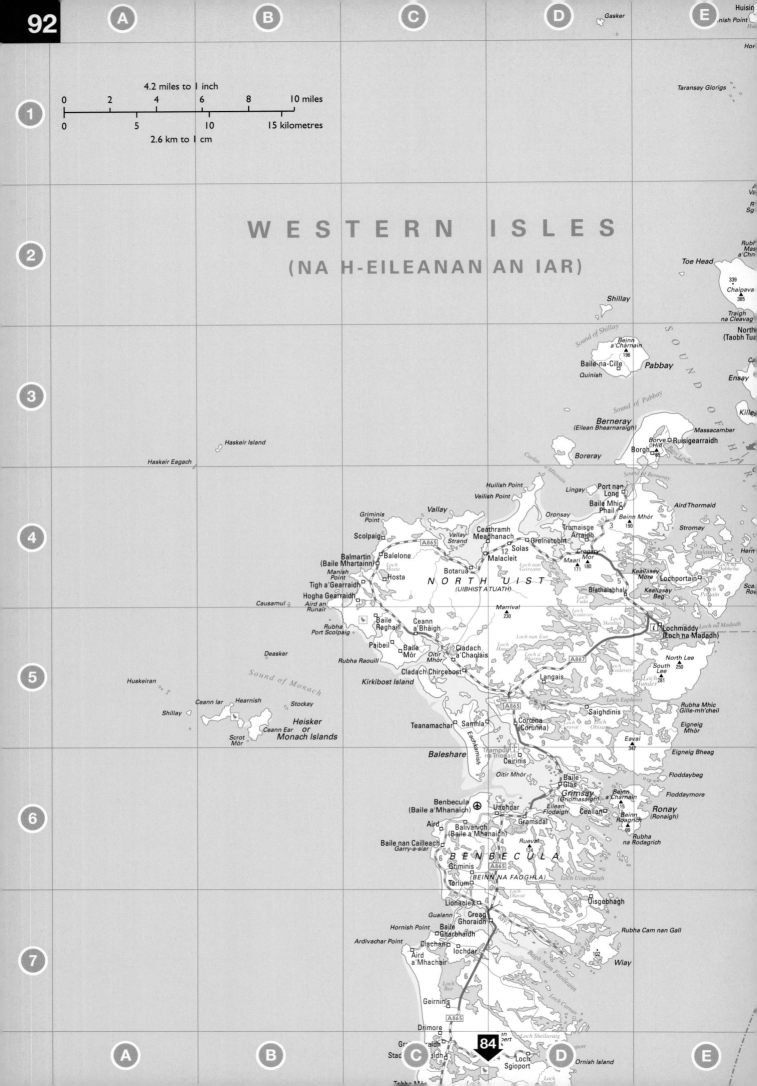

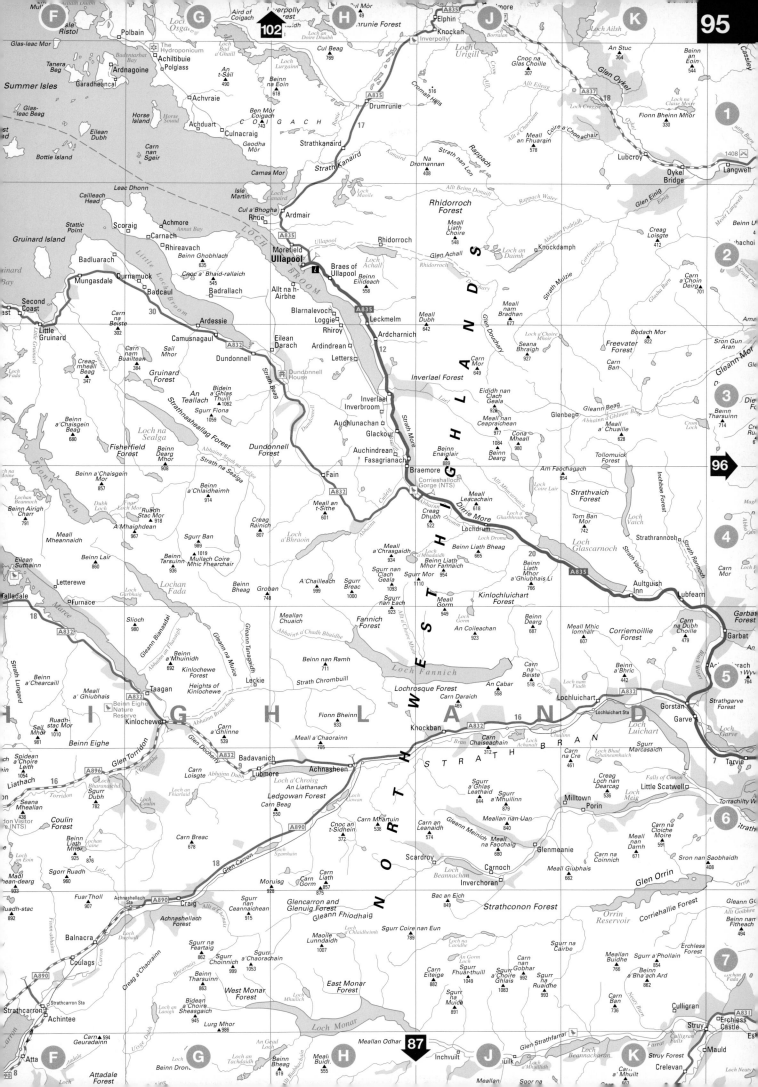

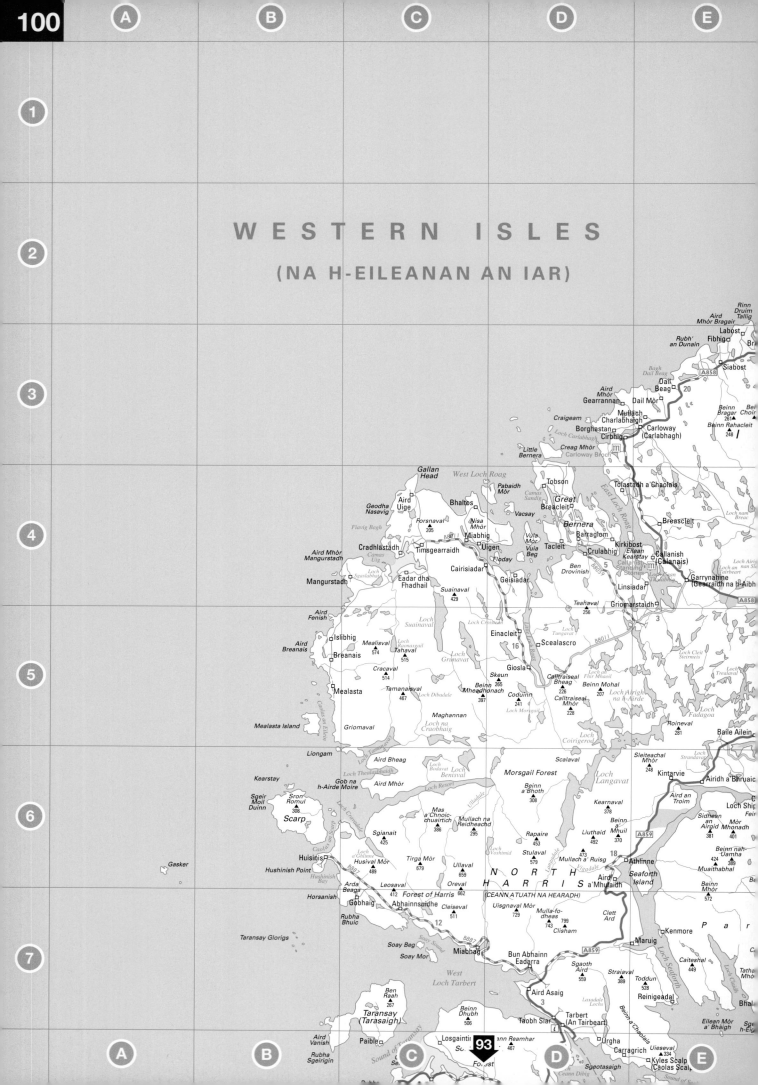

WESTERN ISLES

(NA H-EILEANAN AN IAR)

Butt of Lewis
(Rubha Robhanais)

Port a' Stoth

Cunndal

Teampull Mholuidh
Eoropaidh — Còig Peighinnean
Bad an Fhithich
Lional — Port Nis
Tabost
Suaineabost — Eorodal — *Port Skigersta*
Aird Dhail — Cross — Sgiogarstaigh
Dail Bho Dheas — Dail Bho Thuath
Meall Geal
Toa Galson — Glen Cross — Ness — *Port Alasdair*
Gabhsunn Bho Thuath — A857
Gabhsunn Bho Dheas — *Broch* — Cuidhaseadair
Mealabost — *Laimhrig*
Roinn a' Bhuic — *Airigh na Glaice*
Còig Peighinnean — *Cellar Head*
Siadar Iarach — *Ben Dell*
Siadar Uarach — *Airighean Beinn nan Caorach*
Rubha Leathann — *Airighean Loch Brèihavat*
Baile an Truiseil — *Loch Langavat*
Steinacleit Cairn & Standing Stones — *Diaval* — *Loch Mòr Sandavat*
Goile Broic — *Loch Mòr Bharabhais* — *Port Geiraha*
Black House — A857 — *Torrav*
Barvas *(Barabhas)* — *Loch Gress*
Brú — *Glen Shader* — *Geiraha*
Loch Urrahag — *Muirneag 248* — Tolastadh Ùr
Loch Casgro — Gleann *Mòr Bharabhais* — *Loch Mòr Sandavit* — Tolastadh
Loch Breivat — *Tolsta Head*
Gleann Bhruthadail — 11 — *Loch an Tobair* — *Port nam Bothag*
Loch Sgeireach Mòr — Gleann Tholastaidh
E O F — L E W I S — *Port Ban a' Ghlinne*
Roishal Mòr 174 — Griais — 12
ÌLEAN LEODHAIS) — Bac — *Creag Fhraoich*
Loch na Scuravat — Col
Beinn Mholach 292 — Breibhig — *Rubha Bhataisgeir*
Loch an Stùrr — Col Sands
Loch an Fhearnag — A857 — Tiumpan Head *(Rubha an t-Siumpain)*
Aird Thunga — Portnaguran *(Port nan Giùran)*
Newmarket — Tunga — *Sron Ruadh* — *Rubha Deas*
Stornoway *(Steornabhagh)* — Laxdale *(Lacasdal)* — Melbost Sands — A866
Laxdale — Siulaisiadar
Loch Vatandip — A858 — Stornoway — *Melbost Pt* — Garrabost — Seisiadar
Uraval — Stornoway *(Sanndabhaig)* — Melbost — *Rubha na Grèine*
13 — Lews Castle — *Aignis* — Eye Peninsula *(An Rubha)*
Beinn a'Bhuna — *Columba's Church* — Cnoc — Pabail Uarach
Creed — *Stornoway Harbour* — *Rubha na Bearnaich*
Arnish Pt. — Suardail — *Bagh Phabail*
Achadh Mòr — *Arnish Moor* — *Rubh a'Bhaigh Uaine* — Pabail Iarach
A859 — 6 — *Ceann na Circ*
Loch Thota am Bridein — *Loch Orasay*
Loch Nisreaval
Liurbost — Grimsiadar — *Loch Grimsiadar*
Loch Fada — Crosbost — *Raerinish Point*
Tabhaigh Mhor
12 — Ceos — *Eilean Chaluim Chille* — *Orasaigh*
Lacasaigh — Gleann Ghrabhair — *Torraigh*
Cearsiadar — Cabharstadh
Tabost — Gearraidh Bhaird — Marbhig
13 — Calbost
Loch Sgibacleit — *Rubha Iosal*
Glen Ourn — Grabhair — *Kebock Head*
Loch Shanndabhat — Tom an Fhuadain — *Loch Odhairn*
Leumrabhagh — *Gob na Milaid*
Loch Shell — *Srianach*
Eilean Iubhard
Uisenis 371 — Mulhagery
Mol Truisg
Gob Rubh'Uisenis
Rubha Bhrollum
Rubh a' Bhaird

Cellar Head — *Laimhrig*

T H E   M I N C H

🚢 **Ullapool**................2¾ **hours**

4.2 miles to 1 inch

0 — 2 — 4 — 6 — 8 — 10 miles

0 — 5 — 10 — 15 kilometres

2.6 km to 1 cm

Garbh Eilean 161

Eilean

SOUND OF SHIANT

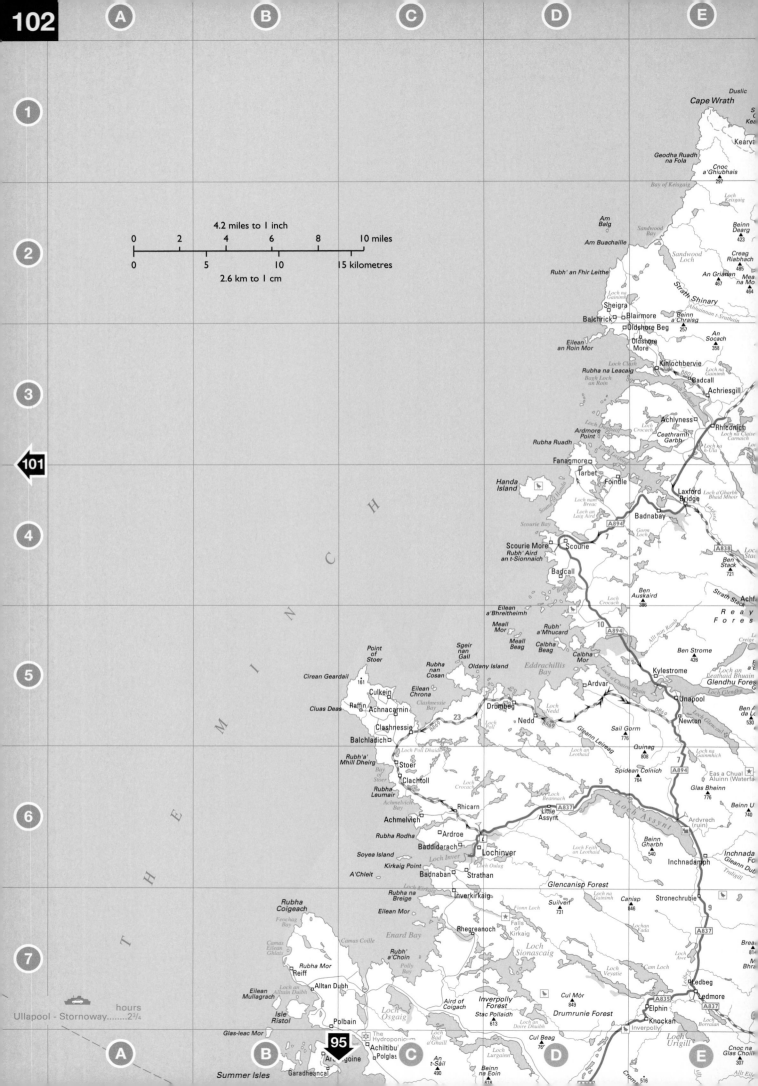

A B C D E

1

Cape Wrath
Duslic

Kearva

Geodha Ruadh
na Fola
Cnoc
a'Ghiubhais
297

2

4.2 miles to 1 inch

0   2   4   6   8   10 miles

0   5   10   15 kilometres

2.6 km to 1 cm

Am
Balg

Am Buachaille

Sandwood
Bay

Sandwood
Loch

Beinn
Dearg
423

Creag
Riabhach

Rubh' an Fhir Leithe

Loch na
Gainimh

Strath Shinary

Abhainn t-Srathain

An Grianan
467

Mea
na Mo
464

Sheigra

Balchrick

Blairmore

Oldshore Beg

Beinn
a'Chraisg
257

An
Socach
358

Eilean
an Roin Mor

Oldshore
More

3

Loch Clash

Kinlochbervie

B801

Loch na
Gainimh

Rubha na Leacaig

Bagh Loch
an Roin

Badcall

Achriesgill

Loch na Claise
Carnaich

Ardmore
Point

Ceathramh
Garbh

Achlyness

Rhiconich

Loch na
h-Ula

Rubha Ruadh

Fanagmore

Loch Laxford

101

Tarbet

Foindle

Laxford
Bridge

Loch a'Gharbh
Bhaid Mhoir

Handa
Island

Loch nam
Brèac

Badnabay

A894

Laxford

4

Scourie Bay

Loch an
Luig Aird

7

A838

Scourie More

Scourie

Gorm
Loch

Ben
Stack
721

Loch
Stac

Rubh' Aird
an t-Sionnaich

Badcall

Loch
Crocach

Ben
Auskaird
386

Strath Stack

Achf

Reay
Fores

Eilean
a'Bhreitheimh

10

A894

Allt nan Ramh

Meall
Mor

Rubh'
a'Mhucard

Calbha
Beag

Ben Strome
426

Loch
Creige

5

Point
of Stoer

Sgeir
nan
Gall

Meall
Beag

Calbha
Mor

Calbha
Beag

Loch an
Leathaid Bhuain

Ben A
da Lo
530

Cirean Geardail

Rubha nan
Cosan

Oldany Island

Eddrachillis
Bay

Kylestrome

Glendhu Fores

161

Culkein

Eilean
Chrona

Loch a'Chuirn Bhuin

Ardvar

Unapool

Loch Glendhu

Cluas Deas

Raffin

Achnacarnin

Clashnessie
Bay

Drumbeg

Loch
Nedd

B869

Newton

Balchladich

Clashnessie

B869

23

Nedd

B869

Gleann Leireag

Sail Gorm
776

Loch
Poll

Loch Poll Dhaidhin

Loch an
Leothaid

Quinag
808

Loch na
Gainimhich

Rubh'a'
Mhill Dheirg

Stoer

A894

Bay
of
Stoer

Clachtoll

Spidean Coinich
764

Eas a' Chual
Aluinn (Waterfa

Rubha
Leumair

Loch
Crocach

9

Glas Bheinn
776

Achmelvich
Bay

Rhicarn

Little
Assynt

A837

Loch Assynt

Ardvreck
(ruin)

Beinn U
740

6

Achmelvich

Rubha Rodha

Ardroe

Beinn
Gharbh
540

Inchnada
Fo
Gleann Dub

Soyea Island

Baddidarach

Lochinver

Loch Inver

Loch Feith
an Leothaid

Inchnadamph

Tralgill

Kirkaig Point

Badnaban

Strathan

Loch Outag

Glencanisp Forest

A'Chleit

Loch Kirkaig

Rubha na
Breige

Inverkirkaig

Loch na
Gainimh

Canisp
846

Stronechrubie

9

A837

Rubha
Coigeach

Eilean Mor

Rhegreanoch

Suilven
731

Feochag
Bay

Fionn Loch

Falls
of
Kirkaig

Lochan
Fada

Beinn
814

M
Bhre

Enard Bay

Camas Coille

Rubh'
a'Choin

Polly
Bay

Aird of
Coigach

Loch
Sionascaig

Cam Loch

Ledbeg

Ledmore

A835

A837

7

Rubha Mor

Reiff

Alltan Dubh

Loch
Veyatie

Loch
Awe

Ullapool - Stornoway........2¾ hours

Eilean
Mullagrach

Loch an
Alltan Duibh

Inverpolly
Forest

Cul Mòr
849

Drumrunie Forest

Elphin

Isle Ristol

Polbain

Loch
Osgaig

Stac Pollaidh
613

Loch an
Doire Dhuibh

Cul Beag
76°

Knockan

Loch
Borralan

Glas-leac Mor

95

The
Hydroponicum

Achiltibu

Polglas

An
t-Sàil

Loch
Lurgainn

Beinn
na Eoin
490

Cul Beag

D

Inverpolly

Loch
Urigill

Cnoc na
Glas Choill
307

Summer Isles

Arc...goine

Garadheancal

A

B

C

Beinn
618

Crom
516

E

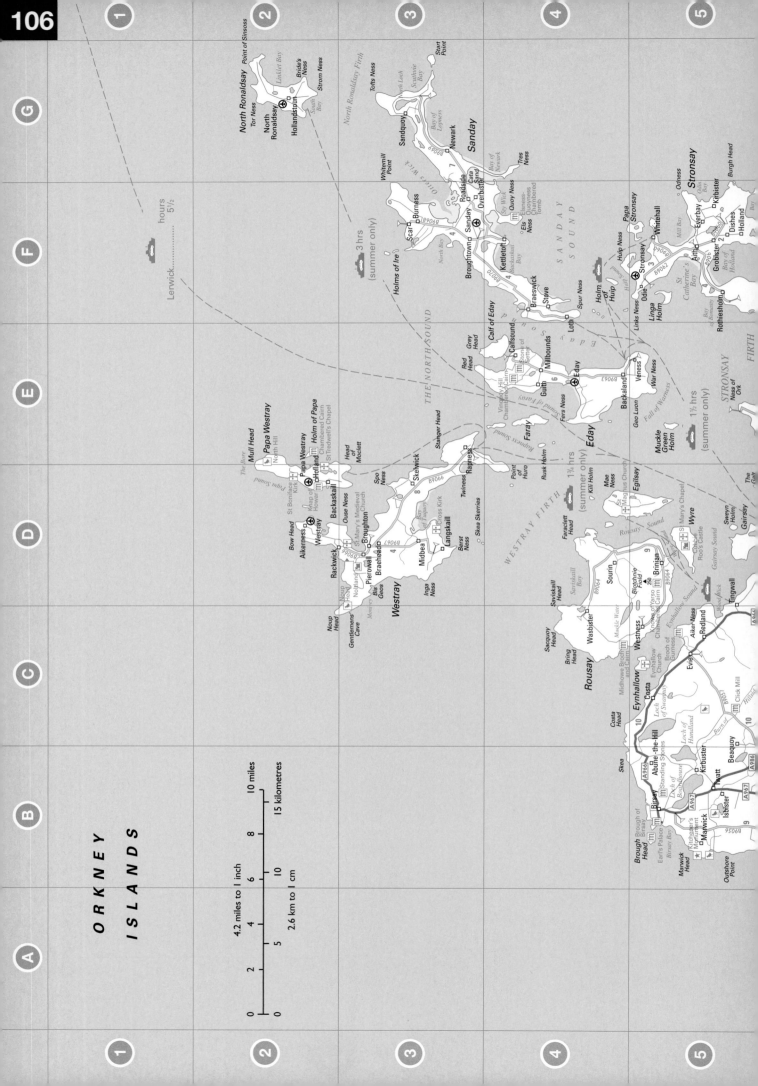

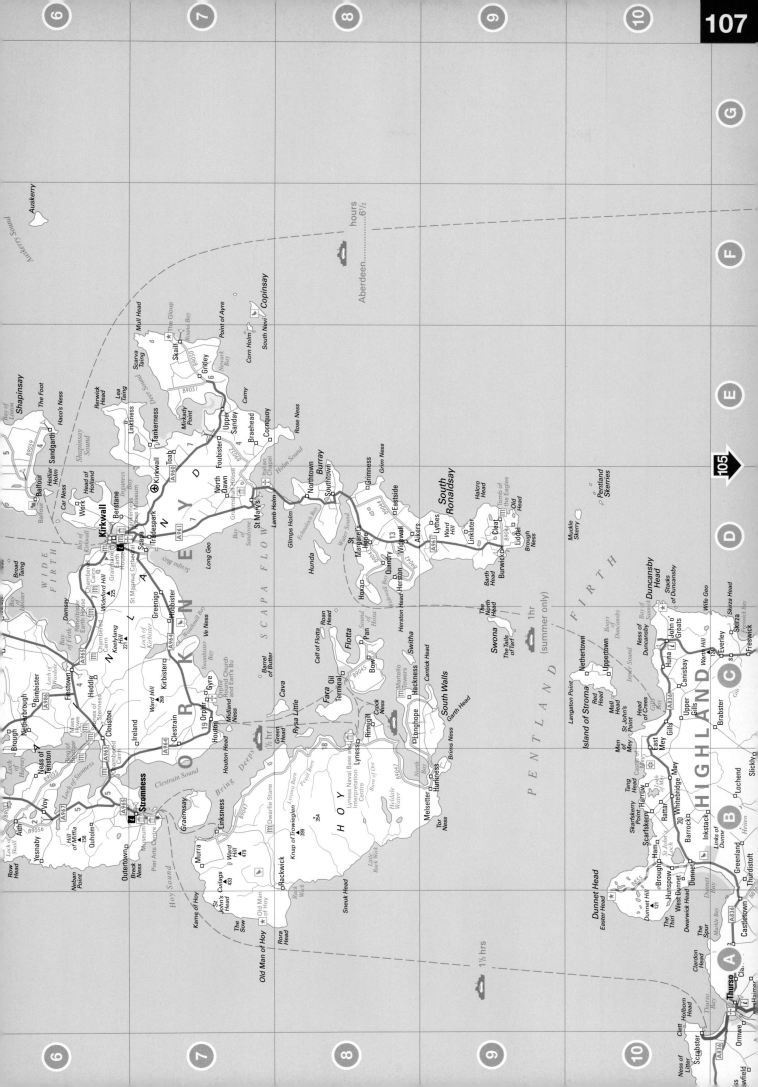

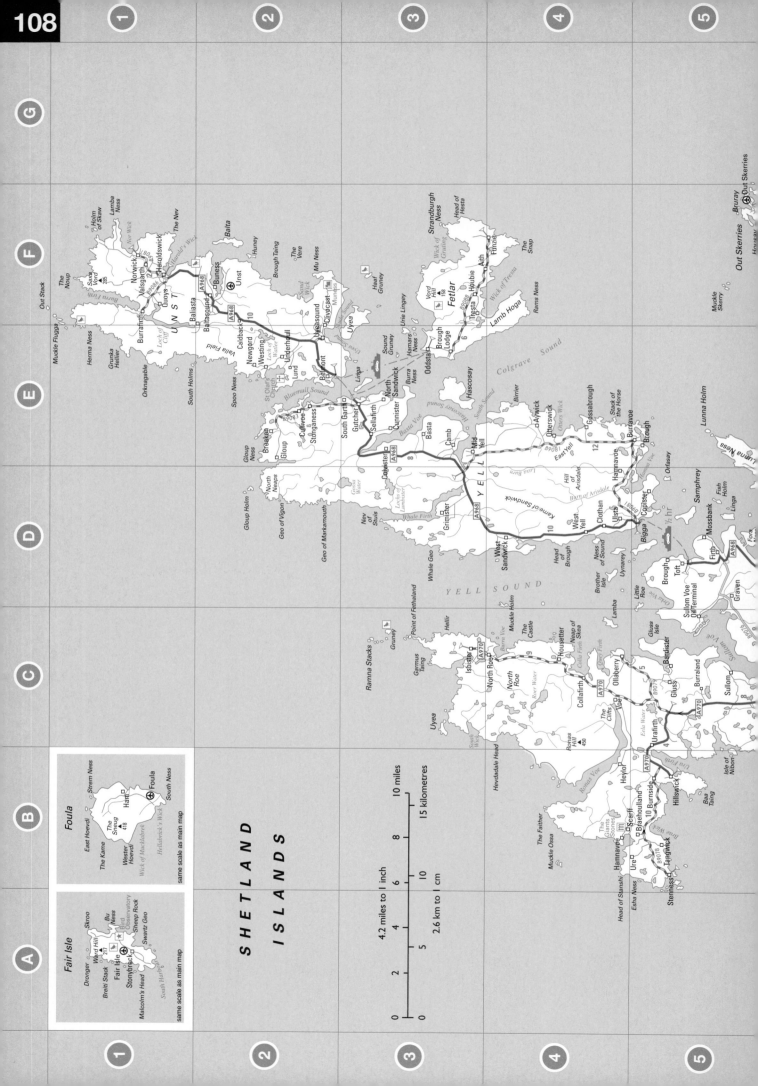

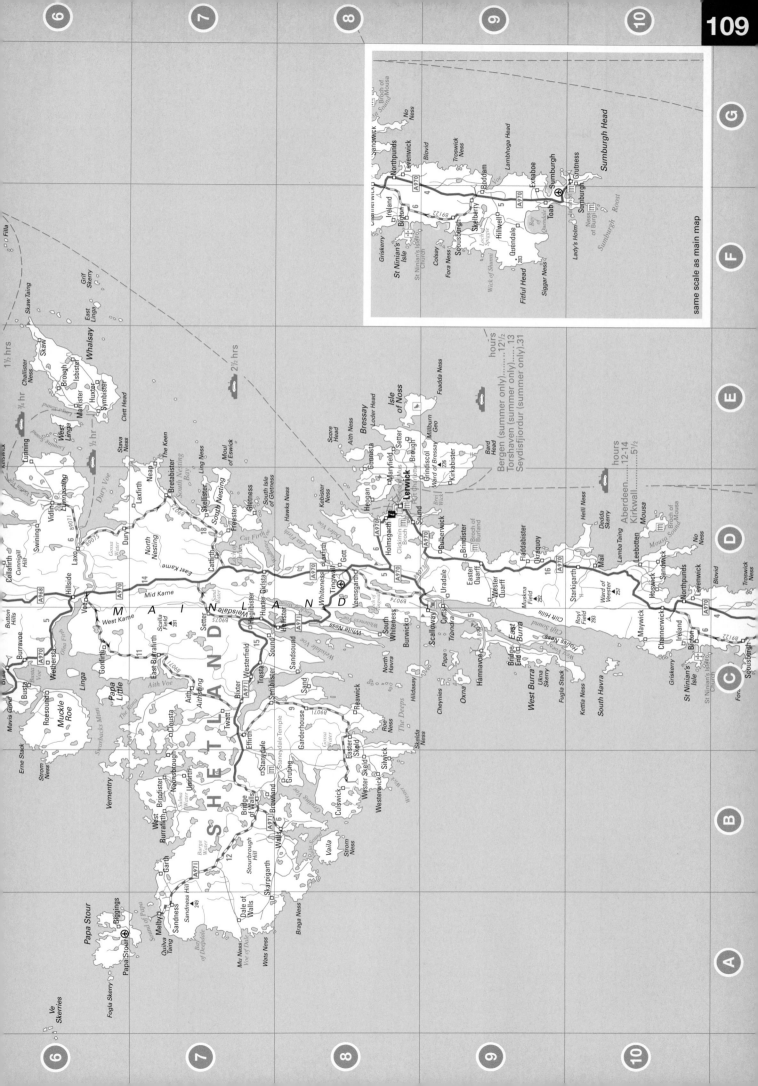

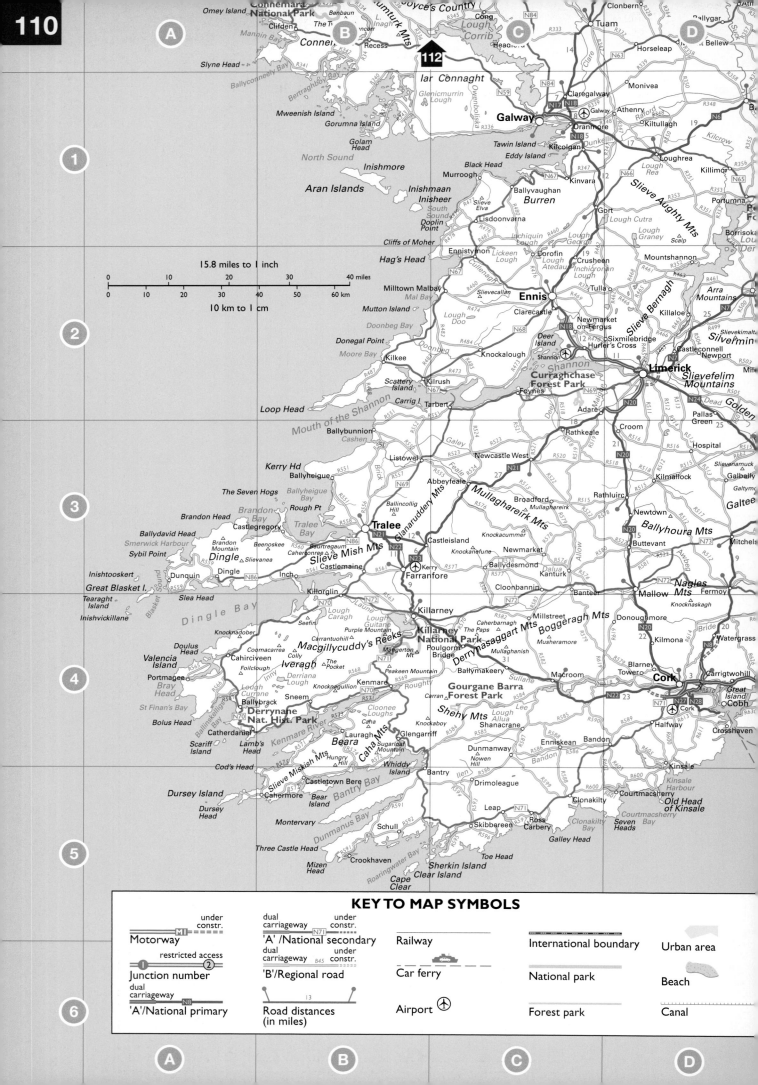

Map labels (County Dublin / East Ireland region)

Ballymahon · Mullingar · R156 · Rush · Lambay Island
Uisneach · 390 · N4 · R161 · Portrane · hours
E · R55 · R391 · N52 · N6 · Kinnegad · Moyvalley · R156 · R154 · N3 · N2 · Malahide · Douglas....2¼-4¾ (summer only) · hours
Athlone · Moate · Kilbeggan · 113 · Dunboyne · Dublin · Ireland's Eye · Holyhead............1¾-3¼
Clara · N62 · N80 · N52 · M4 · Leixlip · Howth · Liverpool............4-9
Tullamore · Edenderry · Celbridge · Lucan · M50 · DUBLIN · Mostyn............6-7½
Cloghan · R357 · Clonygowan · Bog of Allen · Clane · Newcastle · Dublin Bay · Dún Laoghaire
Banagher · N62 · Portarlington · Rathangan · Kildare · M7 · Naas · N11 · Bray
Kilcormac · Mountmellick · Monasterevan · M9 · Kilcullen · Enniskerry · Greystones
Birr · R440 · Portlaoise · M7 · The Curragh · Blessington · Kilcoole · Cherbourg............18 (summer only)
Roscrea · Mountrath · Castletown · Stradbally · Athy · Dunlavin · Wicklow Mts National Park · Newtownmountkennedy
Moneygall · Rathdowney · Abbeyleix · Ballylynan · Baltinglass · Lungnaquilla Mountain · Wicklow · Wicklow Head
Templemore · Durrow · Timolin · Castledermot · Rathvilly · Ardmore Point
Devils Bit Mountain · Ballyragget · Graigue · Carlow · Tullow · Aughrim · Avoca · Brittas Bay · Mizen Head
Thurles · Johnstown · Freshford · Leighlinbridge · Ballon · Shillelagh · Arklow · Kilmichael Point
Holycross · Urlingford · Whitehall · Muine Bheag · Craanford · Gorey · Courtown
Kilkenny · Borris · Mount Leinster · Bunclody · Ferns · Ballycanew · Cahore Point
Sieveardagh Hills · Dungarvan · Ballymurphy · Blackstairs Mountains · Enniscorthy · Wexford Bay
Killenaule · Graiguenamanagh · Thomastown · Drummin · Clonroche · Blackwater
Cashel · Kells · Knocktopher · Ballyhale · Killurin · Castlebridge · Wexford · Wexford Harbour · Rosslare Point
Fethard · Ninemilehouse · Lukeswell · John F. Kennedy Park · Taghmon · Rosslare
Clonmel · Carrick-on-Suir · New Ross · Wellington Bridge · Killinick · Rosslare Harbour · Greenore Point
Knockanaffrin · Portlaw · Waterford · Cheekpoint · Killinick · Cherbourg............17½-19
Ballymacarbery · Croughaun Hill · Duncannon · Duncormick · Lady's Island · Fishguard............1¾-3½
Monavullagh Mountains · Tramore · Dunmore East · Hook Head · Kilmore Quay · Carnsore Point · Pembroke............3¾ · Roscoff (summer only)............19
Cappoquin · Ballymacmague · Tramore Bay · Ballyteige Bay · Saltee Islands
Lismore · Dungarvan · Helvick Head
Tallow · Grange · Mine Head · Ardmore Bay
Youghal · Ballymacoda · Youghal Bay · Knockadoon Head · Ballycotton Bay
Swansea............10
Roscoff (summer only)............14

DUBLIN (inset map)

Grangegorman Upper · Western Way · Dublin Writers Museum · Summerhill · Sheriff St. Lwr.
Constitution Hill · National Wax Museum · James Joyce Centre · McDermott Street · Connolly Station
Dominick St. Upper · Hugh Lane Gallery · Gate Theatre · Gardiner Street Lower · Amiens St.
King's Inns · Rotunda Hospital · O'Connell Street · Marlborough St. · Sean · Talbot Street · Police Station
Cinema · Parnell Street · Moore St. · St. Mary's Cathedral · Bus Station · Custom House
Brunswick Street North · Ilac Shopping Centre · Henry St. · General Post Office · Abbey Theatre · Custom House Quay
King Street North · Old Jameson Distillery · Jervis Shopping Centre · Hot Press Music Hall of Fame · Eden Quay · George's Quay · City Quay · R105
The Chimney · Mary's Lane · Capel Street · Bachelors Wk. · Liffey River · Tara Street Station
Four Courts · Ormond Quay Upper · Ormond Quay Lower · Aston Quay · Burgh Quay · Townsend Street
Arran Quay · Inns Quay · Wellington Quay · Pearse Street · Lombard St. Lwr. · Sandwith St.
Ushers Quay · Merchants Quay · Wood Quay · Essex Quay · Temple Bar · Bank of Ireland · Westland Row · Pearse Station Upr.
Dublin's Viking Adventure · Dame Street · College Grn. · Trinity College - Book of Kells & The Dublin Experience
Christ Church Cathedral · Dvblinia · City Hall · Civic Museum · Suffolk St. · Nassau St. · Heraldic Museum
Thomas St. W. · High St. · Dublin Castle · Police Station · South Great George's St. · Grafton Arcade · National Library
Patrick Street · Golden La. · Drury St. · William St. · Westbury Mall · Mansion House · National Gallery · Leinster House · Natural History Museum
St. Patrick's Cathedral · Aungier St. · Gaiety Theatre · National Museum · Government Buildings
Marsh's Library · Police Station · York Street · St. Stephen's Green Shopping Centre · Dawson St. · Kildare St. · Merrion Sq.
Bishop St. · Kevin St. Upper · Cuffe St. · St. Stephen's Green Park · Newman House Museum · Fenian St.

DUBLIN
N · 0 · 200 · 400 m · 0 · 400 yds

BELFAST

N

| 0 | | 200 yds |
| 0 | | 200 m |

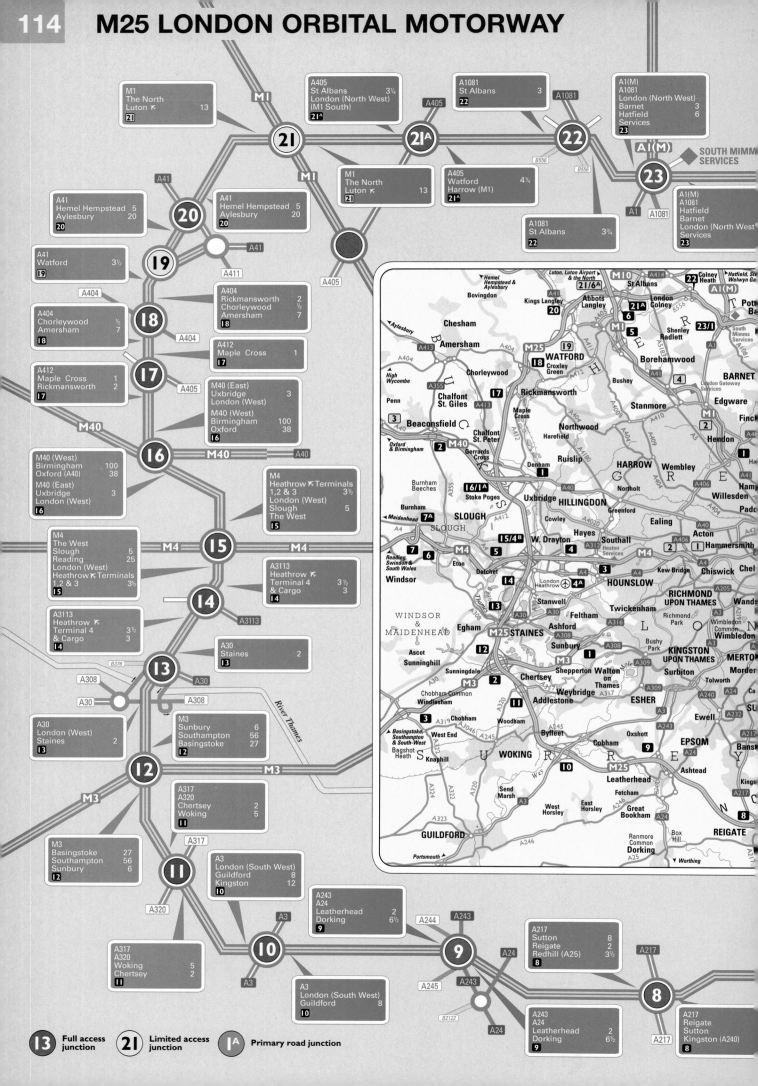

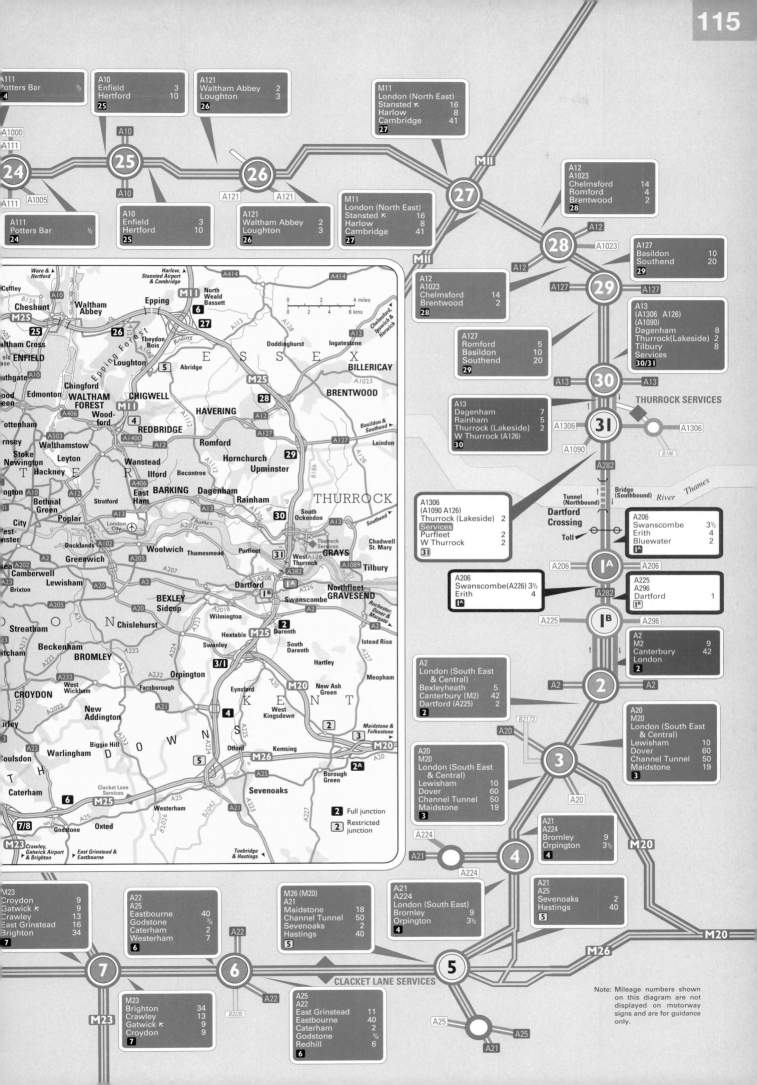

A111	
Potters Bar	½
24	

A10	
Enfield	3
Hertford	10
25	

A121	
Waltham Abbey	2
Loughton	3
26	

M11	
London (North East)	
Stansted ✈	16
Harlow	8
Cambridge	41
27	

A12	
A1023	
Chelmsford	14
Romford	4
Brentwood	2
28	

A111	
Potters Bar	½
24	

A10	
Enfield	3
Hertford	10
25	

A121	
Waltham Abbey	2
Loughton	3
26	

M11	
London (North East)	
Stansted ✈	16
Harlow	8
Cambridge	41
27	

A127	
Basildon	10
Southend	20
29	

A12	
A1023	
Chelmsford	14
Brentwood	2
28	

A13	
(A1306 A126)	
(A1090)	
Dagenham	8
Thurrock (Lakeside)	2
Tilbury	8
Services	
30/31	

A127	
Romford	5
Basildon	10
Southend	20
29	

A13	
Dagenham	7
Rainham	5
Thurrock (Lakeside)	2
W Thurrock (A126)	
30	

THURROCK SERVICES

A1306	
(A1090 A126)	
Thurrock (Lakeside)	2
Services	
Purfleet	2
W Thurrock	2
31	

Tunnel (Northbound)
Bridge (Southbound) River Thames

Dartford Crossing

Toll ↙

A206	
Swanscombe	3½
Erith	4
Bluewater	2
1A	

A206	
Swanscombe(A226) 3½	
Erith	4
1A	

A225	
A296	
Dartford	1
1B	

A2	
M2	9
Canterbury	42
London	
2	

A2	
London (South East & Central)	
Bexleyheath	5
Canterbury (M2)	42
Dartford (A225)	2
2	

A20	
M20	
London (South East & Central)	
Lewisham	10
Dover	60
Channel Tunnel	50
Maidstone	19
3	

A20	
M20	
London (South East & Central)	
Lewisham	10
Dover	60
Channel Tunnel	50
Maidstone	19
3	

A21	
A224	
Bromley	9
Orpington	3½
4	

A21	
A224	
London (South East)	
Bromley	9
Orpington	3½
4	

A21	
A25	
Sevenoaks	2
Hastings	40
5	

M23	
Croydon	9
Gatwick ✈	9
Crawley	13
East Grinstead	16
Brighton	34
7	

A22	
A25	
Eastbourne	40
Godstone	¾
Caterham	2
Westerham	7
6	

M26 (M20)	
A21	
Maidstone	18
Channel Tunnel	50
Sevenoaks	2
Hastings	40
5	

M23	
Brighton	34
Crawley	13
Gatwick ✈	9
Croydon	9
7	

A25	
A22	
East Grinstead	11
Eastbourne	40
Caterham	2
Godstone	¾
Redhill	6
6	

CLACKET LANE SERVICES

2 Full junction
2 Restricted junction

Note: Mileage numbers shown on this diagram are not displayed on motorway signs and are for guidance only.

CENTRAL LONDON

0   ¼   ½ mile

0   0.25   0.5 kilometres

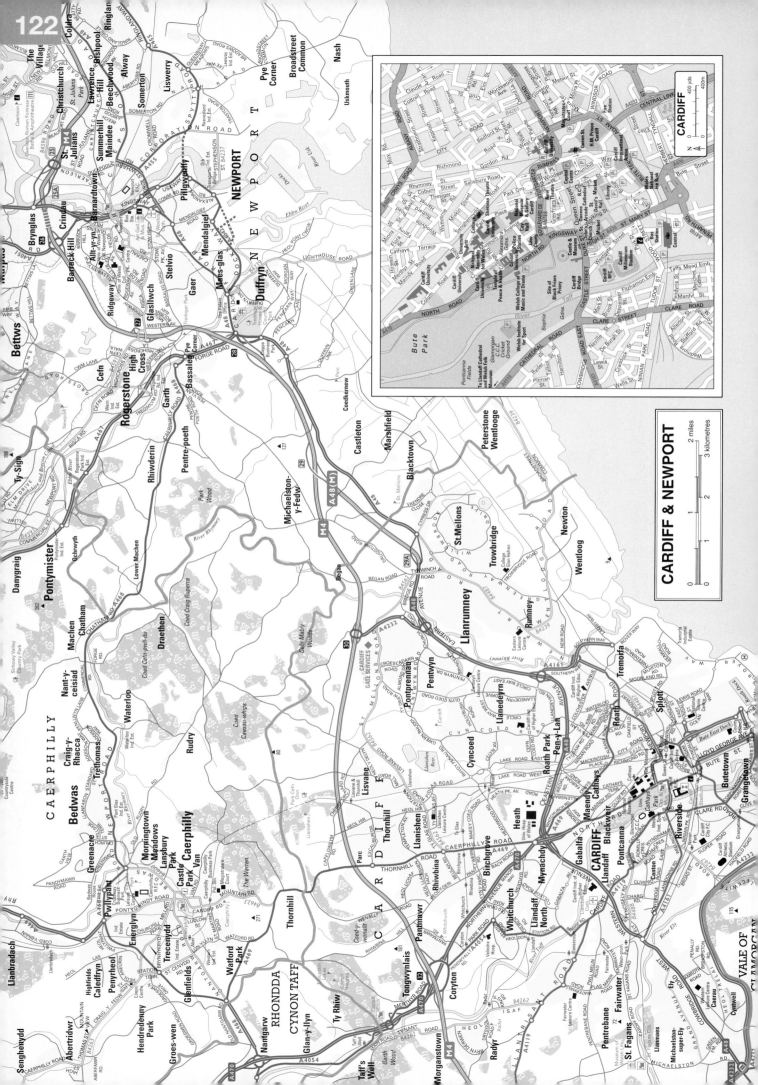

NEWCASTLE UPON TYNE

hours
Amsterdam.........................15
Bergen...........................22-26
Göteborg (summer only)...........25
Haugesund........................21½
Kristiansand.....................17
Stavanger........................19

2 miles
3 kilometres

NEWCASTLE

400 yds
400m

Use of the Index

In this index place names are followed by a page number and a grid reference. The place can be found by searching that grid square.
Where more than one place has the same name, each can be distinguished by the abbreviated county or unitary authority name shown after the place name.
A list of abbreviations for these names is shown below.

Abbreviations

Aber.	Aberdeenshire
Arg. & B.	Argyll & Bute
B'burn.	Blackburn with Darwen
B. & H.	Brighton & Hove
B. & N.E.Som.	Bath & North East Somerset
B.Gwent	Blaenau Gwent
Beds.	Bedfordshire
Bourne.	Bournemouth
Brack.F.	Bracknell Forest
Bucks.	Buckinghamshire
Caerp.	Caerphilly
Cambs.	Cambridgeshire
Carmar.	Carmarthenshire
Cere.	Ceredigion
Chan.I.	Channel Islands
Ches.	Cheshire
Cornw.	Cornwall
Cumb.	Cumbria
D. & G.	Dumfries & Galloway
Darl.	Darlington
Denb.	Denbighshire
Derbys.	Derbyshire
Dur.	Durham
E.Ayr.	East Ayrshire
E.Dun.	East Dunbartonshire
E.Loth.	East Lothian
E.Renf.	East Renfrewshire
E.Riding	East Riding of Yorkshire
E.Suss.	East Sussex
Edin.	Edinburgh
Falk.	Falkirk
Flints.	Flintshire
Glas.	Glasgow
Glos.	Gloucestershire
Gt.Lon.	Greater London
Gt.Man.	Greater Manchester
Gwyn.	Gwynedd
Hants.	Hampshire
Hart.	Hartlepool
Here.	Herefordshire
Herts.	Hertfordshire
High.	Highland
I.o.A.	Isle of Anglesey
I.o.M.	Isle of Man
I.o.S.	Isles of Scilly
I.o.W.	Isle of Wight
Inclyde	Inverclyde
Lancs.	Lancashire
Leic.	Leicester
Leics.	Leicestershire
Lincs.	Lincolnshire
M.K.	Milton Keynes
M.Tyd.	Merthyr Tydfil
Med.	Medway
Mersey.	Merseyside
Middbro.	Middlesbrough
Midloth.	Midlothian
Mon.	Monmouthshire
N.Ayr.	North Ayrshire
N.E.Lincs.	North East Lincolnshire
N.Lan.	North Lanarkshire
N.Lincs.	North Lincolnshire
N.P.T.	Neath Port Talbot
N.Som.	North Somerset
N.Yorks.	North Yorkshire
Norf.	Norfolk
Northants.	Northamptonshire
Northumb.	Northumberland
Nott.	Nottingham
Notts.	Nottinghamshire
Ork.	Orkney
Oxon.	Oxfordshire
P. & K.	Perth & Kinross
Pembs.	Pembrokeshire
Peter.	Peterborough
Plym.	Plymouth
Ports.	Portsmouth
R. & C.	Redcar & Cleveland
R.C.T.	Rhondda Cynon Taff
Read.	Reading
Renf.	Renfrewshire
Rut.	Rutland
S'end	Southend
S'ham.	Southampton
S.Ayr.	South Ayrshire
S.Glos.	South Gloucestershire
S.Lan.	South Lanarkshire
S.Yorks.	South Yorkshire
Sc.Bord.	Scottish Borders
Shet.	Shetland
Shrop.	Shropshire
Slo.	Slough
Som.	Somerset
Staffs.	Staffordshire
Stir.	Stirling
Stock.	Stockton-on-Tees
Stoke	Stoke-on-Trent
Suff.	Suffolk
Surr.	Surrey
Swan.	Swansea
Swin.	Swindon
T. & W.	Tyne & Wear
Tel. & W.	Telford & Wrekin
Thur.	Thurrock
V. of Glam.	Vale of Glamorgan
W'ham	Wokingham
W. & M.	Windsor & Maidenhead
W.Berks.	West Berkshire
W.Dun.	West Dunbartonshire
W.Isles	Western Isles (Na h-Eileanan an Iar)
W.Loth.	West Lothian
W.Mid.	West Midlands
W.Suss.	West Sussex
W.Yorks.	West Yorkshire
Warks.	Warwickshire
Warr.	Warrington
Wilts.	Wiltshire
Worcs.	Worcestershire
Wrex.	Wrexham

A

Ab Kettleby 42 A3
Abbas Combe 9 G2
Abberley 29 G2
Abberton *Essex* 34 E7
Abberton *Worcs.* 29 J3
Abberwick 71 G2
Abbess Roding 33 J7
Abbey Dore 28 C5
Abbey Hulton 40 B1
Abbey St. Bathans 77 F4
Abbey Village 56 B7
Abbey Wood 23 H4
Abbeycwmhir 27 K1
Abbeystead 55 J4
Abbeytown 60 C1
Abbotrule 70 B2
Abbots Bickington 6 B4
Abbots Bromley 40 C3
Abbots Langley 22 D1
Abbots Leigh 19 J4
Abbots Morton 30 B3
Abbots Ripton 33 F1
Abbot's Salford 30 B3
Abbotsbury 8 E6
Abbotsham 6 C3
Abbotskerswell 5 J4
Abbotsley 33 F3
Abbotts Ann 21 G7
Abbottswood 10 E2
Abdon 38 E7
Aber 17 H1
Aber Bargoed 18 E1
Aber Bowlan 17 K2
Aberaeron 26 D2
Aberaman 18 D1
Aberangell 37 H5
Aberarad 17 G2
Aberarder 88 B6
Aberarder House 88 D2
Aberargie 82 C6
Aberarth 26 D2
Aberavon 18 A3
Aber-banc 17 G1
Aberbeeg 19 F1
Abercanaid 18 D1
Abercarn 19 F2
Abercastle 16 B2
Abercegir 37 H5
Aberchalder 87 K4
Aberchirder 98 E5
Abercorn 75 J3
Abercraf 27 H7
Abercrombie 83 G7
Abercrychan 27 G5
Abercwmboi 18 D1
Abercych 17 F1
Abercynafon 27 K7
Abercynon 18 D2
Aber-Cywarch 37 H4
Aberdalgie 82 B5
Aberdare 18 C1
Aberdaron 36 A3
Aberdaugleddau (Milford Haven) 16 C5
Aberdeen 91 H4
Aberdeen Airport 91 G3
Aberdesach 46 C7
Aberdour 75 K2
Aberdovey (Aberdyfi) 37 F6
Aberduhonw 27 K3
Aberdulais 18 A2
Aberdyfi (Aberdovey) 37 F6
Aberedw 27 K4
Abereiddy 16 B2
Abererch 36 D2
Aberfan 18 D1
Aberfeldy 81 K3
Aberffraw 46 B6
Aberffrwd 27 F1
Aberford 57 K6
Aberfoyle 81 G7
Abergarw 18 C3
Abergavenny (Y Fenni) 28 C7
Abergele 47 H5
Abergiar 17 J1
Abergorlech 17 J2
Abergwaun (Fishguard) 16 C2
Abergwesyn 27 H3
Abergwili 17 H3
Abergwydol 37 G5
Abergwynant 37 F4
Abergwynfi 18 B2
Abergwyngregyn 46 E5
Abergynolwyn 37 F5
Aberhafesp 37 K6
Aberhonddu (Brecon) 27 K6
Aberhosan 37 H6
Aberkenfig 18 B3
Aberlady 76 C2
Aberlemno 83 G2
Aberllefenni 37 G5
Aber-Ilia 27 J7
Aberlour (Charlestown of Aberlour) 97 K7
Abermad 26 E1
Abermaw (Barmouth) 37 F4
Abermeurig 26 E3
Abermule 38 A6
Aber-Naint 38 A3
Abernant *Carmar.* 17 G3
Aber-nant *R.C.T.* 18 D1
Abernethy 82 C6
Abernyte 82 D4
Aberpergwm 18 B1
Aberporth 26 B3
Aberriw (Berriew) 38 A5
Aberscross 96 E1
Abersky 88 C2
Abersoch 36 C3
Abersychan 19 F1
Abertawe (Swansea) 17 K6
Aberteifi (Cardigan) 16 E1
Aberthin 18 D4
Abertillery 19 F1
Abertridwr *Caerp.* 18 E3
Abertridwr *Powys* 37 K4
Abertysswg 18 E1
Aberuthven 82 A6
Aberyscir 27 J6
Aberystwyth 36 E7
Abhainnsuidhe 100 C7
Abingdon 21 H2
Abinger Common 22 E7
Abinger Hammer 22 D7
Abington 68 E1
Abington Pigotts 33 G4
Abingworth 12 E5
Ablington 20 E1
Abney 50 E5
Aboyne 90 D5
Abram 49 F2
Abriachan 88 C1
Abridge 23 H2
Abronhill 75 F3
Abson 19 K4
Abthorpe 31 H4
Abune-the-Hill 106 B5
Aby 53 H5
Acaster Malbis 58 B5
Acaster Selby 58 B5
Accrington 56 C7
Accurrach 80 C6
Acha 78 C2
Achacha 80 A3
Achadacaie 73 G4
Achadh Mòr 101 F5
Achadh-chaorrunn 73 F5
Achadunan 80 C6
Achagavel 79 J2
Achaglass 73 F6
Achahoish 73 F3
Achalader 82 C3
Achallader 80 E3
Achamore 72 D3
Achandunie 96 D4
Achany 96 C1
Achaphubuil 87 G7
Acharacle 79 H1
Achargary 104 C3
Acharn *Arg. & B.* 80 C4
Acharn *P. & K.* 81 J3
Acharonich 79 F4
Acharosson 73 H3
Achateny 79 G1
Achath 91 F3
Achavanich 105 G4
Achduart 95 G1
Achentoul 104 D5
Achfary 102 E4
Achgarve 94 E2
Achiemore *High.* 103 F2
Achiemore *High.* 104 D3
Achies 105 G3
A'Chill 85 H4
Achiltibuie 95 G1
Achina 104 C2
Achindown 97 F7
Achinduich 96 C1
Achingills 105 G2
Achintee 95 F7
Achintee House 87 H7
Achintraid 86 E1
Achlean 89 F5
Achleanan 79 G2
Achleek 79 J2
Achlian 80 C5
Achlyness 102 E3
Achmelvich 102 C6
Achmony 88 B1
Achmore *High.* 86 E1
Achmore *High.* 95 G2
Achmore *Stir.* 81 G4
Achnaba 73 H2
Achnabat 88 C1
Achnabourin 104 C3
Achnacairn 80 A4
Achnacarnin 102 C5
Achnaclerach 96 B5
Achnacloich *Arg. & B.* 80 A4
Achnacloich *High.* 86 B4
Achnaclyth 105 F5
Achnacraig 79 F3
Achnacroish 79 K3
Achnadrish 79 F2
Achnafalnich 80 D5
Achnafauld 81 K4
Achnagairn 96 C7
Achnagarron 96 D4
Achnaha *High.* 79 H3
Achnaha *High.* 79 F1
Achnahanat 96 C2
Achnahannet 89 G2
Achnalea 79 K1
Achnamara 73 F2
Achnanellan 79 J1
Achnasaul 87 H6
Achnasheen 95 H6
Achnashellach 73 G1
Achnastank 89 K1
Achorn 105 G5
Achosnich *High.* 96 E2
Achosnich *High.* 79 F1
Achreamie 105 F2
Achriabhach 80 C1
Achriesgill 102 E3
Achrimsdale 97 G1
Achtoty 103 J2
Achurch 42 D7
Achuvoldrach 103 H3
Achvaich 96 E2
Achvarasdal 104 E2
Achvlair 80 A2
Achvraie 95 G1
Ackergill 105 J3
Acklam *Middbro.* 63 F5
Acklam *N.Yorks.* 58 D3
Ackleton 39 G6
Acklington 71 H3
Ackton 57 K7
Ackworth Moor Top 51 G1
Acle 45 J4
Acock's Green 40 D7
Acol 25 J5
Acomb *Northumb.* 70 E7
Acomb *York* 58 B4
Aconbury 28 E5
Acre 56 C7
Acrefair 38 B1
Acrise Place 15 G3
Acton *Ches.* 49 F7
Acton *Gt.Lon.* 22 E4
Acton *Shrop.* 38 C7
Acton *Suff.* 34 C4
Acton *Worcs.* 29 H2
Acton Beauchamp 29 F3
Acton Bridge 48 E5
Acton Burnell 38 E5
Acton Green 29 F3
Acton Pigott 38 E5
Acton Round 39 F6
Acton Scott 38 D7
Acton Trussell 40 B4
Acton Turville 20 B3
Adamhill 74 C7
Adbaston 39 G3
Adber 8 E2
Adderbury 31 F5
Adderley 39 F2
Adderstone 77 K7
Addiewell 75 H4
Addingham 57 F5
Addington *Bucks.* 31 J6
Addington *Gt.Lon.* 23 G5
Addington *Kent* 23 K6
Addlestone 22 D5
Addlethorpe 53 J6
Adel 57 H6
Adeney 39 F4
Adfa 37 K5
Adforton 28 C1
Adisham 15 H2
Adlestrop 30 D6
Adlingfleet 58 E7
Adlington *Ches.* 49 J4
Adlington *Lancs.* 49 F1
Admaston *Staffs.* 40 C3
Admaston *Tel. & W.* 39 F4
Admington 30 C4
Adsborough 8 B2
Adstock 31 J5
Adstone 31 G3
Adversane 12 D4
Advie 89 J1
Adwalton 57 H7
Adwell 21 K2
Adwick le Street 51 H2
Adwick upon Dearne 51 G2
Ae Village 68 E5
Affleck 91 G2
Affpuddle 9 H5
Afon-wen 47 K5
Afton Bridgend 68 B2
Agglethorpe 57 F1
Aigburth 48 C4
Aignis 101 G4
Aike 59 G5
Aikerness 106 D2
Aikers 107 D8
Aiketgate 61 F2
Aikshaw 60 C2
Aikton 60 D1
Aikwood Tower 69 K1
Ailey 28 C4
Ailsworth 42 E6
Aimster 105 G2
Ainderby Quernhow 57 J1
Ainderby Steeple 62 E7
Aingers Green 35 F7
Ainsdale 48 C1
Ainstable 61 G2
Ainsworth 49 G1
Ainthorpe 63 J6
Aintree 48 C3
Aird 92 C6
Aird a' Mhachair 92 C7
Aird a' Mhulaidh 100 D6
Aird Asaig 100 D7
Aird Dhail 101 G1
Aird Leimhe 93 G3
Aird Mhige 93 G2
Aird Mhighe 93 F3
Aird of Sleat 86 B4
Aird Thunga 101 G4
Aird Uige 100 C4
Airdrie *Fife* 83 G7
Airdrie *N.Lan.* 75 F4
Airidh a' Bhruaich 100 E6
Airieland 65 H5
Airies 66 D7
Airigh-drishaig 86 D1
Airmyn 58 D7
Airntully 82 B4
Airor 86 D4
Airth 75 G2
Airton 56 E4
Airyhassen 64 D6
Aisby *Lincs.* 52 B3
Aisby *Lincs.* 42 D2
Aisgernis 84 C2
Aiskew 57 H1
Aislaby *N.Yorks.* 63 K6
Aislaby *N.Yorks.* 58 D1
Aislaby *Stock.* 63 F5
Aisthorpe 52 C4
Aith *Ork.* 107 B6
Aith *Ork.* 106 F5
Aith *Shet.* 109 C7
Aith *Shet.* 108 F3
Aitnoch 89 G1
Akeld 70 E1
Akeley 31 J5
Akenham 35 F4
Albaston 4 E3
Alberbury 38 C4
Albourne 13 F5
Albrighton *Shrop.* 40 A5
Albrighton *Shrop.* 38 D4
Alburgh 45 G7
Albury *Herts.* 33 H6
Albury *Surr.* 22 D7
Albury Heath 22 D7
Alby Hill 45 F2
Alcaig 96 C6
Alcaston 38 D7
Alcester 30 B3
Alciston 13 J6
Alcombe 7 H1
Alconbury 32 E1
Alconbury Hill 32 E1
Alconbury Weston 32 E1
Aldborough *N.Yorks.* 57 K3
Aldborough *Norf.* 45 F2
Aldbourne 21 F4
Aldbrough 59 J6
Aldbrough St. John 62 C5
Aldburgh 57 H2
Aldbury 32 C7
Aldclune 82 A1
Aldeburgh 35 J3
Aldeby 45 J6
Aldenham 22 E2
Alderbury 10 C2
Alderford 45 F4
Alderholt 10 C3
Alderley 20 A2
Alderley Edge 49 H5
Alderman's Green 41 F7
Aldermaston 21 J5
Aldermaston Soke 21 K5
Aldermaston Wharf 21 K5
Alderminster 30 D4
Alderney Airport 3 J4
Aldersey Green 48 D7
Aldershot 22 B6
Alderton *Glos.* 29 J5
Alderton *Northants.* 31 J4
Alderton *Shrop.* 38 D3
Alderton *Suff.* 35 H4
Alderton *Wilts.* 20 B3
Alderwasley 51 F7
Aldfield 57 H3
Aldford 48 D7
Aldham *Essex* 34 D6
Aldham *Suff.* 34 E4
Aldie *Aber.* 91 J1
Aldie *High.* 96 E3
Aldingbourne 12 C6
Aldingham 55 F2
Aldington *Kent* 15 F4
Aldington *Worcs.* 30 B4
Aldivalloch 90 B2
Aldochlay 74 B1
Aldons 67 F5
Aldreth 33 H1
Aldridge 40 C5
Aldringham 35 J2
Aldro 58 E3
Aldsworth 30 C7
Aldunie 90 B2
Aldville 82 A4
Aldwark *Derbys.* 50 E7
Aldwark *N.Yorks.* 57 K3
Aldwick 12 C7
Aldwincle 42 D7
Aldworth 21 J4
Alexandria 74 B3
Alfardisworthy 6 A4
Alfington 7 K6
Alfold 12 D3
Alfold Crossways 12 D3
Alford *Aber.* 90 D3
Alford *Lincs.* 53 H5
Alford *Som.* 9 F1
Alfreton 51 G7
Alfrick 29 G3
Alfriston 13 J6
Algarkirk 43 F2
Alhampton 9 F1
Alkborough 58 E7
Alkerton 30 E4
Alkham 15 H3
Alkington 38 E2
Alkmonton 40 D2
All Cannings 20 D5
All Saints South Elmham 45 H7
All Stretton 38 D6
Allaleigh 5 J5
Allanaquoich 89 J5
Allancreich 90 D5
Allangillfoot 69 H4
Allanton *D. & G.* 68 E5
Allanton *N.Lan.* 75 G5
Allanton *S.Lan.* 75 F5
Allanton *Sc.Bord.* 77 G5
Allardice 91 G7
Allathasdal 84 B4
Allendale Town 61 K1
Allenheads 61 K2
Allen's Green 33 H7
Allensford 62 B1
Allensmore 28 D5
Aller 8 C2
Allerby 60 B3
Allerford *Devon* 6 C7
Allerford *Som.* 7 H1
Allerston 58 E1
Allerthorpe 58 D5
Allerton *Mersey.* 48 D4
Allerton *W.Yorks.* 57 G6
Allerton Bywater 57 K7
Allesley 40 E7
Allestree 41 F2
Allexton 42 B5
Allgreave 49 J6
Allhallows 24 E4
Allhallows-on-Sea 24 E4
Alligin Shuas 94 E6
Allimore Green 40 A4
Allington *Lincs.* 42 B1
Allington *Wilts.* 10 D1
Allington *Wilts.* 20 D5
Allithwaite 55 G2
Allnabad 103 G4
Alloa 75 G1
Allonby 60 B2
Alloway 67 H2
Allscot 39 G6
Allt na h-Airbhe 95 H2
Alltachonaich 79 J2
Alltan Dubh 102 B7
Alltbeithe 87 G2
Alltforgan 37 J3
Alltmawr 27 K4
Alltnacaillich 103 G4
Allt-na-subh 87 F2
Alltsigh 88 B3
Alltwalis 17 H2
Alltwen 18 A1
Alltyblaca 17 J1
Almeley 28 C3
Almer 9 J5
Almington 39 F2
Almiston Cross 6 B3
Almondbank 82 B5
Almondbury 50 D1
Almondsbury 19 J3
Alne 57 K3
Alness 96 D5
Alnham 70 E2
Alnmouth 71 H2
Alnwick 71 G2
Alphamstone 34 C5
Alpheton 34 C3
Alphington 7 H6
Alpington 45 G5
Alport 50 E6
Alpraham 48 E7
Alresford 34 E6
Alrewas 40 D4
Alrick 82 C1
Alsager 49 G7
Alsagers Bank 40 A1
Alsop en le Dale 50 D7
Alston *Cumb.* 61 J2
Alston *Devon* 8 C4
Alstone 29 J5
Alstonefield 50 D7
Alswear 7 F3
Altanduin 104 D6
Altarnun 4 C2
Altass 96 C1
Altens 91 H4
Alterwall 105 H2
Altham 56 C6
Althorne 25 F2
Althorpe 52 B2
Alticry 64 C5
Altnafeadh 80 D2
Altnaharra 103 H5
Altofts 57 J7
Alton *Derbys.* 51 F6
Alton *Hants.* 11 J1
Alton *Staffs.* 40 C1
Alton Barnes 20 E5
Alton Pancras 9 F4
Alton Priors 20 E5
Altonside 97 K6
Altrincham 49 G4
Altura 87 J6
Alva 75 G1
Alvanley 48 D5
Alvaston 41 F2
Alvechurch 30 B1
Alvecote 40 E5
Alvediston 9 J2
Alveley 39 G7
Alverdiscott 6 D3
Alverstoke 11 H5
Alverstone 11 G6
Alverton 42 A1
Alves 97 J5
Alvescot 21 F1
Alveston *S.Glos.* 19 K3
Alveston *Warks.* 30 D3
Alvie 89 F4
Alvingham 53 G3
Alvington 19 K1
Alwalton 42 E6
Alweston 9 F3
Alwinton 70 E3
Alwoodley Gates 57 J5
Alyth 82 D3
Amalebra 2 B5
Amber Hill 43 F1
Ambergate 51 F7
Amberley *Glos.* 20 B1
Amberley *W.Suss.* 12 D5
Amble 71 H3
Amblecote 40 A7
Ambleside 60 E6
Ambleston 16 D3
Ambrismore 73 J5
Ambrosden 31 H7
Amcotts 52 B1
Amersham 22 C2
Amesbury 20 E7
Amington 40 E5
Amisfield 69 F5
Amlwch 46 C3
Amlwch Port 46 C
Ammanford (Rhydaman) 17 K
Amotherby 58 D
Ampfield 10 E
Ampleforth 58 E
Ampleforth College 58 E
Ampney Crucis 20 D
Ampney St. Mary 20 D
Ampney St. Peter 20 D
Amport 21 G
Ampthill 32 D
Ampton 34 C
Amroth 16 E
Amulree 81 K
An Tairbeart (Tarbert) 100 D
An T-òb (Leverburgh) 93 F
Anaboard 89 H
Anaheilt 79 K
Ancaster 42 C
Anchor 38 A
Ancroft 77 H
Ancrum 70 B
Ancton 12 C
Anderby 53 J
Anderson 9 H
Anderton 49 F
Andover 21 G
Andover Down 21 G
Andoversford 30 B
Andreas 54 D
Anelog 36 A
Angarrack 2 C
Angersleigh 7 K
Angerton 60 D
Angle 16 B
Angler's Retreat 37 G
Angmering 12 D
Angram 58 E
Anie 81 G
Ankerville 97 F
Anlaby 59 G
Anmer 44 B
Anna Valley 21 G
Annan 69 G
Annaside 54 D
Annat *Arg. & B.* 80 B
Annat *High.* 94 E
Annbank 67 J
Annesley 51 H
Annesley Woodhouse 51 H
Annfield Plain 62 C
Annscroft 38 D
Ansdell 55 G
Ansford 9 F
Ansley 40 E
Anslow 40 E
Anslow Gate 40 D
Anstey *Herts.* 33 H
Anstey *Leics.* 41 H
Anstruther 83 G
Ansty *W.Suss.* 13 F
Ansty *Warks.* 41 F
Ansty *Wilts.* 9 J
Anthill Common 11 H
Anthorn 60 C
Antingham 45 G
Anton's Gowt 43 F
Antony 4 D
Antrobus 49 F
Anvil Corner 6 B
Anwick 52 E
Anwoth 65 F
Aoradh 72 A
Apethorpe 42 D
Apley 52 E
Apperknowle 51 F
Apperley 29 H
Appin 80 A
Appin House 80 A
Appleby 52 C
Appleby Magna 41 F
Appleby Parva 41 F
Appleby-in-Westmorland 61 H
Applecross 94 D
Appledore *Devon* 6 C
Appledore *Devon* 7 J
Appledore *Kent* 14 E
Appledore Heath 14 E
Appleford 21 J
Appleshaw 21 G
Applethwaite 60 D
Appleton 21 H
Appleton Roebuck 58 B
Appleton Thorn 49 F
Appleton Wiske 62 E
Appleton-le-Moors 58 D
Appleton-le-Street 58 D
Appletreehall 70 A
Appletreewick 57 F

Appley 7 J3
Appley Bridge 48 E1
Apse Heath 11 G6
Apsley 22 D1
Apsley End 32 E5
Apuldram 12 B6
Arberth (Narberth) 16 E4
Arbirlot 83 G3
Arborfield 22 A5
Arborfield Cross 22 A5
Arborfield Garrison 22 A5
Arbroath 83 H3
Arbuthnott 91 G7
Archdeacon Newton 62 D5
Archiestown 97 K7
Arclid 49 G6
Ard a' Chapuill 73 J3
Ardacheanbeg 73 J2
Ardacheranmor 73 J2
Ardachoil 79 J4
Ardachu 96 D1
Ardachvie 87 H5
Ardailly 72 E5
Ardalanish 78 E6
Ardallie 91 J1
Ardanaiseig 80 B5
Ardaneaskan 86 E1
Ardanstur 79 K6
Ardantiobart 79 H2
Ardantrive 79 K5
Ardarroch 86 E1
Ardbeg Arg. & B. 73 J4
Ardbeg Arg. & B. 72 C6
Ardbeg Arg. & B. 73 K2
Ardblair 88 B1
Ardbrecknish 80 B5
Ardcharnich 95 H3
Ardchiavaig 78 E6
Ardchonnel 80 A4
Ardchonnell 80 A6
Ardchrishnish 79 F5
Ardchronie 96 D3
Ardchuilk 87 J1
Ardchullarie More 81 G6
Ardchyle 81 G5
Arddlin 38 B4
Ardeley 33 G6
Ardelve 86 E2
Arden 74 B2
Ardencaple House 79 J6
Ardens Grafton 30 C3
Ardentallan 79 K5
Ardentinny 73 K2
Ardeonaig 81 H4
Ardersier 96 E6
Ardery 79 J1
Ardessie 95 G3
Ardfad 79 J6
Ardfern 79 K7
Ardfin 72 C4
Ardgartan 80 D7
Ardgay 96 C2
Ardgenavan 80 C6
Ardgowan 74 A3
Ardgowse 90 E3
Ardgye 97 J5
Ardhallow 73 K3
Ardheslaig 94 D6
Ardiecow 98 D4
Ardinamar 79 J6
Ardindrean 95 H3
Ardingly 13 G4
Ardington 21 H3
Ardintoul 86 E2
Ardkinglas House 80 C6
Ardlair 90 D2
Ardlamont 73 H4
Ardleigh 34 E6
Ardleish 80 E6
Ardler 82 D3
Ardley 31 G6
Ardlui 80 E6
Ardlussa 72 E2
Ardmaddy 80 B4
Ardmair 95 H2
Ardmaleish 73 J4
Ardmay 80 D7
Ardmenish 72 D3
Ardmhór 84 C4
Ardminish 72 E6
Ardmolich 86 D7
Ardmore Arg. & B. 72 C6
Ardmore Arg. & B. 79 J5
Ardmore Arg. & B. 74 B3
Ardmore High. 96 E3
Ardnackaig 73 F1
Ardnacross 73 K3
Ardnadam 73 K3
Ardnadrochit 79 J4
Ardnagoine 95 F1
Ardnagowan 80 C7
Ardnagrask 96 C7
Ardnahein 74 A1
Ardnahoe 72 C3
Ardnarff 86 E1
Ardnastang 79 K1
Ardnave 72 A3
Ardno 80 C7
Ardo 91 G1
Ardoch D. & G. 68 D3
Ardoch Moray 97 J6
Ardoch P. & K. 82 B4
Ardochrig 74 E6
Ardoyne 90 E2
Ardpatrick 73 F4
Ardpeaton 74 A2
Ardradnaig 81 J3
Ardrishaig 73 G2
Ardroe 102 C6
Ardrossan 74 A6
Ardscalpsie 73 J5
Ardshave 96 E2
Ardshealach 79 H1
Ardshellach 79 J6
Ardsley 51 F2
Ardslignish 79 G1
Ardtalla 72 C5
Ardtalnaig 81 H4
Ardtaraig 73 J2
Ardteatle 80 C5
Ardtoe 86 C7
Ardtornish 79 J3
Ardtrostan 81 H4
Ardtur 80 A3
Ardullie 96 C5
Ardura 79 H4
Ardvar 102 D5
Ardvasar 86 C4
Ardveich 81 H5
Ardverikie 88 C6
Ardvorlich Arg. & B. 80 E6
Ardvorlich P. & K. 81 H5
Ardwall 65 F5
Ardwell D. & G. 64 B6
Ardwell Moray 90 B1
Ardwell S.Ayr. 67 F4

Areley Kings 29 G1
Arford 12 B3
Argaty 81 J7
Argoed 18 E2
Argoed Mill 27 J2
Argrennan 65 H5
Arichamish 80 A7
Arichastlich 80 D4
Arichonan 73 F1
Arienskill 86 D6
Arileod 78 C2
Arinacrinachd 94 D6
Arinafad Beg 73 F2
Arinagour 78 D2
Arinambane 84 C2
Arisaig 86 C6
Arivegaig 79 H1
Arkendale 57 J3
Arkesden 33 H5
Arkholme 55 J2
Arkleby 60 C3
Arkleside 57 F1
Arkleton 69 J4
Arkley 23 F2
Arksey 51 H2
Arkwright 51 G5
Arlary 82 C7
Arlecdon 60 B5
Arlesey 32 E5
Arleston 39 F4
Arley 49 F4
Arlingham 29 G7
Arlington Devon 6 E1
Arlington E.Suss. 13 J6
Arlington Glos. 20 E1
Arlington Beccott 6 E1
Armadale Ches. 48 E6
Armadale High. 104 C2
Armadale High. 86 C4
Armadale W.Loth. 75 H4
Armathwaite 61 G2
Arminghall 45 G5
Armitage 40 C4
Armscote 30 D4
Armston 42 D7
Armthorpe 51 J2
Arnabost 78 D2
Arncliffe 56 E2
Arncliffe Cote 56 E2
Arncroach 83 G7
Arne 9 J6
Arnesby 41 J6
Arngask 82 C6
Arngibbon 74 E1
Arngomery 74 E1
Arnhall 83 H1
Arnicle 73 F7
Arnipol 86 D6
Arnisdale 86 E3
Arnish 94 C7
Arniston Engine 76 B4
Arnol 101 F3
Arnold 41 H1
Arnprior 74 E1
Arowry 38 D2
Arrad Foot 55 G1
Arradoul 98 C4
Arram 59 G5
Arrat 83 H2
Arrathorne 62 C7
Arreton 11 G6
Arrington 33 G3
Arrivain 80 D4
Arrochar 80 E7
Arrow 30 B3
Arscaig 103 H7
Arthington 57 H5
Arthingworth 42 A7
Arthog 37 F4
Arthrath 91 H1
Arthurstone 82 D3
Artrochie 91 J1
Aruadh 72 A4
Arundel 12 D6
Aryhoulan 80 B1
Asby 60 B4
Ascog 73 K4
Ascot 22 C5
Ascott 30 E5
Ascott-under-Wychwood 30 D7
Ascreavie 82 E2
Asenby 57 J2
Asfordby 42 A4
Asfordby Hill 42 A4
Asgarby Lincs. 53 G6
Asgarby Lincs. 42 E1
Ash Kent 15 H2
Ash Kent 24 C5
Ash Som. 8 D2
Ash Surr. 22 B6
Ash Barton 6 D5
Ash Bullayne 7 F5
Ash Magna 38 E2
Ash Mill 7 F3
Ash Priors 7 K3
Ash Thomas 7 J4
Ash Vale 22 B6
Ashampstead 21 J4
Ashbocking 35 F3
Ashbourne 40 D1
Ashbrittle 7 J3
Ashburnham Place 14 K5
Ashburton 5 H4
Ashbury Devon 6 D6
Ashbury Oxon. 21 F3
Ashby 52 C2
Ashby by Partney 53 H6
Ashby cum Fenby 53 F3
Ashby de la Launde 52 D7
Ashby de la Zouch 41 F4
Ashby Folville 42 A4
Ashby Magna 41 H6
Ashby Parva 41 H7
Ashby Puerorum 53 G5
Ashby St. Ledgers 31 G2
Ashby St. Mary 45 H5
Ashchurch 29 J5
Ashcombe 5 K3
Ashcott 8 D1
Ashdon 33 J4
Ashe 21 J7
Asheldham 25 F1
Ashen 34 B4
Ashenden 14 D4
Ashendon 31 J7
Ashens 73 G3
Ashfield Arg. & B. 73 F2
Ashfield Stir. 81 G7
Ashfield Suff. 35 G2
Ashfield Green 35 G1
Ashfield Crossways 13 F4
Ashford Devon 6 D2
Ashford Devon 5 G6
Ashford Hants. 10 C3
Ashford Kent 15 F3
Ashford Surr. 22 D4
Ashford Bowdler 28 E1

Ashford Carbonel 28 E1
Ashford Hill 21 J5
Ashford in the Water 50 E6
Ashgill 75 F5
Ashiestiel 76 C7
Ashill Devon 7 J4
Ashill Norf. 44 C5
Ashingdon 24 E2
Ashington Northumb. 71 H5
Ashington Som. 8 E2
Ashington W.Suss. 12 E5
Ashkirk 69 K1
Ashleworth 29 H6
Ashley Cambs. 33 K2
Ashley Ches. 49 G4
Ashley Devon 6 E4
Ashley Glos. 20 C2
Ashley Hants. 10 E1
Ashley Hants. 10 D5
Ashley Kent 15 H3
Ashley Northants. 42 A6
Ashley Staffs. 39 G2
Ashley Wilts. 20 B5
Ashley Green 22 C1
Ashley Heath 10 C4
Ashmanhaugh 45 H3
Ashmansworth 21 H6
Ashmansworthy 6 B4
Ashmore Dorset 9 J3
Ashmore P.& K. 82 B2
Ashorne 30 E3
Ashover 51 F6
Ashow 30 E1
Ashperton 29 F4
Ashprington 5 J5
Ashreigney 6 E4
Ashtead 22 E6
Ashton Ches. 48 E6
Ashton Cornw. 2 C6
Ashton Cornw. 4 D4
Ashton Here. 28 E2
Ashton Northants. 42 D5
Ashton Northants. 31 J4
Ashton Common 20 B6
Ashton Keynes 20 D2
Ashton under Hill 29 J5
Ashton upon Mersey 49 G3
Ashton-in-Makerfield 48 E3
Ashton-under-Lyne 49 J3
Ashurst Hants. 10 E3
Ashurst Kent 13 J3
Ashurst W.Suss. 12 E5
Ashurstwood 13 H3
Ashwater 6 B6
Ashwell Herts. 33 F5
Ashwell Rut. 42 B4
Ashwellthorpe 45 F6
Ashwick 19 K7
Ashwicken 44 B4
Ashybank 70 A2
Askam in Furness 55 F2
Askern 51 H1
Askerswell 8 E5
Askett 22 B1
Askham Cumb. 61 G4
Askham Notts. 51 K5
Askham Bryan 58 B5
Askham Richard 58 B5
Asknish 73 H1
Askrigg 62 A7
Askwith 57 G5
Aslackby 42 D2
Aslacton 45 F6
Aslockton 42 A1
Asloun 90 D3
Aspall 35 F2
Aspatria 60 C2
Aspenden 33 G6
Aspley Guise 32 C5
Aspull 49 F2
Asselby 58 D7
Assington 34 D5
Astbury 49 H6
Astcote 31 H3
Asterby 53 F5
Asterley 38 C5
Asterton 38 C6
Asthall 30 D7
Asthall Leigh 30 E7
Astley Shrop. 38 E4
Astley Warks. 41 F7
Astley Worcs. 29 G2
Astley Abbotts 39 G6
Astley Bridge 49 G1
Astley Cross 29 G2
Astley Green 49 G3
Aston Ches. 39 F1
Aston Ches. 48 E5
Aston Derbys. 50 D4
Aston Flints. 48 C6
Aston Here. 28 D1
Aston Herts. 33 F6
Aston Oxon. 21 G1
Aston S.Yorks. 51 G4
Aston Shrop. 38 E3
Aston Staffs. 39 G1
Aston Tel. & W. 39 F5
Aston W.Mid. 40 C7
Aston W'ham 22 A3
Aston Abbotts 32 B7
Aston Botterell 39 F7
Aston Cantlow 30 C3
Aston Clinton 32 B7
Aston Crews 29 F6
Aston Cross 29 J5
Aston End 33 F6
Aston Eyre 39 F6
Aston Fields 29 J1
Aston Flamville 41 G6
Aston Ingham 29 F6
Aston juxta Mondrum 49 F7
Aston le Walls 31 F3
Aston Magna 30 C5
Aston Munslow 38 E7
Aston on Clun 38 C7
Aston on Trent 41 G3
Aston Rogers 38 C5
Aston Rowant 22 A2
Aston Sandford 22 A1
Aston Somerville 30 B5
Aston Subedge 30 C4
Aston Tirrold 21 J3
Aston Upthorpe 21 J3
Aston-by-Stone 40 B2
Astwick 33 F5
Astwood 32 C4
Astwood Bank 30 B2
Aswarby 42 D2
Aswardby 53 G5
Aswick Grange 43 G4
Atch Lench 30 B3
Atcham 38 E5
Athelington 35 G1

Athelney 8 C2
Athelstaneford 76 D3
Atherington 6 D3
Atherstone 41 F6
Atherstone on Stour 30 D3
Atherton 49 F2
Athlinne 100 D6
Atlow 40 E1
Attadale 87 F1
Attenborough 41 H2
Atterby 52 C3
Attleborough Norf. 44 E6
Attleborough Warks. 41 F6
Attlebridge 45 F4
Atwick 59 H4
Atworth 20 B5
Aubourn 52 C6
Auch 80 E4
Auchairne 67 F5
Auchallater 89 J6
Auchameanach 73 G5
Auchamore 98 E6
Auchattie 90 E5
Auchavan 82 C1
Auchbraad 73 G2
Auchbreck 89 K2
Auchenblae 91 F7
Auchenbothie 74 B3
Auchenbrack 68 C4
Auchenbreck 73 J2
Auchencairn 65 J5
Auchencrow 77 G4
Auchendinny 76 A4
Auchendolly 65 H4
Auchenfoyle 74 B3
Auchengray 75 H5
Auchenhalrig 98 B4
Auchenhessnane 68 D4
Auchenlochan 73 H3
Auchenmalg 64 C5
Auchenrivock 69 J5
Auchentiber 74 B6
Auchenvennal 74 A2
Auchessan 81 F5
Auchgourish 89 G3
Auchinafaud 73 F5
Auchincruive 67 H1
Auchindarrach 73 G2
Auchindarroch 80 B2
Auchindrain 80 B7
Auchindrean 95 H3
Auchininna 98 E6
Auchinleck 67 K1
Auchinloch 74 E3
Auchinner 81 H6
Auchinroath 97 K6
Auchintoul Aber. 90 D3
Auchintoul Aber. 98 E5
Auchintoul High. 96 C1
Auchiries 91 J1
Auchleven 90 E2
Auchlochan 75 G7
Auchlunachan 95 H3
Auchlunies 91 G5
Auchlunkart 98 B6
Auchlyne 81 G5
Auchmacoy 91 H1
Auchmair 90 B2
Auchmantle 64 B4
Auchmithie 83 H3
Auchmuirbridge 82 D7
Auchmull 90 D7
Auchnabony 65 H6
Auchnabreac 80 B7
Auchnacloich 81 K4
Auchnacraig 79 J5
Auchnacree 83 F1
Auchnafree 81 K4
Auchnagallin 89 H1
Auchnagatt 99 H6
Auchnaha 73 H2
Auchnangoul 80 B7
Aucholzie 90 B5
Auchorrie 90 E4
Auchraw 81 G5
Auchreoch 80 E5
Auchronie 90 C6
Auchterarder 82 A6
Auchtercairn 94 E4
Auchterderran 76 A1
Auchterhouse 82 E4
Auchtermuchty 82 D6
Auchterneed 96 B5
Auchtertool 76 A1
Auchtertyre Angus 82 D3
Auchtertyre Moray 97 J6
Auchtertyre Stir. 80 E5
Auchtubh 81 G5
Auckengill 105 J2
Auckley 51 J2
Audenshaw 49 J3
Audlem 39 F1
Audley 49 G7
Audley End 33 J5
Auds 98 E4
Aughton E.Riding 58 D6
Aughton Lancs. 48 C2
Aughton Lancs. 55 J3
Aughton S.Yorks. 51 G4
Aughton Park 48 D2
Auldearn 97 G6
Aulden 28 D3
Auldgirth 68 E5
Auldhame 76 D2
Auldhouse 74 E5
Aulich 81 H2
Ault a' chruinn 87 F2
Ault Hucknall 51 G6
Aultanrynie 103 F5
Aultbea 94 E3
Aultgrishan 94 D3
Aultguish Inn 95 K4
Aultibea 105 F6
Aultiphurst 104 D2
Aultmore 98 C5
Aultnagoire 88 C2
Aultnamain Inn 96 D3
Aultnapaddock 98 B6
Aulton 90 E2
Aultvoulin 86 D4
Aundorach 89 G3
Aunk 7 J5
Aunsby 42 D2
Auquhorthies 91 G2
Aust 19 J3
Austerfield 51 J3
Austonley 50 D2
Austrey 40 E5
Austwick 56 C3
Authorpe 53 H4
Authorpe Row 53 J5
Avebury 20 D4
Aveley 23 J3
Avening 20 B2
Averham 51 K7

Aveton Gifford 5 G6
Avielochan 89 G3
Aviemore 89 F3
Avington Hants. 11 G1
Avington W.Berks. 21 G5
Avoch 96 D6
Avon 10 C5
Avon Dassett 31 F3
Avonbridge 75 H3
Avonmouth 19 J4
Avonwick 5 H5
Awbridge 10 E2
Awhirk 64 A5
Awkley 19 J3
Awliscombe 7 K5
Awre 20 A1
Awsworth 41 G1
Axbridge 19 H6
Axford Hants. 21 K7
Axford Wilts. 21 F4
Axminster 8 B5
Axmouth 8 B5
Aycliffe 62 D4
Aydon 71 F7
Aylburton 19 K1
Ayle 61 J2
Aylesbeare 7 J6
Aylesbury 32 B7
Aylesby 53 F2
Aylesford 14 C2
Aylesham 15 H2
Aylestone 41 H5
Aylmerton 45 F2
Aylsham 45 F3
Aylton 29 F5
Aymestrey 28 D2
Aynho 31 G5
Ayot St. Lawrence 32 E7
Ayot St. Peter 33 F7
Ayr 67 H1
Aysgarth 57 F1
Ayshford 7 J4
Ayside 55 G1
Ayston 42 B5
Aythorpe Roding 33 J7
Ayton P. & K. 82 C6
Ayton Sc.Bord. 77 H4
Aywick 108 E4
Azerley 57 H2

B

Babbacombe 5 K4
Babbinswood 38 C2
Babcary 8 E2
Babel 27 H5
Babell 47 K5
Babeny 5 G3
Babraham 33 J4
Babworth 51 J4
Bac 101 G3
Back of Keppoch 86 C6
Backaland 106 E4
Backaskaill 106 D2
Backbarrow 55 G1
Backburn 90 D1
Backfolds 99 J5
Backford 48 C5
Backhill 91 F1
Backhill of Clackriach 99 H6
Backhill of Trustach 90 E5
Backies High. 97 F1
Backies Moray 98 C5
Backlass 105 H3
Backside 90 C1
Backwell 19 H5
Backworth 71 H6
Bacon End 33 J7
Baconsthorpe 45 F2
Bacton Here. 28 C5
Bacton Norf. 45 H2
Bacton Suff. 34 E2
Bacup 56 D7
Badachro 94 D4
Badanloch Lodge 104 C5
Badavanich 95 H6
Badbea 105 F7
Badbury 20 E3
Badby 31 G3
Badcall High. 102 E3
Badcall High. 102 E3
Badcaul 95 G2
Baddeley Green 49 J7
Badden 73 G2
Baddesley Ensor 40 E6
Baddidarach 102 C6
Badenscoth 90 E1
Badenyon 90 B3
Badger 39 G6
Badgerbank 49 H5
Badgers Mount 23 H5
Badgeworth 29 J7
Badgworth 19 G6
Badicaul 86 D2
Badingham 35 H2
Badintagairt 103 J2
Badlesmere 15 F2
Badley 34 E3
Badlipster 105 H4
Badluarach 95 F2
Badminton 20 B3
Badnaban 102 C6
Badnabay 102 E4
Badnafrave 89 K3
Badnagie 105 G5
Badnambiast 88 E2
Badninish 96 E2
Badrallach 95 G2
Badsey 30 B4
Badshot Lea 22 B7
Badsworth 51 G1
Badwell Ash 34 D2
Badyo 82 A1
Bae Cinmel (Kinmel Bay) 47 H4
Bae Colwyn (Colwyn Bay) 47 G5
Bae Penrhyn (Penrhyn Bay) 47 G4
Bag Enderby 53 G5
Bagby 57 K1
Bagendon 20 D1
Baggrave Hall 42 A5
Baggrow 60 C2
Bagh a' Chaisteil (Castlebay) 84 B5
Baghasdal 84 C3
Bagillt 48 B5
Baginton 30 E1
Baglan 18 A2
Bagley 38 D3
Bagnall 49 J7
Bagnor 21 H5
Bagshot Surr. 22 C5
Bagshot Wilts. 21 G5

Bagstone 19 K3
Bagthorpe Norf. 44 B2
Bagthorpe Notts. 51 G7
Baguley 49 H4
Bagworth 41 G5
Bagwyllydiart 28 D6
Baildon 57 G6
Baile a' Mhanaich (Balivanich) 92 C6
Baile Ailein 100 E5
Baile an Truiseil 101 F2
Baile Boidheach 73 F3
Baile Gharbhaidh 92 C7
Baile Glas 92 D6
Baile Mhartainn (Balmartin) 92 C4
Baile Mhic Phail 92 D4
Baile Mòr Arg. & B. 78 D5
Baile Mòr W.Isles 92 C5
Baile nan Cailleach 92 C6
Baile Raghaill 92 C5
Bailebeag 88 C3
Baileguish 89 F5
Baile-na-Cille 92 D3
Bailetonach 86 C7
Bailiesward 90 C1
Bainbridge 62 A7
Bainsford 75 G2
Bainshole 90 E1
Bainton E.Riding 59 F4
Bainton Peter. 42 D5
Bairnkine 70 B2
Bakebare 90 B1
Baker Street 24 C3
Baker's End 33 G7
Bakewell 50 E6
Bala 37 J2
Balachuirn 94 B7
Balafark 74 E1
Balaldie 97 F4
Balavil 88 E4
Balbeg High. 88 B1
Balbeg High. 88 B2
Balbeggie 82 C5
Balbithan 91 F3
Balblair High. 96 E5
Balblair High. 96 C2
Balby 51 H2
Balcharn 96 C1
Balchers 99 F5
Balchladich 102 C5
Balchraggan High. 96 C7
Balchraggan High. 88 C1
Balchrick 102 D2
Balcurvie 82 E7
Baldernock 74 D3
Baldersby 57 J2
Balderstone 56 B6
Balderton 52 B7
Baldhu 2 E4
Baldinnie 83 F6
Baldock 33 F5
Baldovie Angus 82 E2
Baldovie Dundee 82 E4
Baldrine 54 D5
Baldslow 14 C6
Baldwin 54 C5
Baldwinholme 60 E1
Baldwin's Gate 39 G1
Bale 44 E2
Balelone 92 C4
Balemartine 78 A3
Balendoch 82 D3
Balephuil 78 A3
Balerno 75 K4
Balernock 74 A2
Baleromindubh 72 B1
Balerominmore 72 B1
Balevulin 79 F5
Balfield 83 G1
Balfour Aber. 90 D5
Balfour Ork. 107 D6
Balfron 74 D2
Balfron Station 74 D2
Balgedie 82 C7
Balgonar 75 J1
Balgove 91 G1
Balgowan D. & G. 64 B6
Balgowan High. 88 D5
Balgown 93 J5
Balgray 83 F4
Balgreen 99 F5
Balgreggan 64 A5
Balgy 94 E6
Balhaldie 81 K7
Balhalgardy 91 F2
Balhary 82 D3
Balhelvie 82 E5
Balhousie 82 E7
Baliasta 108 F2
Baligill 104 D2
Baligrundle 79 K4
Balindore 80 A4
Balintore 97 F4
Balintraid 96 E4
Balintyre 81 H3

Ballimore Stir. 81 G6
Ballinaby 72 A4
Ballindean 82 D5
Ballingdon 34 C4
Ballinger Common 22 C1
Ballingham 28 E5
Ballingry 75 K1
Ballinlick 82 A3
Ballinluig P. & K. 82 A2
Ballinluig P. & K. 82 B2
Ballintuim 82 C2
Balloch Angus 82 E2
Balloch High. 96 E7
Balloch N.Lan. 75 F3
Balloch W.Dun. 74 B2
Ballochan 90 D5
Ballochandrain 73 H2
Ballochford 90 B1
Ballochgair 66 B1
Ballochmartin 73 K5
Ballochmorrie 67 G5
Ballochmyle 67 K1
Ballochroy 73 F5
Ballogie 90 D5
Balls Cross 12 C4
Ballyaurgan 73 F3
Ballygown 79 F3
Ballygrant 72 B4
Ballyhaugh 78 C2
Ballymeanoch 73 G1
Ballymichael 73 H7
Balmacara 86 E2
Balmaclellan 65 G3
Balmacneil 82 A2
Balmadies 83 G3
Balmae 65 G6
Balmaha 74 C1
Balmalcolm 82 E7
Balmartin (Baile Mhartainn) 92 C4
Balmeanach Arg. & B. 79 H3
Balmeanach Arg. & B. 79 F4
Balmedie 91 H3
Balmerino 82 E5
Balmerlawn 10 E4
Balminnoch 64 C4
Balmore E.Dun. 74 E3
Balmore High. 97 F7
Balmore High. 87 K1
Balmore High. 93 H7
Balmore P. & K. 81 J2
Balmullo 83 F5
Balmungie 96 E6
Balmyle 82 B2
Balnaboth 82 E1
Balnabruaich 96 E4
Balnacra 95 F7
Balnafoich 88 D1
Balnagall 97 F3
Balnaguard 82 A2
Balnaguisich 96 D4
Balnahard Arg. & B. 72 C1
Balnahard Arg. & B. 79 H3
Balnain 88 B1
Balnakeil 103 F2
Balnaknock 93 K5
Balnamoon 83 G1
Balnapaling 96 E5
Balnespick 89 F4
Balquhidder 81 G5
Balsall 30 D1
Balsall Common 30 D1
Balscote 30 E4
Balsham 33 J3
Baltasound 108 F2
Balterley 49 G7
Baltersan 64 E4
Balthangie 99 G5
Balthayock 82 C5
Baltonsborough 8 E1
Baluachraig 73 G1
Balulive 72 C4
Balure Arg. & B. 80 B4
Balure Arg. & B. 79 K4
Balvaird 96 C6
Balvarran 82 B1
Balvicar 79 J6
Balvraid High. 86 E3
Balvraid High. 89 F1
Bamber Bridge 55 J7
Bamber's Green 33 J6
Bamburgh 77 K7
Bamff 82 D2
Bamford 50 E4
Bampton Cumb. 61 G5
Bampton Devon 7 H3
Bampton Oxon. 21 G1
Banavie 87 H7
Banbury 31 F4
Bancffosfelen 17 H4
Banchor 97 G7
Banchory 91 F5
Banchory-Devenick 91 H4
Bancyfelin 17 G4
Banc-y-ffordd 17 H2
Bandon 82 D7
Banff 98 E4
Bangor 46 D5
Ball Haye Green 49 J7
Ball Hill 21 H5
Ballabeg 54 B6
Ballacannell 54 D5
Ballacarnane Beg 54 C5
Ballachulish 80 B2
Balladoole 54 B7
Ballafesson 54 B6
Ballagyr 54 B5
Ballajora 54 D4
Ballakilpheric 54 B6
Ballamodha 54 B6
Ballantrae 66 E5
Ballards Gore 25 F2
Ballasalla I.o.M. 54 C4
Ballasalla I.o.M. 54 B6
Ballater 90 C5
Ballaterach 90 C5
Ballaugh 54 C4
Ballaveare 54 C6
Ballechin 81 G7
Balleich 81 G7
Ballencrieff 76 C3
Ballidon 50 E7
Balliekine 54 B7
Balliemeanoch 80 C7
Balliemore Arg. & B. 73 K1
Balliemore Arg. & B. 79 K5
Ballig 54 B5
Ballimeanoch 80 B6
Ballimore Arg. & B. 73 H2
Bangor Teifi 17 G1
Bangor-is-y-coed 38 C1
Banham 44 E7
Bank 10 D4
Bank End 54 E1
Bank Newton 56 E4
Bank Street 29 F2
Bankend D. & G. 69 F7
Bankend S.Lan. 75 G7
Bankfoot 82 B4
Bankglen 67 K2
Bankhead Aber. 90 E3
Bankhead Aber. 90 E4
Bankhead Aberdeen 91 G4
Bankhead D. & G. 65 H6
Banknock 75 F3
Banks Cumb. 70 A7
Banks Lancs. 55 G7
Bankshill 69 G5
Banningham 45 G3
Bannister Green 33 K6
Bannockburn 75 G1
Banstead 23 F6
Bantham 5 G6
Banton 75 F3
Banwell 19 G6
Bapchild 25 F5
Baptiston 74 D2
Bar Hill 33 G2
Barabhas (Barvas) 101 F2
Barachander 80 B5
Barassie 74 B7

Barbaraville 96 E4
Barber Booth 50 D4
Barbon 56 B1
Barbrook 7 F1
Barby 31 G1
Barcaldine 80 A3
Barcaple 65 G5
Barcheston 30 D4
Barcombe 13 H5
Barcombe Cross 13 H5
Barden 62 C7
Bardennoch 67 K4
Bardfield End Green 33 K5
Bardfield Saling 33 K6
Bardister 108 C5
Bardney 52 E6
Bardon *Leics.* 41 G4
Bardon *Moray* 97 K6
Bardon Mill 70 C7
Bardsea 55 G2
Bardsey 57 J5
Bardsley 49 J2
Bardwell 34 D1
Barewood 28 C3
Barfad 73 G4
Barford *Norf.* 45 F5
Barford *Warks.* 30 D2
Barford St. John 31 F5
Barford St. Martin 10 B1
Barford St. Michael 31 F5
Barfrestone 15 H2
Bargaly 64 E4
Bargany Mains 67 G3
Bargoed 18 E2
Bargrennan 64 D3
Barham *Cambs.* 32 E1
Barham *Kent* 15 G2
Barham *Suff.* 35 F3
Barharrow 65 G5
Barholm 42 D4
Barholm Mains 64 E5
Barkby 41 J5
Barkby Thorpe 41 J5
Barkestone-le-Vale 42 A2
Barkham 22 A5
Barking *Gt.Lon.* 23 H3
Barking *Suff.* 34 E3
Barkingside 23 H3
Barkisland 50 C1
Barkston *Lincs.* 42 C1
Barkston *N.Yorks.* 57 K6
Barkway 33 G5
Barlae 64 C4
Barlaston 40 A2
Barlavington 12 C5
Barlborough 51 G5
Barlby 58 C6
Barlestone 41 G5
Barley *Herts.* 33 G5
Barley *Lancs.* 56 D5
Barleycroft End 33 H6
Barleyhill 62 B1
Barleythorpe 42 B5
Barling 25 F3
Barlings 52 D5
Barlow *Derbys.* 51 F5
Barlow *N.Yorks.* 58 C7
Barlow *T. & W.* 71 G7
Barmby Moor 58 D5
Barmby on the Marsh 58 C7
Barmer 44 C2
Barmolloch 73 G1
Barmoor Lane End 77 J6
Barmouth (Abermaw) 37 F4
Barmpton 62 E5
Barmston 59 H4
Barnacabber 73 K2
Barnacarry 73 J1
Barnack 42 D5
Barnacle 41 F7
Barnamuc 80 B3
Barnard Castle 62 B5
Barnard Gate 31 F7
Barnardiston 34 B4
Barnard's Green 29 G4
Barnbarroch *D. & G.* 64 D5
Barnbarroch *D. & G.* 65 J5
Barnburgh 51 G2
Barnby 45 J6
Barnby Dun 51 J2
Barnby in the Willows 52 B7
Barnby Moor 51 J4
Barndennoch 68 D5
Barnes 23 F4
Barnet 23 F2
Barnetby le Wold 52 D2
Barney 44 D2
Barnham *Suff.* 34 C1
Barnham *W.Suss.* 12 C6
Barnham Broom 44 E5
Barnhead 83 H2
Barnhill 97 J6
Barnhills 66 D6
Barningham *Dur.* 62 B5
Barningham *Suff.* 34 D1
Barnoldby le Beck 53 F2
Barnoldswick 56 D5
Barns Green 12 E4
Barnsdale Bar 51 H1
Barnsley *Glos.* 20 D1
Barnsley *S.Yorks.* 51 F2
Barnstaple 6 D2
Barnston *Essex* 33 K7
Barnston *Mersey.* 48 B4
Barnstone 42 A2
Barnt Green 30 B1
Barnton 49 F5
Barnwell All Saints 42 D7
Barnwell St. Andrew 42 D7
Barnwood 29 H7
Barr *Arg. & B.* 72 B4
Barr *High.* 79 H2
Barr *S.Ayr.* 67 G4
Barr Hall 34 B5
Barra (Tràigh Mhòr) Airport 84 C4
Barrackan 79 J7
Barraer 64 D4
Barraglom 100 D4
Barrahormid 73 F2
Barran 80 C5
Barrapoll 78 A3
Barrasford 70 E6
Barravullin 79 K7
Barregarrow 54 C5
Barrhead 74 D5
Barrhill 67 G5
Barrington *Cambs.* 33 G4
Barrington *Som.* 8 C3
Barripper 2 D5
Barrisdale 86 E4
Barrmill 74 B5
Barrnacarry 79 K5
Barrock 105 H1
Barrow *Lancs.* 56 C6
Barrow *Rut.* 42 B4
Barrow *Shrop.* 39 F5
Barrow *Som.* 9 G1
Barrow *Suff.* 34 B2
Barrow Gurney 19 J5
Barrow Haven 59 G7
Barrow Nook 48 D2
Barrow Street 9 H1
Barrow upon Humber 59 G7
Barrow upon Soar 41 H4
Barrow upon Trent 41 F3
Barrowby 42 B2
Barrowden 42 C5
Barrowford 56 D6
Barrow-in-Furness 55 F3
Barry *Angus* 83 G4
Barry *V. of Glam.* 18 E5
Barsby 42 A4
Barsham 45 H6
Barskimming 67 J1
Barsloisnoch 73 G1
Barston 30 D1
Bartestree 28 E4
Barthol Chapel 91 G1
Barthomley 49 G7
Bartley 10 E3
Bartlow 33 J4
Barton *Cambs.* 33 H3
Barton *Ches.* 48 D7
Barton *Glos.* 30 B6
Barton *Lancs.* 55 J6
Barton *Lancs.* 48 C2
Barton *N.Yorks.* 62 D6
Barton *Torbay* 5 K4
Barton *Warks.* 30 C3
Barton Bendish 44 B5
Barton Common 45 H3
Barton End 20 B2
Barton Hartshorn 31 H5
Barton in Fabis 41 H2
Barton in the Beans 41 F5
Barton Mills 34 B1
Barton on Sea 10 D5
Barton St. David 8 E1
Barton Seagrave 32 B1
Barton Stacey 21 H7
Barton Turf 45 H3
Barton-le-Clay 32 D5
Barton-le-Street 58 D2
Barton-le-Willows 58 D3
Barton-on-the-Heath 30 D5
Barton-under-Needwood 40 D4
Barton-upon-Humber 59 G7
Barvas (Barabhas) 101 F2
Barway 33 J1
Barwell 41 G6
Barwhinnock 65 G5
Barwick 8 E3
Barwick in Elmet 57 J6
Barwinnock 64 D6
Baschurch 38 D3
Bascote 31 F2
Basford Green 49 J7
Bashall Eaves 56 B5
Bashall Town 56 C5
Bashley 10 D5
Basildon *Essex* 24 D3
Basildon *W.Berks.* 21 K4
Basingstoke 21 K6
Baslow 50 E5
Bason Bridge 19 G7
Bassaleg 19 F3
Bassenthwaite 60 D3
Basset's Cross 6 D5
Bassett 11 F3
Bassingbourn 33 G4
Bassingfield 41 J2
Bassingham 52 C6
Bassingthorpe 42 C3
Basta 108 E3
Baston 42 E4
Bastwick 45 J4
Batavaime 81 F4
Batchworth 22 D2
Batchworth Heath 22 D2
Batcombe *Dorset* 9 F4
Batcombe *Som.* 9 F1
Bate Heath 49 F5
Bath 20 A5
Bathampton 20 A5
Bathealton 7 J3
Batheaston 20 A5
Bathford 20 A5
Bathgate 75 H4
Bathley 51 K7
Bathpool *Cornw.* 4 C3
Bathpool *Som.* 8 B2
Batley 57 H7
Batsford 30 C5
Battersby 63 G6
Battersea 23 F4
Battisborough Cross 5 G6
Battisford 34 E3
Battisford Tye 34 E3
Battle *E.Suss.* 14 C6
Battle *Powys* 27 K5
Battlefield 38 E4
Battlesbridge 24 D2
Battlesden 32 C6
Battleton 7 H3
Battramsley 10 E5
Batt's Corner 22 B7
Bauds of Cullen 98 C4
Baugh 78 B3
Baughton 29 H4
Baughurst 21 J6
Baulds 90 E5
Baulking 21 G2
Baumber 53 F5
Baunton 20 D1
Baveney Wood 29 F1
Baverstock 10 B1
Bawburgh 45 F5
Bawdeswell 44 E3
Bawdrip 8 C1
Bawdsey 35 H4
Bawtry 51 J3
Baxenden 56 C7
Baxterley 40 E6
Baycliff 55 F2
Baydon 21 F4
Bayford *Herts.* 23 G1
Bayford *Som.* 9 G2
Bayfordbury 33 G7
Bayham Abbey 13 K3
Bayles 61 J2
Baylham 35 F3
Baynards Green 31 G6
Baysham 28 E6
Bayston Hill 38 D5
Baythorn End 34 B4
Bayton 29 F1
Beach 79 J2
Beachampton 31 J5
Beacharr 72 E6
Beachborough 15 G4
Beachley 19 J2
Beacon 7 K5
Beacon End 34 D6
Beacon Hill 12 B3
Beacon's Bottom 22 A2
Beaconsfield 22 C2
Beadlam 58 C1
Beadnell 71 H1
Beaford 6 D4
Beal *N.Yorks.* 58 B7
Beal *Northumb.* 77 J6
Bealach 80 A2
Beambridge 49 F7
Beamhurst 40 C2
Beaminster 8 D4
Beamish 62 D1
Beamsley 57 F4
Bean 23 J4
Beanacre 20 B5
Beanley 71 F2
Beaquoy 106 C5
Beardon 6 D7
Beare Green 22 E7
Bearley 30 C2
Bearnie 91 H1
Bearnock 88 B1
Bearnus 79 F3
Bearpark 62 D2
Bearsbridge 61 J1
Bearsden 74 D3
Bearsted 14 C2
Bearwood 10 B5
Beattock 69 F3
Beauchamp Roding 23 J1
Beauchief 51 F4
Beaudesert 30 C2
Beaufort 28 A7
Beaulieu 10 E4
Beauly 96 C7
Beaumaris (Biwmaris) 46 E5
Beaumont *Cumb.* 60 E1
Beaumont *Essex* 35 F6
Beausale 30 D1
Beauworth 11 G2
Beaworthy 6 C6
Beazley End 34 B6
Bebington 48 C4
Bebside 71 H5
Beccles 45 J6
Becconsall 55 H7
Beck Foot 61 H7
Beck Hole 63 K6
Beck Row 33 K1
Beck Side 55 F1
Beckbury 39 G5
Beckenham 23 G5
Beckermet 60 B6
Beckfoot *Cumb.* 60 C6
Beckfoot *Cumb.* 60 B2
Beckford 29 J5
Beckhampton 20 D5
Beckingham *Lincs.* 52 B7
Beckingham *Notts.* 51 K4
Beckington 20 A6
Beckley *E.Suss.* 14 D5
Beckley *Oxon.* 31 G7
Beckton 23 H3
Beckwithshaw 57 H4
Becontree 23 H3
Bedale 57 H1
Bedburn 62 C3
Bedchester 9 H3
Beddau 18 D3
Beddgelert 36 E1
Beddingham 13 H6
Beddington 23 G5
Beddington Corner 23 F5
Bedfield 35 G2
Bedford 32 D4
Bedgebury Cross 14 C4
Bedhampton 11 J4
Bedingfield 35 F2
Bedlington 71 H5
Bedlinog 18 D1
Bedminster 19 J4
Bedmond 22 E1
Bednall 40 B4
Bedol 48 B5
Bedrule 70 A2
Bedstone 28 C1
Bedwas 18 E3
Bedwellty 18 E1
Bedworth 41 F7
Beeby 41 J5
Beech *Hants.* 11 H1
Beech *Staffs.* 40 A2
Beech Hill 21 K5
Beechamwell 44 B5
Beechingstoke 20 D6
Beedon 21 H4
Beeford 59 H4
Beeley 50 E6
Beelsby 53 F2
Beenham 21 J5
Beer 8 B6
Beer Hackett 8 E3
Beercrocombe 8 C2
Beesands 5 J6
Beesby 53 H4
Beeson 5 J6
Beeston *Beds.* 32 E4
Beeston *Ches.* 48 E7
Beeston *Norf.* 44 D4
Beeston *Notts.* 41 H2
Beeston *W.Yorks.* 57 H6
Beeston Regis 45 F1
Beeston St. Lawrence 45 H3
Beeswing 65 J4
Beetham 55 H2
Beetley 44 D4
Began 19 F3
Begbroke 31 F7
Begelly 16 E5
Beggshill 90 D1
Beguildy 28 A1
Beighton *Norf.* 45 H5
Beighton *S.Yorks.* 51 G4
Beith 74 B5
Bekesbourne 15 G2
Belaugh 45 G4
Belbroughton 29 J1
Belchamp Otten 34 C4
Belchamp St. Paul 34 B4
Belchamp Walter 34 C4
Belchford 53 F5
Belford 77 K7
Belgrave 41 H5
Belhaven 76 E3
Belhelvie 91 H3
Belhinnie 90 C2
Bell Bar 23 F1
Bell Busk 56 E4
Bell End 29 J1
Bellabeg 90 B3
Belladrum 96 C7
Bellanoch 73 G1
Bellasize 58 E7
Bellaty 82 D2
Belleau 53 H5
Bellehiglash 89 J1
Bellerby 62 C7
Bellever 5 G3
Belliehill 83 G1
Bellingdon 22 C1
Bellingham 70 D5
Belloch 72 E7
Bellochantuy 72 E7
Bells Yew Green 13 K3
Bellshill *N.Lan.* 75 F5
Bellshill *Northumb.* 77 K7
Bellside 75 G5
Bellsquarry 75 J4
Belluton 19 K5
Belmaduthy 96 D6
Belmesthorpe 42 D4
Belmont *B'burn.* 49 F1
Belmont *Gt.Lon.* 23 F5
Belmont *Shet.* 108 E2
Belowda 3 G2
Belper 41 F1
Belper Lane End 41 F1
Belsay 71 G6
Belsford 5 H5
Belstead 35 F4
Belston 67 H1
Belstone 6 E6
Belstone Corner 6 E6
Belsyde 75 H3
Belthorn 56 C7
Beltinge 25 H5
Beltoft 52 B2
Belton *Leics.* 41 G3
Belton *Lincs.* 42 C2
Belton *N.Lincs.* 51 K2
Belton *Norf.* 45 J5
Belton *Rut.* 42 B5
Beltring 23 K7
Belvedere 23 H4
Belvoir 42 B2
Bembridge 11 H6
Bemersyde 76 D7
Bempton 59 H2
Ben Alder Cottage 81 F1
Ben Alder Lodge 88 C7
Benacre 45 K7
Benbecula (Baile a' Mhanaich) Airport 92 C6
Benbuie 68 C4
Benderloch 80 A4
Bendish 32 E6
Benenden 14 D4
Benfield 64 D4
Bengate 45 H3
Bengeo 33 G7
Benholm 83 K1
Beningbrough 58 B4
Benington *Herts.* 33 F6
Benington *Lincs.* 43 G1
Benington Sea End 43 H1
Benllech 46 D4
Benmore *Arg. & B.* 73 K2
Benmore *Stir.* 81 F5
Bennacott 4 C1
Bennan Cottage 65 G3
Benniworth 53 F4
Benover 14 C3
Benson 21 K2
Benthall *Northumb.* 71 H1
Benthall *Shrop.* 39 F5
Bentham 29 J7
Benthoul 91 G4
Bentley *E.Riding* 59 G6
Bentley *Hants.* 22 A7
Bentley *S.Yorks.* 51 H2
Bentley *Suff.* 35 F5
Bentley *Warks.* 40 E6
Bentley Heath 30 C1
Benton 6 E2
Benton Square 71 J6
Bentpath 69 J4
Bentworth 21 K7
Benvie 82 E4
Benville Lane 8 E4
Benwick 43 G7
Beoley 30 B2
Bepton 12 B5
Berden 33 H6
Bere Alston 4 E4
Bere Ferrers 4 E4
Bere Regis 9 H5
Berea 16 A3
Berepper 2 D6
Bergh Apton 45 H5
Berinsfield 21 J2
Berkeley 19 K2
Berkhamsted 22 C1
Berkley 20 B7
Berkswell 30 D1
Bermondsey 23 G4
Bernera 86 E2
Berners Roding 24 C1
Bernice 73 K1
Bernisdale 93 K6
Berrick Salome 21 K2
Berriedale 105 G6
Berriew (Aberriw) 38 A5
Berrington *Northumb.* 77 J6
Berrington *Shrop.* 38 E5
Berrow 19 F6
Berrow Green 29 G3
Berry Down Cross 6 D1
Berry Hill *Glos.* 28 E7
Berry Hill *Pembs.* 16 D1
Berry Pomeroy 5 J4
Berryhillock 98 D4
Berrynarbor 6 D1
Bersham 38 C1
Berstane 107 D6
Berwick 13 J6
Berwick Bassett 20 D4
Berwick Hill 71 G6
Berwick St. James 10 B1
Berwick St. John 9 J2
Berwick St. Leonard 9 J1
Berwick-upon-Tweed 77 H5
Bescar 48 C1
Besford *Shrop.* 38 E3
Besford *Worcs.* 29 J4
Bessacarr 51 J2
Bessels Leigh 21 H1
Bessingby 59 H3
Bessingham 45 F2
Best Beech Hill 13 K3
Besthorpe *Norf.* 44 E6
Besthorpe *Notts.* 52 B6
Beswick 59 G5
Betchworth 23 F6
Bethania *Cere.* 26 E2
Bethania *Gwyn.* 37 G1
Bethel *Gwyn.* 46 D6
Bethel *Gwyn.* 37 J2
Bethel *I.o.A.* 46 B5
Bethersden 14 E3
Bethesda *Gwyn.* 46 E6
Bethesda *Pembs.* 16 D4
Bethlehem 17 K3
Bethnal Green 23 G3
Betley 39 G1
Betsham 24 C4
Betteshanger 15 J2
Bettiscombe 8 C5
Bettisfield 38 D2
Betton *Shrop.* 38 C5
Betton *Shrop.* 39 F2
Bettws 19 F2
Bettws Bledrws 26 E3
Bettws Cedewain 38 A6
Bettws Evan 17 G1
Bettws Gwerfil Goch 37 K1
Bettws Newydd 19 G1
Bettws-y-crwyn 38 B7
Bettyhill 104 C2
Betws *Bridgend* 18 C3
Betws *Carmar.* 17 K4
Betws Disserth 28 A3
Betws Garmon 46 D7
Betws-y-coed 47 F7
Betws-yn-Rhos 47 H5
Beulah *Cere.* 17 F1
Beulah *Powys* 27 J3
Bevendean 13 G6
Bevercotes 51 K5
Beverley 59 G6
Beverstone 20 B2
Bevington 19 K2
Bewaldeth 60 D3
Bewcastle 70 A6
Bewdley 29 G1
Bewerley 57 G3
Bewholme 59 H5
Bewley Common 20 C5
Bexhill 14 C7
Bexleyheath 23 H4
Bexwell 44 A5
Beyton 34 D2
Beyton Green 34 D2
Bhalamus 100 E7
Bhaltos 100 C4
Bhatarsaigh (Vatersay) 84 B5
Biallaid 88 E5
Bibury 20 E1
Bicester 31 G6
Bickenhall 8 B3
Bickenhill 40 D7
Bicker 43 F2
Bickerstaffe 48 D2
Bickerton *Ches.* 48 E7
Bickerton *N.Yorks.* 57 K4
Bickford 40 A4
Bickham Bridge 5 H5
Bickham House 7 H7
Bickington *Devon* 6 D2
Bickington *Devon* 5 H3
Bickleigh *Devon* 5 F4
Bickleigh *Devon* 7 H5
Bickleton 6 D2
Bickley 23 H5
Bickley Moss 38 E1
Bickley Town 38 E1
Bicknacre 24 D1
Bicknoller 7 K2
Bicknor 14 D2
Bickton 10 C3
Bicton *Shrop.* 38 D4
Bicton *Shrop.* 38 B7
Bicton Heath 38 D4
Bidborough 23 J7
Biddenden 14 D4
Biddenham 32 D4
Biddestone 20 B4
Biddisham 19 G6
Biddlesden 31 H4
Biddlestone 70 E3
Biddulph 49 H7
Biddulph Moor 49 J7
Bideford 6 C3
Bidford-on-Avon 30 B3
Bidston 48 B3
Bielby 58 D5
Bieldside 91 G4
Bierley *I.o.W.* 11 G7
Bierley *W.Yorks.* 57 G6
Bierton 32 B7
Big Sand 94 D4
Bigbury 5 G6
Bigbury-on-Sea 5 G6
Bigby 52 D2
Bigert Mire 60 C7
Biggar *Cumb.* 54 E3
Biggar *S.Lan.* 75 J7
Biggin *Derbys.* 40 E1
Biggin *Derbys.* 50 D7
Biggin *N.Yorks.* 58 B6
Biggin Hill 23 H6
Biggin Hill Airport 23 H5
Biggings 109 A6
Biggleswade 32 E4
Bigholms 69 J5
Bighouse 104 D2
Bighton 11 H1
Biglands 60 D1
Bignor 12 C5
Bigrigg 60 B5
Bigton 109 C10
Bilberry 4 A4
Bilborough 41 H1
Bilbrook *Som.* 7 J1
Bilbrook *Staffs.* 40 A5
Bilbrough 58 B5
Bilbster 105 H3
Bildershaw 62 C4
Bildeston 34 D4
Billericay 24 C2
Billesdon 42 A5
Billesley 30 C3
Billholm 69 H4
Billingborough 42 E2
Billinge 48 E2
Billingford *Norf.* 35 F1
Billingford *Norf.* 44 E3
Billingham 63 F4
Billinghay 52 E7
Billingley 51 G2
Billingshurst 12 D4
Billingsley 39 G7
Billington *Beds.* 32 C6
Billington *Lancs.* 56 C6
Billockby 45 J4
Billy Row 62 C3
Bilsborrow 55 J5
Bilsby 53 H5
Bilsdean 77 F3
Bilsham 12 C6
Bilsington 15 F4
Bilsthorpe 51 J6
Bilston *Midloth.* 76 A4
Bilston *W.Mid.* 40 B6
Bilstone 41 F5
Bilting 15 F3
Bilton *E.Riding* 59 H6
Bilton *N.Yorks.* 57 K4
Bilton *N.Yorks.* 57 J4
Bilton *Northumb.* 71 H2
Bilton *Warks.* 31 F1
Bimbister 107 C6
Binbrook 53 F3
Bincombe 9 F6
Bindal 97 G3
Binegar 19 K7
Bines Green 12 E5
Binfield 22 B4
Binfield Heath 22 A4
Bingfield 70 E6
Bingham 42 A2
Bingham's Melcombe 9 G4
Bingley 57 G6
Binham 44 D2
Binley *Hants.* 21 H6
Binley *W.Mid.* 30 E1
Binniehill 75 G3
Binsoe 57 H2
Binstead 11 G5
Binsted *Hants.* 22 A7
Binsted *W.Suss.* 12 C6
Binton 30 C3
Bintree 44 E3
Binweston 38 B5
Birch *Essex* 34 D7
Birch *Gt.Man.* 49 H2
Birch Green 34 D7
Birch Heath 48 E6
Birch Vale 50 C4
Bircham Newton 44 B2
Bircham Tofts 44 B2
Birchanger 33 J6
Bircher 28 D2
Birchfield 96 B2
Birchgrove *Cardiff* 18 E3
Birchgrove *Swan.* 18 A2
Birchington 25 J5
Birchover 50 E6
Birchwood 49 F3
Bircotes 51 J3
Bird End 40 C6
Birdbrook 34 B4
Birdfield 73 H1
Birdham 12 B7
Birdingbury 31 F2
Birdlip 29 J7
Birdsall 58 E3
Birdsgreen 39 G7
Birdsmoor Gate 8 C4
Birdwell 51 F2
Birdwood 29 G7
Birgham 77 F7
Birichen 96 E2
Birkby 62 E6
Birkdale *Mersey.* 48 C1
Birkdale *N.Yorks.* 61 K6
Birkenhead 48 C4
Birkenhills 99 F6
Birkenshaw 57 H7
Birkhall 90 B5
Birkhill *Angus* 82 E4
Birkhill *Sc.Bord.* 76 D6
Birkhill *Sc.Bord.* 69 H2
Birkin 58 B7
Birkwood 75 G7
Birley 28 D3
Birley Carr 51 F3
Birling *Kent* 24 C5
Birling *Northumb.* 71 H3
Birling Gap 13 J7
Birlingham 29 J4
Birmingham 40 C7
Birmingham International Airport 40 D7
Birnam 82 B3
Birsay 106 B5
Birse 90 D5
Birsemore 90 D5
Birstall 41 H5
Birstall Smithies 57 H7
Birstwith 57 H4
Birthorpe 42 E2
Birtley *Here.* 28 C2
Birtley *Northumb.* 70 D6
Birtley *T. & W.* 62 D1
Birts Street 29 G5
Bisbrooke 42 B6
Bish Mill 7 F3
Bisham 22 B3
Bishampton 29 J3
Bishop Auckland 62 D3
Bishop Burton 59 F6
Bishop Middleham 62 E3
Bishop Monkton 57 J3
Bishop Norton 52 C3
Bishop Sutton 19 J6
Bishop Thornton 57 H3
Bishop Wilton 58 D4
Bishopbridge 52 D3
Bishopbriggs 74 E4
Bishopmill 97 K5
Bishops Cannings 20 D5
Bishop's Castle 38 C7
Bishop's Caundle 9 F3
Bishop's Cleeve 29 J6
Bishop's Frome 29 F4
Bishop's Green 33 K7
Bishop's Hull 8 B2
Bishop's Itchington 30 E3
Bishop's Lydeard 7 K3
Bishop's Nympton 7 F3
Bishop's Offley 39 G3
Bishop's Stortford 33 H6
Bishop's Sutton 11 H1
Bishop's Tachbrook 30 E2
Bishop's Tawton 6 D2
Bishop's Waltham 11 G3
Bishop's Wood 40 A5
Bishopsbourne 15 G2
Bishopsteignton 5 K3
Bishopstoke 11 F3
Bishopston 17 J7
Bishopstone *Bucks.* 32 B7
Bishopstone *E.Suss.* 13 H6
Bishopstone *Here.* 28 D4
Bishopstone *Swin.* 21 F3
Bishopstone *Wilts.* 10 B2
Bishopstrow 20 B7
Bishopswood 8 B3
Bishopsworth 19 J5
Bishopthorpe 58 B5
Bishopton *Darl.* 62 E4
Bishopton *Renf.* 74 C3
Bishton 19 G3
Bisley *Glos.* 20 C
Bisley *Surr.* 22 C
Bispham 55 G
Bissoe 2 E
Bisterne 10 C
Bisterne Close 10 D
Bitchfield 42 C
Bittadon 6 D
Bittaford 5 G
Bittering 44 D
Bitterley 28 E
Bitterne 11 F
Bitteswell 41 H
Bitton 19 K
Biwmaris (Beaumaris) 46 E
Bix 22 A
Bixter 109 C
Blaby 41 H
Black Bourton 21 F
Black Callerton 71 G
Black Clauchrie 67 G
Black Corries Lodge 80 D
Black Cross 3 G
Black Dog 7 G
Black Heddon 71 F
Black Marsh 38 C
Black Mount 80 D
Black Notley 34 B
Black Pill 17 K
Black Torrington 6 C
Blackacre 69 F
Blackadder 77 G
Blackawton 5 J
Blackborough 7 J
Blackborough End 44 A
Blackboys 13 J
Blackbraes *Aber.* 91 G
Blackbraes *Falk.* 75 H
Blackbrook 39 G
Blackburn *Aber.* 91 G
Blackburn *B'burn.* 56 B
Blackburn *W.Loth.* 75 H
Blackbushe 22 A
Blackcastle 97 F
Blackchambers 91 F
Blackcraig *D. & G.* 64 E
Blackcraig *D. & G.* 68 C
Blackden Heath 49 G
Blackdog 91 H
Blackdown *Devon* 5 F
Blackdown *Dorset* 8 C
Blackfield 11 F
Blackford *Aber.* 90 E
Blackford *Cumb.* 69 J
Blackford *P. & K.* 81 K
Blackford *Som.* 9 F
Blackford *Som.* 19 H
Blackfordby 41 F
Blackgang 11 F
Blackhall 76 A
Blackhall Colliery 63 F
Blackhall Rocks 63 F
Blackham 13 J
Blackheath *Essex* 34 D
Blackheath *Gt.Lon.* 23 G
Blackheath *Suff.* 35 J
Blackheath *Surr.* 22 D
Blackheath *W.Mid.* 40 B
Blackhill *Aber.* 99 J
Blackhill *Aber.* 99 J
Blackhillock 98 C
Blackhills 97 K
Blackland 20 D
Blacklunans 82 C
Blackmill 18 C
Blackmoor *Hants.* 11 J
Blackmoor *Som.* 7 K
Blackmoor Gate 6 E
Blackmore 24 C
Blackmore End *Essex* 34 B
Blackmore End *Herts.* 32 E
Blackness *Aber.* 90 E
Blackness *Falk.* 75 J
Blackness *High.* 105 H
Blacknest 22 A
Blacko 56 D
Blackpool 55 G
Blackpool Airport 55 G
Blackpool Gate 70 A
Blackridge 75 G
Blackrock *Arg. & B.* 72 B
Blackrock *Mon.* 28 B
Blackrod 49 F
Blackshaw 69 F
Blackshaw Head 56 E
Blacksmith's Corner 34 E
Blackstone 13 F
Blackthorn 31 H
Blackthorpe 34 D
Blacktoft 58 E
Blacktop 91 G
Blacktown 19 F
Blackwater *Cornw.* 2 E
Blackwater *Hants.* 22 B
Blackwater *I.o.W.* 11 G
Blackwater *Suff.* 35 J
Blackwaterfoot 66 D
Blackwell *Darl.* 62 D
Blackwell *Derbys.* 50 D
Blackwell *Derbys.* 51 G
Blackwell *Warks.* 30 D
Blackwell *Worcs.* 29 J
Blackwells End 29 G
Blackwood *Caerp.* 18 E
Blackwood *D. & G.* 68 E
Blackwood *S.Lan.* 75 F
Blackwood Hill 49 J
Blacon 48 C
Bladbean 15 G
Blades 62 A
Bladnoch 64 E
Bladon 31 F
Blaen Dyryn 27 J
Blaenannerch 17 F
Blaenau Dolwyddelan 46 E
Blaenau Ffestiniog 37 F
Blaenavon 19 F
Blaenawey 28 B
Blaencwm 18 C
Blaenffos 16 E
Blaengarw 18 C
Blaengweche 17 K
Blaengwrach 18 B
Blaengwynfi 18 B
Blaenos 27 G
Blaenpennal 27 F
Blaenplwyf 26 E
Blaenporth 17 F
Blaenrhondda 18 C
Blaenwaun 17 F
Blaen-y-coed 17 G
Blagdon *N.Som.* 19 H
Blagdon *Torbay* 5 J
Blagdon Hill 8 B

Place	Page	Grid
Blaich	87	G7
Blaina	19	F1
Blair	74	B6
Blair Atholl	81	K1
Blair Drummond	75	F1
Blairannaich	80	E7
Blairbuie	73	K3
Blairgowrie	82	C3
Blairhall	75	J2
Blairhoyle	81	H7
Blairhullichan	81	F7
Blairingone	75	H1
Blairkip	74	D7
Blairlogie	75	G1
Blairmore Arg. & B.	73	K2
Blairmore High.	96	E1
Blairmore High.	102	D2
Blairnairn	74	B2
Blairnamarrow	89	K3
Blairpark	74	A5
Blairquhan	67	H3
Blairquhosh	74	D2
Blair's Ferry	73	H4
Blairshinnoch	98	E4
Blairuskinmore	81	F7
Blairvadach	74	A2
Blairydryne	91	F5
Blairythan Cottage	91	H2
Blaisdon	29	G7
Blake End	33	K6
Blakebrook	29	H1
Blakedown	29	H1
Blakelaw Sc.Bord.	77	F7
Blakelaw T. & W.	71	H7
Blakemere	28	C4
Blakeney Glos.	19	K1
Blakeney Norf.	44	E1
Blakenhall Ches.	39	G1
Blakenhall W.Mid.	40	A7
Blakeshall	40	A7
Blakesley	31	H3
Blanchland	62	A1
Bland Hill	57	H4
Blandford Camp	9	J4
Blandford Forum	9	H4
Blandford St. Mary	9	H4
Blanefield	74	D3
Blankney	52	D6
Blar a' Chaorainn	80	C1
Blargie	88	D5
Blarglas	74	B2
Blarmachfoldach	80	B1
Blarnalevoch	95	H2
Blashford	10	C4
Blaston	42	B6
Blathaisbhal	92	D4
Blatherwycke	42	C6
Blawith	55	F1
Blaxhall	35	H3
Blaxton	51	J2
Blaydon	71	G7
Bleadney	19	H7
Bleadon	19	G6
Bleak Hey Nook	50	C2
Blean	25	H5
Bleasby	42	A1
Bleatarn	61	J5
Blebocraigs	83	F6
Bleddfa	28	B2
Bledington	30	D6
Bledlow	22	A1
Bledlow Ridge	22	A2
Blencarn	61	H3
Blencogo	60	C2
Blencow	61	F3
Blendworth	11	J3
Blennerhasset	60	C2
Blervie Castle	97	H6
Bletchingdon	31	G7
Bletchingley	23	G6
Bletchley M.K.	32	B5
Bletchley Shrop.	39	F2
Bletherston	16	D3
Bletsoe	32	D3
Blewbury	21	J3
Blickling	45	F3
Blidworth	51	H7
Blindburn Aber.	91	H1
Blindburn Northumb.	70	D2
Blindcrake	60	C3
Blindley Heath	23	G7
Blisland	4	B3
Bliss Gate	29	G1
Blissford	10	C3
Blisworth	31	J3
Blithbury	40	C3
Blitterlees	60	C1
Blo Norton	34	E1
Blockley	30	C5
Blofield	45	H5
Blore	40	D1
Blossomfield	30	C1
Blount's Green	40	C2
Bloxham	31	F5
Bloxholm	52	D7
Bloxwich	40	B5
Bloxworth	9	H5
Blubberhouses	57	G4
Blue Anchor Cornw.	3	G3
Blue Anchor Som.	7	J1
Blue Bell Hill	24	D5
Bluewater	23	J4
Blundeston	45	K6
Blunham	32	E3
Blunsdon St. Andrew	20	E2
Bluntisham	33	G1
Blunts	4	D4
Blyborough	52	C3
Blyford	35	J1
Blymhill	40	A4
Blyth Northumb.	71	J5
Blyth Notts.	51	J4
Blyth Bridge	75	K6
Blythburgh	35	J1
Blythe Bridge	40	B1
Blythe Marsh	40	B1
Blyton	52	B3
Boarhills	83	G6
Boarhunt	11	H4
Boars Hill	21	H1
Boarshead	13	J3
Boarstall	31	H7
Boarzell	14	C5
Boasley Cross	6	D6
Boat o' Brig	98	B5
Boat of Garten	89	G3
Boath	96	C4
Bobbing	24	E5
Bobbington	40	A6
Bobbingworth	23	J1
Bocaddon	4	B5
Bochastle	81	H7
Bockhampton	21	G4
Bocking	34	B6
Bocking Churchstreet	34	B6
Boconnoc	4	B4
Boddam Aber.	99	K6
Boddam Shet.	109	F9
Boddington	29	H6
Bodedern	46	B4
Bodelwyddan	47	J5
Bodenham Here.	28	E3
Bodenham Wilts.	10	C2
Bodenham Moor	28	E3
Bodesbeck	69	G3
Bodewryd	46	B3
Bodfari	47	J5
Bodffordd	46	C5
Bodfuan	36	C2
Bodham Street	45	F1
Bodiam	14	C5
Bodicote	31	F5
Bodieve	3	G1
Bodinnick	4	B5
Bodior	46	A5
Bodle Street Green	13	K5
Bodmin	4	A4
Bodney	44	C6
Bodorgan	46	B6
Bodsham Green	15	G3
Bodwen	4	A4
Bogallan	96	D6
Bogbain	96	E7
Bogbrae	91	J1
Bogbuie	96	C6
Bogend	74	B7
Bogfern	90	D4
Bogfields	90	D4
Bogfold	99	G5
Boghall	75	H1
Boghead Aber.	98	E5
Boghead E.Ayr.	68	B1
Boghead S.Lan.	75	F6
Boghole Farm	97	G6
Bogmoor	98	B4
Bogniebrae	98	D6
Bognor Regis	12	C7
Bograxie	91	F3
Bogroy	89	G2
Bogside	75	H1
Bogston	90	B4
Bogton	98	E5
Bogue	68	B5
Bohenie	87	J6
Bohortha	3	F5
Bohuntine	87	J6
Boirseam	93	F3
Bojewyan	2	A5
Bolam	62	C4
Bolberry	5	G7
Bold Heath	48	E4
Bolderwood	10	D4
Boldon	71	J7
Boldre	10	E5
Boldron	62	B5
Bole	51	K4
Bolehill	50	E7
Boleigh	2	B6
Boleside	76	C7
Bolfracks	81	K3
Bolgoed	17	K5
Bolham	7	H4
Bolham Water	7	K4
Bolingey	2	E3
Bollington	49	J5
Bolney	13	F4
Bolnhurst	32	D3
Bolshan	83	H2
Bolsover	51	G5
Bolsterstone	50	E3
Bolstone	28	E5
Boltby	57	K1
Bolter End	22	A2
Bolton Cumb.	61	H4
Bolton E.Loth.	76	D3
Bolton E.Riding	58	D4
Bolton Gt.Man.	49	G2
Bolton Northumb.	71	G2
Bolton Abbey	57	F4
Bolton Bridge	57	F4
Bolton by Bowland	56	C5
Bolton Low Houses	60	D2
Bolton Percy	58	B5
Bolton upon Dearne	51	G2
Boltonfellend	69	K7
Boltongate	60	D2
Bolton-le-Sands	55	H3
Bolton-on-Swale	62	D7
Bolventor	4	B3
Bombie	65	H5
Bomere Heath	38	D4
Bonar Bridge	96	D2
Bonawe	80	B4
Bonawe Quarries	80	B4
Bonby	52	D1
Boncath	17	F2
Bonchester Bridge	70	A2
Bonchurch	11	G7
Bondleigh	6	E5
Bonehill	40	D5
Bo'ness	75	H2
Bonhill	74	B3
Boningale	40	A5
Bonjedward	70	B1
Bonkle	75	G5
Bonnington	15	F4
Bonnybank	82	E7
Bonnybridge	75	G2
Bonnykelly	99	G5
Bonnyrigg	76	B4
Bonnyton Aber.	83	G1
Bonnyton Angus	83	H1
Bonnyton Angus	82	E4
Bonsall	50	E7
Bont	28	C7
Bont Dolgadfan	37	H5
Bont Newydd	37	G3
Bontddu	37	F4
Bont-goch (Elerch)	37	F7
Bontnewydd	46	C6
Bontuchel	47	J7
Bonvilston	18	D4
Bon-y-maen	17	K6
Boohay	5	K5
Booker	22	B2
Booley	38	E3
Boor	94	E3
Boosbeck	63	H5
Boot	60	C6
Booth Wood	50	C1
Boothby Graffoe	52	C7
Boothby Pagnell	42	C2
Boothstown	49	G2
Boothville	31	J2
Bootle Cumb.	54	E1
Bootle Mersey.	48	C3
Booton	45	F3
Boquhan	74	D2
Boraston	29	F1
Bordeaux	3	J5
Borden	24	E5
Bordley	56	E3
Bordon	11	J1
Boreham Essex	24	D1
Boreham Wilts.	20	B7
Boreham Street	13	K5
Borehamwood	22	E2
Boreland D. & G.	69	G4
Boreland D. & G.	64	D4
Boreland Stir.	81	G4
Boreraig	93	G6
Borgh W.Isles	92	E3
Borgh W.Isles	84	B4
Borghastan	100	D3
Borgie	103	J3
Borgue D. & G.	65	G6
Borgue High.	105	G6
Borley	34	C4
Bornais	84	C2
Borness	65	G6
Borough Green	23	K6
Boroughbridge	57	J3
Borras Head	48	C7
Borrowash	41	G2
Borrowby N.Yorks.	63	J5
Borrowby N.Yorks.	57	K1
Borrowdale	60	D5
Borrowfield	91	G5
Borstal	24	D5
Borth	37	F7
Borthwick	76	B5
Borthwickbrae	69	K2
Borthwickshiels	69	K2
Borth-y-Gest	36	E2
Borve	93	K7
Borwick	55	J2
Bosavern	2	A5
Bosbury	29	F4
Boscastle	4	B1
Boscombe Bourne.	10	C5
Boscombe Wilts.	10	D1
Boscoppa	4	A5
Bosham	12	B6
Bosherston	16	C6
Bosley	49	J6
Bossall	58	D3
Bossiney	4	A2
Bossingham	15	G3
Bossington Hants.	10	E1
Bossington Som.	7	G1
Bostock Green	49	F6
Boston	43	G1
Boston Spa	57	K5
Boswinger	3	G4
Botallack	2	A5
Botany Bay	23	F2
Botarua	92	C4
Botcheston	41	G5
Botesdale	34	E1
Bothal	71	H5
Bothamsall	51	J5
Bothel	60	C3
Bothenhampton	8	D5
Bothwell	75	F5
Botley Bucks.	22	C1
Botley Hants.	11	G3
Botley Oxon.	21	H1
Botloe's Green	29	G6
Botolph Claydon	31	J6
Botolphs	12	E6
Bottacks	96	B5
Bottesford Leics.	42	B2
Bottesford N.Lincs.	52	C2
Bottisham	33	J2
Bottom Head	56	B3
Bottomcraig	82	E5
Botusfleming	4	E4
Botwnnog	36	B2
Bough Beech	23	H7
Boughrood	28	A5
Boughspring	19	J2
Boughton Norf.	44	A5
Boughton Northants.	31	J2
Boughton Notts.	51	J6
Boughton Aluph	15	F3
Boughton Green	14	C2
Boughton Lees	15	F3
Boughton Malherbe	14	D3
Boughton Street	15	F2
Boulby	63	J5
Bouldon	38	E7
Boulmer	71	H2
Boulston	16	C4
Boultenstone Hotel	90	C3
Boultham	52	C6
Bourn	33	G3
Bournbrook	40	C7
Bourne	42	D3
Bourne End Beds.	32	C4
Bourne End Bucks.	22	B3
Bourne End Herts.	22	D1
Bournebridge	23	J2
Bournemouth	10	B5
Bournemouth Airport	10	C5
Bournes Green	20	C1
Bournheath	29	J1
Bournmoor	62	E1
Bournville	40	C7
Bourton Dorset	9	G1
Bourton N.Som.	19	G5
Bourton Oxon.	21	F3
Bourton Shrop.	38	E6
Bourton on Dunsmore	31	F1
Bourton-on-the-Hill	30	C5
Bourton-on-the-Water	30	C6
Bousd	78	D1
Boustead Hill	60	D1
Bouth	55	G1
Bouthwaite	57	G2
Bovain	81	G4
Boveney	22	C4
Boveridge	10	B3
Boverton	18	C5
Bovey Tracey	5	J3
Bovingdon	22	D1
Bovinger	23	J1
Bovington Camp	9	H6
Bow Devon	7	F5
Bow Devon	5	J5
Bow Ork.	107	C8
Bow Brickhill	32	C5
Bow of Fife	82	E6
Bow Street	37	F7
Bowbank	62	A4
Bowburn	62	E3
Bowcombe	11	F6
Bowd	7	K6
Bowden Devon	5	J6
Bowden Sc.Bord.	76	D7
Bowden Hill	20	C5
Bowdon	49	G4
Bower	70	C5
Bower Hinton	8	D3
Bowerchalke	10	B2
Bowerhill	20	C5
Bowermadden	105	H2
Bowers Gifford	24	D3
Bowershall	75	J1
Bowertower	105	H2
Bowes	62	A5
Bowgreave	55	H5
Bowland Bridge	55	H1
Bowley	28	E3
Bowlhead Green	12	C3
Bowling	74	C3
Bowling Bank	38	C1
Bowlish	19	K7
Bowmanstead	60	E7
Bowmore	72	B5
Bowness-on-Solway	69	H7
Bowness-on-Windermere	61	F7
Bowsden	77	H6
Bowside Lodge	104	D2
Bowthorpe	45	F5
Bowtrees	75	H2
Box Glos.	20	B1
Box Wilts.	20	B5
Box End	32	D4
Boxbush	29	G7
Boxford Suff.	34	D4
Boxford W.Berks.	21	H4
Boxgrove	12	C6
Boxley	14	C2
Boxmoor	22	D1
Boxted Essex	34	D5
Boxted Suff.	34	C3
Boxted Cross	34	E5
Boxworth	33	G2
Boxworth End	33	G2
Boyden Gate	25	J5
Boydston	74	C7
Boylestone	40	D2
Boyndie	98	E4
Boynton	59	H3
Boysack	83	H3
Boyton Cornw.	6	B6
Boyton Suff.	35	H4
Boyton Wilts.	9	J1
Boyton Cross	24	C1
Bozeat	32	C3
Braaid	54	C6
Braal Castle	105	G2
Brabling Green	35	G2
Brabourne	15	F3
Brabourne Lees	15	F3
Brabster	105	J2
Bracadale	85	J1
Braceborough	42	D4
Bracebridge	52	C6
Bracebridge Heath	52	C6
Braceby	42	D2
Bracewell	56	D5
Brachla	88	C1
Brackenber	61	J4
Brackenfield	51	F7
Brackens	99	F5
Bracklach	90	B2
Bracklamore	99	G5
Brackletter	87	H6
Brackley Arg. & B.	73	G2
Brackley High.	97	F6
Brackley Northants.	31	G5
Bracknell	22	B5
Braco	81	K7
Bracobrae	98	D5
Bracon Ash	45	F6
Bracora	86	D5
Bracorina	86	D5
Bradbourne	50	E7
Bradbury	62	E4
Bradda	54	B6
Bradden	31	H4
Bradenham	22	B2
Bradenstoke	20	D3
Bradfield Devon	7	J5
Bradfield Essex	35	F5
Bradfield Norf.	45	G2
Bradfield W.Berks.	21	K4
Bradfield Combust	34	C3
Bradfield Green	49	F7
Bradfield Heath	35	F6
Bradfield St. Clare	34	D3
Bradfield St. George	34	D3
Bradford Devon	6	C5
Bradford Northumb.	77	K7
Bradford W.Yorks.	57	G6
Bradford Abbas	8	E3
Bradford Leigh	20	B5
Bradford Peverell	9	F5
Bradford-on-Avon	20	B5
Bradford-on-Tone	7	K3
Brading	11	H6
Bradley Derbys.	40	E1
Bradley Hants.	21	K7
Bradley N.E.Lincs.	53	F2
Bradley or Low Bradley N.Yorks.	57	F5
Bradley Staffs.	40	A4
Bradley W.Mid.	40	B6
Bradley in the Moors	40	C1
Bradley Stoke	19	K3
Bradmore Notts.	41	H2
Bradmore W.Mid.	40	A6
Bradninch	7	J5
Bradnop	50	C7
Bradpole	8	D5
Bradshaw	49	G1
Bradstone	6	B7
Bradwall Green	49	G6
Bradwell Derbys.	50	D4
Bradwell Essex	34	C6
Bradwell M.K.	32	B5
Bradwell Norf.	45	K5
Bradwell Waterside	25	F1
Bradwell-on-Sea	25	F1
Bradworthy	6	B4
Brae D. & G.	65	J3
Brae High.	96	B1
Brae Shet.	109	C6
Braeantra	96	C4
Braedownie	89	K7
Braefoot	97	F6
Braegrum	82	B5
Braehead Glas.	74	D4
Braehead Moray	98	B6
Braehead Ork.	107	E7
Braehead Ork.	106	D3
Braehead S.Lan.	75	G7
Braehead S.Lan.	75	H5
Braehead of Lunan	83	H2
Braehoulland	108	B5
Braeleny	81	H6
Braemar	89	J5
Braemore High.	96	C1
Braemore High.	105	F5
Braemore High.	95	H4
Braenaloin	89	K5
Braes of Enzie	98	B5
Braes of Foss	81	J2
Braes of Ullapool	95	H2
Braeswick	106	F4
Braeval	81	G7
Brafferton Darl.	62	D4
Brafferton N.Yorks.	57	K2
Brafield-on-the-Green	32	B3
Bragar	100	D3
Bragbury End	33	F6
Bragleenbeg	80	A5
Braichmelyn	46	E6
Braides	55	H4
Braidley	57	F1
Braidwood	75	G6
Braigo	72	A4
Brailsford	40	E1
Braintree	34	B6
Braiseworth	35	F1
Braishfield	10	E2
Braithwaite Cumb.	60	D4
Braithwaite S.Yorks.	51	J1
Braithwell	51	H3
Bramber	12	E5
Brambletye	13	H3
Bramcote	41	H2
Bramdean	11	H2
Bramerton	45	G5
Bramfield Herts.	33	F7
Bramfield Suff.	35	H1
Bramford	35	F4
Bramhall	49	H4
Bramham	57	K5
Bramhope	57	H5
Bramley Hants.	21	K6
Bramley S.Yorks.	51	G3
Bramley Surr.	22	D7
Bramling	15	H2
Brampford Speke	7	H6
Brampton Cambs.	33	F1
Brampton Cumb.	70	A7
Brampton Cumb.	61	H4
Brampton Derbys.	51	F5
Brampton Lincs.	52	B5
Brampton Norf.	45	G3
Brampton S.Yorks.	51	G2
Brampton Suff.	45	J7
Brampton Abbotts	29	F6
Brampton Ash	42	A7
Brampton Bryan	28	C1
Brampton en le Morthen	51	G4
Bramshall	40	C2
Bramshaw	10	D3
Bramshill	22	A5
Bramshott	12	B3
Bramwell	8	D2
Bran End	33	K6
Branault	79	G1
Brancaster	44	B1
Brancepeth	62	D3
Branchill	97	H6
Brand Green	29	G6
Branderburgh	97	K4
Brandesburton	59	H5
Brandeston	35	G2
Brandis Corner	6	C5
Brandiston	45	F3
Brandon Dur.	62	D3
Brandon Lincs.	42	C1
Brandon Northumb.	71	F2
Brandon Suff.	44	B7
Brandon Warks.	31	F1
Brandon Bank	44	A7
Brandon Creek	44	A6
Brandon Parva	44	E5
Brandsby	58	B2
Brandy Wharf	52	D3
Brane	2	A6
Branksome	10	B5
Branksome Park	10	B5
Bransby	52	B5
Branscombe	7	K7
Bransford	29	G3
Bransgore	10	C5
Branson's Cross	30	B1
Branston Leics.	42	B3
Branston Lincs.	52	D6
Branston Staffs.	40	E3
Branston Booths	52	D6
Branstone	11	G6
Brant Broughton	52	C7
Brantham	35	F5
Branthwaite Cumb.	60	B4
Branthwaite Cumb.	60	D3
Brantingham	59	F7
Branton Northumb.	71	F2
Branton S.Yorks.	51	J2
Brantwood	60	E7
Branxholm	69	K2
Branxholme	69	K2
Branxton	77	G7
Brassington	50	E7
Brasted	23	H6
Brasted Chart	23	H6
Brathens	90	E4
Bratoft	53	H6
Brattleby	52	C4
Bratton Clovelly	6	C6
Bratton Fleming	6	E2
Bratton Seymour	9	F2
Braughing	33	G6
Braunston Rut.	42	B5
Braunstone	6	A4
Braunton	6	C2
Brawby	58	D2
Brawdy	16	B3
Brawith	63	G6
Brawl	104	D2
Brawlbin	105	F3
Bray	22	C4
Bray Shop	4	D3
Bray Wick	22	B4
Braybrooke	42	A7
Brayford	6	E2
Brayshaw	56	C4
Brayton	58	C6
Brazacott	4	C1
Breach	24	E5
Breachwood Green	32	E6
Breacleit	100	D4
Breadsall	41	F2
Breadstone	20	A1
Breage	2	D6
Breakon	108	E2
Bream	19	K1
Breamore	10	C3
Brean	19	F6
Breanais	100	B5
Brearton	57	J3
Breascleit	100	E4
Breaston	41	G2
Brechfa	17	J2
Brechin	83	H1
Brecklate	66	A2
Breckles	44	D6
Brecon (Aberhonddu)	27	K6
Breconside	68	D3
Bredbury	49	J3
Brede	14	D6
Bredenbury	29	F3
Bredfield	35	G3
Bredgar	24	E5
Bredhurst	24	D5
Bredicot	29	J3
Bredon	29	J5
Bredon's Hardwick	29	J5
Bredon's Norton	29	J5
Bredwardine	28	C4
Breedon on the Hill	41	G3
Breibhig	101	G4
Breich	75	H4
Breighton	58	D6
Breinton	28	D4
Bremhill	20	C4
Brenachoille	80	B7
Brenchley	23	K7
Brendon Devon	7	F1
Brendon Devon	6	B4
Brendon Common	51	G5
Brenkley	71	H6
Brent Eleigh	34	D4
Brent Knoll	19	G6
Brent Pelham	33	H5
Brentford	22	E4
Brentingby	42	A4
Brentwood	23	J2
Brenzett	15	F5
Breoch	65	H5
Brereton	40	C4
Brereton Green	49	G6
Brereton Heath	49	H6
Bressingham	44	E7
Bretabister	109	D7
Bretby	40	E3
Bretford	31	F1
Bretforton	30	B4
Bretherdale Head	61	G6
Bretherton	55	H7
Brettenham Norf.	44	D7
Brettenham Suff.	34	D3
Bretton	48	C6
Brewood	40	A5
Briach	97	H6
Briantspuddle	9	H5
Bricket Wood	22	E1
Bricklehampton	29	J4
Bride	54	D3
Bridekirk	60	C3
Bridell	16	E1
Bridestones	49	J6
Bridestowe	6	D7
Brideswell	90	D1
Bridford	7	G7
Bridge Cornw.	2	D4
Bridge Kent	15	G2
Bridge End Lincs.	42	E2
Bridge End Shet.	109	C9
Bridge Hewick	57	J2
Bridge o' Ess	90	D5
Bridge of Alford	90	D3
Bridge of Allan	75	F1
Bridge of Avon	89	J1
Bridge of Balgie	81	G3
Bridge of Bogendreip	90	E5
Bridge of Brewlands	82	C1
Bridge of Brown	89	J2
Bridge of Cally	82	C2
Bridge of Canny	90	E5
Bridge of Craigisla	82	D2
Bridge of Dee Aber.	91	G5
Bridge of Dee Aber.	90	E5
Bridge of Dee D. & G.	65	H4
Bridge of Don	91	H4
Bridge of Dun	83	H2
Bridge of Dye	90	E6
Bridge of Earn	82	C6
Bridge of Ericht	81	G2
Bridge of Feugh	90	E5
Bridge of Forss	105	F2
Bridge of Gairn	90	B5
Bridge of Gaur	81	G2
Bridge of Muchalls	91	G5
Bridge of Muick	90	B5
Bridge of Orchy	80	E4
Bridge of Tynet	98	B4
Bridge of Tyt	81	K1
Bridge of Walls	109	B7
Bridge of Weir	74	B4
Bridge Sollers	28	D4
Bridge Street	34	C4
Bridgefoot Cambs.	33	H4
Bridgefoot Cumb.	60	B4
Bridgehampton	8	E2
Bridgemary	11	G4
Bridgemere	39	G1
Bridgend Aber.	90	D1
Bridgend Angus	83	G1
Bridgend Arg. & B.	72	B4
Bridgend Arg. & B.	73	G1
Bridgend (Pen-y-bont ar Ogwr) Bridgend	18	C4
Bridgend Cornw.	4	B5
Bridgend Cumb.	61	F5
Bridgend Fife	82	E6
Bridgend Moray	90	B1
Bridgend P. & K.	82	C5
Bridgend W.Loth.	75	J3
Bridgend of Lintrathen	82	D2
Bridgerule	6	A5
Bridges	38	C6
Bridgeton	90	C3
Bridgetown Cornw.	6	B7
Bridgetown Som.	7	H2
Bridgeyate	19	K4
Bridgham	44	D7
Bridgnorth	39	G6
Bridgtown	40	B5
Bridgwater	8	B1
Bridlington	59	H3
Bridport	8	D5
Bridstow	28	E6
Brierfield	56	D6
Brierley Glos.	29	F7
Brierley Here.	28	D3
Brierley S.Yorks.	51	G1
Brierley Hill	40	B7
Brig o'Turk	81	G7
Brigehaugh	90	B1
Brigg	52	D2
Brigham Cumb.	60	B3
Brigham E.Riding	59	G4
Brighouse	57	G7
Brighstone	11	F6
Brightgate	50	E7
Brighthampton	21	G1
Brightling	13	K4
Brightlingsea	34	E7
Brighton B. & H.	13	G6
Brighton Cornw.	3	G3
Brightons	75	H3
Brightwalton	21	H4
Brightwell Oxon.	21	J2
Brightwell Suff.	35	G4
Brightwell Baldwin	21	K2
Brignall	62	B5
Brigsley	53	F2
Brigsteer	55	H1
Brigstock	42	C7
Brill Bucks.	31	H7
Brill Cornw.	2	E6
Brilley	28	B4
Brilley Mountain	28	B3
Brimfield	28	E2
Brimington	51	G5
Brimington Common	51	G5
Brimley	5	J3
Brimpsfield	29	J7
Brimpton	21	J5
Brimscombe	20	B1
Brimstage	48	C4
Brind	58	D6
Brindister Shet.	109	D9
Brindister Shet.	109	B7
Brindle	55	J7
Brindley Ford	49	H7
Brineton	40	A4
Bringhurst	42	B6
Brington	32	D1
Brinian	106	D5
Briningham	44	E2
Brinkhill	53	G5
Brinkley	33	K3
Brinklow	31	F1
Brinkworth	20	D3
Brinmore	88	D2
Brinscall	56	B7
Brinsley	41	G1
Brinsop	28	D4
Brinsworth	51	G4
Brinton	44	E2
Brisco	61	F1
Brisley	44	D3
Brislington	19	K4
Bristol	19	J4
Bristol International Airport	19	H5
Briston	44	E2
Britannia	56	D7
Britford	10	C2
Brithdir	37	G4
Brithem Bottom	7	J4
Briton Ferry (Llansawel)	18	A2
Britwell Salome	21	K2
Brixham	5	K5
Brixton	5	F5
Brixton Deverill	9	H1
Brixworth	31	J1
Brize Norton	21	F1
Broad Blunsdon	20	E2
Broad Campden	30	C5
Broad Chalke	10	B2
Broad Green Beds.	32	C4
Broad Green Essex	34	C6
Broad Green Worcs.	29	G3
Broad Haven	16	B4
Broad Hill	33	J1
Broad Hinton	20	E4
Broad Laying	21	H5
Broad Marston	30	C4
Broad Oak Cumb.	60	C7
Broad Oak E.Suss.	14	D6
Broad Oak E.Suss.	13	K4
Broad Oak Here.	28	D6
Broad Street	14	D2
Broad Street Green	24	E1
Broad Town	20	D4
Broadbottom	49	J3
Broadbridge	12	B6
Broadbridge Heath	12	E3
Broadclyst	7	H6
Broadford	86	C2
Broadford Bridge	12	D4
Broadgate	54	E1
Broadgroves	33	K7
Broadhaugh	69	K3
Broadheath Gt.Man.	49	G4
Broadheath Worcs.	29	F2
Broadhembury	7	K5
Broadhempston	5	J4
Broadholme	52	B5
Broadland Row	14	D6
Broadlay	17	G5
Broadley Lancs.	49	H1
Broadley Moray	98	B4
Broadley Common	23	H1
Broadmayne	9	G6
Broadmeadows	69	K1
Broadmere	21	K7
Broadnymett	7	F5
Broadoak Carmar.	17	J3
Broadoak Dorset	8	D5
Broadoak Kent	25	H5
Broadsea	99	G4
Broadstairs	25	K5
Broadstone Poole	10	B5
Broadstone Shrop.	38	E7
Broadstreet Common	19	G3
Broadwas Herts.	33	F6
Broadwater W.Suss.	12	E6
Broadway Carmar.	17	J3
Broadway Carmar.	17	F4
Broadway Pembs.	16	B4
Broadway Som.	8	C3
Broadway Suff.	35	H1
Broadway Worcs.	30	B5
Broadwell Glos.	30	D6
Broadwell Glos.	28	E7
Broadwell Oxon.	21	F1
Broadwell Warks.	31	F2

Place	County	Page	Grid
Broadwell House		62	A1
Broadway		9	F6
Broadwindsor		8	D4
Broadwood Kelly		6	E5
Broadwoodwidger		6	C7
Brobury		28	C4
Brochel		94	B7
Brochloch		67	K4
Brock		78	B3
Brockbridge		11	H3
Brockdish		35	G1
Brockenhurst		10	E4
Brockfield		58	C4
Brockford Street		35	F2
Brockhall		31	H2
Brockham		22	E7
Brockhampton	*Glos.*	30	B6
Brockhampton	*Here.*	28	E5
Brockholes		50	D1
Brockhurst		13	H3
Brocklebank		60	E2
Brocklesby		52	E1
Brockley	*N.Som.*	19	H5
Brockley	*Suff.*	34	C3
Brockton	*Shrop.*	38	E6
Brockton	*Shrop.*	39	G5
Brockton	*Shrop.*	38	C5
Brockton	*Shrop.*	38	C7
Brockweir		19	J1
Brockwood Park		11	H2
Brockworth		29	H7
Brocton		40	B4
Brodick		73	J7
Brodsworth		51	H2
Brogborough		32	C5
Brogyntyn		38	B2
Broken Cross	*Ches.*	49	H5
Broken Cross	*Ches.*	49	F5
Brokenborough		20	C3
Bromborough		48	C4
Brome		35	F1
Brome Street		35	F1
Bromeswell		35	G3
Bromfield	*Cumb.*	60	C2
Bromfield	*Shrop.*	28	D1
Bromham	*Beds.*	32	D3
Bromham	*Wilts.*	20	C5
Bromley		23	H5
Bromley Green		14	E4
Brompton	*Med.*	24	D5
Brompton	*N.Yorks.*	62	E7
Brompton	*N.Yorks.*	59	F1
Brompton on Swale		62	D6
Brompton Ralph		7	J2
Brompton Regis		7	H2
Bromsash		29	F6
Bromsberrow Heath		29	G5
Bromsgrove		29	J1
Bromstead Heath		40	A4
Bromyard		29	F3
Bromyard Downs		29	F3
Bronaber		37	G2
Brongest		17	G1
Bronington		38	D2
Bronllys		28	A5
Bronnant		27	F2
Bronydd		28	B4
Bron-y-Gaer		17	G4
Brongarth		38	B2
Brook	*Carmar.*	17	F5
Brook	*Hants.*	10	D3
Brook	*Hants.*	10	E1
Brook	*I.o.W.*	10	E6
Brook	*Kent*	15	F3
Brook	*Surr.*	12	C3
Brook Street	*Essex*	23	J2
Brook Street	*Kent*	14	E4
Brook Street	*Suff.*	34	C4
Brook Street	*W.Suss.*	13	G4
Brooke	*Norf.*	45	G6
Brooke	*Rut.*	42	B5
Brookend		19	J2
Brookhouse		55	J3
Brookhouse Green		49	H6
Brookland		14	E5
Brooklands		65	J3
Brookmans Park		23	F1
Brooks		38	A6
Brooks Green		12	E4
Brooksby		41	J4
Brookthorpe		29	H7
Brookwood		22	C6
Broom	*Beds.*	32	E4
Broom	*Warks.*	30	B3
Broom Hill		10	B4
Broom of Dalreach		82	B6
Broomcroft		38	E4
Broome	*Norf.*	45	H6
Broome	*Shrop.*	38	C7
Broome	*Worcs.*	29	J1
Broome Wood		71	G2
Broomedge		49	G4
Broomer's Corner		12	E4
Broomfield	*Aber.*	91	H1
Broomfield	*Essex*	34	B7
Broomfield	*Kent*	25	H5
Broomfield	*Kent*	14	D2
Broomfield	*Som.*	8	B1
Broomfleet		58	E7
Broomhaugh		71	F7
Broomhead		99	H4
Broomhill		71	H3
Broom's Green		29	G5
Brora		97	G1
Broseley		39	F5
Brotherlee		62	A3
Brothertoft		43	F1
Brotherton		57	K7
Brotton		63	H4
Broubster		105	F2
Brough	*Cumb.*	61	J5
Brough	*Derbys.*	50	D4
Brough	*E.Riding*	59	F7
Brough	*High.*	105	H1
Brough	*Notts.*	52	B7
Brough	*Ork.*	107	C6
Brough	*Shet.*	109	E8
Brough	*Shet.*	108	D5
Brough	*Shet.*	108	E5
Brough	*Shet.*	108	E6
Brough Lodge		108	E3
Brough Sowerby		61	J5
Broughall		38	E1
Brougham		61	G4
Broughton	*Cambs.*	33	F1
Broughton	*Flints.*	48	C6
Broughton	*Hants.*	10	E1
Broughton	*Lancs.*	55	J6
Broughton	*M.K.*	32	B4
Broughton	*N.Lincs.*	52	C2
Broughton	*N.Yorks.*	58	D2
Broughton	*N.Yorks.*	56	E4
Broughton	*Northants.*	32	B1
Broughton	*Ork.*	106	D3
Broughton	*Oxon.*	31	F5
Broughton	*Sc.Bord.*	75	K7
Broughton	*V. of Glam.*	18	C4
Broughton Astley		41	H6
Broughton Beck		55	F1
Broughton Gifford		20	B5
Broughton Hackett		29	J3
Broughton in Furness		55	F1
Broughton Mills		60	D7
Broughton Moor		60	B3
Broughton Poggs		21	F1
Broughtown		106	F3
Broughty Ferry		83	F4
Browland		109	B7
Brown Candover		11	G1
Brown Edge	*Lancs.*	48	C1
Brown Edge	*Staffs.*	49	J7
Brown Lees		49	H7
Brownhill		99	G6
Brownhills	*Fife*	83	G6
Brownhills	*W.Mid.*	40	C5
Brownieside		71	G1
Brownlow Heath		49	H6
Brownshill Green		41	F7
Brownston		5	G5
Broxa		63	J3
Broxbourne		23	G1
Broxburn	*E.Loth.*	76	D3
Broxburn	*W.Loth.*	75	J3
Broxholme		52	C5
Broxted		33	J6
Broxton		48	D7
Broxwood		28	C3
Bru		101	F2
Bruachmary		97	F7
Bruan		105	J5
Bruichladdich		72	A4
Bruera		48	D6
Bruisyard		35	H2
Bruisyard Street		35	H2
Brund		50	D6
Brundall		45	H5
Brundish		35	G2
Brundish Street		35	G1
Bruntingthorpe		41	J7
Bruntland		90	C2
Brunton	*Fife*	82	E5
Brunton	*Northumb.*	71	H1
Brushford	*Devon*	6	E5
Brushford	*Som.*	7	H3
Bruton		9	F1
Bryanston		9	H4
Brydekirk		69	G6
Brymbo		48	B7
Bryn	*Carmar.*	17	J5
Bryn	*Gt.Man.*	48	E2
Bryn	*N.P.T.*	18	B2
Bryn	*Shrop.*	38	B7
Bryn Gates		48	E2
Brynamman		27	G7
Brynberian		16	E2
Bryncae		18	C3
Bryncethin		18	C3
Bryncir		36	D1
Bryn-côch		18	A2
Bryncroes		36	B2
Bryncrug		37	F5
Bryneglwys		38	A1
Brynford		47	K5
Bryngwran		46	B5
Bryngwyn	*Mon.*	19	G1
Bryngwyn	*Powys*	28	A4
Bryn-henllan		16	D2
Brynhoffnant		26	C3
Brynmawr		28	A7
Brynmelyn		28	A1
Brynmenyn		18	C3
Brynna		18	C3
Brynog		26	E3
Brynrefail	*Gwyn.*	46	D6
Brynrefail	*I.o.A.*	46	C4
Brynsadler		18	D3
Brynsiencyn		46	C6
Bryn-teg	*I.o.A.*	46	C4
Brynteg	*Wrex.*	48	C7
Bryn-y-maen		47	G5
Buaile nam Bodach		84	B4
Bualintur		85	K2
Bualnaluib		94	E3
Bubbenhall		30	E1
Bubwith		58	D6
Buccleuch		69	J2
Buchan		65	H4
Buchanan Castle		74	C2
Buchanhaven		99	K6
Buchanty		82	A5
Buchlyvie		74	D1
Buckabank		60	E2
Buckby Wharf		31	H2
Buckden	*Cambs.*	32	E2
Buckden	*N.Yorks.*	56	E2
Buckenham		45	H5
Buckerell		7	K5
Buckfast		5	H4
Buckfastleigh		5	H4
Buckhaven		76	B1
Buckholm		76	C7
Buckhorn Weston		9	G2
Buckhurst Hill		23	H2
Buckie		98	C4
Buckies		105	G2
Buckingham		31	H5
Buckland	*Bucks.*	32	B7
Buckland	*Devon*	5	G6
Buckland	*Glos.*	30	B5
Buckland	*Herts.*	33	G5
Buckland	*Kent*	15	H3
Buckland	*Oxon.*	21	G2
Buckland	*Surr.*	23	F6
Buckland Brewer		6	C3
Buckland Common		22	C1
Buckland Dinham		20	A6
Buckland Filleigh		6	C5
Buckland in the Moor		5	H3
Buckland Monachorum		4	E4
Buckland Newton		9	G4
Buckland St. Mary		8	B3
Buckland-tout-Saints		5	H6
Bucklebury		21	J4
Bucklerheads		83	F4
Bucklers Hard		11	F4
Bucklesham		35	G4
Buckley (Bwcle)		48	B6
Buckman Corner		12	E4
Buckminster		42	B3
Bucknall	*Lincs.*	52	E6
Bucknall	*Stoke*	40	B1
Bucknell	*Oxon.*	31	G6
Bucknell	*Shrop.*	28	C1
Buck's Cross		6	B3
Bucks Green		12	D3
Bucks Hill		22	D1
Bucks Horn Oak		22	B7
Buck's Mills		6	B3
Buckton	*E.Riding*	59	H2
Buckton	*Here.*	28	C1
Buckton	*Northumb.*	77	J7
Buckworth		32	E1
Budbrooke		30	D2
Budby		51	J6
Buddon		83	G4
Bude		6	A5
Budlake		7	H5
Budle		77	K7
Budleigh Salterton		7	J7
Budock Water		2	E5
Buerton		39	F1
Bugbrooke		31	H3
Bugle		4	A5
Bugthorpe		58	D4
Buildwas		39	F5
Builth Road		27	K3
Builth Wells		27	K3
Buirgh		93	F2
Bulby		42	D3
Buldoo		104	E2
Bulford		20	E7
Bulford Camp		20	E7
Bulkeley		48	E7
Bulkington	*Warks.*	41	F7
Bulkington	*Wilts.*	20	C6
Bulkworthy		6	B4
Bull Bay		46	C3
Bull Green		14	E4
Bulley		29	G7
Bullington		21	H7
Bullpot Farm		56	B1
Bull's Green		33	F7
Bullwood		73	K3
Bulmer	*Essex*	34	C4
Bulmer	*N.Yorks.*	58	C3
Bulmer Tye		34	C5
Bulphan		24	C3
Bulverhythe		14	C7
Bulwark		99	H6
Bulwell		41	H1
Bulwick		42	C6
Bumble's Green		23	H1
Bun Abhainn Eadarra		100	D7
Bun Loyne		87	J4
Bunacaimb		86	C6
Bunarkaig		87	H6
Bunbury		48	E7
Bunchrew		96	D7
Bundalloch		86	E2
Bunessan		78	E5
Bungay		45	H7
Bunlarie		73	F7
Bunloit		88	C2
Bunnahabhainn		72	C3
Bunny		41	H3
Buntait		87	K1
Buntingford		33	G6
Bunwell		45	F6
Bunwell Street		45	F6
Burbage	*Derbys.*	50	C5
Burbage	*Leics.*	41	G6
Burbage	*Wilts.*	21	F5
Burchett's Green		22	B3
Burcombe		10	B1
Burcot		21	J2
Burcott		32	B6
Burdale		58	E3
Burdocks		12	D4
Bures		34	D5
Bures Green		34	D5
Burford		30	D7
Burgate		34	E1
Burgess Hill		13	G5
Burgh		35	G3
Burgh by Sands		60	E1
Burgh Castle		45	J5
Burgh Heath		23	F6
Burgh le Marsh		53	H6
Burgh next Aylsham		45	G3
Burgh on Bain		53	F4
Burgh St. Margaret		45	J4
Burgh St. Peter		45	J6
Burghclere		21	H5
Burghead		97	J5
Burghfield		21	K5
Burghfield Common		21	K5
Burghfield Hill		21	K5
Burghill		28	D4
Burghwallis		51	H1
Burham		24	D5
Buriton		11	J2
Burland		49	F7
Burlawn		3	G1
Burleigh		22	C5
Burlescombe		7	J4
Burleston		9	G5
Burley	*Hants.*	10	D4
Burley	*Rut.*	42	B4
Burley Gate		28	E4
Burley in Wharfedale		57	G5
Burley Street		10	D4
Burleydam		39	F1
Burlingjobb		28	B3
Burlow		13	J5
Burlton		38	D3
Burmarsh		15	G4
Burmington		30	D5
Burn		58	B7
Burn Farm		90	E7
Burn Naze		55	G5
Burn of Cambus		81	J7
Burnage		49	H3
Burnaston		40	E2
Burnby		58	E5
Burndell		12	C6
Burneside		61	G7
Burness		106	F3
Burneston		57	J1
Burnett		19	K5
Burnfoot	*High.*	104	D3
Burnfoot	*P. & K.*	82	A7
Burnfoot	*Sc.Bord.*	70	A2
Burnfoot	*Sc.Bord.*	69	K2
Burnham	*Bucks.*	22	C3
Burnham	*N.Lincs.*	52	D1
Burnham Deepdale		44	C1
Burnham Green		33	F7
Burnham Market		44	C1
Burnham Norton		44	C1
Burnham Overy		44	C1
Burnham Thorpe		44	C1
Burnham-on-Crouch		25	F2
Burnham-on-Sea		19	G7
Burnhaven		99	K7
Burnhead	*D. & G.*	67	K5
Burnhead	*D. & G.*	68	D5
Burnhervie		91	F3
Burnhill Green		39	G5
Burnhope		62	C2
Burnhouse		74	B5
Burniston		63	K3
Burnley		56	D6
Burnmouth		77	H4
Burnopfield		62	C1
Burnsall		57	F3
Burnside	*Aber.*	91	F3
Burnside	*Angus*	83	G2
Burnside	*E.Ayr.*	67	K2
Burnside	*Fife*	82	C7
Burnside	*Shet.*	108	B5
Burnside	*W.Loth.*	75	J3
Burnside of Duntrune		83	F4
Burnstones		61	H1
Burnswark		69	G6
Burnt Houses		62	C4
Burnt Yates		57	H3
Burntcliff Top		49	J6
Burntisland		76	A2
Burnton	*E.Ayr.*	67	J2
Burnton	*E.Ayr.*	67	K2
Burntwood		40	C4
Burntwood Green		40	C5
Burpham	*Surr.*	22	D6
Burpham	*W.Suss.*	12	D6
Burradon	*Northumb.*	70	E3
Burradon	*T. & W.*	71	H6
Burrafirth		108	F1
Burraland		108	C5
Burras		2	D5
Burravoe	*Shet.*	108	E5
Burravoe	*Shet.*	109	C6
Burrells		61	H5
Burrelton		82	C4
Burridge		11	G3
Burrill		57	H1
Burringham		52	B2
Burrington	*Devon*	6	E4
Burrington	*Here.*	28	D1
Burrington	*N.Som.*	19	H6
Burrough End		33	K3
Burrough Green		33	K3
Burrough on the Hill		42	A4
Burrow Bridge		8	C1
Burrowhill		22	C5
Burry Port		17	H5
Burscough		48	D1
Burscough Bridge		48	D1
Bursea		58	E6
Burshill		59	G5
Bursledon		11	F4
Burslem		40	A1
Burstall		35	F4
Burstock		8	D4
Burston	*Norf.*	45	F7
Burston	*Staffs.*	40	B2
Burstow		23	G7
Burstwick		59	J7
Burtersett		56	D1
Burtle		19	H7
Burton	*Ches.*	48	C5
Burton	*Ches.*	48	E6
Burton	*Dorset*	10	C5
Burton	*Dorset*	9	F5
Burton	*Lincs.*	52	C5
Burton	*Northumb.*	77	K7
Burton	*Pembs.*	16	C5
Burton	*Som.*	7	K1
Burton	*Wilts.*	20	B4
Burton Agnes		59	H3
Burton Bradstock		8	D6
Burton Coggles		42	C3
Burton Fleming		59	G2
Burton Green	*Warks.*	30	D1
Burton Green	*Wrex.*	48	C7
Burton Hastings		41	G6
Burton in Lonsdale		56	B2
Burton Joyce		41	J1
Burton Latimer		32	C1
Burton Lazars		42	A4
Burton Leonard		57	J3
Burton on the Wolds		41	H3
Burton Overy		41	J6
Burton Pedwardine		42	E1
Burton Pidsea		59	J6
Burton Salmon		57	K7
Burton upon Stather		52	B1
Burton upon Trent		40	E3
Burton-in-Kendal		55	J2
Burtonwood		48	E3
Burwardsley		48	E7
Burwarton		39	F7
Burwash		13	K4
Burwash Common		13	K4
Burwash Weald		13	K4
Burwell	*Cambs.*	33	J2
Burwell	*Lincs.*	53	G5
Burwen		46	C3
Burwick	*Ork.*	107	D9
Burwick	*Shet.*	109	C8
Bury	*Cambs.*	43	F7
Bury	*Gt.Man.*	49	H1
Bury	*Som.*	7	H3
Bury	*W.Suss.*	12	D5
Bury Green		33	H6
Bury St. Edmunds		34	C2
Buryas Bridge		2	B6
Burythorpe		58	D3
Busbridge		22	C7
Busby	*E.Renf.*	74	D5
Busby	*P. & K.*	82	B5
Buscot		21	F2
Bush Bank		28	D3
Bush Crathie		89	K5
Bush Green		45	G7
Bushbury		40	B5
Bushby		41	J5
Bushey		22	E2
Bushey Heath		22	E2
Bushley		29	H5
Bushton		20	D4
Bussage		20	B1
Busta		109	C6
Butcher's Cross		13	J4
Butcher's Pasture		33	K6
Butcombe		19	J5
Buthill		97	J5
Butleigh		8	E1
Butleigh Wootton		8	E1
Butler's Cross		22	B1
Butler's Hill		41	H1
Butlers Marston		30	E3
Butley		35	H3
Butsfield		62	C2
Butt Green		49	F7
Butt Lane		49	H7
Butterburn		70	B6
Buttercrambe		58	D4
Butterknowle		62	C4
Butterleigh		7	H5
Buttermere	*Cumb.*	60	C5
Buttermere	*Wilts.*	21	G5
Butters Green		49	H7
Buttershaw		57	G7
Butterstone		82	B3
Butterton		50	C7
Butterwick	*Lincs.*	43	G1
Butterwick	*N.Yorks.*	59	F2
Butterwick	*N.Yorks.*	58	D2
Buttington		38	B5
Buttonoak		29	G1
Buxhall		34	E3
Buxted		13	H4
Buxton	*Derbys.*	50	C5
Buxton	*Norf.*	45	G3
Buxton Heath		45	F3
Buxworth		50	C4
Bwlch		28	A6
Bwlch-clawdd		17	G2
Bwlch-derwin		36	D1
Bwlchgwyn		48	B7
Bwlch-llan		26	E3
Bwlchnewydd		17	G3
Bwlchtocyn		36	C3
Bwlch-y-cibau		38	A4
Bwlch-y-ddar		38	A3
Bwlch-y-ffridd		37	K6
Bwlch-y-groes		17	F2
Bwlch-y-sarnau		27	K1
Byers Green		62	D3
Byfield		31	G3
Byfleet		22	D5
Byford		28	C4
Bygrave		33	F5
Byker		71	H7
Bylane End		4	C5
Bylchau		47	H6
Byley		49	G6
Bynea		17	J6
Byrness		70	C3
Bythorn		32	D1
Byton		28	C2
Byworth		12	C4

C

Place	County	Page	Grid
Cabharstadh		101	F5
Cabourne		52	E2
Cabrach	*Arg. & B.*	72	C4
Cabrach	*Moray*	90	B2
Cackle Street		14	D6
Cacrabank		69	J2
Cadboll		97	F4
Cadbury		7	H5
Cadbury Barton		6	E4
Cadbury Heath		19	K4
Cadder		74	E3
Cadderlie		80	B4
Caddington		32	D7
Caddonfoot		76	C7
Cade Street		13	K4
Cadeby	*Leics.*	41	G5
Cadeby	*S.Yorks.*	51	H2
Cadeleigh		7	H5
Cadgwith		2	E7
Cadham		82	D7
Cadishead		49	G3
Cadle		17	K6
Cadley		21	F5
Cadmore End		22	A2
Cadnam		10	E3
Cadney		52	D2
Cadole		48	B6
Cadover Bridge		5	F4
Cadoxton		18	E5
Cadoxton-Juxta-Neath		18	A2
Cae Ddafydd		37	F1
Caeathro		46	D6
Caehopkin		27	H7
Caen		105	F7
Caenby		52	D4
Caenby Corner		52	C4
Caer Llan		19	H1
Caerau	*Bridgend*	18	B2
Caerau	*Cardiff*	18	E4
Caerdeon		37	F4
Caerfarchell		16	A3
Caerfyrddin (Carmarthen)		17	H4
Caergeiliog		46	B5
Caergwrle		48	C7
Caergybi (Holyhead)		46	A4
Caerhun		47	F5
Caer-Lan		27	H7
Caerleon		19	G2
Caernarfon		46	C6
Caerphilly		18	E3
Caersws		37	K6
Caerwedros		26	C3
Caerwent		19	H2
Caerwys		47	K5
Caethle Farm		37	F6
Caggan		89	F3
Caio		17	K2
Cairinis		92	D6
Cairisiadar		100	C4
Cairminis		93	F3
Cairnargat		90	C1
Cairnbaan		73	G1
Cairnbeathie		90	E4
Cairnbrogie		91	G2
Cairnbulg		99	J4
Cairncross		77	G4
Cairncurran		74	B3
Cairndoon		64	D7
Cairndow		80	C6
Cairness		99	J4
Cairneyhill		75	J2
Cairnfield		98	C4
Cairney Lodge		82	E6
Cairnhill	*Aber.*	90	E1
Cairnie	*Aber.*	98	C6
Cairnie	*Aber.*	91	G4
Cairnorrie		99	G6
Cairnryan		64	A4
Cairnsmore		64	E4
Caister-on-Sea		45	K4
Caistor		52	E2
Caistor St. Edmund		45	G5
Caistron		70	E3
Cake Street		44	E6
Calanais (Callanish)		100	E4
Calbost		101	G6
Calbourne		11	F6
Calcot		21	K4
Calcott		25	H5
Caldarvan		74	C2
Caldback		108	F2
Caldbeck		60	E3
Caldbergh		57	F1
Caldecote	*Cambs.*	33	G3
Caldecote	*Cambs.*	42	E7
Caldecote	*Herts.*	33	F5
Caldecote	*Warks.*	41	F6
Caldecott	*Northants.*	32	C2
Caldecott	*Rut.*	42	B6
Calder Bridge		60	B6
Calder Mains		105	F3
Calder Vale		55	J5
Calderbank		75	F4
Calderbrook		49	J1
Caldercruix		75	G4
Calderglen		74	E5
Caldermill		74	E6
Caldhame		83	F3
Caldicot		19	H3
Caldwell	*Derbys.*	40	E4
Caldwell	*E.Renf.*	74	C5
Caldwell	*N.Yorks.*	62	C5
Caldy		48	B4
Caledrhydiau		26	D3
Calfsound		106	E4
Calgary		78	E2
Califer		97	H6
California	*Falk.*	75	H3
California	*Norf.*	45	K4
Calke		41	F3
Callakille		94	C6
Callaly		71	F3
Callander		81	H7
Callanish (Calanais)		100	E4
Callaughton		38	E6
Callendar Lane End		71	G7
Callestick		2	E3
Calliburn		66	B1
Calligarry		86	C4
Callington		4	D4
Callisterhall		69	H5
Callow		28	D5
Callow End		29	H4
Callow Hill	*Wilts.*	20	D3
Callow Hill	*Worcs.*	29	G1
Callows Grave		28	E2
Calmore		10	E3
Calmsden		20	D1
Calne		20	C4
Calow		51	G5
Calrossie		96	E4
Calshot		11	F4
Calstock		4	E4
Calstone Wellington		20	D5
Calthorpe		45	F2
Calthwaite		61	F2
Calton	*N.Yorks.*	56	E4
Calton	*Staffs.*	50	D7
Calveley		48	E7
Calver		50	E5
Calver Hill		28	C4
Calverhall		39	F2
Calverleigh		7	H4
Calverley		57	H6
Calvert		31	H6
Calverton	*M.K.*	31	J5
Calverton	*Notts.*	41	J1
Calvine		81	J1
Calvo		60	C1
Cam		20	A2
Camas-luinie		87	F2
Camasnacroise		79	K2
Camastianavaig		86	B1
Camasunary		86	B3
Camault Muir		96	C7
Camb		108	E3
Camber		14	E6
Camberley		22	B5
Camberwell		23	G4
Camblesforth		58	C7
Cambo		71	F5
Cambois		71	J5
Camborne		2	D4
Cambourne		33	G3
Cambridge	*Cambs.*	33	H3
Cambridge	*Glos.*	20	A1
Cambridge Airport		33	H3
Cambus		75	G1
Cambus o'May		90	C5
Cambusbarron		75	F1
Cambuskenneth		75	G1
Cambuslang		74	E4
Cambusnethan		75	G5
Cameley		19	K6
Camelford		4	B2
Camelon		75	G2
Camelsdale		12	B3
Camer		24	C5
Cameron		74	B2
Camer's Green		29	H1
Cameron	*B. & N.E.Som.*	19	K6
Camerton	*Cumb.*	60	B3
Camghouran		81	G2
Camis Eskan		74	B2
Cammachmore		91	H5
Cammeringham		52	C4
Campbeltown		66	B2
Campbeltown (Machrihanish) Airport		66	A1
Camperdown		71	H6
Camphouse		79	G3
Campmuir		82	D4
Camps End		33	K4
Camps Heath		45	K6
Campsall		51	H1
Campsey Ash		35	H3
Campton		32	E5
Camptown		70	B2
Camquhart		73	H2
Camrose		16	C3
Camserney		81	K3
Camster		105	H4
Camstraddan House		74	B1
Camus Croise		86	C3
Camusnagaul	*High.*	87	G7
Camusnagaul	*High.*	95	G3
Camusrory		86	E5
Camusteel		94	D7
Camusterrach		94	D7
Camusvrachan		81	H3
Canada		10	D3
Candacraig		90	B5
Candlesby		53	H6
Candy Mill		75	J6
Cane End		21	K4
Canewdon		24	E2
Canford Bottom		10	B4
Canford Cliffs		10	B6
Canford Magna		10	B5
Canisbay		105	J1
Cann		9	H2
Cann Common		9	H2
Cannard's Grave		19	K7
Cannich		87	K1
Cannington		8	B1
Cannock		40	B5
Cannock Wood		40	C4
Canon Bridge		28	D4
Canon Frome		29	F4
Canon Pyon		28	D4
Canonbie		69	J6
Canons Ashby		31	G3
Canon's Town		2	C5
Canterbury	*Aber.*	98	D5
Canterbury	*Kent*	15	G2
Cantley	*Norf.*	45	H5
Cantley	*S.Yorks.*	51	J2
Cantlop		38	E5
Canton		18	E4
Cantray		96	E7
Cantraydoune		96	E7
Cantraywood		96	E7
Cantsfield		56	B2
Canvey Island		24	D3
Canwell Hall		40	D5
Canwick		52	C6
Canworthy Water		4	C1
Caol		87	H7
Caolas	*Arg. & B.*	78	B3
Caolas	*W.Isles*	84	B5
Caolas Scalpaigh (Kyles Scalpay)		93	H2
Caolasnacon		80	C1
Capel	*Kent*	23	K7
Capel	*Surr.*	22	E7
Capel Bangor		37	F7
Capel Betws Lleucu		27	F3
Capel Carmel		36	A3
Capel Coch		46	C4
Capel Curig		47	F7
Capel Cynon		17	G1
Capel Dewi	*Carmar.*	17	H3
Capel Dewi	*Cere.*	37	F7
Capel Dewi	*Cere.*	17	H1
Capel Garmon		47	G7
Capel Gwyn	*Carmar.*	17	H3
Capel Gwyn	*I.o.A.*	46	B5
Capel Gwynfe		27	G6
Capel Hendre		17	J4
Capel Isaac		17	J3
Capel Iwan		17	F2
Capel le Ferne		15	H4
Capel Parc		46	C4
Capel St. Andrew		35	H4
Capel St. Mary		34	E5
Capel St. Silin		26	E3
Capel Seion		37	F7
Capel Tygwydd		17	F1
Capeluchaf		36	D1
Capelulo		47	F5
Capel-y-ffin		28	B5
Capenhurst		48	C5
Capernwray		55	J2
Capheaton		71	F5
Caplaw		74	C5
Cappercleuch		69	H1
Capplegill		69	G3
Capstone		24	D5
Capton		5	J5
Caputh		82	B3
Car Colston		42	A1
Carbellow		68	B1
Carbeth		74	D3
Carbis Bay		2	C5
Carbost	*High.*	93	K7
Carbost	*High.*	85	J1
Carbrain		75	F3
Carbrooke		44	D5
Carburton		51	J5
Carcary		83	H2
Carclew		2	E5
Carco		68	C2
Carcroft		51	H1
Cardenden		76	A1
Cardeston		38	C4
Cardiff (Caerdydd)		18	E4
Cardiff International Airport		18	D5
Cardigan (Aberteifi)		16	E1
Cardington	*Beds.*	32	D4
Cardington	*Shrop.*	38	E6
Cardinham		4	B4
Cardno		99	H4
Cardoness		65	F5
Cardow		97	J7
Cardrona		76	A7
Cardross		74	B3
Cardurnock		60	C1
Careby		42	D4
Careston		83	G1
Carew		16	D5
Carew Cheriton		16	D5
Carew Newton		16	D5
Carey		28	E5
Carfrae		76	D4
Carfraemill		76	D5
Cargen		65	K3
Cargenbridge		65	K3
Cargill		82	C4
Cargo		60	E1
Cargo Fleet		63	G5
Cargreen		4	E4
Carham		77	F7
Carhampton		7	J1
Carharrack		2	E4
Carie	*P. & K.*	81	H2
Carie	*P. & K.*	81	H3
Carines		2	E3
Carisbrooke		11	F6
Cark		55	G2
Carkeel		4	E4
Carland Cross		3	F3
Carlby		42	D4
Carlecotes		50	D2
Carleton	*Cumb.*	61	G1
Carleton	*Lancs.*	55	G5
Carleton	*N.Yorks.*	56	E5
Carleton	*W.Yorks.*	57	K7
Carleton Fishery		67	F5
Carleton Forehoe		44	E5
Carleton Rode		45	F6
Carlin How		63	J5
Carlingcott		19	K6
Carlisle		61	F1
Carlops		75	K5

Carloway (Carlabhagh) 100 E3
Carlton Beds. 32 C3
Carlton Cambs. 33 K3
Carlton Leics. 41 F5
Carlton N.Yorks. 58 C7
Carlton N.Yorks. 57 F1
Carlton N.Yorks. 58 C1
Carlton Notts. 41 J1
Carlton S.Yorks. 51 F2
Carlton Stock. 62 E4
Carlton Suff. 35 H2
Carlton W.Yorks. 57 J7
Carlton Colville 45 K6
Carlton Curlieu 41 J6
Carlton Husthwaite 57 K2
Carlton in Lindrick 51 H4
Carlton Miniott 57 J1
Carlton Scroop 42 C1
Carlton-in-Cleveland 63 G6
Carlton-le-Moorland 52 C7
Carlton-on-Trent 52 B6
Carluke 75 G5
Carlyon Bay 4 A5
Carmacoup 68 C1
Carmarthen (Caerfyrddin) 17 H4
Carmel Carmar. 17 J4
Carmel Flints. 47 K5
Carmel Gwyn. 46 C7
Carmel I.o.A. 46 B4
Carmont 91 G6
Carmore 96 E2
Carmunnock 74 E5
Carmyle 74 E4
Carmyllie 83 G3
Carn 72 A5
Carn Brea 2 D4
Carn Dearg 94 D4
Carnaby 59 H3
Carnach High. 87 G2
Carnach High. 95 G2
Carnassarie 79 K7
Carnbee 83 G7
Carnbo 82 B7
Carnduncan 72 A4
Carne 3 G5
Carnforth 55 H2
Carnhell Green 2 D5
Carnichal 99 H5
Carnmore 72 B6
Carno 37 J6
Carnoch High. 87 K1
Carnoch High. 95 J6
Carnoch High. 97 F7
Carnock 75 J2
Carnon Downs 2 E4
Carnousie 98 E5
Carnoustie 83 G4
Carnwath 75 H6
Carnyorth 2 A5
Carperby 62 B7
Carr Shield 61 K2
Carr Vale 51 G5
Carradale 73 G7
Carragrich 93 G2
Carrbridge 89 G2
Carrefour Selous 3 J6
Carreg-lefn 46 B4
Carrick Arg. & B. 73 K1
Carrick Arg. & B. 73 H2
Carrick Fife 83 F5
Carriden 75 J2
Carrine 66 A3
Carrington Gt.Man. 49 G3
Carrington Lincs. 53 G7
Carrington Midloth. 76 B4
Carroch 68 B4
Carrog 38 A1
Carroglen 81 J5
Carrol 97 F1
Carron Arg. & B. 73 H1
Carron Falk. 75 G2
Carron Moray 97 K7
Carron Bridge 75 F2
Carronbridge 68 D4
Carronshore 75 G2
Carrot 83 F3
Carrutherstown 69 G6
Carruthmuir 74 B4
Carrville 62 E2
Carry 73 H4
Carsaig 79 G5
Carscreugh 64 C4
Carse 73 F4
Carse of Ardesier 97 F6
Carsegowan 64 E5
Carseriggan 64 D4
Carsethorn 65 K5
Carsgoe 105 G2
Carshalton 23 F5
Carsington 50 E7
Carsluith 64 E5
Carsphairn 67 K4
Carstairs 75 H6
Carstairs Junction 75 H6
Carswell Marsh 21 G2
Carter's Clay 10 E2
Carterton 21 F1
Carterway Heads 62 B1
Carthew 4 A5
Carthorpe 57 J1
Cartington 71 F3
Cartmel 55 G2
Cartmel Fell 55 H1
Carway 17 H5
Cascob 28 B2
Cashel Farm 74 C1
Cashlie 81 F3
Cashmoor 9 J3
Casnewydd (Newport) 19 G3
Cassencarie 64 E5
Cassington 31 F7
Cassop 62 E3
Castell Gorfod 17 F3
Castell Howell 17 H1
Castell Newydd Emlyn (Newcastle Emlyn) 17 G1
Castellau 18 D3
Castell-Nedd (Neath) 18 A2
Castell-y-bwch 19 F2
Casterton 56 B2
Castle Acre 44 C4
Castle Ashby 32 B3
Castle Bank 40 B3
Castle Bolton 62 B7
Castle Bromwich 40 D7
Castle Bytham 42 C4
Castle Caereinion 38 A5
Castle Camps 33 K4
Castle Carrock 61 G1
Castle Cary 9 F1
Castle Combe 20 B4
Castle Donington 41 G3
Castle Douglas 65 H4
Castle Eaton 20 E2
Castle Eden 63 F3
Castle End 30 D1
Castle Frome 29 F4
Castle Gresley 40 E4
Castle Heaton 77 H6
Castle Hedingham 34 B5
Castle Hill 35 F4
Castle Kennedy 64 B5
Castle Leod 96 B6
Castle Levan 74 A3
Castle Madoc 27 K5
Castle Morris 16 C2
Castle O'er 69 H4
Castle Rising 44 A3
Castle Stuart 96 E6
Castlebay (Bagh a' Chaisteil) 84 B5
Castlebythe 16 D3
Castlecary 75 F3
Castlecraig High. 97 F5
Castlecraig Sc.Bord. 75 K6
Castlefairn 68 C5
Castleford 57 K7
Castlemartin 16 C6
Castlemilk D. & G. 69 G6
Castlemilk Glas. 74 E5
Castlemorton 29 G5
Castleside 62 B2
Castlethorpe 32 B4
Castleton Aber. 99 F5
Castleton Angus 82 E3
Castleton Arg. & B. 73 G2
Castleton Derbys. 50 D4
Castleton Gt.Man. 49 H1
Castleton N.Yorks. 63 H6
Castleton Newport 19 F3
Castleton Sc.Bord. 70 A4
Castletown High. 105 G2
Castletown High. 96 E7
Castletown I.o.M. 54 B7
Castletown T. & W. 62 E1
Castleweary 69 K3
Castlewigg 64 E6
Caston 44 D6
Castor 42 E6
Castramont 65 F4
Cat & Fiddle Inn 50 C5
Catbrain 19 J3
Catchall 2 B6
Catcleugh 70 C3
Catcliffe 51 G4
Catcott 8 C1
Caterham 23 G6
Catesby 31 G3
Catfield 45 H3
Catfirth 109 D7
Catford 23 G4
Catforth 55 H6
Cathedine 28 A6
Catherington 11 H3
Catherton 29 F1
Catlow 56 D6
Catlowdy 69 K6
Catmore 21 H4
Caton Devon 5 H3
Caton Lancs. 55 J3
Cator Court 5 G3
Catrine 67 K1
Catsfield 14 C6
Catshill 29 J1
Cattadale 72 B5
Cattal 57 K4
Cattawade 35 F5
Catterall 55 J5
Catterick 62 D7
Catterick Camp 62 C7
Catterlen 61 F3
Catterline 91 G7
Catterton 58 B5
Cattistock 8 E4
Catton N.Yorks. 57 J2
Catton Norf. 45 G4
Catton Northumb. 61 K1
Catton Hall 40 E4
Catwick 59 H5
Catworth 32 D1
Caudworthy 4 C1
Caulcott 31 G6
Cauldcots 83 H3
Cauldhame Stir. 74 E1
Cauldhame Stir. 81 K7
Cauldon 40 C1
Caulkerbush 65 K5
Caulside 69 K5
Caundle Marsh 9 F3
Caunsall 40 A7
Caunton 51 K6
Causeway End D. & G. 64 E4
Causeway End Essex 33 K7
Causewayhead Cumb. 60 C1
Causewayhead Stir. 75 G1
Causey Park 71 G4
Causeyend 91 H3
Cautley 61 H7
Cavendish 34 C4
Cavenham 34 B2
Cavens 65 K5
Caversfield 31 G6
Caversham 22 A4
Caverswall 40 B1
Cawdor 97 F6
Cawkwell 53 F5
Cawood 58 B6
Cawsand 4 E5
Cawston 45 F3
Cawthorne 50 E2
Cawthorpe 42 D3
Cawton 58 C2
Caxton 33 G3
Caxton Gibbet 33 F3
Caynham 28 E1
Caythorpe Lincs. 42 C1
Caythorpe Notts. 41 J1
Cayton 59 G1
Ceallan 92 D6
Ceann a' Bhàigh W.Isles 92 C5
Ceann a' Bhàigh W.Isles 93 F3
Ceann Loch Shiphoirt 100 E6
Cearsiadar 101 F5
Ceathramh Meadhanach 92 C4
Cedig 37 J3
Cefn Bycharn (Newbridge) 19 F2
Cefn Cantref 27 K6
Cefn Coch 47 K7
Cefn Cribwr 18 B3
Cefn Cross 18 B3
Cefn Einion 38 B7
Cefn Hengoed 18 E2
Cefn-brith 47 H7
Cefn-caer-Ferch 36 D1
Cefn-coch 38 A3
Cefn-coed-y-cymmer 18 D1
Cefn-ddwysarn 37 J2
Cefndeuddwr 37 G3
Cefneithin 17 J4
Cefn-gorwydd 27 J4
Cefn-gwyn 38 A7
Cefn-mawr 38 B1
Cefn-y-bedd 48 C7
Cefn-y-pant 16 E3
Cegidfa (Guilsfield) 38 B4
Ceidio 46 C4
Ceidio Fawr 36 B2
Ceinewydd (New Quay) 26 C3
Ceint 46 C5
Cellan 17 K1
Cellardyke 83 G7
Cellarhead 40 B1
Cemaes 46 B3
Cemmaes 37 H5
Cemmaes Road (Glantwymyn) 37 H5
Cenarth 17 F1
Cennin 36 D1
Ceos 101 F5
Ceres 82 E6
Cerne Abbas 9 F4
Cerney Wick 20 D2
Cerrigceinwen 46 C5
Cerrigydrudion 37 J1
Cessford 70 C1
Chaceley 29 H5
Chacewater 2 E4
Chackmore 31 H5
Chacombe 31 F4
Chad Valley 40 C7
Chadderton 49 J2
Chaddesden 41 F2
Chaddesley Corbett 29 H1
Chaddleworth 21 H4
Chadlington 30 E6
Chadshunt 30 E3
Chadwell 42 A3
Chadwell St. Mary 24 C4
Chadwick End 30 D1
Chaffcombe 8 C3
Chafford Hundred 24 C4
Chagford 7 F7
Chailey 13 G5
Chainhurst 14 C3
Chalbury Common 10 B4
Chaldon 23 G6
Chaldon Herring or East Chaldon 9 G6
Chale 11 F7
Chale Green 11 F7
Chalfont Common 22 D2
Chalfont St. Giles 22 C2
Chalfont St. Peter 22 D2
Chalford 20 B1
Chalgrove 21 K2
Chalk 24 C4
Challacombe 6 E1
Challoch 64 D4
Challock 15 F2
Chalmington 8 E4
Chalton Beds. 32 D6
Chalton Hants. 11 J3
Chalvington 13 J6
Champany 75 J3
Chandler's Cross 22 D2
Chandler's Ford 11 F2
Channerwick 109 D10
Chantry Som. 20 A7
Chantry Suff. 35 F4
Chapel 76 A1
Chapel Allerton Som. 19 H6
Chapel Allerton W.Yorks. 57 J6
Chapel Amble 3 G1
Chapel Brampton 31 J2
Chapel Chorlton 40 A2
Chapel Cross 13 K4
Chapel End 41 F6
Chapel Fields 30 E1
Chapel Haddlesey 58 B7
Chapel Hill Aber. 91 J1
Chapel Hill Lincs. 53 F7
Chapel Hill Mon. 19 J1
Chapel Lawn 28 C1
Chapel of Garioch 91 F2
Chapel Rossan 64 B6
Chapel Row 21 J5
Chapel St. Leonards 53 J5
Chapel Stile 60 E6
Chapel Town 3 F3
Chapelbank 82 B6
Chapeldonan 67 F3
Chapel-en-le-Frith 50 C4
Chapelgate 43 H3
Chapelhall 75 F4
Chapelhill High. 97 F4
Chapelhill P. & K. 82 D5
Chapelhill P. & K. 82 B4
Chapelknowe 69 J6
Chapel-le-Dale 56 C2
Chapelton Aber. 91 G6
Chapelton Angus 83 H3
Chapelton S.Lan. 74 E6
Chapeltown B'burn. 49 G1
Chapeltown Cumb. 69 K6
Chapeltown Moray 89 K2
Chapeltown S.Yorks. 51 F3
Chapmans Well 6 B6
Chapmanslade 20 B7
Chapmore End 33 G7
Chappel 34 C6
Chard 8 C4
Chard Junction 8 C4
Chardstock 8 C4
Charfield 20 A2
Charing 14 E3
Charing Heath 14 E3
Charingworth 30 C4
Charlbury 30 E7
Charlcombe 20 A5
Charlcutt 20 C4
Charlecote 30 D3
Charles 6 E2
Charles Tye 34 E3
Charlesfield 70 A1
Charleshill 22 B7
Charleston 82 E3
Charlestown Aber. 99 J4
Charlestown Aberdeen 91 H4
Charlestown Cornw. 4 A5
Charlestown Dorset 9 F7
Charlestown Fife 75 J2
Charlestown High. 94 E4
Charlestown High. 96 D7
Charlestown of Aberlour (Aberlour) 97 K7
Charlesworth 50 C3
Charleton 83 F7
Charlinch 8 B1
Charlton Gt.Lon. 23 H4
Charlton Hants. 21 G7
Charlton Herts. 32 E6
Charlton Northants. 31 G5
Charlton Northumb. 70 D5
Charlton Oxon. 21 H3
Charlton Som. 19 K6
Charlton W.Suss. 12 B5
Charlton Wilts. 9 J2
Charlton Wilts. 20 C3
Charlton Wilts. 20 E6
Charlton Worcs. 30 B4
Charlton Abbots 30 B6
Charlton Adam 8 E2
Charlton Horethorne 9 F2
Charlton Kings 29 J6
Charlton Mackrell 8 E2
Charlton Marshall 9 H4
Charlton Musgrove 9 G2
Charlton-All-Saints 10 C2
Charlton-on-Otmoor 31 G7
Charltons 63 H5
Charlwood 23 F7
Charminster 9 F5
Charmouth 8 C5
Charndon 31 H6
Charney Bassett 21 G2
Charnock Richard 48 E1
Charsfield 35 G3
Chart Corner 14 C3
Chart Sutton 14 D3
Charter Alley 21 K6
Charterhouse 19 H6
Charterville Allotments 30 E7
Chartham 15 G2
Chartham Hatch 15 F2
Chartridge 22 C1
Charwelton 31 G3
Chase End Street 29 G5
Chase Terrace 40 C4
Chasetown 40 C5
Chastleton 30 D6
Chasty 6 B5
Chatburn 56 C5
Chatcull 39 G2
Chatham 24 D5
Chathill 71 G1
Chattenden 24 D4
Chatteris 43 G7
Chattisham 34 E4
Chatto 70 C2
Chatton 71 F1
Chawleigh 7 F4
Chawley 21 H1
Chawston 32 E3
Chawton 11 J1
Cheadle Gt.Man. 49 H4
Cheadle Staffs. 40 C1
Cheadle Hulme 49 H4
Cheam 23 F5
Cheapside 22 C5
Chearsley 22 A1
Chebsey 40 A3
Checkendon 21 K3
Checkley Ches. 39 G1
Checkley Here. 28 E5
Checkley Staffs. 40 C2
Chedburgh 34 B3
Cheddar 19 H6
Cheddington 32 C7
Cheddleton 49 J7
Cheddon Fitzpaine 8 B2
Chedglow 20 C2
Chedgrave 45 H6
Chedington 8 D4
Chediston 35 H1
Chedworth 30 B7
Chedzoy 8 C1
Cheeklaw 77 F5
Cheesden 49 H1
Cheeseman's Green 15 F4
Cheetham Hill 49 H2
Cheldon 7 F4
Chelford 49 H5
Chellaston 41 F2
Chelmarsh 39 G7
Chelmondiston 35 G5
Chelmorton 50 D6
Chelmsford 24 D1
Chelsea 23 F4
Chelsfield 23 H5
Chelsham 23 G6
Chelsworth 34 D4
Cheltenham 29 J6
Chelveston 32 C2
Chelvey 19 H5
Chelwood 19 K5
Chelwood Gate 13 H4
Chelworth 20 C2
Cheney Longville 38 D7
Chenies 22 D2
Chepstow 19 J2
Cherhill 20 D4
Cherington Glos. 20 C2
Cherington Warks. 30 D5
Cheriton Devon 7 F1
Cheriton Hants. 11 G2
Cheriton Kent 15 H4
Cheriton Pembs. 16 C6
Cheriton Swan. 17 H6
Cheriton Bishop 7 F6
Cheriton Cross 7 F6
Cheriton Fitzpaine 7 G5
Cherrington 39 F4
Cherry Burton 59 F5
Cherry Hinton 33 H3
Cherry Willingham 52 D5
Chertsey 22 D5
Cheselbourne 9 G5
Chesham 22 C1
Chesham Bois 22 C2
Cheshunt 23 G1
Cheslyn Hay 40 B5
Chessington 22 E5
Chester 48 D6
Chesterblade 19 K7
Chesterfield Derbys. 51 F5
Chesterfield Staffs. 40 D5
Chester-le-Street 62 D1
Chesters Sc.Bord. 70 B2
Chesters Sc.Bord. 70 B1
Chesterton Cambs. 33 H3
Chesterton Cambs. 42 E6
Chesterton Oxon. 31 G6
Chesterton Shrop. 39 G6
Chesterton Staffs. 40 A1
Chesterton Green 30 E3
Chestfield 25 H5
Cheswardine 39 G3
Cheswick 77 J6
Chetnole 9 F4
Chettiscombe 7 H4
Chettisham 43 J7
Chettle 9 J3
Chetton 39 F6
Chetwode 31 H6
Chetwynd Aston 39 G4
Cheveley 33 K2
Chevening 23 H6
Cheverell's Green 32 D7
Chevington 34 B3
Chevington Drift 71 H4
Chevithorne 7 H4
Chew Magna 19 J5
Chew Stoke 19 J5
Chewton Keynsham 19 K5
Chewton Mendip 19 J6
Chicheley 32 C4
Chichester 12 B6
Chickerell 9 F6
Chickering 35 G1
Chicklade 9 J1
Chickney 33 J6
Chicksands 32 E5
Chidden 11 H3
Chiddingfold 12 C3
Chiddingly 13 J5
Chiddingstone 23 H7
Chiddingstone Causeway 23 J7
Chiddingstone Hoath 23 H7
Chideock 8 D5
Chidham 11 J4
Chieveley 21 H4
Chignall St. James 24 C1
Chignall Smealy 33 K7
Chigwell 23 H2
Chigwell Row 23 H2
Chilbolton 21 G7
Chilcomb 11 G2
Chilcombe 8 E5
Chilcompton 19 K6
Chilcote 40 E4
Child Okeford 9 H3
Childer Thornton 48 C5
Childerditch 24 C3
Childrey 21 G3
Child's Ercall 39 F3
Childswickham 30 B5
Childwall 48 D4
Childwick Green 32 E7
Chilfrome 8 E5
Chilgrove 12 B5
Chilham 15 F2
Chillaton 6 C7
Chillenden 15 H2
Chillerton 11 F6
Chillesford 35 H3
Chillingham 71 F1
Chillington Devon 5 H6
Chillington Som. 8 C3
Chilmark 9 J1
Chilson 30 E7
Chilsworthy Cornw. 4 E3
Chilsworthy Devon 6 B5
Chilthorne Domer 8 E3
Chilton Bucks. 31 H7
Chilton Dur. 62 D3
Chilton Oxon. 21 H3
Chilton Candover 11 G1
Chilton Cantelo 8 E2
Chilton Foliat 21 G4
Chilton Polden 8 C1
Chilton Street 34 B4
Chilton Trinity 8 B1
Chilvers Coton 41 F6
Chilworth Hants. 11 F3
Chilworth Surr. 22 D7
Chimney 21 G1
Chineham 21 K6
Chingford 23 G2
Chinley 50 C4
Chinley Head 50 C4
Chinnor 22 A1
Chipchase Castle 70 D6
Chipley Park 7 K3
Chipnall 39 G2
Chippenham Cambs. 33 K2
Chippenham Wilts. 20 C4
Chipperfield 22 D1
Chipping Herts. 33 G5
Chipping Lancs. 56 B5
Chipping Campden 30 C5
Chipping Hill 34 C7
Chipping Norton 30 E6
Chipping Ongar 23 J1
Chipping Sodbury 20 A3
Chipping Warden 31 F4
Chipstable 7 J3
Chipstead Kent 23 H6
Chipstead Surr. 23 F6
Chirbury 38 B6
Chirk 38 B2
Chirmorrie 64 C3
Chirnside 77 G5
Chirnsidebridge 77 G5
Chirton 20 D6
Chisbury 21 F5
Chiscan 66 A2
Chiselborough 8 D3
Chiseldon 20 E3
Chislehampton 21 J2
Chislehurst 23 H4
Chislet 25 J5
Chiswell Green 22 E1
Chiswick 23 F4
Chisworth 49 J3
Chithurst 12 B4
Chittering 33 H2
Chitterne 20 C7
Chittlehamholt 6 E3
Chittlehampton 6 E3
Chittoe 20 C5
Chivelstone 5 H7
Chobham 22 C5
Choicelee 77 F5
Cholderton 21 F7
Cholesbury 22 C1
Chollerford 70 E6
Chollerton 70 E6
Cholsey 21 J3
Cholstrey 28 D3
Cholwell B. & N.E.Som. 19 K6
Cholwell Devon 4 E3
Chop Gate 63 G6
Chopwell 62 C1
Chorley Ches. 48 E7
Chorley Lancs. 48 E1
Chorley Shrop. 39 F7
Chorley Staffs. 40 C4
Chorleywood 22 D2
Chorlton 49 G7
Chorlton Lane 38 D1
Chorlton-cum-Hardy 49 H3
Chowley 48 D7
Chrishall 33 H5
Chrishall Grange 33 H4
Chrisswell 74 A3
Christchurch Cambs. 43 H6
Christchurch Dorset 10 C5
Christchurch Glos. 28 E7
Christchurch Newport 19 G3
Christian Malford 20 C4
Christleton 48 D6
Christmas Common 22 A2
Christon 19 G6
Christon Bank 71 H1
Christow 7 G7
Chryston 74 E3
Chudleigh 5 J3
Chudleigh Knighton 5 J3
Chulmleigh 6 E4
Chunal 50 C3
Church 56 C7
Church Aston 39 G4
Church Brampton 31 J2
Church Broughton 40 E2
Church Common 35 H3
Church Crookham 22 B6
Church Eaton 40 A4
Church End Beds. 32 E5
Church End Beds. 32 C6
Church End Beds. 32 E3
Church End Cambs. 43 G5
Church End Cambs. 33 H3
Church End Cambs. 33 G1
Church End E.Riding 59 G4
Church End Essex 33 J4
Church End Essex 34 B6
Church End Hants. 21 K6
Church End Herts. 32 E7
Church End Lincs. 43 F2
Church End Lincs. 53 H3
Church End Warks. 40 E6
Church End Wilts. 20 D4
Church Enstone 30 E6
Church Fenton 58 B6
Church Green 7 K6
Church Gresley 40 E4
Church Hanborough 31 F7
Church Houses 63 H7
Church Knowle 9 J6
Church Langley 23 H1
Church Langton 42 A6
Church Lawford 31 F1
Church Lawton 49 H7
Church Leigh 40 C2
Church Lench 30 B3
Church Minshull 49 F6
Church Norton 12 B7
Church Preen 38 E6
Church Pulverbatch 38 D5
Church Stoke 38 B6
Church Stowe 31 H3
Church Street 24 D4
Church Stretton 38 D6
Church Village 18 D3
Church Warsop 51 H6
Churcham 29 G7
Churchdown 29 H6
Churchend Essex 25 G2
Churchend Essex 33 K6
Churchend S.Glos. 20 A2
Churchgate 23 G1
Churchgate Street 33 H7
Churchill N.Som. 19 H6
Churchill Oxon. 30 D6
Churchill Worcs. 29 J3
Churchill Worcs. 29 H1
Churchingford 8 B3
Churchover 41 H7
Churchstanton 7 K4
Churchstow 5 H6
Churchthorpe 53 G3
Churchtown Devon 6 E1
Churchtown I.o.M. 54 D4
Churchtown Lancs. 55 H5
Churchtown Mersey. 48 C1
Churnsike Lodge 70 B6
Churston Ferrers 5 K5
Churt 12 B3
Churton 48 D7
Churwell 57 H7
Chute Cadley 21 G6
Chute Standen 21 G6
Chwilog 36 D2
Chwitffordd (Whitford) 47 K5
Chyandour 2 B5
Cilan Uchaf 36 C3
Cilcain 47 K6
Cilcennin 26 E2
Cilfrew 18 A1
Cilfynydd 18 D2
Cilgerran 16 E1
Cilgwyn Carmar. 27 G6
Cilgwyn Pembs. 16 D2
Ciliau-Aeron 26 E3
Cille Bhrighde 84 C3
Cille Pheadair 84 C3
Cilmery 27 K3
Cilrhedyn 17 F2
Cilrhedyn Bridge 16 D2
Ciltalgarth 37 H1
Cilwendeg 17 F2
Cilybebyll 18 A1
Cilycwm 27 G4
Cinderford 29 F7
Cippyn 16 E1
Cirbhig 100 D3
Cirencester 20 D1
City 23 G3
City Airport 23 H3
City Dulas 46 C4
Clabhach 78 C2
Clachaig 73 K2
Clachan Arg. & B. 80 C6
Clachan Arg. & B. 79 K3
Clachan Arg. & B. 73 F5
Clachan High. 86 B1
Clachan W.Isles 92 C7
Clachan of Campsie 74 E3
Clachan of Glendaruel 73 J2
Clachan Strachur 80 C7
Clachandhu 79 F4
Clachaneasy 64 D3
Clachanmore 64 A6
Clachan-Seil 79 J6
Clachanturn 89 K5
Clachbreck 73 F3
Clachnabrain 82 E1
Clachnaharry 96 D7
Clachtoll 102 C6
Clackmannan 75 H1
Clacton-on-Sea 35 F7
Cladach a' Chaolais 92 C5
Cladach Chircebost 92 C5
Cladich 80 B5
Claggan High. 87 H7
Claggan High. 79 J3
Claigan 93 H6
Claines 29 H3
Clandown 19 K6
Clanfield Hants. 11 J3
Clanfield Oxon. 21 F1
Clannaborough Barton 7 F5
Clanville 21 G7
Claonaig 73 G5
Claonairigh 80 B7
Claonel 96 C1
Clap Gate 57 J5
Clapgate 10 B4
Clapham Beds. 32 D3
Clapham Gt.Lon. 23 F4
Clapham N.Yorks. 56 C3
Clapham W.Suss. 12 D6
Clapham Hill 25 H5
Clappers 77 H5
Clappersgate 60 E6
Clapton 8 D4
Clapton-in-Gordano 19 H4
Clapton-on-the-Hill 30 C7
Clapworthy 6 E3
Clarach 37 F7
Clarbeston 16 D3
Clarbeston Road 16 D3
Clarborough 51 K4
Clardon 105 G2
Clare 34 B4
Clarebrand 65 H4
Clarencefield 69 F7
Clareton 57 J4
Clarilaw 70 A2
Clarkston 74 D5
Clashban 96 D2
Clashcoig 96 D2
Clashgour 80 D3
Clashindarroch 90 C1
Clashmore 96 E2
Clashnessie 102 C5
Clashnoir 89 K2
Clathy 82 A5
Clatt 90 D2
Clatter 37 J6
Clatterford End 23 J1
Clatterin Brig 90 E7
Clatteringshaws 65 F3
Clatworthy 7 J2
Claughton Lancs. 55 J3
Claughton Lancs. 55 J5
Claverdon 30 C2
Claverham 19 H5
Clavering 33 H5
Claverley 39 G6
Claverton 20 A5
Clawdd-newydd 47 J7
Clawfin 67 K3
Clawthorpe 55 J2
Clawton 6 B6
Claxby Lincs. 53 H5
Claxby Lincs. 52 E3
Claxby Pluckacre 53 G6
Claxton N.Yorks. 58 C3
Claxton Norf. 45 H5
Clay Common 45 J7
Clay Coton 31 G1
Clay Cross 51 F6
Clay of Allan 97 F4
Claybrooke Magna 41 G7
Claybrooke Parva 41 G7
Claydene 23 H7
Claydon Oxon. 31 F3
Claydon Suff. 35 F4
Claygate Kent 14 C3
Claygate Surr. 22 E5
Claygate Cross 23 K6
Clayhanger Devon 7 J3
Clayhanger W.Mid. 40 C5
Clayhidon 7 K4
Clayock 105 G3
Claypole 42 B1
Claythorpe 53 H5
Clayton S.Yorks. 51 G2
Clayton Staffs. 40 A1
Clayton W.Suss. 13 F5
Clayton W.Yorks. 57 G6
Clayton West 50 E1
Clayton-le-Moors 56 C6
Clayton-le-Woods 55 J7
Clayworth 51 K4
Cleadale 85 K6
Cleadon 71 J7
Clearbrook 5 F4
Clearwell 19 J1
Cleasby 62 D5
Cleat 107 D9
Cleatlam 62 C5
Cleatop 56 D3
Cleator 60 B5
Cleator Moor 60 B5
Cleckheaton 57 G7
Clee St. Margaret 38 E7
Cleedownton 38 E7
Cleehill 28 E1
Cleethorpes 53 G2
Cleeton St. Mary 29 F1
Cleeve N.Som. 19 H5
Cleeve Oxon. 21 K3
Cleeve Hill 29 J6
Cleeve Prior 30 B4
Cleghorn 75 H6
Clehonger 28 D5
Cleigh 79 K5
Cleish 75 J1
Cleland 75 F5
Clench Common 20 E5
Clenchwarton 43 J3
Clent 29 J1
Cleobury Mortimer 29 F1
Cleobury North 39 F7
Clephanton 97 F6
Clerklands 70 A1
Clestrain 107 C7
Cleuch Head 70 A2
Cleughbrae 69 F6
Clevancy 20 D4
Clevedon 19 H4
Cleveland Tontine 63 F7
Cleveleys 55 G5
Clevelode 29 H4
Cleverton 20 C3
Clewer 19 H6
Clewer Village 22 C4

Cley next the Sea 44 E1
Cliburn 61 G4
Cliddesden 21 K7
Cliff Carmar. 17 G5
Cliff High. 79 H1
Cliff End 14 D6
Cliffe Med. 24 D4
Cliffe N.Yorks. 58 C6
Cliffe Woods 24 D4
Clifford Here. 28 B4
Clifford W.Yorks. 57 K5
Clifford Chambers 30 C3
Clifford's Mesne 29 G6
Cliffs End 25 K5
Clifton Beds. 32 E5
Clifton Bristol 19 J4
Clifton Cumb. 61 G4
Clifton Derbys. 40 D1
Clifton Lancs. 55 H6
Clifton Northumb. 71 H5
Clifton Nott. 41 H2
Clifton Oxon. 31 F5
Clifton Stir. 80 E4
Clifton Worcs. 29 H4
Clifton Campville 40 E4
Clifton Hampden 21 J2
Clifton Reynes 32 C3
Clifton upon Dunsmore 31 G1
Clifton upon Teme 29 G2
Cliftonville 25 K4
Climping 12 D6
Climpy 75 H5
Clint 57 H4
Clint Green 44 E4
Clinterty 91 G3
Clintmains 76 E7
Clippesby 45 J4
Clipsham 42 C4
Clipston Northants. 42 A7
Clipston Notts. 41 J2
Clipstone 51 H6
Clitheroe 56 C5
Clive 38 E3
Clivocast 108 F2
Clocaenog 47 J7
Clochan 98 C4
Clochtow 91 J1
Clock Face 48 E3
Clockhill 99 G6
Cloddach 97 J6
Clodock 28 C6
Cloford 20 A7
Cloichran 81 H4
Clola 99 J6
Clonrae 68 D4
Clophill 32 D5
Clopton 32 D1
Clopton Green 34 B3
Close Clark 54 B6
Closeburn 68 D4
Closworth 8 E3
Clothall 33 F5
Clothan 108 D4
Clotton 48 E6
Clough Cumb. 61 J7
Clough Gt.Man. 49 J1
Clough Foot 56 E7
Cloughton 63 K3
Cloughton Newlands 63 K3
Clounlaid 79 J2
Clousta 109 C7
Clouston 107 C6
Clova Aber. 90 C2
Clova Angus 90 B7
Clove Lodge 62 A5
Clovelly 6 B3
Clovelly Cross 6 B3
Clovenfords 76 C7
Clovenstone 91 F3
Cloverhill 91 H3
Cloves 97 J5
Clovullin 80 B1
Clowne 51 G5
Clows Top 29 G1
Cloyntie 67 H3
Cluanach 72 B5
Clubworthy 4 C1
Cluer 93 G2
Clun 38 B7
Clunas 97 F7
Clunbury 38 C7
Clune High. 88 E2
Clune Moray 98 D4
Clunes 87 H6
Clungunford 28 C1
Clunie Aber. 98 E5
Clunie P.& K. 82 C3
Clunton 38 C7
Cluny 76 A1
Clutton B.& N.E.Som. 19 K6
Clutton Ches. 48 D7
Clwt-y-bont 46 D6
Clydach Mon. 28 B7
Clydach Swan. 17 K5
Clydach Vale 18 C2
Clydebank 74 D4
Clydey 17 F2
Clyffe Pypard 20 D4
Clynder 74 A2
Clynderwen 16 E4
Clynelish 97 F1
Clynfyw 17 F2
Clynnog-fawr 36 D1
Clyro 28 B4
Clyst Honiton 7 H6
Clyst Hydon 7 J5
Clyst St. George 7 H7
Clyst St. Lawrence 7 J5
Clyst St. Mary 7 H6
Cnewr 27 H6
Cnoc 101 G4
Cnwch Coch 27 F1
Coachford 98 C6
Coad's Green 4 C3
Coal Aston 51 F5
Coalbrookdale 39 F5
Coalbrookvale 18 E1
Coalburn 75 G7
Coalburns 71 G7
Coalcleugh 61 K2
Coaley 20 A1
Coalpit Heath 19 K3
Coalpit Hill 49 H7
Coalport 39 G5
Coalsnaughton 75 H1
Coaltown of Balgonie 76 B1
Coaltown of Wemyss 76 B1
Coalville 41 G4
Coast 95 F2
Coat 8 D2
Coatbridge 75 F4
Coate Swin. 20 E3
Coate Wilts. 20 D5
Coates Cambs. 43 G6
Coates Glos. 20 C1
Coates Lincs. 52 C4
Coates W.Suss. 12 C5
Coatham 63 G4
Coatham Mundeville 62 D4
Cobairdy 98 D6
Cobbaton 6 E3
Coberley 29 J7
Cobham Kent 24 C5
Cobham Surr. 22 E6
Cobleland 74 D1
Cobler's Green 33 K7
Cobnash 28 D2
Coburty 99 H4
Cochno 74 C3
Cock Alley 51 G6
Cock Bridge 89 K4
Cock Clarks 24 E1
Cockayne 63 H7
Cockayne Hatley 33 F4
Cockburnspath 77 F3
Cockenzie & Port Seton 76 C3
Cockerham 55 H4
Cockermouth 60 C3
Cockernhoe 32 E6
Cockett 17 K6
Cockfield Dur. 62 C4
Cockfield Suff. 34 D3
Cockfosters 23 F2
Cocking 12 B5
Cockington 5 J4
Cocklake 19 H7
Cockley Beck 60 D6
Cockley Cley 44 B5
Cockpole Green 22 A3
Cockshutt 38 D3
Cockthorpe 44 D1
Cockwood 7 H7
Codda 4 B3
Coddenham 35 F3
Coddington Ches. 48 D7
Coddington Here. 29 G4
Coddington Notts. 52 B7
Codford St. Mary 9 J1
Codford St. Peter 20 C7
Codicote 33 F7
Codmore Hill 12 D5
Codnor 41 G1
Codrington 20 A4
Codsall 40 A5
Codsall Wood 40 A5
Coed Morgan 28 C7
Coed Ystumgwern 36 E3
Coedcae 19 F1
Coedely 18 D3
Coedkernew 19 F3
Coedpoeth 48 B7
Coed-y-paen 19 G2
Coed-yr-ynys 28 A6
Coelbren 27 H7
Coffinswell 5 J4
Cofton Hackett 30 B1
Cogan 18 E4
Cogenhoe 32 B2
Coggeshall 34 C6
Coggeshall Hamlet 34 C6
Coggins Mill 13 J4
Cóig Peighinnean W.Isles 101 F2
Cóig Peighinnean W.Isles 101 H1
Coilantogle 81 G7
Coileitir 80 C3
Coilessan 80 D7
Coillaig 80 B5
Coille Mhorgil 87 H4
Coille-righ 87 F2
Coillore 85 J1
Coity 18 C3
Col 101 G3
Colaboll 103 H7
Colan 3 F2
Colaton Raleigh 7 J7
Colbost 93 H7
Colbury 10 E3
Colby Cumb. 61 H4
Colby I.o.M. 54 B6
Colby Norf. 45 G2
Colchester 34 D6
Colcot 18 E5
Cold Ash 21 J5
Cold Ashby 31 H1
Cold Ashton 20 A4
Cold Aston 30 C6
Cold Blow 16 E4
Cold Brayfield 32 C3
Cold Chapel 68 E1
Cold Hanworth 52 D4
Cold Hesledon 63 F2
Cold Higham 31 H3
Cold Kirby 58 B1
Cold Newton 42 A5
Cold Norton 24 E1
Cold Overton 42 B5
Coldbackie 103 J2
Coldblow 23 J4
Coldean 13 G6
Coldeast 5 J3
Colden Common 11 F2
Coldfair Green 35 J2
Coldham 43 H5
Coldharbour 22 E7
Coldingham 77 G4
Coldrain 82 B7
Coldred 15 H3
Coldrey 22 A7
Coldridge 6 E5
Coldrife 71 F4
Coldstream 77 G7
Coldwaltham 12 D5
Coldwells 99 K6
Cole 9 F1
Cole Green 33 F7
Colebatch 38 C7
Colebrook 7 J5
Colebrooke 7 F5
Coleby Lincs. 52 C6
Coleby N.Lincs. 52 C1
Coleford Devon 7 F5
Coleford Glos. 28 E7
Coleford Som. 19 K7
Colehill 10 B4
Coleman's Hatch 13 H3
Colemere 38 D2
Colemore 11 J1
Colenden 82 C5
Coleorton 41 G4
Colerne 20 B4
Cole's Cross 5 H6
Colesbourne 30 B7
Colesden 32 E3
Coleshill Bucks. 22 C2
Coleshill Oxon. 21 F2
Coleshill Warks. 40 E7
Colestocks 7 J5
Colfin 64 A5
Colgate 13 F3
Colgrain 74 B2
Colinsburgh 83 F7
Colinton 76 A4
Colintraive 73 J3
Colkirk 44 D3
Collace 82 D4
Collafirth Shet. 109 D6
Collafirth Shet. 108 C4
Collamoor Head 4 B1
Collaton St. Mary 5 J4
Collessie 82 D6
Colleton Mills 6 E4
Collett's Green 29 H3
Collier Row 23 J2
Collier Street 14 C3
Collier's End 33 G6
Colliery Row 62 E1
Collieston 91 J2
Collin 69 F6
Collingbourne Ducis 21 F6
Collingbourne Kingston 21 F6
Collingham Notts. 52 B6
Collingham W.Yorks. 57 J5
Collington 29 F2
Collingtree 31 J3
Collins Green 48 E3
Colliston 83 H3
Colliton 7 J5
Collmuir 90 D4
Collycroft 41 F7
Collynie 91 G1
Collyweston 42 D5
Colmonell 67 F5
Colmworth 32 E3
Coln Rogers 20 D1
Coln St. Aldwyns 20 E1
Coln St. Dennis 30 B7
Colnabaichin 89 K4
Colnbrook 22 D4
Colne Cambs. 33 G1
Colne Lancs. 56 D5
Colne Engaine 34 C5
Colney 45 F5
Colney Heath 23 F1
Colney Street 22 E1
Colonsay 72 B1
Colpy 90 E1
Colquhar 76 B6
Colsterdale 57 G1
Colsterworth 42 C3
Colston Bassett 42 A2
Coltfield 97 J5
Coltishall 45 G4
Colton Cumb. 55 G1
Colton N.Yorks. 58 B5
Colton Norf. 45 F4
Colton Staffs. 40 C3
Colva 28 B3
Colvend 65 J5
Colvister 108 E3
Colwall Green 29 G4
Colwall Stone 29 G4
Colwell 70 E6
Colwich 40 C3
Colwick 41 J1
Colwinston 18 C4
Colworth 12 C6
Colwyn Bay (Bae Colwyn) 47 G5
Colyford 8 B5
Colyton 8 B5
Combe Here. 28 C2
Combe Oxon. 31 F7
Combe W.Berks. 21 G5
Combe Cross 5 H3
Combe Down 20 A5
Combe Florey 7 K2
Combe Hay 20 A5
Combe Martin 6 D1
Combe Raleigh 7 K5
Combe St. Nicholas 8 B3
Combeinteignhead 5 K3
Comberbach 49 F5
Comberford 40 D5
Comberton Cambs. 33 G3
Comberton Here. 28 D2
Combpyne 8 B5
Combrook 30 E3
Combs Derbys. 50 C5
Combs Suff. 34 E3
Combs Ford 34 E3
Combwich 19 F7
Comer 80 E7
Comers 90 E4
Commercial End 33 J2
Commins Coch 37 H5
Common Edge 55 G6
Common Moor 4 C4
Common Side 51 F5
Commondale 63 H5
Commonside 40 E1
Compstall 49 J3
Compton Devon 5 J4
Compton Hants. 11 F2
Compton Surr. 22 C7
Compton W.Berks. 21 J4
Compton W.Suss. 11 J3
Compton Abbas 9 H3
Compton Abdale 30 B7
Compton Bassett 20 D4
Compton Beauchamp 21 F3
Compton Bishop 19 G6
Compton Chamberlayne 10 B2
Compton Dando 19 K5
Compton Dundon 8 D1
Compton Martin 19 J6
Compton Pauncefoot 9 F2
Compton Valence 8 E5
Comra 88 C5
Comrie 81 J5
Conchra Arg.& B. 73 J2
Conchra High. 86 E2
Concraigie 82 C3
Conder Green 55 H4
Conderton 29 J5
Condicote 30 C6
Condorrat 75 F3
Condover 38 D5
Coney Weston 34 D1
Coneyhurst 12 E4
Coneysthorpe 58 D2
Coneythorpe 57 J4
Conford 12 B3
Congash 89 H2
Congdon's Shop 4 C3
Congerstone 41 F5
Congham 44 B3
Congleton 49 H6
Congresbury 19 H5
Conicavel 97 G6
Coningsby 53 F7
Conington Cambs. 42 E7
Conington Cambs. 33 G2
Conisbrough 51 H3
Conisby 72 A4
Conisholme 53 H3
Coniston Cumb. 60 E7
Coniston E.Riding 59 H6
Coniston Cold 56 E4
Conistone 56 E3
Conland 98 E6
Connah's Quay 48 B6
Connel 80 A4
Connel Park 68 B2
Connor Downs 2 C5
Conon Bridge 96 C6
Cononish 80 E5
Cononley 56 E5
Cononsyth 83 G3
Consall 40 B1
Consett 62 C1
Constable Burton 62 C7
Constantine 2 E6
Contin 96 B6
Contlaw 91 G4
Contullich 96 D4
Conwy 47 F5
Conyer 25 F5
Cooden 14 C7
Coodham 74 B7
Cookbury 6 C5
Cookham 22 B3
Cookham Dean 22 B3
Cookham Rise 22 B3
Cookhill 30 B3
Cookley Suff. 35 H1
Cookley Worcs. 40 A7
Cookley Green 21 K3
Cookney 91 G5
Cooksbridge 13 H5
Cookshill 40 B1
Cooksmill Green 24 C1
Cookston 91 H1
Coolham 12 E4
Cooling 24 D4
Coombe Cornw. 3 G3
Coombe Cornw. 6 A4
Coombe Cornw. 2 D4
Coombe Devon 5 H6
Coombe Devon 7 G7
Coombe Bissett 10 C2
Coombe Hill 29 H6
Coombe Keynes 9 H6
Coombes 12 E6
Coombes Moor 28 C2
Cooper's Corner E.Suss. 14 C5
Cooper's Corner Kent 23 H7
Cooper's Hill 22 C4
Coopersale Common 23 H1
Cootham 12 D5
Cop Street 15 H2
Copdock 35 F4
Copford Green 34 D6
Copgrove 57 J3
Copister 108 D5
Cople 32 E4
Copley 62 B4
Coplow Dale 50 D5
Copmanthorpe 58 B5
Coppathorne 6 A5
Coppenhall 40 B4
Coppenhall Moss 49 G7
Coppingford 32 E1
Coppleridge 9 H2
Copplestone 7 F5
Coppull 48 E1
Coppull Moor 48 E1
Copsale 12 E4
Copster Green 56 B6
Copston Magna 41 G7
Copt Heath 30 C1
Copt Hewick 57 J2
Copt Oak 41 G4
Copthorne 13 G3
Copy Lake 6 E4
Copythorne 10 E3
Coralhill 99 J4
Corbiegoe 105 J4
Corbridge 70 E7
Corby 42 B7
Corby Glen 42 D3
Cordach 90 E5
Coreley 29 F1
Corfcott Green 6 B6
Corfe 8 B3
Corfe Castle 9 J6
Corfe Mullen 9 J5
Corfton 38 D7
Corgarff 89 K4
Corhampton 11 H2
Corley 40 E7
Corley Ash 40 E7
Corley Moor 40 E7
Cornabus 72 B6
Corney 60 C7
Cornforth 62 E3
Cornhill 98 D5
Cornhill on Tweed 77 G7
Cornholme 56 E7
Cornish Hall End 33 K5
Cornquoy 107 E7
Cornriggs 61 K2
Cornsay 62 C2
Cornsay Colliery 62 C2
Corntown High. 96 C6
Corntown V. of Glam. 18 C4
Cornwell 30 D6
Cornwood 5 G5
Cornworthy 5 J5
Corpach 87 H7
Corpusty 45 F3
Corrachree 90 C4
Corran Arg.& B. 74 A1
Corran High. 86 E4
Corran High. 80 B1
Corranbuie 73 G4
Corranmore 79 J7
Corrany 54 D5
Corrie 73 J6
Corrie Common 69 H5
Corriechrevie 73 F5
Corriecravie 66 D1
Corriedoo 68 B5
Corrielorne 79 K6
Corrievorrie 88 E2
Corrimony 87 K1
Corringham Lincs. 52 B3
Corringham Thur. 24 D3
Corris 37 G5
Corris Uchaf 37 G5
Corrlarach 87 F7
Corrour Shooting Lodge 81 F1
Corrow 80 C7
Corry 86 C2
Corrychurrachan 80 B1
Corrykinloch 103 F6
Corrylach 66 B1
Corrymuckloch 81 K4
Corsback 105 H2
Corscombe 8 E4
Corse Aber. 98 E6
Corse Glos. 29 G6
Corse Lawn 29 H5
Corse of Kinnoir 98 D6
Corsebank 68 D2
Corsehill 69 G5
Corsewall 64 A4
Corsham 20 B4
Corsindae 90 E4
Corsley 20 B7
Corsley Heath 20 B7
Corsock 65 H3
Corston B.& N.E.Som. 19 K5
Corston Wilts. 20 C3
Corstorphine 75 K3
Cortachy 82 E2
Corton Suff. 45 K6
Corton Wilts. 20 C7
Corton Denham 9 F2
Corúna (Corunna) 92 D5
Corunna (Corúna) 92 D5
Corwar House 67 G5
Corwen 37 K1
Coryton Devon 6 C7
Coryton Thur. 24 D3
Cosby 41 H6
Coseley 40 B6
Cosford 39 G5
Cosgrove 31 J4
Cosham 11 H4
Cosheston 16 D5
Coshieville 81 J3
Cossall 41 G1
Cossington Leics. 41 J4
Cossington Som. 19 G7
Costa 106 C5
Costessey 45 F4
Costock 41 H3
Coston Leics. 42 B3
Coston Norf. 44 E5
Cote Oxon. 21 G1
Cote Som. 19 G7
Cotebrook 48 E6
Cotehill 61 F1
Cotes Cumb. 55 H1
Cotes Leics. 41 H3
Cotes Staffs. 40 A2
Cotesbach 41 H7
Cotgrave 41 J2
Cothall 91 G3
Cotham 42 A1
Cothelstone 7 K2
Cothercott 38 D5
Cotheridge 29 G3
Cotherstone 62 B5
Cothill 21 H2
Cotleigh 8 B4
Coton Cambs. 33 H3
Coton Northants. 31 H1
Coton Staffs. 40 B2
Coton Staffs. 40 D5
Coton Clanford 40 A3
Coton in the Clay 40 D3
Coton in the Elms 40 E4
Cott 5 H4
Cottam E.Riding 59 F3
Cottam Lancs. 55 H6
Cottam Notts. 52 B4
Cottartown 89 H1
Cottenham 33 H2
Cotterdale 61 K7
Cottered 33 G6
Cotteridge 40 C7
Cotterstock 42 D6
Cottesbrooke 31 J1
Cottesmore 42 C4
Cottingham E.Riding 59 G6
Cottingham Northants. 42 B6
Cottisford 31 G5
Cotton 34 E2
Cotton End 32 D4
Cottown Aber. 90 D2
Cottown Aber. 99 G6
Cottown Aber. 91 F3
Cotwalton 40 B2
Couch's Mill 4 B5
Coughton Here. 28 E6
Coughton Warks. 30 B2
Cougie 87 J2
Coulaghailtro 73 F4
Coulags 95 F7
Coulby Newham 63 G5
Coull 90 D4
Coulport 74 A2
Coulsdon 23 G6
Coulston 20 C6
Coulter 75 J7
Coultershaw Bridge 12 C5
Coultings 19 F7
Coulton 58 C2
Coultra 82 E5
Cound 38 E5
Coundon 62 D3
Coundon Grange 62 D4
Countersett 56 E1
Countess 20 E7
Countess Wear 7 H6
Countesthorpe 41 H6
Countisbury 7 F1
County Oak 13 F3
Coupar Angus 82 D3
Coupland Cumb. 61 J5
Coupland Northumb. 77 H7
Cour 73 G6
Court Barton 7 G6
Court Henry 17 J3
Court House Green 41 F7
Court-at-Street 15 F4
Courteenhall 31 J3
Courtsend 25 G2
Courtway 8 B1
Cousland 76 B4
Cousley Wood 13 K3
Coustonn 73 J3
Cove Arg.& B. 74 A2
Cove Devon 7 H4
Cove Hants. 22 B6
Cove High. 94 E2
Cove Sc.Bord. 77 F3
Cove Bay 91 H4
Covehithe 45 K7
Coven 40 B5
Coveney 43 H7
Covenham St. Bartholomew 53 G3
Covenham St. Mary 53 G3
Coventry 30 E1
Coverack 2 E7
Coverham 57 F1
Covesea 97 J4
Covington Cambs. 32 D1
Covington S.Lan. 75 H7
Cowan Bridge 56 B2
Cowbeech 13 K5
Cowbit 43 F4
Cowbridge 18 D4
Cowden 23 H7
Cowden Pound 23 H7
Cowdenbeath 75 K1
Cowes 11 F5
Cowesby 63 F7
Cowfold 13 F4
Cowgill 56 C1
Cowie Aber. 91 G6
Cowie Stir. 75 G2
Cowlam Manor 59 F3
Cowley Devon 7 H6
Cowley Glos. 29 J7
Cowley Gt.Lon. 22 D3
Cowley Oxon. 21 J1
Cowling N.Yorks. 56 E5
Cowling N.Yorks. 57 H1
Cowlinge 34 B3
Cowmes 50 D1
Cowpen 71 H5
Cowpen Bewley 63 F4
Cowplain 11 H3
Cowshill 61 K2
Cowthorpe 57 K4
Cox Common 45 H7
Coxbank 39 F1
Coxbench 41 F1
Coxheath 14 C2
Coxhoe 62 E3
Coxley 19 J7
Coxtie Green 23 J2
Coxwold 58 B2
Coychurch 18 C4
Coylet 73 K2
Coylton 67 J2
Coylumbridge 89 G3
Coynach 90 C4
Coynachie 90 C1
Coytrahen 18 B3
Crabbet Park 13 G3
Crabbs Cross 30 B2
Crabtree Plym. 5 F5
Crabtree W.Suss. 13 F4
Crackaig 72 D4
Crackenthorpe 61 H4
Crackington 4 B1
Crackington Haven 4 B1
Crackleybank 39 G4
Crackpot 62 A7
Cracoe 56 E3
Craddock 7 J4
Cradhlastadh 100 C4
Cradley Here. 29 G4
Cradley W.Mid. 40 B7
Crafthole 4 D5
Cragg 57 F7
Craggan Moray 89 J1
Craggan P.& K. 81 K6
Cragganruar 81 H3
Craggie High. 88 E1
Craggie High. 104 D6
Craghead 62 D1
Craibstone Aberdeen 91 G3
Craibstone Moray 98 C5
Craichie 83 F3
Craig Arg.& B. 80 B4
Craig Arg.& B. 79 G5
Craig D.& G. 65 G4
Craig High. 94 D5
Craig High. 95 G7
Craig S.Ayr. 67 H3
Craigans 73 H1
Craigbeg 88 B6
Craig-cefn-parc 17 K5
Craigcleuch 69 J5
Craigculter 99 H5
Craigdallie 82 D5
Craigdam 91 G1
Craigdarroch D.& G. 68 C4
Craigdarroch E.Ayr. 68 B3
Craigdhu D.& G. 64 D6
Craigdhu High. 96 B7
Craigearn 91 F3
Craigellachie 97 K7
Craigellie 99 J4
Craigencallie 65 F3
Craigend Moray 97 J6
Craigend P.& K. 82 C5
Craigendive 73 J2
Craigendoran 74 B2
Craigengillan 67 J3
Craigenputtock 68 C5
Craigens 72 A4
Craigglas 73 G2
Craighall 83 F6
Craighat 74 C2
Craighead Fife 83 H7
Craighead High. 96 E5
Craighlaw 64 D4
Craighouse 72 D4
Craigie Aber. 91 H3
Craigie P.& K. 82 C3
Craigie S.Ayr. 74 C7
Craigie Brae 91 G1
Craigieburn 69 G3
Craigieholm 82 C4
Craiglockhart 76 A3
Craiglug 91 G5
Craigmaud 99 G5
Craigmillar 76 A3
Craigmore 73 K4
Craigmyle House 90 E4
Craignafeoch 73 H3
Craignant 38 B2
Craignavie 81 G4
Craigneil 67 F5
Craignure 79 J4
Craigo 83 H1
Craigoch 67 H3
Craigow 82 B7
Craigrothie 82 E6
Craigroy 97 J6
Craigroy Farm 89 J1
Craigruie 81 G5
Craigsanquhar 82 E6
Craigton Aberdeen 91 G4
Craigton Angus 83 G4
Craigton Angus 82 E2
Craigton Stir. 74 E2
Craigtown 104 D3
Craig-y-nos 27 H7
Craik Aber. 90 C2
Craik Sc.Bord. 69 J3
Crail 83 H7
Crailing 70 B1
Crailinghall 70 B1
Crakehill 57 K2
Crambe 58 D3
Cramlington 71 H6
Cramond 75 K3
Cranage 49 G6
Cranberry 40 A2
Cranborne 10 B3
Cranbourne 22 C4
Cranbrook 14 C4
Cranbrook Common 14 C4
Cranfield 32 C4
Cranford Devon 6 B3
Cranford Gt.Lon. 22 E4
Cranford St. Andrew 32 C1
Cranford St. John 32 C1
Cranham Glos. 29 H7
Cranham Gt.Lon. 23 J3
Crank 48 E2
Cranleigh 12 D3
Cranmer Green 34 E1
Cranmore I.o.W. 11 F5
Cranmore Som. 19 K7
Cranna 98 E5
Crannach 98 C5
Cranoe 42 A6
Cransford 35 H2
Cranshaws 76 E4
Cranstal 54 D3
Crantock 2 E2
Cranwell 42 D1
Cranwich 44 B6
Cranworth 44 D5
Craobh Haven 79 J7
Crapstone 5 F4
Crarae 73 H1
Crask Inn 103 H6
Crask of Aigas 96 B7
Craskins 90 D4
Craster 71 H1
Craswall 28 B5
Cratfield 35 H1
Crathes 91 F5
Crathie Aber. 89 K5
Crathie High. 88 C5
Crathorne 63 F6
Craven Arms 38 D7
Craw 73 G6
Crawcrook 71 G7
Crawford Lancs. 48 D2
Crawford S.Lan. 68 E1
Crawfordjohn 68 D1
Crawfordton 68 C4
Crawick 68 C2
Crawley Hants. 11 F1
Crawley Oxon. 30 E7
Crawley W.Suss. 13 F3
Crawley Down 13 G3
Crawleyside 62 A2
Crawshawbooth 56 D7
Crawton 91 G7
Crawyn 54 C4
Cray N.Yorks. 56 E2
Cray P.& K. 82 C1
Cray Powys 27 H6
Crayford 23 J4
Crayke 58 B2
Crays Hill 24 D2
Cray's Pond 21 K3
Crazies Hill 22 A3
Creacombe 7 G4
Creag Ghoraidh 92 D7
Creagbheitheachain 80 A1
Creaton 31 J1
Creca 69 H6
Credenhill 28 D4
Crediton 7 G5
Creech Heathfield 8 B2
Creech St. Michael 8 B2
Creed 3 G4
Creedy Park 7 G5
Creekmouth 23 H3
Creeting St. Mary 34 E3
Creeton 42 D3
Creetown 64 E5
Creggans 80 B7
Cregneash 54 A7
Cregrina 28 A3
Creich 82 E5
Creigiau 18 D3
Crelevan 87 K1
Cremyll 4 E5
Cressage 38 E5
Cresselly 16 D5
Cressing 34 B6
Cresswell Northumb. 71 H4
Cresswell Staffs. 40 B2
Cresswell Quay 16 D5
Creswell 51 H5
Cretingham 35 G3
Cretshengan 73 F4
Crewe Ches. 49 G7
Crewe Ches. 48 D7
Crewgreen 38 C4
Crewkerne 8 D4
Crewton 41 F2
Crianlarich 80 E5
Cribbs Causeway 19 J3
Cribyn 26 E3
Criccieth 36 D2
Crich 51 F7
Crich Carr 51 F7
Crichie 99 H6
Crichton 76 B4
Crick Mon. 19 H3
Crick Northants. 31 G1
Crickadarn 27 K4
Cricket Malherbie 8 C3
Cricket St. Thomas 8 C4
Crickheath 38 B3
Crickhowell 28 B7
Cricklade 20 E2
Cridling Stubbs 58 B7
Crieff 81 K5
Criggion 38 B4
Crigglestone 51 F1
Crimdon Park 63 F3
Crimond 99 J5
Crimonmogate 99 J5
Crimplesham 44 A5
Crinan 73 F1
Cringleford 45 F5
Cringletie 76 A6
Crinow 16 E4
Cripplesease 2 B5
Cripp's Corner 14 C5
Crix 34 B7
Croalchapel 68 E4
Croasdale 60 B5
Crock Street 8 C3
Crockenhill 23 J5
Crockernwell 7 F6
Crockerton 20 B7
Crocketford or Ninemile Bar 65 J3
Crockey Hill 58 C5
Crockham Hill 23 H6
Crockhurst Street 23 K7

rockleford Heath 34 E6
roes Hywel 28 C7
roes y pant 19 G1
roesau Bach 38 B3
roeserw 18 B2
roesgoch 16 B3
roes-lan 17 G1
roesor 37 F1
roespenmaen 18 E2
roesyceiliog
Carmar. 17 H4
roesyceiliog
Torfaen 19 G2
roes-y-mwyalch 19 G2
roft *Leics.* 41 H6
roft *Lincs.* 53 J6
roft *Warr.* 49 F3
rofthead 69 J6
roftmore 81 K1
rofton *W.Yorks.* 51 F1
rofton *Wilts.* 21 F5
roft-on-Tees 62 D5
rofts 65 H3
rofts of
Benachielt 105 G5
rofts of Buinach 97 J6
rofts of Haddo 91 G1
rofty 17 J6
rogen 37 K2
roggan 79 J5
roglin 61 G2
roick *High.* 96 B2
roick *High.* 104 D3
roig 79 F2
rois Dughaill 84 C3
roit e Caley 54 B6
romarty 96 E5
rombie Mill 83 G3
romblet 91 F1
romdale 89 H2
romer *Herts.* 33 F6
romer *Norf.* 45 G1
romer Hyde 33 F7
romford 50 E7
romhall 19 K2
romhall Common 19 K3
rompton Fold 49 J2
romwell 52 B6
ronberry 68 B1
rondall 22 A7
ronk-y-Voddy 54 C5
ronton 48 D4
rook *Cumb.* 61 F7
rook *Dur.* 62 C3
rook of Devon 82 B7
rookedholm 74 C7
rookham
Northumb. 77 H7
rookham
W.Berks. 21 J5
rookham Village 22 A6
rooklands 55 J1
ropredy 31 F4
ropston 41 H4
ropthorne 29 J4
ropton 58 D1
ropwell Bishop 41 J2
ropwell Butler 41 J2
ros 101 G1
rosbie 74 A6
rosbost 101 F5
rosby *Cumb.* 60 B3
rosby *I.o.M.* 54 C6
rosby *Mersey.* 48 C3
rosby *N.Lincs.* 52 B1
rosby Court 62 E7
rosby Garrett 61 J6
rosby
Ravensworth 61 H5
roscombe 19 J7
ross 19 H6
ross Ash 28 D7
ross Foxes Inn 37 G4
ross Gates 57 J6
ross Green *Devon* 6 B7
ross Green *Suff.* 34 D3
ross Green *Suff.* 34 C3
ross Hands
Carmar. 17 J4
ross Hands
Pembs. 16 D4
ross Hill 41 G1
ross Hills 57 F5
ross Houses 38 E5
ross in Hand 13 J4
ross Inn *Cere.* 26 C3
ross Inn *Cere.* 26 E2
ross Inn *R.C.T.* 18 D3
ross Keys 20 B4
ross Lane Head 39 G6
ross Lanes *Cornw.* 2 E4
ross Lanes
N.Yorks. 58 B3
ross Lanes *Wrex.* 38 C1
ross o' the Hands 40 E1
ross of Jackson 91 F1
ross Street 35 F1
rossaig 73 G5
rossapol 78 C2
rossapoll 78 A3
ross-at-Hand 14 C3
rossbush 12 D6
rosscanonby 60 B3
rossdale Street 45 G2
rossens 55 G7
rossford *D. & G.* 68 D5
rossford *Fife* 75 J2
rossford *S.Lan.* 75 G6
rossgate 43 F3
rossgatehall 76 B4
rossgates *Fife* 75 K2
rossgates *P. & K.* 82 B5
rossgates *Powys* 27 K2
rossgill 55 J3
rosshands 74 C7
rosshill *Fife* 75 K1
rosshill *S.Ayr.* 67 H3
rosshouse 74 B7
rosskeys 19 F2
rosskirk 105 F1
rosslanes *Cornw.* 2 D6
rosslanes *Shrop.* 38 C4
rosslee *Renf.* 74 C4
rosslee *Sc.Bord.* 69 J2
rosslet 74 C3
rossmichael 65 H4
rossmoor 55 H6
rossroads *Aber.* 91 F5
rossroads *E.Ayr.* 74 C7
rossway *Mon.* 28 D7
rossway *Powys* 27 K3
rossway Green 29 H2
rossways *Dorset* 9 G6
rossways *Glos.* 28 E7
rosswell 16 E2
rosthwaite 61 F7
roston 48 D1
rostwick 45 G4
rostwight 45 H2
Crouch 23 K6
Crouch Hill 9 G3
Croughton 31 G5
Crovie 99 G4
Crow 10 C4
Crow Hill 29 F6
Crowan 2 D5
Crowborough 13 J3
Crowcombe 7 K2
Crowdecote 50 D6
Crowdhill 11 F2
Crowfield
Northants. 31 H4
Crowfield *Suff.* 35 F3
Crowhurst *E.Suss.* 14 C6
Crowhurst *Surr.* 23 G7
Crowhurst Lane
End 23 G7
Crowland *Lincs.* 43 F4
Crowland *Suff.* 34 E1
Crowlas 2 C5
Crowle *N.Lincs.* 51 K1
Crowle *Worcs.* 29 J3
Crowle Green 29 J3
Crowmarsh Gifford 21 K3
Crownhill 4 E5
Crownthorpe 44 E5
Crowntown 2 D5
Crows-an-wra 2 A6
Crowthorne 22 B5
Crowton 48 E5
Croxall 40 D4
Croxdale 62 D3
Croxden 40 C2
Croxley Green 22 D2
Croxton *Cambs.* 33 F3
Croxton *N.Lincs.* 52 E1
Croxton *Norf.* 44 C7
Croxton *Staffs.* 39 G2
Croxton Green 48 E7
Croxton Kerrial 42 B3
Croxtonbank 39 G2
Croy *High.* 96 E7
Croy *N.Lan.* 75 F3
Croyde 6 C2
Croydon *Cambs.* 33 G4
Croydon *Gt.Lon.* 23 G5
Cruach 72 B5
Cruchie 98 D6
Cruckmeole 38 D5
Cruckton 38 D4
Cruden Bay 91 J1
Crudgington 39 F4
Crudwell 20 C2
Crug 28 A1
Crugmeer 3 G1
Crugybar 17 K2
Crulabhig 100 D4
Crumlin 19 F2
Crundale *Kent* 15 F3
Crundale *Pembs.* 16 C4
Crutherland 74 E5
Cruwys Morchard 7 G4
Crux Easton 21 H6
Crwbin 17 H4
Cryers Hill 22 B2
Crymlyn 46 E5
Crymych 16 E2
Crynant 18 A1
Crystal Palace 23 G4
Cuaig 94 D6
Cubbington 30 E2
Cubert 2 E3
Cublington 32 B6
Cuckfield 13 G4
Cucklington 9 G2
Cuckney 51 H5
Cuckoo's Nest 48 C6
Cuddesdon 21 J1
Cuddington *Bucks.* 31 J7
Cuddington *Ches.* 49 F5
Cuddington Heath 38 D1
Cuddy Hill 55 H6
Cudham 23 H6
Cudlipptown 5 F3
Cudworth *S.Yorks.* 51 F2
Cudworth *Som.* 8 C3
Cuffley 23 G1
Cuidhaseadair 101 H2
Cuidhir 84 B4
Cuidhtinis 93 F3
Cuidrach 93 J6
Cuilmuich 73 K1
Cuil-uaine 80 A4
Culag 74 B1
Culbo 96 D5
Culbokie 96 D6
Culbone 7 G1
Culburnie 96 B7
Culcabock 96 D7
Culcharan 80 A4
Culcharry 97 F6
Culcheth 49 F3
Culdrain 90 D1
Culduie 94 D7
Culford 34 C2
Culgaith 61 H4
Culgower 104 E7
Culham 21 J2
Culindrach 73 H5
Culkein 102 C5
Culkerton 20 C2
Cullachie 89 G2
Cullen 98 D4
Cullercoats 71 J6
Cullicudden 96 D5
Culligran 95 K7
Cullingworth 57 F6
Cullipool 79 J6
Cullivoe 108 E2
Culloch 81 J6
Culloden 96 E7
Cullompton 7 J5
Culmaily 97 F2
Culmalzie 64 D5
Culmington 38 D7
Culmstock 7 J4
Culnacraig 95 G1
Culnadalloch 80 A4
Culnaknock 94 B5
Culnamean 85 K2
Culpho 35 G4
Culquhirk 64 E5
Culrain 96 C2
Culross 75 H2
Culroy 67 H2
Culsh 90 B5
Culshabbin 64 D5
Culswick 109 B8
Culter Allers Farm 75 J7
Cultercullen 91 H2
Cults *Aber.* 90 D1
Cults *Aberdeen* 91 G4
Cults *D. & G.* 64 E6
Cultybraggan
Camp 81 J6
Culverhouse Cross 18 E4
Culverstone Green 24 C5
Culverthorpe 42 D1
Culvie 98 D5
Culworth 31 G4
Cumberhead 75 F7
Cumbernauld 75 F3
Cumberworth 53 J5
Cuminestown 99 G5
Cumloden 64 E4
Cummersdale 60 E1
Cummertrees 69 G7
Cummingstown 97 J5
Cumnock 67 K1
Cumnor 21 H1
Cumrew 61 G1
Cumrue 69 F5
Cumstoun 65 G5
Cumwhinton 61 F1
Cumwhitton 61 G1
Cundall 57 K2
Cunninghamhead 74 B6
Cunnister 108 E3
Cunnoquhie 82 E6
Cupar 82 E6
Cupar Muir 82 E6
Curbar 50 E5
Curbridge *Hants.* 11 G3
Curbridge *Oxon.* 21 G1
Curdridge 11 G3
Curdworth 40 D6
Curland 8 B3
Curload 8 C2
Curridge 21 H4
Currie 75 K4
Curry Mallet 8 C2
Curry Rivel 8 C2
Curteis' Corner 14 D4
Curtisden Green 14 C3
Cury 2 D6
Cushnie 99 F4
Cushuish 7 K2
Cusop 28 B4
Cutcloy 64 E7
Cutcombe 7 H2
Cuthill 96 E3
Cutiau 37 F4
Cutnall Green 29 H2
Cutsdean 30 B5
Cutthorpe 51 F5
Cutts 109 D9
Cuttyhill 99 J5
Cuxham 21 K2
Cuxton 24 D5
Cuxwold 52 E2
Cwm *B.Gwent* 18 E1
Cwm *Denb.* 47 J5
Cwm Ffrwd-oer 19 F1
Cwm Gwaun 16 D2
Cwm Irfon 27 H4
Cwmafan 18 A2
Cwmaman 18 D2
Cwmann 17 J1
Cwmbach *Carmar.* 17 F3
Cwmbach *Powys* 28 A5
Cwmbach *Powys* 27 K3
Cwmbach *R.C.T.* 18 D1
Cwmbelan 37 J7
Cwmbrân 19 F2
Cwmbrwyno 37 G7
Cwmcarn 19 F2
Cwmcarvan 19 H1
Cwm-Cewydd 37 H4
Cwmcoy 17 F1
Cwmdare 18 C1
Cwmdu *Carmar.* 17 K2
Cwmdu *Powys* 28 A6
Cwmduad 17 G2
Cwmfelin Boeth 16 E4
Cwmfelin Mynach 17 F3
Cwmfelinfach 18 E2
Cwmffrwd 17 H4
Cwmgiedd 27 G7
Cwmgors 27 G7
Cwmgwrach 18 B1
Cwmisfael 17 H4
Cwm-Llinau 37 H5
Cwmllyfri 17 G4
Cwmllynfell 27 G7
Cwm-Morgan 17 F2
Cwm-parc 18 C2
Cwmpengraig 17 G2
Cwmsychbant 17 H1
Cwmsymlog 37 F7
Cwmtillery 19 F1
Cwm-twrch Isaf 27 G7
Cwm-y-glo 46 D6
Cwmyoy 28 C6
Cwm-yr-Eglwys 16 D1
Cwmystwyth 27 G1
Cwrt 37 F5
Cwrt-newydd 17 H1
Cwrt-y-gollen 28 B7
Cydwelli (Kidwelly) 17 H5
Cyffylliog 47 J7
Cyfronydd 38 A5
Cymmer *N.P.T.* 18 B2
Cymmer *R.C.T.* 18 D2
Cynghordy 27 H5
Cynheidre 17 H5
Cynwyd 37 K1
Cynwyl Elfed 17 G3

D

Dabton 68 D4
Daccombe 5 K4
Dacre *Cumb.* 61 F4
Dacre *N.Yorks.* 57 G3
Dacre Banks 57 G3
Daddry Shield 61 K3
Dadford 31 H5
Dadlington 41 G6
Dafen 17 J5
Daffy Green 44 D5
Dagenham 23 H3
Daggons 10 C3
Daglingworth 20 C1
Dagnall 32 C7
Dail 80 B4
Dail Beag 100 E3
Dail Bho Dheas 101 G1
Dail Bho Thuath 101 G1
Dail Mòr 100 E3
Dailly 67 G3
Dailnamac 80 A4
Dairsie or
Osnaburgh 83 F6
Dalabrog 84 C2
Dalavich 80 A6
Dalballoch 88 D5
Dalbeattie 65 J4
Dalblair 68 B2
Dalbog 90 D7
Dalbreck 104 C7
Dalbury 40 E2
Dalby 54 B6
Dalcairnie 67 J3
Dalchalloch 81 J1
Dalchalm 97 G1
Dalchenna 80 B7
Dalchirach 89 J1
Dalchork 103 H7
Dalchreichart 87 J3
Dalchruin 81 J6
Dalcross 96 E7
Dalderby 53 F6
Daldownie 89 K4
Dale *Derbys.* 41 G2
Dale *Pembs.* 16 B5
Dale Head 61 F5
Dale of Walls 109 A7
Dale Park 12 C6
Dalehouse 63 J5
Dalelia 79 J1
Daless 89 F1
Dalestie 89 J3
Dalfad 90 B4
Dalganachan 105 F4
Dalgarven 74 A6
Dalgety Bay 75 K2
Dalgig 67 K2
Dalginross 81 J5
Dalgonar 68 C3
Dalguise 82 A3
Dalhalvaig 104 D3
Dalham 34 B2
Daligan 74 B2
Dalivaddy 66 A2
Daljarrock 67 F5
Dalkeith 76 B4
Dallas 97 J6
Dallaschyle 97 F7
Dallash 64 E4
Dallinghoo 35 G3
Dallington *E.Suss.* 13 K5
Dallington
Northants. 31 J2
Dalmadilly 91 F3
Dalmally 80 C5
Dalmarnock 82 A3
Dalmary 74 D1
Dalmellington 67 J3
Dalmeny 75 K3
Dalmichy 103 H7
Dalmigavie 88 E3
Dalmore 96 D5
Dalmunzie Hotel 89 H7
Dalnabreck 79 J1
Dalnacarn 82 B1
Dalnaglar Castle 82 C1
Dalnaha 79 H5
Dalnahaitnach 89 F3
Dalnamain 96 E2
Dalnatrat 80 A2
Dalnavie 96 D4
Dalness 80 C2
Dalnessie 103 J7
Dalnigap 64 B3
Dalqueich 82 B7
Dalreoch 67 F5
Dalriech 81 J4
Dalroy 96 E7
Dalrulzian 82 C2
Dalry 74 A6
Dalrymple 67 H2
Dalserf 75 F5
Dalshangan 67 K5
Dalskairth 65 K3
Dalston 60 E1
Dalswinton 68 E5
Daltomach 88 E2
Dalton *D. & G.* 69 G6
Dalton *Lancs.* 48 D2
Dalton *N.Yorks.* 57 K2
Dalton *N.Yorks.* 62 C6
Dalton *Northumb.* 71 G6
Dalton *Northumb.* 62 A1
Dalton *S.Yorks.* 51 G3
Dalton Piercy 63 F3
Dalton-in-Furness 55 F2
Dalton-le-Dale 63 F2
Dalton-on-Tees 62 D6
Daltote 73 F2
Daltra 97 G7
Dalveich 81 H5
Dalvennan 67 H2
Dalvourn 88 D1
Dalwhinnie 88 D6
Dalwood 8 B4
Damerham 10 C3
Damgate 45 J5
Damnaglaur 64 B7
Damside 82 A6
Danbury 24 D1
Danby 63 J6
Danby Wiske 62 E7
Dandaleith 97 K7
Danderhall 76 B4
Dane End 33 G6
Dane Hills 41 H5
Danebridge 49 J6
Danehill 13 H4
Danesmoor 51 G6
Danestone 91 H3
Danskine 76 D4
Darby Green 22 B5
Darenth 23 J4
Daresbury 48 E4
Darfield 51 G2
Dargate 25 G5
Dargues 70 D4
Darite 4 C4
Darlaston 40 B6
Darley 57 H4
Darley Dale 50 E6
Darlingscott 30 D4
Darlington 62 D5
Darliston 38 E2
Darlton 51 K5
Darnabo 99 F6
Darnall 51 F4
Darnconner 67 K1
Darnford 91 F5
Darngarroch 65 G4
Darnick 76 D7
Darowen 37 H5
Darra 99 F6
Darras Hall 71 G6
Darrington 51 G1
Darsham 35 J2
Dartfield 99 J5
Dartford 23 J4
Dartington 5 H4
Dartmeet 5 G3
Dartmouth 5 J5
Darton 51 F2
Darvel 74 D7
Darvell 14 C5
Darwen 56 B7
Datchet 22 C4
Datchworth 33 F7
Datchworth Green 33 F7
Daubhill 49 G2
Daugh of
Kinermony 97 K7
Dauntsey 20 C3
Dava 89 H1
Davaar 66 B2
Davan 90 C4
Davenham 49 F5
Daventry 31 G2
Davidstow 4 B2
Davington 69 H3
Daviot *Aber.* 91 F2
Daviot *High.* 88 E1
Davoch of Grange 98 C5
Dawley 39 F5
Dawlish 5 K3
Dawn 47 G5
Daws Heath 24 E3
Dawsmere 43 H2
Daylesford 30 D6
Ddôl 47 K5
Deadwaters 75 F6
Deal 15 J2
Deal Hall 25 G2
Dean *Cumb.* 60 B4
Dean *Devon* 5 H4
Dean *Dorset* 9 J3
Dean *Hants.* 11 G3
Dean *Oxon.* 30 E6
Dean *Som.* 19 K7
Dean Bank 62 D3
Dean Prior 5 H4
Dean Row 49 H4
Dean Street 14 C2
Deanburnhaugh 69 J2
Deane 21 J7
Deanland 9 J3
Deanscales 60 B4
Deanshanger 31 J4
Deanston 81 J7
Dearham 60 B3
Debach 35 G3
Debate 69 H5
Debden 33 J5
Debden Green 33 J5
Debenham 35 F2
Dechmont 75 J3
Deddington 31 F5
Dedham 34 E5
Deecastle 90 C5
Deene 42 C6
Deenethorpe 42 C6
Deepcar 50 E3
Deepcut 22 C6
Deepdale *Cumb.* 56 C1
Deepdale *N.Yorks.* 56 D2
Deeping Gate 42 E5
Deeping St. James 42 E5
Deeping
St. Nicholas 43 F4
Deerhill 98 C5
Deerhurst 29 H6
Defford 29 J4
Defynnog 27 J6
Deganwy 47 F5
Degnish 79 J6
Deighton *N.Yorks.* 62 E6
Deighton *York* 58 C5
Deiniolen 46 D6
Delabole 4 A2
Delamere 48 E6
Delavorar 89 J3
Delfrigs 91 H2
Dell Lodge 89 H3
Delliefure 89 H1
Delnabo 89 J3
Delny 96 E4
Delph 49 J2
Delphorrie 90 C3
Delves 62 C2
Delvine 82 C3
Dembleby 42 D2
Denaby 51 G3
Denaby Main 51 G3
Denbigh (Dinbych) 47 J6
Denbury 5 J4
Denby 41 F1
Denby Dale 50 E2
Denchworth 21 G2
Dendron 55 F2
Denend 90 D1
Denford 32 C1
Dengie 25 F1
Denham *Bucks.* 22 D3
Denham *Suff.* 35 F1
Denham *Suff.* 34 B2
Denham Green 22 D3
Denhead *Aber.* 91 F3
Denhead *Aber.* 99 H5
Denhead *Dundee* 82 E4
Denhead *Fife* 83 F6
Denhead of
Arbirlot 83 G3
Denholm 70 A2
Denholme 57 F6
Denholme Clough 57 F6
Denio 36 C2
Denmead 11 H3
Denmill 91 G3
Denmoss 98 E6
Dennington 35 G2
Denny 75 G2
Dennyloanhead 75 G2
Denshaw 49 J1
Denside 91 G5
Densole 15 H3
Denston 34 B3
Denstone 40 C1
Dent 56 C1
Denton *Cambs.* 42 E7
Denton *Darl.* 62 D5
Denton *E.Suss.* 13 H6
Denton *Gt.Man.* 49 J3
Denton *Kent* 15 H3
Denton *Lincs.* 42 B2
Denton *N.Yorks.* 57 G5
Denton *Norf.* 45 G7
Denton *Northants.* 32 B3
Denton *Oxon.* 21 J1
Denver 44 A5
Denvilles 11 J4
Denwick 71 H2
Deopham 44 E5
Deopham Green 44 E6
Depden 34 B3
Deptford *Gt.Lon.* 23 G4
Deptford *Wilts.* 10 B1
Derby 41 F2
Derbyhaven 54 B7
Dereham
(East Dereham) 44 D4
Dererach 79 G5
Deri 18 E1
Derringstone 15 G3
Derrington 40 A3
Derry 81 H5
Derry Hill 20 C4
Derrythorpe 52 B2
Dersingham 44 A2
Dervaig 79 F2
Derwen 47 J7
Derwenlas 37 G6
Derwydd 17 K4
Derybruich 73 H3
Desborough 42 B7
Desford 41 G5
Detchant 77 J7
Detling 14 C2
Deuddwr 38 B4
Deunant 47 H6
Deuxhill 39 F7
Devauden 19 H2
Devil's Bridge
(Pontarfynach) 27 G1
Devizes 20 D5
Devonport 4 E5
Devonside 75 H1
Devoran 2 E5
Dewar 76 B6
Dewlish 9 G5
Dewsall Court 28 D5
Dewsbury 57 H7
Dhiseig 79 F4
Dhoon 54 D5
Dhoor 54 D4
Dhowin 54 D3
Dhuhallow 88 C2
Dial Post 12 E5
Dibden 11 F4
Dibden Purlieu 11 F4
Dickleburgh 45 F7
Didbrook 30 B5
Didcot 21 J3
Diddington 32 E2
Diddlebury 38 E7
Didley 28 D5
Didling 12 B5
Didmarton 20 B3
Didsbury 49 H3
Didworthy 5 G4
Digby 52 D7
Digg 93 K5
Diggle 50 C2
Digmoor 48 D2
Digswell 33 F7
Dihewyd 26 D3
Dildawn 65 H5
Dilham 45 H3
Dilhorne 40 B1
Dilston 70 E7
Dilton Marsh 20 B6
Dilwyn 28 D3
Dilwyn Common 28 D3
Dinas *Carmar.* 17 F2
Dinas *Gwyn.* 46 C7
Dinas *Gwyn.* 36 B2
Dinas Cross 16 D2
Dinas Dinlle 46 C7
Dinas Powys 18 E4
Dinas-Mawddwy 37 H4
Dinbych (Denbigh) 47 J6
Dinbych-y-Pysgod
(Tenby) 16 E5
Dinder 19 J7
Dinedor 28 E5
Dingestow 28 D7
Dingley 42 A7
Dingwall 96 C6
Dinlabyre 70 A4
Dinnet 90 C5
Dinnington
S.Yorks. 51 H4
Dinnington *Som.* 8 D3
Dinnington *T. & W.* 71 H6
Dinorwig 46 D6
Dinton *Bucks.* 31 J7
Dinton *Wilts.* 10 B1
Dinvin 64 A5
Dinwoodie Mains 69 G4
Dinworthy 6 B4
Dippen 73 F7
Dippenhall 22 B7
Dippin 66 E1
Dipple *Moray* 98 B5
Dipple *S.Ayr.* 67 G3
Diptford 5 H5
Dipton 62 C1
Dirdhu 89 H2
Dirleton 76 D2
Discoed 28 B2
Diseworth 41 G3
Dishes 106 F5
Dishforth 57 J2
Disley 49 J4
Diss 45 F7
Disserth 27 K3
Distington 60 B4
Ditcheat 9 F1
Ditchingham 45 H6
Ditchley 30 E6
Ditchling 13 G5
Ditteridge 20 B5
Dittisham 5 J5
Ditton *Halton* 48 D4
Ditton *Kent* 14 C2
Ditton Green 33 K3
Ditton Priors 39 F7
Dixton *Glos.* 29 J5
Dixton *Mon.* 28 E7
Dobcross 49 J2
Dobwalls 4 C4
Doc Penfro
(Pembroke Dock) 16 C5
Doccombe 7 F7
Dochgarroch 96 D7
Dockenfield 22 B7
Docking 44 B2
Docklow 28 E3
Dockray 60 E4
Doddinghurst 23 J2
Doddington
Cambs. 43 G6
Doddington *Kent* 14 E2
Doddington *Lincs.* 52 C5
Doddington
Northumb. 77 H7
Doddington
Shrop. 29 F1
Doddiscombsleigh 7 G7
Dodford
Northants. 31 H2
Dodford *Worcs.* 29 J1
Dodington *S.Glos.* 20 A3
Dodington *Som.* 7 K1
Dodington Ash 20 A4
Dodleston 48 C6
Dodworth 51 F2
Doe Lea 51 G6
Dog Village 7 H6
Dogdyke 53 F7
Dogmersfield 22 A6
Dol Fawr 37 H5
Dolanog 37 K4
Dolau 28 A2
Dolbenmaen 36 E1
Dolfach 27 J1
Dolfor 38 A7
Dolgarreg 27 G5
Dolgarrog 47 F6
Dolgellau 37 G4
Dolgoch 37 F5
Dol-gran 17 H2
Doll 97 F1
Dollar 75 H1
Dollarbeg 75 H1
Dolleycanney 28 A4
Dolphinholme 55 J4
Dolphinton 75 K6
Dolton 6 D4
Dolwen *Conwy* 47 G5
Dolwen *Powys* 37 J5
Dolwyddelan 47 F7
Dolybont 37 F7
Dolyhir 28 B3
Dolywern 38 B2
Domgay 38 B4
Doncaster 51 H2
Donhead
St. Andrew 9 J2
Donhead St. Mary 9 J2
Donibristle 75 K2
Doniford 7 J1
Donington 43 F2
Donington le Heath 41 G4
Donington on Bain 53 F4
Donisthorpe 41 F4
Donkey Town 22 C5
Donnington *Glos.* 30 C6
Donnington *Here.* 29 G5
Donnington *Shrop.* 38 E5
Donnington
Tel. & W. 39 G4
Donnington
W.Berks. 21 H5
Donnington
W.Suss. 12 B6
Donyatt 8 C3
Dorchester *Dorset* 9 F5
Dorchester *Oxon.* 21 J2
Dordon 40 E5
Dore 51 F4
Dores 88 C1
Dorket Head 41 H1
Dorking 22 E7
Dormans Park 23 G7
Dormansland 23 H7
Dormanstown 63 G4
Dormington 28 E4
Dorney 22 C4
Dornie 86 E2
Dornoch 96 E3
Dornock 69 H7
Dorrery 105 F3
Dorridge 30 C1
Dorrington *Lincs.* 52 D7
Dorrington *Shrop.* 38 D5
Dorsell 90 D3
Dorsington 30 C3
Dorstone 28 C4
Dorton 31 H7
Dorusduain 87 F2
Dosthill 40 E6
Dotland 62 A1
Dottery 8 D5
Doublebois 4 B4
Dougalston 74 D3
Dougarie 73 G7
Doughton 20 B2
Douglas *I.o.M.* 54 C6
Douglas *S.Lan.* 75 G7
Douglas & Angus 83 F4
Douglas Hall 65 J5
Douglas Water 75 G7
Douglastown 83 F3
Doulting 19 K7
Dounby 106 B5
Doune *Arg. & B.* 74 B1
Doune *Arg. & B.* 80 E6
Doune *High.* 89 F3
Doune *High.* 96 B1
Doune *Stir.* 81 J7
Dounepark 99 F4
Douneside 90 C4
Dounie *High.* 96 D3
Dounie *High.* 96 C2
Dounreay 104 E2
Dousland 5 F4
Dovaston 38 C3
Dove Holes 50 C5
Dovenby 60 B3
Dover 15 J3
Dovercourt 35 G6
Doverdale 29 H2
Doveridge 40 D2
Doversgreen 23 F7
Dowally 82 B3
Dowdeswell 30 B6
Dowhill 67 G3
Dowland 6 D4
Dowlands 8 B5
Dowlish Wake 8 C3
Down Ampney 20 E2
Down End 19 G7
Down Hatherley 29 H6
Down St. Mary 7 F5
Down Thomas 5 F6
Downderry 4 D5
Downe 23 H5
Downend *I.o.W.* 11 G6
Downend *S.Glos.* 19 K4
Downend *W.Berks.* 21 H4
Downfield 82 E4
Downfields 33 J1
Downgate 4 D3
Downham *Essex* 24 D2
Downham *Lancs.* 56 C5
Downham
Northumb. 77 G7
Downham Market 44 A5
Downhead *Cornw.* 4 C2
Downhead *Som.* 19 K7
Downholland Cross 48 C2
Downholme 62 C7
Downies 91 H5
Downing 47 K5
Downley 22 B2
Downside *N.Som.* 19 H5
Downside *Som.* 19 K7
Downside *Surr.* 22 E6
Downton *Devon* 6 D7
Downton *Devon* 5 J5
Downton *Hants.* 10 D5
Downton *Wilts.* 10 C2
Downton on the
Rock 28 D1
Dowsby 42 E3
Dowthwaitehead 60 E4
Doynton 20 A4
Draethen 19 F3
Draffan 75 F6
Drakeland Corner 5 F5
Drakes Broughton 29 J4
Drakes Cross 30 B1
Draughton
N.Yorks. 57 F4
Draughton
Northants. 31 J1
Drax 58 C7
Draycote 31 F1
Draycott *Derbys.* 41 G2
Draycott *Glos.* 30 C5

Draycott Som. 19 H6
Draycott Worcs. 29 H4
Draycott in the Clay 40 D3
Draycott in the Moors 40 B2
Drayton Leics. 42 B6
Drayton Lincs. 43 F2
Drayton Norf. 45 H4
Drayton Oxon. 31 F4
Drayton Oxon. 21 H2
Drayton Ports. 11 H4
Drayton Som. 8 D2
Drayton Worcs. 29 J1
Drayton Bassett 40 D5
Drayton Beauchamp 32 C7
Drayton Parslow 32 B6
Drayton St. Leonard 21 J2
Drebley 57 F4
Dreemskerry 54 D4
Dreenhill 16 C4
Drefach Carmar. 17 G2
Drefach Carmar. 17 J4
Dre-fach Cere. 17 J1
Dreghorn 74 B7
Drellingore 15 H3
Drem 76 D3
Drewsteignton 7 F6
Driby 53 G5
Driffield E.Riding 59 G4
Driffield Glos. 20 D2
Drigg 60 B7
Drighlington 57 H7
Drimfern 80 B6
Drimlee 80 C6
Drimmin 79 G2
Drimore 84 C1
Drimpton 8 D4
Drimsynie 80 C7
Drimvore 73 G1
Drinan 86 B3
Drinkstone 34 D2
Drinkstone Green 34 D3
Drishaig 80 C6
Drissaig 80 A6
Droitton 40 C3
Droitwich 29 H2
Dron 82 C6
Dronfield 51 F5
Dronfield Woodhouse 51 F5
Drongan 67 J2
Dronley 82 E4
Dropmore 22 C3
Droxford 11 H3
Droylsden 49 J3
Druid 37 K1
Druidston 16 B4
Druimarbin 80 B1
Druimavuic 80 B3
Druimdrishaig 73 F3
Druimindarroch 86 C6
Druimkinnerras 96 B7
Drum Arg. & B. 73 H3
Drum P. & K. 82 B7
Drumachloy 73 J4
Drumbeg 102 D5
Drumblade 98 D6
Drumblair 98 E6
Drumbuie D. & G. 68 C2
Drumbuie High. 86 D1
Drumburgh 60 D1
Drumchapel 74 D3
Drumchardine 96 C7
Drumchork 94 E3
Drumclog 74 E7
Drumdelgie 98 C6
Drumderfit 96 D6
Drumeldrie 83 F7
Drumelzier 75 K7
Drumfearn 86 C3
Drumfern 87 F7
Drumgarve 66 B1
Drumgley 83 F3
Drumguish 88 E5
Drumhead 90 E5
Drumin 89 J1
Drumine 96 E6
Drumjohn 67 K4
Drumlamford House 64 C3
Drumlasie 90 E4
Drumlemble 66 A2
Drumlithie 91 F6
Drummond High. 96 D5
Drummond Stir. 81 H7
Drummore 64 B7
Drummuir Castle 98 B6
Drumnadrochit 88 C1
Drumnagorrach 98 D5
Drumnatorran 79 K1
Drumoak 91 F5
Drumore 66 B1
Drumour 82 A3
Drumrash 65 G3
Drumrunie 95 H1
Drums 91 H2
Drumsturdy 83 F4
Drumuie 93 K7
Drumuillie 89 G2
Drumvaich 81 H7
Drumwhindle 91 H1
Drumwhirn 68 C5
Drunkendub 83 H3
Drury 48 B6
Drws-y-nant 37 H3
Dry Doddington 42 C2
Dry Drayton 33 G2
Dry Harbour 94 C6
Dry Sandford 21 H2
Dry Street 24 C3
Drybeck 61 H5
Drybridge Moray 98 C4
Drybridge N.Ayr. 74 B7
Drybrook 29 F7
Drygrange 76 D7
Dryhope 69 H1
Drymen 74 C2
Drymuir 99 H6
Drynoch 85 K1
Dryslwyn 17 J3
Dryton 38 E5
Duachy 79 K5
Dubford 99 F4
Dubhchladach 73 G4
Dubheads 82 A5
Dubton 83 G2
Duchal 74 B4
Duchally 103 F3
Duchray 74 C1
Duck End 33 K6
Duckington 48 D7
Ducklington 21 G1
Duck's Cross 32 E3
Duddenhoe End 33 H5

Duddingston 76 A3
Duddington 42 C5
Duddleswell 13 H4
Duddo 77 H6
Duddon 48 E6
Duddon Bridge 54 E1
Dudleston Heath 38 C2
Dudley T. & W. 71 H6
Dudley W.Mid. 40 B6
Dudley Hill 57 G6
Dudley Port 40 B6
Dudsbury 10 B5
Duffield 41 F1
Duffryn 18 B2
Dufftown 98 B6
Duffus 97 J5
Dufton 61 H4
Duggleby 58 E3
Duiar 89 J1
Duible 104 E6
Duiletter 80 C5
Duinish 81 H1
Duirinish 86 D1
Duisdealmor 86 D3
Duisky 87 G7
Dukestown 28 A7
Dukinfield 49 J3
Dulas 46 C4
Dulax 90 B3
Dulcote 19 J7
Dulford 7 J5
Dull 81 K3
Dullatur 75 F3
Dullingham 33 K3
Dulnain Bridge 89 G2
Duloe Beds. 32 E2
Duloe Cornw. 4 C5
Dulsie 97 G7
Dulverton 7 H3
Dulwich 23 G4
Dumbarton 74 C3
Dumbleton 30 B5
Dumcrieff 69 G3
Dumeath 90 C1
Dumfin 74 B2
Dumfries 65 K3
Dumgoyne 74 D2
Dummer 21 J7
Dun 83 H2
Dunach 79 K5
Dunalastair 81 J2
Dunan Arg. & B. 73 K3
Dunan High. 86 B2
Dunans 73 J1
Dunball 19 G7
Dunbar 76 E3
Dunbeath 105 G6
Dunblane 81 J7
Dunbog 82 D6
Duncanston Aber. 90 D2
Duncanston High. 96 C6
Dunchideock 7 G7
Dunchurch 31 F1
Duncote 31 H3
Duncow 68 E5
Duncraggan 81 G7
Duncrievie 82 C7
Duncroist 81 G4
Duncrub 82 B6
Duncryne 74 C2
Duncton 12 C5
Dundee 83 F4
Dundee Airport 82 E5
Dundon 8 D1
Dundonald 74 B7
Dundonnell 95 G3
Dundraw 60 D2
Dundreggan 87 K3
Dundrennan 65 H6
Dundry 19 J5
Dunearn 76 A2
Dunecht 91 F4
Dunfermline 75 J2
Dunfield 20 E2
Dunford Bridge 50 D2
Dungavel 74 E7
Dunham 52 B5
Dunham Town 49 G4
Dunham-on-the-Hill 48 D5
Dunhampton 29 H2
Dunholme 52 D5
Dunino 83 G6
Dunipace 75 G2
Dunira 81 J5
Dunkeld 82 B3
Dunkerton 20 A6
Dunkeswell 7 K5
Dunkeswick 57 J5
Dunkirk 15 F2
Dunk's Green 23 K6
Dunlappie 83 G1
Dunley 29 G2
Dunlop 74 C6
Dunloskin 73 K3
Dunmere 4 A4
Dunmore Arg. & B. 73 F4
Dunmore Falk. 75 G2
Dunn 105 G3
Dunnabie 69 H5
Dunnet 105 H1
Dunnichen 83 G3
Dunning 82 B6
Dunnington E.Riding 59 H4
Dunnington Warks. 30 B3
Dunnington York 58 C4
Dunnockshaw 56 D7
Dunoon 73 K3
Dunragit 64 B5
Dunrostan 73 F2
Duns 77 F5
Duns Tew 31 F6
Dunsby 42 E3
Dunscore 68 D5
Dunscroft 51 J2
Dunsdale 63 H5
Dunsden Green 22 A4
Dunsfold 12 D3
Dunsford 7 G7
Dunshelt 82 D6
Dunsinnan 82 C4
Dunsland Cross 6 C5
Dunsley 63 J5
Dunsmore 22 B1
Dunsop Bridge 56 B4
Dunstable 32 D6
Dunstall 40 D3
Dunstall Green 34 B2
Dunstan 71 H1
Dunster 7 H1
Dunston Lincs. 52 D6
Dunston Norf. 45 G5
Dunston Staffs. 40 B4
Dunston T. & W. 71 H7
Dunstone Devon 5 H6

Dunstone Devon 5 H3
Dunstone Devon 5 F5
Dunsville 51 J2
Dunswell 59 G6
Dunsyre 75 J6
Dunterton 4 D3
Duntisbourne Abbots 20 C1
Duntisbourne Leer 20 C1
Duntisbourne Rouse 20 C1
Duntish 9 F4
Duntocher 74 C3
Dunton Beds. 33 F4
Dunton Bucks. 32 B6
Dunton Norf. 44 C2
Dunton Green 23 J6
Dunton Wayletts 24 C3
Duntulm 93 K4
Dunure 67 G2
Dunure Mains 67 G2
Dunvant 17 J6
Dunvegan 93 H7
Dunwich 35 J1
Dura 83 F6
Durdar 61 F1
Durgates 13 K3
Durham 62 D2
Durinemast 79 H2
Durisdeer 68 D3
Durleigh 8 B1
Durley Hants. 11 G3
Durley Wilts. 21 F5
Durnamuck 95 G2
Durness 103 F2
Durno 91 F2
Duror 80 A2
Durran Arg. & B. 80 A7
Durran High. 105 G2
Durrington W.Suss. 12 E6
Durrington Wilts. 20 E7
Dursley 20 A2
Durston 8 B2
Durweston 9 H4
Dury 109 D6
Duston 31 J2
Duthil 89 G2
Dutlas 28 B1
Duton Hill 33 K6
Dutton 48 E5
Duxford 33 H4
Dwygyfylchi 47 F5
Dwyran 46 C6
Dyce 91 G3
Dyfatty 17 H5
Dyffryn Bridgend 18 B2
Dyffryn (Valley) I.o.A. 46 A5
Dyffryn Pembs. 16 C2
Dyffryn Ardudwy 36 E3
Dyffryn Castell 37 G7
Dyffryn Ceidrych 27 G6
Dyffryn Cellwen 27 H7
Dyke Devon 6 B3
Dyke Lincs. 42 E3
Dyke Moray 97 G6
Dykehead Angus 82 E1
Dykehead N.Lan. 75 G5
Dykehead Stir. 74 D1
Dykelands 83 J1
Dykends 82 D2
Dykeside 99 F6
Dylife 37 H6
Dymchurch 15 F5
Dymock 29 G5
Dyrham 20 A4
Dysart 76 B1
Dyserth 47 J5

E

Eadar dha Fhadhail 100 C4
Eagland Hill 55 H5
Eagle 52 B6
Eaglescliffe 63 F5
Eaglesfield Cumb. 60 B4
Eaglesfield D. & G. 69 H6
Eaglesham 74 D5
Eaglethorpe 42 D6
Eagley 49 G1
Eairy 54 C6
Eakley 32 B3
Eakring 51 J6
Ealand 51 K1
Ealing 22 E3
Eamont Bridge 61 G4
Earby 56 E5
Earcroft 56 B7
Eardington 39 G6
Eardisland 28 D3
Eardisley 28 C4
Eardiston Shrop. 38 C3
Eardiston Worcs. 29 F2
Earith 33 G1
Earl Shilton 41 G6
Earl Soham 35 G2
Earl Sterndale 50 C6
Earl Stonham 35 F3
Earle 70 E1
Earlestown 48 E3
Earley 22 A4
Earlham 45 F5
Earlish 93 J5
Earls Barton 32 B2
Earls Colne 34 C6
Earl's Common 29 J3
Earl's Croome 29 H4
Earl's Green 34 E2
Earlsdon 30 E1
Earlsferry 83 F7
Earlsford 91 G1
Earlston 76 D7
Earlswood Mon. 19 H2
Earlswood Warks. 30 C1
Earnley 12 B7
Earsairidh 84 B5
Earsdon 71 J6
Earsham 45 H7
Earswick 58 C4
Eartham 12 C6
Earthcott Green 19 K3
Easby 63 G6
Easdale 79 J6
Easebourne 12 B4
Easenhall 31 F1
Eashing 22 C7
Easington Bucks. 21 K1
Easington Dur. 63 F2
Easington E.Riding 53 H1
Easington Northumb. 77 K7
Easington Oxon. 21 K2
Easington R. & C. 63 J5
Easington Colliery 63 F2

Easington Lane 62 E2
Easingwold 58 B3
Easole Street 15 H2
Eassie & Nevay 82 E3
East Aberthaw 18 D5
East Allington 5 H6
East Anstey 7 G3
East Appleton 62 D7
East Ardsley 57 J7
East Ashey 11 G6
East Ashling 12 B6
East Auchronie 91 G4
East Ayton 59 F1
East Barkwith 52 E4
East Barming 14 C2
East Barnby 63 K5
East Barnet 23 F2
East Barsham 44 D2
East Beckham 45 F2
East Bedfont 22 D4
East Bergholt 34 E5
East Bilney 44 D4
East Blatchington 13 H7
East Boldon 71 J7
East Boldre 10 E4
East Bolton 71 G2
East Bradenham 44 D5
East Brent 19 G6
East Bridge 35 J2
East Bridgford 41 J1
East Brora 97 F1
East Buckland 6 E2
East Budleigh 7 J7
East Burnham 22 C3
East Burrafirth 109 C7
East Burton 9 H6
East Cairnbeg 91 F7
East Calder 75 J4
East Carleton 45 F5
East Carlton 42 B7
East Chaldon or Chaldon Herring 9 G6
East Challow 21 G3
East Charleton 5 H6
East Chelborough 8 E4
East Chiltington 13 G5
East Chinnock 8 D3
East Chisenbury 20 E6
East Clandon 22 D6
East Claydon 31 J6
East Clyth 105 H5
East Coker 8 E3
East Cornworthy 5 J5
East Cottingwith 58 D5
East Cowes 11 G5
East Cowick 58 C7
East Cowton 62 E6
East Cranmore 19 K7
East Creech 9 J6
East Croachy 88 D2
East Darlochan 66 A1
East Davoch 90 C4
East Dean E.Suss. 13 J7
East Dean Hants. 10 D2
East Dean W.Suss. 12 C5
East Dereham (Dereham) 44 D4
East Down 6 E1
East Drayton 51 K5
East End Hants. 21 H5
East End Hants. 10 E5
East End Herts. 33 H6
East End Kent 14 D4
East End N.Som. 19 H4
East End Oxon. 30 E7
East End Poole 9 J5
East End Suff. 35 F5
East Farleigh 14 C2
East Farndon 42 A7
East Ferry 52 B3
East Fortune 76 D3
East Garston 21 G4
East Ginge 21 H3
East Goscote 41 J4
East Grafton 21 F5
East Grimstead 10 D2
East Grinstead 13 G3
East Guldeford 14 E5
East Haddon 31 H2
East Hagbourne 21 J3
East Halton 52 E1
East Ham 23 H3
East Hanney 21 H2
East Hanningfield 24 D1
East Hardwick 51 G1
East Harling 44 D7
East Harlsey 63 F7
East Harptree 19 J6
East Hartford 71 H6
East Hatch 9 J2
East Hatley 33 F3
East Hauxwell 62 C7
East Haven 83 G4
East Heckington 42 E1
East Hedleyhope 62 C2
East Helmsdale 105 F7
East Hendred 21 H3
East Heslerton 59 F2
East Hoathly 13 J5
East Horndon 24 C3
East Horrington 19 J7
East Horsley 22 D6
East Horton 77 J7
East Huntspill 19 G7
East Hyde 32 E7
East Ilsley 21 H3
East Keal 53 G6
East Kennett 20 E5
East Keswick 57 J5
East Kilbride 74 E5
East Kirkby 53 G6
East Knapton 58 E2
East Knighton 9 H6
East Knoyle 9 H1
East Lambrook 8 D3
East Langdon 15 J3
East Langton 42 A6
East Langwell 96 E1
East Lavant 12 B6
East Lavington 12 C5
East Layton 62 C5
East Leake 41 H3
East Learmouth 77 G7
East Learney 7 F4
East Leigh 6 E5
East Lexham 44 C4
East Lilburn 71 F1
East Linton 76 D3
East Liss 11 J2
East Lockinge 21 H3
East Looe 4 C5
East Lound 51 K3
East Lulworth 9 H6
East Lutton 59 F3
East Lydford 8 E1
East Mains 90 E5
East Malling 14 C2
East March 83 F4
East Marden 12 B5
East Markham 51 K5

East Marton 56 E4
East Meon 11 H2
East Mere 7 H4
East Mersea 34 E7
East Mey 105 J1
East Midlands Airport 41 G3
East Molesey 22 E5
East Morden 9 J5
East Morton 57 F5
East Ness 58 C2
East Norton 42 A5
East Oakley 21 J7
East Ogwell 5 J3
East Orchard 9 H3
East Ord 77 H5
East Panson 6 B6
East Peckham 23 K7
East Pennard 8 E1
East Portlemouth 5 H7
East Prawle 5 H7
East Preston 12 D6
East Putford 6 B4
East Quantoxhead 7 K1
East Rainton 62 E2
East Ravendale 53 F3
East Raynham 44 C3
East Rigton 57 J5
East Rolstone 19 G5
East Rounton 63 F6
East Rudham 44 C3
East Runton 45 F1
East Ruston 45 H3
East Saltoun 76 C4
East Shefford 21 G4
East Sleekburn 71 H5
East Somerton 45 J4
East Stockwith 51 K3
East Stoke Dorset 9 H6
East Stoke Notts. 42 A1
East Stour 9 G2
East Stourmouth 25 J5
East Stratton 11 G1
East Studdal 15 J3
East Suisnish 86 B1
East Taphouse 4 B4
East Thirston 71 G4
East Tilbury 24 C4
East Tisted 11 J1
East Torrington 52 E4
East Tuddenham 44 E4
East Tytherley 10 D2
East Tytherton 20 C4
East Village 7 G5
East Wall 38 E6
East Walton 44 B4
East Wellow 10 E2
East Wemyss 76 B1
East Whitburn 75 H4
East Wickham 23 H4
East Williamston 16 D5
East Winch 44 A4
East Wittering 11 J5
East Witton 57 G1
East Woodhay 21 H5
East Worldham 11 J1
East Worlington 7 F4
East Youlstone 6 A4
Eastbourne Darl. 62 E5
Eastbourne E.Suss. 13 K7
Eastburn 59 F4
Eastbury Herts. 22 E2
Eastbury W.Berks. 21 G4
Eastby 57 F4
Eastchurch 25 F4
Eastcombe Glos. 20 B1
Eastcombe Som. 7 K2
Eastcote Gt.Lon. 22 E3
Eastcote Northants. 31 H3
Eastcote W.Mid. 30 C1
Eastcott Cornw. 6 A4
Eastcott Wilts. 20 D6
Eastcourt Wilts. 20 C2
Eastcourt Wilts. 21 F5
Eastend 30 E6
Easter Ardross 96 D3
Easter Balmoral 89 K5
Easter Boleskine 88 C2
Easter Borland 81 H7
Easter Brae 96 D5
Easter Buckieburn 75 F2
Easter Compton 19 J3
Easter Drummond 88 C3
Easter Dullater 81 G7
Easter Ellister 72 A5
Easter Fearn 96 D3
Easter Galcantray 97 F7
Easter Howlaws 77 F6
Easter Kinkell 96 C6
Easter Knox 83 G3
Easter Lednathie 82 E1
Easter Moniack 96 C7
Easter Ord 91 G4
Easter Poldar 74 E1
Easter Quarff 109 D9
Easter Skeld 109 C8
Easter Suddie 96 D6
Easter Tulloch 91 F7
Easter Whyntie 98 E4
Eastergate 12 C6
Easterhouse 74 E4
Eastern Green 30 D1
Easterton 20 D6
Eastertown 19 G6
Eastfield N.Lan. 75 G4
Eastfield N.Yorks. 59 G1
Eastfield Hall 71 H3
Eastgate Dur. 62 A3
Eastgate Lincs. 42 E4
Eastgate Norf. 45 F3
Eastham 48 C4
Easthampstead 22 B5
Easthaugh 44 E4
Easthope 38 E6
Easthorpe Essex 34 D6
Easthorpe Leics. 42 B2
Easthorpe Notts. 51 K7
Easthouses 76 B4
Eastington Devon 7 F5
Eastington Glos. 20 C7
Eastington Glos. 30 C7
Eastleach Martin 21 F1
Eastleach Turville 21 F1
Eastleigh Devon 6 C3
Eastleigh Hants. 11 F3
Eastling 14 E2
Eastney 11 H5
Eastnor 29 G5
Eastoft 52 B1
Eastoke 11 J5
Easton Cambs. 32 E1
Easton Cumb. 69 K6
Easton Cumb. 60 D1
Easton Devon 7 F7
Easton Dorset 9 F7
Easton Hants. 11 G1
Easton I.o.W. 11 F6
Easton Lincs. 42 C3
Easton Norf. 45 F4
Easton Som. 19 J7

Easton Suff. 35 G3
Easton Wilts. 20 B4
Easton Maudit 32 B3
Easton on the Hill 42 D5
Easton Royal 21 F5
Easton-in-Gordano 19 J4
Eastrea 43 F6
Eastriggs 69 H7
Eastrington 58 D6
Eastry 15 H2
Eastside 107 D8
East-the-Water 6 C3
Eastville 53 H7
Eastwell 42 A3
Eastwick 33 H7
Eastwood Notts. 41 G1
Eastwood S'end 24 E3
Eastwood W.Yorks. 56 E7
Eathorpe 30 E2
Eaton Ches. 49 H6
Eaton Ches. 48 E6
Eaton Leics. 42 A3
Eaton Norf. 45 G5
Eaton Notts. 51 K5
Eaton Oxon. 21 H1
Eaton Shrop. 38 E6
Eaton Shrop. 38 C7
Eaton Bishop 28 D5
Eaton Bray 32 C6
Eaton Constantine 38 E5
Eaton Ford 32 E3
Eaton Green 32 C6
Eaton Hall 48 D6
Eaton Hastings 21 F2
Eaton Socon 32 E3
Eaton upon Tern 39 F3
Eavestone 57 H3
Ebberston 59 F1
Ebbesborne Wake 9 J2
Ebbw Vale 18 E1
Ebchester 62 C1
Ebford 7 H7
Ebrington 30 C4
Ecchinswell 21 J6
Ecclaw 77 F4
Ecclefechan 69 G6
Eccles Gt.Man. 49 G3
Eccles Kent 24 D5
Eccles Sc.Bord. 77 F6
Eccles Road 44 E6
Ecclesall 51 F4
Ecclesfield 51 F3
Ecclesgreig 83 J1
Eccleshall 40 A3
Eccleshill 57 G6
Ecclesmachan 75 J3
Eccleston Ches. 48 D6
Eccleston Lancs. 48 E1
Eccleston Mersey. 48 D3
Eccup 57 H5
Echt 91 F4
Eckford 70 C1
Eckington Derbys. 51 G5
Eckington Worcs. 29 J4
Ecton Northants. 32 B2
Ecton Staffs. 50 C7
Edale 50 D4
Edburton 13 F5
Edderside 60 C2
Edderton 96 E3
Eddington 21 G5
Eddleston 76 A6
Eddlewood 75 F5
Eden Park 23 G5
Edenbridge 23 H7
Edendonich 80 C5
Edenfield 49 H1
Edenhall 61 G3
Edenham 42 D3
Edensor 50 E6
Edentaggart 74 B1
Edenthorpe 51 J2
Edern 36 B2
Edgarley 8 E1
Edgbaston 40 C7
Edgcott 31 H6
Edgcumbe 2 E5
Edge Glos. 20 B1
Edge Shrop. 38 C5
Edge End 28 E7
Edgebolton 38 E3
Edgefield 45 F2
Edgeley 38 E1
Edgerley 38 C4
Edgeworth 20 C1
Edginswell 5 J4
Edgmond 39 G4
Edgmond Marsh 39 G3
Edgton 38 C7
Edgware 23 F2
Edgworth 49 G1
Edial 40 C5
Edinample 81 H5
Edinbanchory 90 C3
Edinbane 93 J6
Edinbarnet 74 D3
Edinburgh 76 A3
Edinburgh Airport 75 K3
Edinchip 81 G5
Edingale 40 E4
Edingley 51 J7
Edingthorpe 45 H2
Edington Som. 8 C1
Edington Wilts. 20 C6
Edintore 98 C6
Edinvale 97 J6
Edistone 6 A3
Edith Weston 42 C5
Edithmead 19 G7
Edlaston 40 D1
Edlesborough 32 C7
Edlingham 71 G3
Edlington 53 F5
Edmondsham 10 B3
Edmondsley 62 D2
Edmondthorpe 42 B4
Edmonstone 106 E5
Edmonton 23 G2
Edmundbyers 62 B1
Ednam 77 F7
Ednaston 40 E1
Edney Common 24 C1
Edra 81 F6
Edradynate 81 K2
Edrom 77 G5
Edstaston 38 E2
Edstone 30 C2
Edvin Loach 29 F3
Edwalton 41 H2
Edwardstone 34 D4
Edwinsford 17 K2
Edwinstowe 51 J6
Edworth 33 F4
Edwyn Ralph 29 F3
Edzell 83 G1

Effingham 22 E6
Effirth 109 C7
Efford 7 G5
Egbury 21 H6
Egdean 12 C4
Egerton Gt.Man. 49 G1
Egerton Kent 14 E3
Egerton Forstal 14 D3
Egerton Green 48 E7
Egg Buckland 5 F5
Eggerness 64 E6
Eggesford Barton 6 E4
Eggington 32 C6
Egginton 40 E3
Egglescliffe 63 F5
Eggleston 62 B4
Egham 22 D4
Egleton 42 B5
Eglingham 71 G2
Egloshayle 4 A3
Egloskerry 4 C2
Eglwys Cross 38 D1
Eglwys Fach 37 F6
Eglwysbach 47 G5
Eglwys-Brewis 18 D5
Eglwyswrw 16 E2
Egmanton 51 K6
Egmere 44 D2
Egremont 60 B5
Egton 63 J6
Egton Bridge 63 J6
Egypt 21 H6
Eight Ash Green 34 D6
Eignaig 79 J3
Eil 89 F3
Eilanreach 86 E3
Eilean Darach 95 H3
Eilean Iarmain (Isleornsay) 86 C3
Einacleit 100 D5
Eisgean 101 F6
Eisingrug 37 F2
Eisteddfa Gurig 37 G7
Elan Village 27 J2
Elberton 19 J3
Elburton 5 F5
Elcho 82 C5
Elcombe 20 E3
Eldernell 43 G6
Eldersfield 29 G5
Elderslie 74 C4
Eldrick 67 G1
Eldroth 56 C3
Eldwick 57 G5
Elerch (Bont-goch) 37 F7
Elford Northumb. 77 K7
Elford Staffs. 40 D4
Elgin 97 K5
Elgol 86 B3
Elham 15 G3
Elie 83 F7
Elilaw 70 E3
Elim 46 B4
Eling 10 E3
Eliock 68 D3
Elishader 94 B5
Elishaw 70 D4
Elkesley 51 J5
Elkstone 29 J7
Ellan 88 E2
Elland 57 G7
Ellary 73 F3
Ellastone 40 D1
Ellemford 77 F4
Ellenborough 60 B3
Ellenhall 40 A3
Ellen's Green 12 D3
Ellerbeck 63 F7
Ellerby 63 J5
Ellerdine Heath 39 F3
Ellerker 59 F7
Ellerton E.Riding 58 D5
Ellerton N.Yorks. 62 D7
Ellerton Shrop. 39 G3
Ellesborough 22 B1
Ellesmere 38 C2
Ellesmere Port 48 C5
Ellingham Hants. 10 C4
Ellingham Norf. 45 H6
Ellingham Northumb. 71 G1
Ellingstring 57 G1
Ellington Cambs. 32 E1
Ellington Northumb. 71 H4
Ellisfield 21 K7
Ellistown 41 G4
Ellon 91 H1
Ellonby 61 F3
Ellough 45 J7
Elloughton 59 F7
Ellwood 19 J1
Elm 43 H5
Elm Park 23 J3
Elmbridge 29 J2
Elmdon Essex 33 H5
Elmdon W.Mid. 40 D7
Elmdon Heath 40 D7
Elmesthorpe 41 G6
Elmhurst 40 D4
Elmley Castle 29 J4
Elmley Lovett 29 H2
Elmore 29 G7
Elmore Back 29 G7
Elmscott 6 A3
Elmsett 34 E4
Elmstead Market 34 E6
Elmstone 25 J5
Elmstone Hardwicke 29 J6
Elmswell E.Riding 59 F4
Elmswell Suff. 34 D2
Elmton 51 H5
Elphin 102 E7
Elphinstone 76 B3
Elrick Aber. 91 G4
Elrick Moray 90 C2
Elrig 64 D6
Elrigbeag 80 C6
Elsdon 70 E4
Elsecar 51 F2
Elsenham 33 J6
Elsfield 21 J1
Elsham 52 D1
Elsing 44 E4
Elslack 56 E5
Elson 38 C2
Elsrickle 75 J6
Elstead 22 C7
Elsted 11 J2
Elsthorpe 42 D3
Elstob 62 D4
Elston Lancs. 55 J6
Elston Notts. 42 A1
Elstone 6 E4
Elstow 32 D4
Elstree 22 E2
Elstronwick 59 J6
Elswick 55 H6

Elsworth 33 G2
Elterwater 60 E6
Eltham 23 H4
Eltisley 33 F3
Elton *Cambs.* 42 D6
Elton *Ches.* 48 D5
Elton *Derbys.* 50 E6
Elton *Glos.* 29 G7
Elton *Here.* 28 D1
Elton *Notts.* 42 A2
Elton *Stock.* 63 F5
Elvanfoot 68 E2
Elvaston 41 G2
Elveden 34 C1
Elvingston 76 C3
Elvington *Kent* 15 H2
Elvington *York* 58 D5
Elwick *Hart.* 63 F3
Elwick *Northumb.* 77 K7
Elworth 49 G6
Elworthy 7 J2
Ely *Cambs.* 33 J1
Ely *Cardiff* 18 E4
Emberton 32 B4
Embleton *Cumb.* 60 C3
Embleton *Northumb.* 71 H1
Embo 97 F2
Embo Street 97 F2
Emborough 19 K6
Embsay 57 F4
Emery Down 10 D4
Emley 50 E1
Emmer Green 22 A4
Emmington 22 A1
Emneth 43 H5
Emneth Hungate 43 J5
Empingham 42 C5
Empshott 11 J1
Emsworth 11 J4
Enborne 21 H5
Enchmarsh 38 E6
Enderby 41 H6
Endmoor 55 J1
Endon 49 J7
Enfield 23 G2
Enford 20 E6
Engine Common 19 K3
Englefield 21 K4
Englefield Green 22 C4
Englesea-brook 49 G7
English Bicknor 28 E7
English Frankton 38 D3
Englishcombe 20 A5
Enham Alamein 21 G7
Enmore 8 B1
Ennerdale Bridge 60 B5
Ennochdhu 82 B1
Ensay 78 E3
Ensdon 38 D4
Ensis 6 D3
Enstone 30 E6
Enterkinfoot 68 D3
Enterpen 63 F6
Enville 40 A7
Eolaigearraidh 84 C4
Eorabus 78 E5
Eorodal 101 H1
Eoropaidh 101 H1
Epperstone 41 J1
Epping 23 H1
Epping Green *Essex* 23 H1
Epping Green *Herts.* 23 F1
Epping Upland 23 H1
Eppleby 62 C5
Eppleworth 59 G6
Epsom 23 F5
Epwell 30 E4
Epworth 51 K2
Erbistock 38 C1
Erbusaig 86 D2
Erchless Castle 96 B7
Erdington 40 D6
Eredine 80 A7
Eriboll 103 G3
Ericstane 69 F2
Eridge Green 13 J3
Eriff 67 K3
Erines 73 G3
Eriswell 34 B1
Erith 23 J4
Erlestoke 20 C6
Ermington 5 G5
Erpingham 45 F2
Errogie 88 C2
Errol 82 D5
Errollston 91 J1
Erskine 74 C3
Ervie 64 A4
Erwarton 35 G5
Erwood 27 K4
Eryholme 62 E6
Eryrys 48 B7
Escart 73 G4
Escart Farm 73 G5
Escrick 58 C5
Esgair 17 G3
Esgairgeiliog 37 G5
Esh 62 C2
Esh Winning 62 C2
Esher 22 E5
Eshott 71 H4
Eshton 56 E4
Eskadale 88 B1
Eskbank 76 B4
Eskdale Green 60 C6
Eskdalemuir 69 H4
Eskham 53 G3
Esknish 72 B4
Espley Hall 71 G4
Esprick 55 H6
Essendine 42 D4
Essendon 23 F1
Essich 88 D1
Essington 40 B5
Esslemont 91 H2
Eston 63 G5
Etal 77 H7
Etchilhampton 20 D5
Etchingham 14 C5
Etchinghill *Kent* 15 G4
Etchinghill *Staffs.* 40 C4
Ethie Mains 83 H3
Eton 22 C4
Eton Wick 22 C4
Etteridge 88 D5
Ettingshall 40 B6
Ettington 30 D4
Etton *E.Riding* 59 F5
Etton *Peter.* 42 E5
Ettrick 69 H2
Ettrickbridge 69 J1
Ettrickhill 69 H2
Etwall 40 E2
Eurach 79 K7
Euston 34 C1
Euxton 48 E1
Evanton 96 D5
Evedon 42 D1
Evelix 96 E2
Evenjobb 28 B2
Evenley 31 G5
Evenlode 30 D6
Evenwood 62 C4
Everbay 106 F5
Evercreech 9 F1
Everdon 31 G3
Everingham 58 E5
Everleigh 21 F6
Everley *High.* 105 J2
Everley *N.Yorks.* 59 F1
Eversholt 32 C5
Evershot 8 E4
Eversley 22 A5
Eversley Cross 22 A5
Everthorpe 59 F6
Everton *Beds.* 33 F3
Everton *Hants.* 10 D5
Everton *Notts.* 51 J3
Evertown 69 J6
Evesbatch 29 F4
Evesham 30 B4
Evie 106 C5
Evington 41 J5
Ewart Newtown 77 H7
Ewden Village 50 E3
Ewell 23 F5
Ewell Minnis 15 H3
Ewelme 21 K2
Ewen 20 D2
Ewenny 18 C4
Ewerby 42 E1
Ewerby Thorpe 42 E1
Ewhurst *E.Suss.* 14 C5
Ewhurst *Surr.* 22 D7
Ewhurst Green 12 D3
Ewloe 48 B6
Ewood 56 B7
Eworthy 6 C6
Ewshot 22 B7
Ewyas Harold 28 C6
Exbourne 6 E5
Exbury 11 F4
Exebridge 7 H3
Exelby 57 H1
Exeter 7 H6
Exeter Airport 7 H6
Exford 7 G2
Exfords Green 38 D5
Exhall *Warks.* 30 C3
Exhall *Warks.* 41 F7
Exlade Street 21 K3
Exminster 7 H7
Exmouth 7 J7
Exnaboe 109 F9
Exning 33 K2
Exton *Devon* 7 H7
Exton *Hants.* 11 H2
Exton *Rut.* 42 C4
Exton *Som.* 7 H2
Exwick 7 H6
Eyam 50 E5
Eydon 31 G3
Eye *Here.* 28 D2
Eye *Peter.* 43 F5
Eye *Suff.* 35 F1
Eye Green 43 F5
Eyemouth 77 H4
Eyeworth 33 F4
Eyhorne Street 14 D2
Eyke 35 H3
Eynesbury 32 E3
Eynort 85 J2
Eynsford 23 J5
Eynsham 21 H1
Eype 8 D5
Eyre 93 K6
Eythorne 15 H3
Eyton *Here.* 28 D2
Eyton *Shrop.* 38 C7
Eyton *Wrex.* 38 C1
Eyton upon the Weald Moors 39 F4
Eywood 28 C3

F

Faccombe 21 G6
Faceby 63 F6
Fachwen 46 D6
Faddiley 48 E7
Fadmoor 58 C1
Faebait 96 B6
Faifley 74 D3
Fail 67 J1
Failand 19 J4
Failford 67 J1
Failsworth 49 H2
Fain 95 H4
Fair Oak *Hants.* 11 F3
Fair Oak *Hants.* 21 J5
Fairbourne 37 F4
Fairburn 57 K7
Fairfield *Derbys.* 50 C5
Fairfield *Worcs.* 29 J1
Fairford 20 E1
Fairgirth 65 J5
Fairholm 75 F5
Fairley 91 G4
Fairlie 74 A5
Fairlight 14 D6
Fairlight Cove 14 D6
Fairmile 7 J6
Fairmilehead 76 A4
Fairnington 70 B1
Fairoak 39 G2
Fairseat 24 C5
Fairstead *Essex* 34 B7
Fairstead *Norf.* 45 G3
Fairwarp 13 H4
Fairy Cross 6 C3
Fairyhill 17 H6
Fakenham 44 D3
Fala 76 C4
Fala Dam 76 C4
Falahill 76 B5
Faldingworth 52 D4
Falfield *Fife* 83 F7
Falfield *S.Glos.* 19 K2
Falkenham 35 G5
Falkirk 75 G3
Falkland 82 D7
Falla 70 C2
Fallgate 51 F6
Fallin 75 G1
Falmer 13 G6
Falmouth 3 F5
Falsgrave 59 G1
Falstone 70 C5
Fanagmore 102 D3
Fanans 80 B5
Fancott 32 D6
Fangdale Beck 63 G7
Fangfoss 58 D4
Fanmore 79 F3
Fans 76 E6
Far Cotton 31 J3
Far Forest 29 G1
Far Gearstones 56 C1
Farcet 43 F6
Farden 28 E1
Fareham 11 G4
Farewell 40 C4
Farforth 53 G5
Faringdon 21 F2
Farington 55 J7
Farlam 61 G1
Farlary 96 E1
Farleigh *N.Som.* 19 H5
Farleigh *Surr.* 23 G5
Farleigh Hungerford 20 A6
Farleigh Wallop 21 K7
Farlesthorpe 53 H5
Farleton 55 J1
Farley *Shrop.* 38 C5
Farley *Staffs.* 40 C1
Farley *Wilts.* 10 D2
Farley Green 22 D7
Farley Hill 22 A5
Farleys End 29 G7
Farlington 58 C3
Farlow 39 F7
Farmborough 19 K5
Farmcote 30 B6
Farmington 30 C7
Farmoor 21 H1
Farmtown 98 D5
Farnborough *Gt.Lon.* 23 H5
Farnborough *Hants.* 22 B6
Farnborough *W.Berks.* 21 H3
Farnborough *Warks.* 31 F3
Farnborough Green 22 B6
Farncombe 22 C7
Farndish 32 C2
Farndon *Ches.* 48 D7
Farndon *Notts.* 51 K7
Farnell 83 H2
Farnham *Dorset* 9 J3
Farnham *Essex* 33 H6
Farnham *N.Yorks.* 57 J3
Farnham *Suff.* 35 H3
Farnham *Surr.* 22 B7
Farnham Common 22 C3
Farnham Green 33 H6
Farnham Royal 22 C3
Farningham 23 J5
Farnley 57 H5
Farnley Tyas 50 D1
Farnsfield 51 J7
Farnworth *Gt.Man.* 49 G2
Farnworth *Halton* 48 E4
Farr *High.* 104 C2
Farr *High.* 88 D1
Farr *High.* 89 F4
Farr House 88 D1
Farraline 88 C2
Farringdon 7 J6
Farrington Gurney 19 K6
Farsley 57 H6
Farthinghoe 31 G5
Farthingloe 15 H3
Farthingstone 31 H3
Farway 7 K6
Fasag 94 E6
Fasagrianach 95 H3
Fascadale 86 B7
Faslane 74 A2
Fasnacloich 80 B3
Fasnakyle 87 K2
Fassfern 87 G7
Fatfield 62 E1
Fattahead 98 E5
Faugh 61 G1
Fauldhouse 75 H4
Faulkbourne 34 B7
Faulkland 20 A6
Fauls 38 E2
Faversham 25 G5
Favillar 89 K1
Fawdington 57 K2
Fawdon 71 H7
Fawfieldhead 50 C6
Fawkham Green 23 J5
Fawler 30 E7
Fawley *Bucks.* 22 A3
Fawley *Hants.* 11 F4
Fawley *W.Berks.* 21 G3
Fawley Chapel 28 E6
Fawsyde 91 G7
Faxfleet 58 E7
Faxton 31 J1
Faygate 13 F3
Fazeley 40 E5
Fearby 57 G1
Fearn 97 F4
Fearnan 81 J3
Fearnbeg 94 D6
Fearnhead 49 F3
Fearnmore 94 D5
Fearnoch *Arg. & B.* 73 J3
Fearnoch *Arg. & B.* 73 H3
Featherstone *Staffs.* 40 B5
Featherstone *W.Yorks.* 51 G1
Featherstone Castle 70 B7
Feckenham 30 B2
Feering 34 C6
Feetham 62 A7
Feith-hill 98 E6
Feizor 56 C3
Felbridge 13 G3
Felbrigg 45 G2
Felcourt 23 G7
Felden 22 D1
Felindre *Carmar.* 27 G6
Felindre *Carmar.* 17 J3
Felindre *Carmar.* 17 G2
Felindre *Powys* 38 A7
Felindre *Swan.* 17 K5
Felinfach 27 K5
Felinfoel 17 J5
Felingwmuchaf 17 J3
Felixkirk 57 K1
Felixstowe 35 G5
Felixstowe Ferry 35 H5
Felkington 77 H6
Felldownhead 6 B7
Felling 71 H7
Fellonmore 79 H5
Felmersham 32 C3
Felmingham 45 G3
Felpham 12 C7
Felsham 34 D3
Felsted 33 K6
Feltham 22 E4
Felthorpe 45 F4
Felton *Here.* 28 E4
Felton *N.Som.* 19 J5
Felton *Northumb.* 71 G3
Felton Butler 38 C4
Feltwell 44 B7
Fen Ditton 33 H3
Fen Drayton 33 G2
Fen End 30 D1
Fen Street 34 D1
Fence 56 D6
Fence Houses 62 E1
Fencott 31 G7
Fendike Corner 53 H6
Fenhouses 43 F1
Feniscowles 56 B7
Feniton 7 K6
Fenny Bentley 50 D7
Fenny Bridges 7 K6
Fenny Compton 31 F3
Fenny Drayton 41 F6
Fenny Stratford 32 B5
Fenrother 71 G4
Fenstanton 33 G2
Fenton *Cambs.* 33 G1
Fenton *Lincs.* 52 B5
Fenton *Lincs.* 52 B7
Fenton *Northumb.* 77 H7
Fenton *Stoke* 40 A1
Fenwick *E.Ayr.* 74 C6
Fenwick *Northumb.* 71 F6
Fenwick *Northumb.* 77 J6
Fenwick *S.Yorks.* 51 H1
Feochaig 66 B2
Feock 3 F5
Feolin 72 D4
Feolin Ferry 72 C4
Feorlan 66 A3
Feorlin 73 H1
Feriniquarrie 93 G6
Fern 83 F1
Ferndale 18 C2
Ferndown 10 B4
Ferness 97 G7
Fernham 21 F2
Fernhill Heath 29 H3
Fernhurst 12 B4
Fernie 82 E6
Fernilea 85 J1
Fernilee 50 C5
Fernybank 90 D7
Ferrensby 57 J3
Ferring 12 D6
Ferrybridge 57 K7
Ferryden 83 J2
Ferryhill 62 D3
Ferryside 17 G4
Fersfield 44 E7
Fersit 87 K7
Ferwig 16 E1
Feshiebridge 89 F4
Fetcham 22 E6
Fetterangus 99 H5
Fettercairn 90 E7
Fetternear House 91 F3
Feus of Caldhame 83 H1
Fewcott 31 G6
Fewston 57 G4
Ffairfach 17 K3
Ffair-Rhos 27 G2
Ffarmers 17 K1
Ffawyddog 28 B7
Ffestiniog 37 G1
Ffordd-las 47 K6
Fforest 17 J5
Fforest-fach 17 K6
Ffostrasol 17 G1
Ffos-y-ffin 26 D2
Ffridd Uchaf 46 D7
Ffrith 48 B7
Ffrwdgrech 27 K6
Ffynnon Taf (Taff's Well) 18 E3
Ffynnon-ddrain 17 H3
Ffynnongroyw 47 K4
Fibhig 100 E3
Fichlie 90 C3
Fidden 78 E5
Fiddington *Glos.* 29 J5
Fiddington *Som.* 19 F7
Fiddler's Green 28 E5
Fiddlers Hamlet 23 H1
Field 40 C2
Field Broughton 55 G1
Field Dalling 44 E2
Field Head 41 G5
Fife Keith 98 C5
Fifehead Magdalen 9 G2
Fifehead Neville 9 G3
Fifield *Oxon.* 30 D7
Fifield *W. & M.* 22 C4
Fifield Bavant 10 B2
Figheldean 20 E7
Filby 45 J4
Filey 59 H2
Filgrave 32 B4
Filkins 21 F1
Filleigh *Devon* 6 E3
Filleigh *Devon* 7 F4
Fillingham 52 C4
Fillongley 40 E7
Filmore Hill 11 H2
Filton 19 J4
Fimber 59 F3
Finavon 83 F2
Fincham 44 A5
Finchampstead 22 A5
Finchdean 11 J3
Finchingfield 33 K5
Finchley 23 F2
Findern 41 F2
Findhorn 97 H5
Findhorn Bridge 89 F2
Findhuglen 81 J6
Findo Gask 82 B5
Findochty 98 C4
Findon *Aber.* 91 H5
Findon *W.Suss.* 12 E6
Findon Mains 96 D5
Findrassie 97 J5
Findron 89 J3
Finedon 32 C1
Finegand 82 C1
Fingal Street 35 G2
Fingask 91 F2
Fingerpost 29 G1
Fingest 22 A2
Finghall 62 C7
Fingland *Cumb.* 60 D1
Fingland *D. & G.* 69 H3
Fingland *D. & G.* 68 C2
Finglesham 15 J2
Fingringhoe 34 E7
Finlarig 81 G4
Finmere 31 H5
Finnart *Arg. & B.* 74 A1
Finnart *P. & K.* 81 G2
Finningham 34 E2
Finningley 51 J3
Finnygaud 98 E5
Finsbury 23 G3
Finstall 29 J1
Finsthwaite 55 G1
Finstock 30 E7
Finstown 107 C6
Fintry *Aber.* 99 F5
Fintry *Stir.* 74 E2
Finzean 90 D5
Fionnphort 78 E5
Fir Tree 62 C3
Fir Vale 51 F4
Firbank 61 H7
Firbeck 51 H4
Firgrove 49 J1
Firs Road 10 D1
Firsby 53 H6
Firth 108 D5
Fishbourne *I.o.W.* 11 G5
Fishbourne *W.Suss.* 12 B6
Fishburn 62 E3
Fisherford 90 E1
Fisher's Pond 11 F2
Fisher's Row 55 H5
Fisherstreet 12 C3
Fisherton *High.* 96 E6
Fisherton *S.Ayr.* 67 G2
Fisherton de la Mere 10 B1
Fishguard (Abergwaun) 16 C2
Fishlake 51 J1
Fishleigh Barton 6 D3
Fishnish 79 H3
Fishpond Bottom 8 C5
Fishponds 19 K4
Fishpool 49 H1
Fishtoft 43 G1
Fishtoft Drove 43 G1
Fishtown of Usan 83 J2
Fishwick *Lancs.* 55 J6
Fishwick *Sc.Bord.* 77 H5
Fiskerton *Lincs.* 52 D5
Fiskerton *Notts.* 51 K7
Fittleton 20 E6
Fittleworth 12 D5
Fitton End 43 H4
Fitz 38 D4
Fitzhead 7 K3
Fitzwilliam 51 G1
Fiunary 79 H3
Five Ash Down 13 H4
Five Ashes 13 J4
Five Bridges 29 F4
Five Oak Green 23 K7
Five Oaks *Chan.I.* 3 K7
Five Oaks *W.Suss.* 12 D4
Five Roads 17 H5
Five Turnings 28 B1
Five Wents 14 D2
Fivehead 8 C2
Fivelanes 4 C2
Flackwell Heath 22 B3
Fladbury 29 J4
Fladdabister 109 D9
Flagg 50 D6
Flamborough 59 J2
Flamstead 32 D7
Flamstead End 23 G1
Flansham 12 C6
Flasby 56 E4
Flash 50 C6
Flashader 93 J6
Flask Inn 63 J2
Flaunden 22 D1
Flawborough 42 A1
Flawith 57 K3
Flax Bourton 19 J5
Flaxby 57 J4
Flaxley 29 F7
Flaxpool 7 K2
Flaxton 58 C3
Fleckney 41 J6
Flecknoe 31 G2
Fleet *Hants.* 22 B6
Fleet *Lincs.* 43 G3
Fleet Hargate 43 G3
Fleetwood 55 G5
Flemingston 18 D5
Flemington 74 E5
Flempton 34 C2
Fleoideabhagh 93 F3
Fletchertown 60 D2
Fletching 13 H4
Flete 5 G5
Fleuchats 90 B4
Fleur-de-lis 18 E2
Flexbury 6 A5
Flexford 22 C6
Flimby 60 B3
Flimwell 14 C4
Flint (Y Fflint) 48 B5
Flint Cross 33 H4
Flint Mountain 48 B5
Flintham 42 A1
Flinton 59 J6
Flishinghurst 14 C4
Flitcham 44 B3
Flitton 32 D5
Flitwick 32 D5
Flixborough 52 B1
Flixton *Gt.Man.* 49 G3
Flixton *N.Yorks.* 59 G2
Flixton *Suff.* 45 H7
Flockton 50 E1
Flockton Green 50 E1
Flodden 77 H7
Flodigarry 93 K4
Flookburgh 55 G2
Floors 98 C5
Flordon 45 F6
Flore 31 H2
Flotterton 71 F3
Flowton 34 E4
Flushing *Aber.* 99 J6
Flushing *Cornw.* 3 F5
Flyford Flavell 29 J3
Fobbing 24 D3
Fochabers 98 B5
Fochriw 18 E1
Fockerby 52 B1
Fodderletter 89 J2
Fodderty 96 C6
Foel 37 J4
Foggathorpe 58 D6
Fogo 77 F6
Fogorig 77 F6
Foindle 102 D4
Folda 82 C1
Fole 40 C2
Foleshill 41 F7
Folke 9 F3
Folkestone 15 H4
Folkingham 42 D2
Folkington 13 J6
Folksworth 42 E7
Folkton 59 G2
Folla Rule 91 F1
Follifoot 57 J4
Folly *Dorset* 9 G4
Folly *Pembs.* 16 C3
Folly Gate 6 D6
Fonthill Bishop 9 J1
Fonthill Gifford 9 J1
Fontmell Magna 9 H3
Fontwell 12 C6
Foolow 50 D5
Foots Cray 23 H4
Forbestown 90 B3
Force Forge 60 E7
Forcett 62 C5
Forches Cross 7 F5
Ford *Arg. & B.* 79 K7
Ford *Bucks.* 22 A1
Ford *Devon* 5 G5
Ford *Devon* 6 C3
Ford *Devon* 5 H6
Ford *Glos.* 30 B6
Ford *Mersey.* 48 C2
Ford *Midloth.* 76 B4
Ford *Northumb.* 77 H7
Ford *Pembs.* 16 C3
Ford *Shrop.* 38 D4
Ford *Som.* 7 J3
Ford *W.Suss.* 12 C6
Ford *Wilts.* 20 B4
Ford End 33 K7
Ford Street 7 K4
Fordcombe 23 J7
Fordell 75 K2
Forden 38 B5
Forder Green 5 H4
Fordham *Cambs.* 33 K1
Fordham *Essex* 34 D6
Fordham *Norf.* 44 A6
Fordham Abbey 33 K2
Fordingbridge 10 C3
Fordon 59 G2
Fordoun 91 F7
Fordstreet 34 D6
Fordwells 30 E7
Fordwich 15 G2
Fordyce 98 D4
Forebrae 82 A5
Foreland 72 A4
Forest Gate 23 H3
Forest Green 22 E7
Forest Hall *Cumb.* 61 G6
Forest Hall *T. & W.* 71 H7
Forest Head 61 G1
Forest Hill 21 J1
Forest Lodge *Arg. & B.* 80 D3
Forest Lodge *P. & K.* 89 G7
Forest Mill 75 H1
Forest Row 13 H3
Forest Town 51 H6
Forestburn Gate 71 F4
Forest-in-Teesdale 61 K3
Forestside 11 J3
Forfar 83 F2
Forgandenny 82 B6
Forgie 98 B5
Formby 48 B2
Forncett End 45 F6
Forncett St. Mary 45 F6
Forncett St. Peter 45 F6
Forneth 82 B3
Fornham All Saints 34 C2
Fornham St. Martin 34 C2
Fornighty 97 G6
Forres 97 H6
Forrest 75 G4
Forrest Lodge 67 K5
Forsbrook 40 B1
Forse 105 H5
Forsie 105 F2
Forsinain 104 E4
Forsinard 104 D4
Forston 9 F5
Fort Augustus 87 K4
Fort George 96 E6
Fort William 87 H7
Forter 82 C1
Forteviot 82 B6
Forth 75 H5
Forthampton 29 H5
Fortingall 81 J3
Forton *Hants.* 21 H7
Forton *Lancs.* 55 H4
Forton *Shrop.* 38 D4
Forton *Som.* 8 C4
Forton *Staffs.* 39 G3
Fortrie 98 E6
Fortrose 96 E6
Fortuneswell 9 F7
Forty Green 22 C2
Forty Hill 23 G2
Forward Green 34 E3
Fosbury 21 G6
Foscot 30 D6
Fosdyke 43 G2
Foss 81 J2
Foss Cross 20 D1
Fossdale 61 K7
Fossebridge 30 B7
Foster Street 23 H1
Foster's Booth 31 H3
Foston *Derbys.* 40 D2
Foston *Lincs.* 42 B1
Foston *N.Yorks.* 58 C3
Foston on the Wolds 59 H4
Fotherby 53 G3
Fotheringhay 42 D6
Foubister 107 E7
Foul Mile 13 K5
Foulbog 69 H3
Foulden *Norf.* 44 B6
Foulden *Sc.Bord.* 77 H5
Foulridge 56 D5
Foulsham 44 E3
Foulzie 99 F4
Fountainhall 76 C6
Four Ashes *Staffs.* 40 B5
Four Ashes *Suff.* 34 D1
Four Crosses *Denb.* 37 K1
Four Crosses *Powys* 38 B4
Four Crosses *Powys* 37 K5
Four Crosses *Staffs.* 40 B5
Four Elms 23 H7
Four Forks 8 B1
Four Gotes 43 H4
Four Lanes 2 D5
Four Marks 11 H1
Four Mile Bridge 46 A5
Four Oaks *E.Suss.* 14 D5
Four Oaks *W.Mid.* 40 E7
Four Oaks *W.Mid.* 40 D6
Four Roads 17 H5
Four Throws 14 C5
Fourlane Ends 51 F7
Fourlanes End 49 H7
Fourpenny 96 E2
Fourstones 70 D7
Fovant 10 B2
Foveran House 91 H2
Fowey 4 B5
Fowlis 82 E4
Fowlis Wester 82 A5
Fowlmere 33 H4
Fownhope 28 E5
Fox Lane 22 B6
Fox Street 34 E6
Foxcote 30 B7
Foxdale 54 B6
Foxearth 34 C4
Foxfield 55 F1
Foxham 20 C4
Foxhole *Cornw.* 3 G3
Foxhole *High.* 88 C1
Foxholes 59 G2
Foxhunt Green 13 J5
Foxley *Here.* 28 D4
Foxley *Norf.* 44 E3
Foxley *Northants.* 31 H3
Foxley *Wilts.* 20 B3
Foxt 40 C1
Foxton *Cambs.* 33 H4
Foxton *Dur.* 62 E4
Foxton *Leics.* 42 A6
Foxup 56 D2
Foxwist Green 49 F6
Foy 28 E6
Foyers 88 B2
Frachadil 78 E2
Fraddam 2 C5
Fraddon 3 G3
Fradley 40 D4
Fradswell 40 B2
Fraisthorpe 59 H3
Framfield 13 H4
Framingham Earl 45 G5
Framingham Pigot 45 G5
Framlingham 35 G2
Frampton *Dorset* 9 F5
Frampton *Lincs.* 43 G2
Frampton Cotterell 19 K3
Frampton Mansell 20 C1
Frampton on Severn 20 A1
Frampton West End 43 G1
Framsden 35 G3
Framwellgate Moor 62 D2
Franche 29 H1
Frankby 48 B4
Frankley 40 B7
Frankton 31 F1
Frant 13 J3
Fraserburgh 99 H4
Frating 34 E6
Fratton 11 H4
Freathy 4 D5
Freckenham 33 K1
Freckleton 55 H7
Freeby 42 B3
Freefolk 21 H7
Freeland 31 F7
Freemantle 11 F3
Freester 109 D7
Freethorpe 45 J5
Freethorpe Common 45 J5
Freiston 43 G1
Freiston Shore 43 G1
Fremington *Devon* 6 D2
Fremington *N.Yorks.* 62 B7
Frenchay 19 K4
Frenchbeer 6 E7
Frendraught 98 E6
Frenich 81 F7
Frensham 22 B7
Fresgoe 104 E2
Freshfield 48 B2
Freshford 20 A5
Freshwater 10 E6
Freshwater East 16 D6
Fressingfield 35 G1
Freston 35 F5
Freswick 105 J2
Frettenham 45 G4
Freuchie 82 D7
Freystrop Cross 16 C4
Friars Carse 68 E5
Friar's Gate 13 H3
Friarton 82 C5
Friday Bridge 43 H5
Friday Street *E.Suss.* 13 K6
Friday Street *Surr.* 22 E7
Fridaythorpe 58 E4
Friern Barnet 23 F2
Friesthorpe 52 D4
Frieston 42 C1
Frieth 22 A2
Frilford 21 H2
Frilsham 21 J4
Frimley 22 B6
Frimley Green 22 B6
Frindsbury 24 D5
Fring 44 B2
Fringford 31 H6
Frinsted 14 D2
Frinton-on-Sea 35 G7
Friockheim 83 G3
Friog 37 F4
Frisby on the Wreake 41 J4
Friskney 53 H7
Friskney Eaudyke 53 H7
Friston *E.Suss.* 13 J7
Friston *Suff.* 35 J3
Fritchley 51 F7
Frith 14 E2
Frith Bank 43 G1
Frith Common 29 F2
Fritham 10 D3
Frithelstock 6 C4
Frithelstock Stone 6 C4
Frithville 53 G7
Frittenden 14 D3
Fritton *Norf.* 45 G6
Fritton *Norf.* 45 J5
Fritwell 31 G6
Frizington 60 B5
Frocester 20 A1
Frochas 38 B4
Frodesley 38 E5
Frodingham 52 B1
Frodsham 48 E5
Frog End 33 H3
Frog Pool 29 G2
Frogden 70 C1
Froggatt 50 E5
Froghall 40 C1
Frogham 10 C3

Frogmore *Devon* 5 H6
Frogmore *Hants.* 22 B6
Frogmore *Herts.* 22 E1
Frolesworth 41 H6
Frome 20 A7
Frome Market 20 B6
Frome St. Quentin 8 E4
Fromes Hill 29 F4
Fron *Gwyn.* 36 C2
Fron *Powys* 38 B5
Fron *Powys* 27 K2
Froncysyllte 38 B1
Fron-goch 37 J2
Frostenden 45 J7
Frosterley 62 B3
Froxfield 21 F5
Froxfield Green 11 J2
Fryerning 24 C1
Fryton 58 C2
Fugglestone St. Peter 10 C1
Fulbeck 52 C7
Fulbourn 33 J3
Fulbrook 30 D7
Fulford *Som.* 8 B2
Fulford *Staffs.* 40 B2
Fulford *York* 58 C5
Fulham 23 F4
Fulking 13 F5
Full Sutton 58 D4
Fuller Street 34 B7
Fuller's Moor 48 D7
Fullerton 10 E1
Fulletby 53 F5
Fullwood 74 C6
Fulmer 22 C3
Fulmodeston 44 D2
Fulnetby 52 E5
Fulready 30 D4
Fulstow 53 G3
Fulwell *Oxon.* 30 E6
Fulwell *T. & W.* 62 E1
Fulwood *Lancs.* 55 J6
Fulwood *S.Yorks.* 51 F4
Fundenhall 45 F6
Funtington 12 B6
Funtley 11 G4
Funzie 108 F4
Furley 8 B4
Furnace *Arg. & B.* 80 B7
Furnace *Cere.* 37 F6
Furnace *High.* 95 F4
Furness Vale 50 C4
Furneux Pelham 33 H6
Furze Platt 22 B3
Furzehill 7 F1
Fyfett 8 B3
Fyfield *Essex* 23 J1
Fyfield *Glos.* 21 F1
Fyfield *Hants.* 21 F7
Fyfield *Oxon.* 21 H2
Fyfield *Wilts.* 20 E5
Fylingthorpe 63 J2
Fyvie 91 F1

G

Gabhsunn Bho Dheas 101 G2
Gabhsunn Bho Thuath 101 G2
Gablon 96 E2
Gabroc Hill 74 C5
Gaddesby 41 J4
Gaddesden Row 32 D7
Gaer *Newport* 19 F3
Gaer *Powys* 28 A6
Gaerllwyd 19 H2
Gaerwen 46 C5
Gagingwell 31 F6
Gaich 89 H2
Gaick 88 D1
Gaick Lodge 88 E6
Gailey 40 B4
Gainford 62 C5
Gainsborough 52 B3
Gairloch 94 E4
Gairlochy 87 H6
Gairney Bank 75 K1
Gairnshiel Lodge 89 K4
Gaitsgill 60 E2
Galabank 76 C6
Galashiels 76 C7
Galdenoch 64 B4
Galgate 55 H4
Galhampton 9 F2
Gallanach 79 K5
Gallantry Bank 48 E7
Gallatown 76 A1
Gallchoille 73 F2
Gallery 83 H1
Galley Common 41 F6
Galleyend 24 D1
Galleywood 24 D1
Gallowfauld 83 F3
Gallowstree Common 21 K4
Gallowstree Elm 40 A7
Gallt Melyd (Meliden) 47 J4
Galltair 86 E3
Galmisdale 85 K6
Galmpton *Devon* 5 G6
Galmpton *Torbay* 5 J5
Galphay 57 H2
Galston 74 D7
Galtrigill 93 G6
Gamble's Green 34 B7
Gamblesby 61 H3
Gamelsby 60 D1
Gamlingay 33 F3
Gammaton Moor 6 C3
Gammersgill 57 F1
Gamrie 99 F4
Gamston *Notts.* 51 K5
Gamston *Notts.* 41 J2
Ganarew 28 E7
Ganllwyd 37 G3
Gannochy 90 E7
Ganstead 59 H6
Ganthorpe 58 C2
Ganton 59 F2
Gaodhail 79 H4
Gara Bridge 5 H5
Garabal 80 E6
Garadheancal 95 F1
Garbat 96 B5
Garbhallt 73 J1
Garboldisham 44 E7
Garden 74 D1
Garden City 48 C6
Gardenstown 99 F4
Garderhouse 109 C8
Gardham 59 F5
Gare Hill 20 A7
Garelochhead 74 A1
Garford 21 H2
Garforth 57 K6
Gargrave 56 E4
Gargunnock 75 F1
Gariob 73 F2
Garlies Castle 64 E4
Garlieston 64 E6
Garlogie 91 F4
Garmond 99 G5
Garmony 79 H3
Garmouth 98 B4
Garnant 17 K4
Garndolbenmaen 36 D1
Garneddwen 37 G5
Garnett Bridge 61 G7
Garnfadryn 36 B2
Garnswllt 17 K5
Garrabost 101 H4
Garrachra 73 J2
Garralburn 98 C5
Garras 2 D6
Garreg 37 F1
Garreg Bank 38 B4
Garrick 81 K6
Garrigill 61 J2
Garroch 67 K5
Garrochty 73 J5
Garros 94 B5
Garrow 81 K4
Garryhorn 67 K4
Garrynahine (Gearraidh na h-Aibhne) 100 E4
Garsdale Head 61 J7
Garsdon 20 C3
Garshall Green 40 B2
Garsington 21 J1
Garstang 55 H5
Garston 48 D4
Garswood 48 E3
Gartachoil 74 D1
Gartally 88 B1
Gartavaich 73 G5
Gartbreck 72 A5
Gartcosh 74 E4
Garth *Bridgend* 18 B2
Garth *Gwyn.* 46 D5
Garth *I.o.M.* 54 C6
Garth *Powys* 27 J4
Garth *Shet.* 109 B7
Garth *Wrex.* 38 B1
Garthbrengy 27 K5
Gartheli 26 E3
Garthmyl 38 A6
Garthorpe *Leics.* 42 B3
Garthorpe *N.Lincs.* 52 B1
Garths 61 G7
Garthynty 27 G4
Gartincaber 81 H7
Gartly 90 D1
Gartmore 74 D1
Gartnagrenach 73 F5
Gartnatra 72 B5
Gartness 74 D2
Gartocharn 74 C2
Garton 59 J6
Garton-on-the-Wolds 59 F3
Gartymore 105 F7
Garvald 76 D3
Garvamore 88 C5
Garvan 87 F7
Garvard 72 B1
Garve 95 K5
Garveld 66 A3
Garvestone 44 E5
Garvie 73 J2
Garvock *Aber.* 91 F7
Garvock *Inclyde* 74 A3
Garvock *P. & K.* 82 B6
Garwald 69 H3
Garwaldwaterfoot 69 H3
Garway 28 D6
Garway Hill 28 D6
Gask *Aber.* 99 J6
Gask *Aber.* 99 F6
Gask *P. & K.* 82 A6
Gaskan 86 E7
Gass 67 J3
Gastard 20 B5
Gasthorpe 44 D7
Gatcombe 11 F6
Gate Burton 52 B4
Gate Helmsley 58 C4
Gate House 72 D3
Gateacre 48 D4
Gatebeck 55 J1
Gateford 51 H4
Gateforth 58 B7
Gatehead 74 B7
Gatehouse 81 K3
Gatehouse of Fleet 65 G5
Gatelawbridge 68 E4
Gateley 44 D3
Gatenby 57 J1
Gateshaw 70 C1
Gateshead 71 H7
Gatesheath 48 D6
Gateside *Aber.* 90 E3
Gateside *Angus* 83 F3
Gateside *Fife* 82 C7
Gateside *N.Ayr.* 74 B5
Gateslack 68 D3
Gathurst 48 E2
Gatley 49 H4
Gattonside 76 D7
Gatwick Airport 23 F7
Gaufron 27 J2
Gaulby 41 J5
Gauldry 82 E5
Gaunt's Common 10 B4
Gautby 52 E5
Gavinton 77 F5
Gawber 51 F2
Gawcott 31 H5
Gawsworth 49 H6
Gawthrop 56 B1
Gawthwaite 55 F1
Gay Street 12 D4
Gaydon 30 E3
Gayhurst 32 B4
Gayles 62 C6
Gayton *Mersey.* 48 B4
Gayton *Norf.* 44 B4
Gayton *Northants.* 31 J3
Gayton *Staffs.* 40 B3
Gayton le Marsh 53 H4
Gayton le Wold 53 F4
Gayton Thorpe 44 B4
Gaywood 44 A3
Gazeley 34 B2
Geanies House 97 F4
Gearach 72 A5
Gearnsary 104 C5
Gearradh 80 A1
Gearraidh Bhailteas 84 C2
Gearraidh Bhaird 101 F5
Gearraidh na h-Aibhne (Garrynahine) 100 E4
Gearraidh na Monadh 84 C3
Gearrannan 100 D3
Geary 93 H5
Gedding 34 D3
Geddington 42 B7
Gedgrave Hall 35 J4
Gedling 41 J1
Gedney 43 H3
Gedney Broadgate 43 H3
Gedney Drove End 43 H3
Gedney Dyke 43 H3
Gedney Hill 43 G4
Gee Cross 49 J3
Geirninis 92 C7
Geisiadar 100 D4
Geldeston 45 H6
Gell *Conwy* 47 G6
Gell *Gwyn.* 36 D2
Gelli Gynan 47 K7
Gelligaer 18 E2
Gellilydan 37 F2
Gellioedd 37 J1
Gelly 16 D4
Gellyburn 82 B4
Gellywen 17 F3
Gelston 65 H5
Gembling 59 H4
Gemmil 79 J7
Genoch 64 B5
Genoch Square 64 B5
Gentleshaw 40 C4
George Green 22 D3
George Nympton 7 F3
Georgeham 6 C2
Georgetown 74 C4
Gerlan 46 E6
Germansweek 6 C6
Germoe 2 C6
Gerrans 3 F5
Gerrards Cross 22 C3
Gerston 105 G3
Gestingthorpe 34 C5
Geuffordd 38 B4
Geufron 37 H7
Gibbshill 65 H3
Gibraltar 53 J7
Gidea Park 23 J3
Gidleigh 6 E7
Giffnock 74 D5
Gifford 76 D4
Giffordland 74 A6
Giggleswick 56 D3
Gilberdyke 58 E7
Gilchriston 76 C4
Gilcrux 60 C3
Gildersome 57 H7
Gildingwells 51 H4
Gileston 18 D5
Gilfach 18 E2
Gilfach Goch 18 C3
Gilfachrheda 26 D3
Gilgarran 60 B4
Gillamoor 63 H7
Gillen 93 H5
Gillenbie 69 G5
Gillfoot 65 K3
Gilling East 58 C2
Gilling West 62 C6
Gillingham *Dorset* 9 H2
Gillingham *Med.* 24 D5
Gillingham *Norf.* 45 J6
Gillivoan 105 G5
Gillock 105 H3
Gillow Heath 49 H7
Gills 105 J1
Gill's Green 14 C4
Gilmanscleuch 69 J1
Gilmerton *Edin.* 76 A4
Gilmerton *P. & K.* 81 K5
Gilmilnscroft 67 K1
Gilmonby 62 A5
Gilmorton 41 H7
Gilsland 70 B7
Gilsland Spa 70 B7
Gilston 76 C5
Gilston Park 33 H7
Gilwern 28 B7
Gimingham 45 G2
Giosla 100 D5
Gipping 34 E2
Gipsey Bridge 43 F1
Girlsta 109 D7
Girsby 62 E6
Girtford 32 E4
Girthon 65 G5
Girton *Cambs.* 33 H2
Girton *Notts.* 52 B6
Girvan 67 F4
Gisburn 56 D5
Gisleham 45 K7
Gislingham 34 E1
Gissing 45 F7
Gittisham 7 K6
Givons Grove 22 E6
Glackour 95 H3
Gladestry 28 B3
Gladsmuir 76 C3
Glaic 73 J3
Glais 18 A1
Glaisdale 63 J6
Glaister 73 H7
Glame 94 B7
Glamis 82 E3
Glan Conwy 47 G7
Glan Honddu 27 K5
Glanaber Terrace 37 G1
Glanadda 46 D5
Glanaman 17 K4
Glanbran 27 G5
Glanderston 90 D2
Glandford 44 E1
Glandwr *B.Gwent* 19 F1
Glandwr *Pembs.* 16 E3
Glan-Dwyfach 36 D1
Glangrwyne 28 B7
Glanllynfi 18 B2
Glanmule 38 A6
Glanrhyd 16 E1
Glanton 71 F2
Glantwymyn (Cemmaes Road) 37 H5
Glanvilles Wootton 9 F4
Glan-y-don 47 K5
Glan-y-llyn 18 E3
Glan-yr-afon *Gwyn.* 37 J1
Glan-yr-afon *Gwyn.* 37 K1
Glan-y-Wern 37 F2
Glapthorn 42 D7
Glapwell 51 G6
Glasahoile 81 F7
Glasbury 28 A5
Glaschoil 89 H1
Glascoed 19 G1
Glascorrie 90 B5
Glascote 40 E5
Glascwm 28 A3
Glasdrum 80 B3
Glasfryn 47 H7
Glasgow 74 D4
Glasgow Airport 74 C4
Glasgow Prestwick International Airport 67 H1
Glashmore 91 F4
Glasinfryn 46 D6
Glasnacardoch 86 C5
Glasnakille 86 B3
Glaspant 17 F2
Glaspwll 37 G6
Glassburn 87 K1
Glassel 90 E5
Glassenbury 14 C4
Glasserton 64 E7
Glassford 75 F6
Glasshouse Hill 29 G6
Glasshouses 57 G3
Glassingall 81 J7
Glasslie 82 D7
Glasson *Cumb.* 69 H7
Glasson *Lancs.* 55 H4
Glassonby 61 G3
Glasterlaw 83 G2
Glaston 42 B5
Glastonbury 8 D1
Glatton 42 E7
Glazebury 49 F3
Glazeley 39 G7
Gleadless 51 F4
Gleadsmoss 49 H6
Gleann Ghrabhair 101 F5
Gleann Tholastaidh 101 H3
Gleaston 55 F2
Glecknabae 73 J4
Gledhow 57 J6
Gledrid 38 B2
Glemsford 34 C4
Glen *D. & G.* 65 J3
Glen *D. & G.* 65 F5
Glen Auldyn 54 D4
Glen Parva 41 H6
Glen Trool Lodge 67 J5
Glen Vine 54 C6
Glenae 68 E5
Glenaladale 86 E7
Glenald 74 A1
Glenamachrie 80 A5
Glenapp Castle 66 E5
Glenarm 82 E1
Glenbarr 72 E7
Glenbatrick 72 D3
Glenbeg *High.* 95 K3
Glenbeg *High.* 89 H2
Glenbeg *High.* 79 G1
Glenbeich 81 H5
Glenbervie *Aber.* 91 F6
Glenbervie *Falk.* 75 G2
Glenboig 75 F4
Glenborrodale 79 H1
Glenbranter 73 K1
Glenbreck 69 F1
Glenbrittle 85 K2
Glenbuck 68 C1
Glenbyre 79 G5
Glencaple 65 K4
Glencarse 82 C5
Glencat 90 D5
Glenceitlein 80 C3
Glencloy 73 J7
Glencoe 80 C2
Glenconglass 89 J2
Glencraig 75 K1
Glencripesdale 79 H2
Glencrosh 68 C5
Glencruittein 79 K5
Glencuie 90 C3
Glendearg *D. & G.* 69 H3
Glendearg *Sc.Bord.* 76 D7
Glendessary 87 F5
Glendevon 82 A7
Glendoebeg 88 B4
Glendoick 82 D5
Glendoll Lodge 89 K7
Glendoune 67 F4
Glendrissaig 67 F4
Glenduckie 82 D6
Glenduisk 67 G5
Glendye Lodge 90 E6
Gleneagles Hotel 82 A6
Gleneagles House 82 A7
Glenearn 82 C6
Glenegedale 72 B5
Glenelg 86 E3
Glenfarg 82 C6
Glenfeochan 79 K5
Glenfield 41 H5
Glenfinnan 87 F6
Glenfoot 82 C6
Glengalmadale 79 K2
Glengap 65 G5
Glengarnock 74 B5
Glengarrisdale 72 E1
Glengennet 67 G4
Glengolly 105 G2
Glengrasco 93 K7
Glengyle 80 E6
Glenhead 68 D5
Glenhead Farm 82 D1
Glenhurich 79 K1
Glenkerry 69 H2
Glenkiln 73 J7
Glenkin 73 K3
Glenkindie 90 C3
Glenlair 65 H3
Glenlatterach 97 K6
Glenlean 73 J2
Glenlee *Angus* 90 C6
Glenlee *D. & G.* 68 B5
Glenlichorn 81 J6
Glenlivet 89 J2
Glenlochar 65 H4
Glenluce 64 B5
Glenmallan 74 A1
Glenmanna 68 C3
Glenmavis 75 F4
Glenmaye 54 B5
Glenmeanie 95 J6
Glenmore *Arg. & B.* 73 J4
Glenmore *High.* 93 K7
Glenmore Lodge 89 G4
Glenmoy 83 F1
Glenmuick 103 F7
Glennoe 80 B4
Glenochar 68 E2
Glenogil 83 F1
Glenprosen Village 83 E1
Glenquiech 83 F1
Glenramskill 66 B2
Glenrazie 64 D4
Glenridding 60 E5
Glenrisdell 73 G5
Glenrossal 96 B1
Glenrothes 82 D7
Glensanda 79 K3
Glensaugh 90 E7
Glensgaich 96 B5
Glenshalg 90 D4
Glenshellish 73 K1
Glensluain 73 J1
Glentaggart 68 D1
Glentham 52 D3
Glenton 90 E2
Glentress 76 A7
Glentrool 64 D3
Glentruan 54 D3
Glentworth 52 C4
Glenuachdarach 93 K6
Glenuig 86 C7
Glenure 80 B3
Glenurquhart 96 E5
Glenwhilly 64 B3
Glespin 68 D1
Gletness 109 D7
Glewstone 28 E6
Glinton 42 E5
Glooston 42 A6
Glororum 77 K7
Glossop 50 C3
Gloster Hill 71 H3
Gloucester 29 H7
Gloup 108 E2
Gloweth 2 E4
Glusburn 57 F5
Gluss 108 C5
Glympton 31 F6
Glyn 47 F7
Glyn Ceiriog 38 B2
Glynarthen 17 G1
Glyncoch 18 D2
Glyncorrwg 18 B2
Glyn-Cywarch 37 F2
Glynde 13 H6
Glyndebourne 13 H5
Glyndyfrdwy 38 A1
Glynneath 18 B1
Glynogwr 18 C3
Glyntaff 18 D3
Glynteg 17 G2
Gnosall 40 A3
Gnosall Heath 40 A4
Goadby 42 A6
Goadby Marwood 42 A3
Goatacre 20 D4
Goatfield 80 B7
Goathill 9 F3
Goathland 63 K6
Goathurst 8 B1
Gobernuisgeach 104 E5
Gobhaig 100 C7
Gobowen 38 B2
Godalming 22 C7
Godford Cross 7 K5
Godmanchester 33 F2
Godmanstone 9 F5
Godmersham 15 F2
Godolphin Cross 2 D5
Godor 38 B4
Godre'r-graig 18 A1
Godshill *Hants.* 10 C3
Godshill *I.o.W.* 11 G6
Godstone 23 G6
Goetre 19 G1
Goff's Oak 23 G1
Gogar 75 K3
Gogarth 47 F4
Goginan 37 F7
Goirtean a' Chladaich 87 G7
Goirtein 73 H2
Golan 36 E1
Golant 4 B5
Golberdon 4 D3
Golborne 49 F3
Golcar 50 D1
Gold Hill 43 J6
Goldcliff 19 G3
Golden Cross 13 J5
Golden Green 23 K7
Golden Grove 17 J4
Golden Pot 22 A7
Golden Valley 29 J6
Goldenhill 49 H7
Golders Green 23 F3
Goldhanger 24 E1
Goldielea 65 K3
Golding 38 E5
Goldington 32 D3
Goldsborough *N.Yorks.* 63 K5
Goldsborough *N.Yorks.* 57 J4
Goldsithney 2 C5
Goldthorpe 51 G2
Goldworthy 6 B3
Gollanfield 97 F6
Golspie 97 F2
Golval 104 D2
Gomeldon 10 C1
Gomersal 57 H7
Gometra House 78 E3
Gomshall 22 D7
Gonachan Cottage 74 E2
Gonalston 41 J1
Gonfirth 109 C6
Good Easter 33 K7
Gooderstone 44 B5
Goodleigh 6 E2
Goodmanham 58 E5
Goodnestone *Kent* 15 H2
Goodnestone *Kent* 25 G5
Goodrich 28 E7
Goodrington 5 J5
Goodwick (Wdig) 16 C2
Goodworth Clatford 21 G7
Goodyers End 41 F7
Goole 58 D7
Goonbell 2 E4
Goonhavern 2 E3
Goose Green 23 K6
Gooseham 6 A4
Goosewell 5 F5
Goosey 21 G2
Goosnargh 55 J6
Goostrey 49 G5
Gorcott Hill 30 B2
Gorddinog 46 E5
Gordon 76 E6
Gordonbush 97 F1
Gordonstoun 97 J5
Gordonstown *Aber.* 98 D5
Gordonstown *Aber.* 91 F1
Gore Cross 20 D6
Gore Street 25 J5
Gorebridge 76 B4
Gorefield 43 H4
Gorey 3 K7
Goring 21 K3
Goring-by-Sea 12 E6
Gorleston on Sea 45 K5
Gorllwyn 17 G2
Gornalwood 40 B6
Gorrachie 99 F5
Gorran Churchtown 3 G4
Gorran Haven 4 A6
Gors 27 F1
Gorsedd 47 K5
Gorseinon 17 J6
Gorseness 107 D6
Gorsgoch 26 D3
Gorslas 17 J4
Gorsley 29 F6
Gorsley Common 29 F6
Gorstan 95 K5
Gorstanvorran 86 E7
Gorten 79 J4
Gortenbuie 79 G4
Gorteneorn 79 H1
Gorton *Arg. & B.* 78 C2
Gorton *Gt.Man.* 49 H3
Gosbeck 35 F3
Gosberton 43 F2
Goseley Dale 41 F3
Gosfield 34 B6
Gosforth *Cumb.* 60 B6
Gosforth *T. & W.* 71 H7
Gosmore 32 E6
Gospel End 40 B6
Gosport 11 H5
Gossabrough 108 E4
Gossops Green 13 F3
Goswick 77 J6
Gotham 41 H2
Gotherington 29 J6
Gott 109 D8
Goudhurst 14 C4
Goulceby 53 F5
Gourdas 99 F6
Gourdon 91 G7
Gourock 74 A3
Govan 74 D4
Goveton 5 H6
Govilon 28 B7
Gowanhill 99 J4
Gowdall 58 C7
Gowerton 17 J6
Gowkhall 75 J2
Gowthorpe 58 D4
Goxhill *E.Riding* 59 H5
Goxhill *N.Lincs.* 59 H7
Goytre 18 A3
Grabhair 101 F6
Gradbach 49 J6
Grade 2 E7
Graffham 12 C5
Grafham *Cambs.* 32 E2
Grafham *Surr.* 22 D7
Grafton *Here.* 28 D5
Grafton *N.Yorks.* 57 K3
Grafton *Oxon.* 21 F1
Grafton *Shrop.* 38 D4
Grafton *Worcs.* 28 E2
Grafton Flyford 29 J3
Grafton Regis 31 J4
Grafton Underwood 32 C1
Grafty Green 14 D3
Graianrhyd 48 B7
Graig *Conwy* 47 G5
Graig *Denb.* 47 J5
Graig Penllyn 18 C4
Graig-fechan 47 K7
Grain 24 E4
Grainel 72 A4
Grainhow 99 G6
Grainsby 53 F3
Grainthorpe 53 G3
Graiselound 51 K3
Grampound 3 G4
Grampound Road 3 G3
Gramsdal 92 D6
Granborough 31 J6
Granby 42 A2
Grandborough 31 F2
Grandtully 82 A2
Grange *Cumb.* 60 D5
Grange *High.* 87 K1
Grange *Med.* 24 D5
Grange *N.Yorks.* 63 G7
Grange *P. & K.* 82 D5
Grange Crossroads 98 C5
Grange Hall 97 H5
Grange Hill 23 H2
Grange Moor 50 E1
Grange of Lindores 82 D6
Grange Villa 62 D1
Grangemill 50 E7
Grangemouth 75 H2
Grangemuir 83 G7
Grange-over-Sands 55 H2
Grangeston 67 G4
Grangetown *Cardiff* 18 E4
Grangetown *R. & C.* 63 G4
Granish 89 G3
Gransmoor 59 H4
Granston 16 B2
Grantchester 33 H3
Grantham 42 C2
Grantley 57 H2
Grantlodge 91 F3
Granton House 69 F3
Grantown-on-Spey 89 H2
Grantshouse 77 G4
Grappenhall 49 F4
Grasby 52 D2
Grasmere 60 E6
Grasscroft 49 J2
Grassendale 48 C4
Grassholme 62 A4
Grassington 57 F3
Grassmoor 51 G6
Grassthorpe 51 K6
Grateley 21 F7
Gratwich 40 C2
Graveley *Cambs.* 33 F2
Graveley *Herts.* 33 F6
Gravelly Hill 40 D6
Gravels 38 C5
Graven 108 D5
Graveney 25 G5
Gravesend 24 C4
Grayingham 52 C3
Grayrigg 61 G7
Grays 24 C4
Grayshott 12 B3
Grayswood 12 C3
Grazeley 22 A5
Greasbrough 51 G3
Greasby 48 B4
Great Abington 33 J4
Great Addington 32 C1
Great Alne 30 C3
Great Altcar 48 C2
Great Amwell 33 G7
Great Asby 61 H5
Great Ashfield 34 D2
Great Ayton 63 G5
Great Baddow 24 D1
Great Bardfield 33 K5
Great Barford 32 E3
Great Barr 40 C6
Great Barrington 30 D7
Great Barrow 48 D6
Great Barton 34 C2
Great Barugh 58 D2
Great Bavington 70 E5
Great Bealings 35 G4
Great Bedwyn 21 F5
Great Bentley 35 F6
Great Billing 32 B2
Great Bircham 44 B2
Great Blakenham 35 F3
Great Bolas 39 F3
Great Bookham 22 E6
Great Bourton 31 F4
Great Bowden 42 A7
Great Bradley 33 K3
Great Braxted 34 C7
Great Bricett 34 E3
Great Brickhill 32 C5
Great Bridgeford 40 A3
Great Brington 31 H2
Great Bromley 34 E6
Great Broughton *Cumb.* 60 B3
Great Broughton *N.Yorks.* 63 G6
Great Budworth 49 F5
Great Burdon 62 E5
Great Burstead 24 C2
Great Busby 63 G6
Great Canfield 33 J7
Great Canney 24 E1
Great Carlton 53 H4
Great Casterton 42 D5
Great Chart 14 E3
Great Chatwell 39 G4
Great Chesterford 33 J4
Great Cheverell 20 C6
Great Chishill 33 H5
Great Clacton 35 F7
Great Clifton 60 B4
Great Coates 53 F2
Great Comberton 29 J4
Great Corby 61 F1
Great Cornard 34 C4
Great Cowden 59 J5
Great Coxwell 21 F2
Great Crakehall 62 D7
Great Cransley 32 B1
Great Cressingham 44 C5
Great Crosby 48 C2
Great Cubley 40 D2
Great Dalby 42 A4
Great Doddington 32 B2
Great Dunham 44 C4
Great Dunmow 33 K6
Great Durnford 10 C1
Great Easton *Essex* 33 K6
Great Easton *Leics.* 42 B6
Great Eccleston 55 H5
Great Edstone 58 D1
Great Ellingham 44 E6
Great Elm 20 A7
Great Eversden 33 G3
Great Fencote 62 D7
Great Finborough 34 E3
Great Fransham 44 C4
Great Gaddesden 32 D7
Great Gidding 42 E7
Great Givendale 58 E4
Great Glemham 35 H2
Great Glen 41 J6
Great Gonerby 42 B2
Great Gransden 33 F3
Great Green *Norf.* 45 G6
Great Green *Suff.* 34 D3
Great Habton 58 D2
Great Hale 42 E1
Great Hallingbury 33 J7
Great Harrowden 32 B1
Great Harwood 56 C6
Great Haseley 21 K1
Great Hatfield 59 H5
Great Haywood 40 C3
Great Heath 41 F7
Great Heck 58 B7
Great Henny 34 C5
Great Hinton 20 C6
Great Hockham 44 D6
Great Holland 35 G7
Great Horkesley 34 D5
Great Hormead 33 H5
Great Horwood 31 J5
Great Houghton *Northants.* 31 J3
Great Houghton *S.Yorks.* 51 G2
Great Hucklow 50 D5
Great Kelk 59 H4
Great Kimble 22 B1
Great Kingshill 22 B2
Great Langton 62 D7
Great Leighs 34 B7
Great Limber 52 E2
Great Linford 32 B4
Great Livermere 34 C1
Great Longstone 50 E5
Great Lumley 62 D2
Great Lyth 38 D5
Great Malvern 29 G4
Great Maplestead 34 C5
Great Marton 55 G6
Great Massingham 44 B3
Great Melton 45 F5
Great Milton 21 K1
Great Missenden 22 B1
Great Mitton 56 C6
Great Mongeham 15 J2
Great Moulton 45 F6
Great Munden 33 G6
Great Musgrave 61 J5
Great Ness 38 C4
Great Notley 34 B6
Great Oak 28 C7
Great Oakley *Essex* 35 F6
Great Oakley *Northants.* 42 B7
Great Offley 32 E6
Great Ormside 61 J5
Great Orton 60 E1
Great Ouseburn 57 K3
Great Oxendon 42 A7
Great Oxney Green 24 C1
Great Palgrave 44 C4
Great Parndon 23 H1
Great Paxton 33 F2
Great Plumpton 55 G6
Great Plumstead 45 G5
Great Ponton 42 C2
Great Preston 57 J7
Great Raveley 43 F7
Great Rissington 30 C7

Great Rollright 30 E5
Great Ryburgh 44 D3
Great Ryle 71 F2
Great Ryton 38 D5
Great Saling 33 K6
Great Salkeld 61 G3
Great Sampford 33 K5
Great Sankey 48 E4
Great Saxham 34 B2
Great Shefford 21 G4
Great Shelford 33 H3
Great Smeaton 62 E6
Great Snoring 44 D2
Great Somerford 20 C3
Great Stainton 62 E4
Great Stambridge 24 E2
Great Staughton 32 E2
Great Steeping 53 H6
Great Stonar 15 J2
Great Strickland 61 G4
Great Stukeley 33 F1
Great Sturton 53 F5
Great Sutton Ches. 48 C5
Great Sutton Shrop. 38 E7
Great Swinburne 70 E6
Great Tew 30 E6
Great Tey 34 C6
Great Thurlow 33 K4
Great Torrington 6 D4
Great Tosson 71 F3
Great Totham Essex 34 C7
Great Totham Essex 34 C7
Great Urswick 55 F2
Great Wakering 25 F3
Great Waldingfield 34 D4
Great Walsingham 44 D2
Great Waltham 33 K7
Great Warley 23 J2
Great Washbourne 29 J5
Great Welnetham 34 C3
Great Wenham 34 E5
Great Whittington 71 F6
Great Wigborough 34 D7
Great Wilbraham 33 J3
Great Wishford 10 B1
Great Witcombe 29 J7
Great Witley 29 G2
Great Wolford 30 D5
Great Wratting 33 K4
Great Wymondley 33 F6
Great Wyrley 40 B5
Great Wytheford 38 E4
Great Yarmouth 45 K5
Great Yeldham 34 B5
Greatford 42 D4
Greatgate 40 C1
Greatham Hants. 11 J1
Greatham Hart. 63 F4
Greatham W.Suss. 12 D5
Greatstone-on-Sea 15 F5
Greatworth 31 G4
Green End Beds. 32 E3
Green End Herts. 33 G6
Green Hammerton 57 K4
Green Ore 19 J6
Green Street 22 E2
Green Street Green Gt.Lon. 23 H5
Green Street Green Kent 23 J4
Green Tye 33 H7
Greenburn 83 F4
Greencroft 62 C2
Greendams 90 E5
Greendykes 71 F1
Greenfield Beds. 32 D5
Greenfield (Maes-Glas) Flints. 47 K5
Greenfield Gt.Man. 50 C2
Greenfield High. 87 J4
Greenfield Oxon. 22 A2
Greenford 22 E3
Greengairs 75 F3
Greenhalgh 55 H6
Greenhall 90 E2
Greenham Som. 7 J3
Greenham W.Berks. 21 H5
Greenhaugh 70 C5
Greenhead 70 B7
Greenheads 91 J1
Greenhill Gt.Lon. 22 E3
Greenhill High. 97 G1
Greenhill S.Yorks. 51 F4
Greenhithe 23 J4
Greenholm 74 D7
Greenholme 61 G6
Greenhow Hill 57 G3
Greenigo 107 D7
Greenland 105 H2
Greenlands 22 A3
Greenlaw Aber. 98 E5
Greenlaw Sc.Bord. 77 F6
Greenloaning 81 K7
Greenmount 49 G1
Greenmyre 91 G1
Greenock 74 A3
Greenodd 55 G1
Greens Norton 31 H3
Greenscares 81 J6
Greenside 71 G7
Greensted Green 34 C6
Greensted 23 J1
Greenway Pembs. 16 D2
Greenway Som. 8 C2
Greenwich Gt.Lon. 23 G4
Greenwich Gt.Lon. 23 G4
Greet 30 B5
Greete 28 E1
Greetham Lincs. 53 G5
Greetham Rut. 42 C4
Greetland 57 F7
Greinetobht 92 D4
Greinton 8 D1
Grenaby 54 B6
Grendon Northants. 32 B2
Grendon Warks. 40 E6
Grendon Common 40 E6
Grendon Green 28 E3
Grendon Underwood 31 H6
Grenoside 51 F3
Greosabhagh 93 G2
Gresford 48 C7
Gresham 45 F2
Greshornish 93 J6
Gressenhall 44 D4
Gressingham 55 J2
Greta Bridge 62 B5
Gretna 69 J7
Gretna Green 69 J7
Gretton Glos. 30 B5
Gretton Northants. 42 C6
Gretton Shrop. 38 E6
Grewelthorpe 57 H2
Greygarth 57 G2
Greylake 8 C1
Greys Green 22 A3
Greysouthen 60 B4
Greystoke 61 F3
Greystone Aber. 89 K5
Greystone Angus 83 G3
Greystone Lancs. 56 D5
Greywell 22 A6
Griais 101 G3
Gribthorpe 58 D6
Gribton 68 E5
Gridley Corner 6 B6
Griff 41 F7
Griffithstown 19 F2
Grigadale 79 F1
Grigghall 61 F7
Grimeford Village 49 F1
Grimethorpe 51 G2
Griminis 92 C6
Grimister 108 D3
Grimley 29 H2
Grimmet 67 H2
Grimness 107 D8
Grimoldby 53 G4
Grimpo 38 C3
Grimsargh 55 J6
Grimsbury 31 F4
Grimsby 53 F2
Grimscote 31 H3
Grimscott 6 A5
Grimsiadar 101 G5
Grimsthorpe 42 D3
Grimston Leics. 41 J3
Grimston Norf. 44 B3
Grimstone 9 F5
Grindale 59 H2
Grindiscol 109 D9
Grindle 39 G5
Grindleford 50 E5
Grindleton 56 C5
Grindley 40 C3
Grindlow 50 D5
Grindon Northumb. 77 H6
Grindon Staffs. 50 C7
Gringley on the Hill 51 K3
Grinsdale 60 E1
Grinshill 38 E3
Grinton 62 B7
Griomarstaidh 100 E4
Grishipoll 78 C2
Gristhorpe 59 G1
Griston 44 D6
Gritley 107 E7
Grittenham 20 D3
Grittleton 20 B3
Grizebeck 55 F1
Grizedale 60 E7
Grobister 106 F5
Groby 41 H5
Groes 47 J6
Groes-faen 18 D3
Groesffordd 36 B2
Groesffordd Marli 47 J5
Groeslon 46 C7
Groes-lwyd 38 B4
Grogport 73 G6
Groigearraidh 84 C1
Gromford 35 H3
Gronant 47 J4
Groombridge 13 J3
Grosmont Mon. 28 D6
Grosmont N.Yorks. 63 K6
Grotaig 88 B2
Groton 34 D4
Groundistone Heights 69 K2
Grouville 3 K7
Grove Dorset 9 F7
Grove Kent 25 J5
Grove Notts. 51 K5
Grove Oxon. 21 H2
Grove Park 23 H4
Grovesend 17 J5
Gruids 96 C1
Gruinart Flats 72 A4
Gruline 79 G4
Grundcruie 82 B5
Grundisburgh 35 G3
Gruting 109 B8
Grutness 109 G10
Gualachulain 80 C3
Guardbridge 83 F6
Guarlford 29 H4
Guay 82 B3
Gubbergill 60 B7
Guernsey Airport 3 H5
Guestling Green 14 D6
Guestling Thorn 14 D6
Guestwick 44 E3
Guide Post 71 H5
Guilden Morden 33 F4
Guilden Sutton 48 D6
Guildford 22 C7
Guildtown 82 C4
Guilsborough 31 H1
Guilsfield (Cegidfa) 38 B4
Guisborough 63 H5
Guiseley 57 G5
Guist 44 D3
Guith 106 E4
Guiting Power 30 B6
Gulberwick 109 D9
Gullane 76 C2
Gulval 2 B5
Gulworthy 4 E3
Gumfreston 16 E5
Gumley 41 J7
Gunby E.Riding 58 D6
Gunby Lincs. 42 C3
Gundleton 11 H1
Gunn 6 E2
Gunnerside 62 A7
Gunnerton 70 E6
Gunness 52 B1
Gunnislake 4 E3
Gunnista 109 D8
Gunter's Bridge 12 C4
Gunthorpe Norf. 44 E2
Gunthorpe Notts. 41 J1
Gunville 11 F6
Gunwalloe 2 D6
Gurnard 11 F5
Gurney Slade 19 K7
Gurnos 18 A1
Gussage All Saints 10 B3
Gussage St. Michael 9 J3
Guston 15 J3
Gutcher 108 E3
Guthrie 83 G2
Guyhirn 43 G5
Guynd 83 G3
Guy's Head 43 H3
Guy's Marsh 9 H2
Guyzance 71 H3
Gwaelod-y-garth 18 E3
Gwaenysgor 47 J4
Gwaithla 28 B3
Gwalchmai 46 B5
Gwaun-Cae-Gurwen 27 G7
Gwaynynog 47 J6
Gwbert 16 E1
Gweek 2 E6
Gwehelog 19 G1
Gwenddwr 27 K4
Gwennap 2 E4
Gwenter 2 E7
Gwernaffield 48 B6
Gwernesney 19 H1
Gwernogle 17 J2
Gwernymynydd 48 B6
Gwersyllt 48 C7
Gwespyr 47 K4
Gwinear 2 C5
Gwithian 2 C4
Gwyddelwern 37 K1
Gwyddgrug 17 H2
Gwystre 27 K2
Gwytherin 47 G6
Gyfelia 38 C1
Gyffin 47 F5
Gyre 107 C7
Gyrn Goch 36 D1

H

Habberley 38 C5
Habrough 52 E1
Haccombe 5 J3
Hacconby 42 E3
Haceby 42 D2
Hacheston 35 H3
Hackenthorpe 51 G4
Hackford 44 E5
Hackforth 62 D7
Hackland 106 C5
Hackleton 32 B3
Hacklinge 15 J2
Hackness N.Yorks. 63 J3
Hackness Ork. 107 C8
Hackney 23 G3
Hackthorn 52 C4
Hackthorpe 61 G4
Hadden 77 F7
Haddenham Bucks. 22 A1
Haddenham Cambs. 33 H1
Haddington E.Loth. 76 D3
Haddington Lincs. 52 C6
Haddiscoe 45 J6
Haddon 42 E6
Hademore 40 D5
Hadfield 50 C3
Hadham Cross 33 H7
Hadham Ford 33 H6
Hadleigh Essex 24 E3
Hadleigh Suff. 34 E4
Hadley 39 F4
Hadley End 40 D3
Hadley Wood 23 F2
Hadlow 23 K7
Hadlow Down 13 J4
Hadnall 38 E3
Hadstock 33 J4
Hadzor 29 J2
Haffenden Quarter 14 D3
Hafod-Dinbych 47 G7
Hafodunos 47 G6
Haggate 56 D6
Haggbeck 69 K6
Haggs 75 F3
Hagley Here. 28 E4
Hagley Worcs. 40 B7
Hagnaby 53 G6
Hagworthingham 53 G6
Haigh 49 F2
Haighton Green 55 J6
Hail Weston 32 E2
Haile 60 B6
Hailes 30 B5
Hailey Herts. 33 G7
Hailey Oxon. 21 K3
Hailey Oxon. 30 E7
Hailsham 13 J6
Haimer 105 G2
Hainault 23 H2
Hainford 45 G4
Hainton 52 E4
Haisthorpe 59 H3
Halam 51 J7
Halbeath 75 K2
Halberton 7 J4
Halcro 105 H2
Hale Gt.Man. 49 G4
Hale Hants. 10 C3
Hale Surr. 22 B7
Hale Bank 48 D4
Hale Street 23 K7
Halebarns 49 G4
Hales Norf. 45 H6
Hales Staffs. 39 G2
Hales Place 15 G2
Halesowen 40 B7
Halesworth 35 H1
Halewood 48 D4
Half Way Inn 7 J6
Halford Shrop. 38 D7
Halford Warks. 30 D4
Halfpenny Green 40 A6
Halfway Carmar. 17 K2
Halfway Powys 27 H5
Halfway S.Yorks. 51 G4
Halfway W.Berks. 21 H5
Halfway House 38 C4
Halfway Houses 25 F4
Halghton Mill 38 D1
Halifax 57 F7
Halistra 93 H6
Halkirk 105 G3
Halkyn 48 B5
Hall 74 C5
Hall Dunnerdale 60 D7
Hall Green 40 D7
Hall of the Forest 38 B7
Halland 13 J5
Hallaton 42 A6
Hallatrow 19 K6
Hallbankgate 61 G1
Hallen 19 J4
Hallin 93 H6
Halling 24 D5
Hallington Lincs. 53 G4
Hallington Northumb. 70 E6
Halloughton 51 J7
Hallow 29 H3
Hallow Heath 29 H3
Hallrule 70 A2
Halls 76 E3
Hall's Green 33 F6
Hall's Tenement 61 G1
Hallsands 5 J7
Hallworthy 4 B2
Halmer End 39 G1
Halmore 19 K1
Halmyre Mains 75 K6
Halnaker 12 C6
Halsall 48 C1
Halse Northants. 31 G4
Halse Som. 7 K3
Halsetown 2 C5
Halsham 59 J7
Halsinger 6 D2
Halstead Essex 34 C5
Halstead Kent 23 H5
Halstead Leics. 42 A5
Halstock 8 E4
Haltham 53 F6
Haltoft End 43 G1
Halton Bucks. 32 B7
Halton Halton 48 E4
Halton Lancs. 55 J3
Halton Northumb. 71 F7
Halton Wrex. 38 C2
Halton East 57 F4
Halton Gill 56 D2
Halton Holegate 53 H6
Halton Lea Gate 61 H1
Halton West 56 D4
Haltwhistle 70 C7
Halvergate 45 J5
Halwell 5 H5
Halwill 6 C6
Halwill Junction 6 C6
Ham Glos. 19 K2
Ham Gt.Lon. 22 E4
Ham High. 105 H1
Ham Kent 15 J2
Ham Shet. 108 B1
Ham Som. 8 B2
Ham Wilts. 21 G5
Ham Green N.Som. 19 J4
Ham Green Worcs. 30 B2
Ham Hill 24 C5
Ham Street 8 E1
Hambleden 22 A3
Hambledon Hants. 11 H3
Hambledon Surr. 12 C3
Hamble-le-Rice 11 F4
Hambleton Lancs. 55 G5
Hambleton N.Yorks. 58 B6
Hambleton Moss Side 55 G5
Hambridge 8 C2
Hambrook S.Glos. 19 K4
Hambrook W.Suss. 11 J4
Hameringham 53 G6
Hamerton 32 E1
Hamilton 75 F5
Hamlet 7 K6
Hammer 12 B3
Hammerpot 12 D6
Hammersmith 23 F4
Hammerwich 40 C5
Hammerwood 13 H3
Hammond Street 23 G1
Hammoon 9 H3
Hamnavoe Shet. 109 C9
Hamnavoe Shet. 108 D4
Hamnavoe Shet. 108 B4
Hamnavoe Shet. 108 D5
Hampden Park 13 K6
Hampnett 30 C7
Hampole 51 H2
Hampreston 10 B5
Hampstead 23 F3
Hampstead Norreys 21 J4
Hampsthwaite 57 H4
Hampton Gt.Lon. 22 E5
Hampton Shrop. 39 G7
Hampton Worcs. 30 B4
Hampton Bishop 28 E5
Hampton Heath 38 D1
Hampton in Arden 40 E7
Hampton Lovett 29 H2
Hampton Lucy 30 D3
Hampton on the Hill 30 D2
Hampton Poyle 31 G7
Hamptworth 10 D2
Hamsey 13 H5
Hamstall Ridware 40 D4
Hamstead I.o.W. 11 F5
Hamstead W.Mid. 40 C6
Hamstead Marshall 21 H5
Hamsterley Dur. 62 C3
Hamsterley Dur. 62 C1
Hamstreet 15 F4
Hamworthy 9 J5
Hanbury Staffs. 40 D3
Hanbury Worcs. 29 J2
Hanbury Woodend 40 D3
Hanchurch 40 A1
Handbridge 48 D6
Handcross 13 F4
Handforth 49 H4
Handley 48 D7
Handsacre 40 C4
Handsworth S.Yorks. 51 G4
Handsworth W.Mid. 40 C6
Handy Cross 22 B2
Hanford 40 A1
Hanging Bridge 40 D1
Hanging Langford 10 B1
Hangingshaw 69 G5
Hangleton 13 F6
Hanham 19 K4
Hankelow 39 F1
Hankerton 20 C2
Hankham 13 K6
Hanley 40 A1
Hanley Castle 29 H4
Hanley Child 29 F2
Hanley Swan 29 H4
Hanley William 29 F2
Hanlith 56 E3
Hanmer 38 D2
Hannah 53 H5
Hannington Hants. 21 J6
Hannington Northants. 32 B1
Hannington Swin. 20 E2
Hannington Wick 20 E2
Hanslope 32 B4
Hanthorpe 42 D3
Hanwell Gt.Lon. 22 E4
Hanwell Oxon. 31 F4
Hanwood 38 D5
Hanworth Gt.Lon. 22 E4
Hanworth Norf. 45 F2
Happisburgh 45 H2
Happisburgh Common 45 H3
Hapsford 48 D5
Hapton Lancs. 56 C6
Hapton Norf. 45 F6
Harberton 5 H5
Harbertonford 5 H5
Harbledown 15 G2
Harborne 40 C7
Harborough Magna 31 F1
Harbottle 70 E3
Harbourneford 5 H4
Harbridge 10 C3
Harburn 75 J4
Harbury 30 E3
Harby Leics. 42 A2
Harby Notts. 52 B5
Harcombe 7 K6
Harden 57 F6
Hardenhuish 20 C4
Hardgate 91 F4
Hardham 12 D5
Hardingham 44 E5
Hardings Wood 49 H7
Hardingstone 31 J3
Hardington 20 A6
Hardington Mandeville 8 E3
Hardington Marsh 8 E4
Hardley 11 F4
Hardley Street 45 H5
Hardmead 32 C4
Hardraw 61 K7
Hardstoft 51 G6
Hardway Hants. 11 H4
Hardway Som. 9 G1
Hardwick Bucks. 32 B7
Hardwick Cambs. 33 G3
Hardwick Norf. 45 G6
Hardwick Northants. 32 B2
Hardwick Oxon. 21 G1
Hardwick Oxon. 31 G6
Hardwick Village 51 J5
Hardwicke Glos. 29 J6
Hardwicke Glos. 29 G7
Hardwicke Here. 28 B4
Hardy's Green 34 D7
Hare Green 34 E6
Hare Hatch 22 B4
Hare Street Herts. 33 G6
Hare Street Herts. 33 G6
Hareby 53 G6
Hareden 56 B4
Harefield 22 D2
Harehills 57 J6
Harelaw 75 H6
Haresceugh 61 H2
Harescombe 29 H7
Haresfield 29 H7
Hareshaw 74 E6
Harewood 57 J5
Harewood End 28 E6
Harford 5 G5
Hargate 45 F6
Hargrave Ches. 48 D6
Hargrave Northants. 32 D1
Hargrave Suff. 34 B3
Harker 69 J7
Harkstead 35 F5
Harlaston 40 E4
Harlaxton 42 B2
Harle Syke 56 D6
Harlech 36 E2
Harlesden 23 F3
Harleston Norf. 45 G7
Harleston Suff. 34 E3
Harlestone 31 J2
Harley 38 E5
Harleyholm 75 H7
Harlington 32 D5
Harlosh 93 H7
Harlow 33 H7
Harlow Hill 71 F7
Harlthorpe 58 D6
Harlton 33 G3
Harman's Cross 9 J6
Harmby 62 C7
Harmer Green 33 F7
Harmer Hill 38 D3
Harmondsworth 22 D4
Harmston 52 C6
Harnham 10 C2
Harnhill 20 D1
Harold Hill 23 J2
Harold Wood 23 J2
Haroldston West 16 B4
Haroldswick 108 F1
Harome 58 C1
Harpenden 32 E7
Harpford 7 J6
Harpham 59 G3
Harpley Norf. 44 B3
Harpley Worcs. 29 F2
Harpole 31 H2
Harprigg 56 B1
Harpsdale 105 G3
Harpsden 22 A3
Harpswell 52 C3
Harpur Hill 50 C5
Harpurhey 49 H2
Harrapool 86 C2
Harrietfield 82 A4
Harrietsham 14 D2
Harrington Lincs. 53 G5
Harrington Northants. 31 J1
Harringworth 42 C6
Harris 85 J5
Harriseahead 49 H7
Harrogate 57 J4
Harrold 32 C3
Harrow Gt.Lon. 22 E3
Harrow High. 105 H1
Harrow on the Hill 22 E3
Harrow Weald 22 E2
Harrowbarrow 4 E3
Harrowden 32 D4
Harston Cambs. 33 H3
Harston Leics. 42 B2
Hart 63 F3
Hartburn Northumb. 71 F5
Hartburn Stock. 63 F5
Hartest 34 C3
Hartfield E.Suss. 13 H3
Hartfield High. 94 D7
Hartford Cambs. 33 F1
Hartford Ches. 49 F5
Hartford End 33 K7
Hartfordbridge 22 A6
Harthill Ches. 48 D7
Harthill N.Lan. 75 H4
Harthill S.Yorks. 51 G4
Hartington 50 D6
Hartland 6 A3
Hartland Quay 6 A3
Hartlebury 29 H1
Hartlepool 63 G3
Hartley Cumb. 61 J6
Hartley Kent 24 C5
Hartley Kent 14 C4
Hartley Northumb. 71 J6
Hartley Wespall 22 A6
Hartley Wintney 22 A6
Hartlip 24 E5
Harton N.Yorks. 58 D3
Harton Shrop. 38 D7
Harton T. & W. 71 J7
Hartpury 29 G6
Hartrigge 70 B1
Hartshill 41 F6
Hartshorne 41 F3
Hartsop 61 F5
Hartwell Bucks. 31 J7
Hartwell E.Suss. 13 H3
Hartwell Northants. 31 J4
Hartwood 75 G5
Harvel 24 C5
Harvington Worcs. 30 B4
Harvington Worcs. 29 H1
Harwell Notts. 51 J3
Harwell Oxon. 21 H3
Harwich 35 G5
Harwood Dur. 61 K3
Harwood Gt.Man. 49 G1
Harwood Dale 63 J3
Harwood on Teviot 69 K3
Harworth 51 J3
Hasbury 40 B7
Hascombe 12 C3
Haselbech 31 J1
Haselbury Plucknett 8 D3
Haseley 30 D2
Haselor 30 C3
Hasfield 29 H6
Hasguard 16 B5
Haskayne 48 C2
Hasketon 35 G3
Hasland 51 F6
Haslemere 12 C3
Haslingden 56 C7
Haslingden Grane 56 C7
Haslingfield 33 H3
Haslington 49 G7
Hassall 49 G7
Hassall Green 49 G7
Hassell Street 15 F3
Hassendean 70 A1
Hassingham 45 H5
Hassocks 13 F5
Hassop 50 E5
Haster 105 J3
Hastigrow 105 H2
Hastingleigh 15 F3
Hastings 14 D7
Hastingwood 23 H1
Hastoe 22 C1
Haswell 62 E2
Hatch Beds. 32 E4
Hatch Hants. 21 K6
Hatch Beauchamp 8 B2
Hatch End 22 E2
Hatch Green 8 B3
Hatching Green 32 E7
Hatchmere 48 E5
Hatcliffe 53 F2
Hatfield Here. 28 E3
Hatfield Herts. 23 F1
Hatfield S.Yorks. 51 J2
Hatfield Broad Oak 33 J7
Hatfield Heath 33 J7
Hatfield Hyde 33 F7
Hatfield Peverel 34 B7
Hatfield Woodhouse 51 J2
Hatford 21 G2
Hatherden 21 G6
Hatherleigh 6 D5
Hathern 41 G3
Hatherop 20 E1
Hathersage 50 E4
Hatherton Ches. 39 F1
Hatherton Staffs. 40 B4
Hatley St. George 33 F3
Hatt 4 D4
Hattingley 11 H1
Hatton Aber. 91 J1
Hatton Derbys. 40 E3
Hatton Gt.Lon. 22 D4
Hatton Lincs. 52 E5
Hatton Shrop. 38 D6
Hatton Warks. 30 D2
Hatton Warr. 48 E4
Hatton Castle 99 F6
Hatton Heath 48 D6
Hatton of Fintray 91 G3
Hattoncrook 91 G2
Haugh Head 71 F1
Haugh of Glass 90 C1
Haugh of Urr 65 J4
Haugham 53 G4
Haughhead 74 E3
Haughley 34 E2
Haughley Green 34 E2
Haughley New Street 34 E2
Haughs 98 D6
Haughton Notts. 51 J5
Haughton Shrop. 39 F6
Haughton Shrop. 38 E4
Haughton Shrop. 38 C3
Haughton Staffs. 40 A3
Haughton Green 49 J3
Haughton Le Skerne 62 E5
Haughton Moss 48 E7
Haultwick 33 G6
Haunn 84 C3
Haunton 40 E4
Hauxley 71 H3
Hauxton 33 H3
Havant 11 J4
Haven 28 D3
Haven Side 59 K7
Havenstreet 11 G5
Haverfordwest (Hwllfforddd) 16 C4
Haverhill 33 K4
Haverigg 54 E2
Havering-atte-Bower 23 J2
Haversham 32 B4
Haverthwaite 55 G1
Haverton Hill 63 F4
Hawarden 48 C6
Hawbridge 29 J4
Hawbush Green 34 B7
Hawcoat 55 F2
Hawen 17 G1
Hawes 56 D1
Hawford 29 H2
Hawick 70 A2
Hawkchurch 8 C4
Hawkedon 34 B3
Hawkenbury 13 J3
Hawkeridge 20 B6
Hawkerland 7 J7
Hawkes End 41 F7
Hawkesbury 20 A3
Hawkesbury Upton 20 A3
Hawkhill 71 H2
Hawkhurst 14 C4
Hawkinge 15 H3
Hawkley 11 J2
Hawkridge 7 G2
Hawkshead 60 E7
Hawksland 75 G7
Hawkswick 56 E2
Hawksworth Notts. 42 A1
Hawksworth W.Yorks. 57 G5
Hawkwell Essex 24 E2
Hawkwell Northumb. 71 F6
Hawley Hants. 22 B6
Hawley Kent 23 J4
Hawling 30 B6
Hawnby 63 G7
Haworth 57 F6
Hawstead 34 C3
Hawthorn Dur. 63 F2
Hawthorn Wilts. 20 B5
Hawthorn Hill Brack.F. 22 B4
Hawthorn Hill Lincs. 53 F7
Hawthorpe 42 D3
Hawton 51 K7
Haxby 58 C4
Haxey 51 K3
Haxted 23 H7
Hay Mills 40 D7
Hay Street 33 G6
Haydock 48 E3
Haydon 9 F3
Haydon Bridge 70 D7
Haydon Wick 20 E3
Haye 4 D4
Hayes Gt.Lon. 22 D3
Hayes Gt.Lon. 23 H5
Hayfield Arg. & B. 80 B5
Hayfield Derbys. 50 C4
Hayfield High. 105 G2
Hayhillock 83 G3
Haylands 11 G5
Hayle 2 C5
Haynes 32 E4
Haynes Church End 32 D4
Hay-on-Wye 28 B4
Hayscastle 16 B3
Hayscastle Cross 16 C3
Hayton Cumb. 61 G1
Hayton Cumb. 60 C2
Hayton E.Riding 58 E5
Hayton Notts. 51 K4
Hayton's Bent 38 E7
Haytor Vale 5 H3
Haywards Heath 13 G4
Haywood Oaks 51 J7
Hazel End 33 H6
Hazel Grove 49 J4
Hazelbank Arg. & B. 80 B7
Hazelbank S.Lan. 75 G6
Hazelbury Bryan 9 G4
Hazeleigh 24 E1
Hazeley 22 A6
Hazelside 68 D1
Hazelslade 40 C4
Hazelton Walls 82 E5
Hazelwood Derbys. 41 F1
Hazelwood Gt.Lon. 23 H5
Hazlefield 65 H6
Hazlehead 91 G4
Hazlemere 22 B2
Hazlerigg 71 H6
Hazleton 30 B7
Heacham 44 A2
Head Bridge 6 E4
Headbourne Worthy 11 F1
Headcorn 14 D3
Headington 21 J1
Headlam 62 C5
Headless Cross 30 B2
Headley Hants. 12 B3
Headley Hants. 21 J5
Headley Surr. 23 F6
Headley Down 12 B3
Headon 51 K5
Heads Nook 61 F1
Heage 51 F7
Healaugh N.Yorks. 62 B7
Healaugh N.Yorks. 58 B5
Heald Green 49 H4
Heale 6 E1
Healey Lancs. 49 H1
Healey N.Yorks. 57 G1
Healey Northumb. 62 B1
Healeyfield 62 B2
Healing 53 F1
Heamoor 2 B5
Heanish 78 B3
Heanor 41 G1
Heanton Punchardon 6 D2
Heanton Satchville 6 D4
Heapey 56 B7
Heapham 52 B4
Hearthstane 69 G1
Heasley Mill 7 F2
Heast 86 C3
Heath 51 G6
Heath & Reach 32 C6
Heath End Hants. 21 J5
Heath End Surr. 22 B7
Heath Hayes 40 C4
Heath Hill 39 G4
Heath House 19 H7
Heath Town 40 B6
Heathcot 91 G4
Heathcote Derbys. 50 D6
Heathcote Shrop. 39 F3
Heather 41 F4
Heathfield Devon 5 J3
Heathfield E.Suss. 13 J4
Heathfield Som. 7 K3
Heathrow Airport 22 D4
Heathton 40 A6
Heatley 49 G4
Heaton Lancs. 55 H3
Heaton Staffs. 49 J6
Heaton T. & W. 71 H7
Heaton Moor 49 H3
Heaverham 23 J6
Heaviley 49 J4
Hebburn 71 J7
Hebden 57 F3
Hebden Bridge 56 E7
Hebden Green 49 F6
Hebing End 33 G6
Hebron Carmar. 16 E3
Hebron Northumb. 71 G5
Heck 69 F5
Heckfield 22 A5

Heckfield Green 35 F1
Heckfordbridge 34 D6
Heckingham 45 H6
Heckington 42 E1
Heckmondwike 57 H7
Heddington 20 C5
Heddle 107 C6
Heddon-on-the-Wall 71 G7
Hedenham 45 H6
Hedge End 11 F3
Hedgerley 22 C3
Hedging 8 B2
Hedley on the Hill 62 B1
Hednesford 40 C4
Hedon 59 H7
Hedsor 22 C3
Heeley 51 F4
Heglibister 109 C7
Heighington *Darl.* 62 D4
Heighington *Lincs.* 52 D6
Heights of Brae 96 C5
Heilam 103 G3
Heithat 69 G5
Heiton 77 F7
Hele *Devon* 6 D1
Hele *Devon* 7 H5
Hele Bridge 6 D5
Hele Lane 7 F4
Helebridge 6 A5
Helensburgh 74 A2
Helford 2 E6
Helhoughton 44 C3
Helions Bumpstead 33 K4
Helland 4 A3
Hellandbridge 4 A3
Hellesdon 45 F4
Hellidon 31 G3
Hellifield 56 D4
Hellingly 13 J5
Hellington 45 H5
Hellister 109 C8
Helmdon 31 G4
Helmingham 35 G4
Helmsdale 105 F7
Helmshore 56 C7
Helmsley 58 C1
Helperby 57 K2
Helperthorpe 59 F2
Helpringham 42 E5
Helpston 42 E5
Helsby 48 D5
Helston 2 B6
Helstone 4 A2
Helton 61 G4
Helwith Bridge 56 D3
Hemblington 45 H4
Hemborough Post 5 J5
Hemel Hempstead 22 D1
Hemingbrough 58 C6
Hemingby 53 F5
Hemingford Abbots 33 F1
Hemingford Grey 33 F1
Hemingstone 35 F4
Hemington *Leics.* 41 G3
Hemington *Northants.* 42 D7
Hemley 35 G4
Hemlington 63 F5
Hempholme 59 G5
Hempnall 45 G6
Hempnall Green 45 G6
Hempriggs 97 J5
Hempriggs House 105 J4
Hempstead *Essex* 33 K5
Hempstead *Norf.* 45 J3
Hempstead *Norf.* 45 F2
Hempsted 29 H7
Hempton *Norf.* 44 D3
Hempton *Oxon.* 31 F5
Hemsby 45 J4
Hemswell 52 C3
Hemsworth 51 G1
Hemyock 7 K4
Henbury *Bristol* 19 J4
Henbury *Ches.* 49 H5
Henderland 65 J3
Hendersyde Park 77 F7
Hendon *Gt.Lon.* 23 F3
Hendon *T. & W.* 62 E1
Hendy 17 J5
Heneglwys 46 C5
Henfield 13 F5
Henford 6 B6
Hengherst 14 E4
Hengoed *Caerp.* 18 E2
Hengoed *Powys* 28 B3
Hengoed *Shrop.* 38 B2
Hengrave 34 C2
Henham 33 J6
Heniarth 38 A5
Henlade 8 B2
Henley *Shrop.* 28 D1
Henley *Som.* 8 D1
Henley *Suff.* 35 F3
Henley *W.Suss.* 12 B4
Henley Corner 8 D1
Henley Park 22 C6
Henley-in-Arden 30 C2
Henley's Down 14 C6
Henllan *Carmar.* 17 G2
Henllan *Denb.* 47 J6
Henllan Amgoed 16 E3
Henllys 19 F2
Henlow 32 E5
Hennock 7 G7
Henny Street 34 C5
Henryd 47 F5
Henry's Moat 16 D3
Hensall 58 B7
Henshaw 70 C7
Hensingham 60 A5
Henstead 45 J7
Hensting 11 F2
Henstridge 9 G3
Henstridge Ash 9 G3
Henstridge Marsh 9 G2
Henton *Oxon.* 22 A1
Henton *Som.* 19 H7
Henwick 29 H3
Henwood 4 C3
Heogan 109 D8
Heol Senni 27 J6
Heol-ddu 17 J4
Heol-y-Cyw 18 C3
Hepburn 71 F1
Hepple 70 E3
Hepscott 71 H5
Heptonstall 56 E7
Hepworth *Suff.* 34 D1
Hepworth *W.Yorks.* 50 D2
Herbrandston 16 B5
Herdicott 6 B6
Hereford 28 E4

Heriot 76 B5
Hermiston 75 K3
Hermitage *D. & G.* 65 J4
Hermitage *Dorset* 9 F4
Hermitage *Sc.Bord.* 70 A4
Hermitage *W.Berks.* 21 J4
Hermitage *W.Suss.* 11 J4
Hermon *Carmar.* 17 G2
Hermon *I.o.A.* 46 B6
Hermon *Pembs.* 17 F2
Herne 25 H5
Herne Bay 25 H5
Herne Common 25 H5
Herner 6 D3
Hernhill 25 G5
Herodsfoot 4 C4
Herongate 24 C2
Heron's Ghyll 13 H4
Heronsgate 22 D2
Herriard 21 K7
Herringfleet 45 J6
Herring's Green 32 D4
Herringswell 34 B2
Herringthorpe 51 G3
Hersden 25 H5
Hersham *Cornw.* 6 A5
Hersham *Surr.* 22 E5
Herstmonceux 13 K5
Herston *Dorset* 10 B7
Herston *Ork.* 107 D8
Hertford 33 G7
Hertford Heath 33 G7
Hertingfordbury 33 G7
Hesket Newmarket 60 E3
Hesketh Bank 55 H7
Hesketh Lane 56 B5
Heskin Green 48 E1
Hesleden 63 F3
Hesleyside 70 D5
Heslington 58 C4
Hessay 58 B4
Hessenford 4 D5
Hessett 34 D2
Hessle 59 G7
Hest Bank 55 H3
Heston 22 E4
Heswall 48 B4
Hethe 31 G6
Hetherington 70 D6
Hethersett 45 F5
Hethersgill 69 K7
Hethpool 70 D1
Hett 62 D3
Hetton 56 E4
Hetton-le-Hole 62 E2
Heugh 71 F6
Heugh-head *Aber.* 90 B3
Heugh-head *Aber.* 90 B3
Heveningham 35 H1
Hever 23 H7
Heversham 55 H1
Hevingham 45 F3
Hewas Water 3 G4
Hewell Grange 30 B2
Hewell Lane 30 B2
Hewelsfield 19 J1
Hewelsfield Common 19 J1
Hewish *N.Som.* 19 G5
Hewish *Som.* 8 D4
Hewton 6 D6
Hexham 70 E7
Hextable 23 J4
Hexton 32 E5
Hexworthy 5 G3
Heybridge *Essex* 24 C2
Heybridge *Essex* 24 E1
Heybridge Basin 24 E1
Heybrook Bay 5 F6
Heydon *Cambs.* 33 H4
Heydon *Norf.* 45 F3
Heydour 42 D2
Heylipoll 78 A3
Heylor 108 B4
Heysham 55 H3
Heyshaw 57 G3
Heyshott 12 B5
Heytesbury 20 C7
Heythrop 30 E6
Heywood *Gt.Man.* 49 H1
Heywood *Wilts.* 20 B6
Hibaldstow 52 C2
Hickleton 51 G2
Hickling *Norf.* 45 J3
Hickling *Notts.* 41 J3
Hickling Green 45 J3
Hickling Heath 45 J3
Hickstead 13 F4
Hidcote Boyce 30 C4
High Ackworth 51 G1
High Balantyre 80 B6
High Beach 23 H2
High Bentham 56 B3
High Bickington 6 D3
High Birkwith 56 D2
High Blantyre 74 E5
High Bonnybridge 75 G3
High Borgue 65 G5
High Bradfield 50 E3
High Bray 6 E2
High Brooms 23 J7
High Bullen 6 D3
High Burton 57 H1
High Buston 71 H3
High Callerton 71 G6
High Catton 58 D4
High Coniscliffe 62 D5
High Cross *Hants.* 11 J2
High Cross *Herts.* 33 G7
High Cross Bank 40 E4
High Easter 33 K7
High Ellington 57 G1
High Entercommon 62 E6
High Ercall 38 E4
High Etherley 62 C4
High Garrett 34 B6
High Gate 56 E7
High Grange 62 C3
High Green *Norf.* 45 F5
High Green *S.Yorks.* 51 F3
High Green *Worcs.* 29 H4
High Halden 14 D4
High Halstow 24 D4
High Ham 8 D1
High Harrington 60 B4
High Harrogate 57 J4
High Hatton 39 F3
High Hawsker 63 J2
High Heath 39 F3
High Hesket 61 F2
High Hoyland 50 E1
High Hunsley 59 F6
High Hurstwood 13 H4

High Hutton 58 D3
High Ireby 60 D3
High Kilburn 58 B1
High Lane *Derbys.* 41 G1
High Lane *Worcs.* 29 F2
High Laver 23 J1
High Legh 49 G4
High Leven 63 F5
High Littleton 19 K6
High Lorton 60 C4
High Melton 51 H2
High Newton 55 H1
High Newton by-the-Sea 71 H1
High Nibthwaite 60 D7
High Offley 39 G3
High Ongar 23 J1
High Onn 40 A4
High Risby 52 C1
High Roding 33 K7
High Salvington 12 E6
High Shaw 61 K7
High Spen 71 G7
High Street *Cornw.* 3 G3
High Street *Kent* 14 C4
High Street *Suff.* 35 J3
High Street Green 34 E3
High Toynton 53 F6
High Trewhitt 71 F3
High Wollaston 19 J2
High Wray 60 E7
High Wych 33 H7
High Wycombe 22 B2
Higham *Derbys.* 51 F7
Higham *Kent* 24 D4
Higham *Lancs.* 56 D6
Higham *Suff.* 34 B2
Higham *Suff.* 34 E5
Higham Dykes 71 G6
Higham Ferrers 32 C2
Higham Gobion 32 E5
Higham on the Hill 41 F6
Higham Wood 23 K7
Highampton 6 C5
Highbridge 19 G7
Highbrook 13 G3
Highburton 50 D1
Highbury 19 K7
Highbury Vale 41 H1
Highclere 21 H5
Highcliffe 10 D5
Higher Ansty 9 G4
Higher Ashton 7 G7
Higher Ballam 55 G6
Higher Blackley 49 H2
Higher Brixham 5 K5
Higher Cheriton 7 J5
Higher Gabwell 5 K4
Higher Green 49 G3
Higher Kingcombe 8 E5
Higher Tale 7 J5
Higher Thrushgill 56 B3
Higher Town 2 C1
Higher Walreddon 4 E3
Higher Walton *Lancs.* 55 J7
Higher Walton *Warr.* 48 E4
Higher Whatcombe 9 H4
Higher Whitley 49 F4
Higher Wych 38 D1
Highfield *E.Riding* 58 D6
Highfield *N.Ayr.* 74 B5
Highfield *T. & W.* 62 C1
Highfields 33 G3
Highgreen Manor 70 D4
Highlane *Ches.* 49 H6
Highlane *Derbys.* 51 G4
Highlaws 60 C2
Highleadon 29 G6
Highleigh 12 B7
Highley 39 G7
Highmead 17 J1
Highmoor Cross 21 K3
Highmoor Hill 19 H3
Highnam 29 G7
Highstead 25 J5
Highsted 25 F5
Highstreet Green 35 B5
Hightae 69 F6
Hightown *Ches.* 49 H6
Hightown *Mersey.* 48 B2
Highway 5 J3
Highweek 21 F2
Highworth 44 C5
Hilborough 44 C5
Hilcott 20 E6
Hilden Park 23 J7
Hildenborough 23 J7
Hildersham 33 J4
Hilderstone 40 B2
Hilderthorpe 59 H3
Hilfield 9 F4
Hilgay 44 A6
Hill 19 K2
Hill Brow 11 J2
Hill Chorlton 39 G2
Hill Dyke 43 G1
Hill End *Dur.* 62 B3
Hill End *Fife* 75 J1
Hill End *N.Yorks.* 57 F4
Hill Head 11 G4
Hill of Beath 75 K1
Hill of Fearn 97 F4
Hill Ridware 40 C4
Hill Top *Hants.* 11 F4
Hill Top *W.Yorks.* 51 F1
Hill View 9 J5
Hillam 58 B7
Hillberry 54 C5
Hillborough 25 J5
Hillbrae *Aber.* 98 E6
Hillbrae *Aber.* 91 F2
Hillbrae *Aber.* 91 G1
Hillend *Aber.* 98 C6
Hillend *Fife* 75 K2
Hillend *Midloth.* 76 A4
Hillesden 31 H6
Hillesley 20 A3
Hillfarrance 7 K3
Hillhead 5 K5
Hillhead of Auchentumb 99 H5
Hillhead of Cocklaw 99 J6
Hilliard's Cross 40 D4
Hilliclay 105 G2
Hillingdon 22 D3
Hillington 44 B3
Hillmorton 31 G1
Hillockhead *Aber.* 90 B4
Hillockhead *Aber.* 90 C3
Hillowton 65 H4
Hillpound 11 G3
Hills Town 51 G6
Hillsford Bridge 7 F1
Hillside *Aber.* 91 H5
Hillside *Angus* 83 J1

Hillside *Moray* 97 J5
Hillside *Shet.* 109 D6
Hillswick 108 B5
Hillway 11 H6
Hillwell 109 F9
Hilmarton 20 C4
Hilperton 20 B6
Hilsea 11 H4
Hilton *Cambs.* 33 F2
Hilton *Cumb.* 61 J4
Hilton *Derbys.* 40 E2
Hilton *Dorset* 9 G4
Hilton *Dur.* 62 C4
Hilton *High.* 97 G3
Hilton *Shrop.* 39 G6
Hilton *Stock.* 63 F5
Hilton Croft 91 H1
Hilton of Cadboll 97 F4
Hilton of Delnies 97 F6
Himbleton 29 J3
Himley 40 A6
Hincaster 55 J1
Hinckley 41 G6
Hinderclay 34 E1
Hinderwell 63 J5
Hindford 38 C2
Hindhead 12 B3
Hindley 49 F2
Hindley Green 49 F2
Hindlip 29 H3
Hindolveston 44 E3
Hindon 9 J1
Hindringham 44 D2
Hingham 44 E5
Hinstock 39 F3
Hintlesham 34 E4
Hinton *Hants.* 10 D5
Hinton *Here.* 28 C5
Hinton *Northants.* 31 G3
Hinton *S.Glos.* 20 A4
Hinton *Shrop.* 38 D5
Hinton Admiral 10 D5
Hinton Ampner 11 G2
Hinton Blewett 19 J6
Hinton Charterhouse 20 A6
Hinton Martell 10 B4
Hinton on the Green 30 B4
Hinton Parva 21 F3
Hinton St. George 8 D3
Hinton St. Mary 9 G3
Hinton Waldrist 21 G2
Hinton-in-the-Hedges 31 G5
Hints *Shrop.* 29 F1
Hints *Staffs.* 40 D5
Hinwick 32 C2
Hinxhill 15 F3
Hinxton 33 H4
Hinxworth 33 H4
Hipperholme 57 G7
Hirn 91 F4
Hirnant 37 K3
Hirst 71 H5
Hirst Courtney 58 C7
Hirwaen 47 K6
Hirwaun 18 C1
Hiscott 6 D3
Histon 33 H2
Hitcham *Bucks.* 22 C3
Hitcham *Suff.* 34 D3
Hitchin 32 E6
Hither Green 23 G4
Hittisleigh 7 F6
Hixon 40 C3
Hoaden 25 J5
Hoaldalbert 28 C6
Hoar Cross 40 D3
Hoarwithy 28 E6
Hoath 25 H5
Hobarris 28 C1
Hobbister 107 C7
Hobbs Lots Bridge 43 G5
Hobkirk 70 A2
Hobland Hall 45 K5
Hobson 62 C1
Hoby 41 J4
Hockering 44 E4
Hockerton 51 K7
Hockley 24 E2
Hockley Heath 30 C1
Hockliffe 32 C6
Hockwold cum Wilton 44 B7
Hockworthy 7 J4
Hoddesdon 23 G1
Hoddlesden 56 C7
Hodgeston 16 D6
Hodnet 39 F3
Hodthorpe 51 H5
Hoe 44 D4
Hoe Gate 11 H3
Hoff 61 H5
Hoffleet Stow 43 F2
Hoggeston 32 B6
Hoggie 98 D4
Hogha Gearraidh 92 C4
Hoghton 56 B7
Hognaston 50 E7
Hogsthorpe 53 J5
Holbeach 43 G3
Holbeach Bank 43 G3
Holbeach Clough 43 G3
Holbeach Drove 43 G4
Holbeach Hurn 43 G3
Holbeach St. Johns 43 G4
Holbeach St. Marks 43 G2
Holbeach St. Matthew 43 H2
Holbeck 51 H5
Holberrow Green 30 B3
Holbeton 5 G5
Holborough 24 D5
Holbrook *Derbys.* 41 F1
Holbrook *Suff.* 35 F5
Holburn 77 J7
Holbury 11 F4
Holcombe *Devon* 5 K3
Holcombe *Som.* 19 K7
Holcombe Rogus 7 J4
Holcot 31 J2
Holden 56 C5
Holdenby 31 H2
Holdenhurst 10 C5
Holdgate 38 E7
Holdingham 42 D1
Holditch 8 C4
Hole Park 14 D4
Hole Street 12 E5
Hole-in-the-Wall 29 F6
Holford 7 K1
Holker 55 G2
Holkham 44 C1
Hollacombe *Devon* 6 B5
Hollacombe *Devon* 6 E4
Holland *Ork.* 106 D2
Holland *Ork.* 106 F5
Holland *Surr.* 23 H6

Holland-on-Sea 35 F7
Hollandstoun 106 G2
Hollee 69 H7
Hollesley 35 H4
Hollingbourne 14 D2
Hollingbury 13 G6
Hollington *Derbys.* 40 E2
Hollington *E.Suss.* 14 C6
Hollington *Staffs.* 40 C2
Hollingworth 50 C3
Hollins 49 H2
Hollins Green 49 F3
Hollinsclough 50 C6
Hollinswood 39 G5
Hollinwood 38 E2
Holloway 51 F7
Hollowell 31 H1
Holly End 43 J5
Holly Green 29 H4
Hollybush *Caerp.* 18 E1
Hollybush *E.Ayr.* 67 H2
Hollybush *Worcs.* 29 G5
Hollym 59 K7
Holm 69 H4
Holm of Drumlanrig 68 D7
Holmbury St. Mary 22 E7
Holmbush *Cornw.* 4 A5
Holmbush *W.Suss.* 13 F3
Holme *Cambs.* 42 E7
Holme *Cumb.* 55 J2
Holme *Notts.* 52 B7
Holme *W.Yorks.* 50 D2
Holme Chapel 56 D7
Holme Hale 44 C5
Holme Lacy 28 E5
Holme Marsh 28 C3
Holme next the Sea 44 B1
Holme on the Wolds 59 F5
Holme Pierrepont 41 J2
Holmebridge 9 H6
Holme-on-Spalding-Moor 58 E6
Holmer 28 E4
Holmer Green 22 C2
Holmes Chapel 49 G6
Holme's Hill 13 J5
Holmesfield 51 F5
Holmeswood 48 D1
Holmewood 51 G6
Holmfield 57 F7
Holmfirth 50 D2
Holmhead *D. & G.* 68 C5
Holmhead *E.Ayr.* 67 K1
Holmpton 59 K7
Holmrook 60 B6
Holmsgarth 109 D8
Holmside 62 D2
Holmston 67 H1
Holmwrangle 61 G2
Holne 5 H4
Holnest 9 F4
Holsworthy 6 B5
Holsworthy Beacon 6 B5
Holt *Dorset* 10 B4
Holt *Norf.* 44 E2
Holt *Wilts.* 20 B5
Holt *Worcs.* 29 H2
Holt *Wrex.* 48 D7
Holt End *Hants.* 11 H1
Holt End *Worcs.* 30 B2
Holt Fleet 29 H2
Holt Heath *Dorset* 10 B4
Holt Heath *Worcs.* 29 H2
Holtby 58 C4
Holton *Oxon.* 21 K1
Holton *Som.* 9 F2
Holton *Suff.* 35 H1
Holton cum Beckering 52 E4
Holton Heath 9 J5
Holton le Clay 53 F2
Holton le Moor 52 D3
Holton St. Mary 34 E5
Holtspur 22 C2
Holtye Common 13 H3
Holwell *Dorset* 9 G3
Holwell *Herts.* 32 E5
Holwell *Leics.* 42 A3
Holwell *Oxon.* 21 F1
Holwell *Som.* 20 A7
Holwick 62 A4
Holworth 9 G6
Holy Cross 29 J1
Holy Island 77 K6
Holybourne 22 A7
Holyhead (Caergybi) 46 A4
Holymoorside 51 F6
Holyport 22 B4
Holystone 70 E3
Holytown 75 F4
Holywell *Cambs.* 33 G1
Holywell *Cornw.* 2 E3
Holywell *Dorset* 8 E4
Holywell *E.Suss.* 13 J7
Holywell (Treffynnon) *Flints.* 47 K5
Holywell Green 50 C1
Holywell Lake 7 K3
Holywell Row 34 B1
Holywood 68 E5
Hom Green 28 E6
Homer 39 F5
Homersfield 45 G7
Homington 10 C2
Honey Hill 25 H5
Honey Tye 34 D5
Honeyborough 16 C5
Honeybourne 30 C4
Honeychurch 6 E5
Honiley 30 D1
Honing 45 H3
Honingham 45 F4
Honington *Lincs.* 42 C1
Honington *Suff.* 34 D1
Honington *Warks.* 30 D4
Honiton 7 K5
Honley 50 D1
Hoo *Med.* 24 D4
Hoo *Suff.* 35 G3
Hooe *E.Suss.* 13 K6
Hooe *Plym.* 5 F5
Hooe Common 13 K5
Hook *E.Riding* 58 D7
Hook *Gt.Lon.* 22 E5
Hook *Hants.* 22 A6
Hook *Pembs.* 16 C4
Hook *Wilts.* 20 D3
Hook Green *Kent* 13 K3
Hook Green *Kent* 24 C5
Hook Green *Kent* 24 C4
Hook Norton 30 E5
Hook-a-Gate 38 D5
Hooke 8 E4
Hookgate 39 G2
Hookway 7 G6

Hookwood 23 F7
Hoole 48 D6
Hooley 23 F6
Hooton 48 C5
Hooton Levitt 51 H3
Hooton Pagnell 51 G2
Hooton Roberts 51 G3
Hope *Derbys.* 50 D4
Hope *Devon* 5 G7
Hope *Flints.* 48 C7
Hope *Powys* 38 B5
Hope *Shrop.* 38 C5
Hope Bagot 28 E1
Hope Bowdler 38 D6
Hope End Green 33 J7
Hope Mansell 29 F7
Hope under Dinmore 28 E3
Hopehouse 69 H2
Hopeman 97 J5
Hope's Green 24 D3
Hopesay 38 C7
Hopkinstown 18 D2
Hopton *Derbys.* 50 E7
Hopton *Norf.* 45 K5
Hopton *Shrop.* 38 B3
Hopton *Staffs.* 40 B3
Hopton *Suff.* 34 D1
Hopton Cangeford 38 E7
Hopton Castle 28 C1
Hopton Wafers 29 F1
Hoptonheath 28 C1
Hopwas 40 D5
Hopwood 30 B1
Horam 13 J5
Horbling 42 E2
Horbury 50 E1
Horden 62 F2
Horderley 38 D7
Hordle 10 D5
Hordley 38 C2
Horeb *Carmar.* 17 H5
Horeb *Cere.* 17 G1
Horfield 19 J4
Horham 35 G1
Horkesley Heath 34 D6
Horkstow 52 C1
Horley *Oxon.* 31 F4
Horley *Surr.* 23 F7
Horn Hill 22 D2
Hornblotton Green 8 E1
Hornby *Lancs.* 55 J3
Hornby *N.Yorks.* 62 D7
Hornby *N.Yorks.* 62 E6
Horncastle 53 F6
Hornchurch 23 J3
Horncliffe 77 H5
Horndean *Hants.* 11 J3
Horndean *Sc.Bord.* 77 G6
Horndon 6 D7
Horndon on the Hill 24 C3
Horne 23 G7
Horniehaugh 83 F1
Horning 45 H4
Horninghold 42 B6
Horninglow 40 E3
Horningsea 33 H2
Horningsham 20 B7
Horningtoft 44 D3
Horns Cross *Devon* 6 B3
Horns Cross *E.Suss.* 14 D5
Hornsby 61 G2
Hornsea 59 J5
Hornsey 23 G3
Hornton 30 E4
Horrabridge 5 F4
Horridge 5 H3
Horringer 34 C2
Horse Bridge 49 J7
Horsebridge *Devon* 4 E3
Horsebridge *Hants.* 10 E1
Horsebrook 40 A4
Horsehay 39 F5
Horseheath 33 K4
Horsehouse 57 F1
Horsell 22 C6
Horseman's Green 38 D1
Horseway 43 H7
Horsey 45 J3
Horsford 45 F4
Horsforth 57 H6
Horsham *W.Suss.* 12 E3
Horsham *Worcs.* 29 G3
Horsham St. Faith 45 G4
Horsington *Lincs.* 52 E6
Horsington *Som.* 9 F2
Horsley *Derbys.* 41 F1
Horsley *Glos.* 20 B2
Horsley *Northumb.* 71 F7
Horsley *Northumb.* 70 D4
Horsley Cross 35 F6
Horsley Woodhouse 41 F1
Horsleycross Street 35 F6
Horsmonden 14 C3
Horspath 21 J1
Horstead 45 G4
Horsted Keynes 13 G4
Horton *Bucks.* 32 C7
Horton *Dorset* 10 B4
Horton *Lancs.* 56 D4
Horton *Northants.* 32 B3
Horton *S.Glos.* 20 A3
Horton *Som.* 8 C3
Horton *Staffs.* 49 J7
Horton *Swan.* 17 H7
Horton *W. & M.* 22 D4
Horton *Wilts.* 20 D5
Horton Cross 8 C3
Horton Grange 71 H6
Horton Green 38 D1
Horton Heath 11 F3
Horton in Ribblesdale 56 D2
Horton Inn 10 B4
Horton Kirby 23 J5
Horton-cum-Studley 31 G7
Horwich 49 F1
Horwich End 50 C4
Horwood 6 D3
Hose 42 A3
Hoses 60 D7
Hosh 81 K5
Hosta 92 C4
Hoswick 109 D10
Hotham 58 E6
Hothfield 14 E3
Hoton 41 H3

Hough 49 G2
Hough Green 48 D4
Hougham 42 B1
Hough-on-the-Hill 42 C1
Houghton *Cambs.* 33 F1
Houghton *Cumb.* 61 F1
Houghton *Devon* 5 G6
Houghton *Hants.* 10 E1
Houghton *Pembs.* 16 C5
Houghton *W.Suss.* 12 D5
Houghton Bank 62 D4
Houghton Conquest 32 D4
Houghton le Spring 62 E2
Houghton on the Hill 41 J5
Houghton Regis 32 D6
Houghton St. Giles 44 D2
Houghton-le-Side 62 D4
Houlsyke 63 J6
Hound 11 F4
Hound Green 22 A6
Houndslow 76 A5
Houndwood 77 G4
Hounslow 23 F4
Hounslow Green 33 K7
Househill 97 F6
Housetter 108 C4
Houston 74 C4
Houstry 105 G5
Houstry of Dunn 105 H4
Houton 107 C7
Hove 13 F6
Hoveringham 41 J1
Hoveton 45 H4
Hovingham 58 C2
How 61 G2
How Caple 29 F5
How End 32 D4
How Man 60 A5
Howden 58 D7
Howden-le-Wear 62 C3
Howe *Cumb.* 55 H1
Howe *High.* 105 J2
Howe *N.Yorks.* 57 J1
Howe *Norf.* 45 G5
Howe Green 24 D1
Howe of Teuchar 99 F6
Howe Street *Essex* 33 K6
Howe Street *Essex* 33 K5
Howell 42 E1
Howey 27 K3
Howgate 76 A5
Howgill 57 F5
Howick 71 H2
Howle 39 F3
Howle Hill 29 F6
Howlett End 33 J5
Howley 8 B4
Hownam 70 C2
Hownam Mains 70 C1
Howpasley 69 J3
Howsham *N.Lincs.* 52 D2
Howsham *N.Yorks.* 58 D3
Howtel 77 G7
Howton 28 D6
Howwood 74 C4
Hoxa 107 D8
Hoxne 35 F1
Hoy 105 H1
Hoylake 48 B4
Hoyland 51 F2
Hoyland Swaine 50 E2
Hubberholme 56 E2
Hubbert's Bridge 43 F1
Huby *N.Yorks.* 58 B3
Huby *N.Yorks.* 57 H4
Hucclecote 29 H7
Hucking 14 D2
Hucknall 41 H1
Huddersfield 50 D1
Huddington 29 J3
Hudscott 6 E3
Hudswell 62 C6
Huggate 58 E4
Hugglescote 41 G4
Hugh Town 2 C1
Hughenden Valley 22 B2
Hughley 38 E6
Hugmore 48 C7
Huish *Devon* 6 D4
Huish *Wilts.* 20 E5
Huish Champflower 7 J3
Huish Episcopi 8 D2
Huisinis 100 B7
Hulcote 32 B4
Hulcott 32 B7
Hull 59 H7
Hulland 40 E1
Hullavington 20 B3
Hullbridge 24 E2
Hulme End 50 D7
Hulme Walfield 49 H6
Hulver Street 45 J7
Humber 28 E3
Humberside International Airport 52 E2
Humberston 53 G2
Humberstone 41 J5
Humbie 76 C4
Humbleton *E.Riding* 59 J6
Humbleton *Northumb.* 70 E1
Humby 42 D2
Hume 77 F7
Humehall 77 F7
Humshaugh 70 E6
Huna 105 J1
Huncoat 56 C6
Huncote 41 H6
Hundalee 70 B2
Hunderthwaite 62 A4
Hundleby 53 G6
Hundleton 16 C5
Hundon 34 B4
Hundred Acres 11 G3
Hundred End 55 H7
Hundred House 28 A3
Hungarton 41 J5
Hungerford *Hants.* 10 C3
Hungerford *W.Berks.* 21 G5
Hungerford Newtown 21 G4
Hunglader 93 J4
Hunmanby 59 H2
Hunningham 30 E2
Hunny Hill 11 F6
Hunsdon 33 H7
Hunsingore 57 K4
Hunsonby 61 G3
Hunspow 105 H1
Hunstanton 44 A1
Hunstanworth 62 A2
Hunston *Suff.* 34 D2
Hunston *W.Suss.* 12 B6
Hunstrete 19 K5
Hunt End 30 B2

Hunt House 63 K7
Huntercombe End 21 K3
Hunters Forstal 25 H5
Hunter's Inn 6 E1
Hunter's Quay 73 K3
Hunterston 73 K5
Huntford 70 B3
Huntingdon 33 F1
Huntingfield 35 H1
Huntingford 9 H1
Huntington *Here.* 28 B3
Huntington *Staffs.* 40 B4
Huntington *York* 58 C4
Huntingtower 82 B5
Huntley 29 G7
Huntly 98 D6
Huntlywood 76 E6
Hunton *Hants.* 11 F1
Hunton *Kent* 14 C3
Hunton *N.Yorks.* 62 C7
Hunton Bridge 22 D1
Hunt's Cross 48 D4
Huntsham 7 J3
Huntshaw Cross 6 D3
Huntspill 19 G7
Huntworth 8 C1
Hunwick 62 C3
Hunworth 44 E2
Hurdsfield 49 J5
Hurley *W. & M.* 22 B3
Hurley *Warks.* 40 E6
Hurley Bottom 22 B3
Hurlford 74 C7
Hurliness 107 B9
Hurn 10 C5
Hursley 11 F2
Hurst *Gt.Man.* 49 J2
Hurst *N.Yorks.* 62 B6
Hurst *W'ham* 22 A4
Hurst Green
  E.Suss. 14 C5
Hurst Green
  Lancs. 56 B6
Hurst Green
  Surr. 23 G6
Hurstbourne
  Priors 21 H7
Hurstbourne
  Tarrant 21 G6
Hurstpierpoint 13 F5
Hurstway Common 28 B4
Hurstwood 56 D6
Hurtmore 22 C7
Hurworth-on-Tees 62 E5
Hury 62 A4
Husabost 93 H6
Husbands
  Bosworth 41 J7
Husborne Crawley 32 C5
Husthwaite 58 B2
Huthwaite 51 G7
Huttoft 53 J5
Hutton *Cumb.* 61 F4
Hutton *Essex* 24 C2
Hutton *Lancs.* 55 H7
Hutton *N.Som.* 19 G6
Hutton *Sc.Bord.* 77 H5
Hutton Bonville 62 E6
Hutton Buscel 59 F1
Hutton Conyers 57 J2
Hutton Cranswick 59 G4
Hutton End 61 F3
Hutton Henry 63 F3
Hutton Magna 62 C5
Hutton Roof
  Cumb. 55 J2
Hutton Roof
  Cumb. 60 E3
Hutton Rudby 63 F6
Hutton Sessay 57 K2
Hutton Wandesley 58 B4
Hutton-le-Hole 63 J7
Huxley 48 E6
Huxter *Shet.* 109 C7
Huxter *Shet.* 109 E6
Huyton 48 D3
Hwllffordd
  (Haverfordwest) 16 C4
Hycemoor 54 D1
Hyde *Glos.* 20 B1
Hyde *Gt.Man.* 49 J3
Hyde Heath 22 C1
Hyde Lea 40 B4
Hydestile 22 C7
Hyndford Bridge 75 H6
Hyndlee 70 A3
Hynish 78 A4
Hyssington 38 C6
Hythe *Hants.* 11 F4
Hythe *Kent* 15 G4
Hythe End 22 D4
Hythie 99 J5
Hyton 54 D1

I

Ianstown 98 C4
Ibberton 9 G4
Ible 50 E7
Ibsley 10 C4
Ibstock 41 G4
Ibstone 22 A2
Ibthorpe 21 G6
Ibworth 21 J6
Icelton 19 G5
Ickburgh 44 C6
Ickenham 22 D3
Ickford 21 K1
Ickham 15 H2
Ickleford 32 E5
Icklesham 14 D6
Ickleton 33 H4
Icklingham 34 B1
Ickwell Green 32 E4
Icomb 30 D6
Idbury 30 D6
Iddesleigh 6 D5
Ide 7 H6
Ide Hill 23 H6
Iden 14 E5
Iden Green *Kent* 14 D4
Iden Green *Kent* 14 D4
Idlicote 30 D4
Idmiston 10 C1
Idridgehay 40 E1
Idrigil 93 J5
Idstone 21 F3
Idvies 83 G3
Iffley 21 J1
Ifield or Singlewell
  Kent 24 C4
Ifield *W.Suss.* 13 F3
Ifieldwood 13 F3
Ifold 12 D3
Iford 13 H6
Ifton Heath 38 C2
Ightfield 38 E2

Ightham 23 J6
Iken 35 J3
Ilam 50 D7
Ilchester 8 E2
Ilderton 71 F1
Ilford 23 H3
Ilfracombe 6 D1
Ilkeston 41 G1
Ilketshall
  St. Andrew 45 H7
Ilketshall
  St. Lawrence 45 H7
Ilketshall
  St. Margaret 45 H7
Ilkley 57 G5
Illey 40 B7
Illington 44 D7
Illingworth 57 F7
Illogan 2 D4
Illston on the Hill 42 A6
Ilmer 22 A1
Ilmington 30 D4
Ilminster 8 C3
Ilsington 5 H3
Ilston 17 J6
Ilton *N.Yorks.* 57 G2
Ilton *Som.* 8 C3
Imachar 73 G6
Immeroin 81 G6
Immingham 52 E1
Immingham Dock 53 F1
Impington 33 H2
Ince 48 D5
Ince Blundell 48 C2
Ince-in-Makerfield 48 E2
Inch of Arnhall 90 E7
Inchbare 83 H1
Inchberry 98 B5
Inchbraoch 83 J2
Inchgrundle 90 C7
Inchindown 96 D4
Inchinnan 74 C4
Inchkinloch 103 J4
Inchlaggan 87 H4
Inchlumpie 96 C4
Inchmarlo 90 E5
Inchnabobart 90 C6
Inchnacardoch
  Hotel 87 K3
Inchnadamph 102 E6
Inchock 83 H3
Inchrory 89 J4
Inchture 82 D5
Inchvuilt 87 J1
Inchyra 82 C6
Indian Queens 3 G3
Inerval 72 B6
Ingatestone 24 C1
Ingbirchworth 50 E2
Ingerthorpe 57 H3
Ingestre 40 B3
Ingham *Lincs.* 52 C4
Ingham *Norf.* 45 H3
Ingham *Suff.* 34 C1
Ingleby *Derbys.* 41 F3
Ingleby *Lincs.* 52 B5
Ingleby Arncliffe 63 F6
Ingleby Barwick 63 F6
Ingleby Cross 63 F6
Ingleby Greenhow 63 G6
Inglesbatch 19 K5
Inglesham 21 F2
Ingleton *Dur.* 62 C4
Ingleton *N.Yorks.* 56 B2
Inglewhite 55 J6
Ingmire Hall 61 H7
Ingoe 71 F6
Ingoldisthorpe 44 A2
Ingoldmells 53 J6
Ingoldsby 42 D2
Ingon 30 D3
Ingram 71 F2
Ingrave 24 C2
Ingrow 57 F6
Ings 61 F7
Ingst 19 J3
Ingworth 45 F3
Inistrynich 80 B5
Injebreck 54 C5
Inkberrow 30 B3
Inkhorn 91 H1
Inkpen 21 G5
Inkstack 105 H1
Innellan 73 K4
Innergellie 83 G7
Innerleithen 76 B7
Innerleven 82 E7
Innermessan 64 A4
Innerwick *E.Loth.* 77 F3
Innerwick *P. & K.* 81 G3
Inninbeg 79 J3
Innsworth 29 H6
Insch 90 E2
Insh 89 F4
Inshore 103 F2
Inskip 55 H6
Instow 6 C2
Intake 51 F4
Intwood 45 F5
Inver *Aber.* 89 K5
Inver *Arg. & B.* 80 A3
Inver *High.* 97 F3
Inver *High.* 105 G3
Inver *P. & K.* 82 B3
Inver Mallie 87 H6
Inverailort 86 D6
Inverallgin 94 E6
Inverallochy 99 J4
Inveran 96 C2
Inveraray 80 B7
Inverardoch Mains 81 J7
Inverardran 80 E5
Inverarish 86 B1
Inverarity 83 F3
Inverarnan 80 E6
Inverasdale 94 D6
Inverbain 94 D6
Inverbeg 74 B1
Inverbervie 91 G7
Inverboyndie 98 E4
Inverbroom 95 H3
Inverbrough 89 F2
Invercassley 96 B1
Inverchaolain 73 J3
Invercharnan 80 C3
Inverchorachan 80 D6
Inverchoran 95 J6
Invercreran 80 B3
Inverdruie 89 G3
Inverebrie 91 H1
Invereen 89 F1
Inverernan 97 H5
Inveresk 76 B3
Inverey 89 H6
Inverfarigaig 88 C2
Invergarry 87 K4
Invergelder 89 K5
Invergeldie 81 J5
Invergloy 87 J6
Invergordon 96 E5

Invergowrie 82 E4
Inverguseran 86 D4
Inverhadden 81 H2
Inverharroch 90 B1
Inverherive 80 E5
Inverhope 103 G2
Inverie 86 D4
Inverinan 80 A6
Inverinate 87 F2
Inverkeilor 83 H3
Inverkeithing 75 K2
Inverkeithny 98 E6
Inverkip 74 A3
Inverkirkaig 102 C7
Inverlael 95 H3
Inverlauren 74 B2
Inverliever 79 K7
Inverliver 80 B4
Inverlochlarig 81 F6
Inverlochy 80 C5
Inverlussa 72 E2
Invermay 82 B6
Invermoriston 88 B3
Invernaver 104 C2
Inverneil 73 G2
Inverness 96 D7
Inverness Airport 96 E6
Invernettie 99 K6
Invernoaden 73 K1
Inveroran Hotel 80 D3
Inverquharity 83 F2
Inverquhomery 99 J6
Inverroy 87 J6
Inversanda 80 A2
Invershiel 87 F3
Inversnaid Hotel 80 E7
Invertrossachs 81 G7
Inveruglas 80 E7
Inveruglass 89 F4
Inverurie 91 F2
Invervar 81 H3
Invervegain 73 J3
Invery House 90 E5
Inverythan 99 F6
Inwardleigh 6 D6
Inworth 34 C7
Iochdar 92 C7
Iping 12 B4
Ipplepen 5 J4
Ipsden 21 K3
Ipstones 50 C7
Ipswich 35 F4
Irby 48 B4
Irby in the Marsh 53 H6
Irby upon Humber 52 E2
Irchester 32 C2
Ireby *Cumb.* 60 D3
Ireby *Lancs.* 56 B2
Ireland *Ork.* 107 C7
Ireland *Shet.* 109 C10
Ireleth 55 F2
Ireshopeburn 61 K3
Irlam 49 G3
Irnham 42 D3
Iron Acton 19 K3
Iron Cross 30 B3
Ironbridge 39 F5
Ironside 99 G5
Ironville 51 G7
Irstead 45 H4
Irthington 69 K7
Irthlingborough 32 C1
Irton 59 G1
Irvine 74 B7
Isauld 104 E2
Isbister *Ork.* 107 C6
Isbister *Ork.* 106 B5
Isbister *Shet.* 109 E6
Isbister *Shet.* 108 C3
Isfield 13 H5
Isham 32 B1
Ishriff 79 H4
Islay Airport 72 B5
Islay House 72 B4
Isle Abbotts 8 C2
Isle Brewers 8 C2
Isle of Man Airport 54 B7
Isle of Whithorn 64 E7
Isleham 33 K1
Isleornsay
  (Eilean Iarmain) 86 C3
Islesburgh 109 C6
Isleworth 22 E4
Isley Walton 41 G3
Islibhig 100 B5
Islip *Northants.* 32 C1
Islip *Oxon.* 31 G7
Isombridge 39 F4
Istead Rise 24 C5
Itchen 11 F3
Itchen Abbas 11 G1
Itchen Stoke 11 G1
Itchingfield 12 E4
Itchington 19 K3
Itteringham 45 F2
Itton 6 E6
Itton Common 19 H2
Ivegill 61 F2
Ivelet 62 A7
Iver 22 D3
Iver Heath 22 D3
Iveston 62 C1
Ivinghoe 32 C7
Ivinghoe Aston 32 C7
Ivington 28 D3
Ivington Green 28 D3
Ivy Hatch 23 J6
Ivy Todd 44 C5
Ivybridge 5 G5
Ivychurch 15 F5
Iwade 25 F5
Iwerne Courtney
  (Shroton) 9 H3
Iwerne Minster 9 H3
Ixworth 34 D1
Ixworth Thorpe 34 D1

J

Jack Hill 57 G4
Jackstown 91 F1
Jackton 74 D5
Jacobstow 4 B1
Jacobstowe 6 D5
Jameston 16 D6
Jamestown
  D. & G. 69 J4
Jamestown
  High. 96 A6
Jamestown
  W.Dun. 74 B2
Janefield 96 E6
Janetstown 105 F2
Jarrow 71 J7
Jarvis Brook 13 J3
Jasper's Green 34 B6
Jawcraig 75 G3

Jayes Park 22 E7
Jaywick 35 F7
Jedburgh 70 B1
Jeffreyston 16 D5
Jemimaville 96 E5
Jersay 75 G4
Jersey Airport 3 J7
Jerviswood 75 G6
Jesmond 71 H7
Jevington 13 J6
Jodrell Bank 49 G5
John o' Groats 105 J1
Johnby 61 F3
John's Cross 14 C5
Johnshaven 83 J1
Johnston 16 C4
Johnston Mains 83 H1
Johnstone 74 C4
Johnstone Castle 74 C4
Johnstonebridge 69 F4
Johnstown
  Carmar. 17 G4
Johnstown *Wrex.* 38 C1
Joppa *Edin.* 76 B3
Joppa *S.Ayr.* 67 J2
Jordans 22 C2
Jordanston 16 C2
Jordanstone 82 D3
Jump 51 F2
Juniper Green 75 K4
Jura House 72 C4
Jurby East 54 C4
Jurby West 54 C4

K

Kaber 61 J5
Kaimes 76 A4
Kames *Arg. & B.* 73 H3
Kames *Arg. & B.* 79 K6
Kames *E.Ayr.* 68 B1
Kea 3 F4
Keadby 52 B1
Keal Cotes 53 G6
Kearsley 49 G2
Kearstwick 56 B1
Kearton 62 B7
Kearvaig 102 E1
Keasden 56 C3
Kebholes 98 E5
Keckwick 48 E4
Keddington 53 G4
Kedington 34 B4
Kedleston 41 F1
Keelby 52 E2
Keele 40 A1
Keeley Green 32 D4
Keeres Green 33 J7
Keeston 16 C4
Keevil 20 C6
Kegworth 41 G3
Kehelland 2 D4
Keig 90 E3
Keighley 57 F5
Keil *Arg. & B.* 66 A3
Keil *High.* 80 A2
Keilhill 99 F5
Keillmore 72 E2
Keillor 82 D3
Keillour 82 A5
Keills 72 C4
Keils 72 D4
Keinton Mandeville 8 E1
Keir House 75 F1
Keir Mill 68 D4
Keisby 42 D3
Keisley 61 J4
Keiss 105 J2
Keith 98 C5
Keithick 82 D4
Keithmore 90 B1
Keithock 83 H1
Kelbrook 56 E5
Kelby 42 D1
Keld *Cumb.* 61 G5
Keld *N.Yorks.* 61 K6
Keldholme 58 D1
Keldy Castle 63 J7
Kelfield *N.Lincs.* 52 B2
Kelfield *N.Yorks.* 58 B6
Kelham 51 K7
Kellan 79 G3
Kellas *Angus* 83 F4
Kellas *Moray* 97 J6
Kellaton 5 J7
Kelleth 61 H6
Kelleythorpe 59 G4
Kelling 44 E1
Kellington 58 B7
Kelloe 62 E3
Kelloholm 68 C2
Kelly *Cornw.* 4 A3
Kelly *Devon* 6 B7
Kelly Bray 4 D3
Kelmarsh 31 J1
Kelmscott 21 F2
Kelsale 35 H2
Kelsall 48 E6
Kelsay 72 A2
Kelshall 33 G5
Kelsick 60 C1
Kelso 77 F7
Kelstedge 51 F6
Kelstern 53 F3
Kelston 19 K5
Keltneyburn 81 J3
Kelton 65 K3
Kelton Hill or
  Rhonehouse 65 H5
Kelty 75 K1
Kelvedon 34 C7
Kelvedon Hatch 23 J2
Kelynack 2 A5
Kemback 83 F6
Kemberton 39 G5
Kemble 20 C2
Kemerton 29 J5
Kemeys
  Commander 19 G1
Kemeys Inferior 19 G2
Kemnay 91 F3
Kemp Town 13 G6
Kempley 29 F6
Kempley Green 29 F6
Kempsey 29 H4
Kempsford 20 E2
Kempshott 21 K7
Kempston 32 D4
Kempston
  Church End 32 D4
Kempston
  Hardwick 32 D4
Kempton 38 C7
Kemsing 23 J6
Kemsley 25 F5
Kenardington 14 E4
Kenchester 28 D4
Kencott 21 F1

Kendal 61 G7
Kenderchurch 28 D6
Kenfig 18 B3
Kenfig Hill 18 B3
Kenilworth 30 D1
Kenknock P. & B. 81 G3
Kenknock *Stir.* 81 F4
Kenley *Gt.Lon.* 23 G6
Kenley *Shrop.* 38 E5
Kenmore
  Arg. & B. 80 B7
Kenmore *High.* 94 D6
Kenmore *P. & K.* 81 J3
Kenmore *W.Isles* 100 E1
Kenn *Devon* 7 H7
Kenn *N.Som.* 19 H5
Kennacraig 73 G4
Kennards House 4 C2
Kennavay 93 H2
Kennerleigh 7 G5
Kennerty 90 E5
Kennet 75 H1
Kennethmont 90 D2
Kennett 33 K2
Kennford 7 H7
Kenninghall 44 E7
Kennington *Kent* 15 F3
Kennington *Oxon.* 21 J1
Kennoway 82 E7
Kennyhill 33 K1
Kennythorpe 58 D3
Kensaleyre 93 K6
Kensington 23 F4
Kensworth 32 D7
Kensworth
  Common 32 D7
Kent Street
  E.Suss. 14 C6
Kent Street *Kent* 23 K6
Kentallen 80 B2
Kentchurch 28 D6
Kentford 34 B2
Kentisbeare 7 J5
Kentisbury 6 E1
Kentisbury Ford 6 E1
Kentmere 61 F6
Kenton *Devon* 7 H7
Kenton *Suff.* 35 F2
Kenton *T. & W.* 71 H7
Kentra 79 H1
Kents Bank 55 H2
Kent's Green 29 G6
Kent's Oak 10 E2
Kenwick 38 D2
Kenwyn 3 F4
Keoldale 103 F2
Keppanach 80 B2
Keppoch *Arg. & B.* 74 B3
Keppoch *High.* 86 E2
Keprigan 66 A2
Kepwick 63 F7
Keresley 41 F7
Kerne Bridge 28 E7
Kerridge 49 J5
Kerris 2 B6
Kerry 38 A7
Kerrycroy 73 K4
Kerry's Gate 28 C5
Kerrysdale 94 E4
Kersall 51 K6
Kersey 34 E4
Kershopefoot 69 K5
Kerswell 7 J5
Kerswell Green 29 H4
Kesgrave 35 G4
Kessingland 45 K7
Kessingland Beach 45 K7
Kestle Mill 3 F3
Keston 23 H5
Keswick *Cumb.* 60 D4
Keswick *Norf.* 45 G5
Keswick *Norf.* 45 H2
Ketsby 53 G5
Kettering 32 B1
Ketteringham 45 F5
Kettins 82 D4
Kettlebaston 34 D4
Kettlebridge 82 E7
Kettlebrook 40 E5
Kettleburgh 35 G2
Kettleholm 69 G6
Kettleness 63 K5
Kettleshulme 49 J5
Kettlesing 57 H4
Kettlesing Bottom 57 H4
Kettlestone 44 D2
Kettlethorpe 52 B5
Kettletoft 106 F4
Kettlewell 56 E2
Ketton 42 C5
Kew 22 E4
Kewstoke 19 G5
Kexbrough 51 F2
Kexby *Lincs.* 52 B4
Kexby *York* 58 D4
Key Green 49 H6
Keyham 41 J5
Keyhaven 10 E5
Keyingham 59 J7
Keymer 13 G5
Keynsham 19 K5
Key's Toft 53 H7
Keysoe 32 D2
Keysoe Row 32 D2
Keyston 32 D1
Keyworth 41 J2
Kibblesworth 62 D1
Kibworth
  Beauchamp 41 J6
Kibworth Harcourt 41 J6
Kidbrooke 23 H4
Kiddal Lane End 57 K6
Kiddemore Green 40 A5
Kidderminster 29 H1
Kiddington 31 F6
Kidmore End 21 K4
Kidsdale 64 E7
Kidsgrove 49 H7
Kidstones 56 E1
Kidwelly (Cydweli) 17 H5
Kiel Crofts 80 A4
Kielder 70 B4
Kilbarchan 74 C4
Kilbeg 86 C4
Kilberry 72 E3
Kilbirnie 74 B5
Kilblaan 80 D5
Kilbraur 104 D1
Kilbrennan 79 F3
Kilbride *Arg. & B.* 79 K5
Kilbride *Arg. & B.* 80 B5
Kilbride *High.* 86 B2
Kilbride Farm 73 H4
Kilbridemore 73 J1
Kilburn *Derbys.* 41 F1
Kilburn *N.Yorks.* 58 B2
Kilby 41 J6
Kilchamaig 73 G4
Kilchattan 73 K5

Kilchattan 72 A5
Kilchenzie 66 A2
Kilcheran 66 K4
Kilchiaran 72 A5
Kilchoan *Arg. & B.* 79 J2
Kilchoan *High.* 79 F1
Kilchoman 72 A4
Kilchrenan 80 B5
Kilchrist 66 A2
Kilconquhar 83 F7
Kilcot 29 F6
Kilcoy 96 C6
Kilcreggan 74 A2
Kildale 63 H6
Kildary 96 E4
Kildavie 66 B2
Kildermorie Lodge 96 C4
Kildonan 66 E1
Kildonan Lodge 104 E6
Kildonnan 85 K6
Kildrochet House 64 A5
Kildrummy 90 C3
Kildwick 57 F5
Kilfinan 73 H3
Kilfinnan 87 J5
Kilgetty 16 E5
Kilgwrrwg
  Common 19 H2
Kilham *E.Riding* 59 G3
Kilham *Northumb.* 77 G7
Kilkenneth 78 A3
Kilkenny 30 B7
Kilkerran
  Arg. & B. 66 B2
Kilkerran *S.Ayr.* 67 H3
Kilkhampton 6 A4
Killamarsh 51 G4
Killay 17 K6
Killbeg 79 H3
Killean *Arg. & B.* 72 E6
Killean *Arg. & B.* 80 B7
Killearn 74 D2
Killellan 66 A2
Killerby 62 C4
Killichonan 81 G2
Killichonate 87 J6
Killiechonan 79 G3
Killiecrankie 82 A1
Killiehuntly 88 E5
Killiemor 79 F4
Killilan 87 F1
Killimster 105 J3
Killin *High.* 97 F1
Killin *Stir.* 81 G4
Killinallan 72 B3
Killinghall 57 H4
Killington 56 B1
Killingworth 71 H6
Killochyett 76 C6
Killocraw 66 A1
Killunaig 79 F5
Killundine 79 G3
Kilmacolm 74 B4
Kilmaha 80 A7
Kilmahog 81 H7
Kilmalieu 79 K2
Kilmaluag 93 K4
Kilmany 82 E5
Kilmarie 86 B3
Kilmarnock 74 C7
Kilmartin 73 G1
Kilmaurs 74 C6
Kilmelford 79 K6
Kilmeny 72 B4
Kilmersdon 19 K6
Kilmeston 11 G2
Kilmichael 66 A1
Kilmichael Glassary 73 G1
Kilmichael of
  Inverlussa 73 F2
Kilmington *Devon* 8 B5
Kilmington *Wilts.* 9 G1
Kilmington Street 9 G1
Kilmorack 96 B7
Kilmore *Arg. & B.* 79 K5
Kilmore *High.* 86 C4
Kilmory *Arg. & B.* 73 F3
Kilmory *Arg. & B.* 79 F3
Kilmory *High.* 85 J4
Kilmory *High.* 79 J1
Kilmote 104 E1
Kilmuir *High.* 93 H7
Kilmuir *High.* 96 D6
Kilmuir *High.* 96 E4
Kilmuir *High.* 96 D5
Kilmun 73 K2
Kilmux 82 E7
Kiln Green 22 B4
Kiln Pit Hill 62 B1
Kilnave 72 A3
Kilncadzow 75 G6
Kilndown 14 C4
Kilnhurst 51 G3
Kilninian 79 F3
Kilninver 79 K5
Kilnsea 53 H1
Kilnsey 56 E3
Kilnwick 59 G5
Kiloran 72 B1
Kilpatrick 66 D1
Kilpeck 28 D5
Kilphedir 104 E1
Kilpin 58 D7
Kilrenny 83 G7
Kilsby 31 G1
Kilspindie 82 D5
Kilstay 64 B7
Kilsyth 75 F3
Kiltarlity 96 C7
Kilton *R. & C.* 63 H5
Kilton *Som.* 7 K1
Kiltyrie 81 H4
Kilvaxter 93 J5
Kilve 7 K1
Kilverstone 44 C7
Kilvington 42 B1
Kilwinning 74 B6
Kimberley *Norf.* 44 E5
Kimberley *Notts.* 41 H1
Kimble Wick 22 B1
Kimblesworth 62 D2
Kimbolton *Cambs.* 32 E2
Kimbolton *Here.* 28 E2
Kimcote 41 H7
Kimmeridge 9 H7
Kimmerston 77 H7
Kimpton *Hants.* 21 F7
Kimpton *Herts.* 32 E7
Kinaldy 83 G6
Kinblethmont 83 H3
Kinbrace 104 D3
Kinbreack 87 G5
Kinbuck 81 J7
Kincaldrum 83 F3
Kincaple 83 F6
Kincardine *Fife* 75 H2
Kincardine *High.* 96 C3
Kincardine O'Neil 90 D5
Kinclaven 82 C4

Kincorth 91 H4
Kincraig *Aber.* 91 H2
Kincraig *High.* 89 F4
Kincraigie 82 A3
Kindallachan 82 A2
Kindrogan Field
  Centre 82 B1
Kinellar 91 G3
Kineton *Glos.* 30 B6
Kineton *Warks.* 30 E3
Kineton Green 40 D7
Kinfauns 82 C5
King Sterndale 50 C5
Kingarth 73 J5
Kingcoed 19 H1
Kingerby 52 D3
Kingham 30 D6
Kingholm Quay 65 K3
Kinghorn 76 A2
Kinglassie 76 A1
Kingoodie 82 E5
King's Bromley 40 D4
Kings Caple 28 E6
King's Cliffe 42 D6
King's Coughton 30 B3
King's Green 29 G5
King's Heath 40 C7
King's Hill *Kent* 23 K6
King's Hill *W.Mid.* 40 B6
Kings Langley 22 D1
King's Lynn 44 A3
Kings Meaburn 61 H4
King's Mills 3 H5
Kings Muir 76 A7
King's Newton 41 F3
King's Norton
  Leics. 41 J5
King's Norton
  W.Mid. 30 B1
King's Nympton 6 E4
King's Pyon 28 D3
Kings Ripton 33 F1
King's Somborne 10 E1
King's Stag 9 G3
King's Stanley 20 B1
King's Sutton 31 F5
King's Walden 32 E6
Kings Worthy 11 F1
Kingsand 7 J4
Kingsbarns 83 G6
Kingsbridge *Devon* 5 H6
Kingsbridge *Som.* 7 H2
Kingsburgh 93 J6
Kingsbury *Gt.Lon.* 22 E3
Kingsbury *Warks.* 40 E6
Kingsbury Episcopi 8 D2
Kingscavil 75 J3
Kingsclere 21 J6
Kingscote 20 B2
Kingscott 6 D4
Kingscross 66 E1
Kingsdale 82 E7
Kingsdon 8 E2
Kingsdown 15 J3
Kingseat 75 K1
Kingsey 22 A1
Kingsfold *Pembs.* 16 C6
Kingsfold *W.Suss.* 12 E3
Kingsford *Aber.* 99 F6
Kingsford *Aber.* 90 D3
Kingsford
  Aberdeen 91 G4
Kingsford *E.Ayr.* 74 C6
Kingsford *Worcs.* 40 A7
Kingsforth 52 D1
Kingsgate 25 K4
Kingsheanton 6 D2
Kingshouse 81 G5
Kingshouse Hotel 80 D2
Kingskerswell 5 J4
Kingskettle 82 E7
Kingsland *Here.* 28 D2
Kingsland *I.o.A.* 46 A4
Kingsley *Ches.* 48 E5
Kingsley *Hants.* 11 J1
Kingsley *Staffs.* 40 C1
Kingsley Green 12 B3
Kingsmuir 83 F3
Kingsnorth 15 F4
Kingsnorth Power
  Station 24 E4
Kingstanding 40 C6
Kingsteignton 5 J3
Kingsteps 97 G6
Kingsthorne 28 E5
Kingsthorpe 31 J2
Kingston *Cambs.* 33 G3
Kingston *Devon* 5 G6
Kingston *Dorset* 9 G4
Kingston *Dorset* 9 H7
Kingston *E.Loth.* 76 D2
Kingston *Hants.* 10 C4
Kingston *I.o.W.* 11 F6
Kingston *Kent* 15 G2
Kingston *Moray* 98 B4
Kingston *W.Suss.* 12 D6
Kingston Bagpuize 21 H2
Kingston Blount 22 A2
Kingston by Sea 13 F6
Kingston Deverill 9 H1
Kingston Lisle 21 G3
Kingston near
  Lewes 13 G6
Kingston on Soar 41 H3
Kingston Russell 8 E5
Kingston St. Mary 8 B2
Kingston Seymour 19 G5
Kingston Upon
  Hull 59 G7
Kingston upon
  Thames 22 E5
Kingston Warren 21 G3
Kingstone *Here.* 28 D5
Kingstone *Som.* 8 C3
Kingstone *Staffs.* 40 C3
Kingstown 60 E1
Kingswear 5 J5
Kingswell 74 D6
Kingswells 91 G4
Kingswinford 40 A7
Kingswood *Bucks.* 31 H7
Kingswood *Glos.* 20 A2
Kingswood *Here.* 28 B3
Kingswood *Kent* 14 D2
Kingswood *Powys* 38 B5
Kingswood *S.Glos.* 19 K4
Kingswood *Surr.* 23 F6
Kingswood *Warks.* 30 C1
Kingthorpe 52 E5
Kington *Here.* 28 B3
Kington *Worcs.* 29 J3
Kington Langley 20 C4
Kington Magna 9 G2
Kington St. Michael 20 B4
Kingussie 88 E4

Kingweston 8 E1
Kinharrachie 91 H1
Kinharvie 65 K4
Kinkell 74 E3
Kinkell Bridge 82 A6
Kinknockie 99 J6
Kinlet 39 G7
Kinloch *Fife* 82 D6
Kinloch *High.* 103 F5
Kinloch *High.* 79 H2
Kinloch *High.* 85 K5
Kinloch *High.* 96 C4
Kinloch *P. & K.* 82 D3
Kinloch *P. & K.* 82 D3
Kinloch Hourn 87 F4
Kinloch Laggan 88 C6
Kinloch Rannoch 81 H2
Kinlochan 79 K1
Kinlochard 81 F7
Kinlocharkaig 87 F5
Kinlochbeoraid 86 E6
Kinlochbervie 102 E3
Kinlocheil 87 F7
Kinlochetive 80 C3
Kinlochewe 95 G5
Kinlochlaich 80 A3
Kinlochleven 80 C1
Kinlochmoidart 86 E7
Kinlochmorar 86 E5
Kinlochmore 80 C1
Kinlochspelve 79 H5
Kinloss 97 H5
Kinmel Bay (Bae Cinmel) 47 H4
Kinmuck 91 G3
Kinnadie 99 H6
Kinnaird 82 D5
Kinneff 91 G7
Kinnelhead 69 F3
Kinnell *Angus* 83 H2
Kinnell *Stir.* 81 H7
Kinnerley 38 C3
Kinnersley *Here.* 28 D2
Kinnersley *Worcs.* 29 H4
Kinnerton 28 B2
Kinnesswood 82 C7
Kinnettles 83 F3
Kinninvie 62 B4
Kinnordy 82 E2
Kinoulton 41 J2
Kinrara 89 F4
Kinross 82 C7
Kinrossie 82 D4
Kinsbourne Green 32 E7
Kinsham 28 C2
Kinsley 51 G1
Kinson 10 B5
Kintarvie 100 E6
Kintbury 21 G5
Kintessack 97 G5
Kintillo 82 C6
Kintocher 90 D4
Kinton *Here.* 28 D1
Kinton *Shrop.* 38 C4
Kintore 91 F3
Kintour 72 C5
Kintra *Arg. & B.* 72 B6
Kintra *Arg. & B.* 78 E5
Kintradwell 97 G1
Kintraw 79 K7
Kinuachdrachd 73 F1
Kinveachy 89 G3
Kinver 40 A7
Kiplaw Croft 91 J1
Kiplin 62 D7
Kiplingcotes 59 F5
Kipp 81 G6
Kippax 57 K6
Kippen *P. & K.* 82 B6
Kippen *Stir.* 74 E1
Kippenross House 81 J7
Kippford or Scaur 65 J5
Kipping's Cross 23 K7
Kirbister *Ork.* 107 C7
Kirbister *Ork.* 106 F5
Kirbuster 106 B5
Kirby Bedon 45 G5
Kirby Cane 45 H6
Kirby Corner 30 D1
Kirby Cross 35 G7
Kirby Grindalythe 59 F3
Kirby Hill *N.Yorks.* 62 C6
Kirby Hill *N.Yorks.* 57 J3
Kirby Knowle 57 K1
Kirby le Soken 35 G6
Kirby Misperton 58 D2
Kirby Muxloe 41 H5
Kirby Row 45 H6
Kirby Sigston 63 F7
Kirby Underdale 58 E4
Kirby Wiske 57 J1
Kirdford 12 D4
Kirk 105 H3
Kirk Bramwith 51 J1
Kirk Deighton 57 J4
Kirk Ella 59 G7
Kirk Hallam 41 G1
Kirk Hammerton 57 K4
Kirk Ireton 50 E7
Kirk Langley 40 E2
Kirk Merrington 62 D3
Kirk Michael 54 C4
Kirk of Shotts 75 G4
Kirk Sandall 51 J2
Kirk Smeaton 51 H1
Kirk Yetholm 70 D1
Kirkabister 109 D9
Kirkandrews 65 G6
Kirkandrews-upon-Eden 60 E1
Kirkbampton 60 E1
Kirkbean 65 K5
Kirkbride 60 D1
Kirkbridge 62 D7
Kirkbuddo 83 G3
Kirkburn *E.Riding* 59 F4
Kirkburn *Sc.Bord.* 76 A7
Kirkburton 50 D1
Kirkby *Lincs.* 52 D3
Kirkby *Mersey.* 48 D3
Kirkby *N.Yorks.* 63 G6
Kirkby Bellars 42 A4
Kirkby Fleetham 62 D7
Kirkby Green 51 G7
Kirkby in Ashfield 51 G7
Kirkby la Thorpe 42 D1
Kirkby Lonsdale 56 B2
Kirkby Malham 56 D3
Kirkby Mallory 41 G5
Kirkby Malzeard 57 H2
Kirkby Mills 58 D1
Kirkby on Bain 53 F6
Kirkby Overblow 57 J5
Kirkby Stephen 61 J6
Kirkby Thore 61 H4
Kirkby Underwood 42 D3

Kirkby Wharfe 58 B5
Kirkbymoorside 58 C1
Kirkcaldy 76 A1
Kirkcambeck 70 A7
Kirkcolm 64 A4
Kirkconnel 68 C2
Kirkconnell 65 K4
Kirkcowan 64 D4
Kirkcudbright 65 G5
Kirkdale House 65 F5
Kirkdean 75 K6
Kirkfieldbank 75 G6
Kirkgunzeon 65 J4
Kirkham *Lancs.* 55 H6
Kirkham *N.Yorks.* 58 D3
Kirkhamgate 57 H7
Kirkharle 71 F5
Kirkhaugh 61 H2
Kirkheaton *Northumb.* 71 F6
Kirkheaton *W.Yorks.* 50 D1
Kirkhill *Angus* 83 H1
Kirkhill *High.* 96 C7
Kirkhill *Moray* 98 B5
Kirkhope 69 J1
Kirkibost *High.* 86 B3
Kirkibost *W.Isles* 100 D4
Kirkinch 82 E3
Kirkinner 64 E5
Kirkintilloch 74 E3
Kirkland *Cumb.* 61 H3
Kirkland *Cumb.* 60 B5
Kirkland *D. & G.* 68 D4
Kirkland *D. & G.* 68 C2
Kirkland *D. & G.* 69 F5
Kirkland of Longcastle 64 D6
Kirkleatham 63 G4
Kirklevington 63 F5
Kirkley 45 K6
Kirklington *N.Yorks.* 57 J1
Kirklington *Notts.* 51 J7
Kirklinton 69 K7
Kirkliston 75 K3
Kirkmaiden 64 B7
Kirkmichael *P.& K.* 82 C2
Kirkmichael *S.Ayr.* 67 H3
Kirkmuirhill 75 F6
Kirknewton *Northumb.* 70 E1
Kirknewton *W.Loth.* 75 K4
Kirkney 90 D1
Kirkoswald *Cumb.* 61 G2
Kirkoswald *S.Ayr.* 67 G3
Kirkpatrick Durham 65 H3
Kirkpatrick-Fleming 69 H6
Kirksanton 54 E1
Kirkstall 57 H6
Kirkstead 52 E6
Kirkstile *Aber.* 90 D1
Kirkstile *D. & G.* 69 J4
Kirkton *Aber.* 90 E1
Kirkton *Aber.* 98 E5
Kirkton *Aber.* 90 E3
Kirkton *Angus* 83 F3
Kirkton *Arg. & B.* 79 J7
Kirkton *D. & G.* 68 E5
Kirkton *Fife* 82 E5
Kirkton *High.* 88 D1
Kirkton *High.* 96 E2
Kirkton *High.* 104 D2
Kirkton *High.* 86 E2
Kirkton *P. & K.* 82 A6
Kirkton *Sc.Bord.* 70 A2
Kirkton Manor 76 A7
Kirkton of Airlie 82 E2
Kirkton of Auchterhouse 82 E4
Kirkton of Barevan 97 F7
Kirkton of Bourtie 91 G2
Kirkton of Collace 82 C4
Kirkton of Craig 83 J2
Kirkton of Culsalmond 90 E1
Kirkton of Durris 91 F5
Kirkton of Glenbuchat 90 B3
Kirkton of Glenisla 82 D1
Kirkton of Kingoldrum 82 E2
Kirkton of Lethendy 82 C3
Kirkton of Logie Buchan 91 H2
Kirkton of Maryculter 91 G5
Kirkton of Menmuir 83 G1
Kirkton of Monikie 83 G4
Kirkton of Rayne 90 E1
Kirkton of Skene 91 G4
Kirkton of Strathmartine 82 E4
Kirkton of Tealing 83 F4
Kirktonhill 83 H1
Kirktown 99 J5
Kirktown of Alvah 98 D4
Kirktown of Auchterless 99 F6
Kirktown of Deskford 98 D4
Kirktown of Fetteresso 91 G6
Kirktown of Slains 91 J2
Kirkwall 107 D6
Kirkwall Airport 107 D7
Kirkwhelpington 70 E5
Kirmington 52 E1
Kirmond le Mire 52 E3
Kirn 73 K3
Kirriemuir 82 E2
Kirstead Green 45 G6
Kirtlebridge 69 H6
Kirtling 33 K3
Kirtling Green 33 K3
Kirtlington 31 F7
Kirtomy 104 C2
Kirton *Lincs.* 43 G2
Kirton *Notts.* 51 J6
Kirton *Suff.* 35 G5
Kirton End 43 F1
Kirton Holme 43 F1
Kirton in Lindsey 52 C3
Kiscadale 66 E1
Kislingbury 31 H3
Kismeldon Bridge 6 B4
Kites Hardwick 31 F2
Kitley 5 F5
Kittisford 7 J3
Kitwood 11 H1
Kiveton Park 51 G4
Klibreck 103 H5
Knabbygates 98 D5
Knaith 52 B4
Knap Corner 9 H2

Knaphill 22 C6
Knapp *P. & K.* 82 D4
Knapp *Som.* 8 B2
Knapton *Norf.* 45 H2
Knapton *York* 58 B4
Knapton Green 28 D3
Knapwell 33 G2
Knaresborough 57 J4
Knarsdale 61 H1
Knaven 99 G6
Knayton 57 K1
Knebworth 33 F7
Knedlington 58 D7
Kneesall 51 K6
Kneesworth 33 G4
Kneeton 42 A1
Knelston 17 H7
Knettishall 34 D1
Knightacott 6 E2
Knightcote 31 F3
Knighton *Devon* 5 F6
Knighton *Leic.* 41 J5
Knighton *Powys* 28 B1
Knighton *Som.* 7 K1
Knighton *Staffs.* 39 G3
Knighton *Staffs.* 39 G2
Knighton *Wilts.* 21 F4
Knightwick 29 G3
Knill 28 B2
Knipoch 79 K5
Knipton 42 B2
Knitsley 62 C2
Kniveton 50 E7
Knock *Arg. & B.* 79 G4
Knock *Cumb.* 61 H4
Knock *Moray* 98 D5
Knock of Auchnahannet 89 H1
Knockalava 73 H1
Knockally 105 G6
Knockaloe Moar 54 B5
Knockan 102 E7
Knockandhu 89 K2
Knockando 97 J7
Knockbain 96 D6
Knockban 95 J5
Knockbreck 96 E3
Knockbrex 65 F6
Knockdamph 95 J2
Knockdee 105 G2
Knockdow 73 K3
Knockdown 20 B3
Knockenkelly 66 E1
Knockentiber 74 C7
Knockfin 87 J2
Knockgray 67 K4
Knockholt 23 H6
Knockholt Pound 23 H6
Knockin 38 C3
Knocklearn 65 H3
Knocknaha 66 A2
Knocknain 66 D7
Knocknalling 67 K5
Knockrome 72 D3
Knocksharry 54 B5
Knockville 64 D3
Knockvologan 78 E6
Knodishall 35 J2
Knolls Green 49 H5
Knolton 38 C2
Knook 20 C7
Knossington 42 B5
Knott End-on-Sea 55 G5
Knotting 32 D2
Knotting Green 32 D2
Knottingley 58 B7
Knotty Ash 48 D3
Knotty Green 22 C2
Knowbury 28 E1
Knowe 64 D3
Knowes of Elrick 98 E5
Knowesgate 70 E5
Knoweside 67 G2
Knowetownhead 70 A2
Knowhead 99 H5
Knowl Green 34 B4
Knowl Hill 22 B4
Knowl Wall 40 A2
Knowle *Bristol* 19 K4
Knowle *Devon* 7 F5
Knowle *Devon* 6 C2
Knowle *Devon* 7 J7
Knowle *Shrop.* 28 E1
Knowle *W.Mid.* 30 C1
Knowle Green 56 B6
Knowle Hall 19 G7
Knowlton *Dorset* 10 B3
Knowlton *Kent* 15 H2
Knowsley 48 D3
Knowstone 7 G3
Knucklas 28 B1
Knutsford 49 G5
Knypersley 49 H7
Kuggar 2 E7
Kyle of Lochalsh 86 D2
Kyleakin 86 D2
Kylerhea 86 D2
Kyles Scalpay (Caolas Scalpaigh) 93 H2
Kylesbeg 86 C7
Kylesknoydart 86 E5
Kylesmorar 86 E5
Kylestrome 102 E5
Kyloag 96 D2
Kynnersley 39 F4
Kyre Park 29 F2

L

Labost 100 E3
Lacasaigh 101 F5
Lacasdal (Laxdale) 101 G4
Laceby 53 F2
Lacey Green 22 B1
Lach Dennis 49 G5
Lackford 34 B1
Lacock 20 C5
Ladbroke 31 F3
Laddingford 23 K7
Lade Bank 53 G7
Ladock 3 F3
Lady Hall 54 E1
Ladybank 82 E6
Ladycross 6 B7
Ladyfield 80 B6
Ladykirk 77 G6
Lady's Green 34 B3
Ladysford 99 H4
Laga 79 H1
Lagalochan 79 K6
Lagavulin 72 C6
Lagg *Arg. & B.* 72 C3
Lagg *N.Ayr.* 66 D1
Lagg *S.Ayr.* 67 G5
Laggan *Arg. & B.* 72 A5
Laggan *High.* 87 J5
Laggan *High.* 88 D5

Laggan *Moray* 90 B1
Laggan *Stir.* 81 G6
Lagganulva 79 F3
Lagganvoulin 89 J3
Laglingarten 80 C7
Lagnalean 96 D7
Lagrae 68 C2
Laguna 82 C4
Laid 103 G3
Laide 94 E2
Laig 85 K6
Laight 68 B2
Lainchoil 89 H3
Laindon 24 C3
Lair 82 C1
Lairg 96 C1
Lairg Lodge 96 C1
Lairgmor 80 C1
Laithers 98 E6
Laithes 61 F3
Lake 10 C1
Lakenham 45 G5
Lakenheath 44 B7
Lakesend 43 J6
Lakeside *Cumb.* 55 G1
Lakeside *Thur.* 23 J4
Laleham 22 D5
Laleston 18 B4
Lamachan 76 A5
Lamarsh 34 C5
Lamas 45 G3
Lamb Corner 34 E5
Lamberton 77 H5
Lambeth 23 G4
Lambfell Moar 54 B5
Lambley *Northumb.* 61 H1
Lambley *Notts.* 41 J1
Lambourn 21 G4
Lambourn Woodlands 21 G4
Lambourne End 23 H2
Lambs Green 13 F3
Lambston 16 C4
Lamellion 4 C4
Lamerton 4 E3
Lamesley 62 D1
Lamington *High.* 96 E4
Lamington *S.Lan.* 75 H7
Lamlash 73 J7
Lamloch 67 K4
Lamonby 61 F3
Lamorran 3 F4
Lampert 70 B6
Lampeter 17 J1
Lampeter Velfrey 16 E4
Lamphey 16 D5
Lamplugh 60 B4
Lamport 31 J1
Lamyatt 9 F1
Lana 6 B6
Lanark 75 G6
Lancaster 55 H3
Lanchester 62 C2
Lancing 12 E6
Landbeach 33 H2
Landcross 6 C3
Landerberry 91 F4
Landewednack 2 E7
Landford 10 D3
Landimore 17 H6
Landkey 6 D2
Landore 17 K6
Landrake 4 D4
Landscove 5 H4
Landshipping 16 D4
Landulph 4 E4
Landwade 33 K2
Landywood 40 B5
Lane End *Bucks.* 22 B2
Lane End *Cumb.* 60 C7
Lane End *Derbys.* 51 G6
Lane End *Dorset* 9 H5
Lane End *Kent* 23 J4
Lane Green 40 A5
Lane Head *Dur.* 62 C5
Lane Head *Gt.Man.* 49 F3
Lane Head *W.Yorks.* 50 D2
Laneast 4 C2
Lane-end 4 A4
Laneham 52 B5
Lanehead 70 C5
Laneshawbridge 56 E5
Langais 92 D5
Langamull 78 E2
Langar 42 A2
Langbank 74 B3
Langbar 57 F4
Langcliffe 56 D3
Langdale End 63 J3
Langdon 4 C1
Langdon Beck 61 K3
Langdon Hills 24 C3
Langdon House 5 K3
Langdyke 82 E7
Langenhoe 34 D7
Langford *Beds.* 32 E4
Langford *Devon* 7 J5
Langford *Essex* 24 E1
Langford *Notts.* 52 B7
Langford *Oxon.* 21 F1
Langford Budville 7 K3
Langham *Essex* 34 E5
Langham *Norf.* 44 E1
Langham *Rut.* 42 B4
Langham *Suff.* 34 D2
Langham Moor 34 E5
Langho 56 B6
Langholm 69 J5
Langlands 65 G5
Langlee 70 B2
Langleeford 70 E1
Langley *Ches.* 49 J5
Langley *Derbys.* 41 G1
Langley *Essex* 33 H5
Langley *Hants.* 11 F4
Langley *Herts.* 33 F6
Langley *Kent* 14 D2
Langley *Northumb.* 70 D7
Langley *Slo.* 22 D4
Langley *Som.* 7 J3
Langley *W.Suss.* 12 B4
Langley *Warks.* 30 C2
Langley Burrell 20 C4
Langley Green 40 E7
Langley Heath 14 D2
Langley Marsh 7 J3
Langley Mill 41 G1
Langley Moor 62 D2
Langley Park 62 D2
Langley Street 45 H5
Langney 13 K6
Langold 51 H4
Langore 4 C2
Langport 8 D2
Langrick 43 F1

Langridge *B. & N.E.Som.* 20 A5
Langridge *Devon* 6 D3
Langridgeford 6 D3
Langrigg 60 C2
Langrish 11 J2
Langsett 50 E2
Langshaw 69 H3
Langshawburn 69 H3
Langside 81 J6
Langskaill 106 D3
Langstone 11 J4
Langthorne 62 D7
Langthorpe 57 J3
Langthwaite 62 B6
Langtoft *E.Riding* 59 G3
Langtoft *Lincs.* 42 E4
Langton *Dur.* 62 C5
Langton *Lincs.* 53 G5
Langton *Lincs.* 53 F6
Langton *N.Yorks.* 58 D3
Langton by Wragby 52 E5
Langton Green 13 J3
Langton Herring 9 F6
Langton Long Blandford 9 J4
Langton Matravers 10 B7
Langtree 6 C4
Langwathby 61 G3
Langwell 96 B1
Langwell House 105 G6
Langworth 52 D5
Lanivet 4 A4
Lanlivery 4 A5
Lanner 2 E4
Lanreath 4 B5
Lansallos 4 B5
Lansdown 20 A5
Lanteglos 4 A2
Lanton *Northumb.* 77 H7
Lanton *Sc.Bord.* 70 B1
Lapford 7 F5
Laphroaig 72 B6
Lapley 40 A4
Lapworth 30 C1
Larach na Gaibhre 73 F4
Larachbeg 79 H3
Larbert 75 G2
Larden Green 48 E7
Larg 64 D3
Largie 90 E1
Largiemore 73 H2
Largoward 83 F7
Largs 74 A5
Largue 98 E6
Largybaan 66 A2
Largybeg 66 E1
Largymore 66 E1
Lark Hall 33 J3
Larkhall 75 F5
Larkhill 20 E7
Larling 44 D7
Larriston 70 A4
Lartington 62 B5
Lary 90 B4
Lasborough 20 B2
Lasham 21 K7
Lassington 29 G6
Lassintullich 81 J2
Lassodie 75 K1
Lasswade 76 B4
Lastingham 63 J7
Latcham 19 H7
Latchford 49 F4
Latchingdon 24 E1
Latchley 4 E3
Lately Common 49 F3
Lathallan Mill 83 F7
Lathbury 32 B4
Latheron 105 G5
Latheronwheel 105 G5
Lathockar 83 F6
Lathones 83 F7
Lathrisk 82 D7
Latimer 22 D2
Latteridge 19 K3
Lattiford 9 F2
Latton 20 D2
Lauchentyre 65 F5
Lauchintilly 91 F3
Lauder 76 D6
Laugharne 17 G4
Laughterton 52 B5
Laughton *E.Suss.* 13 J5
Laughton *Leics.* 41 J7
Laughton *Lincs.* 42 D2
Laughton *Lincs.* 52 B3
Laughton en le Morthen 51 H4
Launcells 6 A5
Launcells Cross 6 A5
Launceston 6 B7
Launde Abbey 42 B5
Launton 31 H6
Laurencekirk 91 F7
Laurieston *D. & G.* 65 G4
Laurieston *Falk.* 75 H3
Lavendon 32 C3
Lavenham 34 D4
Laverhay 69 G4
Lavernock 18 E5
Laversdale 69 K7
Laverstock 10 C1
Laverstoke 21 H7
Laverton *Glos.* 30 B5
Laverton *N.Yorks.* 57 H2
Laverton *Som.* 20 A6
Lavister 48 C7
Law 75 G5
Lawers *P. & K.* 81 J5
Lawers *P. & K.* 81 H4
Lawford 34 E5
Lawhitton 6 B7
Lawkland 56 C3
Lawley 39 F5
Lawnhead 40 A3
Lawrenny 16 D5
Laws 83 F4
Lawshall 34 C3
Lawton 28 D3
Laxdale (Lacasdal) 101 G4
Laxey 54 D5
Laxfield 35 G1
Laxfirth *Shet.* 109 D7
Laxfirth *Shet.* 109 D7
Laxford Bridge 102 E4
Laxo 109 D6
Laxton *E.Riding* 58 D7
Laxton *Northants.* 42 C6
Laxton *Notts.* 51 K6
Laycock 57 F5
Layer Breton 34 D7
Layer de la Haye 34 D7
Layer Marney 34 D7
Layham 34 E4
Laytham 58 D6
Lazenby 63 G4

Lazonby 61 G3
Lea *Derbys.* 51 F7
Lea *Here.* 29 F6
Lea *Lincs.* 52 B4
Lea *Shrop.* 38 C7
Lea *Shrop.* 38 D5
Lea *Wilts.* 20 C3
Lea Marston 40 E6
Lea Town 56 C1
Lea Yeat 56 C1
Leac a' Li 93 G2
Leachd 73 J1
Leachkin 96 D7
Leadburn 76 A5
Leaden Roding 33 J7
Leadgate *Cumb.* 61 J2
Leadgate *Dur.* 62 C1
Leadgate *T. & W.* 62 C1
Leadhills 68 D2
Leafield 30 E7
Leagrave 32 D6
Leake Common Side 53 G7
Leake Hurn's End 43 H1
Lealands 13 J5
Lealholm 63 J6
Lealt *Arg. & B.* 72 E1
Lealt *High.* 94 B5
Leamington Hastings 31 F2
Leamington Spa 30 E2
Leanach *Arg. & B.* 73 J1
Leanach *High.* 96 E7
Leanaig 96 C6
Leanoch 97 J6
Leargybreck 72 D3
Leasgill 55 H1
Leasingham 42 D1
Leask 91 J1
Leatherhead 22 E6
Leathley 57 H5
Leaton 38 D4
Leaveland 15 F2
Leavenheath 34 D5
Leavening 58 D3
Leaves Green 23 H5
Lebberston 59 G1
Lechlade 21 F2
Leck 56 B2
Leckford 10 E1
Leckfurin 104 C3
Leckgruinart 72 A4
Leckhampstead *Bucks.* 31 J5
Leckhampstead *W.Berks.* 21 H4
Leckhampton 29 J7
Leckie *High.* 95 G5
Leckie *Stir.* 74 E1
Leckmelm 95 H2
Leckroy 87 K5
Leckuary 73 G1
Leckwith 18 E4
Leconfield 59 G5
Ledaig 80 A4
Ledard 81 F7
Ledbeg 102 E7
Ledburn 32 B6
Ledbury 29 G5
Ledcharrie 81 G5
Ledgemoor 28 D3
Ledicot 28 D2
Ledmore *Arg. & B.* 79 G3
Ledmore *High.* 102 E7
Lednagullin 104 C2
Ledsham *Ches.* 48 C5
Ledsham *W.Yorks.* 57 K7
Ledston 57 K7
Ledstone 5 H6
Ledwell 31 F6
Lee *Arg. & B.* 79 F5
Lee *Devon* 6 C1
Lee *Hants.* 10 E3
Lee *Lancs.* 55 J4
Lee *Shrop.* 38 D2
Lee Brockhurst 38 E3
Lee Clump 22 C1
Lee Mill Bridge 5 F4
Lee Moor 5 F4
Leebotten 109 D10
Leebotwood 38 D6
Leece 55 F3
Leeds *Kent* 14 D2
Leeds *W.Yorks.* 57 H6
Leeds Bradford International Airport 57 H5
Leedstown 2 D5
Leegomery 39 F4
Leek 49 J7
Leek Wootton 30 D2
Leeming *N.Yorks.* 57 H1
Leeming *W.Yorks.* 57 F6
Leeming Bar 62 D7
Lee-on-the-Solent 11 G4
Lees *Derbys.* 40 E2
Lees *Gt.Man.* 49 J2
Leeswood 48 B7
Legars 77 F6
Legbourne 53 G4
Legerwood 76 D6
Legsby 52 E4
Leicester 41 H5
Leideag 84 B5
Leigh *Dorset* 9 F4
Leigh *Glos.* 29 H6
Leigh *Gt.Man.* 49 F2
Leigh *Kent* 23 J7
Leigh *Shrop.* 38 C5
Leigh *Surr.* 23 F7
Leigh *Wilts.* 20 D2
Leigh *Worcs.* 29 G3
Leigh Beck 24 E3
Leigh Common 9 G2
Leigh Delamere 20 B4
Leigh Green 14 E4
Leigh Sinton 29 G3
Leigh upon Mendip 19 K7
Leigh Woods 19 J4
Leigh-on-Sea 24 E3
Leighterton 20 B2
Leighton *N.Yorks.* 57 G2
Leighton *Powys* 38 B5
Leighton *Shrop.* 39 F5
Leighton *Som.* 20 A7
Leighton Bromswold 32 E1
Leighton Buzzard 32 C6
Leinthall Earls 28 D2
Leinthall Starkes 28 D2
Leintwardine 28 D1
Leire 41 H7
Leirinmore 103 G2
Leiston 35 J2
Leitfie 82 D3
Leith 76 A3
Leitholm 77 F6
Lelant 2 C5
Lelley 59 J6

Lem Hill 29 G1
Lemington 71 G7
Lemnas 99 G4
Lempitlaw 77 F7
Lemsford 33 F7
Lenchwick 30 B4
Lendalfoot 67 F5
Lendrick Lodge 81 G7
Lenham 14 D2
Lenham Heath 14 E3
Lenie 88 C2
Lenimore 73 G6
Lennel 77 G6
Lennox Plunton 65 G5
Lenton *Lincs.* 42 D2
Lenton 41 H1
Lenwade 45 F4
Lenzie 74 E3
Leoch 82 E4
Leochel-Cushnie 90 D3
Leominster 28 D2
Leonard Stanley 20 B1
Leorin 72 B6
Lepe 11 F5
Lephinchapel 73 H1
Lephinmore 73 H1
Leppington 58 D3
Lepton 50 E1
Lerags 79 K5
Lerryn 4 B5
Lerwick 109 D8
Lesbury 71 H2
Leschangie 91 F3
Lescrow 4 B5
Leslie *Aber.* 90 D2
Leslie *Fife* 82 D7
Lesmahagow 75 G7
Lesnewth 4 B1
Lessendrum 98 D6
Lessingham 45 H3
Lessonhall 60 D1
Leswalt 64 A4
Letchmore Heath 22 E2
Letchworth Garden City 33 F5
Letcombe Bassett 21 G3
Letcombe Regis 21 G3
Leth Meadhanach 84 C3
Letham *Angus* 83 G3
Letham *Fife* 82 E6
Lethanhill 67 J2
Lethenty 99 G6
Letheringham 35 G3
Letheringsett 44 E2
Lettaford 7 F7
Letter Finlay 87 J5
Letterewe 95 F4
Letterfearn 86 E2
Lettermorar 86 D6
Lettermore *Arg. & B.* 79 G3
Lettermore *High.* 103 J3
Letters 95 H3
Lettershaws 68 D1
Letterston 16 C3
Lettoch *High.* 89 H3
Lettoch *High.* 89 H1
Letton *Here.* 28 C1
Letton *Here.* 28 C4
Letty Green 33 F7
Letwell 51 H4
Leuchars 83 F5
Leumrabhagh 101 F6
Levedale 40 A4
Leven *E.Riding* 59 H5
Leven *Fife* 82 E7
Levencorroch 66 E1
Levenhall 76 B3
Levens 55 H1
Levenshulme 49 H3
Levenwick 109 D10
Leverburgh (An T-òb) 93 F3
Leverington 43 H4
Leverstock Green 22 D1
Leverton 43 H1
Leverton Outgate 43 H1
Levington 35 G5
Levisham 63 K7
Levishie 88 B3
Lew 21 G1
Lewannick 4 C2
Lewdown 6 C7
Lewes 13 H5
Leweston 16 C3
Lewisham 23 G4
Lewiston 88 C2
Lewknor 22 A2
Leworthy 6 E2
Lewtrenchard 6 C7
Ley *Aber.* 90 D3
Ley *Cornw.* 4 B4
Ley Green 32 E6
Leybourne 23 K6
Leyburn 62 C7
Leycett 39 G1
Leyland 55 J7
Leylodge 91 F3
Leys *Aber.* 99 J5
Leys *Aber.* 90 C4
Leys of Cossans 82 E3
Leysdown-on-Sea 25 G4
Leysmill 83 H3
Leysters 28 E2
Leyton 23 G3
Lezant 4 D3
Lhanbryde 97 K5
Liatrie 87 J1
Libanus 27 J6
Libberton 75 H6
Liberton 76 A4
Liceasto 93 G2
Lichfield 40 D5
Lickey 29 J1
Lickey End 29 J1
Lickfold 12 C4
Liddel 107 D9
Liddesdale 79 J2
Liddington 21 F3
Lidgate *Derbys.* 51 F5
Lidgate *Suff.* 34 B3
Lidlington 32 C5
Lidsing 24 D5
Lidstone 30 E6
Lienassie 87 F2
Lieurary 105 F2
Liff 82 E4
Lifton 6 B7
Liftondown 6 B7
Lighthorne 30 E3
Lightwater 22 C5
Lightwood 40 B1
Lightwood Green *Ches.* 39 F1
Lightwood Green *Wrex.* 38 C1
Lilbourne 31 G1
Lilburn Tower 71 F1

Lilleshall 39 G4
Lilley Herts. 32 E6
Lilley W.Berks. 21 H4
Lilliesleaf 70 A1
Lillingstone Dayrell 31 J5
Lillingstone Lovell 31 J4
Lillington 9 F3
Lilliput 10 B5
Lilstock 7 K1
Limbrick 49 F1
Limbury 32 D6
Limefield 49 H1
Limehillock 98 D5
Limekilnburn 75 F5
Limekilns 75 J2
Limerigg 75 G3
Limerstone 11 F6
Limington 8 E2
Limpenhoe 45 H5
Limpley Stoke 20 A5
Limpsfield 23 H6
Linbriggs 70 D3
Linby 51 H7
Linchmere 12 B3
Lincoln 52 C5
Lincomb 29 H2
Lincombe 5 H5
Lindal in Furness 55 F2
Lindale 55 H1
Lindean 76 C7
Lindertis 82 E2
Lindfield 13 G4
Lindford 12 B3
Lindifferon 82 E6
Lindley 50 D1
Lindores 82 D6
Lindridge 29 F2
Lindsaig 73 H3
Lindsell 33 K6
Lindsey 34 D4
Linford Hants. 10 C4
Linford Thur. 24 C4
Lingague 54 B6
Lingdale 63 H5
Lingen 28 C2
Lingfield 23 G7
Lingwood 45 H5
Linhead 98 E5
Linhope 69 K3
Linicro 93 J5
Linkenholt 21 G6
Linkhill 14 D5
Linkinhorne 4 D3
Linklater 107 D9
Linksness Ork. 107 B7
Linksness Ork. 107 E6
Linktown 76 A1
Linley 38 C6
Linley Green 29 G3
Linlithgow 75 H3
Linlithgow Bridge 75 H3
Linn of Muick Cottage 90 B6
Linnels 70 E7
Linney 16 B6
Linshiels 70 D3
Linsiadar 100 E4
Linsidemore 96 C2
Linslade 32 C6
Linstead Parva 35 H1
Linstock 61 F1
Linthwaite 50 D1
Lintlaw 77 G5
Lintmill 98 D4
Linton Cambs. 33 J4
Linton Derbys. 40 E4
Linton Here. 29 F6
Linton Kent 14 C3
Linton N.Yorks. 56 E3
Linton Sc.Bord. 70 C1
Linton W.Yorks. 57 J5
Linton-on-Ouse 57 K3
Lintzford 62 C1
Linwood Hants. 10 C4
Linwood Lincs. 52 E4
Linwood Renf. 74 C4
Lionacleit 92 C7
Lional 101 H1
Liphook 12 B3
Liscombe 7 G2
Liskeard 4 C4
L'Islet 3 J5
Liss 11 J2
Liss Forest 11 J2
Lissett 59 H4
Lissington 52 E4
Liston 34 C4
Lisvane 18 E3
Liswerry 19 G3
Litcham 44 C4
Litchborough 31 H3
Litchfield 21 H6
Litherland 48 C3
Litlington Cambs. 33 G4
Litlington E.Suss. 13 J6
Little Abington 33 J4
Little Addington 32 C1
Little Alne 30 C2
Little Amwell 33 G7
Little Assynt 102 D6
Little Aston 40 C6
Little Atherfield 11 F7
Little Ayton 63 G5
Little Baddow 24 D1
Little Badminton 20 A3
Little Ballinluig 82 A2
Little Bampton 60 D1
Little Bardfield 33 K5
Little Barford 32 E3
Little Barningham 45 F2
Little Barrington 30 D7
Little Barugh 58 D2
Little Bealings 35 G4
Little Bedwyn 21 F5
Little Bentley 35 F6
Little Berkhamsted 23 F1
Little Billing 32 B2
Little Birch 28 E5
Little Bispham 55 G5
Little Blakenham 35 F4
Little Bollington 49 G4
Little Bookham 22 E6
Little Bradley 33 K3
Little Brampton 38 C7
Little Braxted 34 C7
Little Brechin 83 G1
Little Brickhill 32 C5
Little Bridgeford 40 A3
Little Brington 31 F3
Little Bromley 34 E6
Little Broughton 60 B3
Little Budworth 48 E6
Little Burstead 24 C2
Little Burton 59 H5
Little Carlton Lincs. 53 H4

Little Carlton Notts. 51 K7
Little Casterton 42 D5
Little Catwick 59 H5
Little Cawthorpe 53 G4
Little Chalfont 22 C2
Little Chart 14 E3
Little Chesterford 33 J4
Little Cheverell 20 C6
Little Chishill 33 H5
Little Clacton 35 F7
Little Clifton 60 B4
Little Comberton 29 J4
Little Common 14 C7
Little Compton 30 D5
Little Corby 61 F1
Little Cowarne 29 F3
Little Coxwell 21 F2
Little Crakehall 62 D7
Little Creich 96 D3
Little Cressingham 44 C6
Little Crosby 48 C2
Little Cubley 40 D2
Little Dalby 42 A4
Little Dens 99 J6
Little Dewchurch 28 E5
Little Downham 43 J7
Little Driffield 59 G4
Little Dunham 44 C4
Little Dunkeld 82 B3
Little Dunmow 33 K6
Little Easton 33 K6
Little Eaton 41 F1
Little Ellingham 44 E6
Little End 23 J1
Little Eversden 33 G3
Little Fakenham 34 D1
Little Faringdon 21 F1
Little Fencote 62 D7
Little Fenton 58 B6
Little Finborough 34 E3
Little Fransham 44 C4
Little Gaddesden 32 C7
Little Garway 28 D6
Little Gidding 42 E7
Little Glemham 35 H3
Little Glenshee 82 A4
Little Gorsley 29 F6
Little Gransden 33 F3
Little Green 34 E1
Little Grimsby 53 G3
Little Gruinard 95 F3
Little Habton 58 D2
Little Hadham 33 H6
Little Hale 42 E1
Little Hallingbury 33 H7
Little Hampden 22 B1
Little Harrowden 32 B1
Little Haseley 21 K1
Little Hautbois 45 G3
Little Haven 16 B4
Little Hay 40 D5
Little Hayfield 50 C4
Little Haywood 40 C3
Little Heath 41 F7
Little Hereford 28 E2
Little Horkesley 34 D5
Little Hormead 33 H6
Little Horsted 13 H5
Little Horwood 31 J5
Little Houghton 32 B3
Little Hucklow 50 D5
Little Hulton 49 G2
Little Hungerford 21 J4
Little Idoch 99 F6
Little Kimble 22 B1
Little Kineton 30 E3
Little Kingshill 22 B2
Little Langford 10 B1
Little Laver 23 J1
Little Lawford 31 F1
Little Leigh 49 F5
Little Leighs 34 B7
Little Lever 49 G2
Little Ley 90 E3
Little Linford 32 B4
Little London E.Suss. 13 J5
Little London Hants. 21 G6
Little London Hants. 21 K6
Little London I.o.M. 54 C5
Little London Lincs. 43 H3
Little London Lincs. 43 F3
Little London Lincs. 53 G5
Little London Norf. 43 H3
Little London Norf. 44 B6
Little Longstone 50 D5
Little Malvern 29 G4
Little Maplestead 34 C5
Little Marcle 29 F5
Little Marlow 22 B3
Little Massingham 44 B3
Little Melton 45 F5
Little Mill 19 G1
Little Milton 21 K1
Little Missenden 22 C2
Little Musgrave 61 J5
Little Neston 48 B5
Little Newcastle 16 C3
Little Newsham 62 C5
Little Oakley Essex 35 G6
Little Oakley Northants. 42 B7
Little Orton 60 E1
Little Ouseburn 57 K3
Little Parndon 33 H1
Little Paxton 32 E2
Little Petherick 3 G1
Little Plumstead 45 H4
Little Ponton 42 C2
Little Raveley 33 F1
Little Ribston 57 J4
Little Rissington 30 C6
Little Rogart 96 E1
Little Ryburgh 44 D3
Little Ryle 71 F2
Little Salkeld 61 G3
Little Sampford 33 K5
Little Saxham 34 B2
Little Scatwell 95 K6
Little Shelford 33 H3
Little Smeaton 51 H1
Little Snoring 44 D2
Little Sodbury 20 A3
Little Somborne 10 E1
Little Somerford 20 C3
Little Stainton 62 E4
Little Stanney 48 D5

Little Staughton 32 E2
Little Steeping 53 H6
Little Stonham 35 F3
Little Stretton Leics. 41 J6
Little Stretton Shrop. 38 D6
Little Strickland 61 G4
Little Stukeley 33 F1
Little Sutton 48 C5
Little Swinburne 70 E6
Little Tew 30 E6
Little Tey 34 C6
Little Thetford 33 J1
Little Thirkleby 57 K2
Little Thorpe 63 F2
Little Thurlow 33 K3
Little Thurrock 24 C4
Little Torboll 96 E2
Little Torrington 6 C4
Little Totham 34 C7
Little Town 60 D5
Little Urswick 55 F2
Little Wakering 25 F3
Little Walden 33 J4
Little Waldingfield 34 D4
Little Walsingham 44 D2
Little Waltham 34 B7
Little Warley 24 C2
Little Weighton 59 F6
Little Welland 29 H5
Little Welnetham 34 C3
Little Wenham 34 E5
Little Wenlock 39 F5
Little Whittingham Green 35 G1
Little Whittington 70 E7
Little Wilbraham 33 J3
Little Witcombe 29 J7
Little Witley 29 G2
Little Wittenham 21 J2
Little Wolford 30 D5
Little Wratting 33 K4
Little Wymondley 33 F6
Little Wyrley 40 C5
Little Yeldham 34 B5
Littlebeck 63 K6
Littleborough Gt.Man. 49 J1
Littleborough Notts. 52 B4
Littlebourne 15 G2
Littlebredy 8 E6
Littlebury 33 J5
Littlebury Green 33 H5
Littledean 29 F7
Littleferry 97 F2
Littleham Devon 6 C3
Littleham Devon 7 J7
Littlehampton 12 D6
Littlehempston 5 J4
Littlehoughton 71 H2
Littlemill E.Ayr. 67 J2
Littlemill High. 97 G6
Littlemoor 21 J1
Littleover 41 F2
Littleport 43 J7
Littlestone-on-Sea 15 F5
Littlethorpe 57 J3
Littleton Ches. 48 D6
Littleton Hants. 11 F1
Littleton P.& K. 82 D4
Littleton Som. 8 D1
Littleton Surr. 22 D5
Littleton Drew 20 B3
Littleton Panell 20 D6
Littleton-on-Severn 19 J3
Littletown 62 E2
Littlewick Green 22 B4
Littleworth Oxon. 21 G2
Littleworth Staffs. 40 C4
Littleworth Worcs. 29 H3
Littley Green 33 K7
Litton Derbys. 50 D5
Litton N.Yorks. 56 E2
Litton Som. 19 J6
Litton Cheney 8 E5
Liurbost 101 F5
Liverpool 48 C3
Liverpool John Lennon Airport 48 D4
Liversedge 57 G7
Liverton Devon 5 J3
Liverton R.& C. 63 J5
Liverton Street 14 D3
Livingston 75 J4
Livingston Village 75 J4
Lixwm 47 K5
Lizard 2 D7
Llaingoch 46 A4
Llaithddu 37 K7
Llan 37 H5
Llanaber 37 F4
Llanaelhaearn 36 C1
Llanaeron 26 D2
Llanafan 27 F1
Llanafan-fawr 27 J3
Llanafan-fechan 27 J3
Llanallgo 46 C4
Llanarmon 36 D2
Llanarmon Dyffryn Ceiriog 38 A2
Llanarmon-yn-Ial 47 K7
Llanarth Cere. 26 D3
Llanarth Mon. 28 C7
Llanarthney 17 J3
Llanasa 47 K4
Llanbabo 46 B4
Llanbadarn Fawr 36 E7
Llanbadarn Fynydd 27 K1
Llanbadarn-y-garreg 28 A4
Llanbadoc 19 G1
Llanbadrig 46 B3
Llanbeder 19 G2
Llanbedr Gwyn. 36 E3
Llanbedr Powys 28 B6
Llanbedr Powys 28 A4
Llanbedr-Dyffryn-Clwyd 47 K7
Llanbedrgoch 46 D4
Llanbedrog 36 C2
Llanbedr-y-cennin 47 F6
Llanberis 46 D6
Llanbethery 18 D5
Llanbister 28 A1
Llanblethian 18 C4
Llanboidy 17 F3
Llanbradach 18 E2
Llanbrynmair 37 H5
Llancarfan 18 D4
Llancayo 19 G1
Llancynfelyn 37 F6
Llan-dafal 18 E1
Llandaff 18 E4
Llandaff North 18 E4
Llandanwg 36 E3
Llandawke 17 F4

Llanddaniel Fab 46 C5
Llanddarog 17 J4
Llanddeiniol 26 E1
Llanddeiniolen 46 D6
Llanddderfel 37 J2
Llanddeusant Carmar. 27 G6
Llanddeusant I.o.A. 46 B4
Llanddew 27 K5
Llanddewi 17 H7
Llanddewi Rhydderch 28 C7
Llanddewi Skirrid 28 C7
Llanddewi Velfrey 16 E4
Llanddewi Ystradenni 28 A2
Llanddoged 47 F7
Llanddona 46 D5
Llanddowror 17 F4
Llanddulas 47 H5
Llanddwywe 36 E3
Llanddyfnan 46 D5
Llandefaelog 17 J4
Llandefaelog Fach 27 K5
Llandefaelog-tre'r-graig 28 A6
Llandefalle 28 A5
Llandegfan 46 D5
Llandegla 47 K7
Llandegley 28 A2
Llandegveth 19 G2
Llandegwning 36 B2
Llandeilo 17 K3
Llandeilo Abercywyn 17 G4
Llandeilo Graban 27 K4
Llandeilo'r-Fan 27 H5
Llandeloy 16 B3
Llandenny 19 H1
Llandevenny 19 H3
Llandinabo 28 E6
Llandinam 37 K7
Llandissilio 16 E3
Llandogo 19 J1
Llandough V. of Glam. 18 E4
Llandough V. of Glam. 18 C4
Llandovery 27 G5
Llandow 18 C4
Llandre Carmar. 17 K1
Llandre Carmar. 16 E3
Llandre Cere. 37 F7
Llandrillo 37 K2
Llandrillo-yn-Rhôs 47 G4
Llandrindod Wells 27 K2
Llandrinio 38 B4
Llandudno 47 F4
Llandudno Junction 47 F5
Llandwrog 46 C7
Llandybie 17 K4
Llandyfriog 17 G1
Llandyfrydog 46 C4
Llandygai 46 D5
Llandygwydd 17 F1
Llandynog 47 K6
Llandysilio 38 B4
Llandyssil 38 A6
Llandysul 17 H1
Llanedeyrn 19 F3
Llanegryn 37 F5
Llanegwad 17 J3
Llaneilian 46 C3
Llanelian-yn-Rhôs 47 G5
Llanelidan 47 K7
Llanelieu 28 A5
Llanellen 28 C7
Llanelli 17 J5
Llanelltyd 37 G4
Llanelly 28 B7
Llanelly Hill 28 B7
Llanelwedd 27 K3
Llanelwy (St. Asaph) 47 J5
Llanenddwyn 36 E3
Llanengan 36 B3
Llanerch-y-medd 46 C4
Llanerfyl 37 K5
Llanfachraeth 46 B4
Llanfachreth 37 G3
Llanfaelog 46 B5
Llanfaelrhys 36 B3
Llan-faes I.o.A. 46 E5
Llanfaes Powys 27 K6
Llanfaethlu 46 B4
Llanfaglan 46 C6
Llanfair 36 E3
Llanfair Caereinion 38 A5
Llanfair Clydogau 27 F3
Llanfair Dyffryn Clwyd 47 K7
Llanfair Talhaiarn 47 H6
Llanfair Waterdine 28 B1
Llanfairfechan 46 E5
Llanfair-Nant-Gwyn 16 E2
Llanfair-Orllwyn 17 G1
Llanfairpwllgwyngyll 46 D5
Llanfairynghornwy 46 B3
Llanfair-yn-neubwll 46 B5
Llanfallteg 16 E4
Llanfallteg West 16 E4
Llanfaredd 27 K3
Llanfarian 26 E1
Llanfechain 38 A3
Llanfechell 46 B3
Llanfendigaid 36 E5
Llanferres 47 K6
Llanfflewyn 46 B3
Llanfigael 46 B4
Llanfihangel ar-arth 17 H2
Llanfihangel Crucorney 28 C6
Llanfihangel Glyn Myfyr 37 J1
Llanfihangel Nant Bran 27 J5
Llanfihangel Rhydithon 28 A2
Llanfihangel Rogiet 19 H3
Llanfihangel uwch-gwili 17 H3
Llanfihangel-nant-Melan 28 A3
Llanfihangel-Tal-y-llyn 28 A6
Llanfihangel-y-Creuddyn 27 F1
Llanfihangel-yng-Ngwynfa 37 K4
Llanfihangel-y-pennant Gwyn. 36 E1
Llanfihangel-y-pennant Gwyn. 37 F5

Llanfilo 28 A5
Llanfoist 28 B7
Llanfor 37 J2
Llanfrechfa 19 G2
Llanfrothen 37 F1
Llanfrynach 27 K6
Llanfwrog Denb. 47 K7
Llanfwrog I.o.A. 46 B4
Llanfyllin 38 A4
Llanfynydd Carmar. 17 J3
Llanfynydd Flints. 48 B7
Llanfyrnach 17 F2
Llangadfan 37 K4
Llangadog 27 G6
Llangadwaladr I.o.A. 46 B6
Llangadwaladr Powys 38 A2
Llangaffo 46 C6
Llangain 17 G4
Llangammarch Wells 27 J4
Llangan 18 C4
Llangarron 28 E6
Llangasty-Talyllyn 28 A6
Llangathen 17 J3
Llangattock 28 B7
Llangattock Lingoed 28 C6
Llangattock-Vibon-Avel 28 D7
Llangedwyn 38 A3
Llangefni 46 C5
Llangeinor 18 C3
Llangeitho 27 F3
Llangeler 17 G2
Llangelynin 36 E5
Llangendeirne 17 H4
Llangennech 17 J5
Llangennith 17 H6
Llangenny 28 B7
Llangernyw 47 G6
Llangian 36 B3
Llangiwg 18 A1
Llanglydwen 16 E3
Llangoed 46 E5
Llangoedmor 16 E1
Llangollen 38 B1
Llangolman 16 E3
Llangorse 28 A6
Llangorwen 37 F7
Llangovan 19 H1
Llangower 37 J2
Llangrannog 26 C3
Llangristiolus 46 C5
Llangrove 28 E7
Llangua 28 C6
Llangunllo 28 B1
Llangunnor 17 H3
Llangurig 27 J1
Llangwm Conwy 37 J1
Llangwm Mon. 19 H1
Llangwm Pembs. 16 C5
Llangwnnadl 36 B2
Llangwyfan 47 K6
Llangwyllog 46 C5
Llangwyryfon 26 E1
Llangybi Cere. 27 F3
Llangybi Gwyn. 36 D1
Llangybi Mon. 19 G2
Llangyfelach 17 K6
Llangynhafal 47 K6
Llangynidr 28 A7
Llangyniew 38 A5
Llangynin 17 F4
Llangynog Carmar. 17 G4
Llangynog Powys 37 K3
Llangynwyd 18 B3
Llanhamlach 27 K6
Llanharan 18 D3
Llanharry 18 D3
Llanhennock 19 G2
Llanhilleth 19 F1
Llanidloes 37 J7
Llaniestyn 36 B2
Llanigon 28 B5
Llanilar 27 F1
Llanilid 18 C3
Llanishen Cardiff 18 E3
Llanishen Mon. 19 H1
Llanllawddog 17 H3
Llanllechid 46 E6
Llanlleonfel 27 J4
Llanllugan 37 K5
Llanllwch 17 G4
Llanllwchaiarn 38 A6
Llanllwni 17 H1
Llanllyfni 46 C7
Llanllywel 19 G2
Llanmadoc 17 H6
Llanmaes 18 C5
Llanmartin 19 G3
Llanmerewig 38 A6
Llanmihangel 18 C4
Llanmiloe 17 F5
Llanmorlais 17 J6
Llannefydd 47 H5
Llannerch 47 H5
Llannerch-y-Môr 47 K5
Llannon 17 J5
Llanon 26 E2
Llanover 19 G1
Llanpumsaint 17 H3
Llanreithan 16 B3
Llanrhaeadr 47 J6
Llanrhaeadr-ym-Mochnant 38 A3
Llanrhian 16 B2
Llanrhidian 17 H6
Llanrhos 47 F4
Llanrhyddlad 46 B3
Llanrhystud 26 E2
Llanrothal 28 D7
Llanrug 46 D6
Llanrumney 19 F3
Llanrwst 47 F6
Llansadurnen 17 F4
Llansadwrn Carmar. 17 K2
Llansadwrn I.o.A. 46 D5
Llansaint 17 G5
Llansamlet 17 K6
Llansanffraid Glan Conwy 47 G5
Llansannan 47 H6
Llansannor 18 C4
Llansantffraed 28 A6
Llansantffraed-Cwmdeuddwr 27 J2
Llansantffraed-in-Elvel 27 K3
Llansantffraid-ym-Mechain 38 A3
Llansawel Carmar. 17 K2

Llansawel (Briton Ferry) N.P.T. 18 A2
Llansilin 38 B3
Llansoy 19 H1
Llanspyddid 27 K6
Llanstadwell 16 C5
Llansteffan 17 G4
Llanstephan 28 A4
Llantarnam 19 G2
Llanteg 16 E4
Llanthony 28 B6
Llantilio Crossenny 28 C7
Llantilio Pertholey 28 C7
Llantood 16 E1
Llantrisant Mon. 19 G2
Llantrisant R.C.T. 18 D3
Llantrithyd 18 D4
Llantwit Fardre 18 D3
Llantwit Major 18 C5
Llantysilio 38 A1
Llanuwchllyn 37 H2
Llanvaches 19 H2
Llanvair-Discoed 19 H2
Llanvapley 28 C7
Llanvetherine 28 C7
Llanveynoe 28 C5
Llanvihangel Gobion 19 G1
Llanvihangel-Ystern-Llewern 28 D7
Llanwarne 28 E6
Llanwddyn 37 K4
Llanwenog 17 H1
Llanwern 19 G3
Llanwinio 17 F3
Llanwnda Gwyn. 46 C7
Llanwnda Pembs. 16 C2
Llanwnnen 17 H1
Llanwnog 37 K6
Llanwonno 18 D2
Llanwrda 27 G5
Llanwrin 37 G5
Llanwrthwl 27 J2
Llanwrtyd 27 H4
Llanwrtyd Wells 27 H4
Llanwyddelan 37 K5
Llanyblodwel 38 B3
Llanybri 17 G4
Llanybydder 17 J1
Llanycefn 16 D3
Llanychaer Bridge 16 C2
Llanycil 37 J2
Llanycrwys 17 K1
Llanymawddwy 37 J4
Llanymynech 38 B3
Llanynghenedl 46 B4
Llanynys 47 K6
Llan-y-pwll 48 C7
Llanyre 27 K2
Llanystumdwy 36 D2
Llanywern 28 A6
Llawhaden 16 D4
Llawnt 38 B2
Llawr-y-dref 36 B3
Llawryglyn 37 J6
Llay 48 C7
Llechcynfarwy 46 B4
Llechfaen 27 K6
Llechryd Caerp. 18 E1
Llechryd Cere. 17 F1
Llechrydau 38 B2
Lledrod Cere. 27 F1
Lledrod Powys 38 B2
Llethr 16 B3
Llidiadnenog 17 J2
Llidiardau 37 H2
Llithfaen 36 C1
Lloc 47 K5
Llong 48 B6
Llowes 28 A4
Lloyney 28 B1
Llwydcoed 18 C1
Llwydiarth 37 K4
Llwyn 38 B7
Llwyncelyn 26 D3
Llwyndafydd 26 C3
Llwynderw 38 B5
Llwyndyrys 36 C1
Llwyngwril 36 E5
Llwyn-Madoc 27 J3
Llwynmawr 38 B2
Llwyn-onn 26 D3
Llwyn-y-brain Carmar. 17 F4
Llwyn-y-brain Carmar. 27 G5
Llwynypia 18 C2
Llynclys 38 B3
Llynfaes 46 C5
Llysfaen 47 G5
Llyswen 28 A5
Llysworney 18 C4
Llys-y-fran 16 D3
Llywel 27 H5
Loandhu 97 F4
Loanhead Aber. 91 H1
Loanhead Midloth. 76 A4
Loans 74 B7
Loch Baghasdail (Lochboisdale) 84 C3
Loch Coire Lodge 103 J5
Loch Eil Outward Bound 87 G7
Loch Head D.& G. 64 D6
Loch Head D.& G. 67 J4
Loch na Madadh (Lochmaddy) 92 D1
Loch Sgioport 84 D1
Lochailort 86 D6
Lochaline 79 H3
Lochans 64 A5
Locharbriggs 68 E5
Lochawe 80 C5
Lochboisdale (Loch Baghasdail) 84 C3
Lochbuie 79 H5
Lochcarron 86 E1
Lochdhu Hotel 105 F4
Lochdon 79 J4
Lochdrum 95 J4
Lochearnhead 81 F5
Lochee 82 E4
Lochend High. 88 C1
Lochend High. 105 H2
Lochfoot 65 K3
Lochgair 73 H1
Lochgarthside 88 C3
Lochgelly 75 K1
Lochgilphead 73 G2
Lochgoilhead 80 D7
Lochhill E.Ayr. 68 B2
Lochhill Moray 97 K5
Lochinch Castle 64 B4
Lochinver 102 C6

Lochlair 83 G3
Lochlane 81 K5
Lochlea 67 J1
Lochluichart 95 K5
Lochmaben 69 F5
Lochmaddy (Loch na Madadh) 92 D1
Lochore 75 K1
Lochportain 92 E4
Lochranza 73 H6
Lochside Aber. 83 J1
Lochside High. 103 G3
Lochside High. 104 D5
Lochside High. 105 H2
Lochslin 97 F3
Lochton 67 G5
Lochty 83 G7
Lochuisge 79 J2
Lochurr 68 C5
Lochussie 96 B6
Lochwinnoch 74 B5
Lockengate 4 A4
Lockerbie 69 G5
Lockeridge 20 E5
Lockerley 10 D2
Locking 19 G6
Lockington E.Riding 59 G5
Lockington Leics. 41 G3
Lockleywood 39 F3
Locks Heath 11 G4
Locksbottom 23 H5
Lockton 63 K7
Loddington Leics. 42 A5
Loddington Northants. 32 B1
Loddiswell 5 H6
Loddon 45 H6
Lode 33 J2
Loders 8 D5
Lodsworth 12 C4
Lofthouse N.Yorks. 57 F2
Lofthouse W.Yorks. 57 J7
Loftus 63 J5
Logan D.& G. 64 A6
Logan E.Ayr. 67 K1
Loganlea 75 H4
Loggerheads 39 G2
Loggie 95 H2
Logie Angus 83 H1
Logie Angus 82 E2
Logie Fife 83 F5
Logie Moray 97 H6
Logie Coldstone 90 C4
Logie Hill 96 E4
Logie Newton 90 E1
Logie Pert 83 H1
Logierait 82 A2
Login 16 E3
Lolworth 33 G2
Lonbain 94 C6
Londesborough 58 E5
London 23 G3
London Beach 14 D4
London Biggin Hill Airport 23 H5
London City Airport 23 H3
London Colney 22 E1
London Gatwick Airport 23 F7
London Heathrow Airport 22 D4
London Luton Airport 32 E6
London Southend Airport 24 E3
London Stansted Airport 33 J6
Londonderry 57 H1
Londonthorpe 42 C2
Londubh 94 E3
Lonemore 96 E3
Long Ashton 19 J4
Long Bennington 42 B1
Long Bredy 8 E5
Long Buckby 31 H2
Long Clawson 42 A3
Long Common 11 G3
Long Compton Staffs. 40 A3
Long Compton Warks. 30 D5
Long Crendon 21 K1
Long Crichel 9 J3
Long Ditton 22 E5
Long Downs 2 E5
Long Drax 58 C7
Long Duckmanton 51 G5
Long Eaton 41 G2
Long Gill 56 C4
Long Hanborough 31 F7
Long Itchington 31 F2
Long Lawford 31 F1
Long Load 8 D2
Long Marston Herts. 32 B7
Long Marston N.Yorks. 58 B4
Long Marston Warks. 30 C4
Long Marton 61 H4
Long Melford 34 C4
Long Newnton 20 C2
Long Preston 56 D4
Long Riston 59 H5
Long Stratton 45 F6
Long Street 31 J4
Long Sutton Hants. 22 A7
Long Sutton Lincs. 43 H3
Long Sutton Som. 8 D2
Long Thurlow 34 E2
Long Waste 39 F4
Long Whatton 41 G3
Long Wittenham 21 J2
Longbenton 71 H7
Longborough 30 C6
Longbridge W.Mid. 30 B1
Longbridge Warks. 30 D2
Longbridge Deverill 20 B7
Longburgh 60 E1
Longburton 9 F3
Longcliffe 50 E7
Longcot 21 F2
Longcroft 75 F3
Longcross Devon 4 E3
Longcross Surr. 22 C5
Longden 38 D5

Longdon *Staffs.* 40 C4
Longdon *Worcs.* 29 H5
Longdon upon Tern 39 F4
Longdown 7 G6
Longdrum 91 H3
Longfield 24 C5
Longfield Hill 24 C5
Longfleet 10 B5
Longford *Derbys.* 40 E2
Longford *Glos.* 29 H6
Longford *Gt.Lon.* 22 D4
Longford *Shrop.* 39 F2
Longford *Tel. & W.* 39 G4
Longford *W.Mid.* 41 F7
Longforgan 82 E5
Longformacus 76 E5
Longframlington 71 G3
Longham *Dorset* 10 B5
Longham *Norf.* 44 D4
Longhill 99 H5
Longhirst 71 H5
Longhope *Glos.* 29 F7
Longhope *Ork.* 107 C8
Longhorsley 71 G4
Longhoughton 71 H2
Longlands *Aber.* 90 C2
Longlands *Cumb.* 60 D3
Longlane *Derbys.* 40 E2
Longlane *W.Berks.* 21 J4
Longley Green 29 G3
Longmanhill 99 F4
Longmoor Camp 11 J1
Longmorn 97 K6
Longnewton *Sc.Bord.* 70 A1
Longnewton *Stock.* 62 E5
Longney 29 G7
Longniddry 76 C3
Longnor *Shrop.* 38 D5
Longnor *Staffs.* 50 C6
Longparish 21 H7
Longridge *Lancs.* 56 B6
Longridge *W.Loth.* 75 H4
Longridge Towers 77 H5
Longrock 75 G3
Longsdon 2 B5
Longside 49 J7
Longside 99 J6
Longslow 39 F2
Longstanton 33 G2
Longstock 10 E1
Longstowe 33 G3
Longstreet 20 E6
Longthorpe 42 E6
Longton *Lancs.* 55 H7
Longton *Stoke* 40 B1
Longtown *Cumb.* 69 J7
Longtown *Here.* 28 C6
Longville in the Dale 38 E6
Longwell Green 19 K4
Longwick 22 A1
Longwitton 71 F5
Longworth 21 G2
Longyester 76 D4
Lonmore 93 H7
Looe 4 C5
Loose 14 C2
Loosegate 43 G3
Loosley Row 22 B1
Lopcombe Corner 10 D1
Lopen 8 D3
Loppington 38 D3
Lorbottle 71 F3
Lorbottle Hall 71 F3
Lorgill 93 G7
Lorn 74 B2
Lornty 82 C3
Loscoe 41 G1
Losgaintir 93 F2
Lossiemouth 97 K4
Lossit 72 A2
Lostock Gralam 49 F5
Lostock Green 49 F5
Lostock Junction 49 F2
Lostwithiel 4 B5
Loth 106 F4
Lothbeg 104 E7
Lothersdale 56 E5
Lothmore 104 E7
Loudwater 22 C2
Loughborough 41 H4
Loughor 17 J6
Loughton *Essex* 23 H2
Loughton *M.K.* 32 B5
Loughton *Shrop.* 39 F7
Lound *Lincs.* 42 D4
Lound *Notts.* 51 J4
Lound *Suff.* 45 K6
Lount 41 F4
Lour 83 F3
Louth 53 G4
Love Clough 56 D7
Lovedean 11 H3
Lover 10 D2
Loversall 51 H3
Loves Green 24 C1
Loveston 16 D5
Lovington 8 E1
Low 55 H1
Low Ballevain 66 A1
Low Barlay 65 F5
Low Bentham 56 B3
Low Bolton 62 B7
Low Bradfield 50 E3
Low Bradley or Bradley 57 F5
Low Braithwaite 61 F2
Low Brunton 70 E6
Low Burnham 51 K2
Low Burton 57 H1
Low Catton 58 D4
Low Coniscliffe 62 D5
Low Craighead 67 G3
Low Crosby 61 F1
Low Dinsdale 62 E5
Low Eggborough 58 B7
Low Entercommon 62 E6
Low Etherley 62 C4
Low Gate 70 E7
Low Habberley 29 H1
Low Ham 8 D2
Low Hawsker 63 J2
Low Hesket 61 F2
Low Hesleyhurst 71 F4
Low Hutton 58 D3
Low Laithe 57 G3
Low Leighton 50 C4
Low Marishes 58 E2
Low Mill 63 H7
Low Moor 56 C5
Low Newton-by-the-Sea 71 H1
Low Risby 52 C1

Low Row *Cumb.* 70 A7
Low Row *N.Yorks.* 62 A7
Low Santon 52 C1
Low Stillaig 73 H4
Low Street 45 H3
Low Torry 75 J2
Low Toynton 53 F5
Low Waters 75 F5
Low Wood 55 G1
Low Worsall 62 E5
Lowdham 41 J1
Lower Achachenna 80 B5
Lower Aisholt 7 K2
Lower Apperley 29 H6
Lower Ashton 7 G5
Lower Assendon 22 A3
Lower Auchalick 73 H3
Lower Beeding 13 F4
Lower Benefield 42 C7
Lower Berry Hill 28 E7
Lower Bockhampton 9 G5
Lower Boddington 31 F3
Lower Boscaswell 2 A5
Lower Bourne 22 B7
Lower Brailes 30 E5
Lower Breakish 86 C2
Lower Broadheath 29 H3
Lower Broughton 49 H3
Lower Brynamman 27 G7
Lower Bullingham 28 E5
Lower Burgate 10 C3
Lower Caldecote 32 E4
Lower Cam 20 A1
Lower Chapel 27 K5
Lower Chute 21 G6
Lower Crossings 50 C4
Lower Darwen 56 B7
Lower Dean 32 D2
Lower Diabaig 94 D5
Lower Dicker 13 J5
Lower Dinchope 38 D7
Lower Down 38 C7
Lower Drift 2 B6
Lower Dunsforth 57 K3
Lower Earley 22 A4
Lower Egleton 29 F4
Lower End 32 B2
Lower Everleigh 20 E6
Lower Failand 19 J4
Lower Farringdon 11 J1
Lower Freystrop 16 C4
Lower Froyle 22 A7
Lower Gabwell 5 K4
Lower Gledfield 96 C2
Lower Godney 19 H7
Lower Green *Kent* 23 K7
Lower Green *Norf.* 44 D2
Lower Green *Staffs.* 40 B5
Lower Green Bank 55 J4
Lower Halstow 24 E5
Lower Hardres 15 G2
Lower Hawthwaite 55 F1
Lower Hayton 38 E7
Lower Hergest 28 B3
Lower Heyford 31 F6
Lower Higham 24 D4
Lower Holbrook 35 F5
Lower Hordley 38 C3
Lower Horsebridge 13 J5
Lower Kilchattan 72 B1
Lower Killeyan 72 A6
Lower Kingcombe 8 E5
Lower Kinnerton 48 C6
Lower Langford 19 H5
Lower Largo 83 F7
Lower Lemington 30 D5
Lower Lovacott 6 D3
Lower Lydbrook 28 E7
Lower Lye 28 D2
Lower Machen 19 F3
Lower Maes-coed 28 C5
Lower Moor 29 J4
Lower Nazeing 23 G1
Lower Oakfield 75 K1
Lower Oddington 30 D6
Lower Ollach 86 B1
Lower Penarth 18 E4
Lower Penn 40 A6
Lower Pennington 10 E5
Lower Peover 49 G5
Lower Quinton 30 C4
Lower Seagry 20 C3
Lower Shelton 32 C4
Lower Shiplake 22 A4
Lower Shuckburgh 31 F2
Lower Slaughter 30 C6
Lower Stanton St. Quintin 20 C3
Lower Stoke 24 E4
Lower Stondon 32 E5
Lower Street 14 C6
Lower Sundon 32 D6
Lower Swanwick 11 F4
Lower Swell 30 C6
Lower Tean 40 C2
Lower Thurlton 45 J6
Lower Thurnham 55 H4
Lower Town *I.o.S.* 2 C1
Lower Town *Pembs.* 16 C2
Lower Tysoe 30 E4
Lower Upham 11 G3
Lower Vexford 7 K2
Lower Wallop 38 C5
Lower Walton 49 F4
Lower Weare 19 H6
Lower Welson 28 B3
Lower Whitley 49 F5
Lower Wield 21 K7
Lower (Nether) Winchendon 31 J7
Lower Withington 49 H6
Lower Woodend 22 B3
Lower Woodford 10 C1
Lower Wraxall 29 G4
Lowesby 42 A5
Lowestoft 45 K6
Lowestoft End 45 K6
Loweswater 60 C4
Lowfield Heath 23 F7
Lowgill *Cumb.* 61 H7
Lowgill *Lancs.* 56 B3
Lowick *Cumb.* 55 F1
Lowick *Northants.* 42 C7
Lowick *Northumb.* 77 J7
Lownie Moor 83 F3
Lowsonford 30 C2
Lowther 61 G4
Lowther Castle 61 G4
Lowthorpe 59 G4
Lowton 49 F3
Lowton Common 49 F3

Loxbeare 7 H4
Loxhill 12 D3
Loxhore 6 E2
Loxley 30 D3
Loxton 19 G6
Loxwood 12 D3
Lubachoinnich 96 B2
Lubcroy 95 K1
Lubenham 42 A7
Lubfearn 95 K4
Lubmore 95 G6
Lubreoch 81 F3
Luccombe 7 H1
Luccombe Village 11 G7
Lucker 77 K7
Luckett 4 D3
Luckington 20 B3
Lucklawhill 83 F5
Luckwell Bridge 7 H2
Lucton 28 D2
Ludag 84 C3
Ludborough 53 F3
Ludchurch 16 E4
Luddenden 57 F7
Luddenden Foot 57 F7
Luddenham Court 25 F5
Luddesdown 24 C5
Luddington *N.Lincs.* 52 B1
Luddington *Warks.* 30 C3
Luddington in the Brook 42 E7
Ludford 28 E1
Ludford Magna 53 F4
Ludford Parva 52 E4
Ludgershall *Bucks.* 31 H7
Ludgershall *Wilts.* 21 F6
Ludgvan 2 B5
Ludham 45 H4
Ludlow 28 E1
Ludney 53 G3
Ludstock 29 F5
Ludwell 9 J2
Ludworth 62 E2
Luffincott 6 B6
Luffness 76 C2
Lugar 67 K1
Luggiebank 75 F3
Lugton 74 C5
Lugwardine 28 E4
Luib 86 B2
Luibeilt 86 D1
Lulham 28 D4
Lullington *Derbys.* 40 E4
Lullington *Som.* 20 A6
Lulsgate Bottom 19 J5
Lulsley 29 G3
Lulworth Camp 9 H6
Lumb 57 F7
Lumbutts 56 E7
Lumby 57 K6
Lumphanan 90 D4
Lumphinnans 75 K1
Lumsdaine 77 G4
Lumsden 90 C2
Lunan 83 H2
Lunanhead 83 F2
Luncarty 82 B5
Lund *E.Riding* 59 F5
Lund *N.Yorks.* 58 C6
Lund *Shet.* 108 E2
Lundavra 80 B1
Lunderton 99 K6
Lundie *Angus* 82 D4
Lundie *High.* 87 H3
Lundin Links 83 F7
Lunga 79 J7
Lunna 109 D6
Lunning 109 E6
Lunsford's Cross 14 C6
Lunt 48 C2
Luntley 28 C3
Luppitt 7 K5
Lupton 55 J1
Lurgashall 12 C4
Lurignich 80 A2
Lusby 53 G6
Luss 74 B1
Lussagiven 72 E2
Lusta 93 H6
Lustleigh 7 F7
Luston 28 D2
Luthermuir 83 H1
Luthrie 82 E6
Luton *Devon* 7 J5
Luton *Devon* 5 K3
Luton *Luton* 32 D6
Luton *Med.* 24 D5
Luton Airport 32 E6
Lutterworth 41 H7
Lutton *Devon* 5 F5
Lutton *Lincs.* 43 H3
Lutton *Northants.* 42 E7
Luxborough 7 H2
Luxulyan 4 A5
Lybster *High.* 105 F2
Lybster *High.* 105 H5
Lydacott 6 C5
Lydbury North 38 C7
Lydcott 6 E2
Lydd 15 F5
Lydd Airport 15 F5
Lydden 15 H3
Lyddington 42 B6
Lydd-on-Sea 15 F5
Lydeard St. Lawrence 7 K2
Lydford 6 D7
Lydford-on-Fosse 8 E1
Lydgate 56 E7
Lydham 38 C6
Lydiard Millicent 20 D3
Lydiate 48 C2
Lydlinch 9 G3
Lydney 19 K1
Lydstep 16 D6
Lye 40 B7
Lye Green 22 C1
Lyford 21 G2
Lymbridge Green 15 G3
Lyme Regis 8 C5
Lymekilns 74 E5
Lyminge 15 G3
Lymington 10 E5
Lyminster 12 D6
Lymm 49 F4
Lymore 10 D5
Lympne 15 G4
Lympsham 19 G6
Lympstone 7 H7
Lynaberack 88 E4
Lynchat 88 E4
Lyndhurst 10 E4
Lyndon 42 C5
Lyne *Aber.* 90 E4
Lyne *Sc.Bord.* 76 A6
Lyne *Surr.* 22 D5

Lyne of Gorthleck 88 C2
Lyne of Skene 91 F3
Lyne Station 76 A7
Lyneal 38 D2
Lynedale House 93 J6
Lynegar 105 H3
Lyneham *Oxon.* 30 D6
Lyneham *Wilts.* 20 D4
Lyneholmeford 70 A6
Lynemore *High.* 89 H2
Lynemore *Moray* 89 J1
Lynemouth 71 H4
Lyness 107 C8
Lyng *Norf.* 44 E4
Lyng *Som.* 8 C2
Lynmouth 7 F1
Lynsted 25 F5
Lynton 7 F1
Lyon's Gate 9 F4
Lyonshall 28 C3
Lyrabus 72 A4
Lytchett Matravers 9 J5
Lytchett Minster 9 J5
Lyth 105 H2
Lytham 55 G7
Lytham St. Anne's 55 G7
Lythe 63 K5
Lythe Hill 12 C3
Lythes 107 D9
Lythmore 105 F2

M

Mabe Burnthouse 2 E5
Mabie 65 K3
Mablethorpe 53 J4
Macclesfield 49 J5
Macclesfield Forest 49 J5
Macduff 99 F4
Machan 75 F5
Machany 82 A6
Macharioch 66 B3
Machen 19 F3
Machrie *Arg. & B.* 72 B4
Machrie *Arg. & B.* 72 B6
Machrie *N.Ayr.* 73 H7
Machrihanish 66 A2
Machrins 72 B1
McInroy's Point 74 A3
Mackworth 41 F2
Macmerry 76 C3
Macterry 99 F6
Madderty 82 A5
Maddiston 75 H3
Madehurst 12 C5
Madeley *Staffs.* 39 G1
Madeley *Tel. & W.* 39 G5
Madeley Heath 39 G1
Madford 7 K4
Madingley 33 G3
Madjeston 9 H2
Madley 28 D5
Madresfield 29 H4
Madron 2 B5
Maen Porth 2 E6
Maenaddwyn 46 C4
Maenclochog 16 D3
Maendy 18 D4
Maentwrog 37 F1
Maer 39 G2
Maerdy *Carmar.* 17 K3
Maerdy *Carmar.* 17 K3
Maerdy *Conwy* 37 K1
Maerdy *Mon.* 19 G1
Maerdy *R.C.T.* 18 C2
Maesbrook 38 B3
Maesbury Marsh 38 C3
Maes-Glas (Greenfield) *Flints.* 47 K5
Maes-glas *Newport* 19 F3
Maesgwynne 17 F3
Maeshafn 48 B6
Maesllyn 17 G1
Maesmynis 27 K4
Maesteg 18 B2
Maes-Treylow 28 B2
Maesybont 17 J4
Maesycrugiau 17 H1
Maesycwmmer 18 E2
Magdalen Laver 23 J1
Maggieknockater 98 B6
Magham Down 13 K5
Maghull 48 C2
Magor 19 H3
Maiden Bradley 9 G1
Maiden Law 62 C2
Maiden Newton 8 E5
Maiden Wells 16 C6
Maidencombe 5 K4
Maidenhead 22 B3
Maidens 67 G3
Maiden's Green 22 C4
Maidensgrove 22 A3
Maidenwell *Cornw.* 4 B3
Maidenwell *Lincs.* 53 G5
Maidford 31 H3
Maids' Moreton 31 J5
Maidstone 14 C2
Maidwell 31 J1
Mail 109 D10
Mains of Ardestie 83 G4
Mains of Balgavies 83 G2
Mains of Ballindarg 83 F2
Mains of Burgie 97 H6
Mains of Culsh 99 G6
Mains of Dillavaird 91 G7
Mains of Drum 91 G4
Mains of Dudwick 91 H1
Mains of Faillie 88 E1
Mains of Fedderate 99 G6
Mains of Glack 91 F2
Mains of Glassaugh 98 D4
Mains of Glenbuchat 90 B3
Mains of Linton 91 G4
Mains of Melgund 83 G2
Mains of Pitfour 99 H6
Mains of Pittrichie 91 G2
Mains of Sluie 97 G6
Mains of Tannachy 98 B4
Mains of Thornton 91 F7
Mains of Tig 67 F5
Mains of Watten 105 H3
Mainsriddle 65 K5
Mainstone 38 B7
Maisemore 29 H6
Makendon 70 D3
Makerstoun 76 D7
Malacleit 92 C4
Malborough 5 H7
Malden Rushett 22 E5

Maldon 24 E1
Malham 56 E3
Maligar 93 K5
Maligar 86 C5
Mallaig 86 D5
Mallaigmore 86 D5
Mallaigvaig 86 C5
Malleny Mills 75 K4
Malletsheugh 74 D5
Malling 81 G7
Malltraeth 46 C6
Mallwyd 37 H4
Malmesbury 20 C3
Malmsmead 7 F1
Malpas *Ches.* 38 D1
Malpas *Cornw.* 3 F4
Malpas *Newport* 19 G2
Maltby *S.Yorks.* 51 H3
Maltby *Stock.* 63 F5
Maltby le Marsh 53 H4
Maltman's Hill 14 D3
Malton 58 D2
Malvern Link 29 G4
Malvern Wells 29 G4
Mambeg 74 A2
Mamble 29 F1
Mamhead 7 H7
Mamhilad 19 G1
Manaccan 2 E6
Manafon 38 A5
Manais 93 G3
Manaton 7 F7
Manby 53 G4
Mancetter 41 F6
Manchester 49 H3
Manchester Airport 49 H4
Mancot Royal 48 C6
Mandally 87 J4
Manea 43 H7
Maneight 67 K3
Manfield 62 D5
Mangaster 108 C5
Mangotsfield 19 K4
Mangurstadh 100 C4
Mankinholes 56 E7
Manley 48 E5
Manmoel 18 E1
Mannal 78 A3
Manningford Abbots 20 E6
Manningford Bohune 20 E6
Manningford Bruce 20 E6
Mannings Heath 13 F4
Mannington 10 B4
Manningtree 35 F5
Mannofield 91 H4
Manorbier 16 D6
Manordeifi 17 F1
Manordeilo 17 K3
Manorowen 16 C2
Mansell Gamage 28 C4
Mansell Lacy 28 D4
Mansergh 56 B1
Mansfield 51 H6
Mansfield Woodhouse 51 H6
Mansriggs 55 F1
Manston *Dorset* 9 H3
Manston *Kent* 25 K5
Manswood 9 J4
Manthorpe *Lincs.* 42 D4
Manthorpe *Lincs.* 42 C2
Manton *N.Lincs.* 52 C2
Manton *Rut.* 42 B5
Manton *Wilts.* 20 E5
Manuden 33 H6
Maolachy 79 K6
Maperton 9 F2
Maple Cross 22 D2
Maplebeck 51 K6
Mapledurham 21 K4
Mapledurwell 21 K6
Maplehurst 12 E4
Mapleton 40 D1
Mapperley 41 G1
Mapperton 8 E5
Mappleborough Green 30 B2
Mappleton 59 J5
Mapplewell 51 F2
Mappowder 9 G4
Mar Lodge 89 H5
Marazion 2 C5
Marbhig 101 G6
Marbury 38 E1
March 43 H6
Marcham 21 H2
Marchamley 38 E3
Marchington 40 D2
Marchington Woodlands 40 D3
Marchwiel 38 C1
Marchwood 10 E3
Marcross 18 C5
Marcus 83 G2
Marden *Here.* 28 E4
Marden *Kent* 14 C3
Marden *T. & W.* 71 J6
Marden *Wilts.* 20 D6
Marden Beech 14 C3
Marden Thorn 14 C3
Mardy 28 C7
Mare Green 8 C2
Marefield 42 A5
Mareham le Fen 53 F6
Mareham on the Hill 53 F6
Maresfield 13 H4
Marfleet 59 H7
Marford 48 C7
Margam 18 A3
Margaret Marsh 9 H3
Margaret Roding 33 J7
Margaretting 24 C1
Margate 25 K4
Margnaheglish 73 J7
Margreig 65 J3
Margrove Park 63 H5
Marham 44 B5
Marhamchurch 6 A5
Marholm 42 E5
Marian Cwm 47 J5
Marian-Glas 46 D4
Mariansleigh 7 F3
Marishader 93 K5
Maristow House 4 E4
Mark *S. & G.* 19 G6
Mark Causeway 19 G7
Mark Cross 13 J3
Markbeech 23 H4
Markby 53 H5
Markdhu 64 B3
Market Bosworth 41 G5
Market Deeping 42 E4
Market Harborough 42 A7

Market Lavington 20 D6
Market Overton 42 B4
Market Rasen 52 E4
Market Stainton 53 F5
Market Street 45 G3
Market Warsop 51 H6
Market Weighton 58 E5
Market Weston 34 D1
Markethill 82 D4
Markfield 41 G4
Markham 18 E1
Markham Moor 51 K5
Markinch 82 D7
Markington 57 H3
Marks Gate 23 H3
Marks Tey 34 D6
Marksbury 19 K5
Markwell 4 D5
Markyate 32 D7
Marlborough 20 E5
Marldon 5 J4
Marlesford 35 H3
Marley Green 38 E1
Marley Hill 62 D1
Marlingford 45 F5
Marloes 16 A5
Marlow 22 B3
Marlpit Hill 23 H7
Marlpool 41 G1
Marnhull 9 G3
Marnoch 98 D5
Marple 49 J4
Marr 51 H2
Marrel 105 F7
Marrick 62 B7
Marrister 109 E6
Marros 17 F5
Marsden *T. & W.* 71 K7
Marsden *W.Yorks.* 50 C1
Marsett 56 E1
Marsh 8 B3
Marsh Baldon 21 J2
Marsh Benham 21 H5
Marsh Chapel 53 G3
Marsh Gibbon 31 H6
Marsh Green *Devon* 7 J6
Marsh Green *Kent* 23 H7
Marsh Green *Tel. & W.* 39 F4
Marsh Lane 51 G5
Marsh Street 7 H1
Marshall's Heath 32 E7
Marshalsea 8 C4
Marsham 45 F3
Marshaw 55 J4
Marshborough 15 H2
Marshbrook 38 D7
Marshfield *Newport* 19 F3
Marshfield *S.Glos.* 20 A4
Marshgate 4 B1
Marshside 48 C1
Marshwood 8 C5
Marske 62 C6
Marske-by-the-Sea 63 H4
Marston *Ches.* 49 F5
Marston *Here.* 28 C3
Marston *Lincs.* 42 B1
Marston *Oxon.* 21 J1
Marston *Staffs.* 40 B3
Marston *Staffs.* 40 A4
Marston *Warks.* 40 E6
Marston *Wilts.* 20 C6
Marston Green 40 D7
Marston Magna 8 E2
Marston Meysey 20 E2
Marston Montgomery 40 D2
Marston Moretaine 32 C4
Marston on Dove 40 E3
Marston St. Lawrence 31 G4
Marston Stannett 28 E3
Marston Trussell 41 J7
Marstow 28 E7
Marsworth 32 C7
Marten 21 F5
Martham 45 J4
Marthall 49 H5
Martin *Hants.* 10 B3
Martin *Lincs.* 52 E6
Martin *Lincs.* 53 F6
Martin Drove End 10 B2
Martin Hussingtree 29 H2
Martinhoe 6 E1
Martinscroft 49 F4
Martinstown 9 F6
Martlesham 35 G4
Martlesham Heath 35 G4
Martletwy 16 D4
Martley 29 G2
Martock 8 D3
Marton *Ches.* 49 H5
Marton *Cumb.* 55 F2
Marton *E.Riding* 59 H6
Marton *Lincs.* 52 B4
Marton *Middbro.* 63 G5
Marton *N.Yorks.* 57 K3
Marton *N.Yorks.* 58 D1
Marton *Shrop.* 38 B5
Marton *Warks.* 31 F2
Marton Abbey 58 B3
Marton-le-Moor 57 J2
Martyr Worthy 11 G1
Martyr's Green 22 D6
Maruig 100 E7
Marwick 106 B5
Marwood 6 D2
Mary Tavy 5 F3
Marybank 96 B6
Maryburgh 96 C6
Maryfield 109 D8
Marygold 77 G4
Maryhill *Aber.* 99 G6
Maryhill *Glas.* 74 D4
Marykirk 83 H1
Marylebone *Gt.Lon.* 23 F3
Marylebone *Gt.Man.* 48 E2
Marypark 89 J1
Maryport *Cumb.* 60 B3
Maryport *D. & G.* 64 B7
Marystow 6 C7
Maryton 83 H2
Marywell *Aber.* 90 D5
Marywell *Aber.* 91 H5
Marywell *Angus* 83 H3
Masham 57 H1
Mashbury 33 K7
Mastrick 91 H4
Matching 33 J7
Matching Green 33 J7
Matching Tye 33 J7
Matfen 71 F6
Matfield 23 K7
Mathern 19 J2

Mathon 29 G4
Mathry 16 B2
Matlaske 45 F2
Matlock 51 F6
Matlock Bank 50 E6
Matlock Bath 50 E7
Matson 29 H7
Matterdale End 60 E4
Mattersey 51 J4
Mattingley 22 A6
Mattishall 44 E4
Mattishall Burgh 44 E4
Mauchline 67 K1
Maud 99 H6
Maufant 3 K7
Maugersbury 30 C6
Maughold 54 D4
Mauld 87 K1
Maulden 32 D5
Maulds Meaburn 61 H5
Maunby 57 J1
Maund Bryan 28 E3
Maundown 7 J3
Mautby 45 J4
Mavesyn Ridware 40 C4
Mavis Enderby 53 G6
Maw Green 40 C6
Mawbray 60 B2
Mawdesley 48 D1
Mawdlam 18 B3
Mawgan 2 E6
Mawla 2 D4
Mawnan 2 E6
Mawnan Smith 2 E6
Mawsley 32 B1
Maxey 42 E5
Maxstoke 40 E7
Maxton *Kent* 15 H3
Maxton *Sc.Bord.* 70 B1
Maxwellheugh 77 F7
Maxwelltown 65 K3
Maxworthy 4 C1
Maybole 67 H3
Mayen 98 D6
Mayfield *E.Suss.* 13 J4
Mayfield *Midloth.* 76 B4
Mayfield *Staffs.* 40 D1
Mayford 22 C6
Mayland 25 F1
Maylandsea 25 F1
Maynard's Green 13 J5
Maypole *I.o.S.* 2 C1
Maypole *Kent* 25 H5
Maypole Green 109 C10
Maywick 109 C10
Meabhag 93 G2
Mead End 10 B2
Meadle 22 B1
Meadow Hall 51 F3
Meadowmill 51 F3
Meadowtown 38 C5
Meal Bank 61 G7
Mealabost 101 G2
Mealasta 100 B5
Meals 53 H3
Mealsgate 60 D2
Meanley 56 C5
Mearbeck 56 D3
Meare 19 H7
Mearns 74 D5
Mears Ashby 32 B2
Measham 41 F4
Meathop 55 H1
Meavy 5 F4
Medbourne 42 B6
Meddon 6 A4
Meden Vale 51 H6
Medlam 53 G6
Medmenham 22 B3
Medomsley 62 C1
Medstead 11 H1
Meer End 30 D1
Meerbrook 49 J6
Meeth 6 D5
Meggethead 69 G1
Meidrim 17 F3
Meifod *Denb.* 47 J7
Meifod *Powys* 38 A4
Meigle 82 D3
Meikle Earnock 75 F5
Meikle Grenach 73 J4
Meikle Kilmory 73 J4
Meikle Rahane 74 A2
Meikle Strath 90 E7
Meikle Tarty 91 H2
Meikle Wartle 91 F1
Meikleour 82 C4
Meinciau 17 H4
Meir 40 B1
Meirheath 40 B2
Melbost 101 G4
Melbourne *Derbys.* 41 F3
Melbourne *E.Riding* 58 D5
Melbury 6 B4
Melbury Abbas 9 H3
Melbury Bubb 8 E4
Melbury Osmond 8 E4
Melbury Sampford 8 E4
Melby 109 A7
Melchbourne 32 D2
Melchet Court 10 D2
Melcombe Bingham 9 G4
Melcombe Regis 9 F6
Meldon *Devon* 6 D6
Meldon *Northumb.* 71 G5
Meldreth 33 G4
Melfort 79 K6
Melgarve 88 B5
Melgum 90 C4
Meliden (Gallt Melyd) 47 J4
Melincourt 18 B1
Melincryddan 18 A2
Melin-y-coed 47 G6
Melin-y-ddol 37 K5
Melin-y-grug 37 K5
Melin-y-Wig 37 K1
Melkinthorpe 61 H4
Melkridge 70 C7
Melksham 20 C5
Melksham Forest 20 C5
Melldalloch 73 H3
Melling *Lancs.* 55 J2
Melling *Mersey.* 48 C2
Melling Mount 48 D2
Mellis 34 E1
Mellon Charles 94 E2
Mellon Udrigle 94 E2
Mellor *Gt.Man.* 49 J4
Mellor *Lancs.* 56 B6
Mellor Brook 56 B6
Mells 20 A7
Melmerby *Cumb.* 61 H3

Nether Compton 8 E3
Nether Crimond 91 G2
Nether Dalgliesh 69 H3
Nether Dallachy 98 B4
Nether End 50 E5
Nether Exe 7 H6
Nether Glasslaw 99 G5
Nether Handwick 82 E3
Nether Haugh 51 G3
Nether Headon 51 K5
Nether Heselden 56 D2
Nether Heyford 31 H3
Nether Kellet 55 J3
Nether Kinmundy 99 J6
Nether Langwith 51 H5
Nether Lenshie 98 E6
Nether Moor 51 F6
Nether Padley 50 E5
Nether Pitforthie 91 G7
Nether Poppleton 58 B4
Nether Silton 63 F7
Nether Stowey 7 K2
Nether Urquhart 82 C7
Nether Wallop 10 E1
Nether Wasdale 60 C6
Nether Wellwood 68 B1
Nether Whitacre 40 E6
Nether (Lower) Winchendon 31 J7
Nether Worton 31 F5
Netheravon 20 E7
Netherbrae 99 F5
Netherbrough 107 C6
Netherburn 75 G6
Netherbury 8 D5
Netherby *Cumb.* 69 J6
Netherby *N.Yorks.* 57 J5
Nethercott 31 F6
Netherend 19 J2
Netherfield *E.Suss.* 14 C6
Netherfield *Notts.* 41 J1
Netherfield *S.Lan.* 75 F6
Netherhall 74 A4
Netherhampton 10 C1
Netherley 91 G5
Nethermill 69 F5
Nethermuir 99 H6
Netherseal 40 E4
Nethershield 67 K1
Netherstreet 20 C5
Netherthird *D. & G.* 65 H5
Netherthird *E.Ayr.* 67 K2
Netherthong 50 D2
Netherthorpe 51 H4
Netherton *Angus* 83 G2
Netherton *Ches.* 48 E5
Netherton *Devon* 5 J3
Netherton *Mersey.* 48 C2
Netherton *Northumb.* 70 E3
Netherton *Oxon.* 21 H2
Netherton *P. & K.* 82 C2
Netherton *S.Lan.* 75 H5
Netherton *W.Mid.* 40 B7
Netherton *W.Yorks.* 50 E1
Netherton *W.Yorks.* 50 D1
Netherton *Worcs.* 29 J4
Nethertown *Cumb.* 60 A6
Nethertown *Ork.* 105 J1
Netherwitton 71 G5
Netherwood *D. & G.* 65 K3
Netherwood *E.Ayr.* 68 B1
Nethy Bridge 89 H2
Netley Abbey 11 F4
Netley Marsh 10 E3
Nettlebed 22 A3
Nettlebridge 19 K7
Nettlecombe *Dorset* 8 E5
Nettlecombe *Som.* 7 J2
Nettleden 32 D7
Nettleham 52 D5
Nettlestead *Kent* 23 K6
Nettlestead *Suff.* 34 E4
Nettlestead Green 23 K6
Nettlestone 11 H5
Nettleton *Lincs.* 52 E2
Nettleton *Wilts.* 20 B4
Netton *Devon* 5 F6
Netton *Wilts.* 10 C1
Neuadd *Cere.* 26 D3
Neuadd *I.o.A.* 46 B3
Neuadd *Powys* 27 J4
Nevendon 24 D2
Nevern 16 D2
Nevill Holt 42 B6
New Abbey 65 K4
New Aberdour 99 G4
New Addington 23 G5
New Alresford 11 G1
New Alyth 82 D3
New Arley 40 E6
New Ash Green 24 C5
New Barn 24 C5
New Barnet 23 F2
New Belses 70 A1
New Bewick 71 F1
New Bolingbroke 53 G7
New Bradwell 32 B4
New Bridge 65 K3
New Brighton *Hants.* 11 J4
New Brighton *Mersey.* 48 C3
New Brinsley 51 G7
New Broughton 48 C7
New Buckenham 44 E6
New Byth 99 G5
New Cheriton 11 G2
New Costessey 45 F5
New Cross 27 F1
New Cumnock 68 B2
New Deer 99 G6
New Duston 31 J2
New Earswick 58 C4
New Edlington 51 H3
New Elgin 97 K5
New Ellerby 59 H6
New Eltham 23 H4
New End 30 B2
New England 42 E5
New Farnley 57 H6
New Ferry 48 C4
New Fryston 57 K7
New Galloway 65 G3
New Gilston 83 F7
New Grimsby 2 B1
New Hartley 71 J6
New Haw 22 D5
New Hedges 16 E5
New Holland 59 G7
New Houghton *Derbys.* 51 H6
New Houghton *Norf.* 44 B3
New Houses 56 D2
New Hutton 61 G7
New Hythe 14 C2
New Inn *Carmar.* 17 H2
New Inn *Fife* 82 D7
New Inn *Mon.* 19 H1
New Inn *Torfaen* 19 F2
New Invention *Shrop.* 28 B1
New Invention *W.Mid.* 40 B5
New Lanark 75 G6
New Lane 48 D1
New Leake 53 H7
New Leeds 99 H5
New Leslie 90 D2
New Longton 55 J7
New Luce 64 B4
New Mains 75 G7
New Mains of Ury 91 G6
New Malden 23 F5
New Marske 63 H4
New Marton 38 C2
New Mill *Cornw.* 2 B5
New Mill *Herts.* 32 C7
New Mill *W.Yorks.* 50 D2
New Mill End 32 E7
New Mills *Cornw.* 3 F3
New Mills *Derbys.* 49 J4
New Mills *Mon.* 19 J1
New Mills *Powys* 37 K5
New Milton 10 D5
New Mistley 35 F5
New Moat 16 D3
New Orleans 66 B2
New Park 4 B2
New Pitsligo 99 G5
New Polzeath 3 G1
New Quay (Ceinewydd) 26 C3
New Rackheath 45 G4
New Radnor 28 B2
New Rent 61 F3
New Romney 15 F5
New Rossington 51 J3
New Row 56 B6
New Sawley 41 G2
New Silksworth 62 E1
New Town *E.Loth.* 76 C3
New Town *E.Suss.* 13 H4
New Town *Glos.* 30 B5
New Tredegar 18 E1
New Tupton 51 F6
New Ulva 73 F2
New Walsoken 43 H5
New Waltham 53 F2
New Winton 76 C3
New Yatt 30 E7
New York *Lincs.* 53 F7
New York *T. & W.* 71 J6
Newark *Ork.* 106 G3
Newark *Peter.* 43 F5
Newark-on-Trent 52 B7
Newarthill 75 F5
Newbarn 15 G3
Newbarns 55 F2
Newbiggin *Cumb.* 61 F4
Newbiggin *Cumb.* 61 H4
Newbiggin *Cumb.* 61 G2
Newbiggin *Cumb.* 55 F3
Newbiggin *Dur.* 62 A4
Newbiggin *N.Yorks.* 57 F1
Newbiggin *N.Yorks.* 62 A7
Newbiggin *Northumb.* 70 E7
Newbiggin-by-the-Sea 71 J5
Newbigging *Aber.* 91 G5
Newbigging *Aber.* 89 J6
Newbigging *Angus* 83 F4
Newbigging *Angus* 83 F4
Newbigging *Angus* 82 D3
Newbigging *S.Lan.* 75 J6
Newbiggin-on-Lune 61 J6
Newbold *Derbys.* 51 F5
Newbold *Leics.* 41 G4
Newbold on Avon 31 F1
Newbold on Stour 30 D4
Newbold Pacey 30 D3
Newbold Verdon 41 G5
Newborough *I.o.A.* 46 C6
Newborough *Peter.* 43 F5
Newborough *Staffs.* 40 D3
Newbottle 31 G5
Newbourne 35 G4
Newbridge (Cefn Bychan) *Caerp.* 19 F2
Newbridge *Cornw.* 2 B5
Newbridge *Cornw.* 4 D4
Newbridge *Edin.* 75 K3
Newbridge *Hants.* 10 E3
Newbridge *I.o.W.* 11 F6
Newbridge *Oxon.* 21 H1
Newbridge *Pembs.* 16 C2
Newbridge *Wrex.* 38 B1
Newbridge on Wye 27 K3
Newbridge-on-Usk 19 G2
Newbrough 70 D7
Newburgh *Aber.* 99 H5
Newburgh *Aber.* 91 H2
Newburgh *Fife* 82 D6
Newburgh *Lancs.* 48 D1
Newburgh *Sc.Bord.* 69 J2
Newburn 71 G7
Newbury 21 H5
Newby *Cumb.* 61 G4
Newby *Lancs.* 56 D5
Newby *N.Yorks.* 63 G5
Newby *N.Yorks.* 56 C2
Newby Bridge 55 G1
Newby East 61 F1
Newby West 60 E1
Newby Wiske 57 J1
Newcastle *Bridgend* 18 C4
Newcastle *Mon.* 28 D7
Newcastle *Shrop.* 38 B7
Newcastle Emlyn (Castell Newydd Emlyn) 17 G1
Newcastle International Airport 71 G6
Newcastle upon Tyne 71 H7
Newcastleton 69 K5
Newcastle-under-Lyme 40 A1
Newchapel *Pembs.* 17 F2
Newchapel *Stoke* 49 H7
Newchapel *Surr.* 23 G7
Newchurch *Carmar.* 17 G3
Newchurch *I.o.W.* 11 G6
Newchurch *Kent* 15 F4
Newchurch *Lancs.* 56 D7
Newchurch *Lancs.* 56 D6
Newchurch *Mon.* 19 H2
Newchurch *Powys* 28 B3
Newcott 8 B4
Newcraighall 76 B3
Newdigate 22 E7
Newell Green 22 B4
Newenden 14 D5
Newent 29 G6
Newerne 19 K1
Newfield *Dur.* 62 D3
Newfield *Dur.* 62 D1
Newfield *High.* 96 E4
Newgale 16 B3
Newgate 44 E1
Newgate Street 23 G1
Newgord 108 E2
Newhall *Ches.* 39 F1
Newhall *Derbys.* 40 E3
Newham 71 G1
Newham Hall 71 G1
Newhaven 13 H6
Newhey 49 J1
Newholm 63 K5
Newhouse 75 F4
Newick 13 H4
Newington *Kent* 15 G4
Newington *Kent* 24 E5
Newington *Oxon.* 21 K2
Newington Bagpath 20 B2
Newland *Glos.* 19 J1
Newland *N.Yorks.* 58 C7
Newland *Worcs.* 29 G4
Newlandrig 76 B4
Newlands *Northumb.* 62 B1
Newlands *Sc.Bord.* 70 A4
Newland's Corner 22 D7
Newlands of Geise 105 F2
Newlyn 2 B6
Newlyn East 3 F3
Newmachar 91 G3
Newmains 75 G5
Newmarket *Suff.* 33 K2
Newmarket *W.Isles* 101 G4
Newmill *Aber.* 91 F6
Newmill *Aber.* 99 G6
Newmill *Aber.* 91 G2
Newmill *Moray* 98 C5
Newmill *Sc.Bord.* 69 K2
Newmill of Inshewan 83 F1
Newmills 96 D5
Newmiln *P. & K.* 82 C4
Newmiln *P. & K.* 82 B5
Newmilns 74 D7
Newnham *Glos.* 29 F7
Newnham *Hants.* 22 A6
Newnham *Herts.* 33 F5
Newnham *Kent* 14 E2
Newnham *Northants.* 31 G3
Newnham *Worcs.* 29 F2
Newnham Paddox 41 G7
Newnoth 90 D1
Newport *Cornw.* 6 B7
Newport *Devon* 6 D2
Newport *E.Riding* 58 E6
Newport *Essex* 33 J5
Newport *Glos.* 19 K2
Newport *High.* 105 G6
Newport *I.o.W.* 11 G6
Newport (Casnewydd) *Newport* 19 G3
Newport *Norf.* 45 K4
Newport *Pembs.* 16 D2
Newport *Tel. & W.* 39 G4
Newport Pagnell 32 B4
Newport-on-Tay 83 F5
Newpound Common 12 D4
Newquay 3 F2
Newquay Cornwall Airport 3 F2
Newseat 91 F1
Newsham *Lancs.* 55 J6
Newsham *N.Yorks.* 62 C5
Newsham *N.Yorks.* 57 J1
Newsham *Northumb.* 71 H6
Newsholme *E.Riding* 58 D7
Newsholme *Lancs.* 56 D4
Newstead *Northumb.* 71 G1
Newstead *Notts.* 51 H7
Newstead *Sc.Bord.* 76 D7
Newthorpe 57 K6
Newton *Aber.* 98 C6
Newton *Aber.* 99 J6
Newton *Arg. & B.* 73 J1
Newton *Bridgend* 18 B4
Newton *Cambs.* 43 H4
Newton *Cambs.* 33 H4
Newton *Ches.* 48 D7
Newton *Ches.* 48 E5
Newton *Cumb.* 55 F2
Newton *D. & G.* 69 G4
Newton *Gt.Man.* 49 J3
Newton *Here.* 28 C2
Newton *High.* 105 J4
Newton *High.* 96 E7
Newton *High.* 105 H3
Newton *High.* 102 E5
Newton *High.* 96 C6
Newton *High.* 96 E5
Newton *Lancs.* 56 B4
Newton *Lancs.* 55 J2
Newton *Lincs.* 42 D2
Newton *Moray* 98 B4
Newton *N.Ayr.* 73 H5
Newton *Norf.* 44 C4
Newton *Northants.* 42 B7
Newton *Northumb.* 71 F7
Newton *Notts.* 41 J1
Newton *P. & K.* 81 K4
Newton *Pembs.* 16 C3
Newton *Pembs.* 16 C5
Newton *S.Lan.* 75 H7
Newton *Sc.Bord.* 70 B1
Newton *Staffs.* 40 C3
Newton *Suff.* 34 D4
Newton *Swan.* 17 K7
Newton *W.Loth.* 75 J3
Newton *W.Yorks.* 57 K7
Newton *Warks.* 31 G1
Newton *Wilts.* 10 D2
Newton Abbot 5 J3
Newton Arlosh 60 C1
Newton Aycliffe 62 D4
Newton Bewley 63 F4
Newton Blossomville 32 C3
Newton Bromswold 32 D2
Newton Burgoland 41 F5
Newton by Toft 52 D4
Newton Ferrers 5 F6
Newton Flotman 45 G6
Newton Harcourt 41 J6
Newton Kyme 57 K5
Newton Longville 32 B5
Newton Mearns 74 D5
Newton Morrell 62 D6
Newton Mountain 16 C5
Newton Mulgrave 63 J5
Newton of Affleck 83 F4
Newton of Ardtoe 86 C7
Newton of Balcanquhal 82 C6
Newton of Dalvey 97 H6
Newton of Falkland 82 D7
Newton of Leys 96 D7
Newton on Trent 52 B5
Newton Poppleford 7 J7
Newton Purcell 31 H5
Newton Regis 40 E5
Newton Reigny 61 F3
Newton St. Cyres 7 G6
Newton St. Faith 45 G4
Newton St. Loe 20 A5
Newton St. Petrock 6 C4
Newton Solney 40 E3
Newton Stacey 21 H7
Newton Stewart 64 E4
Newton Tony 21 F7
Newton Tracey 6 D3
Newton under Roseberry 63 G5
Newton upon Derwent 58 D5
Newton Valence 11 J1
Newtonairds 68 D5
Newtongrange 76 B4
Newtonhill 91 H5
Newton-le-Willows *Mersey.* 48 E3
Newton-le-Willows *N.Yorks.* 57 H1
Newtonmill 83 H1
Newtonmore 88 E5
Newton-on-Ouse 58 B3
Newton-on-Rawcliffe 63 K7
Newton-on-the-Moor 71 G3
Newtown *B.Gwent* 28 A7
Newtown *Bucks.* 22 C1
Newtown *Ches.* 48 D7
Newtown *Cumb.* 70 A7
Newtown *Derbys.* 49 J4
Newtown *Hants.* 11 H3
Newtown *Hants.* 21 H5
Newtown *Hants.* 10 D3
Newtown *Hants.* 10 E2
Newtown *Hants.* 11 G3
Newtown *Here.* 29 G5
Newtown *Here.* 29 F4
Newtown *High.* 87 K4
Newtown *I.o.M.* 54 C6
Newtown *I.o.W.* 11 F5
Newtown *Northumb.* 71 F3
Newtown *Northumb.* 71 F1
Newtown *Poole* 10 B5
Newtown (Y Drenewydd) *Powys* 38 A6
Newtown *Shrop.* 38 D2
Newtown *Staffs.* 49 J6
Newtown *Staffs.* 50 C6
Newtown *Wilts.* 9 J2
Newtown in St. Martin 2 E6
Newtown Linford 41 H4
Newtown St. Boswells 76 D7
Newtown Unthank 41 G5
Newtyle 82 D3
Neyland 16 C5
Nibley *Glos.* 19 K1
Nibley *S.Glos.* 19 K3
Nicholashayne 7 K4
Nicholaston 17 J7
Nidd 57 J3
Niddrie 76 A3
Nigg *Aberdeen* 91 H4
Nigg *High.* 97 F4
Nightcott 7 G3
Nilig 47 J7
Nimlet 20 A4
Nine Ashes 23 J1
Nine Elms 20 E3
Nine Mile Burn 75 K5
Ninebanks 61 J1
Ninemile Bar or Crocketford 65 J3
Ninfield 14 C6
Ningwood 11 F6
Nisbet 70 B1
Niton 11 G7
Nitshill 74 D4
Nizels 23 J6
No Man's Heath *Ches.* 38 E1
No Man's Heath *Warks.* 40 E5
Noak Hill 23 J2
Noblehill 65 K3
Nobottle 31 H2
Nocton 52 D6
Noddsdale 74 A4
Noke 31 G7
Nolton 16 B4
Nomansland *Devon* 7 G4
Nomansland *Wilts.* 10 D3
Noneley 38 D3
Nonington 15 H2
Nook *Cumb.* 69 K6
Nook *Cumb.* 55 J1
Noonsbrough 109 B7
Noranside 83 F1
Norbiton 22 E5
Norbreck 55 G5
Norbury *Ches.* 38 E1
Norbury *Derbys.* 40 D1
Norbury *Shrop.* 38 C6
Norbury *Staffs.* 39 G3
Norchard 29 H2
Nordelph 43 J5
Norden 9 J6
Nordley 39 F6
Norham 77 H6
Norland Town 57 F7
Norley 48 E5
Norleywood 10 E5
Norman Cross 42 E6
Normanby *N.Lincs.* 52 B1
Normanby *N.Yorks.* 58 D1
Normanby *R. & C.* 63 G5
Normanby by Stow 52 B4
Normanby le Wold 52 E3
Normanby-by-Spital 52 D4
Normandy 22 C6
Normann's Ruh 79 F3
Norman's Bay 13 K6
Norman's Green 7 J5
Normanton *Derby* 41 F2
Normanton *Leics.* 42 B1
Normanton *Lincs.* 42 C1
Normanton *Notts.* 51 K7
Normanton *Rut.* 42 C5
Normanton *W.Yorks.* 57 J7
Normanton le Heath 41 F4
Normanton on Soar 41 H3
Normanton on Trent 51 K6
Normanton-on-the-Wolds 41 J2
Normoss 55 G6
Norrington Common 20 B5
Norris Hill 41 F4
North Anston 51 H4
North Ascot 22 C5
North Aston 31 F6
North Baddesley 10 E2
North Ballachulish 80 B1
North Balloch 67 H4
North Barrow 9 F2
North Barsham 44 D2
North Benfleet 24 D3
North Bersted 12 C6
North Berwick 76 D2
North Boarhunt 11 H3
North Bogbain 98 B5
North Bovey 7 F7
North Bradley 20 B6
North Brentor 6 C7
North Brewham 9 G1
North Buckland 6 C1
North Burlingham 45 H4
North Cadbury 9 F2
North Cairn 66 D6
North Camp 22 B6
North Carlton *Lincs.* 52 C5
North Carlton *Notts.* 51 H4
North Cave 58 E6
North Cerney 20 D1
North Chailey 13 G4
North Charford 10 D2
North Charlton 71 G1
North Cheriton 9 F2
North Cliffe 58 E6
North Clifton 52 B5
North Cockerington 53 G3
North Coker 8 E3
North Connel 80 A4
North Cornelly 18 B3
North Cotes 53 G2
North Cove 45 J7
North Cowton 62 D6
North Crawley 32 C4
North Cray 23 H4
North Creake 44 C2
North Curry 8 C2
North Dallens 80 A3
North Dalton 59 F4
North Dawn 107 D7
North Deighton 57 J4
North Duffield 58 C6
North Elkington 53 F3
North Elmham 44 D3
North Elmsall 51 G1
North End *Bucks.* 32 B6
North End *Essex* 33 K7
North End *Hants.* 21 H5
North End *N.Som.* 19 H5
North End *Norf.* 44 E6
North End *Northumb.* 71 G3
North End *Ports.* 11 H4
North End *W.Suss.* 12 E5
North Erradale 94 D3
North Essie 99 J5
North Ferriby 59 F7
North Frodingham 59 H4
North Gorley 10 C3
North Green 45 G7
North Grimston 58 E3
North Hayling 11 J4
North Hazelrigg 77 J7
North Heasley 7 F2
North Heath 12 D4
North Hill 4 C3
North Hinksey 21 H1
North Holmwood 22 E7
North Huish 5 H5
North Hykeham 52 C6
North Johnston 16 C4
North Kelsey 52 D2
North Kessock 96 D7
North Killingholme 52 E1
North Kilvington 57 K1
North Kilworth 41 J7
North Kyme 52 E7
North Lancing 12 E6
North Lee 22 B1
North Leigh 30 E7
North Leverton with Habblesthorpe 51 K4
North Littleton 30 B4
North Lopham 44 E7
North Luffenham 42 C5
North Marden 12 B5
North Marston 31 J6
North Middleton 76 B5
North Millbrex 99 G6
North Molton 7 F3
North Moreton 21 J3
North Mundham 12 B6
North Muskham 51 K7
North Newbald 59 F6
North Newington 31 F5
North Newnton 20 E6
North Newton 8 B1
North Nibley 20 A2
North Oakley 21 J6
North Ockendon 23 J3
North Ormesby 63 G4
North Ormsby 53 F3
North Otterington 62 E7
North Owersby 52 D3
North Perrott 8 D4
North Petherton 8 B1
North Petherwin 4 C2
North Pickenham 44 C5
North Piddle 29 J3
North Poorton 8 E5
North Queensferry 75 K2
North Radworthy 7 F2
North Rauceby 42 D1
North Reston 53 G4
North Rigton 57 H5
North Rode 49 H6
North Roe 108 C4
North Runcton 44 A4
North Sandwick 108 E3
North Scale 54 E3
North Scarle 52 B6
North Seaton 71 H5
North Shian 80 A3
North Shields 71 J7
North Shoebury 25 F3
North Side 43 F6
North Skelton 63 H5
North Somercotes 53 H3
North Stainley 57 H2
North Stainmore 61 K5
North Stifford 24 C3
North Stoke *B. & N.E.Som.* 19 K5
North Stoke *Oxon.* 21 K3
North Stoke *W.Suss.* 12 D5
North Stoneham 11 F3
North Street *Hants.* 11 H1
North Street *Kent* 15 F2
North Street *W.Berks.* 21 K4
North Sunderland 77 K4
North Tamerton 6 B6
North Tarbothill 91 H3
North Tawton 6 E5
North Third 75 F2
North Thoresby 53 F3
North Tidworth 21 F7
North Togston 71 H3
North Town *Devon* 6 D5
North Town *Hants.* 22 B6
North Tuddenham 44 E4
North Walsham 45 G2
North Waltham 21 J7
North Warnborough 22 A6
North Watten 105 H3
North Weald Bassett 23 H1
North Wheatley 51 K4
North Whilborough 5 J4
North Wick 19 J5
North Widcombe 19 J6
North Willingham 52 E4
North Wingfield 51 G6
North Witham 42 C3
North Wootton *Dorset* 9 F3
North Wootton *Norf.* 44 A3
North Wootton *Som.* 19 J7
North Wraxall 20 B4
North Wroughton 20 E3
North Yardhope 70 E3
Northacre 44 D6
Northall Green 44 E4
Northallerton 62 E7
Northam *Devon* 6 C3
Northam *S'ham.* 11 F3
Northampton 31 J2
Northaw 23 F1
Northay 8 B3
Northborough 42 E5
Northbourne 15 J2
Northbrook 31 F6
Northburnhill 99 G6
Northchapel 12 C4
Northchurch 22 C1
Northcote Manor 6 E4
Northcott 6 B6
Northdyke 106 B5
Northend *B. & N.E.Som.* 20 A5
Northend *Bucks.* 22 A2
Northend *Warks.* 30 E3
Northfield *Aber.* 99 G4
Northfield *Aberdeen* 91 G4
Northfield *High.* 105 J4
Northfield *Sc.Bord.* 77 H4
Northfield *W.Mid.* 30 B1
Northfleet 24 C4
Northhouse 69 K3
Northiam 14 D5
Northill 32 E4
Northington 11 G1
Northlands 53 G7
Northleach 30 C7
Northleigh *Devon* 7 K6
Northleigh *Devon* 6 E2
Northlew 6 D6
Northmoor 21 H1
Northmoor Green or Moorland 8 C1
Northmuir 82 E2
Northney 11 J4
Northolt 22 E3
Northop 48 B6
Northop Hall 48 B6
Northorpe *Lincs.* 43 F2
Northorpe *Lincs.* 52 B3
Northorpe *Lincs.* 42 D4
Northover 8 E2
Northowram 57 G7
Northpunds 109 D10
Northrepps 45 G2
Northton (Taobh Tuath) 92 E3
Northtown 107 D8
Northway 29 J5
Northwich 49 F5
Northwick 19 J3
Northwold 44 B6
Northwood *Gt.Lon.* 22 D2
Northwood *I.o.W.* 11 F5
Northwood *Shrop.* 38 D2
Northwood Green 29 G
Norton *Glos.* 29 H
Norton *Halton* 48 E
Norton *Herts.* 33 F
Norton *I.o.W.* 10 E
Norton *N.Yorks.* 58 D
Norton *Northants.* 31 H
Norton *Notts.* 51 H
Norton *Powys* 28 C
Norton *S.Yorks.* 51 H
Norton *S.Yorks.* 51 F
Norton *Shrop.* 38 E
Norton *Shrop.* 39 G
Norton *Shrop.* 38 D
Norton *Stock.* 63 F
Norton *Suff.* 34 D
Norton *W.Mid.* 40 A
Norton *W.Suss.* 12 C
Norton *W.Suss.* 12 B
Norton *Wilts.* 20 B
Norton *Worcs.* 29 H
Norton *Worcs.* 30 B
Norton Bavant 20 C
Norton Bridge 40 A
Norton Canes 40 C
Norton Canon 28 C
Norton Disney 52 B
Norton Ferris 9 G
Norton Fitzwarren 7 K
Norton Green 10 E
Norton Hawkfield 19 J
Norton Heath 24 C
Norton in Hales 39 F
Norton in the Moors 49 H
Norton Lindsey 30 D
Norton Malreward 19 J
Norton Mandeville 23 J
Norton St. Philip 20 A
Norton sub Hamdon 8 D
Norton Subcourse 45 J
Norton Wood 28 C
Norton-Juxta-Twycross 41 F
Norton-le-Clay 57 J
Norwell 51 K
Norwell Woodhouse 51 K
Norwich 45 G
Norwich Airport 45 G
Norwick 108 F
Norwood Green 22 E
Norwood Hill 23 F
Noseley 42 A
Noss Mayo 5 F
Nosterfield 57 H
Nostie 86 E
Notgrove 30 C
Nottage 18 B
Nottingham *High.* 105 H
Nottingham *Nott.* 41 H
Notton *W.Yorks.* 51 F
Notton *Wilts.* 20 C
Nounsley 24 D
Noutard's Green 29 G
Nowton 34 C
Nox 38 D
Noyadd Trefawr 17 F
Nuffield 21 K
Nun Monkton 58 B
Nunburnholme 58 E
Nuneaton 41 F
Nuneham Courtenay 21 J
Nunney 20 A
Nunnington 58 C
Nunnington Park 7 J
Nunthorpe 63 G
Nunton 10 C
Nunwick *N.Yorks.* 57 J
Nunwick *Northumb.* 70 D
Nup End *Bucks.* 32 B
Nup End *Glos.* 29 H
Nursling 10 E
Nursted 11 J
Nurton 40 A
Nutbourne *W.Suss.* 12 D5
Nutbourne *W.Suss.* 11 J4
Nutfield 23 G
Nuthall 41 H
Nuthampstead 33 H5
Nuthurst *W.Suss.* 12 E4
Nuthurst *Warks.* 30 C
Nutley *E.Suss.* 13 H4
Nutley *Hants.* 21 K7
Nutwell 51 J2
Nyadd 75 F1
Nybster 105 J2
Nyetimber 12 B7
Nyewood 12 B4
Nymet Rowland 7 F5
Nymet Tracey 7 F5
Nympsfield 20 B1
Nynehead 7 K3
Nythe 8 D
Nyton 12 C6

O

Oad Street 24 E5
Oadby 41 J5
Oak Cross 6 D6
Oakamoor 40 C1
Oakbank *Arg. & B.* 79 J4
Oakbank *W.Loth.* 75 J4
Oakdale 18 E2
Oake 7 K3
Oaken 40 A5
Oakenclough 55 J5
Oakengates 39 F4
Oakenhead 97 K5
Oakenshaw *Dur.* 62 D3
Oakenshaw *W.Yorks.* 57 G7
Oakford *Cere.* 26 D3
Oakford *Devon* 7 H3
Oakfordbridge 7 H3
Oakgrove 49 J6
Oakham 42 B5
Oakhanger 11 J1
Oakhill 19 K7
Oakington 33 H2
Oaklands *Conwy* 47 G7
Oaklands *Herts.* 33 F7
Oakle Street 29 G7
Oakley *Beds.* 32 D3
Oakley *Bucks.* 31 H7
Oakley *Fife* 75 J2
Oakley *Hants.* 21 J6
Oakley *Suff.* 35 F1
Oakley Green 22 C4
Oakley Park 37 J7
Oakridge Lynch 20 C1
Oaks 38 D5
Oaksey 20 C2

akshaw Ford 70 A6
akthorpe 41 F4
aktree Hill 62 E7
akwoodhill 12 E3
akworth 57 F6
alinlongart 73 K2
are Kent 25 G5
are Som. 7 G1
are Wilts. 20 E5
asby 42 D2
atfield 66 A2
athlaw 83 F2
ban 79 K5
bley 28 C1
borne 9 F3
cclestone Green 49 F6
ccold 35 F1
ccumster 105 H5
chiltree 67 K1
chr-y-Mynydd 18 D1
chtermuthill 81 K6
chtertyre P. & K. 81 K5
chtertyre Stir. 75 F1
ckbrook 41 G2
ckham 22 D6
ckle 86 B7
ckley 12 E3
cle Pychard 28 E4
cton 59 G3
dcombe 8 E3
dd Down 20 A5
ddingley 29 J3
ddington 31 G7
ddsta 108 E3
dell 32 C3
die 106 F5
diham 22 A6
dstock 10 C2
dstone 41 F5
ffchurch 30 B4
ffenham 30 B4
fferton 49 J4
ffham E.Suss. 13 H5
ffham Kent 23 K6
fford Cluny 33 F2
fford D'Arcy 34 E4
ffton 34 E4
ffwell 7 K6
gbourne Maizey 20 E4
gbourne
  St. Andrew 20 E4
gbourne
  St. George 20 E4
gden 57 F6
gil 83 F1
gle 71 G6
gmore 18 B4
gmore Vale 18 C2
gmore-by-Sea 18 B4
il Terminal 107 C8
keford Fitzpaine 9 H3
kehampton 6 D6
kehampton Camp 6 D6
kraquoy 109 D9
ld 31 J1
ld Aberdeen 91 G4
ld Alresford 11 G1
ld Arley 40 E6
ld Basford 41 H1
ld Basing 21 K6
ld Belses 70 A1
ld Bewick 71 F1
ld Bolingbroke 53 G6
ld Brampton 51 F5
ld Bridge of Urr 65 H4
ld Buckenham 44 E6
ld Burghclere 21 H6
ld Byland 58 B1
ld Cleeve 7 J1
ld Clipstone 51 J6
ld Colwyn 47 G5
ld Craig 91 H2
ld Craighall 76 B3
ld Crombie 98 D5
ld Dailly 67 G4
ld Dalby 41 J3
ld Deer 99 H6
ld Ellerby 59 H6
ld Felixstowe 35 H5
ld Fletton 42 E6
ld Glossop 50 C3
ld Goginan 37 F7
ld Goole 58 D7
ld Gore 29 F6
ld Grimsby 2 B1
ld Hall 53 F1
ld Heath 34 E6
ld Hill 40 B7
ld Hutton 55 J1
ld Kea 3 F4
ld Kilpatrick 74 C3
ld Kinnernie 91 F4
ld Knebworth 33 F6
ld Leake 53 H7
ld Leslie 90 D2
ld Malton 58 D2
ld Micklefield 57 K6
ld Milverton 30 D2
ld Montsale 25 G2
ld Netley 11 F3
ld Newton 34 E2
ld Philpstoun 75 J3
ld Poltalloch 79 K7
ld Radnor 28 B3
ld Rattray 99 J5
ld Rayne 90 E2
ld Romney 15 F5
ld Scone 82 C5
ld Shields 75 G3
ld Sodbury 20 A3
ld Somerby 42 C2
ld Stratford 31 J4
ld Sunderlandwick 59 G4
ld Swarland 71 G3
ld Swinford 40 B7
ld Town Cumb. 55 J1
ld Town I.o.S. 2 C1
ld Town
  Northumb. 70 D4
ld Tupton 51 F6
ld Warden 32 E4
ld Weston 32 E1
ld Windsor 22 C4
ld Wives Lees 15 F2
ld Woking 22 D6
ld Wolverton 32 B4
ld Woods 38 D3
ldberrow 30 C2
ldborough 7 F5
ldbury Kent 23 J6
ldbury Shrop. 39 G6
ldbury W.Mid. 40 B6
ldbury Warks. 41 F6
ldbury Naite 19 K2
ldbury on the Hill 20 B3
ldbury-on-Severn 19 K2
ldcastle 28 C6
ldcastle Heath 38 D1
ldcotes 51 H4

Oldfield W.Yorks. 57 F6
Oldfield Worcs. 29 H2
Oldford 20 A6
Oldhall Aber. 90 C5
Oldhall High. 105 H3
Oldham 49 J2
Oldhamstocks 77 F3
Oldhurst 33 F1
Oldland 19 K4
Oldmeldrum 91 G2
Oldmill 90 D4
Oldpark 39 F5
Oldridge 7 G6
Oldshore Beg 102 D3
Oldshore More 102 D3
Oldstead 58 B1
Oldtown of Aigas 96 B7
Oldtown of Ord 98 E5
Oldwalls 17 H6
Oldways End 7 G3
Oldwhat 99 G5
Olgrinmore 105 F3
Oliver 69 G1
Oliver's Battery 11 F2
Ollaberry 108 C4
Ollerton Ches. 49 G5
Ollerton Notts. 51 J6
Ollerton Shrop. 39 F3
Olmstead Green 33 K4
Olney 32 B3
Olrig House 105 G2
Olton 40 D7
Olveston 19 J3
Ombersley 29 H2
Ompton 51 J6
Onchan 54 C6
Onecote 50 C7
Ongar Hill 43 J3
Ongar Street 28 C2
Onibury 28 D1
Onich 80 B1
Onllwyn 27 H7
Onneley 39 G1
Onslow Village 22 C7
Onthank 74 C6
Openwoodgate 41 F1
Opinan High. 94 E2
Opinan High. 94 D4
Orange Lane 77 F6
Orbliston 98 B5
Orbost 93 H7
Orby 53 H6
Orcadia 73 K4
Orchard 73 K2
Orchard Portman 8 B2
Orchard Wyndham 7 J1
Orcheston 20 D7
Orcop 28 D6
Orcop Hill 28 D6
Ord 86 C3
Ordhead 90 E3
Ordie 90 C4
Ordiequish 98 B5
Ordsall 51 K5
Ore 14 D6
Oreham Common 13 F5
Oreston 5 F5
Oreton 39 F7
Orford Suff. 35 J4
Orford Warr. 49 F3
Orgreave 40 D4
Orleton Here. 28 D2
Orleton Worcs. 29 F2
Orleton Common 28 D2
Orlingbury 32 B1
Ormacleit 84 C1
Ormesby 63 G5
Ormesby
  St. Margaret 45 J4
Ormesby
  St. Michael 45 J4
Ormiscaig 94 E2
Ormiston 76 C4
Ormsaigmore 79 F1
Ormsary 79 F1
Ormsdale 73 J2
Ormskirk 48 D2
Ormwe 105 G2
Orphir 107 C7
Orpington 23 H5
Orrell 48 E2
Orrisdale 54 C4
Orrok House 91 H3
Orroland 65 H6
Orsett 24 C3
Orslow 40 A4
Orston 42 A1
Orthwaite 60 D3
Orton Cumb. 61 H6
Orton Northants. 32 B1
Orton Longueville 42 E6
Orton Waterville 42 E6
Orton-on-the-Hill 41 F5
Orwell 33 G4
Osbaldeston 56 B6
Osbaldwick 58 C4
Osbaston Leics. 41 G5
Osbaston
  Tel. & W. 38 E4
Osborne 11 G5
Osbournby 42 D2
Oscroft 48 E6
Ose 93 J7
Osgathorpe 41 G4
Osgodby Lincs. 52 D3
Osgodby N.Yorks. 58 C6
Osgodby N.Yorks. 59 G1
Oskaig 86 B1
Osmaston Derby 41 F2
Osmaston Derbys. 40 D1
Osmington 9 G6
Osmington Mills 9 G6
Osmotherley 63 F7
Osnaburgh or
  Dairsie 83 F6
Osney 21 J1
Ospringe 15 F2
Ossett 57 H7
Ossington 51 K6
Ostend 25 F2
Osterley 22 E4
Oswaldkirk 58 C2
Oswaldtwistle 56 C7
Oswestry 38 B3
Otford 23 J6
Otham 14 C2
Othery 8 C1
Otley Suff. 35 G3
Otley W.Yorks. 57 H5
Otter 73 H3
Otter Ferry 73 H2
Otterbourne 11 F2
Otterburn
  N.Yorks. 56 D4
Otterburn
  Northumb. 70 D4
Otterburn Camp 70 D4
Otterden Place 14 E2
Otterham 4 B1
Otterhampton 19 F7
Ottershaw 22 D5
Otterswick 108 E4
Otterton 7 J7

Ottery St. Mary 7 J6
Ottinge 15 G3
Ottringham 59 J7
Oughterby 60 D1
Oughtershaw 56 D1
Oughtibridge 51 F3
Oulston 58 B2
Oulton Cumb. 60 D1
Oulton Norf. 45 F3
Oulton Staffs. 40 B2
Oulton Suff. 45 K6
Oulton W.Yorks. 57 J7
Oulton Broad 45 K6
Oulton Street 45 F3
Oundle 42 D7
Ousby 61 H3
Ousdale 105 F6
Ousden 34 B3
Ousefleet 58 E7
Ouston Dur. 62 D1
Ouston Northumb. 71 F6
Out Newton 59 K7
Out Rawcliffe 55 H5
Outertown 107 B6
Outgate 60 E7
Outhgill 61 J6
Outlands 39 G3
Outlane 50 C1
Outwell 43 J5
Outwood Surr. 23 G7
Outwood W.Yorks. 57 J7
Ovenden 57 F7
Over Cambs. 33 G2
Over Ches. 49 F6
Over S.Glos. 19 J3
Over Compton 8 E3
Over End 50 E5
Over Haddon 50 E6
Over Kellet 55 J2
Over Kiddington 31 F6
Over Norton 30 E6
Over Peover 49 G5
Over Rankeilour 82 E6
Over Silton 63 F7
Over Stowey 7 K2
Over Stratton 8 D3
Over Tabley 49 G4
Over Wallop 10 D1
Over Whitacre 40 E6
Over (Upper)
  Winchendon 31 J7
Over Worton 31 F6
Overbister 106 F3
Overbrae 99 G5
Overbury 29 J5
Overcombe 9 F6
Overleigh 8 D1
Overpool 48 C5
Overscaig Hotel 103 G6
Overseal 40 E4
Oversland 15 F2
Oversley Green 30 B3
Overstone 32 B2
Overstrand 45 G1
Overton Aber. 91 F3
Overton Aberdeen 91 G3
Overton Hants. 21 J7
Overton Lancs. 55 H4
Overton N.Yorks. 58 B4
Overton Shrop. 28 E1
Overton Swan. 17 H7
Overton Wrex. 38 C1
Overtown 75 G5
Overy Staithe 44 C1
Oving Bucks. 31 J6
Oving W.Suss. 12 C6
Ovingdean 13 G6
Ovingham 71 F7
Ovington Dur. 62 C5
Ovington Essex 34 B4
Ovington Hants. 11 G1
Ovington Norf. 44 D5
Ovington
  Northumb. 71 F7
Ower 10 E3
Owermoigne 9 G6
Owlswick 22 A1
Owmby 52 D2
Owmby-by-Spital 52 D4
Owslebury 11 G2
Owston 42 A5
Owston Ferry 52 B2
Owstwick 59 J6
Owthorpe 41 J2
Oxborough 44 B5
Oxcliffe Hill 55 H3
Oxcombe 53 G5
Oxen End 33 K6
Oxen Park 55 G1
Oxenhall 29 G6
Oxenholme 61 G7
Oxenhope 57 F6
Oxenton 29 J5
Oxenwood 21 G6
Oxford 21 J1
Oxhill 30 E4
Oxley 40 B5
Oxley Green 34 D7
Oxley's Green 13 K4
Oxnam 70 B2
Oxnead 45 G3
Oxnop Ghyll 62 A7
Oxshott 22 E5
Oxspring 50 E2
Oxted 23 G6
Oxton Mersey. 48 C4
Oxton Notts. 51 J7
Oxton Sc.Bord. 76 C5
Oxwich 17 H7
Oxwich Green 17 H7
Oxwick 44 D3
Oykel Bridge 95 K1
Oyne 90 E2
Ozleworth 20 A2

P

Pabail Iarach 101 H4
Pabail Uarach 101 H4
Packington 41 F4
Padanaram 83 F2
Padbury 31 J5
Paddington 23 F3
Paddlesworth 15 G3
Paddock Wood 23 K7
Paddockhaugh 97 K6
Paddockhole 69 H5
Paddolgreen 38 E2
Padeswood 48 B6
Padiham 56 C6
Padside 57 G4
Padstow 3 G1
Padworth 21 K5
Pagham 12 B7
Paglesham
  Churchend 25 F2
Paglesham
  Eastend 25 F2
Paibeil 92 C5

Paible 93 F2
Paignton 5 J4
Pailton 41 G7
Painscastle 28 A4
Painshawfield 71 F7
Painswick 20 B1
Paisley 74 C4
Pakefield 45 K6
Pakenham 34 D2
Pale 37 J2
Palestine 21 F7
Paley Street 22 B4
Palgowan 67 H5
Palgrave 35 F1
Pallinsburn House 77 G7
Palmerscross 97 K5
Palmerstown 18 E5
Palnackie 65 J5
Palnure 64 E4
Palterton 51 G6
Pamber End 21 K6
Pamber Green 21 K6
Pamber Heath 21 K5
Pamington 29 J5
Pamphill 9 J4
Pampisford 33 H4
Pan 107 C8
Panborough 19 H7
Panbride 83 G4
Pancrasweek 6 A5
Pandy Gwyn. 37 F5
Pandy Mon. 28 C6
Pandy Powys 37 J5
Pandy Wrex. 38 A2
Pandy Tudur 47 G6
Panfield 34 B6
Pangbourne 21 K4
Pannal 57 J4
Panpunton 28 B1
Pant Shrop. 38 B3
Pant Wrex. 38 C1
Pant Glas 36 D1
Pant Gwyn 37 H3
Pant Mawr 37 H7
Pantasaph 47 K5
Pantglas 37 F6
Pantgwyn 17 F1
Pant-lasau 17 K5
Panton 52 E5
Pant-pastynog 47 J6
Pantperthog 37 G5
Pant-y-dwr 27 J1
Pant-y-ffridd 38 A5
Pantyffynnon 17 K4
Panxworth 45 H4
Papcastle 60 C3
Papple 76 D3
Papplewick 51 H7
Papworth Everard 33 F2
Papworth
  St. Agnes 33 F2
Par 4 A5
Parbold 48 D1
Parbrook 8 E1
Parc 37 H2
Parcllyn 26 B3
Parcrhydderch 27 F3
Parc-Seymour 19 H2
Pardshaw 60 B4
Parham 35 H2
Parish Holm 68 C1
Park 98 D5
Park Corner 21 K3
Park End 70 D6
Park Gate 11 G4
Park Lane 38 D2
Park Street 22 E1
Parkend Cumb. 60 D3
Parkend Glos. 19 K1
Parkeston 35 G5
Parkford 83 F2
Parkgate Ches. 48 B5
Parkgate D. & G. 69 F5
Parkgate S.Yorks. 51 G3
Parkgate Surr. 23 F7
Parkham 6 B3
Parkham Ash 6 B3
Parkhill Angus 83 H3
Parkhill P. & K. 82 C3
Parkhouse 19 J1
Parkhurst 11 F5
Parkmill 17 J7
Parkmore 98 B6
Parkneuk 91 F7
Parkstone 10 B5
Parley Cross 10 B5
Parracombe 6 E1
Parrog 16 D2
Parson Drove 43 G5
Parsonby 60 C3
Partick 74 D4
Partington 49 G3
Partney 53 H6
Parton Cumb. 60 A4
Parton D. & G. 65 G3
Partridge Green 12 E5
Parwich 50 D7
Passenham 31 J5
Passfield 12 B3
Passingford
  Bridge 23 H2
Paston 45 H2
Patcham 13 G6
Patching 12 D6
Patchole 6 E1
Patchway 19 J3
Pateley Bridge 57 G3
Path of Condie 82 B6
Pathe 8 C1
Pathfinder Village 7 G6
Pathhead Aber. 83 J1
Pathhead E.Ayr. 68 B2
Pathhead Fife 76 A1
Pathhead Midloth. 76 B4
Patmore Heath 33 H6
Patna 67 J2
Patney 20 D6
Patrick 54 B5
Patrick Brompton 62 D7
Patrington 59 K7
Patrishow 28 B6
Patrixbourne 15 G2
Patterdale 60 E5
Pattingham 40 A6
Pattishall 31 H3
Pattiswick 34 C6
Paul 2 B6
Paulerspury 31 J4
Paull 59 H7
Paulton 19 K6
Pauperhaugh 71 F4
Pavenham 32 C3
Pawlett 19 G7
Pawston 77 G7
Paxford 30 C5
Paxhill Park 13 G4
Paxton 77 H5
Payhembury 7 J5

Paynes Hall 33 G7
Paythorne 56 D4
Peacehaven 13 H6
Peacemarsh 9 H2
Peachley 29 H3
Peak Dale 50 C5
Peak Forest 50 D5
Peakirk 42 E5
Pean Hill 25 H5
Pearsie 82 E2
Pease Pottage 13 F3
Peasedown
  St. John 20 A6
Peasemore 21 H4
Peasenhall 35 H2
Peaslake 22 D7
Peasmarsh 14 D5
Peaston 76 C4
Peastonbank 76 C4
Peat Inn 83 F7
Peathill 99 H4
Peatling Magna 41 H6
Peatling Parva 41 H7
Peaton 38 E7
Pebble Coombe 23 F6
Pebmarsh 34 C5
Pebworth 30 C4
Pecket Well 56 E7
Peckforton 48 E7
Peckham 23 G4
Peckleton 41 G5
Pedmore 40 B7
Pedwell 8 D1
Peebles 76 A6
Peel 54 B5
Pegswood 71 H5
Peighinn nan
  Aoireann 84 C1
Peinchorran 86 B1
Peinlich 93 K6
Pelaw 71 H7
Pelcomb Bridge 16 C4
Pelcomb Cross 16 C4
Peldon 34 D7
Pelsall 40 C5
Pelton 62 D1
Pelutho 60 C2
Pelynt 4 C5
Pembrey 17 H5
Pembridge 28 C3
Pembroke (Penfro) 16 C5
Pembroke Dock
  (Doc Penfro) 16 C5
Pembury 23 K7
Pen-bont
  Rhydybeddau 37 F7
Penboyr 17 G2
Penbryn 26 B3
Pencader 17 H2
Pencaenewydd 36 D1
Pencaitland 76 C4
Pencarreg 17 J1
Pencelli 27 K6
Pen-clawdd 17 J6
Pencoed 18 C3
Pencombe 28 E3
Pencoyd 28 E6
Pencraig Here. 28 E6
Pencraig Powys 37 K3
Pendeen 2 A5
Penderyn 18 C1
Pendine 17 F5
Pendlebury 49 G2
Pendleton 56 C6
Pendock 29 G5
Pendoggett 4 A3
Pendomer 8 E3
Pendoylan 18 D4
Penegoes 37 G5
Pen-ffordd 16 D3
Penfro (Pembroke) 16 C5
Pengam 18 E2
Penge 23 G4
Pengenffordd 28 A5
Pengorffwysfa 46 C3
Pengover Green 4 C4
Pen-groes-oped 19 G1
Pengwern 47 J5
Penhale 2 D7
Penhallow 2 E3
Penhalvean 2 E5
Penhow 19 H2
Penhurst 13 K5
Peniarth 37 F5
Penicuik 76 A4
Penifiler 93 K7
Peniner 66 B1
Penisa'r Waun 46 D6
Penisarcwn 37 K4
Penistone 50 E2
Penjerrick 2 E5
Penketh 48 E4
Penkill 67 G4
Penkridge 40 B4
Penley 38 D2
Penllech 36 B2
Penllergaer 17 K6
Pen-llyn I.o.A. 46 B4
Penllyn
  V. of Glam. 18 C4
Penmachno 47 J7
Penmaen 17 J7
Penmaenmawr 47 F5
Penmaenpool 37 F4
Penmark 18 D5
Penmon 46 E4
Penmorfa 36 E1
Penmynydd 46 D5
Penn Bucks. 22 C2
Penn W.Mid. 40 A6
Penn Street 22 C2
Pennal 37 F5
Pennan 99 G4
Pennance 2 E4
Pennant Cere. 26 E2
Pennant Powys 37 H6
Pennant Melangell 37 K3
Pennard 17 J7
Pennerley 38 C6
Penninghame 64 D4
Pennington 55 F2
Pennsylvania 20 A4
Penny Bridge 55 G1
Pennycross 79 H5
Pennyfuir 79 K4
Pennyghael 79 H5
Pennyglen 67 G2
Pennygown 79 H3
Pennymoor 7 G4
Penparc Cere. 17 F1
Penparc Pembs. 16 B2
Penparcau 36 E7
Penperlleni 19 G1
Penpillick 4 A5
Penpol 3 F5
Penpoll 4 B5

Penpont D. & G. 68 D4
Penpont Powys 27 J6
Penprysg 18 C3
Penrherber 17 F2
Penrhiwceiber 18 D2
Penrhiwgoch 17 J4
Penrhiw-llan 17 G1
Penrhiw-pal 17 G1
Penrhos Gwyn. 36 C2
Penrhos I.o.A. 46 A4
Penrhos Mon. 28 D7
Penrhos Powys 27 H7
Penrhos-garnedd 46 D5
Penrhyn Bay
  (Bae Penrhyn) 47 G4
Penrhyn-coch 37 F7
Penrhyndeudraeth 37 F2
Penrhyn-side 47 G4
Penrhys 18 D2
Penrice 17 H7
Penrith 61 G3
Penrose 3 F1
Penruddock 61 F4
Penryn 2 E5
Pensarn Carmar. 17 H4
Pensarn Conwy 47 H5
Pen-sarn Gwyn. 36 E3
Pen-sarn Gwyn. 36 D1
Pensax 29 G2
Pensby 48 B4
Penselwood 9 G1
Pensford 19 K5
Pensham 29 J4
Penshaw 62 E1
Penshurst 23 J7
Pensilva 4 C4
Pensnett 40 B7
Pentewan 4 A6
Pentir 46 D6
Pentire 2 E2
Pentireglaze 3 G1
Pentlepoir 16 E5
Pentlow 34 C4
Pentney 44 B4
Penton Mewsey 21 G7
Pentraeth 46 D5
Pentre Powys 37 K3
Pentre Powys 37 K7
Pentre Powys 28 B2
Pentre Powys 38 B6
Pentre R.C.T. 18 C2
Pentre Shrop. 38 C4
Pentre Wrex. 38 B1
Pentre Berw 46 C5
Pentre Galar 16 E2
Pentre Gwenlais 17 K4
Pentre Gwynfryn 36 E3
Pentre Halkyn 48 B5
Pentre Isaf 47 G6
Pentre Llanrhaeadr 47 J6
Pentre Maelor 38 C1
Pentre Saron 47 J6
Pentrebach M.Tyd. 18 D1
Pentre-bach
  Powys 27 J5
Pentrebach Swan. 17 K5
Pentre-bont 47 G7
Pentrebwlch 38 A1
Pentrecagal 17 G1
Pentre-celyn
  Denb. 47 K7
Pentre-celyn
  Powys 37 H5
Pentre-chwyth 17 K6
Pentreclwydau 18 B1
Pentre-cwrt 17 G2
Pentre-Dolau-
  Honddu 27 J4
Pentredwr Denb. 38 A1
Pentre-dwr Swan. 17 K6
Pentrefelin Carmar. 17 J3
Pentrefelin Cere. 17 K1
Pentrefelin Conwy 47 G5
Pentrefelin Gwyn. 36 E2
Pentrefelin Powys 38 A3
Pentrefoelas 47 G7
Pentregat 26 C3
Pentreheyling 38 B6
Pentre-Llwyn-
  llwyd 27 J3
Pentre-llyn-cymmer 47 H7
Pentre-piod 37 H2
Pentre-Poeth 19 F3
Pentre'r beirdd 38 A4
Pentre'r-felin 27 J5
Pentre-tafarn-y-
  fedw 47 G6
Pentre-ty-gwyn 27 H5
Pentrich 51 F7
Pentridge 10 B3
Pentwyn Cardiff 19 F3
Pen-twyn Mon. 19 J1
Pentyrch 18 E3
Penuwch 26 E2
Penwithick 4 A5
Penwortham 55 J7
Penwyllt 27 H7
Pen-y-bont
  Carmar. 27 G5
Pen-y-bont Powys 37 K4
Pen-y-bont Powys 38 A2
Penybont Powys 28 A2
Pen-y-bont ar Ogwr
  (Bridgend) 18 C4
Penybontfawr 37 K3
Pen-y-bryn Caerp. 18 E2
Pen-y-bryn Gwyn. 37 F4
Pen-y-cae Powys 27 H7
Pen-y-cae-mawr 19 H2
Penycae Wrex. 38 B1
Pen-y-cefn 47 K5
Pen-y-clawdd 19 H1
Pen-y-coedcae 18 D3
Pencwm 18 B3
Pen-y-fai 18 B3
Penyffordd 48 C6
Pen-y-garn 17 J2
Penygarnedd 38 A3
Pen-y-garreg 27 K4
Penygraig 18 C2
Penygroes Carmar. 17 J4
Penygroes Gwyn. 46 C7
Pen-y-Park 28 C4
Pen-y-sarn 46 C3
Pen-y-stryt 47 K7
Penywaun 18 C1
Penzance 2 B5
Penzance Heliport 2 B5
Peopleton 29 J3
Peover Heath 49 G5
Peper Harow 22 C7
Percie 90 D5
Percyhorner 99 H4
Perham Down 21 F7
Perivale 22 E3

Perkhill 90 D4
Perkins Beach 38 C5
Perlethorpe 51 J5
Perranarworthal 2 E5
Perranporth 2 E3
Perranuthnoe 2 C6
Perranzabuloe 2 E3
Perry Barr 40 C6
Perry Green 33 H7
Perry Street 24 C4
Pershall 40 A3
Pershore 29 J4
Persie House 82 C2
Pert 83 H1
Pertenhall 32 D2
Perth 82 C5
Perthy 38 C2
Perton 40 A6
Peter Tavy 5 F3
Peterborough 42 E6
Peterburn 94 D3
Peterchurch 28 C5
Peterculter 91 G4
Peterhead 99 K6
Peterlee 63 F2
Peter's Green 32 E7
Peters Marland 6 C4
Petersfield 11 J2
Peterstone
  Wentlooge 19 F3
Peterston-super-Ely 18 D4
Peterstow 28 E6
Petham 15 G2
Petrockstow 6 D5
Pett 14 D6
Pettaugh 35 F3
Pettinain 75 H6
Pettistree 35 G3
Petton Devon 7 J3
Petton Shrop. 38 D3
Petty 91 F1
Pettycur 76 A2
Pettymuick 91 H2
Petworth 12 C4
Pevensey 13 K6
Pevensey Bay 13 K6
Pewsey 20 E5
Phesdo 90 E7
Philham 6 A3
Philiphaugh 69 K1
Phillack 2 C5
Philleigh 3 F5
Philpstoun 75 J3
Phoenix Green 22 A6
Phones 88 E5
Phorp 97 H3
Pibsbury 8 D2
Pica 60 B4
Piccadilly Corner 45 G7
Piccotts End 22 D1
Pickerells 23 J1
Pickering 58 C1
Picket Piece 21 G7
Picket Post 10 C4
Pickford Green 40 E7
Pickhill 57 J1
Picklescott 38 D6
Pickletillem 83 F5
Pickmere 49 F5
Pickstock 39 G3
Pickston 82 A5
Pickwell Devon 6 C1
Pickwell Leics. 42 A4
Pickworth Lincs. 42 D2
Pickworth Rut. 42 C4
Picton Ches. 48 D5
Picton N.Yorks. 63 F6
Piddinghoe 13 H6
Piddington
  Northants. 32 B3
Piddington Oxon. 31 H7
Piddlehinton 9 G5
Piddletrenthide 9 G5
Pidley 33 G1
Piercebridge 62 D5
Pierowall 106 D3
Pigdon 71 G5
Pikehall 50 D7
Pilgrims Hatch 23 J2
Pilham 52 B3
Pill 19 J4
Pillaton 4 D4
Pillerton Hersey 30 D4
Pillerton Priors 30 D4
Pilleth 28 B2
Pilley Glos. 29 J7
Pilley Hants. 10 E5
Pilley S.Yorks. 51 F2
Pilling 55 H5
Pilling Lane 55 G5
Pillowell 19 K1
Pilning 19 J3
Pilsbury 50 D6
Pilsdon 8 D5
Pilsgate 42 D5
Pilsley Derbys. 51 G6
Pilsley Derbys. 50 E5
Piltdown 13 H4
Pilton Devon 6 D2
Pilton Northants. 42 D7
Pilton Rut. 42 C5
Pilton Som. 19 J7
Pimperne 9 J4
Pinchbeck 43 F3
Pinchbeck Bars 43 F3
Pinchbeck West 43 F3
Pinchinthorpe 63 G5
Pinfold 48 C1
Pinhay 8 C5
Pinhoe 7 H6
Pinkneys Green 22 B3
Pinley Green 30 D2
Pinminnoch 67 F4
Pinmore 67 G4
Pinn 7 K7
Pinner 22 E3
Pinner Green 22 E3
Pinvin 29 J4
Pinwherry 67 F5
Pinxton 51 G7
Pipe & Lyde 28 E4
Pipe Gate 39 G1
Pipe Ridware 40 C4
Piperhall 73 J5
Piperhill 97 F6
Pipers Pool 4 C2
Pipewell 42 B7
Pippacott 6 D2
Pipton 28 A5
Pirbright 22 C6
Pirnmill 73 G6
Pirton Herts. 32 E5
Pirton Worcs. 29 H4
Pisgah 37 F7
Pishill 22 A3
Pistyll 36 C1

Name	Pg	Grid
Pitagowan	81	K1
Pitblae	99	H4
Pitcairngreen	82	B5
Pitcairns	82	B6
Pitcaple	91	F2
Pitch Green	22	A1
Pitch Place	22	C6
Pitchcombe	20	B1
Pitchcott	31	J7
Pitchford	38	E5
Pitcombe	9	F1
Pitcot	18	B4
Pitcox	76	E3
Pitcur	82	D4
Pitfichie	90	E3
Pitgrudy	96	E2
Pitinnan	91	F1
Pitkennedy	83	G2
Pitkevy	82	D7
Pitlessie	82	E7
Pitlochry	82	A2
Pitmedden	91	G2
Pitmuies	83	G3
Pitmunie	90	E3
Pitnacree	82	A2
Pitney	8	D2
Pitroddie	82	D5
Pitscottie	83	F6
Pitsea	24	D3
Pitsford	31	J2
Pitsford Hill	7	J2
Pitstone	32	C7
Pitstone Green	32	C7
Pitt *Devon*	7	J4
Pitt *Hants.*	11	F2
Pittendreich	97	J5
Pittentrail	96	E1
Pittenweem	83	G7
Pittington	62	E2
Pittodrie House	90	E2
Pitton	10	D1
Pity Me	62	D2
Pityme	3	G1
Pixey Green	35	G1
Place Newton	58	E2
Plaidy	99	F5
Plains	75	F4
Plaish	38	E6
Plaistow	12	D3
Plaitford	10	D3
Plas	17	H3
Plas Gogerddan	37	F7
Plas Gwynant	46	E2
Plas Isaf	37	K1
Plas Llwyd	47	H5
Plas Llwyngwern	37	G5
Plas Llysyn	37	J6
Plas Nantyr	38	A2
Plasisaf	47	H6
Plas-rhiw-Saeson	37	J5
Plastow Green	21	J5
Plas-yn-Cefn	47	J5
Platt	23	K6
Platt Bridge	49	F2
Platt Lane	38	E2
Plawsworth	62	D2
Plaxtol	23	K6
Play Hatch	22	A4
Playden	14	E5
Playford	35	G4
Playing Place	3	F4
Plealey	38	D5
Plean	75	G4
Pleasance	82	D6
Pleasington	56	B7
Pleasley	51	H6
Plenmeller	70	C7
Pleshey	33	K7
Plockton	86	E1
Ploughfield	28	C4
Plowden	38	C7
Ploxgreen	38	C5
Pluckley	14	E3
Pluckley Thorne	14	E3
Plumbland	60	C3
Plumley	49	G5
Plumpton *Cumb.*	61	F3
Plumpton *E.Suss.*	13	G5
Plumpton End	31	J4
Plumpton Green	13	G5
Plumpton Head	61	G3
Plumstead *Gt.Lon.*	23	H4
Plumstead *Norf.*	45	F2
Plumtree	41	J2
Plungar	42	A2
Plush	9	G4
Plwmp	26	C3
Plym Bridge	5	F5
Plymouth	5	F5
Plymouth City Airport	5	F4
Plympton	5	F5
Plymstock	5	F5
Plymtree	7	J5
Pockley	58	C1
Pocklington	58	E5
Pocombe Bridge	7	G6
Pode Hole	43	F3
Podimore	8	E2
Podington	32	C2
Podmore	39	G2
Poffley End	30	E7
Pointon	42	E2
Pokesdown	10	C5
Polanach	80	A2
Polapit Tamar	6	B7
Polbae	64	C3
Polbain	102	B7
Polbathic	4	D5
Polbeth	75	J4
Polchar	89	F4
Poldean	69	G4
Pole Moor	50	C1
Polebrook	42	D7
Polegate	13	J6
Poles	96	E2
Polesworth	40	E5
Polglass	95	G1
Polgooth	3	G3
Polgown	68	C3
Poling	12	D6
Poling Corner	12	D6
Polkerris	4	A5
Poll a' Charra	84	C3
Polla	103	F3
Polldubh	80	C1
Pollie	104	C1
Pollington	51	J1
Polloch	79	J1
Pollokshaws	74	D4
Polmassick	3	G4
Polmont	75	H3
Polnoon	74	D5
Polperro	4	C5

Name	Pg	Grid
Polruan	4	B5
Polsham	19	J7
Polstead	34	D5
Poltalloch	73	G1
Poltimore	7	H6
Polton	76	A4
Polwarth	77	F5
Polyphant	4	C2
Polzeath	3	G1
Pond Street	33	H5
Ponders End	23	G2
Pondersbridge	43	F6
Ponsanooth	2	E5
Ponsonby	60	B6
Ponsworthy	5	H3
Pont Aber	27	G6
Pont Aberglaslyn	36	E1
Pont Ceri	17	F1
Pont Crugnant	37	H6
Pont Cyfyng	47	F7
Pont Dolgarrog	47	F6
Pont Nedd Fechan	18	C1
Pont Pen-y-benglog	46	E6
Pont Rhyd-sarn	37	H3
Pont Rhyd-y-cyff	18	B3
Pont Walby	18	B1
Pont yr Alwen	47	H7
Pontamman	17	K4
Pontantwn	17	H4
Pontardawe	18	A1
Pontarddulais	17	J5
Pontarfynach (Devil's Bridge)	27	G1
Pontargothi	17	J3
Pontarsais	17	H3
Pontblyddyn	48	B6
Pontbren Llwyd	18	C1
Pontefract	57	K7
Ponteland	71	G6
Ponterwyd	37	G7
Pontesbury	38	D5
Pontesford	38	D5
Pontfadog	38	B2
Pontfaen *Pembs.*	16	D2
Pont-faen *Powys*	27	J5
Pont-Henri	17	H5
Ponthir	19	G2
Ponthirwaun	17	F1
Pontllanfraith	18	E2
Pontlliw	17	K5
Pontllyfni	46	C7
Pontlottyn	18	E1
Pontnewydd	19	F2
Pontnewynydd	19	F1
Pontrhydfendigaid	27	G2
Pont-rhyd-y-groes	27	G2
Pontrhydyrun	19	F2
Pontrilas	28	C6
Pont-rug	46	D6
Ponts Green	13	K5
Pontshaen	17	H1
Pontshill	29	F6
Pontsticill	27	K7
Pontwelly	17	H2
Pontyates	17	H5
Pontyberem	17	J4
Pontybodkin	48	B7
Pontyclun	18	D3
Pontycymer	18	C2
Pontygwaith	18	D2
Pontymister	19	F3
Pont-y-pant	47	F7
Pontypool	19	F1
Pontypridd	18	D3
Pontywaun	19	F2
Pooksgreen	10	E3
Pool *Cornw.*	2	D4
Pool *W.Yorks.*	57	H5
Pool Bank	55	H1
Pool of Muckhart	82	B7
Pool Quay	38	B4
Pool Street	34	B5
Poole	10	B5
Poole Keynes	20	C2
Poolewe	94	E3
Pooley Bridge	61	F4
Poolhill	29	G6
Pope Hill	16	C4
Popeswood	22	B5
Popham	21	J7
Poplar	23	G3
Porchfield	11	F5
Porin	95	K6
Poringland	45	G5
Porkellis	2	D5
Porlock	7	G1
Porlock Weir	7	G1
Port Allen	82	D5
Port Appin	80	A3
Port Askaig	72	C4
Port Bannatyne	73	J4
Port Carlisle	69	H7
Port Charlotte	72	A5
Port Clarence	63	G4
Port Driseach	73	H3
Port e Vullen	54	D4
Port Ellen	72	B6
Port Elphinstone	91	F3
Port Erin	54	B7
Port Erroll	91	J1
Port Eynon	17	H7
Port Gaverne	4	A2
Port Glasgow	74	B3
Port Henderson	94	D4
Port Isaac	4	A2
Port Logan	64	A6
Port Mòr	85	K7
Port Mulgrave	63	J5
Port na Craig	82	A2
Port nan Giùran (Portnaguran)	101	H4
Port nan Long	92	D4
Port Nis	101	H1
Port o' Warren	65	J5
Port of Menteith	81	G7
Port Penrhyn	46	D5
Port Quin	3	G1
Port Ramsay	79	K3
Port St. Mary	54	B7
Port Solent	11	H4
Port Sunlight	48	C4
Port Talbot	18	A3
Port Wemyss	72	A5
Port William	64	D6
Portachoillan	73	F5
Portavadie	73	H4
Portbury	19	J4
Portchester	11	H4
Portencross	73	K6
Portesham	9	F6
Portfield	79	J5
Portfield Gate	16	C4
Portgate	6	C7
Portgordon	98	B4
Portgower	105	F7

Name	Pg	Grid
Porth *Cornw.*	3	F2
Porth *R.C.T.*	18	D2
Porth Colmon	36	A2
Porth Mellin	2	D7
Porth Navas	2	E6
Porthaethwy (Menai Bridge)	46	D5
Porthallow *Cornw.*	2	E6
Porthallow *Cornw.*	4	C5
Porthcawl	18	B4
Porthcothan	3	F1
Porthcurno	2	A6
Porthgain	16	B2
Porthkerry	18	D5
Porthleven	2	D6
Porthmadog	36	E2
Porthmeor	2	B5
Portholland	3	G4
Porthoustock	3	F6
Porthpean	4	A5
Porthtowan	2	D4
Porthyrhyd *Carmar.*	27	G5
Porthyrhyd *Carmar.*	17	J4
Porth-y-waen	38	B3
Portincaple	74	A1
Portington	58	D6
Portinnisherrich	80	A6
Portinscale	60	D4
Portishead	19	H4
Portknockie	98	C4
Portlethen	91	H5
Portlethen Village	91	H5
Portloe	3	G5
Portmahomack	97	G3
Portmeirion	36	E2
Portmellon	3	G4
Portmore	10	E5
Port-na-Con	103	G2
Portnacroish	80	A3
Portnaguran (Port nan Giùran)	101	H4
Portnahaven	72	A2
Portnalong	85	J1
Portnaluchaig	86	C6
Portobello	76	B3
Porton	10	C1
Portpatrick	64	A5
Portreath	2	D4
Portree	93	K7
Portscatho	3	F5
Portsea	11	H4
Portskerra	104	D2
Portskewett	19	J3
Portslade	13	F6
Portslade-by-Sea	13	F6
Portslogan	64	A5
Portsmouth	11	H5
Portsonachan	80	B5
Portsoy	98	D4
Portswood	11	F3
Portuairk	79	F1
Portway *Here.*	28	C4
Portway *Worcs.*	30	B1
Portwrinkle	4	D5
Portyerrock	64	E7
Poslingford	34	B4
Postbridge	5	G3
Postcombe	22	A2
Postling	15	G4
Postwick	45	G5
Potarch	90	E5
Potsgrove	32	C6
Pott Row	44	B3
Pott Shrigley	49	J5
Potten End	22	D1
Potter Heigham	45	J3
Potter Street	23	H1
Potterhanworth	52	D6
Potterhanworth Booths	52	D6
Potterne	20	C6
Potterne Wick	20	C6
Potters Bar	23	F1
Potter's Cross	40	A7
Potters Crouch	22	E1
Potterspury	31	J4
Potterton	91	H3
Potto	63	F6
Potton	33	F4
Poughill *Cornw.*	6	A5
Poughill *Devon*	7	G5
Poulner	10	C4
Poulshot	20	C6
Poulton	20	E1
Poulton-le-Fylde	55	G6
Pound Bank	29	G1
Pound Green	13	J4
Pound Hill	13	F3
Poundffald	17	J6
Poundgate	13	H4
Poundland	67	F5
Poundon	31	H6
Poundsbridge	23	J7
Poundstock	4	C1
Povey Cross	23	F7
Pow Green	29	G4
Powburn	71	F2
Powderham	7	H7
Powerstock	8	E5
Powfoot	69	G7
Powick	29	H3
Powler's Piece	6	B4
Powmill	75	J1
Poxwell	9	G6
Poyle	22	D4
Poynings	13	F5
Poyntington	9	F2
Poynton *Ches.*	49	J4
Poynton *Tel. & W.*	38	E4
Poynton Green	38	E4
Poyntzfield	96	E5
Poys Street	35	H1
Poyston Cross	16	C4
Poystreet Green	34	D3
Praa Sands	2	C6
Pratis	82	E7
Pratt's Bottom	23	H5
Praze-an-Beeble	2	D5
Predannack Wollas	2	D7
Prees	38	E2
Prees Green	38	E2
Prees Higher Heath	38	E2
Preesall	55	G5
Preesgweene	38	B2
Prenbrigog	48	B6
Prendergast	16	C4
Prendwick	71	F2
Pren-gwyn	17	H1
Prenteg	36	E1
Prenton	48	C4
Prescot	48	D3
Prescott	38	D3
Presley	97	H6
Pressen	77	G7
Prestatyn	47	J4
Prestbury *Ches.*	49	H5

Name	Pg	Grid
Prestbury *Glos.*	29	J6
Presteigne	28	C2
Presthope	38	E6
Prestleigh	19	K7
Prestolee	49	G2
Preston *B. & H.*	13	G6
Preston *Devon*	5	J3
Preston *Dorset*	9	G6
Preston *E.Loth.*	76	D3
Preston *E.Riding*	59	H6
Preston *Glos.*	29	F5
Preston *Glos.*	20	D1
Preston *Herts.*	32	E6
Preston *Kent*	25	G5
Preston *Kent*	25	J5
Preston *Lancs.*	55	J7
Preston *Northumb.*	71	G1
Preston *Sc.Bord.*	77	F5
Preston *T. & W.*	71	J7
Preston *Wilts.*	20	D4
Preston Bagot	30	C2
Preston Bissett	31	H6
Preston Brockhurst	38	E3
Preston Brook	48	E4
Preston Candover	21	K7
Preston Capes	31	G3
Preston Deanery	31	J3
Preston Gubbals	38	D4
Preston on Stour	30	D3
Preston on the Hill	48	E4
Preston on Wye	28	C4
Preston Plucknett	8	E3
Preston upon the Weald Moors	39	F4
Preston Wynne	28	E4
Prestonpans	76	B3
Preston-under-Scar	62	B7
Prestwich	49	H2
Prestwick *Northumb.*	71	G6
Prestwick *S.Ayr.*	67	H1
Prestwick International Airport	67	H1
Prestwold	41	H3
Prestwood	22	B1
Price Town	18	C2
Prickwillow	43	J7
Priddy	19	J6
Priest Hill	56	B6
Priest Hutton	55	J2
Priestland	74	D7
Priestweston	38	B6
Primethorpe	41	H6
Primrose Green	44	E4
Princes End	40	B6
Princes Gate	16	E4
Princes Risborough	22	B1
Princethorpe	31	F1
Princetown *Caerp.*	28	A7
Princetown *Devon*	5	F3
Prior Muir	83	G6
Prior's Frome	28	E5
Priors Hardwick	31	F3
Priors Marston	31	F3
Priory Wood	28	B4
Priston	19	K5
Prittlewell	24	E3
Privett	11	H2
Prixford	6	D2
Proaig	72	C5
Probus	3	F4
Protstonhill	99	G4
Prudhoe	71	G7
Pubil	81	F3
Publow	19	K5
Puckeridge	33	G6
Puckington	8	C3
Pucklechurch	19	K4
Puddinglake	49	G6
Puddington *Ches.*	48	C5
Puddington *Devon*	7	G4
Puddlebrook	29	F7
Puddledock	44	E6
Puddletown	9	G5
Pudleston	28	E3
Pudsey	57	H6
Pulborough	12	D5
Puldagon	105	J4
Puleston	39	G3
Pulford	48	C7
Pulham	9	G4
Pulham Market	45	F7
Pulham St. Mary	45	G7
Pulloxhill	32	D5
Pulrossie	96	E3
Pulverbatch	38	D5
Pumpherston	75	J4
Pumsaint	17	K1
Puncheston	16	D3
Puncknowle	8	E6
Punnett's Town	13	K4
Purbrook	11	H4
Purfleet	23	J4
Puriton	19	G7
Purleigh	24	E1
Purley	23	G5
Purley on Thames	21	K4
Purlogue	28	B1
Purls Bridge	43	H7
Purslow	38	C7
Purston Jaglin	51	G1
Purton *Glos.*	19	K1
Purton *Wilts.*	20	D3
Purton Stoke	20	D2
Purves Hall	77	F6
Pury End	31	J4
Pusey	21	G2
Putley	29	F5
Putloe	20	A1
Putney	23	F4
Putsborough	6	C1
Puttenham *Herts.*	32	B7
Puttenham *Surr.*	22	C7
Puttock End	34	C4
Putts Corner	7	K6
Puxton	19	H5
Pwll	17	H5
Pwll Trap	17	F4
Pwllcrochan	16	C5
Pwlldefaid	36	A3
Pwllgloyw	27	K5
Pwllheli	36	C2
Pwllmeyric	19	J2
Pwll-y-glaw	18	A2
Pye Corner *Herts.*	33	H7
Pye Corner *Newport*	19	G3
Pye Green	40	B4
Pyecombe	13	F5
Pyle *Bridgend*	18	B3

Name	Pg	Grid
Pyle *I.o.W.*	11	F7
Pylle	9	F1
Pymore	43	H7
Pyrford	22	D6
Pyrton	21	K2
Pytchley	32	B1
Pyworthy	6	B5

Q

Name	Pg	Grid
Quabbs	38	B7
Quadring	43	F2
Quadring Eaudike	43	F2
Quainton	31	J7
Quarley	21	F7
Quarmby	50	D1
Quarndon	41	F1
Quarr Hill	11	G5
Quarrier's Village	74	B4
Quarrington	42	D1
Quarrington Hill	62	E3
Quarry Bank	40	B7
Quarrybank	48	E6
Quarrywood	97	J5
Quarter	75	F5
Quatford	39	G6
Quatt	39	G7
Quebec	62	C2
Quedgeley	29	H7
Queen Adelaide	43	J7
Queen Camel	8	E2
Queen Charlton	19	K5
Queen Street	23	K7
Queenborough	25	F4
Queensbury	57	G6
Queensferry	48	C6
Queenzieburn	74	E3
Quemerford	20	D4
Quendale	109	F9
Quendon	33	J5
Queniborough	41	J4
Quenington	20	E1
Quernmore	55	J3
Queslett	40	C6
Quethiock	4	D4
Quholm	107	B6
Quidenham	44	E7
Quidhampton *Hants.*	21	J6
Quidhampton *Wilts.*	10	C1
Quilquox	91	H1
Quina Brook	38	E2
Quindry	107	D8
Quinhill	73	F5
Quinton *Northants.*	31	J3
Quinton *W.Mid.*	40	B7
Quintrell Downs	3	F2
Quoditch	6	C6
Quoig	81	K5
Quoigs House	81	K7
Quoisley	38	E1
Quoyloo	106	B5
Quoys	108	F1
Quoys of Reiss	105	J3

R

Name	Pg	Grid
Raby	48	C5
Rachan	75	K7
Rachub	46	E6
Rackenford	7	G4
Rackham	12	D5
Rackheath	45	G4
Racks	69	F6
Rackwick *Ork.*	107	B8
Rackwick *Ork.*	106	D4
Radbourne	40	E2
Radcliffe *Gt.Man.*	49	G2
Radcliffe *Northumb.*	71	H3
Radcliffe on Trent	41	J2
Radclive	31	H5
Radcot	20	E2
Radford *Oxon.*	31	F6
Radford *W.Mid.*	30	E1
Radford Semele	30	E2
Radipole	9	F6
Radlett	22	E1
Radley	21	J2
Radstock	19	K6
Radstone	31	G4
Radway	30	E4
Radway Green	49	G7
Radwell *Beds.*	32	D3
Radwell *Herts.*	33	F5
Radwinter	33	K5
Radyr	18	E3
Raechester	70	E5
Raemoir House	90	E5
Raffin	102	C5
Rafford	97	H6
Ragdale	41	J4
Raglan	19	H1
Ragnall	52	B5
Rahoy	79	H2
Rainford	48	D2
Rainham *Gt.Lon.*	23	J3
Rainham *Med.*	24	E5
Rainhill	48	D3
Rainhill Stoops	48	E3
Rainow	49	J5
Rainton	57	J2
Rainworth	51	H7
Raisbeck	61	H6
Raise	61	J2
Rait	82	D5
Raithby *Lincs.*	53	G6
Raithby *Lincs.*	53	G5
Rake	12	B4
Raleigh's Cross	7	J2
Ram	17	J1
Ram Lane	14	E3
Ramasaig	93	G7
Rampisham	8	E4
Rampside	55	F3
Rampton *Cambs.*	33	H2
Rampton *Notts.*	52	B5
Ramsbottom	49	G1
Ramsbury	21	F4
Ramscraigs	105	G6
Ramsdean	11	J2
Ramsdell	21	J6
Ramsden	30	E7
Ramsden Bellhouse	24	D2
Ramsden Heath	24	D2
Ramsey *Cambs.*	43	F7
Ramsey *Essex*	35	G6
Ramsey *I.o.M.*	54	D4
Ramsey Forty Foot	43	G7

Name	Pg	Grid
Ramsey Heights	43	F7
Ramsey Island	25	F1
Ramsey Mereside	43	F7
Ramsey St. Mary's	43	F7
Ramsgate	25	K5
Ramsgate Street	44	E2
Ramsgill	57	G2
Ramsholt	35	H4
Ramshorn	40	C1
Ramsnest Common	12	C3
Ranachan	79	J1
Ranby *Lincs.*	53	F5
Ranby *Notts.*	51	J4
Rand	52	E5
Randwick	20	B1
Rangemore	40	D3
Rangeworthy	19	K3
Rankinston	67	J2
Rank's Green	34	B7
Rannoch School	81	G2
Ranochan	86	E6
Ranskill	51	J4
Ranton	40	A3
Ranworth	45	H4
Rapness	106	E3
Rascarrel	65	J6
Rassau	28	A7
Rastrick	57	G7
Ratby	41	H5
Ratcliffe Culey	41	F6
Ratcliffe on Soar	41	G3
Ratcliffe on the Wreake	41	J4
Ratford Bridge	16	C4
Rathen	99	J4
Rathillet	82	E5
Rathliesbeag	87	J6
Rathmell	56	D3
Ratho	75	K3
Ratho Station	75	K3
Rathven	98	C4
Ratley	30	E4
Ratlinghope	38	D6
Rattar	105	H1
Ratten Row	55	H5
Rattery	5	H4
Rattlesden	34	D3
Rattray	82	C3
Raughton Head	60	E2
Raunds	32	D1
Ravenfield	51	G3
Ravenglass	60	B7
Raveningham	45	H6
Ravenscar	63	J2
Ravensdale	54	C4
Ravensden	32	D3
Ravenshayes	7	H5
Ravenshead	51	H7
Ravensmoor	49	F7
Ravensthorpe *Northants.*	31	H1
Ravensthorpe *W.Yorks.*	50	E1
Ravenstone *Leics.*	41	G4
Ravenstone *M.K.*	32	B4
Ravenstonedale	61	J6
Ravenstruther	75	H6
Ravensworth	62	C6
Raw	63	J2
Rawcliffe *E.Riding*	58	C7
Rawcliffe *York*	58	B4
Rawcliffe Bridge	58	C7
Rawdon	57	H6
Rawmarsh	51	G3
Rawreth	24	D2
Rawridge	7	K5
Rawtenstall	56	D7
Rawyards	75	F4
Raxton	91	G1
Raydon	34	E5
Raylees	70	E4
Rayleigh	24	E2
Raymond's Hill	8	C5
Rayne	34	B6
Reach	33	J2
Read	56	C6
Reading	22	A4
Reading Street	14	E4
Reagill	61	H5
Rearquhar	96	E2
Rearsby	41	J4
Rease Heath	49	F7
Reaster	105	H2
Reaveley	71	F2
Reawick	109	C8
Reay	104	E2
Reculver	25	J5
Red Dial	60	D2
Red Hill *Hants.*	11	J3
Red Hill *Warks.*	30	C3
Red Lodge	33	K1
Red Oaks Hill	33	J5
Red Point	94	D5
Red Post *Cornw.*	6	A5
Red Post *Devon*	5	J4
Red Rock	48	E1
Red Roses	17	F4
Red Row	71	H4
Red Street	49	H7
Red Wharf Bay	46	D4
Redberth	16	D5
Redbourn	32	E7
Redbourne	52	C2
Redbrook	19	J1
Redbrook Street	14	E4
Redburn *High.*	96	C5
Redburn *High.*	97	G7
Redcar	63	H4
Redcastle *Angus*	83	H2
Redcastle *High.*	96	C7
Redcliff Bay	19	H4
Redcloak	91	G6
Reddish	49	H3
Redditch	30	B2
Rede	34	C3
Redenhall	45	G7
Redesmouth	70	D5
Redford *Aber.*	83	J1
Redford *Angus*	83	G3
Redford *Dur.*	62	B3
Redford *W.Suss.*	12	B4
Redgrave	34	E1
Redheugh	83	F1
Redhill *Aber.*	90	E4
Redhill *Aber.*	91	F1
Redhill *Moray*	98	B5
Redhill *N.Som.*	19	H5
Redhill *Notts.*	41	H1
Redhill *Surr.*	23	F6
Redhill *Tel. & W.*	39	G4
Redhill Aerodrome & Heliport	23	F7
Redhouse *Aber.*	90	D2
Redhouse *Arg. & B.*	73	G4
Redhouses	72	B4
Redisham	45	J7

Name	Pg	Grid
Redland *Bristol*	19	J4
Redland *Ork.*	106	C5
Redlingfield	35	F1
Redlynch *Som.*	9	F1
Redlynch *Wilts.*	10	D2
Redmarley D'Abitot	29	G5
Redmarshall	62	E4
Redmile	42	B2
Redmire	62	B7
Redmoor	4	A4
Rednal *Shrop.*	38	C3
Rednal *W.Mid.*	30	B1
Redpath	76	D7
Redruth	2	D4
Redscarhead	76	A6
Redshaw	68	D1
Redstone Bank	16	E4
Redwick *Newport*	19	H3
Redwick *S.Glos.*	19	J3
Redworth	62	D4
Reed	33	G5
Reedham	45	J5
Reedness	58	D7
Reepham *Lincs.*	52	D5
Reepham *Norf.*	44	E3
Reeth	62	B7
Regaby	54	D4
Regil	19	J5
Regoul	97	F6
Reiff	102	B7
Reigate	23	F6
Reighton	59	H2
Reinigeadal	100	E7
Reisgill	105	H5
Reiss	105	J3
Rejerrah	2	E3
Relubbus	2	C5
Relugas	97	G7
Remenham	22	A3
Remenham Hill	22	A3
Remony	81	J3
Rempstone	41	H3
Rendcomb	30	B7
Rendham	35	H2
Rendlesham	35	H3
Renfrew	74	D4
Renhold	32	D3
Renishaw	51	G5
Rennington	71	H2
Renton	74	B3
Renwick	61	G2
Repps	45	J4
Repton	41	F3
Rescobie	83	G2
Resipole	79	J1
Resolis	96	D5
Resolven	18	B1
Resourie	86	E7
Reston	77	G4
Reswallie	83	G2
Retew	3	G3
Retford	51	K4
Rettendon	24	D2
Rettendon Place	24	D2
Retyn	3	F3
Revesby	53	F6
Rew	5	H3
Rewe	7	H6
Reydon	35	J1
Reymerston	44	E5
Reynalton	16	D5
Reynoldston	17	H7
Rezare	4	D3

Name	Pg	Grid
Rhandirmwyn	27	G4
Rhaoine	96	D1
Rhayader	27	J2
Rhedyn	36	B2
Rhegreanoch	102	C7
Rheindown	96	C7
Rhelonie	96	C2
Rhemore	79	G2
Rhes-y-cae	47	K6
Rhewl *Denb.*	38	A1
Rhewl *Denb.*	47	K6
Rhewl *Shrop.*	38	C2
Rhian	103	H7
Rhicarn	102	C6
Rhiconich	102	E3
Rhiculen	96	D5
Rhidorroch	95	H2
Rhifail	104	C4
Rhigos	18	C1
Rhilochan	96	E1
Rhinduie	96	C7
Rhireavach	95	G2
Rhiroy	95	H3
Rhiw	36	B3
Rhiwargor	37	J3
Rhiwbryfdir	37	F1
Rhiwderin	19	F3
Rhiwlas *Gwyn.*	46	D6
Rhiwlas *Gwyn.*	37	J2
Rhiwlas *Powys*	38	A2
Rhodes Minnis	15	G3
Rhodesia	51	H5
Rhodiad-y-Brenin	16	A3
Rhodmad	26	E1
Rhonadale	73	F7
Rhonehouse or Kelton Hill	65	H5
Rhoose	18	D5
Rhos *Carmar.*	17	G1
Rhos *N.P.T.*	18	A1
Rhos-berse	48	B7
Rhoscolyn	46	A5
Rhoscrowther	16	C5
Rhos-ddu	48	C7
Rhosesmor	48	B6
Rhos-fawr	36	B2
Rhosgadfan	46	D7
Rhos-goch *I.o.A.*	46	C4
Rhosgoch *Powys*	28	B4
Rhos-hill	16	E1
Rhoshirwaun	36	A3
Rhoslan	36	D1
Rhoslefain	36	B5
Rhosllanerchrugog	38	B1
Rhosmaen	17	K3
Rhosmeirch	46	C5
Rhosneigr	46	B5
Rhosnesni	48	C7
Rhôs-on-Sea	47	G4
Rhossili	17	H7
Rhosson	16	A3
Rhostryfan	46	C7
Rhostyllen	38	C1
Rhos-y-bol	46	C4
Rhos-y-brwyner	48	C7
Rhos-y-garth	27	F1
Rhos-y-gwaliau	37	J2
Rhos-y-llan	36	B2
Rhos-y-mawn	47	G6
Rhos-y-Meirch	28	B2
Rhu	74	A2
Rhuallt	47	J5
Rhubodach	73	H3
Rhuddlan	47	J5
Rhue	95	G2

Place	Ref		Place	Ref		Place	Ref
...ulen	28 A4		Rivenhall End	34 C7		Roseden	71 F1
numach	86 C6		River	12 C4		Rosehall	96 B1
nunahaorine			River Bank	33 J2		Rosehearty	99 H4
nuthun (Ruthin)	47 K7		River Bridge	19 G7		Rosehill Aber.	90 D5
...yd Gwyn.	37 F1		Riverford Bridge	5 H4		Rosehill Shrop.	39 F2
...yd Powys	37 J5		Riverhead	23 J6		Roseisle	97 J5
...ydaman (Ammanford)	17 K4		Rivington	49 F1		Rosemarket	16 C5
...ydargaeau	17 H3		Roa Island	55 F3		Rosemarkie	96 E6
...ydcymerau	17 J2		Roade	31 J3		Rosemary Lane	7 K4
...ydd	29 H4		Roadhead	70 A6		Rosemount P. & K.	82 C3
...yd-Ddu	46 D7		Roadside High.	105 G2		Rosemount S.Ayr.	67 H1
...ydding	18 A2		Roadside Ork.	106 F3		Rosepool	16 B4
...ydlanfair	47 G7		Roadside of Kinneff	91 G7		Rosewarne	2 D5
...ydlewis	17 G1		Roadwater	7 J2		Rosewell	76 A4
...ydlios	36 A2		Roag	93 H7		Roseworthy	2 D5
...Conwy	47 G7		Roath	19 F4		Rosgill	61 G5
...ydlydan Powys	37 K6		Roberton S.Lan.	68 E1		Roshven	86 D7
...ydolion	36 B3		Roberton Sc.Bord.	69 K2		Roskhill	93 H7
...ydowen	17 H1		Robertsbridge	14 C5		Rosley	60 E2
...yd-rosser	26 E2		Robertstown	97 K7		Roslin	76 A4
...ydspence	28 B4		Roberttown	57 G7		Rosliston	40 E4
...ydtalog	48 B7		Robeston Cross	16 B5		Rosneath	74 A2
...yd-uchaf	37 J2		Robeston Wathen	16 D4		Ross D. & G.	65 G6
...yd-wen	37 J3		Robin Hood Derbys.	50 E5		Ross Northumb.	77 K7
...yd-wyn	46 B4		Robin Hood W.Yorks.	57 J7		Ross P. & K.	81 J5
...ydy-clafdy	36 C2		Robin Hood's Bay	63 J2		Ross Priory	74 C2
...ydycroesau	38 B2		Robins	12 B4		Rossdhu House	74 B2
...ydyfelin Cere.	26 E1		Roborough Devon	6 D4		Rossett	48 C7
...ydyfelin R.C.T.	18 D3		Roborough Plym.	5 F4		Rossie Farm School	83 H2
...yd-y-foel	47 H5		Roby	48 D3		Rossie Ochill	82 B6
...yd-y-fro	18 A1		Roby Mill	48 E2		Rossie Priory	82 D4
...ydymain	37 G3		Rocester	40 D2		Rossington	51 J3
...ydymwyn	48 B6		Roch	16 B3		Rosskeen	96 D5
...yd-yr-onnen	37 F5		Rochallie	82 C2		Ross-on-Wye	29 F6
...ydywrach	16 E4		Rochdale	49 H1		Roster	105 H5
...yl	47 J4		Roche	3 G3		Rostherne	49 G4
...ymney	18 E1		Rochester Med.	24 D5		Rosthwaite Cumb.	60 D5
...yn	38 C2		Rochester Northumb.	70 D4		Rosthwaite Cumb.	55 F1
...ynd	82 C5		Rochford Essex	24 E2		Roston	40 D1
...ynie Aber.	90 C2		Rochford Worcs.	29 F2		Rosyth	75 K2
...ynie High.	97 F4		Rock Caerp.	18 E2		Rothbury	71 F3
...bbesford	29 G1		Rock Cornw.	3 G1		Rotherby	41 J4
...bbleton	55 J6		Rock Northumb.	71 H1		Rotherfield	13 J4
...bchester	56 B6		Rock Worcs.	29 G1		Rotherfield Greys	22 A3
...bigill	103 H3		Rock Ferry	48 C4		Rotherfield Peppard	22 A3
...by	52 E2		Rockbeare	7 J6		Rotherham	51 G3
...ccall	58 C6		Rockbourne	10 C3		Rothersthorpe	31 J3
...ccarton	74 C7		Rockcliffe Cumb.	69 J7		Rotherwick	22 A6
...chard's Castle	28 D2		Rockcliffe D. & G.	65 J5		Rothes	97 K7
...chings Park	22 D4		Rockfield Arg. & B.	73 G5		Rothesay	73 J4
...chmond Gt.Lon.	22 E4		Rockfield High.	97 G3		Rothiebrisbane	91 F1
...chmond N.Yorks.	62 C6		Rockfield Mon.	28 D7		Rothienorman	91 F1
...ckarton	91 G6		Rockhampton	19 K2		Rothiesholm	106 F5
...ckford	19 H6		Rockhead	4 A2		Rothley Leics.	41 H4
...ckinghall	34 E1		Rockingham	42 B6		Rothley Northumb.	71 F5
...ckling	33 H5		Rockland All Saints	44 D6		Rothwell Lincs.	52 E3
...ckling Green	33 J6		Rockland St. Mary	45 H5		Rothwell Northants.	42 B7
...ckmansworth	22 D2		Rockland St. Peter	44 D6		Rothwell W.Yorks.	57 J7
...ddell	70 A1		Rockley	20 E4		Rotsea	59 G4
...ddings	51 G7		Rockside	72 A4		Rottal	82 E1
...ddlecombe	6 E4		Rockwell End	22 A3		Rottingdean	13 G6
...ddlesden	57 F5		Rockwell Green	7 K4		Rottington	60 A5
...dge Dorset	9 J6		Rodborough	20 B1		Roud	11 G6
...dge Herts.	23 F1		Rodbourne	20 C3		Roudham	44 D7
...dge Wilts.	9 J1		Rodbridge Corner	34 C4		Rough Close	40 B2
...dge Lane	40 E6		Rodd	28 C2		Rough Common	15 G2
...dgebourne	27 K2		Roddam	71 F1		Rougham Norf.	44 C3
...dgeway	51 G4		Rodden	9 F6		Rougham Suff.	34 D2
...dgeway Cross	29 G4		Rode	20 B6		Rougham Green	34 D2
...dgewell	34 B4		Rode Heath	49 H7		Roughburn	87 K6
...dgewood	13 H4		Rodeheath	49 H6		Roughlee	56 D5
...dgmont	32 C5		Rodel (Roghadal)	93 F3		Roughley	40 D6
...ding Mill	71 F7		Roden	38 E4		Roughton Lincs.	53 F6
...dley	24 C6		Rodhuish	7 J2		Roughton Norf.	45 G2
...dleywood	48 C7		Rodington	38 E4		Roughton Shrop.	39 G6
...dlington Norf.	45 H2		Rodley	29 G7		Roundhay	57 J6
...dlington Rut.	42 B5		Rodmarton	20 C2		Roundstreet Common	12 D4
...dsdale	70 E5		Rodmell	13 H6		Roundway	20 C5
...echip	82 B3		Rodmersham	25 F5		Rous Lench	30 B3
...evaulx	58 B1		Rodney Stoke	19 H6		Rousdon	8 B5
...gg D. & G.	69 H7		Rodsley	40 E1		Rousham	31 F6
...gg High.	94 B6		Rodway	19 F7		Rousham Gap	31 F6
...ggend	75 F4		Roe Green	33 G5		Routenburn	74 A4
...gmaden Park	56 B1		Roecliffe	57 J3		Routh	59 G5
...gsby	53 H5		Roehampton	23 F4		Row Cornw.	4 A3
...gside	75 G7		Roesound	109 C6		Row Cumb.	55 H1
...leyhill	40 D4		Roffey	12 E3		Row Cumb.	61 H3
...lla Mill	4 C3		Rogart	96 E1		Row Heath	35 F7
...illington	58 E2		Rogate	12 B4		Row Town	22 D5
...imington	56 D5		Rogerstone	19 F3		Rowanburn	69 K6
...impton	9 F2		Roghadal (Rodel)	93 F3		Rowardennan Lodge	74 B1
...imswell	59 K7		Rogiet	19 H3		Rowberrow	19 H6
...inaston	16 C3		Roker	63 F1		Rowchoish	80 E7
...ingford	65 G5		Rollesby	45 J4		Rowde	20 C5
...ingland	45 F4		Rolleston Leics.	42 A5		Rowen	47 F5
...ingles Cross	13 H4		Rolleston Notts.	51 K7		Rowfoot	70 B7
...ingmer	13 H5		Rolleston Staffs.	40 E3		Rowhedge	34 E6
...ingmore	5 G6		Rollestone	20 D7		Rowhook	12 E3
...ingorm	97 K7		Rolston	59 J5		Rowington	30 D2
...ing's End	43 G5		Rolvenden	14 D4		Rowington Green	30 D1
...ingsfield	45 J7		Rolvenden Layne	14 D4		Rowland	50 E5
...ingshall Corner	45 J7		Romaldkirk	62 A4		Rowland's Castle	11 J3
...ingshall Herts.	32 C7		Romanby	62 E7		Rowlands Gill	62 C1
...ingshall Suff.	34 E3		Romannobridge	75 K6		Rowledge	22 B7
...ingshall Stocks	34 E3		Romansleigh	7 F3		Rowley Devon	7 F4
...ingstead Norf.	44 B1		Romford Dorset	10 B4		Rowley Dur.	62 B2
...ingstead Northants.	32 C1		Romford Gt.Lon.	23 J3		Rowley E.Riding	59 F6
...ingwood	10 C4		Romiley	49 J3		Rowley Shrop.	38 C5
...ingwould	15 J3		Romney Street	23 J5		Rowley Regis	40 B7
...inloan	89 K4		Romsey	10 E2		Rowlstone	28 C6
...inmore	90 C3		Romsley Shrop.	39 G7		Rowly	22 D7
...innigill	107 C8		Romsley Worcs.	40 B7		Rowner	11 G4
...insey	2 C6		Ronachan	73 F5		Rowney Green	30 B1
...ipe	13 J6		Ronague	54 B6		Rownhams	10 E3
...ipley Derbys.	51 G7		Ronnachmore	72 B5		Rowrah	60 B5
...ipley Hants.	10 C5		Rookhope	62 A2		Rowsham	32 B7
...ipley N.Yorks.	57 H3		Rookley	11 G6		Rowsley	50 E6
...ipley Surr.	22 D6		Rooks Bridge	19 G6		Rowstock	21 H3
...iplingham	59 F6		Rookwith	57 H1		Rowston	52 D7
...ipon	57 J2		Roos	59 J6		Rowthorne	51 G6
...ippingale	42 E3		Roosecote	55 F3		Rowton Ches.	48 D6
...ipple Kent	15 J2		Rootpark	75 H5		Rowton Shrop.	38 C4
...ipple Worcs.	29 H5		Ropley	11 H1		Rowton Tel. & W.	39 F4
...ipponden	50 C1		Ropley Dean	11 H1		Roxburgh	76 E7
...isabus	72 B6		Ropley Soke	11 H1		Roxby N.Lincs.	52 C1
...isbury	28 E3		Ropsley	42 C2		Roxby N.Yorks.	63 J5
...isby	34 B2		Rora	99 J5		Roxton	32 E3
...isca	73 F2		Rorandle	90 E3		Roxwell	24 C1
...ise	59 H5		Rorrington	38 B5		Royal British Legion Village	14 C2
...isegate	43 F2		Rosarie	98 B5		Royal Leamington Spa	30 E2
...iseley Beds.	32 D2		Rose	2 E3		Royal Tunbridge Wells	13 J3
...iseley W'ham	22 A5		Rose Ash	7 F3		Roybridge	87 J6
...ishangles	35 F2		Rose Green	34 C6		Roydon Essex	33 H7
...ishton	56 C6		Roseacre	55 H6		Roydon Norf.	44 E7
...ishworth	50 C1		Rosebank	75 G6			
...isley Derbys.	41 G2		Rosebrough	71 G1			
...isley Warr.	49 F3		Rosebush	16 D3			
...isplith	57 H3		Rosedale Abbey	63 J7			
...ispond	103 G1						
...ivar	21 G5						
...ivenhall	34 C7						

Place	Ref		Place	Ref		Place	Ref
Roydon Norf.	44 B3		Saddell	73 F7		St. Lawrence I.o.W.	11 G7
Roydon Hamlet	23 H1		Saddington	41 J6		St. Leonards Bucks.	22 C1
Royston Herts.	33 G4		Saddle Bow	44 A4		St. Leonards Dorset	10 C4
Royston S.Yorks.	51 F1		Sadgill	61 F6		St. Leonards E.Suss.	14 D7
Royton	49 J2		Saffron Walden	33 J5		St. Leonards Grange	11 F5
Ruabon	38 C1		Sageston	16 D5		St. Leonard's Street	23 K6
Ruaig	78 B3		Saham Toney	44 C5		St. Levan	2 A6
Ruan Lanihorne	3 F4		Saighdinis	92 D5		St. Lythans	18 E4
Ruan Major	2 D7		Saighton	48 D6		St. Mabyn	4 A3
Ruan Minor	2 E7		St. Abbs	77 H4		St. Margaret South Elmham	45 H7
Ruanaich	78 D5		St. Agnes	2 E3		St. Margarets Here.	28 C5
Ruardean	29 F7		St. Albans	22 E1		St. Margarets Herts.	33 G7
Ruardean Woodside	29 F7		St. Allen	3 F3		St. Margaret's at Cliffe	15 J3
Rubery	29 J1		St. Andrews	83 G6		St. Margaret's Hope	107 D8
Ruckcroft	61 G2		St. Andrews Major	18 E4		St. Mark's	54 C6
Ruckinge	15 F4		St. Anne	3 K4		St. Martin Chan.I.	3 K5
Ruckland	53 G5		St. Anne's	55 G7		St. Martin Chan.I.	3 K7
Ruckley	38 E5		St. Ann's	69 F4		St. Martin Cornw.	4 C5
Rudby	63 F6		St. Ann's Chapel Cornw.	4 E3		St. Martin Cornw.	2 E6
Rudchester	71 G7		St. Ann's Chapel Devon	5 G6		St. Martins P. & K.	82 C4
Ruddington	41 H2		St. Anthony Cornw.	2 E6		St. Martin's Shrop.	38 C2
Ruddlemoor	4 A5		St. Anthony Cornw.	3 F5		St. Mary Bourne	21 H6
Rudford	29 G6		St. Arvans	19 J2		St. Mary Church	18 D4
Rudge	20 B6		St. Asaph (Llanelwy)	47 J5		St. Mary Cray	23 H5
Rudgeway	19 K3		St. Athan	18 D5		St. Mary Hill	18 C4
Rudgwick	12 D3		St. Aubin	3 J7		St. Mary in the Marsh	15 F5
Rudhall	29 F6		St. Audries	7 K1		St. Marychurch	5 K4
Rudheath	49 F5		St. Austell	4 A5		St. Mary's	107 D7
Rudley Green	24 E1		St. Bees	60 A5		St. Mary's Airport	2 C1
Rudry	18 E3		St. Blazey	4 A5		St. Mary's Bay	15 F5
Rudston	59 G3		St. Blazey Gate	4 A5		St. Mary's Croft	64 A4
Rudyard	49 J7		St. Boswells	76 D7		St. Mary's Grove	19 H5
Rufford	48 D1		St. Brelade	3 J7		St. Mary's Hoo	24 D4
Rufforth	58 B4		St. Breock	3 G1		St. Mawes	3 F5
Ruffside	62 A1		St. Breward	4 A3		St. Mawgan	3 F2
Rugby	31 G1		St. Briavels	19 J1		St. Mellion	4 D4
Rugeley	40 C4		St. Brides	16 B4		St. Mellons	19 F3
Ruilick	96 C7		St. Brides Major	18 B4		St. Merryn	3 F1
Ruishton	8 B2		St. Brides Netherwent	19 H3		St. Mewan	3 G3
Ruisigearraidh	92 E3		St. Brides Wentlooge	19 F3		St. Michael Caerhays	3 G4
Ruislip	22 D3		St. Bride's-super-Ely	18 D4		St. Michael Penkevil	3 F4
Rumbling Bridge	75 J1		St. Budeaux	4 E5		St. Michael South Elmham	45 H7
Rumburgh	45 H7		St. Buryan	2 B6		St. Michaels Kent	14 D4
Rumford	3 F1		St. Catherine	20 A4		St. Michaels Worcs.	28 E2
Rumney	19 F4		St. Catherines	80 C7		St. Michael's on Wyre	55 H5
Rumwell	7 K3		St. Clears	17 F4		St. Minver	3 G1
Runacraig	81 G6		St. Cleer	4 C4		St. Monans	83 G7
Runcorn	48 E4		St. Clement	3 F4		St. Neot	4 B4
Runcton	12 B6		St. Clether	4 C2		St. Neots	32 E3
Runcton Holme	44 A5		St. Columb Major	3 G2		St. Nicholas Pembs.	16 C2
Rundlestone	5 F3		St. Columb Minor	3 F2		St. Nicholas V. of Glam.	18 D4
Runfold	22 B7		St. Columb Road	3 G3		St. Nicholas at Wade	25 J5
Runhall	44 E5		St. Combs	99 J4		St. Ninians	75 F1
Runham	45 J4		St. Cross South Elmham	45 G7		St. Osyth	35 F7
Runnington	7 K3		St. Cyrus	83 J1		St. Ouen	3 J6
Runsell Green	24 D1		St. Davids Fife	75 K2		St. Owen's Cross	28 E6
Runswick Bay	63 K5		St. David's P. & K.	82 A5		St. Paul's Cray	23 H5
Runtaleave	82 D1		St. David's (Tyddewi) Pembs.	16 A3		St. Paul's Walden	32 E6
Runwell	24 D2		St. Day	2 E4		St. Peter	3 J7
Ruscombe	22 A4		St. Decumans	7 J1		St. Peter Port	3 J5
Rush Green	23 J3		St. Dennis	3 G3		St. Peter's	25 K5
Rushall Here.	29 F5		St. Dogmaels	16 E1		St. Petrox	16 C6
Rushall Norf.	45 F7		St. Dogwells	16 C3		St. Pinnock	4 C4
Rushall W.Mid.	40 C5		St. Dominick	4 E4		St. Quivox	67 H1
Rushall Wilts.	20 E6		St. Donats	18 C5		St. Sampson	3 J5
Rushbrooke	34 C2		St. Edith's Marsh	20 C5		St. Saviour	3 H5
Rushbury	38 E6		St. Endellion	3 G1		St. Stephen	3 G3
Rushden Herts.	33 G5		St. Enoder	3 F3		St. Stephens Cornw.	4 E5
Rushden Northants.	32 C2		St. Erme	3 F4		St. Stephens Cornw.	6 B7
Rushford	44 D7		St. Erney	4 D5		St. Stephens Herts.	22 E1
Rushlake Green	13 K5		St. Erth	2 C5		St. Teath	4 A2
Rushmere	45 J7		St. Erth Praze	2 C5		St. Tudy	4 A3
Rushmere St. Andrew	35 F4		St. Ervan	3 F1		St. Twynnells	16 C6
Rushmoor Surr.	22 B7		St. Eval	3 F2		St. Veep	4 B5
Rushmoor Tel. & W.	39 F4		St. Ewe	3 G4		St. Vigeans	83 H3
Rushock	29 H1		St. Fagans	18 E4		St. Wenn	3 G2
Rusholme	49 H3		St. Fergus	99 K5		St. Weonards	28 D6
Rushton Ches.	48 E6		St. Fillans	81 H5		Saintbury	30 C4
Rushton Northants.	42 B7		St. Florence	16 D5		Salachail	80 B2
Rushton Shrop.	39 F5		St. Gennys	4 B1		Salcombe	5 H7
Rushton Spencer	49 J6		St. George	47 H5		Salcombe Regis	7 K7
Rushwick	29 H3		St. Georges N.Som.	19 G5		Salcott	34 D7
Rushyford	62 D4		St. George's V. of Glam.	18 D4		Sale	49 G3
Ruskie	81 H7		St. Germans	4 D5		Sale Green	29 J3
Ruskington	52 D7		St. Giles in the Wood	6 D4		Saleby	53 H5
Rusko	65 F5		St. Giles on the Heath	6 B6		Salehurst	14 C5
Rusland	55 G1		St. Harmon	27 J1		Salem Carmar.	17 K3
Rusper	13 F3		St. Helen Auckland	62 C4		Salem Cere.	37 F7
Ruspidge	29 F7		St. Helena	45 F4		Salem Gwyn.	46 D7
Russel	94 E7		St. Helen's E.Suss.	14 D6		Salen Arg. & B.	79 G3
Russell's Water	22 A3		St. Helens I.o.W.	11 H6		Salen High.	79 H1
Rusthall	23 J7		St. Helens Mersey.	48 E3		Salesbury	56 B6
Rustington	12 D6		St. Helier	3 J7		Salford Beds.	32 C5
Ruston	59 F1		St. Hilary Cornw.	2 C5		Salford Gt.Man.	49 H3
Ruston Parva	59 G3		St. Hilary V. of Glam.	18 D4		Salford Oxon.	30 D6
Ruswarp	63 K6		St. Hill	13 G3		Salford Priors	30 B3
Rutherend	74 E5		St. Illtyd	19 F1		Salfords	23 F7
Rutherford	70 B1		St. Ippollitts	33 F6		Salhouse	45 H4
Rutherglen	74 E4		St. Ishmael	17 G5		Saline	75 J1
Ruthernbridge	4 A4		St. Ishmael's	16 B5		Salisbury	10 C1
Ruthin (Rhuthun)	47 K7		St. Issey	3 G1		Salkeld Dykes	61 G3
Ruthrieston	91 H4		St. Ive	4 D4		Sall	45 F3
Ruthven Aber.	98 D6		St. Ives Cambs.	33 G1		Sallachan	80 A1
Ruthven Angus	82 D3		St. Ives Cornw.	2 C4		Sallachy High.	96 B1
Ruthven High.	89 F1		St. Ives Dorset	10 C4		Sallachy High.	87 F1
Ruthven High.	88 E5		St. James South Elmham	45 H7		Salmonby	53 G5
Ruthvoes	3 G2		St. John Chan.I.	3 J6		Salmond's Muir	83 G4
Ruthwaite	60 D3		St. John Cornw.	4 E5		Salperton	30 B6
Ruthwell	69 G7		St. John's I.o.M.	54 B5		Salph End	32 D3
Ruyton-XI-Towns	38 C3		St. John's Surr.	22 C6		Salsburgh	75 G4
Ryal	71 F6		St. John's Worcs.	29 H3		Salt	40 B3
Ryal Fold	56 B7		St. John's Chapel Devon	6 D3		Salt Hill	22 C3
Ryall	8 D5		St. John's Chapel Dur.	61 K3		Saltash	4 E5
Ryarsh	23 K6		St. John's Fen End	43 J4		Saltburn	96 E4
Rydal	60 E6		St. Johns Hall	62 B3		Saltburn-by-the-Sea	63 H4
Ryde	11 G5		St. John's Highway	43 J4		Saltby	42 B3
Rydon	6 B5		St. John's Kirk	75 H7		Saltcoats	74 A6
Rye	14 E5		St. John's Town of Dalry	68 A5		Saltcotes	55 G7
Rye Foreign	14 D5		St. Judes	54 C4		Saltdean	13 G6
Rye Harbour	14 E6		St. Just	2 A5		Salterforth	56 D5
Rye Park	23 G1		St. Just in Roseland	3 F5		Saltergate	63 K7
Ryhall	42 D4		St. Katherines	91 F1		Salterhill	97 K5
Ryhill	51 F1		St. Keverne	2 E6			
Ryhope	62 E1		St. Kew	3 G1			
Ryland	52 D4		St. Kew Highway	4 A3			
Rylstone	56 E4		St. Keyne	4 C4			
Ryme Intrinseca	8 E3		St. Lawrence Cornw.	4 A4			
Ryther	58 B6		St. Lawrence Essex	25 F1			
Ryton Glos.	29 G5						
Ryton N.Yorks.	58 D2						
Ryton Shrop.	39 G5						
Ryton T. & W.	71 G7						
Ryton-on-Dunsmore	30 E1						

Place	Ref
Salterswall	49 F6
Saltfleet	53 H3
Saltfleetby All Saints	53 H3
Saltfleetby St. Clements	53 H3
Saltfleetby St. Peter	53 H4
Saltford	19 K5
Salthaugh Grange	59 J7
Salthouse	44 E1
Saltley	40 C7
Saltmarshe	58 D7
Saltney	48 C6
Salton	58 D1
Saltwick	71 G6
Saltwood	15 G4
Salvington	12 E6
Salwarpe	29 H2
Salwayash	8 D5
Sambourne	30 B2
Sambrook	39 G3
Samhla	92 C5
Samlesbury	55 J6
Samlesbury Bottoms	56 B7
Sampford Arundel	7 K4
Sampford Brett	7 J1
Sampford Courtenay	6 E5
Sampford Peverell	7 J4
Sampford Spiney	5 F3
Samuelston	76 C3
Sanaigmore	72 A4
Sancreed	2 B6
Sancton	59 F6
Sand	109 C8
Sand Hole	58 E6
Sand Hutton	58 C4
Sand Side	55 F1
Sandaig Arg. & B.	78 A3
Sandaig High.	86 D3
Sandaig High.	86 D3
Sandbach	49 G6
Sandbank	73 K2
Sandbanks	10 B6
Sandend	98 D4
Sanderstead	23 G5
Sandford Cumb.	61 J5
Sandford Devon	7 G5
Sandford Dorset	9 J5
Sandford I.o.W.	11 G6
Sandford N.Som.	19 H6
Sandford S.Lan.	75 F6
Sandford Orcas	9 F2
Sandford St. Martin	31 F6
Sandfordhill	99 K6
Sandford-on-Thames	21 J1
Sandgarth	107 E6
Sandgate	15 H4
Sandgreen	65 F5
Sandhaven	99 H4
Sandhead	64 A5
Sandhills Dorset	9 F3
Sandhills Surr.	12 C3
Sandhoe	70 E7
Sandholme E.Riding	58 E6
Sandholme Lincs.	43 G2
Sandhurst Brack.F.	22 B5
Sandhurst Glos.	29 H6
Sandhurst Kent	14 C5
Sandhutton	57 J1
Sandiacre	41 G2
Sandilands	53 J4
Sandiway	49 F5
Sandleheath	10 C3
Sandleigh	21 H1
Sandling	14 C2
Sandness	109 A7
Sandon Essex	24 D1
Sandon Herts.	33 G5
Sandon Staffs.	40 B3
Sandown	11 G6
Sandplace	4 C5
Sandquoy	106 G3
Sandridge Herts.	32 E7
Sandridge Wilts.	20 C5
Sandringham	44 A3
Sandrocks	13 G4
Sandsend	63 K5
Sandside House	104 E2
Sandsound	109 C8
Sandtoft	51 K2
Sanduck	7 F2
Sandway	14 D2
Sandwich	15 J2
Sandwick Cumb.	61 F5
Sandwick Shet.	109 D10
Sandwick W.Isles	101 G4
Sandwith	60 A5
Sandy	32 E4
Sandy Haven	16 B5
Sandy Lane W.Yorks.	57 G6
Sandy Lane Wilts.	20 C5
Sandycroft	48 C6
Sandygate Devon	5 J3
Sandygate I.o.M.	54 C4
Sandylands	55 H3
Sandyway	28 D6
Sangobeg	103 G2
Sanna	79 F1
Sannaig	72 D3
Sanndabhaig (Sandwick)	101 G4
Sanquhar	68 C3
Santon Bridge	60 C6
Santon Downham	44 C7
Sapcote	41 G6
Sapey Common	29 G2
Sapiston	34 D1
Sapperton Glos.	20 C1
Sapperton Lincs.	42 D2
Saracen's Head	43 G3
Sarclet	105 J4
Sardis	16 C5
Sarisbury	11 G4
Sarn Bridgend	18 C3
Sarn Powys	38 B6
Sarn Bach	36 B3
Sarn Meyllteyrn	36 B2
Sarnau Carmar.	17 G3
Sarnau Cere.	26 C3
Sarnau Gwyn.	37 J2
Sarnau Powys	38 B4
Sarnesfield	28 C3
Saron Carmar.	17 K4
Saron Carmar.	17 G2
Saron Gwyn.	46 D6
Sarratt	22 D2
Sarre	25 J5
Sarsden	30 D6

S

Place	Ref
Sabden	56 C6
Sackers Green	34 D5
Sacombe	33 G7
Sacriston	62 D2
Sadberge	62 E5

Sarsgrum 103 F2
Sartfield 54 C4
Satley 62 C2
Satterleigh 6 E3
Satterthwaite 60 E7
Sauchen 90 E3
Saucher 82 C4
Sauchie 75 G1
Sauchieburn 83 H1
Sauchrie 67 H2
Saughall 48 C6
Saughall Massie 48 B4
Saughtree 70 A4
Saul 20 A1
Saundby 51 K4
Saundersfoot 16 E5
Saunderton 22 A1
Saunton 6 C2
Sausthorpe 53 G6
Savalbeg 96 C1
Savalmore 96 C1
Sawbridgeworth 33 H7
Sawdon 59 F1
Sawley Derbys. 41 G2
Sawley Lancs. 56 C5
Sawley N.Yorks. 57 H3
Sawston 33 H4
Sawtry 42 E7
Saxby Leics. 42 B4
Saxby Lincs. 52 D4
Saxby All Saints 52 C1
Saxelbye 42 A3
Saxilby 52 B5
Saxlingham 44 E2
Saxlingham Green 45 G6
Saxlingham Nethergate 45 G6
Saxlingham Thorpe 45 G6
Saxmundham 35 H2
Saxon Street 33 K3
Saxondale 41 J2
Saxtead Green 35 G2
Saxtead Little Green 35 G2
Saxthorpe 45 F2
Saxton 57 K6
Sayers Common 13 F5
Scackleton 58 C2
Scadabhagh 93 G2
Scaftworth 51 J3
Scagglethorpe 58 E2
Scalasaig 72 B1
Scalby E.Riding 58 E7
Scalby N.Yorks. 59 G1
Scaldwell 31 J1
Scale Houses 61 G2
Scaleby 69 K7
Scalebyhill 69 K7
Scales Cumb. 60 E4
Scales Cumb. 55 F2
Scalford 42 A3
Scaling 63 J5
Scallasaig 86 E3
Scallastle 79 J4
Scalloway 109 C9
Scamblesby 53 F5
Scammadale 79 K5
Scamodale 86 E7
Scampston 58 E2
Scampton 52 C5
Scaniport 88 D1
Scapa 107 D7
Scar 106 F3
Scarborough 59 G1
Scarcewater 3 G3
Scarcliffe 51 G6
Scarcroft 57 J5
Scardroy 95 J6
Scarff 108 B4
Scarfskerry 105 H1
Scargill 62 B5
Scarinish 78 B3
Scarisbrick 48 C1
Scarning 44 D4
Scarrington 42 A1
Scarth Hill 48 D2
Scartho 53 F2
Scatraig 88 E1
Scaur D. & G. 65 J3
Scaur or Kippford D. & G. 65 J5
Scawby 52 C2
Scawton 58 B1
Scayne's Hill 13 G4
Scealascro 100 D5
Scethrog 28 A6
Schaw 67 J1
Scholar Green 49 H7
Scholes W.Yorks. 57 J6
Scholes W.Yorks. 50 D2
Sciberscross 104 C7
Scleddau 16 C2
Sco Ruston 45 G3
Scofton 51 J4
Scole 35 F1
Scolpaig 92 C4
Scone 82 C5
Scones Lethendy 82 C5
Sconser 86 B1
Scoor 79 F6
Scopwick 52 D7
Scoraig 95 G2
Scorborough 59 G5
Scorrier 2 E4
Scorriton 5 H4
Scorton Lancs. 55 J5
Scorton N.Yorks. 62 D6
Scotby 61 F1
Scotch Corner 62 D6
Scotforth 55 H4
Scothern 52 D5
Scotland Gate 71 H5
Scotlandwell 82 C7
Scotnish 73 F2
Scots' Gap 71 F5
Scotsburn 96 E4
Scotston Aber. 91 F7
Scotston P. & K. 82 A3
Scotstown 79 K1
Scotter 52 B2
Scotterthorpe 52 B2
Scottlethorpe 42 D3
Scotton Lincs. 52 B3
Scotton N.Yorks. 62 C7
Scotton N.Yorks. 57 J4
Scottow 45 G3
Scoulton 44 D5
Scourie 102 D4
Scourie More 102 D4
Scousburgh 109 F9
Scrabster 105 F1
Scrainwood 70 E3
Scrane End 43 G1
Scraptoft 41 J5

Scratby 45 K4
Scrayingham 58 D3
Scredington 42 D1
Scremby 53 H6
Scremerston 77 J6
Screveton 42 A1
Scriven 57 J4
Scrooby 51 J3
Scropton 40 D2
Scrub Hill 53 F7
Scruton 62 D7
Sculthorpe 44 C2
Scunthorpe 52 B1
Scurlage 17 H7
Sea Palling 45 J3
Seabank 80 A3
Seaborough 8 D4
Seacombe 48 B3
Seacroft Lincs. 53 J6
Seacroft W.Yorks. 57 J6
Seafield Arg. & B. 73 F2
Seafield S.Ayr. 67 H3
Seafield W.Loth. 75 J4
Seaford 13 H7
Seaforth 48 C3
Seagrave 41 J4
Seaham 63 F2
Seahouses 77 K4
Seal 23 J6
Sealand 48 C6
Seale 22 B7
Seamer N.Yorks. 63 F5
Seamer N.Yorks. 59 G1
Seamill 74 A6
Searby 52 D2
Seasalter 25 G5
Seascale 60 B6
Seathwaite Cumb. 60 D7
Seathwaite Cumb. 60 D7
Seatoller 60 D7
Seaton Cornw. 4 D5
Seaton Cumb. 60 B3
Seaton Devon 8 B5
Seaton Dur. 63 F2
Seaton E.Riding 59 H5
Seaton Northumb. 71 J6
Seaton Rut. 42 C6
Seaton Burn 71 H6
Seaton Carew 63 G3
Seaton Delaval 71 J6
Seaton Junction 8
Seaton Ross 58 D5
Seaton Sluice 71 J6
Seatown Aber. 99 K5
Seatown Dorset 8 D5
Seatown Moray 98 C4
Seatown Moray 98 D4
Seave Green 63 G6
Seaview 11 H5
Seaville 60 C1
Seavington St. Mary 8 D3
Seavington St. Michael 8 D3
Seawick 35 F7
Sebastopol 19 F2
Sebergham 60 E2
Seckington 40 E5
Second Coast 95 F2
Sedbergh 61 H7
Sedbury 19 J2
Sedbusk 61 K7
Sedgeberrow 30 B5
Sedgebrook 42 B2
Sedgefield 62 E4
Sedgeford 44 B2
Sedgehill 9 H2
Sedgley 40 B6
Sedgwick 55 J1
Sedlescombe 14 C6
Sedlescombe Street 14 C6
Seend 20 C5
Seend Cleeve 20 C5
Seer Green 22 C2
Seething 45 H6
Sefton 48 C2
Seghill 71 H6
Seifton 38 D7
Seighford 40 A3
Seilebost 93 F2
Seion 46 D6
Seisdon 40 A6
Seisiadar 101 H4
Selattyn 38 B2
Selborne 11 J1
Selby 58 C6
Sellack 28 E6
Sellafield 60 B6
Sellafirth 108 E3
Sellindge 15 F4
Selling 15 F2
Sells Green 20 C5
Selly Oak 40 C7
Selmeston 13 J6
Selsdon 23 G5
Selsey 12 B7
Selsfield Common 13 G3
Selside 56 C2
Selstead 15 H3
Selston 51 G7
Selworthy 7 H1
Semblister 109 C7
Semer 34 D4
Semington 20 B5
Semley 9 H2
Send 22 D6
Send Marsh 22 D6
Senghenydd 18 E2
Sennen 2 A6
Sennen Cove 2 A6
Sennybridge 27 J6
Senwick 65 G6
Sequer's Bridge 5 G5
Sessay 57 K2
Setchey 44 A4
Setley 10 E4
Setter Shet. 109 E8
Setter Shet. 109 C7
Settiscarth 107 C6
Settle 56 D3
Settrington 58 E2
Seven Bridges 20 E2
Seven Kings 23 H3
Seven Sisters 18 B1
Seven Springs 29 J7
Sevenhampton Glos. 30 B6
Sevenhampton Swin. 21 F2
Sevenoaks 23 J6
Sevenoaks Weald 23 J6
Severn Beach 19 J3

Severn Stoke 29 H4
Sevington 15 F3
Sewards End 33 J5
Sewardstone 23 G2
Sewerby 59 J3
Seworgan 2 E5
Sewstern 42 B3
Sexhow 63 F6
Sgarasta Mhòr 93 F2
Sgiogarstaigh 101 H1
Sgodachail 96 B2
Shabbington 21 K1
Shackerley 40 A5
Shackerstone 41 F5
Shackleford 22 C7
Shadfen 71 H5
Shadforth 62 E2
Shadingfield 45 J7
Shadoxhurst 14 E4
Shadwell 44 D7
Shaftesbury 9 H2
Shafton 51 F1
Shalbourne 21 G5
Shalcombe 11 F6
Shalden 21 K7
Shaldon 5 K3
Shalfleet 11 F6
Shalford Essex 34 B6
Shalford Surr. 22 D7
Shalford Green 34 B6
Shallowford 7 F1
Shalmsford Street 15 F2
Shalmstry 105 G2
Shalstone 31 H5
Shalunt 73 J3
Shambellie 65 K4
Shamley Green 22 D7
Shandon 74 A2
Shandwick 97 F4
Shangton 42 A6
Shankend 70 A3
Shankhouse 71 H6
Shanklin 11 G6
Shannochie 66 D1
Shantron 74 B2
Shantullich 96 D6
Shanzie 82 D2
Shap 61 G5
Shapwick Dorset 9 J4
Shapwick Som. 8 D1
Shardlow 41 G2
Shareshill 40 B5
Sharlston 51 F1
Sharnbrook 32 D3
Sharnford 41 G6
Sharoe Green 55 J6
Sharow 57 J2
Sharpenhoe 32 D5
Sharperton 70 E3
Sharpham House 5 J5
Sharpness 19 K1
Sharpthorne 13 G3
Sharrington 44 E2
Shatterford 39 G7
Shaugh Prior 5 F4
Shavington 49 F7
Shaw Gt.Man. 49 J2
Shaw Swin. 20 E3
Shaw W.Berks. 21 H5
Shaw Wilts. 20 B5
Shaw Mills 57 H3
Shawbury 38 E3
Shawclough 49 H1
Shawell 41 H7
Shawford 11 F2
Shawforth 56 D7
Shawhead 65 J3
Shawtonhill 74 E6
Sheanachie 66 B2
Sheandow 89 K1
Shear Cross 20 B7
Shearington 69 F7
Shearsby 41 J6
Shebbear 6 C5
Shebdon 39 G3
Shebster 105 F2
Shedfield 11 G3
Sheen 50 D6
Sheepscombe 29 H7
Sheepstor 5 F4
Sheepwash Devon 6 C5
Sheepwash Northumb. 71 H5
Sheepway 19 H4
Sheepy Magna 41 F5
Sheepy Parva 41 F5
Sheering 33 J7
Sheerness 25 F4
Sheet 11 J2
Sheffield 51 F4
Sheffield Bottom 21 K5
Sheffield City Airport 51 G4
Sheffield Green 13 H4
Shefford 32 E5
Shefford Woodlands 21 G4
Sheigra 102 D2
Sheinton 39 F5
Shelderton 28 D1
Sheldon Derbys. 50 D6
Sheldon Devon 7 K5
Sheldon W.Mid. 40 D7
Sheldwich 15 F2
Shelf 57 G7
Shelfanger 45 F7
Shelfield 40 C5
Shelford 41 J1
Shellachan Arg. & B. 79 K6
Shellachan Arg. & B. 80 B5
Shellbrook Hill 38 C1
Shelley Essex 23 J1
Shelley Suff. 34 E5
Shelley W.Yorks. 50 E1
Shellingford 21 G2
Shellow Bowells 24 C1
Shelsley Beauchamp 29 G2
Shelsley Walsh 29 G2
Shelton Beds. 32 D2
Shelton Norf. 45 G6
Shelton Notts. 42 A1
Shelton Shrop. 38 D4
Shelton Green 45 G6
Shelve 38 C6
Shelwick 28 E4
Shenington 30 E4
Shenley 22 E1
Shenley Brook End 32 B5
Shenley Church End 32 B5
Shenleybury 22 E1
Shenmore 28 C5
Shennanton 64 D4

Shenstone Staffs. 40 D5
Shenstone Worcs. 29 H1
Shenstone Woodend 40 D5
Shenton 41 F5
Shenval 89 K2
Shepeau Stow 43 G4
Shephall 33 F6
Shepherd's Green 22 A3
Shepherdswell (Sibertswold) 15 H3
Shepley 50 D2
Sheppardstown 105 H5
Shepperdine 19 K2
Shepperton 22 D5
Shepreth 33 G4
Shepshed 41 G4
Shepton Beauchamp 8 D3
Shepton Mallet 19 K7
Shepton Montague 9 F1
Shepway 14 C2
Sheraton 63 F3
Sherborne Dorset 9 F3
Sherborne Glos. 30 C7
Sherborne St. John 21 K6
Sherbourne 30 D2
Sherburn Dur. 62 E2
Sherburn N.Yorks. 59 F2
Sherburn in Elmet 57 K6
Shere 22 D7
Shereford 44 C3
Sherfield English 10 D2
Sherfield on Loddon 21 K6
Sherford 5 H6
Sheriff Hutton 58 C3
Sheriffhales 39 G4
Sheringham 45 F1
Sherington 32 B4
Shernborne 44 B2
Sherramore 88 C5
Sherrington 9 J1
Sherston 20 B3
Sherwood Green 6 D3
Shettleston 74 E4
Shevington 48 E2
Shevington Moor 48 E1
Sheviock 4 D5
Shiel Bridge 87 F3
Shieldaig High. 94 E6
Shieldaig High. 94 E4
Shieldhill 75 G3
Shielfoot 86 C7
Shielhill 83 F2
Shiels 90 E4
Shifford 21 G1
Shifnal 39 G5
Shilbottle 71 G3
Shildon 62 D4
Shillingford Devon 7 H3
Shillingford Oxon. 21 J2
Shillingford St. George 7 H7
Shillingstone 9 H3
Shillington 32 E5
Shillmoor 70 D3
Shilstone 6 D5
Shilton Oxon. 21 F1
Shilton Warks. 41 G7
Shimpling Norf. 45 F7
Shimpling Suff. 34 C3
Shimpling Street 34 C3
Shincliffe 62 D2
Shiney Row 62 E1
Shinfield 22 A5
Shingay 33 G4
Shingle Street 35 H4
Shinner's Bridge 5 H4
Shinness Lodge 103 H1
Shipbourne 23 J6
Shipdham 44 D5
Shipham 19 H6
Shiphay 5 J4
Shiplake 22 A4
Shipley Northumb. 71 G2
Shipley Shrop. 40 A6
Shipley W.Suss. 12 E4
Shipley W.Yorks. 57 G6
Shipley Bridge Devon 5 G4
Shipley Bridge Surr. 23 G7
Shipmeadow 45 H6
Shippon 21 H2
Shipston on Stour 30 D4
Shipton Glos. 30 B7
Shipton N.Yorks. 58 B4
Shipton Shrop. 38 E6
Shipton Bellinger 21 F7
Shipton Gorge 8 D5
Shipton Green 12 B7
Shipton Moyne 20 B3
Shipton-on-Cherwell 31 F7
Shiptonthorpe 58 E5
Shipton-under-Wychwood 30 D7
Shira 80 C6
Shirburn 21 K2
Shirdley Hill 48 C1
Shire Oak 40 C5
Shirebrook 51 H6
Shiremoor 71 H6
Shirenewton 19 H2
Shireoaks 51 H4
Shirl Heath 28 D3
Shirland 51 G7
Shirley Derbys. 40 E1
Shirley Gt.Lon. 23 G5
Shirley Hants. 10 C5
Shirley S'ham. 11 F3
Shirley W.Mid. 30 C1
Shirrell Heath 11 G3
Shirwell 6 D2
Shirwell Cross 6 D2
Shiskine 66 D1
Shobdon 28 C2
Shobrooke 7 G5
Shocklach 38 D1
Shoeburyness 25 F3
Sholden 15 J2
Sholing 11 F3
Shoot Hill 38 D4
Shooter's Hill 23 H4
Shop Cornw. 3 F1
Shop Cornw. 6 A4
Shop Corner 35 G5
Shoreditch 23 G3
Shoreham 23 J5
Shoreham-by-Sea 13 F6
Shoremill 96 E5
Shoresdean 77 H6
Shoreswood 77 H6
Shoretown 96 D5

Shorncote 20 D2
Shorne 24 C4
Shorne Ridgeway 24 C4
Short Cross 38 B5
Short Green 44 E7
Short Heath Derbys. 41 F4
Short Heath W.Mid. 40 C6
Shortacombe 6 D7
Shortgate 13 H5
Shortgrove 33 J5
Shortlanesend 3 F4
Shorwell 11 F6
Shoscombe 20 A6
Shotesham 45 G6
Shotgate 24 D2
Shotley 35 G5
Shotley Bridge 62 B1
Shotley Gate 35 G5
Shotleyfield 62 B1
Shottenden 15 F2
Shottermill 12 B3
Shottery 30 C3
Shotteswell 31 F4
Shottisham 35 H4
Shottle 51 F7
Shottlegate 41 F1
Shotton Dur. 63 F3
Shotton Flints. 48 C6
Shotton Northumb. 77 G7
Shotton Colliery 62 E2
Shotts 75 G4
Shotwick 48 C5
Shoughlaige-e-Caine 54 C5
Shouldham 44 A5
Shouldham Thorpe 44 A5
Shoulton 29 H3
Shover's Green 13 K3
Shrawardine 38 C4
Shrawley 29 H2
Shrewley 30 D2
Shrewsbury 38 D4
Shrewton 20 D7
Shripney 12 C6
Shrivenham 21 F3
Shropham 44 D6
Shroton (Iwerne Courtney) 9 H3
Shrub End 34 D6
Shucknall 28 E4
Shudy Camps 33 K4
Shurdington 29 J7
Shurlock Row 22 B4
Shurrery 105 F3
Shurrery Lodge 105 F3
Shurton 7 K1
Shustoke 40 E6
Shut Heath 40 A3
Shute 8 B4
Shutford 30 E4
Shuthonger 29 H5
Shutlanger 31 J3
Shuttington 40 E5
Shuttlewood 51 G5
Shuttleworth 49 H1
Siabost 100 E3
Siadar Iarach 101 F2
Siadar Uarach 101 F2
Sibbaldbie 69 G5
Sibbertoft 41 J7
Sibdon Carwood 38 D7
Sibertswold (Shepherdswell) 15 H3
Sibford Ferris 30 E5
Sibford Gower 30 E5
Sible Hedingham 34 B5
Sibsey 53 G7
Sibson Cambs. 42 D6
Sibson Leics. 41 F5
Sibster 105 J3
Sibthorpe 42 A1
Sibton 35 H2
Sicklesmere 34 C3
Sicklinghall 57 J5
Sidbury Devon 7 K6
Sidbury Shrop. 39 F7
Sidcot 19 H6
Sidcup 23 H4
Siddington Ches. 49 H5
Siddington Glos. 20 D2
Sidemoor 29 J1
Sidestrand 45 G2
Sidford 7 K6
Sidlesham 12 B7
Sidley 14 C7
Sidlow 23 F7
Sidmouth 7 K7
Sigford 5 H3
Sigglesthorne 59 H5
Sigingstone 18 C4
Silchester 21 K5
Sileby 41 J4
Silecroft 54 E1
Silfield 45 F6
Silian 26 E3
Silk Willoughby 42 D1
Silkstone 50 E2
Silkstone Common 50 E2
Silksworth 62 E1
Silloth 60 C1
Sills 70 D3
Sillyearn 98 D5
Silpho 63 J3
Silsden 57 F5
Silsoe 32 D5
Silton 9 G2
Silver End 34 C7
Silver Hill 14 C5
Silverburn 76 A4
Silvercraigs 73 G2
Silverdale Lancs. 55 H2
Silverdale Staffs. 40 A1
Silverley's Green 35 G1
Silvermoss 91 G1
Silverstone 31 H4
Silverton 7 H5
Silvington 29 F1
Silwick 109 B8
Simonburn 70 D6
Simonsbath 7 F2
Simonstone 56 C6
Simprim 77 G6
Simpson 32 B5
Sinclair's Hill 77 G5
Sinclairston 67 J2
Sinderby 57 J1
Sinderhope 61 K1
Sindlesham 22 A5
Singdean 70 A3
Singleton Lancs. 55 G6
Singleton W.Suss. 12 B5
Singlewell or Ifield 24 C4
Sinnahard 90 C3
Sinnington 58 D1
Sinton Green 29 H2

Sipson 22 D4
Sirhowy 28 A7
Sisland 45 H6
Sissinghurst 14 C4
Siston 19 K4
Sithney 2 D6
Sittingbourne 25 F5
Siulaisiadar 101 H4
Six Ashes 39 G7
Six Mile Bottom 33 J3
Sixhills 52 E4
Sixmile Cottages 15 G3
Sixpenny Handley 9 J3
Sizewell 35 J2
Skail 104 C4
Skaill Ork. 107 B6
Skaill Ork. 107 E7
Skares Aber. 90 E1
Skares E.Ayr. 67 K2
Skarpigarth 109 A7
Skateraw 77 F3
Skaw 109 E6
Skeabost 93 K7
Skeabrae 106 B5
Skeeby 62 C6
Skeffington 42 A5
Skeffling 53 G1
Skegby 51 H6
Skegness 53 J6
Skelberry 109 F9
Skelbo 96 E2
Skeldon 67 H2
Skeldyke 43 G2
Skellingthorpe 52 C5
Skellister 109 D7
Skellow 51 H1
Skelmanthorpe 50 E1
Skelmersdale 48 D2
Skelmonae 91 G1
Skelmorlie 73 K4
Skelmuir 99 H6
Skelton Cumb. 61 F3
Skelton E.Riding 58 D7
Skelton N.Yorks. 62 B6
Skelton N.Yorks. 57 J3
Skelton R. & C. 63 H5
Skelton Green 63 H5
Skelwick 106 D3
Skelwith Bridge 60 E6
Skendleby 53 H6
Skenfrith 28 D6
Skerne 59 G4
Skeroblingarry 66 B1
Skerray 103 J2
Sketty 17 K6
Skewen 18 A2
Skewsby 58 C2
Skeyton 45 G3
Skidbrooke 53 H3
Skidby 59 G6
Skilgate 7 H3
Skillington 42 C3
Skinburness 60 C1
Skinflats 75 H2
Skinidin 93 H7
Skinnet 105 G2
Skinningrove 63 J4
Skipness 73 H5
Skipsea 59 H4
Skipton 56 E4
Skipton-on-Swale 57 J1
Skipwith 58 C6
Skirbeck 43 G1
Skirlaugh 59 H6
Skirling 75 J7
Skirmett 22 A3
Skirpenbeck 58 D4
Skirwith Cumb. 61 H3
Skirwith N.Yorks. 56 C2
Skirza 105 J2
Skulamus 86 C2
Skullomie 103 J2
Skye of Curr 89 G2
Slack 90 D1
Slackhall 50 C4
Slackhead 98 C4
Slad 20 B1
Slade 6 D1
Slade Green 23 J4
Slaggyford 61 H1
Slaidburn 56 C4
Slains Park 91 G7
Slaithwaite 50 C1
Slaley 62 A1
Slamannan 75 G3
Slapton Bucks. 32 C6
Slapton Devon 5 J6
Slapton Northants. 31 H4
Slate Haugh 98 C4
Slatenber 56 C2
Slattadale 94 E4
Slattocks 49 H2
Slaugham 13 F4
Slaughden 35 J3
Slaughterford 20 B4
Slawston 42 A6
Sleaford Hants. 12 B3
Sleaford Lincs. 42 D1
Sleagill 61 G5
Sleapford 39 F4
Sledge Green 29 H5
Sledmere 59 F3
Sleights 63 K6
Slepe 9 J5
Slickly 105 H2
Sliddery 66 D1
Sliemore 89 H2
Sligachan 85 K2
Slimbridge 20 A1
Slindon Staffs. 40 A2
Slindon W.Suss. 12 C6
Slinfold 12 E3
Slingsby 58 C2
Slioch 90 D1
Slip End Beds. 32 D7
Slip End Herts. 33 F5
Slipton 32 C1
Slochd 89 F2
Slockavullin 73 G1
Slogarie 65 G4
Sloley 45 G3
Sloothby 53 H5
Slough 22 C4
Sluggan 89 F2
Slyne 55 H3
Smailholm 76 E7
Small Dole 13 F5
Small Hythe 14 D4
Smallburgh 45 H3
Smallburn Aber. 99 J6
Smallburn E.Ayr. 68 B1
Smalley 41 G1
Smallfield 23 G7
Smallridge 8 B4
Smallthorne 49 H7

Smallworth 44 E
Smannell 21 G
Smardale 61 J
Smarden 14 D
Smaull 72 A
Smeale Farm 54 D
Smeatharpe 7 K
Smeeth 15 F
Smeeton Westerby 41 J
Smelthouses 57 G
Smerral 105 G
Smethwick 40 C
Smirisary 86 C
Smisby 41 F
Smith End Green 29 G
Smithfield 69 K
Smithincott 7 J
Smith's Green 33 J
Smithton 96 E
Smithy Green 49 G
Smug Oak 22 E
Smyrton 67 F
Smythe's Green 34 D
Snailbeach 38 C
Snailwell 33 K
Snainton 59 F
Snaith 58 C
Snape N.Yorks. 57 H
Snape Suff. 35 H
Snape Green 48 C
Snarestone 41 F
Snarford 52 D
Snargate 14 E
Snave 15 F
Sneachill 29 J
Snead 38 C
Sneaton 63 K
Sneatonthorpe 63 J
Snelland 52 D
Snellings 60 A
Snelston 40 D
Snetterton 44 A
Snettisham 44 A
Snibston 41 G
Snishival 84 C
Snitter 71 F
Snitterby 52 C
Snitterfield 30 D
Snitton 28 E
Snodhill 28 C
Snodland 24 D
Snowshill 30 B
Soar Carmar. 17 K
Soar Devon 5 H
Soberton 11 H
Soberton Heath 11 H
Sockburn 62 E
Sodylt Bank 38 C
Soham 33 J
Solas 92 D
Soldon Cross 6 B
Soldridge 11
Sole Street Kent 15 F
Sole Street Kent 24 C
Solihull 30 C
Solihull Lodge 30 B
Sollers Dilwyn 28 D
Sollers Hope 29 F
Sollom 48 D
Solsgirth 75 H
Solva 16 A
Solwaybank 69 H
Somerby 42 A
Somercotes 51 G
Somerford Keynes 20 D
Somerley 12 B
Somerleyton 45 J
Somersal Herbert 40 D
Somersby 53 G
Somersham Cambs. 33 G
Somersham Suff. 34 E
Somerton Oxon. 31 F
Somerton Som. 8 D
Somerton Suff. 34 C
Sompting 12 E
Sonning 22 A
Sonning Common 22 A
Sonning Eye 22 A
Sopley 10 C
Sopworth 20 B
Sorbie 64 E
Sordale 105 G
Sorisdale 78 D
Sorn 67 K
Sornhill 74 D
Soroba 79 K
Sortat 105 H
Sotby 52 E
Sots Hole 52 E
Sotterly 45 J
Soudley 39 G
Soughton 48 B
Soulbury 32 B
Soulby 61 J
Souldern 31 G
Souldrop 32 C
Sound Ches. 39 F
Sound Shet. 109 D8
Sound Shet. 109 C
Soundwell 19 K
Sourhope 70 D
Sourin 106 D
Sourton 6 D
Soutergate 55 F
South Acre 44 C
South Allington 5 H
South Alloa 75 G
South Ambersham 12 C
South Anston 51 H
South Ascot 22 C
South Ballachulish 80 B
South Balloch 67 H
South Bank 63 G
South Barrow 9 F
South Beddington 23 F
South Bellsdyke 75 H
South Benfleet 24 D
South Bersted 12 C
South Blackbog 91 F
South Bowood 8 D
South Brent 5 G
South Brentor 6 C
South Brewham 9 G
South Broomhill 71 H
South Burlingham 45 H
South Cadbury 9 F
South Carlton 52 C
South Cave 59 F
South Cerney 20 D
South Chard 8 C
South Cheriton 9 F
South Cliffe 58 E
South Clifton 52 B
South Cockerington 53 G
South Common 13 G

outh Cornelly 18 B4
outh Corrygills 73 J7
outh Cove 45 J7
outh Creagan 80 A3
outh Creake 44 C2
outh Croxton 41 J4
outh Dalton 59 F5
outh Darenth 23 J5
outh Duffield 58 C6
outh Elkington 53 F4
outh Elmsall 51 G1
outh End Bucks. 32 B6
outh End Cumb. 55 F3
outh End
  N.Lincs. 52 E1
outh Erradale 94 D4
outh Fambridge 24 E2
outh Fawley 21 G3
outh Ferriby 59 F7
outh Flobbets 91 F1
outh Garth 108 E3
outh Godstone 23 G7
outh Gorley 10 C3
outh Green
  Essex 24 C2
outh Green
  Norf. 44 E4
outh Hall 73 J3
outh
  Hanningfield 24 D2
outh Harting 11 J3
outh Hayling 11 J5
outh Hazelrigg 77 J7
outh Heath 22 C1
outh Heighton 13 H6
outh Hetton 62 E2
outh Hiendley 51 F1
outh Hill 4 D3
outh Hinksey 21 J1
outh Hole 6 A4
outh Holmwood 22 E7
outh Hornchurch 23 J3
outh Hourat 74 A5
outh Huish 5 G6
outh Hykeham 52 C6
outh Hylton 62 E1
outh Kelsey 52 D3
outh Kessock 96 D7
outh
  Killingholme 52 E1
outh Kilvington 5 K1
outh Kilworth 41 J7
outh Kirkby 51 G1
outh Kirkton 91 F1
outh Kyme 42 E1
outh Lancing 12 E6
outh Ledaig 80 A4
outh Leigh 21 G1
outh Leverton 51 K4
outh Littleton 30 B4
outh Lopham 44 E7
outh Luffenham 42 C5
outh Malling 13 H5
outh Marston 20 E3
outh Milford 57 K6
outh Milton 5 H6
outh Mimms 23 F1
outh Molton 7 F3
outh Moor 62 C1
outh Moreton 21 J3
outh Mundham 12 B6
outh Muskham 51 K7
outh Newbald 59 F6
outh Newington 11 F5
outh Newton 10 B1
outh Normanton 51 G7
outh Norwood 23 G5
outh Nutfield 23 G7
outh Ockendon 23 J3
outh Ormsby 53 G5
outh Otterington 57 J1
outh Oxhey 22 E2
outh Park 23 F7
outh Perrott 8 D4
outh Petherton 8 D3
outh Petherwin 6 B7
outh Pickenham 44 C5
outh Pool 5 H6
outh Queensferry 75 K3
outh Radworthy 7 F2
outh Rauceby 42 D1
outh Raynham 44 C3
outh Redbriggs 99 F6
outh Reston 53 H4
outh Runcton 44 A5
outh Scarle 52 B6
outh Shian 80 A3
outh Shields 71 J7
outh Somercotes 53 H3
outh Stainley 57 J3
outh Stoke
  Oxon. 21 K3
outh Stoke
  W.Suss. 12 D6
outh Street
  E.Suss. 13 G5
outh Street Kent 24 C5
outh Tawton 6 E6
outh Thoresby 53 H5
outh Tidworth 21 F7
outh Town 11 H1
outh Upper
  Barrack 99 H6
outh Walsham 45 H4
outh Warnborough 22 A7
outh Weald 23 J2
outh Weston 22 A2
outh Wheatley
  Cornw. 4 C1
outh Wheatley
  Notts. 51 K4
outh Whiteness 109 C8
outh Widcombe 19 J6
outh Wigston 41 H6
outh
  Willesborough 15 F3
outh Willingham 52 E4
outh Wingate 63 F3
outh Wingfield 51 F7
outh Witham 45 F2
outh Wonston 11 F1
outh Woodham
  Ferrers 24 E2
outh Wootton 44 A3
outh Wraxall 20 B5
outh Yardley 40 D7
outhall
outham Glos. 29 J6
outham Warks. 31 F2
outhampton 11 F3
outhampton
  Airport 11 F3
outhbar 74 C4
outhborough 23 J7
outhbourne
  Bourne. 10 C5
outhbourne
  W.Suss. 11 J4

Southburgh 44 E5
Southburn 59 F4
Southchurch 25 F3
Southcott 6 D6
Southdean 70 B3
Southease 13 H6
Southend Aber. 99 F6
Southend
  Arg. & B. 66 A3
Southend
  W.Berks. 21 K4
Southend Airport 24 E3
Southend-on-Sea 24 E3
Southerndown 18 B4
Southerness 65 K5
Southfleet 23 J5
Southgate Gt.Lon. 23 F2
Southgate Norf. 45 F3
Southgate Norf. 44 A2
Southgate Swan. 17 J2
Southill 32 E4
Southington 21 J7
Southleigh 8 B5
Southminster 25 F2
Southmuir 82 E2
Southoe 32 E2
Southolt 35 F2
Southorpe 42 D5
Southowram 57 G7
Southport 48 C1
Southrepps 45 G2
Southrey 52 E6
Southrop 20 E1
Southrope 21 K7
Southsea Ports. 11 H5
Southsea Wrex. 48 B7
Southstoke 20 A5
Southtown Norf. 45 K5
Southtown Ork. 107 D8
Southwaite Cumb. 61 J6
Southwaite Cumb. 61 F2
Southwark 23 J4
Southwater 12 E4
Southway 19 J7
Southwell Dorset 9 F7
Southwell Notts. 51 K7
Southwick
  Northants. 42 D6
Southwick T. & W. 62 E1
Southwick W.Suss. 13 F6
Southwick Wilts. 20 B6
Southwold 35 K1
Southwood N.Yorks. 45 H5
Southwood Som. 8 E1
Sowerby N.Yorks. 57 K1
Sowerby W.Yorks. 57 F7
Sowerby Bridge 57 F7
Sowerby Row 60 E2
Sowton 7 H6
Soyal 96 C2
Spa Common 45 G2
Spadeadam 70 A6
Spalding 43 F3
Spaldington 58 D6
Spaldwick 32 E1
Spalefield 83 G7
Spalford 52 B6
Spanby 42 D2
Sparham 44 E4
Spark Bridge 55 G1
Sparkford 9 F2
Sparkwell 5 F5
Sparrowpit 50 C4
Sparrow's Green 13 K3
Sparsholt Hants. 11 F1
Sparsholt Oxon. 21 G3
Spartylea 61 K2
Spaunton 63 J7
Spaxton 8 B1
Spean Bridge 87 J6
Speddoch 68 D5
Speen Bucks. 22 B1
Speen W.Berks. 21 H5
Speeton 59 H2
Speke 48 D4
Speldhurst 23 J7
Spellbrook 33 H7
Spelsbury 30 E6
Spen Green 49 H6
Spencers Wood 22 A5
Spennithorne 57 G1
Spennymoor 62 D3
Spetchley 29 H3
Spetisbury 9 J4
Spexhall 45 H7
Spey Bay 98 B4
Speybridge 89 H2
Speyview 97 K3
Spilsby 53 H6
Spindlestone 77 K7
Spinkhill 51 G5
Spinningdale 96 D2
Spirthill 20 C4
Spital High. 105 G3
Spital W. & M. 22 C4
Spital in the
  Street 52 C3
Spitalbrook 23 G1
Spithurst 13 H5
Spittal D. & G. 64 E4
Spittal D. & G. 64 D5
Spittal E.Loth. 76 C3
Spittal Northumb. 77 J5
Spittal Pembs. 16 C3
Spittal of
  Glenmuick 90 B6
Spittal of
  Glenshee 82 C1
Spittalfield 82 C3
Spixworth 45 G4
Spofforth 57 J4
Spondon 41 G2
Spooner Row 44 E6
Spooley 39 F2
Sporle 44 C4
Sportsman's Arms 47 G7
Spott 76 E3
Spratton 31 J2
Spreakley 22 B7
Spreyton 6 E6
Spridlington 52 D4
Springburn 74 E4
Springfield
  Arg. & B. 73 J3
Springfield D. & G. 69 J7
Springfield Moray 97 H6
Springfield P. & K. 82 E6
Springfield W.Mid. 40 C7
Springholm 65 J4
Springkell 69 H6
Springleys 91 F1
Springside 74 B7
Springthorpe 52 B4
Springwell 62 D1
Sproatley 59 H6
Sproston Green 49 G6

Sprotbrough 51 H2
Sproughton 35 F4
Sprouston 77 F7
Sprowston 45 G4
Sproxton Leics. 42 B3
Sproxton N.Yorks. 58 C1
Spurstow 48 E7
Square Point 65 H3
Squires Gate 55 G6
Sròndoire 73 G3
Sronphadruig
  Lodge 88 E7
Stableford 40 A2
Stackhouse 56 D3
Stackpole 16 C6
Stacksteads 56 D7
Staddiscombe 5 F5
Staddlethorpe 58 E7
Stadhampton 21 K2
Stadhlaigearraidh 84 C1
Staffield 61 G2
Staffin 93 K5
Stafford 40 B3
Stagden Cross 33 K7
Stagsden 32 C4
Stagshaw Bank 70 E7
Stain 105 J2
Stainburn 57 H5
Staincross 51 F2
Staindrop 62 C4
Staines 22 D4
Stainfield Lincs. 42 D3
Stainfield Lincs. 52 E5
Stainforth
  N.Yorks. 56 D3
Stainforth
  S.Yorks. 51 J1
Staining 55 G6
Stainland 50 C1
Stainsacre 63 J2
Stainton Cumb. 55 J1
Stainton Cumb. 61 F4
Stainton Dur. 62 B5
Stainton Middbro. 63 F5
Stainton N.Yorks. 62 B7
Stainton S.Yorks. 51 H3
Stainton by
  Langworth 52 D5
Stainton le Vale 52 E3
Stainton with
  Adgarley 55 F2
Staintondale 63 J3
Stair Cumb. 60 D4
Stair E.Ayr. 67 J1
Staithes 63 J5
Stake Pool 55 H5
Stakeford 71 H5
Stalbridge 9 G3
Stalbridge Weston 9 G3
Stalham 45 H3
Stalham Green 45 H3
Stalisfield Green 14 E2
Stalling Busk 56 E1
Stallingborough 53 F1
Stalmine 55 G5
Stalybridge 49 J3
Stambourne 34 B5
Stamford Lincs. 42 D5
Stamford
  Northumb. 71 H2
Stamford Bridge 58 D4
Stamfordham 71 F6
Stanborough 33 F7
Stanbridge Beds. 32 C6
Stanbridge Dorset 10 B4
Stanbridge Earls 10 E2
Stanbury 57 F6
Stand 75 F4
Standburn 75 H3
Standeford 40 B5
Standen 21 G1
Standford 12 B3
Standingstone 60 B5
Standish 48 E1
Standlake 21 G1
Standon Hants. 11 F2
Standon Herts. 33 G6
Standon Staffs. 40 A2
Stane 75 G5
Stanfield 44 D3
Stanford Beds. 32 E4
Stanford Kent 15 G4
Stanford Bishop 29 F3
Stanford Bridge 29 G2
Stanford Dingley 21 J4
Stanford in the Vale 21 G2
Stanford on Avon 31 G1
Stanford on Soar 41 H3
Stanford on Teme 29 G2
Stanford Rivers 23 J1
Stanford-le-Hope 24 C3
Stanghow 63 H5
Stanground 43 F6
Stanhoe 44 C2
Stanhope Dur. 62 A3
Stanhope Sc.Bord. 69 G1
Stanion 42 C7
Stanley Derbys. 41 G1
Stanley Dur. 62 C1
Stanley P. & K. 82 C4
Stanley Staffs. 49 J7
Stanley W.Yorks. 57 J7
Stanley Wilts. 20 C4
Stanley Common 41 G1
Stanlow 48 D5
Stanmer 13 G6
Stanmore Gt.Lon. 22 E2
Stanmore
  W.Berks. 21 H4
Stannersburn 70 C5
Stanningfield 34 C3
Stannington
  Northumb. 71 H6
Stannington
  S.Yorks. 51 F4
Stansbatch 28 C2
Stansfield 34 B3
Stanstead 34 C4
Stanstead Abbotts 33 G7
Stansted 24 C5
Stansted Airport 33 J6
Stansted
  Mountfitchet 33 J6
Stanton Derbys. 40 E4
Stanton Glos. 30 B5
Stanton
  Northumb. 71 G4
Stanton Staffs. 40 D1
Stanton Suff. 34 D1
Stanton by Bridge 41 F3
Stanton by Dale 41 G2
Stanton Drew 19 J5
Stanton Fitzwarren 20 E2
Stanton Harcourt 21 H1
Stanton Hill 51 G6
Stanton in Peak 50 E6
Stanton Lacy 28 D1
Stanton Prior 19 K5

Stanton
  St. Bernard 20 D5
Stanton St. John 21 J1
Stanton St. Quintin 20 C4
Stanton Street 34 D2
Stanton under
  Bardon 41 G4
Stanton upon Hine
  Heath 38 E3
Stanton Wick 19 K5
Stanton-on-the-
  Wolds 41 J2
Stanwardine in the
  Fields 38 D3
Stanway Essex 34 D6
Stanway Glos. 30 B5
Stanwell 22 D4
Stanwell Moor 22 D4
Stanwick 32 C1
Stanydale 109 B7
Staoinebrig 84 C1
Stape 63 J7
Stapehill 10 B4
Stapeley 39 F1
Staple 15 H2
Staple Fitzpaine 8 B3
Staplecross 14 C5
Staplefield 13 F4
Stapleford Cambs. 33 H3
Stapleford Herts. 33 G7
Stapleford Leics. 42 B4
Stapleford Lincs. 52 B7
Stapleford Notts. 41 G2
Stapleford Wilts. 10 B1
Stapleford Abbotts 23 H2
Stapleford Tawney 23 J2
Staplegrove 8 B2
Staplehurst 14 C3
Staplers 11 G6
Stapleton Bristol 19 J4
Stapleton Cumb. 70 A6
Stapleton Here. 28 C2
Stapleton Leics. 41 G6
Stapleton N.Yorks. 62 D5
Stapleton Shrop. 38 D5
Stapleton Som. 8 D2
Stapley 7 K4
Staploe 32 E2
Staplow 29 F2
Star Fife 82 E7
Star Pembs. 17 F2
Star Som. 19 H6
Starbotton 56 E2
Starcross 7 H7
Starkigarth 109 D10
Starling's Green 33 H5
Starr 67 J4
Starston 45 G7
Startforth 62 B5
Startley 20 C3
Statham 49 F4
Stathe 8 C2
Stathern 42 A2
Station Town 62 E3
Staughton Green 32 E2
Staughton Highway 32 E2
Staunton Glos. 28 E7
Staunton Glos. 29 G6
Staunton Harold
  Hall 41 F3
Staunton on Arrow 28 C2
Staunton on Wye 28 C4
Staveley Cumb. 61 F7
Staveley Derbys. 51 G5
Staveley N.Yorks. 57 J3
Staveley-in-
  Cartmel 55 G1
Staverton Devon 5 H4
Staverton Glos. 29 H6
Staverton
  Northants. 31 G2
Staverton Wilts. 20 B5
Staverton Bridge 29 H6
Stawell 8 C1
Stawley 7 J3
Staxigoe 105 J3
Staxton 59 G2
Staylittle 37 H6
Staynall 55 G5
Staythorpe 51 K7
Stean 57 F2
Steane 31 G5
Stearsby 58 C2
Steart 19 F7
Stebbing 33 K6
Stebbing Green 33 K6
Stedham 12 B4
Steel Cross 13 J3
Steele Road 70 A4
Steen's Bridge 28 E3
Steep 11 J2
Steep Marsh 11 J2
Steeple Dorset 9 J6
Steeple Essex 25 F1
Steeple Ashton 20 C6
Steeple Aston 31 F6
Steeple Barton 31 F6
Steeple Bumpstead 33 K4
Steeple Claydon 31 H6
Steeple Gidding 42 E7
Steeple Langford 10 B1
Steeple Morden 33 F4
Steeton 57 F5
Stein 93 H6
Steinmanhill 99 F6
Stella 71 G7
Stelling Minnis 15 G3
Stembridge 8 D2
Stemster High. 105 G2
Stemster High. 105 H2
Stemster House 105 G2
Stenalees 4 A5
Stenhousemuir 75 G2
Stenigot 53 F4
Stenness 108 B5
Stenscholl 93 K5
Stenton E.Loth. 76 E3
Stenton P. & K. 82 B3
Steornabhagh
  (Stornoway) 101 G4
Stepaside 16 E5
Stepney 23 G3
Steppingley 32 D5
Stepps 74 E4
Sternfield 35 H2
Sterridge 6 D1
Stert 20 D6
Stetchworth 33 K3
Stevenage 33 F6
Stevenston 74 A6
Steventon Hants. 21 J7
Steventon Oxon. 21 H2
Stevington 32 C3
Stewartby 32 D4
Stewarton D. & G. 64 D6
Stewarton E.Ayr. 74 C6
Stewkley 32 B6
Stewton 53 G4
Steynton 16 C5
Steyning 12 E5

Steynton 16 C5
Stibb 6 A4
Stibb Cross 6 C4
Stibb Green 21 F5
Stibbard 44 D3
Stibbington 42 D6
Stichill 77 F7
Sticker 3 G3
Stickford 53 G6
Sticklepath 6 E6
Stickney 53 G7
Stiffkey 44 D1
Stifford's Bridge 29 G4
Stillingfleet 58 B5
Stillington
  N.Yorks. 58 B3
Stillington Stock. 62 E4
Stilton 42 E7
Stinchcombe 20 A2
Stinsford 9 G5
Stirchley Tel. & W. 39 G5
Stirchley W.Mid. 40 C7
Stirkoke House 105 J3
Stirling Aber. 99 K6
Stirling Stir. 75 F1
Stirton 56 E4
Stisted 34 B6
Stithians 2 E5
Stittenham 96 D4
Stivichall 30 E1
Stix 81 J3
Stixwould 52 E6
Stoak 48 D5
Stobo 75 K7
Stoborough 9 J6
Stoborough Green 9 J6
Stobwood 75 H5
Stock 24 C2
Stock Green 29 J3
Stock Lane 21 F4
Stock Wood 30 B3
Stockbridge Hants. 10 E1
Stockbridge Stir. 81 J7
Stockbury 24 E5
Stockcross 21 H5
Stockdalewath 60 E2
Stockerston 42 B6
Stocking Pelham 33 H6
Stockingford 41 F6
Stockland 8 B4
Stockland Bristol 19 F7
Stockleigh English 7 G5
Stockleigh Pomeroy 7 G5
Stockley 20 C5
Stocklinch 8 C3
Stockport 49 H4
Stocksbridge 50 E3
Stocksfield 71 F7
Stockton Here. 28 E2
Stockton Norf. 45 H6
Stockton Shrop. 39 G6
Stockton Warks. 31 F2
Stockton Wilts. 9 J1
Stockton Heath 49 F4
Stockton on Teme 29 G2
Stockton on the
  Forest 58 C4
Stockton-on-Tees 63 F4
Stockwood 8 E4
Stodday 55 H4
Stodmarsh 25 J5
Stody 44 E2
Stoer 102 C6
Stoford Som. 8 E3
Stoford Wilts. 10 B1
Stogumber 7 J2
Stogursey 19 F7
Stoke Devon 6 A3
Stoke Hants. 11 H4
Stoke Hants. 21 H6
Stoke Med. 24 E4
Stoke W.Mid. 30 E1
Stoke Abbott 8 D4
Stoke Albany 42 B7
Stoke Ash 35 F1
Stoke Bardolph 41 J1
Stoke Bliss 29 F2
Stoke by Clare 34 B4
Stoke Canon 7 H6
Stoke Charity 11 F1
Stoke Climsland 4 D3
Stoke D'Abernon 22 E6
Stoke Doyle 42 D7
Stoke Dry 42 B6
Stoke Ferry 44 A6
Stoke Fleming 5 J6
Stoke Gabriel 5 J5
Stoke Gifford 19 K4
Stoke Golding 41 F6
Stoke Goldington 32 B4
Stoke Hammond 32 B6
Stoke Heath 39 F3
Stoke Holy Cross 45 G5
Stoke Lacy 29 F3
Stoke Lyne 31 G6
Stoke Mandeville 22 B1
Stoke Newington 23 G3
Stoke on Tern 39 F3
Stoke Orchard 29 J6
Stoke Poges 22 C3
Stoke Prior Here. 28 E3
Stoke Prior Worcs. 29 J2
Stoke Rivers 6 E2
Stoke Rochford 42 C3
Stoke Row 21 K3
Stoke St. Gregory 8 C2
Stoke St. Mary 8 B2
Stoke St. Michael 19 K7
Stoke
  St. Milborough 38 E7
Stoke sub Hamdon 8 D3
Stoke Talmage 21 K2
Stoke Trister 9 G2
Stoke Wake 9 G4
Stoke-by-Nayland 34 D5
Stokeford 9 H6
Stokeham 51 K5
Stokeinteignhead 5 K3
Stokenchurch 22 A2
Stokenham 5 J6
Stoke-on-Trent 40 A1
Stokesay 38 D7
Stokesby 45 J4
Stokesley 63 G6
Stolford 19 F7
Ston Easton 19 K6
Stonar Cut 25 K5
Stondon Massey 23 J1
Stone Bucks. 31 J7
Stone Glos. 19 K2
Stone Kent 14 E5
Stone Kent 23 J4
Stone Staffs. 40 A2
Stone Worcs. 29 H1
Stone Allerton 19 G6
Stone Cross
  E.Suss. 13 K6
Stone Cross Kent 15 F4

Stone Cross Kent 13 J3
Stone House 56 C1
Stone Street Kent 23 J6
Stone Street Suff. 45 H7
Stonebridge
  E.Suss. 13 J4
Stonebridge
  Warks. 40 E7
Stonebroom 51 G7
Stoneferry 59 H6
Stonefield
  Arg. & B. 73 G3
Stonefield S.Lan. 74 E5
Stonegate 13 K4
Stonegrave 58 C2
Stonehaugh 70 C6
Stonehaven 91 G6
Stonehouse
  D. & G. 65 J2
Stonehouse Glos. 20 B1
Stonehouse
  Northumb. 61 H1
Stonehouse Plym. 4 E5
Stonehouse S.Lan. 75 F6
Stoneleigh 30 E1
Stonely 32 E2
Stoner Hill 11 J2
Stones Green 35 F6
Stonesby 42 B3
Stonesfield 30 E7
Stonestreet Green 15 F4
Stonethwaite 60 D5
Stoney Cross 10 D3
Stoney Middleton 50 E5
Stoney Stanton 41 G6
Stoney Stoke 9 G1
Stoney Stratton 9 F1
Stoney Stretton 38 C5
Stoneyburn 75 H4
Stoneygate 41 J5
Stoneyhills 25 F2
Stoneykirk 64 A5
Stoneywood 91 G3
Stonganess 108 E2
Stonham Aspal 35 F3
Stonnall 40 C5
Stonor 22 A3
Stonton Wyville 42 A6
Stony Houghton 51 G6
Stony Stratford 31 J4
Stonybreck 108 A11
Stoodleigh 7 H4
Stopham 12 D5
Stopsley 32 E6
Stoptide 3 G1
Storeton 48 C4
Stornoway
  (Steornabhagh) 101 G4
Stornoway Airport 101 G4
Storridge 29 G4
Storrington 12 D5
Storth 55 H1
Storwood 58 D5
Stotfield 97 K4
Stotfold 33 F5
Stottesdon 39 F7
Stoughton Leics. 41 J5
Stoughton Surr. 22 C6
Stoughton
  W.Suss. 12 B5
Stoul 86 D5
Stoulton 29 J3
Stour Provost 9 G2
Stour Row 9 H2
Stourbridge 40 A7
Stourpaine 9 H4
Stourport-on-
  Severn 29 H1
Stourton Staffs. 40 A7
Stourton Warks. 30 D5
Stourton Wilts. 9 G1
Stourton Caundle 9 G3
Stove 106 F4
Stoven 45 J7
Stow Lincs. 52 B4
Stow Sc.Bord. 76 C6
Stow Bardolph 44 A5
Stow Bedon 44 D6
Stow cum Quy 33 J2
Stow Longa 32 E1
Stow Maries 24 E2
Stowbridge 44 A5
Stowe Glos. 19 J1
Stowe Shrop. 28 C1
Stowe Staffs. 40 C3
Stowell Glos. 30 B7
Stowell Som. 9 F2
Stowey 19 J6
Stowford 6 C7
Stowlangtoft 34 D2
Stowmarket 34 E3
Stow-on-the-Wold 30 C6
Stowting 15 G3
Stowupland 34 E3
Stracathro 83 H1
Strachan 90 E5
Strachur 80 B7
Stradbroke 35 G1
Stradishall 34 B3
Stradsett 44 A5
Stragglethorpe 52 C7
Straiton Edin. 76 A4
Straiton S.Ayr. 67 H3
Straloch Aber. 91 G2
Straloch P. & K. 82 B1
Stramshall 40 C2
Strang 54 C6
Stranraer 64 A4
Strata Florida 27 G2
Stratfield Mortimer 21 K5
Stratfield Saye 21 K5
Stratfield Turgis 21 K6
Stratford 23 H3
Stratford
  St. Andrew 35 H3
Stratford St. Mary 34 E5
Stratford sub Castle 10 C1
Stratford Tony 10 B2
Stratford-upon-
  Avon 30 C3
Strath 105 H3
Strathan High. 102 C5
Strathan High. 87 F5
Strathaven 75 F6
Strathblane 74 D3
Strathcarron 95 F7
Strathdon 90 B3
Strathgirnock 90 B5
Strathkanaird 95 H1
Strathkinness 83 F6
Strathmiglo 82 D7
Strathpeffer 96 B6
Strathrannoch 95 K4
Strathtay 82 A2
Strathwhillan 73 J7
Strathy 104 D2
Strathyre 81 G6

Stratton Glos. 20 D1
Stratton Audley 31 H6
Stratton
  St. Margaret 20 E3
Stratton
  St. Michael 45 G6
Stratton Strawless 45 G3
Stratton-on-the-
  Fosse 19 K6
Stravanan 73 J5
Stravithie 83 G6
Streat 13 G5
Streatham 23 F4
Streatley Beds. 32 D6
Streatley W.Berks. 21 J3
Street Lancs. 55 J4
Street N.Yorks. 63 H6
Street Som. 8 D1
Street Dinas 38 C2
Street End Kent 15 G2
Street End
  W.Suss. 12 B7
Street on the Fosse 9 F1
Streethay 40 D4
Streetlam 62 E1
Streetly 40 C6
Strefford 38 D7
Strensall 58 C3
Strensham 29 J4
Stretcholt 19 F7
Strete 5 J6
Stretford 49 G3
Stretford Court 28 D3
Strethall 33 H5
Stretham 33 J1
Strettington 12 B6
Stretton Ches. 48 E7
Stretton Derbys. 51 F6
Stretton Rut. 42 C4
Stretton Staffs. 40 A4
Stretton Staffs. 40 E3
Stretton Warr. 49 F4
Stretton en le Field 41 F4
Stretton Grandison 29 F4
Stretton Heath 38 C4
Stretton Sugwas 28 D4
Stretton under
  Fosse 41 G7
Stretton Westwood 38 E6
Stretton-on-
  Dunsmore 31 F1
Stretton-on-Fosse 30 D5
Stribers 55 G1
Strichen 99 H5
Stringston 7 K1
Strixton 32 C2
Stroat 19 J2
Stromeferry 86 E1
Stromemore 86 E1
Stromness 107 B7
Stronachlachar 81 F6
Stronaba 87 J6
Stronlonag 73 K2
Stronmilchan 80 C5
Strontian 79 K1
Strontoiller 80 A5
Stronvar 81 G6
Strood 24 D5
Strood Green 68 D5
Stroquhan 68 D5
Stroud Glos. 20 B1
Stroud Hants. 11 J2
Stroud Common 22 D7
Stroud Green 23 F2
Stroul 74 A2
Stroxton 42 C2
Struan High. 85 J1
Struan P & K. 81 K1
Strubby 53 H4
Strumpshaw 45 H5
Struthers 82 E7
Struy 96 B7
Stryt-issa 38 B1
Stryt-yr-hwch 38 C1
Stuartfield 99 H6
Stub Place 60 B1
Stubbings 22 B3
Stubbins 49 G1
Stubhampton 9 J3
Stubley 51 F5
Stubton 42 B1
Stuck Arg. & B. 73 J4
Stuck Arg. & B. 73 K1
Stuckbeg 73 K1
Stuckgowan 80 E7
Stuckindroin 80 E6
Stuckreoch 73 J1
Stuckton 10 C3
Stud Green 22 B4
Studdon 61 K1
Studfold 56 D2
Studham 32 D7
Studholme 60 D1
Studland 10 B6
Studley Warks. 30 B2
Studley Wilts. 20 C4
Studley Common 30 B2
Studley Roger 57 H2
Stuggadhoo 54 C6
Stump Cross 33 J4
Stuntney 33 J1
Stunts Green 13 K5
Sturbridge 40 A2
Sturmer 34 B4
Sturminster
  Common 9 G3
Sturminster
  Marshall 9 J4
Sturminster
  Newton 9 G3
Sturry 25 H5
Sturton by Stow 52 B4
Sturton le Steeple 51 K4
Stuston 35 F1
Stutton N.Yorks. 57 K5
Stutton Suff. 35 F5
Styal 49 H4
Styrrup 51 J3
Suainebost 101 H1
Suardail 101 G4
Succoth Aber. 90 C1
Succoth Arg. & B. 80 D7
Succothmore 80 C7
Suckley 29 G3
Sudborough 42 C7
Sudbourne 35 J3
Sudbrook Lincs. 42 C1
Sudbrook Mon. 19 J3
Sudbrooke 52 D5
Sudbury Derbys. 40 D2
Sudbury Gt.Lon. 22 E3

Sudbury Suff. 34 C4
Sudgrove 20 C1
Suffield N.Yorks. 63 J3
Suffield Norf. 45 G2
Sugarloaf 14 E4
Sugnall 39 G2
Suie Lodge Hotel 81 F5
Sulby 54 C4
Sulgrave 31 G4
Sulham 21 K4
Sulhamstead 21 K5
Sullington 12 D5
Sullom 108 C5
Sullom Voe Oil Terminal 108 C5
Sully 18 E5
Sumburgh 109 G10
Sumburgh Airport 109 F9
Summer Bridge 57 H3
Summercourt 3 F3
Summerfield 44 B2
Summerhill 48 C7
Summerhouse 62 D5
Summerleaze 19 H3
Summerseat 49 G1
Summertown 21 J1
Summit 49 J1
Sunadale 73 G6
Sunbury 22 E5
Sundaywell 68 D5
Sunderland Cumb. 60 C3
Sunderland T. & W. 62 E1
Sunderland Bridge 62 D3
Sundhope 69 J1
Sundon Park 32 D6
Sundridge 23 H6
Sunhill 20 E1
Sunipol 78 E2
Sunk Island 53 F1
Sunningdale 22 C5
Sunninghill 22 C5
Sunningwell 21 H2
Sunniside Dur. 62 D1
Sunniside T. & W. 62 D1
Sunny Bank 60 D7
Sunnylaw 75 F1
Sunnymead 21 J1
Sunnyside Aber. 91 G5
Sunnyside Northumb. 70 E7
Sunnyside W.Suss. 13 G3
Sunwick 77 G5
Surbiton 22 E5
Surfleet 43 F3
Surfleet Seas End 43 F3
Surlingham 45 H5
Sustead 45 F2
Susworth 52 B2
Sutcombe 6 B4
Suton 44 E6
Sutors of Cromarty 97 F5
Sutterton 43 F2
Sutton Beds. 33 F4
Sutton Cambs. 33 H1
Sutton Gt.Lon. 23 F5
Sutton Kent 15 J3
Sutton Lincs. 52 B7
Sutton Norf. 45 H3
Sutton Notts. 42 A2
Sutton Notts. 51 J4
Sutton Oxon. 21 H1
Sutton Pembs. 16 C4
Sutton Peter. 42 E6
Sutton S.Yorks. 51 H1
Sutton Shrop. 39 G7
Sutton Shrop. 39 F2
Sutton Shrop. 38 E4
Sutton Staffs. 39 G3
Sutton Suff. 35 H4
Sutton W.Suss. 12 C5
Sutton Abinger 22 E7
Sutton at Hone 23 J4
Sutton Bassett 42 A7
Sutton Benger 20 C4
Sutton Bonington 41 H3
Sutton Bridge 43 H3
Sutton Cheney 41 G5
Sutton Coldfield 40 D6
Sutton Courtenay 21 H2
Sutton Crosses 43 H3
Sutton Grange 57 H2
Sutton Green 22 D6
Sutton Holms 10 B3
Sutton Howgrave 57 J2
Sutton in Ashfield 51 G7
Sutton in the Elms 41 H6
Sutton Lane Ends 49 J5
Sutton le Marsh 53 J4
Sutton Leach 48 E3
Sutton Maddock 39 G5
Sutton Mallet 8 C1
Sutton Mandeville 9 J2
Sutton Montis 9 F2
Sutton on Sea 53 J4
Sutton on the Hill 40 E2
Sutton on Trent 51 K6
Sutton Poyntz 9 G6
Sutton St. Edmund 43 G4
Sutton St. James 43 H4
Sutton St. Nicholas 28 E4
Sutton Scarsdale 51 G6
Sutton Scotney 11 F1
Sutton upon Derwent 58 D5
Sutton Valence 14 D3
Sutton Veny 20 B7
Sutton Waldron 9 H3
Sutton Weaver 48 E5
Sutton Wick 21 H2
Sutton-in-Craven 57 F5
Sutton-on-Hull 59 H6
Sutton-on-the-Forest 58 B3
Sutton-under-Braies 30 D5
Sutton-under-Whitestonecliffe 57 K1
Swaby 53 G5
Swadlincote 41 F4
Swaffham 44 C5
Swaffham Bulbeck 33 J2
Swaffham Prior 33 J2
Swafield 45 G2
Swainby 63 F6
Swainshill 28 D4
Swainsthorpe 45 G5
Swainswick 20 A5
Swalcliffe 30 E5
Swalecliffe 25 H5
Swallow 52 E2
Swallow Beck 52 C6
Swallowcliffe 9 J2
Swallowfield 22 A5

Swalwell 71 H7
Swampton 21 H6
Swan Street 34 C6
Swanage 10 B7
Swanbach 39 F1
Swanbourne 32 B6
Swanbridge 18 E5
Swancote 39 G6
Swanland 59 F7
Swanlaws 70 C2
Swanley 23 J5
Swanmore 11 G3
Swannington Leics. 41 G4
Swannington Norf. 45 F4
Swanscombe 24 C4
Swansea (Abertawe) 17 K6
Swanton Abbot 45 G3
Swanton Morley 44 E4
Swanton Novers 44 E2
Swanwick Derbys. 51 G7
Swanwick Hants. 11 G4
Swarby 42 D1
Swardeston 45 F5
Swarkestone 41 F3
Swarland 71 G3
Swaton 42 E2
Swavesey 33 G2
Sway 10 D5
Swayfield 42 C3
Swaythling 11 F3
Swaythorpe 59 G3
Sweetshouse 4 A4
Sweffling 35 H2
Swell 8 C2
Swepstone 41 F4
Swerford 30 E5
Swettenham 49 H6
Swffryd 19 F2
Swiftsden 14 C5
Swilland 35 F3
Swillbrook 55 H6
Swillington 57 J6
Swimbridge 6 E3
Swimbridge Newland 6 E2
Swinbrook 30 D7
Swincliffe 57 H4
Swinderby 52 B6
Swindon Staffs. 40 A6
Swindon Swin. 20 E3
Swindon Village 29 J6
Swine 59 H6
Swinefleet 58 D7
Swineshead Beds. 32 D2
Swineshead Lincs. 43 F1
Swineshead Bridge 43 F1
Swiney 105 H5
Swinford Leics. 31 G1
Swinford Oxon. 21 H1
Swingfield Minnis 15 H3
Swinhoe 71 H1
Swinhope 53 F3
Swining 109 D6
Swinithwaite 57 F1
Swinscoe 40 D1
Swinside Hall 70 C2
Swinstead 42 D3
Swinton Gt.Man. 49 G2
Swinton N.Yorks. 58 D2
Swinton N.Yorks. 57 H1
Swinton S.Yorks. 51 G3
Swinton Sc.Bord. 77 G6
Swintonmill 77 G6
Swithland 41 H4
Swordale 96 C5
Swordland 86 D5
Swordle 79 G1
Swordly 104 C2
Sworton Heath 49 F4
Swydd-ffynnon 27 F2
Swynnerton 40 A2
Swyre 8 E6
Syde 29 J7
Sydenham Gt.Lon. 23 G4
Sydenham Oxon. 22 A1
Sydenham Damerel 4 E3
Syderstone 44 C2
Sydling St. Nicholas 9 F5
Sydmonton 21 H6
Syerston 42 A1
Syke 49 H1
Sykehouse 51 J1
Sykes 56 B4
Sylen 7 K2
Symbister 109 E6
Symington S.Ayr. 74 B7
Symington S.Lan. 75 H7
Symonds Yat 28 E7
Symondsbury 8 D5
Synod Inn 26 D3
Syre 103 J4
Syreford 30 B6
Syresham 31 H4
Syston Leics. 41 J4
Syston Lincs. 42 C1
Sytchampton 29 H2
Sywell 32 B2

T

Taagan 95 G5
Tabost W.Isles 101 F6
Tabost W.Isles 101 H1
Tacher 105 G4
Tackley 31 F7
Tacleit 100 D4
Tacolneston 45 F6
Tadcaster 57 K5
Tadden 9 J4
Taddington 50 D5
Taddiport 6 C4
Tadley 21 K5
Tadlow 33 F4
Tadmarton 30 E5
Tadworth 23 F6
Tafarnaubach 28 A7
Tafarn-y-bwlch 16 D2
Tafarn-y-Gelyn 47 K6
Taff's Well (Ffynnon Taf) 18 E3
Tafolwern 37 H5
Taibach N.P.T. 18 A3
Tai-bach Powys 37 K4
Taicynhaeaf 37 F4
Tain High. 105 H2
Tain High. 96 E3
Tai'n Lôn 46 C7
Tai'r Bull 27 J6
Tairgwaith 27 G7
Tairlaw 67 J3
Takeley 33 J6
Takeley Street 33 J6
Talachddu 27 K5
Talacre 47 K4

Talardd 37 H3
Talaton 7 J6
Talbenny 16 B4
Talbot Green 18 D3
Talerddig 37 J5
Talgarreg 26 D3
Talgarth 28 A5
Taliesin 37 F6
Talisker 85 J1
Talke 49 H7
Talkin 61 G1
Talla Linnfoots 69 G1
Talladale 95 F4
Talladh-a-Bheithe 81 G2
Tallarn Green 38 D1
Tallentire 60 C3
Talley 17 K2
Tallington 42 D5
Talmine 103 H2
Talog 17 G3
Tal-sarn 26 E3
Talsarnau 37 F2
Talskiddy 3 G2
Talwrn I.o.A. 46 C5
Talwrn Wrex. 38 B1
Talybont Cere. 37 F7
Tal-y-bont Conwy 47 F6
Tal-y-bont Gwyn. 36 E3
Tal-y-bont Gwyn. 46 E5
Talybont-on-Usk 28 A6
Tal-y-Cae 46 E6
Tal-y-cafn 47 F5
Tal-y-llyn Gwyn. 37 G5
Talyllyn Powys 28 A6
Talysarn 46 C7
Tal-y-wern 37 H5
Tamavoid 74 D1
Tamerton Foliot 4 E4
Tamworth 40 E5
Tandridge 23 G6
Tanerdy 17 H3
Tanfield 62 C1
Tangiers 16 C4
Tanglandford 91 G1
Tangley 21 G6
Tangmere 12 C6
Tangwick 108 B5
Tangy 66 A1
Tankerness 107 E7
Tankersley 51 F2
Tan-lan 37 F1
Tannach 105 J4
Tannachie 91 F6
Tannachy 96 E1
Tannadice 83 F2
Tannington 35 G2
Tannochside 75 F4
Tansley 51 F7
Tansor 42 D6
Tantobie 62 C1
Tanton 63 G5
Tanworth in Arden 30 C1
Tan-y-fron 47 H6
Tan-y-graig 36 C2
Tangyrisiau 37 F1
Tan-y-groes 17 F1
Tan-y-pistyll 37 K3
Taobh a' Deas Loch Baghasdail 84 C3
Taobh Siar 100 D7
Taobh Tuath (Northton) 92 E3
Tapeley 6 C3
Taplow 22 C3
Taraphocain 80 B3
Tarbat House 96 E4
Tarbert Arg. & B. 73 G4
Tarbert Arg. & B. 72 E5
Tarbert Arg. & B. 72 E2
Tarbert High. 79 H1
Tarbert (An Tairbeart) W.Isles 100 D7
Tarbet Arg. & B. 80 E7
Tarbet High. 86 D5
Tarbet High. 102 D4
Tarbolton 67 J1
Tarbrax 75 J5
Tardebigge 29 J2
Tarfside 90 C6
Tarland 90 C4
Tarleton 55 H7
Tarlscough 48 D1
Tarlton 20 C2
Tarnbrook 55 J4
Tarnock 19 G6
Tarporley 48 E6
Tarr 7 K2
Tarrant Crawford 9 J4
Tarrant Gunville 9 J3
Tarrant Hinton 9 J3
Tarrant Keyneston 9 J4
Tarrant Launceston 9 J4
Tarrant Monkton 9 J4
Tarrant Rawston 9 J4
Tarrant Rushton 9 J4
Tarrel 97 F3
Tarring Neville 13 H6
Tarrington 29 F4
Tarrnacraig 73 H7
Tarsappie 82 C5
Tarskavaig 86 B4
Tarves 91 G1
Tarvie High. 96 B6
Tarvie P. & K. 82 B1
Tarvin 48 D6
Tarvin Sands 48 D6
Tasburgh 45 G6
Tasley 39 F6
Taston 30 E6
Tatenhill 40 E3
Tatham 56 B3
Tathwell 53 G4
Tatsfield 23 H6
Tattenhall 48 D7
Tatterford 44 C3
Tattersett 44 C3
Tattershall 53 F7
Tattershall Bridge 52 E7
Tattershall Thorpe 53 F7
Tattingstone 35 F5
Tatworth 8 C4
Tauchers 98 B5
Taunton 8 B2
Tavelty 91 F3
Tavernspite 16 E4
Tavistock 4 E3
Taw Bridge 6 E5
Taw Green 6 E6
Tawstock 6 D3
Taxal 50 C5
Tayburn 74 D6
Taychreggan 80 B5
Tayinloan 72 E6
Taylors Cross 6 A4
Taynafead 80 B6
Taynish 73 F2
Taynton Glos. 29 G6

Taynton Oxon. 30 D7
Taynuilt 80 B4
Tayock 83 H2
Tayovullin 72 A3
Tayport 83 F5
Tayvallich 73 F2
Tealby 52 E3
Team Valley 71 H7
Teanamachar 92 C5
Teangue 86 C4
Teasses 83 F7
Tebay 61 H6
Tebworth 32 C6
Tedburn St. Mary 7 G6
Teddington Glos. 29 J5
Teddington Gt.Lon. 22 E4
Tedstone Delamere 29 F3
Tedstone Wafre 29 F3
Teeton 31 H1
Teffont Evias 9 J1
Teffont Magna 9 J1
Tegryn 17 F2
Teigh 42 B4
Teigngrace 5 J3
Teignmouth 5 K3
Telford 39 F5
Telham 14 C6
Tellisford 20 A6
Telscombe 13 H6
Telscombe Cliffs 13 H6
Tempar 81 H2
Templand 69 F5
Temple Cornw. 4 B3
Temple Midloth. 76 B5
Temple Bar 26 E3
Temple Cloud 19 K6
Temple Ewell 15 H3
Temple Grafton 30 C3
Temple Guiting 30 B6
Temple Hirst 58 C7
Temple Normanton 51 G6
Temple Sowerby 61 H4
Templecombe 9 G2
Templeton Devon 7 G4
Templeton Pembs. 16 E4
Templeton Bridge 7 G4
Templewood 83 H1
Tempsford 32 E3
Ten Mile Bank 43 J6
Tenbury Wells 28 E2
Tenby (Dinbych-y-Pysgod) 16 E5
Tendring 35 F6
Tenga 79 G3
Tenterden 14 D4
Tepersie Castle 90 D2
Terally 64 B6
Terling 34 B7
Ternhill 39 F2
Terregles 65 K3
Terrington 58 C2
Terrington St. Clement 43 J3
Terrington St. John 43 J4
Tervieside 89 K1
Teston 14 C2
Testwood 10 E3
Tetbury 20 B2
Tetbury Upton 20 B2
Tetchill 38 C2
Tetcott 6 B6
Tetford 53 G5
Tetney 53 G2
Tetney Lock 53 G2
Tetsworth 21 K1
Tettenhall 40 A5
Tettenhall Wood 40 A6
Tetworth 33 F3
Teuchan 91 J1
Teversal 51 G6
Teversham 33 H3
Teviothead 69 K3
Tewel 91 G6
Tewin 33 F7
Tewkesbury 29 H5
Teynham 25 F5
Thainston 90 E7
Thainstone House 91 F3
Thakeham 12 E5
Thame 22 A1
Thames Ditton 22 E5
Thames Haven 24 D3
Thamesmead 23 H3
Thanington 15 G2
Thankerton 75 H7
Tharston 45 F6
Thatcham 21 J5
Thatto Heath 48 E3
Thaxted 33 K5
The Apes Hall 43 J7
The Bage 28 B4
The Balloch 81 K6
The Banking 91 F1
The Bar 12 E4
The Belfry 40 D6
The Birks 91 F4
The Bog 38 C6
The Bourne 22 B7
The Bratch 40 A6
The Bryn 19 G1
The Burf 29 H2
The Burn 90 D7
The Camp 20 C1
The Chequer 38 D1
The City 22 A3
The Common 10 D1
The Craigs 96 B2
The Cronk 54 C4
The Den 74 B5
The Dicker 13 J6
The Drums 82 E1
The Eaves 19 K1
The Flatt 70 A6
The Folly 32 E7
The Grange Shrop. 38 C2
The Grange Surr. 23 G7
The Green Arg. & B. 78 A3
The Green Wilts. 9 H1
The Haven 12 D3
The Headland 63 G3
The Hermitage 23 F6
The Howe 54 B7
The Isle 38 D4
The Knowle 48 C3
The Laurels 45 H6
The Leacon 14 E4
The Lee 22 C1
The Lhen 54 C3
The Lodge 73 K1
The Marsh 38 C6
The Moor E.Suss. 14 C5
The Moor Kent 14 C5
The Mumbles 17 K7

The Mythe 29 H5
The Neuk 91 F5
The Node 33 F7
The Oval 20 A5
The Rhos 16 D4
The Rowe 40 A2
The Sands 22 B7
The Shoe 20 B4
The Smithies 39 F6
The Stocks 14 E5
The Vauld 28 E4
The Wrythe 23 F5
The Wyke 39 G5
Theakston 57 H1
Thealby 52 B1
Theale Som. 19 H7
Theale W.Berks. 21 K4
Thearne 59 G6
Theberton 35 J2
Thedden Grange 11 H1
Theddingworth 41 J7
Theddlethorpe All Saints 53 H4
Theddlethorpe St. Helen 53 H4
Thelbridge Barton 7 F4
Thelnetham 34 E1
Thelveton 45 F7
Thelwall 49 F4
Themelthorpe 44 E3
Thenford 31 G4
Therfield 33 G5
Thetford 44 C7
Theydon Bois 23 H2
Thickwood 20 B4
Thimbleby Lincs. 53 F5
Thimbleby N.Yorks. 63 F7
Thirkleby 57 K2
Thirlby 57 K1
Thirlestane 76 D6
Thirn 57 H1
Thirsk 57 K1
Thistleton Lancs. 55 H6
Thistleton Rut. 42 C4
Thistley Green 33 K1
Thixendale 58 E3
Thockrington 70 E6
Tholomas Drove 43 G5
Tholthorpe 57 K3
Thomas Chapel 16 E5
Thomastown 90 D1
Thompson 44 D6
Thomshill 97 K6
Thong 24 C4
Thoralby 57 F1
Thoresby 51 J5
Thoresway 52 E3
Thorganby Lincs. 53 F3
Thorganby N.Yorks. 58 C5
Thorgill 63 J7
Thorington 35 J1
Thorington Street 34 E5
Thorlby 56 E4
Thorley 33 H7
Thorley Street Herts. 33 H7
Thorley Street I.o.W. 10 E6
Thormanby 57 K2
Thorn Falcon 8 B2
Thornaby-on-Tees 62 E5
Thornage 44 E2
Thornborough Bucks. 31 J5
Thornborough N.Yorks. 57 H1
Thornbury Devon 6 C5
Thornbury Here. 29 F3
Thornbury S.Glos. 19 K3
Thornby 31 H1
Thorncliff 50 C7
Thorncombe 8 C4
Thorncombe Street 22 C7
Thorncote Green 32 E4
Thorndon 35 F2
Thorndon Cross 6 D6
Thorne 51 J1
Thorne St. Margaret 7 J3
Thorner 57 J5
Thornes 40 C5
Thorney Bucks. 22 D4
Thorney Notts. 52 B5
Thorney Peter. 43 F5
Thorney Som. 8 D2
Thorney Hill 10 D4
Thornford 8 E3
Thorngrove 8 C1
Thorngumbald 59 J7
Thornham 44 B1
Thornham Magna 35 F1
Thornham Parva 35 F1
Thornhaugh 42 D5
Thornhill Cardiff 18 E3
Thornhill D. & G. 68 D4
Thornhill Derbys. 50 D4
Thornhill S'ham. 11 F3
Thornhill Stir. 81 H7
Thornhill W.Yorks. 50 E1
Thornholme 59 H3
Thornicombe 9 H4
Thornley Dur. 62 E3
Thornley Dur. 62 D3
Thornliebank 74 D5
Thorns 34 B3
Thornsett 50 C4
Thornthwaite Cumb. 60 D4
Thornthwaite N.Yorks. 57 G4
Thornton Angus 82 E3
Thornton Bucks. 31 J5
Thornton E.Riding 58 D5
Thornton Fife 76 A1
Thornton Lancs. 55 G5
Thornton Leics. 41 G5
Thornton Lincs. 53 F6
Thornton Mersey. 48 C2
Thornton Middbro. 63 F5
Thornton Northumb. 77 H6
Thornton P. & K. 82 C4
Thornton Pembs. 16 C5
Thornton W.Yorks. 57 F6
Thornton Curtis 52 D1
Thornton Hough 48 C4
Thornton le Moor 52 D3
Thornton-le-Moor N.Yorks. 57 H1
Thornton-le-Moors 48 D5
Thornton-le-Street 57 K1
Thornton Park 56 E1
Thornton Rust 56 E1
Thornton Steward 57 G1
Thornton Watlass 57 H1
Thorntonhall 74 D5
Thornton-in-Craven 56 E5
Thornton-le-Beans 62 E7
Thornton-le-Clay 58 C3
Thornton-le-Dale 58 E1
Thornton-le-Moor 57 J1

Thornton-le-Moors 48 D5
Thornton-le-Street 57 K1
Thorntonloch 77 F3
Thornwood Common 23 H1
Thornyhill 90 E7
Thornylee 76 C7
Thoroton 42 A1
Thorp Arch 57 K5
Thorpe Derbys. 50 D7
Thorpe E.Riding 59 G5
Thorpe Lincs. 53 H4
Thorpe N.Yorks. 57 F3
Thorpe Norf. 45 J6
Thorpe Notts. 51 K7
Thorpe Surr. 22 D5
Thorpe Abbotts 35 F1
Thorpe Acre 41 H3
Thorpe Arnold 42 A3
Thorpe Audlin 51 G1
Thorpe Bassett 58 E2
Thorpe Bay 25 F3
Thorpe by Water 42 B6
Thorpe Constantine 40 E5
Thorpe Culvert 53 H6
Thorpe End Garden Village 45 G4
Thorpe Green 34 D3
Thorpe Hall 58 B2
Thorpe Hesley 51 F3
Thorpe in Balne 51 H1
Thorpe in the Fallows 52 C4
Thorpe Langton 42 A6
Thorpe Larches 62 E4
Thorpe le Street 58 E5
Thorpe Malsor 32 B1
Thorpe Mandeville 31 G4
Thorpe Market 45 G2
Thorpe Morieux 34 D3
Thorpe on the Hill Lincs. 52 C6
Thorpe on the Hill W.Yorks. 57 J7
Thorpe St. Andrew 45 G4
Thorpe St. Peter 53 H6
Thorpe Salvin 51 H4
Thorpe Satchville 42 A4
Thorpe Thewles 62 E4
Thorpe Tilney Dales 52 E7
Thorpe Underwood 57 K4
Thorpe Waterville 42 D7
Thorpe Willoughby 58 B6
Thorpe-le-Soken 35 F6
Thorpeness 35 J3
Thorpland 44 A5
Thorrington 34 E5
Thorverton 7 H5
Thrandeston 35 F1
Thrapston 32 C1
Threapland 56 E3
Threapwood 38 D1
Three Bridges 13 F3
Three Burrows 2 E4
Three Chimneys 14 D4
Three Cocks 28 A5
Three Crosses 17 J6
Three Cups Corner 13 K4
Three Holes 43 J5
Three Leg Cross 13 K3
Three Legged Cross 10 B4
Three Mile Cross 22 A5
Threekingham 42 D2
Threemilestone 2 E4
Threlkeld 60 E4
Threshers Bush 23 H1
Threshfield 56 E3
Threxton Hill 44 C5
Thriepley 82 E4
Thrigby 45 J4
Thringarth 62 A4
Thringstone 41 G4
Thrintoft 62 E7
Thriplow 33 H4
Throcking 33 G5
Throckley 71 G7
Throckmorton 29 J3
Throphill 71 G5
Thropton 71 F3
Throwleigh 6 E6
Throwley 14 E2
Throws 33 K6
Thrumpton 41 H2
Thrumster 105 J4
Thrunton 71 F2
Thrupp Glos. 20 B1
Thrupp Oxon. 31 F7
Thrushelton 6 C7
Thrussington 41 J4
Thruxton Hants. 21 F7
Thruxton Here. 28 D5
Thrybergh 51 G3
Thulston 41 G2
Thundergay 73 G6
Thundersley 24 E3
Thunderton 99 J6
Thundridge 33 G7
Thurcaston 41 H4
Thurcroft 51 H4
Thurdistoft 105 H2
Thurgarton Norf. 45 F2
Thurgarton Notts. 41 J1
Thurgoland 50 E2
Thurlaston Leics. 41 H6
Thurlaston Warks. 31 F1
Thurlbear 8 B2
Thurlby Lincs. 42 D4
Thurlby Lincs. 52 C6
Thurleigh 32 D3
Thurlestone 5 G6
Thurloxton 8 B1
Thurlstone 50 E2
Thurlton 45 J6
Thurlwood 49 H7
Thurmaston 41 J5
Thurnby 41 J5
Thurne 45 J4
Thurnham 14 D2
Thurning Norf. 44 E3
Thurning Northants. 42 D7
Thurnscoe 51 G2
Thursby 60 E1
Thursden 56 E6
Thursford 44 D2
Thursley 12 C3
Thurso 105 G2
Thurstaston 48 B4
Thurston 34 D2
Thurstonfield 60 E1
Thurstonland 50 D1
Thurton 45 H5
Thurvaston 40 E2
Thuster 105 H3
Thwaite N.Yorks. 61 K7
Thwaite Suff. 35 F2
Thwaite Head 60 E1
Thwaite St. Mary 45 H6
Thwing 59 G2

Tibbermore 82 B5
Tibberton Glos. 29 G6
Tibberton Tel. & W. 39 F3
Tibberton Worcs. 29 J3
Tibbie Shiels Inn 69 H1
Tibenham 45 F6
Tibertich 79 K1
Tibshelf 51 G6
Tibthorpe 59 F4
Ticehurst 13 K3
Tichborne 11 G2
Tickencote 42 C5
Tickenham 19 H4
Tickhill 51 H3
Ticklerton 38 D6
Ticknall 41 F3
Tickton 59 G5
Tidcombe 21 G6
Tiddington Oxon. 21 K1
Tiddington Warks. 30 D3
Tiddleywink 20 B4
Tidebrook 13 K4
Tideford 4 D5
Tidenham 19 J2
Tidenham Chase 19 J2
Tideswell 50 D5
Tidmarsh 21 K4
Tidmington 30 D5
Tidpit 10 B3
Tidworth 21 F7
Tiers Cross 16 C4
Tiffield 31 H3
Tifty 99 F6
Tigerton 83 G1
Tigh a' Gearraidh 92 C4
Tighachnoic 79 H3
Tighnablair 81 J6
Tighnabruaich 73 H3
Tighnacomaire 80 A2
Tigley 5 H4
Tilbrook 32 D2
Tilbury 24 C4
Tile Cross 40 D7
Tile Hill 30 D1
Tilehurst 21 K4
Tilford 22 B7
Tillathrowie 90 C1
Tillers' Green 29 F5
Tillery 91 H1
Tilley 38 E3
Tillicoultry 75 H1
Tillingham 25 F1
Tillington Here. 28 D4
Tillington W.Suss. 12 C4
Tillington Common 28 D4
Tillyarblet 83 G1
Tillybirloch 90 E4
Tillycairn Castle 90 E3
Tillycorthie 91 H2
Tillydrine 90 E5
Tillyfar 99 G6
Tillyfour 90 D3
Tillyfourie 90 E3
Tillygarmond 90 E5
Tillygreig 91 G2
Tillypronie 90 C4
Tilmanstone 15 H2
Tilney All Saints 43 J4
Tilney High End 43 J4
Tilney St. Lawrence 43 J4
Tilshead 20 D7
Tilstock 38 E2
Tilston 48 D7
Tilstone Fearnall 48 E6
Tilsworth 32 C6
Tilton on the Hill 42 A5
Tiltups End 20 B2
Timberland 52 E7
Timberland Dales 52 E6
Timbersbrook 49 H6
Timberscombe 7 H1
Timble 57 G4
Timperley 49 G4
Timsbury B. & N.E.Som. 19 K6
Timsbury Hants. 10 E2
Timsgearraidh 100 C4
Timworth Green 34 C2
Tincleton 9 G5
Tindale 61 H1
Tingewick 31 H5
Tingley 57 H7
Tingrith 32 D5
Tingwall 106 C5
Tinhay 6 C7
Tinney 4 C1
Tinshill 57 H6
Tinsley 51 G3
Tinsley Green 13 F3
Tintagel 4 A2
Tintern Parva 19 J1
Tintinhull 8 D3
Tintwistle 50 C3
Tinwald 69 F5
Tinwell 42 D5
Tippacott 7 F1
Tipperty Aber. 91 H1
Tipperty Aber. 91 H1
Tiptoe 10 D5
Tipton 40 B6
Tipton St. John 7 J6
Tiptree 34 C7
Tiptree Heath 34 C7
Tirabad 27 H4
Tirdeunaw 17 K5
Tiree Airport 78 B3
Tirindrish 87 J6
Tirley 29 H6
Tirphil 18 E1
Tirril 61 G4
Tir-y-dail 17 K4
Tisbury 9 J2
Tissington 50 D7
Tister 105 G2
Titchberry 6 A3
Titchfield 11 G4
Titchmarsh 32 D1
Titchwell 44 B1
Tithby 41 J2
Titley 28 C2
Titsey 23 H6
Titson 6 A5
Tittensor 40 A2
Tittleshall 44 C3
Tiverton Ches. 48 E6
Tiverton Devon 7 H4
Tivetshall St. Margaret 45 F7
Tivetshall St. Mary 45 F7
Tixall 40 B3
Tixover 42 C5
Toab Ork. 107 E7
Toab Shet. 109 F9
Tobermory 79 G2
Toberonochy 79 J1
Tobha Mòr 84 C1

obson 100 D4
cher 90 E1
ockenham 20 D3
ockenham Wick 20 D3
ockholes 56 B7
ockington 19 K3
ockwith 57 K4
odber 9 G2
oddington *Beds.* 32 D6
oddington *Glos.* 30 B5
oddington *W.Suss.* 12 D6
odenham 30 D5
odhills *Angus* 83 F4
odhills *Cumb.* 69 J7
odlachie 90 E3
odmorden 56 E7
odwick 51 G4
oft *Cambs.* 33 G3
oft *Lincs.* 42 D4
oft *Shet.* 108 D5
oft Hill 62 C4
oft Monks 45 J6
oft next Newton 52 D4
oftcarl 105 J4
oftrees 44 C3
ofts 105 J2
oftwood 44 D4
ogston 71 H3
okavaig 86 C3
okers Green 22 A4
olastadh 101 H3
olastadh a' Chaolais 100 D4
olastadh Ur 101 H3
oll of Birness 91 J1
olland 7 K2
ollard Royal 9 J3
olcross 7 K2
oller Down Gate 8 E4
oller Fratrum 8 E5
oller Porcorum 8 E5
oller Wholme 8 E4
ollerton *N.Yorks.* 58 B3
ollerton *Notts.* 41 J2
ollesbury 25 F1
ollesby 63 G5
olleshunt D'Arcy 34 D7
olleshunt Knights 34 C7
olleshunt Major 34 C7
olpuddle 9 G5
olvah 89 F5
olworth 22 E5
om an Fhuadain 101 F6
omatin 88 D1
ombreck 88 D1
omchrasky 87 J3
omdoun 87 H4
omdow 97 H7
omich *High.* 87 K2
omich *High.* 96 D4
omich *High.* 96 D1
omintoul 89 J3
omnacross 96 C7
omnamoon 97 H6
omnaven 90 C1
omnavoulin 89 K2
omvaich 89 H1
on Pentre 18 C2
onbridge 23 J7
ondu 18 B3
onfanau 36 E5
ong Norton 39 G5
ong Street 57 G6
onge 41 G3
ongham 22 B7
ongland 65 H6
ongue 103 H3
ongue House 103 H3
ongwynlais 18 E3
onna 18 A2
on-teg 18 D3
onwell 33 G7
onypandy 18 C2
onyrefail 18 D3
oot Baldon 21 J1
oot Hill 23 J1
oothill 10 E3
op End 32 D2
opcliffe 57 J2
opcroft 45 G6
opcroft Street 45 G6
oppesfield 34 B5
oppings 49 G1
opsham 7 H7
opsham Bridge 5 H5
orastan 78 D1
orbain 89 J3
orbeg *Aber.* 90 C1
orbeg *N.Ayr.* 66 D1
orbryan 5 J4
orcastle 87 H7
orcross 5 J6
ordarroch 88 D1
oreduff 97 F5
oremore *High.* 89 J1
oremore *High.* 105 G5
orgyle 87 K3
orksey 92 C6
orlum 87 H7
orlundy 20 A4
ormarton 72 A2
ormisdale 73 G7
ormore 105 G3
ormsdale *High.* 103 J2
orrance *E.Dun.* 74 E3
orrance *S.Lan.* 74 E6
orrancroy 90 B3
orrich 97 F6
orridon 95 F6
orrin 86 B2
orrisdale *Arg. & B.* 73 F7
orrisdale *High.* 103 J2
orrish 104 E7
orrisholme 55 H3
orry *Aber.* 98 C6
orry Aberdeen 91 H4
orryburn 75 J2
orsonce 77 F6
orthorwald 69 F6

Tortington 12 C6
Tortworth 20 A2
Torvaig 93 K7
Torver 60 D7
Torwood 75 G2
Torworth 51 J4
Tosberry 6 A3
Toscaig 86 D1
Toseland 33 F2
Tosside 56 C4
Tostarie 78 E3
Tostock 34 D2
Totaig 93 H6
Totamore 78 C2
Tote 93 K7
Totegan 104 D2
Totford 11 G1
Tothill 53 H4
Totland 10 E6
Totley 51 F4
Totnes 5 J4
Totnor 41 H2
Totronald 78 C2
Totternhoe 32 C6
Tottenham 23 G2
Tottenhill 44 A4
Totteridge 23 F2
Tottington *Gt.Man.* 49 G1
Tottington *Norf.* 44 C6
Totton 10 E3
Touchen-End 22 B4
Toulton 7 K2
Toux 99 H5
Tovil 14 C2
Tow Law 62 C3
Toward 73 K4
Towcester 31 H4
Towednack 22 B5
Towersey 22 A1
Towie *Aber.* 99 G4
Towie *Aber.* 90 C3
Towie *Aber.* 90 C3
Towiemore 98 B6
Town End *Cambs.* 43 H6
Town End *Cumb.* 55 H1
Town Green 48 D2
Town Row 13 J3
Town Street 44 B7
Town Yetholm 70 D1
Townend 74 C3
Townhead 65 G6
Townhead of Greenlaw 65 H4
Townhill 75 K2
Townshend 2 C5
Towthorpe *E.Riding* 59 F3
Towthorpe *York* 58 C4
Towton 57 K6
Towyn 47 H5
Toynton All Saints 53 G6
Toynton Fen Side 53 G6
Toynton St. Peter 53 H6
Toy's Hill 23 H6
Trabboch 67 J1
Traboe 2 E6
Tradespark *High.* 97 F6
Tradespark *Ork.* 107 D7
Trafford Centre 49 G3
Trafford Park 49 G3
Trallong 27 J6
Trallwn 17 K6
Tranch 19 F1
Tranent 76 C3
Trantlebeg 104 D3
Trantlemore 104 D3
Tranwell 71 G5
Trap 17 K4
Traprain 76 D3
Traquair 76 B7
Trawden 56 E6
Trawsfynydd 37 G2
Trealaw 18 C2
Treales 55 H6
Trearddur 46 A5
Treaslane 93 J6
Trebanog 18 D2
Trebanos 18 A1
Trebarrow 4 C1
Trebartha 4 C3
Trebarwith 4 A2
Trebetherick 3 G1
Treborough 7 J2
Trebudannon 3 F2
Trebullett 4 D3
Treburley 4 D3
Trebyan 4 A4
Trecastle 27 H6
Trecwn 16 C2
Trecynon 18 C1
Tredavoe 2 B6
Tre-ddiog 16 B3
Tredegar 18 E1
Tredington *Glos.* 29 J6
Tredington *Warks.* 30 D4
Tredinnick *Cornw.* 3 G1
Tredinnick *Cornw.* 4 C5
Tredomen 28 A5
Tredrissi 16 D1
Tredunnock 19 G2
Treen 2 A6
Treeton 51 G4
Trefaldwyn (Montgomery) 38 B6
Trefasser 16 B2
Trefdraeth 46 C5
Trefecca 28 A5
Trefeglwys 37 J6
Trefenter 27 F2
Treffgarne 16 C3
Treffynnon (Holywell) *Flints.* 47 K5
Treffynnon *Pembs.* 16 B3
Trefgarn Owen 16 B3
Trefil 18 E1
Trefilan 26 E3
Treflach 38 B3
Trefnanney 38 B4
Trefnant 47 J5
Trefonen 38 B3
Trefor *Gwyn.* 36 C1
Trefor *I.o.A.* 46 B4
Treforest 18 D3
Treforest Industrial Estate 18 E3
Trefriw 47 F6
Trefynwy (Monmouth) 28 E7
Tregadillett 6 B3
Tregaian 46 C5
Tregare 28 D7
Tregaron 27 F3
Tregarth 46 E6
Tregavethan 2 E4
Tregear 3 F3
Tregeare 4 C2
Tregeiriog 38 A2

Tregele 46 B3
Tregidden 2 E6
Treglemais 16 B3
Tregolds 3 F1
Tregole 4 B1
Tregonetha 3 G2
Tregony 3 G4
Tregoyd 28 A5
Tre-groes 17 H1
Treguff 18 D4
Tregurrian 3 F2
Tregynon 37 K6
Trehafod 18 D2
Treharris 18 D2
Treherbert 18 C2
Trekenner 4 D3
Treknow 4 A2
Trelash 4 B1
Trelassick 3 F3
Trelawnyd 47 J5
Trelech 17 F2
Trelech a'r Betws 17 G3
Treleddyd-fawr 16 A3
Trelewis 18 E2
Treligga 4 A2
Trelights 3 G1
Trelill 4 A3
Trelissick 3 F5
Trelleck 19 J1
Trelleck Grange 19 H1
Trelogan 47 K4
Trelystan 38 B5
Tremadog 36 E1
Tremail 4 B2
Tremain 17 F1
Tremaine 4 C2
Tremar 4 C4
Trematon 4 D5
Tremeirchion 47 J5
Trenance 3 F2
Trenarren 4 A6
Trench *Tel. & W.* 39 F4
Trench *Wrex.* 38 C2
Treneglos 4 C2
Trenewan 4 B5
Trent 8 E3
Trentham 40 A1
Trentishoe 6 E1
Treoes 18 C4
Treorchy 18 C2
Tre'r-ddol 37 F6
Tre-Rhys 16 E1
Trerulefoot 4 D5
Tresaith 26 B3
Trescott 40 A6
Trescowe 2 C5
Tresham 20 A2
Treshnish 78 E3
Tresillian 3 F4
Tresinney 4 B2
Tresinwen 16 C1
Treskinnick Cross 4 C1
Tresmeer 4 C2
Tresparrett 4 B1
Tresparrett Posts 4 B1
Tressait 81 K1
Tresta *Shet.* 108 F3
Tresta *Shet.* 109 C7
Treswell 51 K5
Trethurgy 4 A5
Tretio 16 A3
Tretire 28 E6
Tretower 28 A6
Treuddyn 48 B7
Trevalga 4 A2
Trevalyn 48 C7
Trevanson 3 G1
Trevarren 3 G2
Trevarrick 3 G4
Tre-vaughan *Carmar.* 17 H3
Trevaughan *Carmar.* 17 F4
Trevellas 2 E3
Trevelmond 4 C4
Treverva 2 E5
Trevescan 2 A6
Trevethin 19 F1
Trevigro 4 D4
Trevine *Arg. & B.* 80 B5
Trevine *Pembs.* 16 B2
Treviscoe 3 G3
Trevone 3 F1
Trevor 38 B1
Trewalder 4 A2
Trewarmett 4 A2
Trewarthenick 3 G4
Trewassa 4 B2
Trewellard 2 A5
Trewen 4 C2
Trewern 38 B4
Trewidland 4 C5
Trewilym 16 E1
Trewint 4 B1
Trewithian 3 F5
Trewoon 3 G3
Treworga 3 G1
Treyarnon 3 F1
Treyford 12 B5
Triangle 57 F7
Trickett's Cross 10 B4
Trimdon 62 E3
Trimdon Colliery 62 E3
Trimdon Grange 62 E3
Trimingham 45 G2
Trimley St. Mary 35 G5
Trimley St. Mary 35 G5
Trimpley 29 G1
Trimsaran 17 H5
Trimstone 6 D1
Trinafour 81 J1
Trinant 19 F2
Tring 32 C7
Trinity 83 H1
Trislaig 87 G7
Trispen 3 F3
Tritlington 71 H4
Trochry 82 A3
Troedyraur 17 G1
Troedyrhiw 18 D1
Trondavoe 108 C5
Troon *Cornw.* 2 D5
Troon *S.Ayr.* 74 B7
Trosaraidh 84 C4
Troston 34 C1
Troswell 4 C1
Trottiscliffe 23 K6
Trotton 12 B4
Troughend 70 D4
Troustan 73 J3
Troutbeck 61 F6
Troutbeck Bridge 61 F6
Trow Green 19 J1
Trowbridge 20 B6
Trowle Common 20 B6
Trowley Bottom 32 D7
Trows 76 E7
Trowse Newton 45 G5

Trudernish 72 C5
Trudoxhill 20 A7
Trull 8 B2
Trumaisge Arraidh 92 D4
Trumpan 93 H5
Trumpet 29 F5
Trumpington 33 H3
Trunch 45 G2
Trunnah 55 G5
Truro 3 F4
Trusham 7 G6
Trusley 40 E2
Trusthorpe 53 J4
Truthan 3 F3
Trysull 40 A6
Tubney 21 H2
Tuckenhay 5 J5
Tuckingmill 2 D4
Tuddenham *Suff.* 35 H3
Tuddenham *Suff.* 34 B1
Tudeley 23 K7
Tudhoe 62 D3
Tudweiliog 36 B2
Tuffley 29 H7
Tufton *Hants.* 21 H1
Tufton *Pembs.* 16 D3
Tugby 42 A5
Tugford 38 E7
Tughall 71 H1
Tuirnaig 94 E3
Tulchan 82 B4
Tullibody 75 G1
Tullich *Arg. & B.* 80 B1
Tullich *Arg. & B.* 79 K6
Tullich *High.* 97 F4
Tullich *High.* 88 D2
Tullich *Moray* 98 B6
Tullich *Stir.* 81 G4
Tullich Muir 96 E4
Tulliemet 82 A2
Tulloch *Aber.* 91 H1
Tulloch *High.* 96 D2
Tulloch *Moray* 97 H7
Tullochgorm 73 H1
Tullochgribban High 89 G2
Tullochvenus 90 D4
Tulloes 83 G3
Tullybannocher 81 J5
Tullybelton 82 B4
Tullyfergus 82 D3
Tullymurdoch 82 C2
Tullynessle 90 D3
Tumble 17 J4
Tumby 53 F7
Tumby Woodside 53 F7
Tummel Bridge 81 J2
Tunbridge Wells 13 J3
Tundergarth Mains 69 G5
Tunga 101 G4
Tunstall *E.Riding* 59 K6
Tunstall *Kent* 25 F5
Tunstall *Lancs.* 56 B2
Tunstall *N.Yorks.* 62 D7
Tunstall *Norf.* 45 J5
Tunstall *Stoke* 49 H7
Tunstall *Suff.* 35 H3
Tunstead 45 G3
Tunworth 21 K7
Tupsley 28 E4
Tupton 51 F6
Tur Langton 42 A6
Turbiskill 73 F2
Turclossie 99 G5
Turgis Green 21 K6
Turin 83 G2
Turkdean 30 C7
Turnastone 28 C5
Turnberry 67 G3
Turnchapel 4 E5
Turnditch 40 E1
Turner's Green 30 C1
Turners Hill 13 G3
Turners Puddle 9 H5
Turnford 23 G1
Turnworth 9 H4
Turret Bridge 87 K5
Turriff 99 F5
Turton Bottoms 49 G1
Turvey 32 C3
Turville 22 A2
Turville Heath 22 A2
Turweston 31 H5
Tutbury 40 E3
Tutnall 29 J1
Tutshill 19 J2
Tuttington 45 G3
Tuxford 51 K5
Twatt *Ork.* 106 B5
Twatt *Shet.* 109 C7
Twechar 74 E3
Tweedmouth 77 H5
Tweedsmuir 69 F1
Twelveheads 2 E4
Twenty 42 E3
Twerton 20 A5
Twickenham 22 E4
Twigworth 29 H6
Twineham 13 F4
Twinhoe 20 A6
Twinstead 34 C5
Twiss Green 49 F3
Twitchen *Devon* 7 F2
Twitchen *Shrop.* 28 C1
Twizell House 71 G1
Two Bridges 5 G3
Two Dales 50 E6
Two Gates 40 E5
Twycross 41 F5
Twyford *Bucks.* 31 H6
Twyford *Derbys.* 41 F3
Twyford *Dorset* 9 H3
Twyford *Hants.* 11 F2
Twyford *Leics.* 42 A5
Twyford *Norf.* 44 E3
Twyford *Oxon.* 31 F5
Twyford *W'ham* 22 A4
Twyford Common 28 E5
Twynholm 65 G5
Twyning 29 H5
Twyning Green 29 H5
Twynllanan 27 G6
Twyn-yr-odyn 18 E4
Twyn-y-Sheriff 19 H1
Twywell 32 C1
Tyberton 28 C5
Tyburn 40 D6
Tycroes 17 K4
Tycrwyn 38 A4
Tydd Gote 43 H4
Tydd St. Giles 43 H4
Tydd St. Mary 43 H4
Tyddewi (St. David's) 16 A3
Tye Common 24 C2
Tye Green 34 B6
Ty-hen 17 K2
Tyldesley 49 F2
Tyle-garw 18 D3

Tyler Hill 25 H5
Tylers Green *Bucks.* 22 C2
Tyler's Green *Essex* 23 J1
Tylorstown 18 D2
Tylwch 27 J1
Ty-Mawr *Conwy* 37 J1
Ty-mawr *Denb.* 38 A1
Ty-nant *Conwy* 37 J1
Ty-nant *Gwyn.* 37 J3
Tyndrum 80 E4
Tyneham 9 H6
Tynehead 76 B5
Tynemouth 71 J7
Tynewydd 18 C2
Tyninghame 76 E3
Tynron 68 D4
Tyn-y-cefn 37 K1
Tyn-y-Cwm 37 H7
Tyn-y-ffridd 38 A2
Tyn-y-graig *Cere.* 27 F2
Tyn-y-graig *Powys* 27 K4
Ty'n-y-groes 47 F5
Tyringham 32 B4
Tythegston 18 B4
Tytherington *Ches.* 49 J5
Tytherington *S.Glos.* 19 K3
Tytherington *Som.* 20 A7
Tytherington *Wilts.* 20 C7
Tytherleigh 8 C4
Tytherton Lucas 20 C4
Ty-uchaf 37 J3
Tywardreath 4 A5
Tywardreath Highway 4 A5
Tywyn 36 E5

U

Uachdar 92 D6
Uags 86 D1
Ubbeston Green 35 H1
Ubley 19 J6
Uckerby 62 D6
Uckfield 13 H4
Uckinghall 29 H5
Uckington 29 J6
Uddingston 74 E4
Uddington 75 G7
Udimore 14 D6
Udny Green 91 G2
Udny Station 91 H2
Udstonhead 75 F6
Uffcott 20 E4
Uffculme 7 J4
Uffington *Lincs.* 42 D5
Uffington *Oxon.* 21 G3
Uffington *Shrop.* 38 E4
Ufford *Peter.* 42 D5
Ufford *Suff.* 35 G3
Ufton 30 E2
Ufton Nervet 21 K5
Ugborough 5 G5
Uggeshall 35 J1
Ugglebarnby 63 K6
Ugley 33 J6
Ugley Green 33 J6
Ugthorpe 63 J5
Uig *Arg. & B.* 78 C2
Uig *Arg. & B.* 73 K2
Uig *High.* 93 J5
Uig *High.* 93 G6
Uigen 100 C4
Uiginish 93 H7
Uigshader 93 K7
Uisgebhagh 92 D7
Uisken 78 E6
Ulbster 105 J4
Ulcat Row 61 F4
Ulceby *Lincs.* 53 H5
Ulceby *N.Lincs.* 52 E1
Ulceby Cross 53 H5
Ulcombe 14 D3
Uldale 60 D3
Uldale House 61 J7
Uley 20 A2
Ulgham 71 H4
Ullapool 95 H2
Ullenhall 30 C2
Ullenwood 29 J7
Ulleskelf 58 B5
Ullesthorpe 41 H7
Ulley 51 G4
Ullingswick 28 E4
Ullinish 85 J1
Ullock 60 B4
Ulpha 60 C7
Ulrome 59 H4
Ulsta 108 D4
Ulting 24 E1
Uluvalt 79 G5
Ulverston 55 F2
Ulwell 10 B6
Ulzieside 68 C3
Umberleigh 6 E3
Unapool 102 E5
Underbarrow 61 F7
Underhoull 108 E2
Underriver 23 J6
Underwood *Newport* 19 G3
Underwood *Notts.* 51 G7
Undy 19 H3
Unifirth 109 B7
Union Croft 91 G5
Union Mills 54 C6
Unstone 51 F5
Unthank 61 F3
Up Cerne 9 F4
Up Exe 7 H5
Up Hatherley 29 J6
Up Holland 48 E2
Up Marden 11 J3
Up Nately 21 K6
Up Somborne 10 E1
Up Sydling 9 F4
Upavon 20 E6
Upchurch 24 E5
Upcott *Devon* 6 C6
Upcott *Here.* 28 C3
Upend 33 K3
Uphall *Dorset* 8 E4
Uphall *W.Loth.* 75 J3
Uphall Station 75 J3
Upham *Devon* 7 G5
Upham *Hants.* 11 G2
Uphampton 29 H2
Uphill 19 G6
Uplawmoor 74 C5
Upleadon 29 G6
Upleatham 63 H4
Uplees 25 G5

Uploders 8 E5
Uplowman 7 J4
Uplyme 8 C5
Upminster 23 J3
Upottery 7 K5
Upper Affcot 38 D7
Upper Ardroscadale 73 J4
Upper Arley 39 G7
Upper Arncott 31 H7
Upper Aston 40 A6
Upper Astrop 31 G5
Upper Basildon 21 K4
Upper Beeding 12 E5
Upper Benefield 42 C7
Upper Bighouse 104 D3
Upper Boat 18 E3
Upper Boddington 31 F3
Upper Borth 37 F7
Upper Boyndlie 99 H4
Upper Brailes 30 E4
Upper Breakish 86 C2
Upper Breinton 28 D4
Upper Broughton 41 J3
Upper Bucklebury 21 J5
Upper Burgate 10 C3
Upper Burnhaugh 91 G5
Upper Caldecote 32 E4
Upper Camster 105 H4
Upper Catshill 29 J1
Upper Chapel 27 K4
Upper Chute 21 F6
Upper Clatford 21 G7
Upper Coberley 29 J7
Upper Cound 38 E5
Upper Cumberworth 50 E2
Upper Cwmbran 19 F2
Upper Dallachy 98 B4
Upper Dean 32 D2
Upper Denby 50 E2
Upper Derraid 89 H1
Upper Diabaig 94 E5
Upper Dicker 13 J5
Upper Dovercourt 35 G6
Upper Dunsforth 57 K3
Upper Eastern Green 40 E7
Upper Eathie 96 E5
Upper Elkstone 50 C7
Upper End 50 C5
Upper Farringdon 11 J1
Upper Framilode 29 G7
Upper Froyle 22 A7
Upper Gills 105 J1
Upper Glendessarry 87 F5
Upper Godney 19 H7
Upper Gornal 40 B6
Upper Gravenhurst 32 E5
Upper Green *Essex* 33 H5
Upper Green *Mon.* 28 C7
Upper Green *W.Berks.* 21 G5
Upper Gylen 79 K5
Upper Hackney 50 E6
Upper Halliford 22 D5
Upper Halling 24 C5
Upper Hambleton 42 C5
Upper Hardres Court 15 G2
Upper Hartfield 13 H3
Upper Hawkhillock 91 J1
Upper Hayton 38 E7
Upper Heath 38 E7
Upper Helmsley 58 C4
Upper Hergest 28 B3
Upper Heyford 31 F6
Upper Hill 28 D3
Upper Hopton 50 D1
Upper Horsebridge 13 J5
Upper Hulme 50 C6
Upper Inglesham 21 F2
Upper Kilchattan 72 B1
Upper Killay 17 J6
Upper Knockando 97 J7
Upper Lambourn 21 G3
Upper Langwith 51 H6
Upper Largo 83 F7
Upper Lochton 90 E5
Upper Longdon 40 C4
Upper Longwood 39 F5
Upper Ludstone 40 A6
Upper Lybster 105 H5
Upper Lydbrook 29 F7
Upper Maes-coed 28 C5
Upper Midhope 50 E3
Upper Minety 20 D2
Upper Mitton 29 H1
Upper Muirskie 91 G5
Upper North Dean 22 B2
Upper Norwood 23 G4
Upper Obney 82 B4
Upper Oddington 30 D6
Upper Ollach 86 B1
Upper Poppleton 58 B4
Upper Quinton 30 C4
Upper Ridinghill 99 J5
Upper Rissington 30 D6
Upper Rochford 29 F2
Upper Sanday 107 E7
Upper Sapey 29 F2
Upper Scolton 16 C3
Upper Seagry 20 C3
Upper Shelton 32 C4
Upper Sheringham 45 F1
Upper Skelmorlie 74 A4
Upper Slaughter 30 C6
Upper Sonachan 80 B5
Upper Soudley 29 F7
Upper Stoke 41 F7
Upper Stondon 32 E5
Upper Stowe 31 H3
Upper Street *Hants.* 10 C3
Upper Street *Norf.* 45 F5
Upper Street *Suff.* 35 H5
Upper Sundon 32 D6
Upper Swell 30 C6
Upper Tean 40 C2
Upper Thurnham 55 H4
Upper Tillyrie 82 C7
Upper Tooting 23 F4
Upper Town 19 J5
Upper Tysoe 30 E4
Upper Upham 21 F4
Upper Upnor 24 D4
Upper Victoria 83 G4
Upper Wardington 31 F4
Upper Weald 32 B5
Upper Weedon 31 H3
Upper Welson 28 C3
Upper Wield 11 H1
Upper Winchendon 31 J7
Upper Woodford 10 C1
Upper Wootton 21 J6
Upper Wraxall 20 A4
Upper Wyche 29 G4
Uppermill 49 J2

Upperthong 50 D2
Upperton 12 C4
Uppertown 105 J1
Uppingham 42 B6
Uppington *Dorset* 10 B4
Uppington *Shrop.* 38 E5
Upsall 57 K1
Upsettlington 77 G6
Upshire 23 H1
Upstreet 25 J5
Upton *Bucks.* 31 J7
Upton *Cambs.* 32 E1
Upton *Ches.* 48 D6
Upton *Cornw.* 4 C3
Upton *Devon* 7 J7
Upton *Devon* 5 H6
Upton *Dorset* 9 J5
Upton *Hants.* 21 G6
Upton *Hants.* 10 E3
Upton *Lincs.* 52 B4
Upton *Mersey.* 48 B4
Upton *Norf.* 45 H4
Upton *Northants.* 31 J2
Upton *Notts.* 51 K5
Upton *Notts.* 51 K7
Upton *Oxon.* 21 J3
Upton *Peter.* 42 E5
Upton *Slo.* 22 C4
Upton *Som.* 7 H3
Upton *W.Yorks.* 51 G1
Upton Bishop 29 F6
Upton Cheyney 19 K5
Upton Cressett 39 F6
Upton Cross 4 C3
Upton End 32 E5
Upton Green 45 H4
Upton Grey 21 K7
Upton Hellions 7 G5
Upton Lovell 20 C7
Upton Magna 38 E4
Upton Noble 9 G1
Upton Pyne 7 H6
Upton St. Leonards 29 H7
Upton Scudamore 20 B7
Upton Snodsbury 29 J3
Upton upon Severn 29 H4
Upton Warren 29 J2
Upwaltham 12 C5
Upware 33 J2
Upwell 43 J5
Upwey 9 F6
Upwood 43 F7
Uradale 109 D9
Urafirth 108 C5
Urchany 97 F7
Urchfont 20 D6
Urdimarsh 28 E4
Ure 108 B5
Urgha 93 G2
Urlay Nook 62 E5
Urmston 49 G3
Urquhart *High.* 96 C6
Urquhart *Moray* 97 K5
Urra 63 G6
Urray 96 C6
Ushaw Moor 62 D2
Usk 19 G1
Usselby 52 D3
Utley 57 F5
Uton 7 G6
Utterby 53 G3
Uttoxeter 40 C2
Uwchmynydd 36 A3
Uxbridge 22 D3
Uyeasound 108 E2
Uzmaston 16 C4

V

Valley (Dyffryn) 46 A5
Valley Truckle 4 B2
Valleyfield *D. & G.* 65 G5
Valleyfield *Fife* 75 J2
Valsgarth 108 F1
Vange 24 D3
Vardre 17 K5
Varteg 19 F1
Vatersay (Bhatarsaigh) 84 B5
Vatten 93 H7
Vaul 78 B3
Vaynor 27 K7
Vaynor Park 38 A5
Veaullt 28 A3
Veensgarth 109 D8
Velindre *Pembs.* 16 E2
Velindre *Powys* 28 A5
Vellow 7 J2
Veness 106 E5
Venn 5 H6
Venn Ottery 7 J6
Vennington 38 C5
Ventnor 11 G7
Vernham Dean 21 G6
Vernham Street 21 G6
Vernolds Common 38 D7
Verwood 10 B4
Veryan 3 G5
Vicarage 8 B6
Vickerstown 54 E3
Victoria 3 G2
Vidlin 109 D6
Viewfield 105 G2
Viewpark 75 F4
Vigo 40 C5
Vigo Village 24 C5
Villavin 6 D4
Vinehall Street 14 C5
Vine's Cross 13 J5
Viney Hill 19 K1
Virginia Water 22 C5
Virginstow 6 B6
Virley 34 D7
Vobster 20 A7
Voe *Shet.* 109 C4
Voe *Shet.* 108 D5
Vowchurch 28 C5
Voy 107 B6

W

Wackerfield 62 C4
Wacton 45 F6
Wadborough 29 J4
Waddesdon 31 J7
Waddingham 52 C3
Waddington *Lancs.* 56 C5
Waddington *Lincs.* 52 C6
Waddingworth 52 E5
Wadebridge 3 G1
Wadeford 8 C3
Wadenhoe 42 D7

Wadesmill 33 G7
Wadhurst 13 K3
Wadshelf 51 F3
Wadsley Bridge 51 F3
Wadworth 51 H3
Wadworth Hill 59 J7
Waen 47 K6
Waen-fach 38 B4
Waen-wen 46 D6
Wag 105 F6
Wainfleet All Saints 53 H7
Wainfleet Bank 53 H7
Wainhouse Corner 4 B1
Wainscott 24 D4
Wainstalls 57 F7
Waitby 61 J6
Wakefield 57 J7
Wakerley 42 C6
Wakes Colne 34 C6
Walberswick 35 J1
Walberton 12 C6
Walcot Lincs. 42 D2
Walcot Lincs. 52 E7
Walcot N.Lincs. 58 E7
Walcot Shrop. 38 C7
Walcot Tel. & W. 38 E4
Walcot Green 45 F7
Walcote Leics. 41 H7
Walcote Warks. 30 C3
Walcott 45 H2
Walcott Dales 52 E7
Walden 57 F1
Walden Head 56 E1
Walden Stubbs 51 H1
Walderton 11 J3
Walditch 8 D5
Waldley 40 D2
Waldridge 62 D1
Waldringfield 35 G4
Waldron 13 J5
Wales 51 G4
Walesby Lincs. 52 E3
Walesby Notts. 51 J5
Walford Here. 28 C1
Walford Here. 28 E6
Walford Shrop. 38 D3
Walgherton 39 F1
Walhampton 10 E5
Walk Mill 56 D6
Walkden 49 G2
Walker 71 H7
Walker Fold 56 B5
Walkerburn 76 B7
Walkeringham 51 K3
Walkerith 51 K3
Walkern 33 F6
Walker's Green 28 E4
Walkhampton 5 F4
Walkington 59 G6
Walkwood 30 B2
Wall Northumb. 70 E7
Wall Staffs. 40 D5
Wall Bank 38 E6
Wall Heath 40 A7
Wall under Heywood 38 E6
Wallacehall 69 H6
Wallacetown 67 G3
Wallasey 48 B3
Wallbottle 71 G7
Wallend 24 E4
Waller's Green 29 F5
Wallingford 21 K2
Wallington Gt.Lon. 23 F5
Wallington Hants. 11 G4
Wallington Herts. 33 F5
Wallis 16 D3
Wallisdown 10 B5
Walliswood 12 E3
Walls 109 B8
Wallsend 71 J7
Wallyford 76 B3
Walmer 15 J2
Walmer Bridge 55 H7
Walmersley 49 H1
Walmley 40 D6
Walpole 35 H1
Walpole Cross Keys 43 J4
Walpole Highway 43 J4
Walpole St. Andrew 43 J4
Walpole St. Peter 43 J4
Walsall 40 C6
Walsall Wood 40 C5
Walsden 56 E7
Walsgrave on Sowe 41 F7
Walsham le Willows 34 E1
Walsoken 43 H4
Walston 75 J6
Walsworth 32 E5
Walterstone 28 C6
Waltham Kent 15 G3
Waltham N.E.Lincs. 53 F2
Waltham Abbey 23 G1
Waltham Chase 11 G3
Waltham Cross 23 G1
Waltham on the Wolds 42 B3
Waltham St. Lawrence 22 B4
Walthamstow 23 G3
Walton Bucks. 32 B7
Walton Cumb. 70 A7
Walton Derbys. 51 F6
Walton Leics. 41 H7
Walton M.K. 32 B5
Walton Mersey. 48 C3
Walton Peter. 42 E5
Walton Powys 28 B3
Walton Som. 8 D1
Walton Staffs. 40 A2
Walton Suff. 35 G5
Walton Tel. & W. 38 E4
Walton W.Yorks. 51 F1
Walton W.Yorks. 57 K5
Walton Warks. 30 D3
Walton Cardiff 29 J5
Walton East 16 D3
Walton on the Hill 23 F6
Walton on the Naze 35 G6
Walton on the Wolds 41 H4
Walton Park 65 H3
Walton West 16 B4
Walton-in-Gordano 19 H4
Walton-le-Dale 55 J7
Walton-on-Thames 22 E5
Walton-on-the-Hill 40 B3
Walton-on-Trent 40 E4

Walwen Flints. 47 K5
Walwen Flints. 48 B5
Walwick 70 E6
Walworth 62 D5
Walwyn's Castle 16 B4
Wambrook 8 B4
Wanborough Surr. 22 C7
Wanborough Swin. 21 F3
Wandel 68 E1
Wandon 71 F1
Wandsworth 23 F4
Wandylaw 71 G1
Wangford Suff. 35 J1
Wangford Suff. 44 B7
Wanlip 41 J4
Wanlockhead 68 D2
Wannock 13 J6
Wansford E.Riding 59 G4
Wansford Peter. 42 D6
Wanstead 23 H3
Wanstrow 20 A7
Wanswell 19 K1
Wantage 21 G3
Wapley 20 A4
Wappenbury 30 E2
Wappenham 31 H4
Warblebank 60 D2
Warbleton 13 K5
Warborough 21 J2
Warboys 33 G1
Warbstow 4 C1
Warburton 49 F4
Warcop 61 J5
Ward End 40 D7
Ward Green 34 E2
Warden Kent 25 G4
Warden Northumb. 70 E7
Wardgate 40 E1
Wardhouse 90 D1
Wardington 31 F4
Wardle Ches. 49 F7
Wardle Gt.Man. 49 J1
Wardley 42 B5
Wardlow 50 D5
Wardy Hill 43 H7
Ware Herts. 33 G7
Ware Kent 25 J5
Wareham 9 J6
Warehorne 14 E4
Waren Mill 77 K7
Warenford 71 G1
Warenton 77 K7
Wareside 33 G7
Waresley 33 F3
Warfield 22 B4
Wargrave 22 A4
Warham 44 D1
Wark Northumb. 70 D6
Wark Northumb. 77 G7
Warkleigh 6 E3
Warkton 32 B1
Warkworth Northants. 31 F4
Warkworth Northumb. 71 H3
Warlaby 62 E7
Warland 56 E7
Warleggan 4 B4
Warley 40 C7
Warley Town 57 F7
Warlingham 23 G6
Warmfield 57 J7
Warmingham 49 G6
Warminghurst 12 E5
Warmington Northants. 42 D6
Warmington Warks. 31 F4
Warminster 20 B7
Warmlake 14 D2
Warmley 19 K4
Warmsworth 51 H2
Warmwell 9 G6
Warndon 29 H3
Warnford 11 H2
Warnham 12 E3
Warningcamp 12 D6
Warninglid 13 F4
Warren Ches. 49 H5
Warren Pembs. 16 C6
Warren House 6 E7
Warren Row 22 B3
Warren Street 14 E2
Warrenby 63 G4
Warrington M.K. 32 B3
Warrington Warr. 49 F4
Warroch 82 B7
Warsash 11 F4
Warslow 50 C7
Warter 58 E4
Warthill 58 C4
Wartle 90 D4
Wartling 13 K6
Wartnaby 42 A3
Warton Lancs. 55 J2
Warton Lancs. 55 H1
Warton Northumb. 71 F3
Warton Warks. 40 E5
Warwick Cumb. 61 F1
Warwick Warks. 30 D2
Warwick Bridge 61 F1
Wasbister 106 C4
Wash Common 21 H5
Washaway 4 A4
Washbourne 5 H5
Washfield 7 H4
Washfold 62 B6
Washford 7 J1
Washford Pyne 7 G4
Washingborough 52 D5
Washington T. & W. 62 E1
Washington W.Suss. 12 E5
Washmere Green 34 D4
Wasing 21 J5
Waskerley 62 B2
Wasperton 30 D3
Wass 58 B2
Watchet 7 J1
Watchfield Oxon. 21 F2
Watchfield Som. 19 G7
Watchgate 61 G1
Watendlath 60 D5
Water 56 D7
Water Eaton 31 G7
Water End E.Riding 58 E5
Water End Herts. 32 D7
Water Newton 42 E6
Water Orton 40 D6
Water Stratford 31 H5
Water Yeat 55 F1
Waterbeach 33 H2
Waterbeck 69 H6

Waterfoot E.Renf. 74 D5
Waterfoot Lancs. 56 D7
Waterford 33 G7
Waterhead Cumb. 60 E6
Waterhead D. & G. 68 C5
Waterhill of Bruxie 99 H6
Waterhouses Dur. 62 C2
Waterhouses Staffs. 50 C7
Wateringbury 23 K6
Waterloo Aber. 91 J1
Waterloo Mersey. 48 C3
Waterloo N.Lan. 75 G5
Waterloo Norf. 45 G4
Waterloo P. & K. 82 B4
Waterloo Pembs. 16 C5
Waterloo Poole 10 B5
Waterloo Cross 7 J4
Waterloo Port 46 C6
Waterlooville 11 H3
Watermeetings 68 E2
Watermillock 61 F4
Waterperry 21 K1
Waterrow 7 J3
Watersfield 12 D5
Waterside Aber. 90 B3
Waterside Aber. 91 J2
Waterside Bucks. 22 C1
Waterside E.Ayr. 67 J3
Waterside E.Ayr. 74 C6
Waterside E.Dun. 74 E3
Waterstock 21 K1
Waterston 16 C5
Waterthorpe 51 G4
Watford Herts. 22 E2
Watford Northants. 31 H2
Wath N.Yorks. 57 J2
Wath N.Yorks. 57 G3
Wath Brow 60 B5
Wath upon Dearne 51 G2
Watlington Norf. 44 A4
Watlington Oxon. 21 K2
Watnall 41 H1
Watten 105 H3
Wattisfield 34 E1
Wattisham 34 E3
Watton E.Riding 59 G5
Watton Norf. 44 D5
Watton at Stone 33 G7
Watton Green 44 D5
Wattston 75 F4
Wattstown 18 D2
Wattsville 18 E2
Waun Fawr 37 F7
Waun y Clyn 17 H5
Waunarlwydd 17 K6
Waunclunda 17 K2
Waunfawr 46 D7
Wavendon 32 C5
Waverbridge 60 C2
Waverton Ches. 48 D6
Waverton Cumb. 60 D2
Wawne 59 G6
Waxham 45 J3
Waxholme 59 K7
Way Gill 56 E3
Way Village 7 G4
Wayford 8 D4
Waytown 8 D5
Wdig (Goodwick) 16 C2
Weachyburn 98 E5
Weald 21 G1
Wealdstone 22 E3
Weare 19 H6
Weare Giffard 6 C3
Wearhead 61 K2
Wearne 8 D2
Weasenham All Saints 44 C3
Weasenham St. Peter 44 C3
Weathercote 56 C2
Weatheroak Hill 30 B1
Weaverham 49 F5
Weaverthorpe 59 F2
Webheath 30 B2
Webton 28 D5
Wedderlairs 91 G1
Weddington 41 F6
Wedhampton 20 D6
Wedmore 19 H7
Wednesbury 40 B6
Wednesfield 40 B5
Weedon 32 B7
Weedon Bec 31 H3
Weedon Lois 31 H4
Weeford 40 D5
Week 7 F4
Week Orchard 6 A5
Week St. Mary 4 C1
Weekley 42 B7
Weeley 35 F6
Weeley Heath 35 F6
Weem 81 K3
Weeping Cross 40 B3
Weethley 30 B3
Weeting 44 B7
Weeton E.Riding 59 K7
Weeton Lancs. 55 G6
Weeton N.Yorks. 57 H5
Weir Essex 24 E3
Weir Lancs. 56 D7
Weirbrook 38 C3
Welbeck Abbey 51 H5
Welborne 44 E5
Welbourn 52 C7
Welburn 58 D3
Welbury 62 E6
Welby 42 C2
Welches Dam 43 H7
Welcombe 6 A4
Weldon 42 C7
Welford Northants. 41 J7
Welford W.Berks. 21 H4
Welford-on-Avon 30 C3
Welham Leics. 42 A6
Welham Notts. 51 K4
Welham Green 23 F1
Well Hants. 22 A7
Well Lincs. 53 H5
Well N.Yorks. 57 H1
Well End 22 B3
Well Hill 23 H5
Well Town 7 H5
Welland 29 G4
Wellbank 83 F4
Welldale 69 H7
Wellesbourne 30 D3
Wellhill 97 F1
Welling 23 H4
Wellingborough 32 B2
Wellingham 44 C3
Wellingore 52 C7
Wellington Cumb. 60 B6
Wellington Here. 28 D4
Wellington Som. 7 K3
Wellington Tel. & W. 39 F4

Wellington Heath 29 G4
Wellington Marsh 28 E4
Wellow B. & N.E.Som. 20 A6
Wellow I.o.W. 10 E6
Wellow Notts. 51 J6
Wells 19 J7
Wellsborough 41 F5
Wells-next-the-Sea 44 D1
Wellwood 75 J2
Welney 43 J6
Welsh Bicknor 28 E7
Welsh End 38 E2
Welsh Frankton 38 C2
Welsh Hook 16 C3
Welsh Newton 28 E7
Welsh St. Donats 18 D4
Welshampton 38 D2
Welshpool (Y Trallwng) 38 B5
Welton B. & N.E.Som. 19 K6
Welton Cumb. 60 E2
Welton E.Riding 59 F7
Welton Lincs. 52 D4
Welton Northants. 31 G2
Welton le Marsh 53 H6
Welton le Wold 53 F4
Welwick 59 K7
Welwyn 33 F7
Welwyn Garden City 33 F7
Wem 38 E3
Wembdon 8 B1
Wembley 22 E3
Wembury 5 F6
Wembworthy 6 E5
Wenallt 37 J1
Wendens Ambo 33 J5
Wendlebury 31 G7
Wendling 44 D4
Wendover 22 B1
Wendron 2 D5
Wendy 33 G4
Wenfordbridge 4 A3
Wenhaston 35 J1
Wenlli 47 G6
Wennington Cambs. 33 F1
Wennington Gt.Lon. 23 J3
Wennington Lancs. 56 B2
Wensley Derbys. 50 E6
Wensley N.Yorks. 62 B7
Wentbridge 51 G1
Wentnor 38 C6
Wentworth Cambs. 33 H1
Wentworth S.Yorks. 51 F3
Wentworth Castle 51 F2
Wenvoe 18 E4
Weobley 28 C3
Weobley Marsh 28 D3
Wepham 12 D6
Wepre 48 B6
Wereham 44 A5
Wergs 40 A5
Wernyrheolydd 28 C7
Werrington Cornw. 6 B7
Werrington Peter. 42 E5
Werrington Staffs. 40 B1
Wervil Brook 26 C3
Wervin 48 D5
Wesham 55 H6
Wessington 51 F7
West Aberthaw 18 D5
West Acre 44 B4
West Allerdean 77 H6
West Alvington 5 H6
West Amesbury 20 E7
West Anstey 7 G3
West Ashby 53 F5
West Ashling 12 B6
West Ashton 20 B6
West Auckland 62 C4
West Ayton 59 F1
West Bagborough 7 K2
West Barkwith 52 E4
West Barnby 63 K5
West Barns 76 E3
West Barsham 44 D2
West Bay 8 D5
West Beckham 45 F2
West Benhar 75 G4
West Bergholt 34 D6
West Bexington 8 E6
West Bilney 44 B4
West Blatchington 13 F6
West Boldon 71 J7
West Bradenham 44 D5
West Bradford 56 C5
West Bradley 8 E1
West Bretton 50 E1
West Bridgford 41 H2
West Bromwich 40 C6
West Buckland Devon 6 E2
West Buckland Som. 7 K3
West Burrafirth 109 B7
West Burton N.Yorks. 57 F1
West Burton W.Suss. 12 C5
West Butterwick 52 B2
West Byfleet 22 D5
West Cairncake 99 G6
West Caister 45 K4
West Calder 75 J4
West Camel 8 E2
West Cauldcoats 74 E6
West Challow 21 G3
West Charleton 5 H6
West Chelborough 8 E4
West Chevington 71 H4
West Chiltington 12 D5
West Chiltington Common 12 D5
West Chinnock 8 D3
West Chisenbury 20 E6
West Clandon 22 D6
West Cliffe 15 J3
West Clyne 97 F1
West Coker 8 E3
West Compton Dorset 8 E5
West Compton Som. 19 J7
West Cross 17 K7
West Curry 4 C1
West Curthwaite 60 E2
West Dean W.Suss. 12 B5
West Deeping 42 E5
West Derby 48 C3
West Dereham 44 A5

West Ditchburn 71 G1
West Down 6 D1
West Drayton Gt.Lon. 22 D4
West Drayton Notts. 51 K5
West Dullater 81 G7
West Dunnet 105 H1
West Edington 71 G5
West Ella 59 G7
West End Beds. 32 C3
West End E.Riding 59 G3
West End Hants. 11 F3
West End Kent 25 H5
West End Lancs. 53 G3
West End Lincs. 53 G3
West End N.Som. 19 H5
West End N.Yorks. 57 G4
West End Norf. 45 J4
West End Oxon. 21 H1
West End S.Lan. 75 H6
West End Suff. 45 J7
West End Surr. 22 C5
West End Surr. 22 C5
West End Green 21 K5
West Farleigh 14 C2
West Farndon 31 G3
West Felton 38 C3
West Firle 13 H6
West Fleetham 71 G1
West Garforth 57 J6
West Ginge 21 H3
West Glen 73 J3
West Grafton 21 F5
West Green 22 A6
West Grimstead 10 D2
West Grinstead 12 E4
West Haddlesey 58 B7
West Haddon 31 H1
West Hagbourne 21 J3
West Hagley 40 B7
West Hall 70 A7
West Hallam 41 G1
West Halton 59 F7
West Ham 23 H3
West Handley 51 F5
West Hanney 21 H2
West Hanningfield 24 D2
West Hardwick 51 G1
West Harptree 19 J6
West Harting 11 J2
West Hatch Hants. 8 B2
West Heath Hants. 22 B6
West Helmsdale 105 F7
West Hendred 21 H3
West Heslerton 59 F2
West Hill Devon 7 J6
West Hill N.Som. 19 H4
West Hoathly 13 G3
West Holme 9 H6
West Horndon 24 C3
West Horrington 19 J7
West Horsley 22 D6
West Horton 77 J7
West Hougham 15 H3
West Huntspill 19 G7
West Hyde 22 D2
West Hythe 15 G4
West Ilsley 21 H3
West Itchenor 11 J4
West Keal 53 G6
West Kennett 20 E5
West Kilbride 74 A6
West Kingsdown 23 J5
West Kington 20 B4
West Kirby 48 B4
West Knapton 58 E2
West Knighton 9 G6
West Knoyle 9 H1
West Kyloe 77 J6
West Lambrook 8 D3
West Langdon 15 J3
West Langwell 96 D1
West Lavington W.Suss. 12 B4
West Lavington Wilts. 20 D6
West Layton 62 C5
West Leake 41 H3
West Lexham 44 C4
West Lilling 58 C3
West Lingo 83 F7
West Linton 75 K5
West Littleton 20 A4
West Lockinge 21 H3
West Looe 4 C5
West Lulworth 9 H6
West Lutton 59 F3
West Lydford 8 E1
West Lyng 8 C2
West Lynn 44 A4
West Mains 77 J6
West Malling 23 K6
West Malvern 29 G4
West Marden 11 J3
West Markham 51 K5
West Marsh 53 F2
West Marton 56 D4
West Melton 51 G2
West Meon 11 H2
West Meon Hut 11 H2
West Mersea 34 E7
West Milton 8 D5
West Minster 25 F4
West Molesey 22 E5
West Monkton 8 B2
West Moors 10 B4
West Mostard 61 J7
West Muir 83 G1
West Ness 58 C2
West Newton E.Riding 59 J6
West Newton Norf. 44 A3
West Norwood 23 G4
West Ogwell 5 J3
West Orchard 9 H3
West Overton 20 E5
West Park Aber. 91 F5
West Park Mersey. 48 E3
West Parley 10 B5
West Peckham 23 K6
West Pennard 8 E1
West Pentire 2 E2
West Perry 32 E2
West Porlock 7 G1
West Putford 6 B4
West Quantoxhead 7 K1
West Rainton 62 D2
West Rasen 52 D4
West Raynham 44 D3
West Row 33 K1
West Rudham 44 C3
West Runton 45 F1
West Saltoun 76 C4

West Sandwick 108 D4
West Scrafton 57 F1
West Shinness Lodge 103 H7
West Somerton 45 J3
West Stafford 9 G6
West Stockwith 51 K3
West Stoke 12 B6
West Stonesdale 61 K6
West Stoughton 19 H7
West Stour 9 G2
West Stourmouth 25 J5
West Stow 34 C1
West Stowell 20 E5
West Stratton 21 J7
West Street 14 E2
West Tanfield 57 H2
West Taphouse 4 B4
West Tarbert 73 G4
West Tarring 12 E6
West Thorney 11 J4
West Thurrock 23 J4
West Tilbury 24 C4
West Tisted 11 H2
West Tofts Norf. 44 C6
West Tofts P. & K. 82 C4
West Torrington 52 E4
West Town Hants. 11 J5
West Town N.Som. 19 H5
West Tytherley 10 D1
West Walton 43 H4
West Walton Highway 43 H4
West Wellow 10 D2
West Wemyss 76 B1
West Wick 19 G5
West Wickham Cambs. 33 K4
West Wickham Gt.Lon. 23 G5
West Williamston 16 D5
West Winch 44 A4
West Winterslow 10 D1
West Wittering 11 J5
West Witton 57 F1
West Woodburn 70 D5
West Woodhay 21 G5
West Woodlands 20 A7
West Worldham 11 J1
West Worlington 7 F4
West Worthing 12 E6
West Wratting 33 J3
West Wycombe 22 B2
West Yell 108 D4
Westbere 25 H5
Westborough 42 B1
Westbourne B. & N.E.Som. 10 B5
Westbourne W.Suss. 11 J4
Westbrook 21 H4
Westbury Bucks. 31 H5
Westbury Shrop. 38 C5
Westbury Wilts. 20 B6
Westbury Leigh 20 B6
Westbury on Trym 19 J4
Westbury-on-Severn 29 G7
Westbury-sub-Mendip 19 J7
Westby 55 G6
Westcliff-on-Sea 24 E3
Westcombe 9 F1
Westcote 30 D6
Westcott Bucks. 31 J7
Westcott Devon 7 J5
Westcott Surr. 22 E7
Westcott Barton 31 F6
Westdean 13 J7
Westdowns 4 A2
Wester Aberchalder 88 C2
Wester Badentyre 99 F5
Wester Culbeuchly 98 E4
Wester Dechmont 75 J3
Wester Fintray 91 G3
Wester Foffarty 83 F3
Wester Greenskares 99 F4
Wester Gruinards 96 C2
Wester Lealty 96 D4
Wester Lonvine 96 E4
Wester Newburn 83 F7
Wester Ord 91 G4
Wester Quarff 109 D9
Wester Skeld 109 B8
Westerdale High. 105 G3
Westerdale N.Yorks. 63 H6
Westerfield Shet. 109 C7
Westerfield Suff. 35 F4
Westergate 12 C6
Westerham 23 H6
Westerleigh 19 K4
Westerton Aber. 91 F5
Westerton Angus 83 G2
Westerton Dur. 62 D3
Westerton P. & K. 81 K6
Westerwick 109 B8
Westfield Cumb. 60 A4
Westfield E.Suss. 14 D6
Westfield High. 105 F2
Westfield Norf. 44 D5
Westfield W.Loth. 75 H3
Westgate Dur. 62 A3
Westgate N.Lincs. 51 K2
Westgate Norf. 44 D1
Westgate Northumb. 71 G6
Westgate Hill 57 H7
Westgate on Sea 25 K4
Westhall Aber. 90 E2
Westhall Suff. 45 J7
Westham Dorset 9 F7
Westham E.Suss. 13 K6
Westham Som. 19 G7
Westhampnett 12 B6
Westhay 19 H7
Westhead 48 D2
Westhide 28 E4
Westhill Aber. 91 G4
Westhill High. 96 E7
Westhope Here. 28 D3
Westhope Shrop. 38 D7
Westhorpe Lincs. 43 F2
Westhorpe Suff. 34 E2
Westhoughton 49 F2
Westhouse 56 B2
Westhouses 51 G7
Westhumble 22 E6
Westing 108 E2
Westlake 5 G5
Westleigh Devon 6 C3
Westleigh Devon 7 J4
Westleigh Gt.Man. 49 F2
Westleton 35 J2
Westley Shrop. 38 C5
Westley Suff. 34 C2
Westley Heights 24 C3
Westley Waterless 33 K3

Westlington 31 J1
Westlinton 69 J6
Westloch 76 A5
Westmarsh 25 J5
Westmeston 13 G5
Westmill 33 G6
Westminster 23 F4
Westmuir 82 E2
Westness 106 C5
Westnewton Cumb. 60 C2
Westnewton Northumb. 77 G7
Weston B. & N.E.Som. 20 A5
Weston Ches. 49 G5
Weston Devon 7 K5
Weston Dorset 9 F7
Weston Halton 48 E4
Weston Hants. 11 J2
Weston Herts. 33 F5
Weston Lincs. 43 F3
Weston Moray 98 C4
Weston N.Yorks. 57 G5
Weston Northants. 31 G4
Weston Notts. 51 K6
Weston Shrop. 38 E3
Weston Shrop. 38 E6
Weston Staffs. 40 B3
Weston W.Berks. 21 H4
Weston Beggard 28 E4
Weston by Welland 42 A6
Weston Colville 33 K3
Weston Corbett 21 K7
Weston Coyney 40 B1
Weston Favell 31 J2
Weston Green Cambs. 33 K3
Weston Green Norf. 45 F4
Weston Green Surr. 22 E5
Weston Heath 39 G4
Weston Hills 43 F3
Weston Jones 39 G3
Weston Lullingfields 38 D3
Weston Patrick 21 K7
Weston Point 48 D4
Weston Rhyn 38 B2
Weston Subedge 30 C4
Weston Turville 32 B7
Weston under Penyard 29 F6
Weston under Wetherley 30 E2
Weston Underwood Derbys. 40 E1
Weston Underwood M.K. 32 B3
Westonbirt 20 B3
Westoning 32 D5
Weston-in-Gordano 19 H4
Weston-on-the-Green 31 G6
Weston-on-Trent 41 G3
Weston-super-Mare 19 G5
Weston-under-Lizard 40 A4
Westonzoyland 8 C1
Westow 58 D3
Westport Arg. & B. 66 A2
Westport Som. 8 C2
Westrigg 75 H4
Westruther 76 E6
Westry 43 G6
Westside 91 G1
Westward 60 D2
Westward Ho! 6 C2
Westwell Kent 14 E3
Westwell Oxon. 30 D7
Westwell Leacon 14 E3
Westwick Cambs. 33 H2
Westwick Dur. 62 B5
Westwick Norf. 45 G3
Westwood Devon 7 J6
Westwood Wilts. 20 B6
Westwood Heath 30 D1
Westwoodside 51 K3
Wether Cote Farm 58 C1
Wetheral 61 F1
Wetherby 57 K5
Wetherden 34 E2
Wetheringsett 35 F2
Wethersfield 34 B5
Wethersta 109 C6
Wetherup Street 35 F2
Wetley Rocks 40 B1
Wettenhall 49 F6
Wettenhall Green 49 F6
Wetton 50 D7
Wetwang 59 F4
Wetwood 39 G2
Wexcombe 21 F6
Weybourne Norf. 45 F1
Weybread 45 G7
Weybridge 22 D5
Weycroft 8 C4
Weydale 105 G2
Weyhill 21 G7
Weymouth 9 F7
Whaddon Bucks. 32 B5
Whaddon Cambs. 33 G4
Whaddon Glos. 29 H7
Whaddon Wilts. 10 C2
Whaddon Gap 33 G4
Whale 61 G4
Whaley 51 H5
Whaley Bridge 50 C4
Whaligoe 105 J4
Whalley 56 C6
Whalton 71 G5
Wham 56 C3
Whaplode 43 G3
Whaplode Drove 43 G4
Whaplode St. Catherine 43 G3
Wharfe 56 C3
Wharles 55 H6
Wharncliffe Side 51 F3
Wharram le Street 58 E3
Wharram Percy 58 E3
Wharton Ches. 49 F6
Wharton Here. 28 E3
Whashton 62 C6
Whatcote 30 E4
Whatfield 34 E4
Whatley 20 A7
Whatlington 14 C6
Whatstandwell 51 F7
Whatton 42 A2
Whauphill 64 E6
Whaw 62 A6
Wheatacre 45 J6
Wheatenhurst 20 A1
Wheathampstead 32 E7

Wheathill 39 F7
Wheatley Hants. 11 J1
Wheatley Oxon. 21 K1
Wheatley Hill 62 E3
Wheatley Lane 56 D6
Wheaton Aston 40 A4
Wheddon Cross 7 H2
Wheedlemont 90 C2
Wheelerstreet 22 C7
Wheelock 49 G7
Wheelton 56 B7
Wheen 90 B7
Wheldrake 58 C5
Whelford 20 E2
Whelpley Hill 22 D1
Whelpo 60 E3
Whenby 58 C3
Whepstead 34 C3
Wherstead 35 F4
Wherwell 21 G7
Wheston 50 D5
Whetley Cross 8 D4
Whetsted 23 K7
Whetstone 41 H6
Whicham 54 E1
Whichford 30 E1
Whickham 71 H7
Whiddon Down 6 E6
Whifflet 75 F4
Whigstreet 83 F3
Whilton 31 H2
Whim 76 A5
Whimple 7 J6
Whimpwell Green 45 H2
Whin Lane End 55 G5
Whinburgh 44 E5
Whinnyfold 91 J1
Whippingham 11 G5
Whipsnade 32 D7
Whipton 7 H6
Whisby 52 C6
Whissendine 42 B4
Whissonsett 44 D3
Whistley Green 22 A4
Whiston Mersey. 48 D3
Whiston Northants. 32 B2
Whiston S.Yorks. 51 G4
Whiston Staffs. 40 C1
Whiston Staffs. 40 A4
Whitbeck 54 E1
Whitbourne 29 G3
Whitburn T. & W. 71 K7
Whitburn W.Loth. 75 H4
Whitby Ches. 48 C5
Whitby N.Yorks. 63 K5
Whitchurch B. & N.E.Som. 19 K5
Whitchurch Bucks. 32 B6
Whitchurch Cardiff 18 E4
Whitchurch Devon 4 E3
Whitchurch Hants. 21 H7
Whitchurch Here. 28 E7
Whitchurch Pembs. 16 B3
Whitchurch Shrop. 38 E1
Whitchurch Canonicorum 8 C5
Whitchurch Hill 21 K4
Whitchurch-on-Thames 21 K4
Whitcombe 9 G6
Whitcott Keysett 38 C4
White Colne 34 C6
White Coppice 49 F1
White Cross Cornw. 3 F3
White Cross Devon 7 J6
White Cross Here. 28 D4
White End 29 H6
White Lackington 9 G5
White Ladies Aston 29 J3
White Mill 17 H3
White Moor 41 F1
White Notley 34 B7
White Pit 53 G5
White Roding 33 J7
White Waltham 22 B4
Whiteacen 97 K7
Whiteash Green 34 B5
Whitebog 99 H5
Whitebridge High. 105 H1
Whitebridge High. 88 B3
Whitebrook 19 J1
Whiteburn 76 D6
Whitecairn 64 C5
Whitecairns 91 H3
Whitecastle 75 J6
Whitechapel 55 J5
Whitechurch 16 B2
Whitecraig 76 B3
Whitecroft 19 K1
Whitecross 2 C5
Whiteface 96 E3
Whitefield Aber. 91 F2
Whitefield Gt.Man. 49 H2
Whitefield High. 88 C2
Whitefield High. 105 H3
Whitefield P. & K. 82 C4
Whiteford 91 F2
Whitegate 49 F6
Whitehall 106 F5
Whitehaven 60 A5
Whitehill Hants. 11 J1
Whitehill Kent 14 E2
Whitehill N.Ayr. 74 A5
Whitehills 98 E4
Whitehouse Aber. 90 E3
Whitehouse Arg. & B. 73 G4
Whitekirk 76 D2
Whitelackington 8 C3
Whitelaw 77 G5
Whiteleen 105 J4
Whitelees 74 B7
Whiteley 11 G4
Whiteley Bank 11 G6
Whiteley Village 22 D5
Whiteleys 64 A5
Whitemans Green 13 G4
Whitemire 97 G6
Whiteparish 10 D2
Whiterashes 91 G2
Whiterow 105 J4
Whiteshill 20 B1
Whiteside Northumb. 70 C7
Whiteside W.Loth. 75 H4
Whitesmith 13 J5
Whitestaunton 8 B3
Whitestone Aber. 90 E5
Whitestone Arg. & B. 73 F7
Whitestone Devon 7 G6
Whitestripe 99 H5
Whiteway 29 J7
Whitewell Aber. 99 H4
Whitewell Lancs. 56 B5
Whiteworks 5 G3
Whitewreath 97 K6

Whitfield Here. 28 D5
Whitfield Kent 15 H3
Whitfield Northants. 31 H4
Whitfield Northumb. 61 J1
Whitfield S.Glos. 8 B5
Whitford Devon 8 B5
Whitford (Chwitffordd) Flints. 47 K5
Whitgift 58 E7
Whitgreave 40 A3
Whithorn 64 E6
Whiting Bay 66 E1
Whitkirk 57 J6
Whitlam 91 G2
Whitland 17 F4
Whitland Abbey 17 F4
Whitletts 67 H1
Whitley N.Yorks. 58 B7
Whitley Read. 22 A5
Whitley Wilts. 20 B5
Whitley Bay 71 J6
Whitley Chapel 62 A1
Whitley Lower 50 E1
Whitley Row 23 H6
Whitlock's End 30 C1
Whitminster 20 A1
Whitmore Dorset 10 B4
Whitmore Staffs. 40 A1
Whitnage 7 J4
Whitnash 30 E2
Whitney 28 B4
Whitrigg Cumb. 60 D1
Whitrigg Cumb. 60 D3
Whitsbury 10 C3
Whitsome 77 G5
Whitson 19 G3
Whitstable 25 H5
Whitstone 4 C1
Whittingham 71 F2
Whittingslow 38 D7
Whittington Derbys. 51 F5
Whittington Glos. 30 B6
Whittington Lancs. 56 B2
Whittington Norf. 44 B6
Whittington Shrop. 38 C1
Whittington Staffs. 40 D5
Whittington Staffs. 40 A4
Whittington Worcs. 29 H3
Whittlebury 31 H4
Whittle-le-Woods 55 J7
Whittlesey 43 F6
Whittlesford 33 H4
Whitton N.Lincs. 58 E7
Whitton Northumb. 71 F3
Whitton Powys 28 B2
Whitton Shrop. 28 E1
Whitton Stock. 62 E4
Whitton Suff. 35 F4
Whittonditch 21 F4
Whittonstall 62 B1
Whitway 21 H6
Whitwell Derbys. 51 H5
Whitwell Herts. 32 E6
Whitwell Derbys. 40 E3
Whitwell Dur. 62 C3
Whitwell I.o.W. 11 G7
Whitwell N.Yorks. 62 D7
Whitwell T. & W. 71 J7
Whitwell Norf. 45 F3
Whitwell Rut. 42 C5
Whitwell-on-the-Hill 58 D3
Whitwick 41 G4
Whitwood 57 K7
Whitworth 49 H1
Whixall 38 E2
Whixley 57 K4
Whorlton Dur. 62 C5
Whorlton N.Yorks. 63 F6
Whygate 70 C6
Whyle 28 E2
Whyteleafe 23 G6
Wibdon 19 J2
Wibsey 57 G6
Wibtoft 41 G7
Wichenford 29 G2
Wichling 14 E2
Wick Bourne. 10 C5
Wick High. 105 J3
Wick S.Glos. 20 A4
Wick V. of Glam. 18 C4
Wick W.Suss. 12 D6
Wick Wilts. 10 C2
Wick Worcs. 29 J4
Wick Airport 105 J3
Wick Hill Kent 14 D4
Wick Hill W'ham 22 A5
Wick St. Lawrence 19 G5
Wicken Cambs. 33 J1
Wicken Northants. 31 J5
Wicken Bonhunt 33 H5
Wickenby 52 D4
Wickerslack 61 H5
Wickersley 51 G3
Wickford 24 D2
Wickham Hants. 11 G3
Wickham W.Berks. 21 G4
Wickham Bishops 34 C7
Wickham Heath 21 H5
Wickham Market 35 G3
Wickham St. Paul 34 C5
Wickham Skeith 34 E2
Wickham Street Suff. 34 B3
Wickham Street Suff. 34 E2
Wickhambreaux 15 H2
Wickhambrook 34 B3
Wickhamford 30 B4
Wickhampton 45 J5
Wicklewood 44 E5
Wickmere 45 F2
Wickwar 20 A3
Widdington 33 J5
Widdop 56 E6
Widdrington 71 H4
Wide Open 71 H6
Widecombe in the Moor 5 H3
Widegates 4 C5
Widemouth Bay 6 A5
Widewall 107 D8
Widford Essex 24 C1
Widford Herts. 33 H7
Widmerpool 41 J3
Widnes 48 E4
Widworthy 8 B5
Wigan 48 E2
Wiggaton 7 K6
Wiggenhall St. Germans 44 A4
Wiggenhall St. Mary Magdalen 44 A4
Wiggenhall St. Mary the Virgin 43 J4
Wiggenhall St. Peter 44 A4

Wiggington 58 C4
Wigginton Herts. 32 C7
Wigginton Oxon. 30 E5
Wigginton Staffs. 40 E5
Wigglesworth 56 D4
Wiggonby 60 D1
Wiggonholt 12 D5
Wighill 57 K5
Wighton 44 D2
Wightwizzle 50 E3
Wigmore Here. 28 D2
Wigmore Med. 24 E5
Wigsley 52 B5
Wigsthorpe 42 D7
Wigston 41 J6
Wigston Parva 41 G6
Wigthorpe 51 H4
Wigtoft 43 F2
Wigton 60 D2
Wigtown 64 E5
Wilbarston 42 B7
Wilberfoss 58 D4
Wilburton 33 H1
Wilby Norf. 44 E6
Wilby Northants. 32 B2
Wilby Suff. 35 G1
Wilcot 20 E5
Wilcott 38 C4
Wilcrick 19 H3
Wildboarclough 49 J6
Wilden Beds. 32 D3
Wilden Worcs. 29 H1
Wildhern 21 G6
Wildhill 23 F1
Wildsworth 52 B3
Wilford 41 H2
Wilkesley 39 F1
Wilkhaven 97 G3
Wilkieston 75 K4
Willand 7 J4
Willaston Ches. 48 C5
Willaston Ches. 49 F7
Willen 32 B4
Willenhall W.Mid. 40 B6
Willenhall W.Mid. 30 E1
Willerby E.Riding 59 G7
Willerby N.Yorks. 59 G2
Willersey 30 C4
Willersley 28 C4
Willesborough 15 F3
Willesborough Lees 15 F3
Willesden 23 F3
Willesley 20 B3
Willett 7 K2
Willey Shrop. 39 F6
Willey Warks. 41 G7
Williamscot 31 F4
Williamthorpe 51 G6
Willian 33 F5
Willimontswick 70 C7
Willingale 23 J1
Willingdon 13 J6
Willingham Cambs. 33 H2
Willingham Lincs. 52 B4
Willington Beds. 32 E4
Willington Derbys. 40 E3
Willington Dur. 62 C3
Willington T. & W. 71 J7
Willington Warks. 30 D5
Willington Corner 48 E6
Willisham 34 E3
Willitoft 58 D6
Williton 7 J1
Willoughby Lincs. 53 H5
Willoughby Warks. 31 G2
Willoughby Waterleys 41 H6
Willoughby-on-the-Wolds 41 J3
Willoughton 52 C3
Willows Green 34 B7
Willsworthy 6 D7
Wilmcote 30 C3
Wilmington Devon 8 B4
Wilmington E.Suss. 13 J6
Wilmington Kent 23 J4
Wilmslow 49 H4
Wilnecote 40 E5
Wilpshire 56 B6
Wilsden 57 F6
Wilsford Lincs. 42 D1
Wilsford Wilts. 20 E7
Wilsford Wilts. 20 D6
Wilsill 57 G3
Wilsley Green 14 C4
Wilson 41 G3
Wilstead 32 D4
Wilsthorpe 42 D4
Wilstone 32 C7
Wilton Cumb. 60 B5
Wilton N.Yorks. 58 E1
Wilton R. & C. 63 G4
Wilton Sc.Bord. 69 K2
Wilton Som. 8 B2
Wilton Wilts. 21 F5
Wilton Wilts. 10 B1
Wimbish 33 J5
Wimbish Green 33 K5
Wimblebury 40 C4
Wimbledon 23 F4
Wimblington 43 H6
Wimborne Minster 10 B4
Wimborne St. Giles 10 B3
Wimbotsham 44 A5
Wimpole 33 G4
Wimpstone 30 D4
Wincanton 9 G2
Wincham 49 F5
Winchburgh 75 J3
Winchcombe 30 B6
Winchelsea 14 E6
Winchelsea Beach 14 E6
Winchester 11 F2
Winchet Hill 14 C3
Winchfield 22 A6
Winchmore Hill Bucks. 22 C2
Winchmore Hill Gt.Lon. 23 G2
Wincle 49 J6
Wincobank 51 F3
Windermere 61 F7
Winderton 30 E4
Windhill 96 C7
Windlesham 22 C5
Windley 41 F1
Windmill Meadows 41 F1
Windmill Hill E.Suss. 13 K5
Windmill Hill Som. 8 C3
Windrush 30 C7
Windsor 22 C4
Windy Yet 74 C5
Windygates 82 E7
Wineham 13 F4
Winestead 59 K7
Winewall 56 E5

Winfarthing 45 F7
Winford 19 J5
Winforton 28 B4
Winfrith Newburgh 9 H6
Wing Bucks. 32 B6
Wing Rut. 42 B5
Wingate 63 F3
Wingates Gt.Man. 49 F2
Wingates Northumb. 71 F4
Wingerworth 51 F6
Wingfield Beds. 32 D6
Wingfield Suff. 35 G1
Wingfield Wilts. 20 B6
Wingham 15 H2
Wingmore 15 G3
Wingrave 32 B7
Winkburn 51 K7
Winkfield 22 C4
Winkfield Row 22 B4
Winkhill 50 C7
Winkleigh 6 E5
Winksley 57 H2
Winksley Banks 57 H2
Winkton 10 C5
Winlaton 71 G7
Winlaton Mill 71 G7
Winless 105 H3
Winmarleigh 55 H5
Winnards Perch 3 G2
Winnersh 22 A4
Winscombe 19 H6
Winsford Ches. 49 F6
Winsford Som. 7 H2
Winsham 8 C4
Winshill 40 E3
Winsh-wen 17 K6
Winskill 61 G3
Winslade 21 K7
Winsley 20 A5
Winslow 31 J6
Winson 20 D1
Winsor 10 E3
Winster Cumb. 61 F7
Winster Derbys. 50 E6
Winston Dur. 62 C5
Winston Suff. 35 F2
Winstone 20 C1
Winswell 6 C4
Winterborne Came 9 G6
Winterborne Clenston 9 H4
Winterborne Houghton 9 H4
Winterborne Kingston 9 H5
Winterborne Monkton 9 F6
Winterborne Stickland 9 H4
Winterborne Whitechurch 9 H4
Winterborne Zelston 9 H5
Winterbourne S.Glos. 19 K3
Winterbourne W.Berks. 21 H4
Winterbourne Abbas 9 F5
Winterbourne Bassett 20 D4
Winterbourne Dauntsey 10 C1
Winterbourne Earls 10 C1
Winterbourne Gunner 10 C1
Winterbourne Monkton 20 D4
Winterbourne Steepleton 9 F6
Winterbourne Stoke 20 D7
Winterburn 56 E4
Wintercleugh 68 E2
Winteringham 59 F7
Winterley 49 G7
Wintersett 51 F1
Wintershill 11 G3
Winterslow 10 D1
Winterton 52 C1
Winterton-on-Sea 45 J4
Winthorpe Lincs. 53 J6
Winthorpe Notts. 52 B7
Winton Bourne. 10 B5
Winton Cumb. 61 J3
Wintringham 58 E2
Winwick Cambs. 42 E7
Winwick Northants. 31 H1
Winwick Warr. 49 F3
Wirksworth 50 E7
Wirswall 38 E1
Wisbech 43 H5
Wisbech St. Mary 43 H5
Wisborough Green 12 D4
Wiseton 51 K4
Wishaw N.Lan. 75 F5
Wishaw Warks. 40 D6
Wisley 22 D6
Wispington 53 F5
Wissett 35 H1
Wissington 34 D5
Wistanstow 38 D7
Wistanswick 39 F3
Wistaston 49 F7
Wiston Pembs. 16 D4
Wiston S.Lan. 75 H1
Wistow Cambs. 43 F7
Wistow N.Yorks. 58 B6
Wiswell 56 C6
Witcham 33 H1
Witchampton 9 J4
Witchburn 66 B2
Witchford 33 J1
Witcombe 8 D2
Witham 34 C7
Witham Friary 20 A7
Witham on the Hill 42 D4
Withcote 42 B5
Witherenden Hill 13 K4
Witherhurst 13 K4
Witheridge 7 G4
Witherley 41 F6
Withern 53 H4
Withernsea 59 K7
Withernwick 59 H5
Withersdale Street 45 G7
Withersfield 33 K4
Witherslack 55 H1
Witherslack Hall 55 H1
Withiel 3 G2
Withiel Florey 7 H2
Withington Glos. 30 B7
Withington Gt.Man. 49 H3
Withington Here. 28 E4
Withington Shrop. 38 E4

Withington Staffs. 40 C2
Withington Green 49 H5
Withleigh 7 H4
Withnell 56 B7
Withybrook 41 G7
Withycombe 7 J1
Withycombe Raleigh 7 J7
Withyham 13 H3
Withypool 7 G2
Witley 12 C3
Witnesham 35 F3
Witney 30 E7
Wittering 42 D5
Wittersham 14 D5
Witton 83 G1
Witton Bridge 45 H2
Witton Gilbert 62 D2
Witton Park 62 C3
Witton-le-Wear 62 C3
Wiveliscombe 7 J3
Wivelsfield 13 G4
Wivelsfield Green 13 G5
Wivenhoe 34 E6
Wiveton 44 E1
Wix 35 F6
Wixford 30 B3
Wixoe 34 B4
Woburn 32 C5
Woburn Sands 32 C5
Wokefield Park 21 K5
Woking 22 D6
Wokingham 22 B5
Wolborough 5 J3
Wold Newton E.Riding 59 G2
Wold Newton N.E.Lincs. 53 F3
Woldingham 23 G6
Wolfelee 70 A3
Wolferlow 29 F2
Wolferton 44 A3
Wolfhampcote 31 G2
Wolfhill 82 C4
Wolfpits 28 B3
Wolf's Castle 16 C3
Wolfsdale 16 C3
Woll 69 K1
Wollaston Northants. 32 C2
Wollaston Shrop. 38 C4
Wollaston W.Mid. 40 A7
Wollerton 39 F3
Wolsingham 62 B3
Wolstenholme 49 H1
Wolston 31 F1
Wolvercote 21 H1
Wolverhampton 40 B6
Wolverley Shrop. 38 D2
Wolverley Worcs. 29 H1
Wolverton Hants. 21 J6
Wolverton M.K. 32 B4
Wolverton Warks. 30 D2
Wolvesnewton 19 H2
Wolvey 41 G7
Wolviston 63 F4
Wombleton 58 C1
Wombourne 40 A6
Wombwell 51 G2
Womenswold 15 H2
Womersley 51 H1
Wonastow 28 D7
Wonersh 22 D7
Wonson 6 E7
Wonston 11 F1
Wooburn 22 C3
Wooburn Green 22 C3
Wood Burcote 31 H4
Wood Dalling 44 E3
Wood End Beds. 32 D4
Wood End Herts. 33 G6
Wood End Warks. 40 E6
Wood End Warks. 30 C1
Wood Enderby 53 F6
Wood Green 23 G2
Wood Hayes 40 B5
Wood Norton 44 E3
Wood Street Village 22 C6
Woodale 57 F2
Woodbastwick 45 H4
Woodbeck 51 K5
Woodbine 16 C4
Woodborough Notts. 41 J1
Woodborough Wilts. 20 E5
Woodbridge 35 G4
Woodbury 7 J7
Woodbury Salterton 7 J7
Woodchester 20 B1
Woodchurch Kent 14 E4
Woodchurch Mersey. 48 B4
Woodcote Oxon. 21 K3
Woodcote Tel. & W. 39 G4
Woodcott 21 H6
Woodcroft 19 J2
Woodcutts 9 J3
Woodditton 33 K3
Woodeaton 31 G7
Woodend Aber. 90 E3
Woodend Cumb. 60 C7
Woodend High. 88 E2
Woodend High. 79 J1
Woodend Northants. 31 H4
Woodend P. & K. 81 J3
Woodend W.Suss. 12 B6
Woodfalls 10 D2
Woodford Cornw. 6 A4
Woodford Glos. 19 K2
Woodford Gt.Lon. 23 H2
Woodford Gt.Man. 49 H4
Woodford Northants. 32 C1
Woodford Bridge 23 H2
Woodford Green 23 H2
Woodford Halse 31 G3
Woodgate Norf. 44 E4
Woodgate W.Mid. 40 B7
Woodgate W.Suss. 12 C6
Woodgate Worcs. 29 J2
Woodgreen 10 C3
Woodhall 62 A7
Woodhall Spa 52 E6
Woodham Dur. 62 D4
Woodham Surr. 22 D5
Woodham Ferrers 24 D2
Woodham Mortimer 24 E1
Woodham Walter 24 E1
Woodhaven 83 F5
Woodhead 91 F1
Woodhill 39 G7
Woodhorn 71 H5
Woodhouse Cumb. 55 J1

Woodhouse Leics. 41 H4
Woodhouse S.Yorks. 51 G4
Woodhouse Eaves 41 H4
Woodhouses 40 D4
Woodhuish 5 B3
Woodhurst 33 G1
Woodingdean 13 G6
Woodland Devon 5 H4
Woodland Dur. 62 B4
Woodlands Dorset 10 B4
Woodlands Hants. 10 E3
Woodlands Shrop. 39 G7
Woodlands Park 22 B4
Woodleigh 5 H6
Woodlesford 57 J7
Woodley 22 A4
Woodmancote Glos. 20 D1
Woodmancote Glos. 29 J6
Woodmancote W.Suss. 13 F5
Woodmancote W.Suss. 11 J4
Woodmancott 21 J7
Woodmansey 59 G6
Woodmansterne 23 F6
Woodminton 10 B2
Woodmoor 38 B5
Woodnesborough 15 H2
Woodnewton 42 D6
Woodplumpton 55 J6
Woodrising 44 D5
Woodseaves Shrop. 39 F2
Woodseaves Staffs. 39 G3
Woodsend 21 F4
Woodsetts 51 H4
Woodsford 9 G5
Woodside Aberdeen 91 H4
Woodside Brack.F. 22 C4
Woodside D. & G. 69 F6
Woodside Fife 83 F7
Woodside Fife 82 D7
Woodside Herts. 23 F1
Woodside N.Ayr. 74 B5
Woodside P. & K. 82 C4
Woodside Shrop. 28 C1
Woodside W.Mid. 40 B7
Woodstock 31 F7
Woodstock Slop 16 D3
Woodthorpe Derbys. 51 G5
Woodthorpe Leics. 41 H4
Woodton 45 G6
Woodtown 6 C3
Woodville 41 F4
Woodyates 10 B3
Woofferton 28 E2
Wookey 19 J7
Wookey Hole 19 J7
Wool 9 H6
Woolacombe 6 C1
Woolaston 19 J2
Woolavington 19 G7
Woolbeding 12 B4
Wooler 70 E1
Woolfardisworthy Devon 7 G5
Woolfardisworthy Devon 6 B3
Woolfords Cottages 75 J6
Woolhampton 21 J5
Woolhope 29 F5
Woollage Green 15 H3
Woolland 9 G4
Woollard 19 K5
Woollaton 6 C4
Woolley B. & N.E.Som. 20 A5
Woolley Cambs. 32 E1
Woolley W.Yorks. 51 F1
Woolmer Green 33 F7
Woolmere Green 29 J2
Woolmersdon 8 B1
Woolpit 34 D2
Woolscott 31 F2
Woolstaston 38 D6
Woolsthorpe Lincs. 42 B2
Woolsthorpe Lincs. 42 C3
Woolston S'ham. 11 F3
Woolston Shrop. 38 C3
Woolston Shrop. 38 D7
Woolston Warr. 49 F4
Woolston Green 5 H4
Woolstone M.K. 32 B5
Woolstone Oxon. 21 F3
Woolton 48 D4
Woolton Hill 21 H5
Woolverstone 35 F5
Woolverton 20 A6
Woolwich 23 H4
Woonton 28 C3
Wooperton 71 F1
Woore 39 G1
Wootton Beds. 32 D4
Wootton Hants. 10 D5
Wootton Kent 15 H3
Wootton N.Lincs. 52 D1
Wootton Northants. 31 J3
Wootton Oxon. 31 F7
Wootton Oxon. 21 H1
Wootton Shrop. 38 C2
Wootton Staffs. 40 A3
Wootton Staffs. 40 D1
Wootton Bassett 20 D3
Wootton Bridge 11 G5
Wootton Common 11 G5
Wootton Courtenay 7 H1
Wootton Fitzpaine 8 C5
Wootton Rivers 20 E5
Wootton St. Lawrence 21 J6
Wootton Wawen 30 C2
Worcester 29 H3
Worcester Park 23 F5
Wordsley 40 A7
Wordwell 34 C1
Worfield 39 G6
Work 107 D6
Workington 60 B4
Worksop 51 H5
Worlaby 52 D1
Worlds End Hants. 11 H3
World's End W.Berks. 21 H4
Worle 19 G5
Worleston 49 F7
Worlingham 45 J6
Worlington 33 K1

Worlingworth 35 G2
Wormbridge 28 D5
Wormegay 44 A4
Wormelow Tump 28 D5
Wormhill 50 D5
Wormiehills 83 H4
Wormingford 34 D5
Worminghall 21 K1
Wormington 30 B5
Worminster 19 J7
Wormit 83 H7
Wormleighton 31 F3
Wormley Herts. 23 G1
Wormley Surr. 12 C3
Wormshill 14 D2
Wormsley 28 D4
Worplesdon 22 C6
Worrall 51 F3
Worsbrough 51 F2
Worsley 49 G2
Worstead 45 H3
Worsted Lodge 33 J3
Worsthorne 56 D6
Worston 56 C5
Worswell 5 F6
Worth Kent 15 J2
Worth W.Suss. 13 G3
Worth Matravers 9 J7
Wortham 34 E1
Worthen 38 C5
Worthenbury 38 D1
Worthing Norf. 44 E4
Worthing W.Suss. 12 E6
Worthington 41 G3
Wortley Glos. 20 A2
Wortley S.Yorks. 51 F3
Worton 20 C6
Wortwell 45 G7
Wotherton 38 B5
Wotton 22 E7
Wotton Underwood 31 H7
Wotton-under-Edge 20 A2
Woughton on the Green 32 B5
Wouldham 24 D5
Wrabness 35 F5
Wrae 99 F5
Wrafton 6 C2
Wragby 52 E5
Wragholme 53 G3
Wrangham 90 E1
Wrangle 53 H7
Wrangle Lowgate 53 H7
Wrangway 7 K4
Wrantage 8 C2
Wrawby 52 D2
Wraxall N.Som. 19 H4
Wraxall Som. 9 F1
Wray 56 B3
Wray Castle 60 E6
Wraysbury 22 D4
Wrea Green 55 G6
Wreay Cumb. 61 F4
Wreay Cumb. 60 F2
Wrecclesham 22 B7
Wrecsam (Wrexham) 38 C1
Wrekenton 62 D1
Wrelton 58 D1
Wrenbury 38 E1
Wreningham 45 F6
Wrentham 45 J7
Wrenthorpe 51 F1
Wrentnall 38 D5
Wressle 58 D6
Wrestlingworth 33 F4
Wretham 44 D6
Wretton 44 A6
Wrexham (Wrecsam) 38 C1
Wrexham Industrial Estate 38 C1
Wribbenhall 29 G1
Wrightington Bar 48 E1
Wrightpark 74 E1
Wrinehill 39 G1
Wrington 19 H5
Writhlington 19 K6
Wrockwardine 39 F4
Wroot 51 K2
Wrotham 23 K6
Wrotham Heath 23 K6
Wrotham Hill 24 C5
Wrotham Park 23 F2
Wroughton 20 E3
Wroxall I.o.W. 11 G7
Wroxall Warks. 30 D1
Wroxeter 38 E5
Wroxham 45 H4
Wroxton 31 F4
Wstrws 17 G1
Wyaston 40 D1
Wyberton 43 G1
Wyboston 32 E3
Wybunbury 39 F1
Wych Cross 13 H3
Wychbold 29 J2
Wyck 11 J1
Wyck Rissington 30 C6
Wycliffe 62 C5
Wycoller 56 E6
Wycomb 42 A3
Wycombe Marsh 22 B2
Wyddial 33 G5
Wyke 15 F3
Wyke Dorset 9 G2
Wyke Shrop. 39 F5
Wyke W.Yorks. 57 G7
Wyke Regis 9 F7
Wykeham N.Yorks. 59 F1
Wykeham N.Yorks. 58 E2
Wyken 39 G6
Wykey 38 C3
Wylam 71 G7
Wylde Green 40 D6
Wyllie 18 E2
Wylye 10 B1
Wymering 11 H4
Wymeswold 41 J3
Wymington 32 C2
Wymondham Leics. 42 B4
Wymondham Norf. 45 F5
Wyndham 18 C2
Wynford Eagle 8 E5
Wynnstay Park 38 C1
Wynyard 63 F4
Wyre Piddle 29 J4
Wyresdale Tower 56 B4
Wysall 41 J3

Wyson 28 E2
Wythall 30 B1
Wytham 21 H1
Wythburn 60 E5
Wyton 33 F1
Wyverstone 34 E2
Wyverstone Street 34 E2
Wyville 42 B3
Wyvis Lodge 96 B4

Y
Y Bryn 37 H3
Y Drenewydd (Newtown) 38 A6
Y Fan 37 J7
Y Felinheli 46 D6
Y Fenni (Abergavenny) 28 C7

Y Fflint (Flint) 48 B5
Y Ffôr 36 C2
Y Trallwng (Welshpool) 38 B5
Yaddlethorpe 52 B2
Yafford 11 F6
Yafforth 62 E7
Yalding 23 K7
Yanworth 30 B7
Yapham 58 D4
Yapton 12 C6
Yarburgh 53 G3
Yarcombe 8 B4
Yardley 40 D7
Yardley Gobion 31 J4
Yardley Hastings 32 B3
Yardro 28 B3
Yarkhill 29 F4
Yarlet 40 B3
Yarley 19 J7
Yarlington 9 F2
Yarm 63 F5

Yarmouth 10 E6
Yarnacott 6 E2
Yarnbrook 20 B6
Yarnfield 40 A2
Yarnscombe 6 D3
Yarnton 31 F7
Yarpole 28 D2
Yarrow 69 J1
Yarrow Feus 69 J1
Yarrowford 69 K1
Yarsop 28 D4
Yarwell 42 D6
Yate 20 A3
Yateley 22 B5
Yatesbury 20 D4
Yattendon 21 J4
Yatton Here. 28 D2
Yatton N.Som. 19 H5
Yatton Keynell 20 B4
Yaverland 11 H6
Yaxham 44 E4
Yaxley Cambs. 42 E6
Yaxley Suff. 35 F1

Yazor 28 D4
Yeading 22 E3
Yeadon 57 H5
Yealand Conyers 55 J2
Yealand Redmayne 55 J2
Yealmpton 5 F5
Yearby 63 H4
Yearsley 58 B2
Yeaton 38 D4
Yeaveley 40 D1
Yedingham 58 E2
Yelford 21 G1
Yelland Devon 6 C2
Yelland Devon 6 D6
Yelling 33 F2
Yelvertoft 31 G1
Yelverton Devon 5 F4
Yelverton Norf. 45 G5
Yenston 9 G2
Yeo Vale 6 C3
Yeoford 7 F6
Yeolmbridge 6 B7

Yeomadon 6 B5
Yeovil 8 E3
Yeovil Marsh 8 E3
Yeovilton 8 E2
Yerbeston 16 D5
Yesnaby 107 B6
Yetlington 71 F2
Yetminster 8 E3
Yettington 5 J7
Yetts o'Muckhart 82 B7
Yielden 32 D2
Yiewsley 22 D4
Ynys 36 E2
Ynysboeth 18 D2
Ynysddu 18 E2
Ynyshir 18 D2
Ynyslas 37 F6
Ynysmeudwy 18 A1
Ynystawe 17 K5
Ynysybwl 18 D2
Yockenthwaite 56 E2
Yockleton 38 C4
Yokefleet 58 E7

Yoker 74 D4
Yonder Bognie 98 D6
York 58 C4
Yorkletts 25 G5
Yorkley 19 K1
Yorton 38 E3
Youldon 6 B5
Youldonmoor Cross 6 B5
Youlgreave 50 E6
Youlthorpe 58 D4
Youlton 57 K3
Young's End 34 B7
Yoxall 40 D4
Yoxford 35 H2

Ystrad 18 D1
Ystrad Aeron 26 E1
Ystrad Meurig 27 G1
Ystrad Mynach 18 E2
Ystradfellte 27 J1
Ystradffin 27 G1
Ystradgynlais 27 G1
Ystradowen N.P.T. 27 G1
Ystradowen V. of Glam. 18 D3
Ythanwells 90 E1
Ythsie 91 G1

Z
Zeal Monachorum 7 F5
Zeals 9 G1
Zelah 3 F3
Zennor 2 B5

INDEX TO PLACE NAMES IN IRELAND

Abbreviations

Ant.	Antrim	Kilk.	Kilkenny	Tyr.	Tyrone	Wexf. Wexford
Dub.	Dublin	Tipp.	Tipperary	Water.	Waterford	

A
Aasleagh 112 B6
Abbeyfeale 110 C3
Abbeyleix 111 F2
Achill 112 B5
Adare 110 C2
Annahilt 113 G4
Annalong 113 H5
Antrim 113 G3
Ardara 112 D3
Ardee 113 G5
Ardglass 113 H4
Arklow (Antinbhear Mór) 111 G2
Armagh 113 G4
Armoy 113 G2
Arvagh 113 E5
Ashbourne 113 G6
Athboy 113 F6
Athenry 110 D1
Athleague 112 D6
Athlone (Baile Átha Luain) 113 E6
Athy 111 F1
Augher 113 F4
Aughnacloy 113 F4
Aughrim 111 G2
Avoca 111 G2

B
Balbriggan 113 G6
Bailieborough 113 F5
Ballaghaderreen 112 D5
Ballina (Béal an Átha) 112 C5
Ballinafad 112 D5
Ballinalack 113 E6
Ballinamore 113 E5
Ballinasloe (Béal Átha na Sluaighe) 110 D1
Ballindine 112 C6
Ballinrobe 112 C6
Ballon 111 F2
Ballybay 113 F5
Ballybofey 113 E3
Ballybrack 110 A4
Ballybunnion 110 B3
Ballycanew 111 G2
Ballycastle Ant. 113 G2
Ballycastle Mayo 112 C4
Ballyclare 113 G3
Ballyconnell 113 E5
Ballycroy 112 B5
Ballydesmond 110 C3
Ballygar 112 D6
Ballygawley 113 F4
Ballygorman 113 F2
Ballyhale 111 F3
Ballyhaunis 112 D6
Ballyheigue 110 B3
Ballyjamesduff 113 F5
Ballykelly 113 F3
Ballylynan 111 F2
Ballymacarberry 111 E3
Ballymacmague 111 E4
Ballymacoda 113 E6
Ballymahon 113 E6
Ballymakeery 110 C4
Ballymena 113 G3
Ballymoney 113 G3
Ballymote 112 D5
Ballymurphy 111 F2
Ballynahinch 113 H4
Ballyragget 111 F2
Ballyshannon 112 D4
Ballyvaughan 110 C1
Ballyward 113 G4
Baltinglass 111 F1
Banagher 111 E1
Banbridge 113 G4
Bandon 110 D4
Bangor 113 H4
Bangor Erris 112 B5
Banteer 110 C3
Bantry 110 B5
Belcoo 113 E4

Belderg 112 B4
Belfast 113 H4
Belfast City Airport 113 H4
Belfast International Airport 113 G4
Belmullet 112 B5
Beragh 113 F4
Bessbrook 113 G6
Bettystown 113 G6
Birr 111 E1
Blackrock 113 G5
Blackwater 111 G3
Blarney 110 D4
Blessington 111 G1
Bohola 112 C5
Borris 111 F2
Borrisokane 110 D1
Borrisoleigh 111 E2
Boyle 112 D5
Bray (Bré) 111 G1
Broadford 110 C3
Broughshane 113 G3
Bunbeg 112 D3
Bunclody 111 G2
Buncrana 113 F2
Bundoran 112 D4
Burtonport 112 D3
Bushmills 113 G2
Butlers Bridge 113 F5
Buttevant 110 D3

C
Cahermore 110 B5
Cahir 111 E3
Cahirciveen 110 A4
Callan 111 F3
Cappoquin 111 E3
Carlingford 113 G5
Carlow (Ceatharlach) 111 F2
Carndonagh 113 F2
Carnlough 113 G3
Carraroe 110 B1
Carrick-on-Shannon 113 E5
Carrick-on-Suir (Carraig na Siuire) 111 F3
Carrickfergus 113 H3
Carrickmacross 113 F5
Carrigallen 113 E5
Carrigtwohill 110 D4
Carrowdore 113 H4
Carrowkeel 113 F2
Cashel 113 E2
Castlebar (Caisleán an Bharraigh) 112 C5
Castlebellingham 113 F5
Castleblayney 113 F5
Castlebridge 111 G3
Castlecomer 111 F2
Castleconnell 110 D2
Castlederg 113 E3
Castledermot 111 F2
Castlegregory 110 B3
Castleisland 110 B3
Castlemaine 110 B3
Castlemartyr 111 E4
Castlepollard 113 F6
Castlerea 112 D6
Castletown 111 E1
Castletown Bere 110 A4
Catherdaniel 110 A4
Cavan 113 F5
Celbridge 111 G1
Charlestown 112 D5
Cheekpoint 111 F3
City of Derry Airport 113 F3
Clady 113 E3
Clane 111 G1
Clara 111 E1
Clarecastle 110 C2
Claregalway 110 C1
Claremorris 112 C6
Clashmore 111 E4
Claudy 113 F3
Clifden 112 B6
Cliffony 112 D4

Cloghan 111 E1
Clogheen 111 E3
Clonakilty 110 C5
Clonbern 112 D6
Clones 113 F5
Clonmel (Cluain Meala) 111 E3
Clonroche 111 G3
Clonygowan 111 F1
Cloonbannin 110 C3
Clooneagh 113 E5
Cobh (An Cóbh) 110 D4
Coleraine 113 F2
Collooney 112 D5
Comber 113 H4
Cong 110 C6
Cookstown 113 F4
Cootehill 113 F5
Cork (Corcaigh) 110 D4
Cork Airport 110 D4
Corofin 110 C2
Courtmacsherry 110 D5
Courtown 111 G2
Craanford 111 G2
Craigavon 113 G4
Creeslough 113 E2
Cregganbaun 112 B6
Crookhaven 110 B5
Croom 110 D3
Crossgar 113 H4
Crosshaven 110 D4
Crossmaglen 113 G5
Crumlin 113 G4
Crusheen 110 C2
Cullybackey 113 G3
Cushendall 113 G3
Cushendun 113 G2

D
Delvin 113 F6
Dingle 110 A3
Donaghadee 113 H4
Donaghmore 113 F4
Donegal 112 D4
Donoughmore 110 D4
Dooagh 112 B5
Downpatrick 113 H4
Draperstown 113 F3
Drimoleague 110 C5
Drogheda (Droichead Átha) 113 G6
Dromod 113 E5
Dromore Down 113 G4
Dromore Tyr. 113 E4
Dromore West 112 C5
Drumfree 113 E2
Drumkeeran 112 D5
Drummin 111 F3
Dublin (Baile Átha Cliath) 111 G1
Dublin Airport 113 G6
Dún Laoghaire 111 G1
Dunboyne 113 G6
Duncannon 111 F3
Duncormick 111 G3
Dundalk (Dún Dealgan) 113 G5
Dundonald 113 H4
Dundrum 113 H4
Dungannon 113 F4
Dungarvan Kilk. 111 F2
Dungarvan (Dún Garbhán) Water. 111 E4
Dungiven 113 F3
Dungloe 112 D3
Dunleer 113 G5
Dunlavin 111 G1
Dunloy 113 G3
Dunmanway 110 C4
Dunmore 112 D6
Dunmore East 111 F3
Dunmurry 113 G4
Dunquin 110 A3
Durrow 111 F2

E
Edenderry 111 F1
Edgeworthstown 113 E6

Eglinton 113 F3
Ennis (Inis) 110 C2
Enniscorthy (Inis Córthaidh) 111 G3
Enniskean 110 C4
Enniskerry 111 G1
Enniskillen 113 E4
Ennistymon 110 C2

F
Farranfore 110 B3
Fermoy 110 D3
Ferns 111 G2
Fethard 111 E3
Fintona 113 F4
Fintown 112 D3
Fivemiletown 113 F4
Foxford 112 C5
Foynes 110 C2
Frenchpark 112 D5
Freshford 111 F2

G
Galbally 110 D3
Galway (Gaillimh) 110 C1
Galway Airport 110 C1
Garvagh 113 F3
Glenamaddy 112 D6
Glengarriff 110 B4
Glengavlen 113 E5
Glenties 112 D3
Gorey 111 G2
Gort 110 C1
Gortahork 112 D2
Graigue 111 F2
Graiguenamanagh 111 F2
Granard 113 E6
Grange 111 E4
Greenore 113 G5
Greystones 111 G1
Gweedore 112 D3

H
Halfway 110 D4
Headford 112 C6
Holycross 111 E2
Horseleap 112 D6
Hospital 110 D3
Howth 113 G6
Hurler's Cross 110 C2

I
Inch Kerry 110 B3
Inch Wexf. 111 G2

J
Johnstown 111 E2

K
Kanturk 110 C3
Keady 113 F5
Kells Kilk. 111 F3
Kells (Ceanannus Mór) Meath 113 F6
Kenmare 110 B4
Kerry Airport 110 B3
Kilbeggan 111 E1
Kilcolgan 110 C1
Kilcoole 111 G1
Kilcormac 111 E1
Kilcullen 111 F1
Kildare 111 F1
Kilkee 110 B2
Kilkeel 113 G5
Kilkenny (Cill Chainnigh) 111 F2
Killala 112 C5
Killaloe (Cill Dalua) 110 D2
Killarney (Cill Airne) 110 B4
Killenaule 111 E2
Killimor 110 D1

Killinchy 113 H4
Killinick 111 G3
Killorglin 110 B4
Killurin 111 G3
Killybegs 112 D4
Kilmacrenan 113 E2
Kilmaine 112 C6
Kilmallock 110 D3
Kilmona 110 D4
Kilmore Quay 111 G3
Kilrea 113 G3
Kilrush 110 B2
Kilteel 111 G1
Kiltimagh 112 C5
Kiltullagh 110 D1
Kingscourt 113 F5
Kinnegad 113 F6
Kinsale 110 D4
Kinvara 110 C1
Kircubbin 113 H4
Knock 112 C6
Knock International Airport 112 C5
Knockalough 110 C2
Knocktopher 111 F3

L
Lanesborough 113 E6
Larne 113 H3
Lauragh 110 B4
Laytown 113 G6
Leap 110 C5
Leighlinbridge 111 F2
Leixlip 111 G1
Letterkenny 113 E3
Lifford 113 E3
Limavady 113 F3
Limerick (Luimneach) 110 D2
Lisbellaw 113 E4
Lisburn 113 G4
Lisdoonvarna 110 C1
Lismore 111 E3
Lisnarrick 113 E4
Lisnaskea 113 E5
Listowel 110 B3
Londonderry (Derry) 113 F3
Longford 113 E6
Loughrea 110 D1
Louisburgh 112 B6
Lucan 111 G1
Lukeswell 111 F3
Lurgan 113 G4

M
Macroom 110 C4
Maghera 113 F3
Magherafelt 113 G3
Malahide 113 G6
Malin More 112 D3
Mallow (Mala) 110 D3
Manorhamilton 112 D4
Markethill 113 G4
May's Corner 113 G4
Middletown 113 F4
Midleton 110 D4
Milestone 111 E2
Milford 113 E2
Millstreet 110 C4
Milltown Malbay 110 C2
Mitchelstown 110 D3
Moate 111 E1
Mohill 113 E5
Moira 113 G4
Monaghan (Muineachán) 113 F5
Monasterevan 111 F1
Moneygall 111 E2
Moneymore 113 G3
Monivea 110 D1
Mount Bellew 112 D6
Mountmellick 111 F1
Mountrath 111 E1
Mountshannon 110 D2
Moville 113 F2
Moyvalley 111 F1
Muine Bheag 111 F2

Mullany's Cross 112 C5
Mullingar (An Muileann gCearr) 113 F6
Mulrany 112 B5
Murrisk 112 B6
Murroogh 110 C1

N
Naas (An Nás) 111 G1
Navan (An Uaimh) 113 G6
Nenagh (An tAonach) 110 D2
New Ross 111 F3
Newbridge (Droichead Nua) 111 F1
Newcastle Down 113 H5
Newcastle Dub. 111 G1
Newcastle West 110 C3
Newinn 111 E3
Newmarket 110 C3
Newmarket-on-Fergus 110 C2
Newport Mayo 112 B5
Newport Tipp. 110 D2
Newry 113 G5
Newtown 110 D3
Newtownabbey 113 H4
Newtownards 113 H4
Newtownbutler 113 F5
Newtownmount-kennedy 111 G1
Newtownstewart 113 F3
Ninemilehouse 111 E3
Nobber 113 F5

O
Oldcastle 113 F6
Omagh 113 F4
Oranmore 110 C1

P
Pallas Green 110 D2
Park 113 F3
Partry 112 C6
Pettigo 113 E4
Pomeroy 113 F4
Pontoon 112 C5
Portadown 113 G4
Portaferry 113 H4
Portarlington 111 F1
Portavogie 113 H4
Portlaoise 111 F1
Portlaw 111 F3
Portmagee 110 A4
Portrane 113 G6
Portrush 113 G2
Portsalon 113 E2
Portstewart 113 F2
Portumna 110 D1
Poulgorm Bridge 110 C4

R
Randalstown 113 G3
Raphoe 113 E3
Rathangan 111 F1
Rathdowney 111 E2
Rathdrum 111 G2
Rathfriland 113 G5
Rathkeale 110 C3
Rathkeevin 111 E3
Rathluirc (Charleville) 110 D3
Rathvilly 111 F2
Recess 112 B6
Ringsend 113 F3
Roscommon 112 D6
Roscrea 111 E2
Ross Carbery 110 C5
Rosslare Harbour 111 G3
Rosslea 113 F5
Rush 113 G6

S
Saintfield 113 H4

Schull 110 B5
Shanacrane 110 C4
Shannon Airport 110 C2
Shercock 113 F5
Shillelagh 111 G2
Sion Mills 113 E3
Sixmilebridge 110 C2
Sixmilecross 113 F4
Skerries 113 G6
Skibbereen 110 C5
Slane 113 G6
Sligo (Sligeach) 112 D4
Sneem 110 B4
Strabane 113 E3
Stradbally 111 F1
Strangford 113 H4
Stranorlar 113 E3
Strokestown 112 D5
Swinford 112 C5
Swords 113 G6

T
Taghmon 111 G3
Tallow 111 E4
Tandragee 113 G4
Tarbert 110 C3
Templemore 111 E2
Templetuohy 111 E2
Thomastown 111 F3
Thurles (Durlas) 111 E2
Timolin 111 F1
Tipperary 110 D2
Tower 110 D4
Tralee (Trá Lí) 110 B3
Tramore (Trá Mhór) 111 F3
Trim 113 F6
Tuam 112 C6
Tubbercurry 112 D5
Tulla 110 D2
Tullamore (Tulach Mhór) 111 E1
Tullow 111 F2
Tully 113 E3
Tulsk 112 D5

U
Urlingford 111 E2

V
Virginia 113 F5

W
Warrenpoint 113 G5
Waterford (Port Láirgé) 111 F3
Waterford Regional Airport 111 F3
Watergrasshill 110 D4
Wellington Bridge 111 G3
Westport 112 B5
Wexford (Loch Garman) 111 G3
Whitehall 111 E2
Whitehead 113 H3
Wicklow (Cill Mhantáin) 111 H2

Y
Youghal (Eochaill) 111 E4